T0338579

Handbook of Research on Data Science and Cybersecurity Innovations in Industry 4.0 Technologies

Thangavel Murugan
United Arab Emirates University, Al Ain, UAE

Nirmala E.
VIT Bhopal University, India

A volume in the Advances in Information Security, Privacy, and Ethics (AISPE) Book Series

Published in the United States of America by
    IGI Global
    Information Science Reference (an imprint of IGI Global)
    701 E. Chocolate Avenue
    Hershey PA, USA 17033
    Tel: 717-533-8845
    Fax: 717-533-8661
    E-mail: cust@igi-global.com
    Web site: http://www.igi-global.com

Copyright © 2023 by IGI Global. All rights reserved. No part of this publication may be reproduced, stored or distributed in any form or by any means, electronic or mechanical, including photocopying, without written permission from the publisher. Product or company names used in this set are for identification purposes only. Inclusion of the names of the products or companies does not indicate a claim of ownership by IGI Global of the trademark or registered trademark.

Library of Congress Cataloging-in-Publication Data

Names: Thangavel, M., 1989- editor. I E., Nirmala, 1975- editor.
Title: Handbook of research on data science and cybersecurity innovations
    in industry 4.0 technologies / edited by Thangavel M, Nirmala E.
Description: Hershey, PA : Information Science Reference, [2023] I Includes
    bibliographical references and index. I Summary: "This book aims to
    introduce readers to cybersecurity, data science and its impact on the
    realization of the Industry 4.0 applications. The focus of the book is
    to cover the technological foundations of cybersecurity and data science
    within the scope of the Industry 4.0 landscape and to detail the
    existing cybersecurity and data science innovations with Industry 4.0
    applications, as well as state-of-the-art solutions with regard to both
    academic research and practical implementations"-- Provided by
    publisher.
Identifiers: LCCN 2023029673 (print) I LCCN 2023029674 (ebook) I ISBN
    9781668481455 (h/c) I ISBN 9781668481462 (s/c) I ISBN 9781668481479
    (ebook)
Subjects: LCSH: Industry 4.0--Security measures--Handbooks, manuals, etc. I
    Computer security--Handbooks, manuals, etc.
Classification: LCC T59.6 .H35 2023 (print) I LCC T59.6 (ebook) I DDC
    005.8--dc23/eng/20230918
LC record available at https://lccn.loc.gov/2023029673
LC ebook record available at https://lccn.loc.gov/2023029674

This book is published in the IGI Global book series Advances in Information Security, Privacy, and Ethics (AISPE) (ISSN: 1948-9730; eISSN: 1948-9749)

British Cataloguing in Publication Data
A Cataloguing in Publication record for this book is available from the British Library.

All work contributed to this book is new, previously-unpublished material. The views expressed in this book are those of the authors, but not necessarily of the publisher.

For electronic access to this publication, please contact: eresources@igi-global.com.

Advances in Information Security, Privacy, and Ethics (AISPE) Book Series

Manish Gupta
State University of New York, USA

ISSN:1948-9730
EISSN:1948-9749

MISSION

As digital technologies become more pervasive in everyday life and the Internet is utilized in ever increasing ways by both private and public entities, concern over digital threats becomes more prevalent.

The **Advances in Information Security, Privacy, & Ethics (AISPE) Book Series** provides cutting-edge research on the protection and misuse of information and technology across various industries and settings. Comprised of scholarly research on topics such as identity management, cryptography, system security, authentication, and data protection, this book series is ideal for reference by IT professionals, academicians, and upper-level students.

COVERAGE

- Risk Management
- Technoethics
- Access Control
- Network Security Services
- Cookies
- Telecommunications Regulations
- Data Storage of Minors
- Global Privacy Concerns
- CIA Triad of Information Security
- Information Security Standards

IGI Global is currently accepting manuscripts for publication within this series. To submit a proposal for a volume in this series, please contact our Acquisition Editors at Acquisitions@igi-global.com or visit: http://www.igi-global.com/publish/.

The Advances in Information Security, Privacy, and Ethics (AISPE) Book Series (ISSN 1948-9730) is published by IGI Global, 701 E. Chocolate Avenue, Hershey, PA 17033-1240, USA, www.igi-global.com. This series is composed of titles available for purchase individually; each title is edited to be contextually exclusive from any other title within the series. For pricing and ordering information please visit http://www.igi-global.com/book-series/advances-information-security-privacy-ethics/37157. Postmaster: Send all address changes to above address. Copyright © 2023 IGI Global. All rights, including translation in other languages reserved by the publisher. No part of this series may be reproduced or used in any form or by any means – graphics, electronic, or mechanical, including photocopying, recording, taping, or information and retrieval systems – without written permission from the publisher, except for non commercial, educational use, including classroom teaching purposes. The views expressed in this series are those of the authors, but not necessarily of IGI Global.

Titles in this Series

For a list of additional titles in this series, please visit: www.igi-global.com/book-series

Protecting User Privacy in Web Search Utilization
Rafi Ullah Khan (The University of Agriculture, Peshawar, Pakistan)
Information Science Reference • © 2023 • 336pp • H/C (ISBN: 9781668469149) • US $240.00

Information Security and Privacy in Smart Devices Tools, Methods, and Applications
Carlos Rabadão (Computer Science and Communication Research Centre, Polytechnic of Leiria, Portugal) Leonel Santos (Computer Science and Communication Research Centre, Polytechnic of Leiria, Portugal) and Rogério Luís de Carvalho Costa (Computer Science and Communication Research Centre, Polytechnic of Leiria, Portugal)
Information Science Reference • © 2023 • 328pp • H/C (ISBN: 9781668459911) • US $250.00

Applications of Encryption and Watermarking for Information Security
Boussif Mohamed (University of Tunis El Manar, Tunisia)
Information Science Reference • © 2023 • 245pp • H/C (ISBN: 9781668449455) • US $240.00

Handbook of Research on Cybersecurity Risk in Contemporary Business Systems
Festus Fatai Adedoyin (Bournemouth University, UK) and Bryan Christiansen (Southern New Hampshire University, USA)
Information Science Reference • © 2023 • 446pp • H/C (ISBN: 9781668472071) • US $295.00

Fraud Prevention, Confidentiality, and Data Security for Modern Businesses
Arshi Naim (King Kalid University, Saudi Arabia) Praveen Kumar Malik (Lovely Professional University, India) and Firasat Ali Zaidi (Tawuniya Insurance, Saudi Arabia)
Business Science Reference • © 2023 • 347pp • H/C (ISBN: 9781668465813) • US $250.00

Handbook of Research on Cybersecurity Issues and Challenges for Business and FinTech Applications
Saqib Saeed (Department of Computer Information Systems, College of Computer Science and Information Technology, Imam Abdulrahman Bin Faisal University, Dammam, Saudi Arabia) Abdullah M. Almuhaideb (Department of Networks and Communications, College of Computer Science and Information Technology, Imam Abdulrahman Bin Faisal University, Dammam, Saudi Arabia) Neeraj Kumar (Thapar Institute of Engineering and Technology, India) Noor Zaman (Taylor's University, Malaysia) and Yousaf Bin Zikria (Yeungnam University, South Korea)
Business Science Reference • © 2023 • 552pp • H/C (ISBN: 9781668452844) • US $315.00

701 East Chocolate Avenue, Hershey, PA 17033, USA
Tel: 717-533-8845 x100 • Fax: 717-533-8661
E-Mail: cust@igi-global.com • www.igi-global.com

List of Contributors

Table of Contents

Section 1
Data Science Innovations in Industry 4.0

Section 2
Cybersecurity Innovations in Industry 4.0

Detailed Table of Contents

Section 1
Data Science Innovations in Industry 4.0

Chapter 1

    R. K. Kavitha, Kumaraguru College of Technology, India
    W. Jaisingh, Presidency University, India
    V. Kaarthiekheyan, Kumaraguru College of Technology, India

The advent of artificial intelligence (AI) and data sciences has disrupted our society in terms of fast and proactive technical development. The field of artificial intelligence embeds itself with multidisciplinary proficiency where the ultimate objective is to systematize all human actions and responses that currently need human intelligence. On the other hand, data science is a trending field that rationally tries to solve complicated problems. In addition, data science enables the mining of knowledge from data which includes the study of theories and techniques to collect, process and communicate with data during its life cycle once the data is obtained. This chapter establishes a futuristic analysis and applications of artificial intelligence (AI) and data science (DS), which includes fields like healthcare, education, building and construction, industrial design, and agriculture. Ironically, AI in industrial design remains unexplored in enhancing the utility, benefit, and aesthetics of manufactured goods to enhance client satisfaction.

Chapter 2

    Shyam Sunder Gupta, Amity University, Gwalior, India
    Rajeev Goyal, Amity University, Gwalior, India
    Deepak Gupta, ITM University, Gwalior, India

Artificial intelligence (AI) provides appropriate information for decision-making and alerting people of possible malfunctions. Industries will use AI to process data transmitted from the internet of things (IoT) devices and connected machines based on their desire to integrate them into their equipment. It provides companies with the ability to track their entire end-to-end activities and processes fully. Accordingly, the research objectives are crafted to facilitate researchers, practitioners, students, and industry professionals. It includes key features, how industrial AI distinguishes itself within the field of AI, major components in Industrial AI, Industrial AI eco-system, various tools and traits of AI, cyber physical applications, AI technologies and tools, Industrial IoT (IIoT) and data analytics, benefits of adopting an Industry 4.0 model, benefits of deploying AI models, significant advancements, and challenges of industrial artificial intelligence. Furthermore, this technology seeks correlations to avoid errors and eventually to anticipate them.

Chapter 3

Vijaya Kumar Reddy R., Koneru Lakshmaiah Education Foundation, India
U. Rahamathunnisa, Vellore Institute of Technology, India
P. Subhashini, Vel Tech Multi Tech Dr. Rangarajan Dr. Sakunthala Engineering College, India
H. Mickle Aancy, Panimalar Engineering College, India
S. Meenakshi, RMK Engineering College, India
S. Boopathi, Muthayammal Engineering College, India

Software projects have a very high probability of failure, and a major reason for this is a poor requirement engineering process. Requirement elicitation and documentation are the primary and most vital steps in the software development life cycle. There is a lack of a model or framework that deals with these risks in parallel, and a lot of work is needed to manage them holistically. This chapter includes the identification of factors that affect successful software development and explores various sources of requirement risks. It intends to create an intelligent framework for managing VUCA risks in software requirements. The relationship between VUCA and terrorism risks identification at an early stage using fuzzy logic, ANFIS, and intelligent Bayesian network models. The framework includes a model for volatile requirement prioritization and a model for requirement ambiguity and uncertainty management.

Chapter 4

Izzati Zaidi, Universiti Teknologi Brunei, Brunei
Mohamed Saleem Haja Nazmudeen, Universiti Teknologi Brunei, Brunei
Fadzliwati Mohiddin, Universiti Teknologi Brunei, Brunei

Technologies for the Fourth Industrial Revolution (IR 4.0) are widespread due to their significant advantages for various industries, including productivity performance, efficiency, and adaptability. Brunei Darussalam is a developing country that has recently considered the significance of IR 4.0. The maturity level on technology adoption for IR4.0 technologies are crucial to determine its operation performance and effectiveness. Data is collected from 40 micro, small, medium enterprises (MSMEs) from different industries of Brunei Darussalam. The model is from K-means clustering that can show the level of technology adoption in different sectors and sizes of businesses which in turn will help to determine the impact of technology on the performance of the firm. This study is to compare the difference on IR4.0 technology adoption between developed, developing countries, and Brunei Darussalam and their current interest and investment level for future adoption.

Chapter 5

V. Saranya, Hindusthan College of Engineering and Technology, India
S. Uma, HIndusthan College of Engineering and Technology, India

Internet of things, data science, deep learning, augmented reality, edge computing, and digital twins present new opportunities, challenges, and solutions for agriculture, plant sciences, animal sciences, food sciences, and social sciences. These disruptive technologies are at the centre of the fourth industrial revolution. The chapter discusses knowledge engineering to intellectualize higher education. Also, it explains how knowledge engineering (KE) can be utilized to construct intelligent learning and smart tutoring systems (STSs). The intersection of AI, web science, and data science enables a new generation of online-based educational and training tools to determine and examine the benefits of such computational paradigms for smart tutoring systems. Built on this architecture, data science courses should be user-, tool-, and application-based.

Chapter 6

M M. Nirmala Devi, Department of Computer Science and Engineering, Thiagarajar
College of Engineering, India
B. Subbulakshmi, Department of Computer Science and Engineering, Thiagarajar College of
Engineering, India
G. Naga Nivedithaa, Department of Computer Science and Engineering, Thiagarajar
College of Engineering, India
R. Swathi, Department of Computer Science and Engineering, Thiagarajar College of
Engineering, India

Analysis of campus recruitment data and career counseling in the engineering sector can offer insights about the job market trends, company preferences, and student preferences. These insights will improve career counseling services for students. The effectiveness and impact of career counseling services in the engineering sector can be significantly improved by a thorough analysis of college recruitment data. This research can also assist career counselors in adjusting their offerings to meet the shifting demands of the labor market and guarantee that they are offering engineering students useful and pertinent advice. In this study, an online service application is developed to provide all the information needed by the students about internships industry recruitment, higher education, and government employment. In order to provide career counseling services in the engineering field, it is vital to build a model for campus recruitment data. Linear regression outperforms other traditional models and produces an accuracy of 95.7%.

Chapter 7

D. Kavitha, Thiagarajar College of Engineering, India
D. Anitha, Thiagarajar College of Engineering, India
C. Jeyamala, Thiagarajar College of Engineering, India

As the current education scenario has transformed itself to online mode, all learning and assessment activities including quizzes, report submissions, problem solving, peer assessment are done online. Identification of students' characteristics in terms of their academic performance and attitude is the need of the hour for personal tutoring. Also, collaborative learning, which forms an integral part of learning, has group formation as an influential activity for the success of learning. This work proposes an intelligent solution to group learners based on their outcomes and participation in various online assessment activities. This chapter considers the online assessment results of the learners and uses Kohonen self-organizing map neural network (SOM) to group the learners. The proposed method is experimented with a student set in the course "Digital Systems" (n=84). MATLAB is used for implementing SOM and the results obtained from simulations confirm the efficacy of the proposed network with 93.33% performance metric.

Chapter 8
    P. Karthikeyan, Thiagarajar College of Engineering, India
    Vivek A. R., Thiagarajar College of Engineering, India

This work focuses on Industry 4.0 and the contemporary tendencies that it has spawned. The readers gain knowledge on what Industry 4.0 is, how it affects current manufacturing technologies, and its potential in the future. The authors improve comprehension of the effects imposed by Industry 4.0 by using a bibliometric method. Using web-scraping Python code and the YouTube Data API, this is accomplished using randomly selected 45–50 YouTube videos and 25–30 Medium blogs. Spreadsheets are used to organize the information that the web scraping programme has obtained. Following data organization, it is divided with the parameters serving as the key based on how well they coincide with the outcomes. To improve visualization, the results can be shown in a variety of graphs. The knowledge linked to Industry 4.0 that is provided in blogs and videos will provide readers with a better understanding of its impact.

Chapter 9
    A. M. Abirami, Thiagarjar College of Engineering, India
    S. Sumitra, Indian Institute of Space Science and Technology, India

People use social media platforms like Facebook, Twitter, and blog sites for expressing their views and criticising the products purchased and movies watched. They use these platforms for getting information like blood donation requirements and job opportunities. During the disastrous situations like floods and earthquakes, these platforms act as powerful media for passing messages to all people. During this COVID-19 pandemic period, all social media platforms are effectively used by all businesses for the instant communication and interactions between the groups of people. In all these scenarios, the information gets diffused and reaches different levels of people. Sometimes this diffusion gives positive aspects to the readers; sometimes it creates negative impacts to them, which has its own cascading effects. It becomes essential to monitor the rate of flow of information and stop spreading the fake or false messages. The application of suitable graph network modelling and theories would support this research issue and recommend the appropriate model for the social media data.

    Sandeep Kumar Hegde, NMAM Institute of Technology, Nitte University (Deemed), India
    Rajalaxmi Hegde, NMAM Institute of Technology, Nitte University (Deemed), India

Heart disease is the primary cause of death of humankind nowadays. Text summarization is currently a major research topic in natural language processing, and it is an important activity in the analysis of high-volume text documents. In the chapter, an automated summarization of text has been implemented using sentence scoring approach, which includes finding the frequent terms and sentence ranking method. This technique mainly focuses on summarizing medical reports. The proposed approach also uses three algorithms, namely SVM (support vector machine), KNN (k-nearest neighbor), and random forest algorithm, for disease prediction. Experimental results are carried out on several data sets, and they show that the proposed approach provides best accuracy compared to traditional techniques.

    Poorani Marimuthu, CMR Institute of Technology, India
    Santhanalakshmi S. T., Panimalar Engineering College, India
    C. Christlin Shanuja, CMR Institute of Technology, India

The travel and tourism sector is one among the important sectors that contribute or generate income to a country, which in turn raise the economy. More than one billion tourists travel to their desired international destinations as normal tourist, for their business, medical, study purpose, etc. every year contributes 9.8% of global GDP. This value represents 7% of the world total exports. Today with the natural language processing (NLP), most of the major challenges in these sectors have been addressed, which results in the increased revenue generation to the country. Moreover, NLP tries to provide a hassle-free experience to the tourist and thus improves the revenue generation. It helps to streamline the business opportunities and benefits all the interconnected industries. This chapter tries to provide the role of NLP in travel and tourism along with the challenges in this field.

    S. Arun Kamaraj, Thiagarajar College of Engineering, India
    M. Gautham, Thiagarajar College of Engineering, India
    S. Karthikeyan, Thiagarajar College of Engineering, India
    R. Parkavi, Thiagarajar College of Engineering, India

Communication between speakers of many languages is made possible by cutting-edge technologies like spoken language translation. The process of automatically recognizing, translating speech in real life is still a particularly challenging part of spoken language translation. Because it necessitates a fundamental modification of both linguistic and non-linguistic attributes, interpreting spoken words directly from one language to another is difficult. Numerous basic modules, like Google Translate and Text-to-Speech, are capable of achieving this. This speech recognition model not only demonstrates technological proficiency, but also offers a helpful platform for those who have hearing challenges. The majority of hearing-impaired people find it difficult to communicate because they rely on lipreading or other specialized treatments and struggle to understand broad information in this modern era. For those who have hearing impairments, speech recognition software would offer a comprehensive long-term answer because live speech-to-text translations will improve their communication skills.

Floods are one of the most common natural disasters that occur, destroying human life and the environment. Flash floods can cause catastrophic damage to society. The impacts of the flood on society include loss of human life, worsening of health conditions due to waterborne diseases, loss of livestock, and many other factors. It could be difficult to set things back after a huge flood. The main aim of this work is to develop a flood prediction system by reading the rainfall that occurs and to predict the possibilities of floods as well as to recommend the nearby evacuation area for the people to move immediately. Thus, the idea of this chapter is to predict the occurrence of a flood using the rainfall data and recommend nearby evacuation areas away from flood hazard areas. Providing the utmost safety has been the major idea in working on this chapter. Perfect accuracy for rainfall data was obtained using the random forest algorithm. Five algorithms were chosen and applied to the training data set. Accuracy was found precisely while using random forest algorithm.

Section 2
Cybersecurity Innovations in Industry 4.0

#### Chapter 14

Blockchain technology binds the idea of distributed ledgers and decentralization of assets into providing secure and fully ensured transparency of the data history. This technology consists of a P2P or peer-to-peer architecture of nodes that keeps a copy of the blockchain thereby enabling them to validate every transaction that is taking place in the network and has influenced developers and enthusiasts alike to adopt a decentralised mechanism. It is a robust architecture and makes hacking impossible. Consensus mechanisms, smart contracts, gas fees, different security protocols, Web3 wallets, oracles are some of the concepts and features that make blockchains immutable and secure. This chapter covers major contemporary concepts and terms profoundly. Ethereum blockchain network is dealt as the basic and foundational example that can be explained comfortably with it. Content and examples are related to solidity programming language so that even a novice can write his or her first smart contract on the Ethereum blockchain.

Chapter 15

R. Parkavi, Thiagarajar College of Engineering, India
S. Vigneshwaran, Thiagarajar College of Engineering, India
N. Sambath, Thiagarajar College of Engineering, India
P. Sanjai, Thiagarajar College of Engineering, India

Beneficiaries have no confidence in the way donated money is spent. Humanitarian organizations are at a similar risk to the forms of fraud that plague businesses, such as money laundering. Recently, blockchain technology has been implemented in various fields. The use of blockchain technology allows you to perform the process of giving and receiving money openly. It is necessary to build a single donation tracking platform that will track all information about gifts, transactions, and sponsors. The purpose of this work is to explain building blockchain-based infrastructure tracking donations. Based on blockchain technology, the system provides a clear accounting of donor performance, foundations of giving, and recipients. The donation channel should be available from the charity platform, which allows community users and donors to follow and monitor where, when, and to whom donations are made. This work summarizes the activities carried out in the design and implementation of the web-based blockchain management system.

Chapter 16

R. Sasikumar, K. Ramakrishnan College of Engineering, India
P. Karthikeyan, Thiagarajar College of Engineering, India
Thangavel Murugan, United Arab Emirates University, Al Ain, UAE

The name Industry 4.0 describes a synthesis of modern manufacturing techniques that help producers to hit targets more quickly. The manufacturing sector's trend is changing significantly because of digitalization and technological improvements. Technology that aids in comprehensive integration, such as IoT, cybersecurity, blockchain, big data, etc. Due to the internet's open nature as a means of data transmission, security and privacy must be given top priority. The integration of blockchain is currently taking place as part of Industry 4.0. Blockchain enables Industry 4.0 through bringing a variety of processing activities in a protected environment. The inherent characteristics of decentralization, blockchain technology is a promising platform for cybersecurity. This chapter's purpose is to highlight the issues on traditional production sectors, evaluation blockchain application in Industry 4.0, limitations of blockchain, privacy and security requirements, and adoption of blockchain inside this context of Industry 4.0.

Chapter 17

Yuvraj Singh, VIT Bhopal University, India
Subhash Chandra Patel, VIT Bhopal University, India
Jyoti Chauhan, VIT Bhopal University, India

To effectively regulate the energy supply, advanced metering infrastructure (AMI) deployment is gaining momentum in various parts of the world. Energy distributors, service providers, and consumers must work together to address several issues. All the transactions need to be documented properly and securely. Third parties can be trusted in those transactions by using blockchain. With the deployment of advanced metering infrastructure (AMI) and distributed ledgers, blockchain may aid in safeguarding and facilitating the movement of data. This chapter discusses the viability of utilizing blockchain for advanced metering infrastructure and the security risks and threat landscape.

Chapter 18

Hariharasitaraman S., VIT Bhopal University, India
Rounak Yadav, VIT Bhopal University, India
Preksha Agrawal, VIT Bhopal University, India

Cyber-physical systems (CPS) facilitate the incorporation of humans, objects, and computing systems in their physical environment. These systems operate in real-time and are used to enable the systems and devices to self-organize and reconfigure to respond to their changing environments. They help to realize data-intensive interconnected platforms that allow data streams to run continuously on an autonomous basis. CPSs in the context of tourism and travel are considered important elements for developing efficient and effective smart tourism services. This research explores various facets of CPSs and proposes a blockchain-based framework to offer a smart tourism ecosystem, catering to the dynamic preferences and needs of the tourists. The key idea is to use a novel blockchain-based data security mechanism, which uses a set of policies to enforce data security for smart tourism services.

Chapter 19

Subhash Chandra Patel, VIT Bhopal University, India
Santhoshini Sahu, VIT Bhopal University, India

This chapter will give a clear idea of what cyber-crime is and cyber terrorism's causes and types and how these are done and what is the main difference between cyber-crimes and cyber terrorism. It will also explore what precautions can be taken that may help a user with these attacks.

Chapter 20

Sharad Shandhi Ravi, VelTech Rangarajan Dr. Sagunthala R&D Institute of Science and Technology, India

Children and teens often use the internet today. Because kids and teens are using the internet more frequently, a new kind of bullying (harassment) called cyberbullying has emerged. The schoolyard is no longer a place where harassment is accepted. Cyberbullying is the term used to describe harassment that takes place online. Cyberbullying has commonly been described as a "extreme, deliberate activity or action carried out by an individual or a group utilising electronic forms of contact, repeatedly and over time against a victim who cannot quickly defend himself or herself." In addition to mail, pictures, messages, smartphones, internet, and social media sites, bullying may also happen through other avenues. A 22-year-old girl in Kerala, India, who was a famous TikToker, supported the Kerala minister's approaches towards cyberbullying. Only because of that has she been continuously bullied by her followers. The followers used bad commends and threatened her by saying she will be raped by them. Impact of cyberbullying, preventive measures, and law support are discussed here.

R. Parkavi, Thiagarajar College of Engineering, India
M. R. Jeya Iswarya, Thiagarajar College of Engineering, India
G. Kirithika, Thiagarajar College of Engineering, India
M. Madhumitha, Thiagarajar College of Engineering, India
O. Varsha, Thiagarajar College of Engineering, India

Computers, mobile devices, tablets, and other electronic devices are essential in our daily lives so the data plays a major role in it. Data is a valuable thing that might be stolen or leaked. Our ability to secure emerging technology is outpacing their development. Data storage is a critical component in any industry. Data security must be ensured across all industries, which is crucial. Data breaches, with an emphasis on the healthcare industry, are still on the rise as a result of inefficient data storage techniques like paperwork. Digital data storage is therefore becoming more secure. To store the data digitally, the proper software is needed. EHR (electronic health records) is the relevant program; information about patients, doctors, and medical histories is kept in the EHR. Blockchain technology might offer a way to safeguard this software, in particular if you desire more data security. The secure sharing of electronic data with patients, other doctors, and healthcare providers is made possible by blockchain-powered EHR systems.

Section 3
Industry 4.0 Technologies

U. Annaamalai, Thiagarajar College of Engineering, India
A. Dhiyaneshwar, Thiagarajar College of Engineering, India
Indira Suthakar, Thiagarajar College of Engineering, India
S. Karthiga, Thiagarajar College of Engineering, India
Nisha Angeline C. V., Thiagarajar College of Engineering, India

Recently, augmented reality (AR) has gained a lot of popularity. The fundamental tenet of augmented reality is to effectively facilitate interactive communication between people and computers. With the aid of specific tools, a person in the real world can enter the electronically produced reality. These days, this technology is included in every mobile filter we use, including those seen in Pokémon Go and the Instagram and Snapchat apps. Wearable versions of numerous miniature augmented reality models have been created. Numerous industries have been investigated using AR technology, including those in the realms of medicine, education, business, architecture, commerce, tourism, navigation, translation, the visual arts, fitness, flying training, the military, industrial manufacturing, etc. The roots of AR in Industry 4.0 are deepening day by day. The immense potential of AR can be utilized in an infinite number of ways to fulfill the objectives of Industry 4.0. This chapter shows the impact of AR in our society.

Kaustubh Laturkar, Michigan State University, USA
Kasturi Laturkar, Validation Associates LLC, USA

With the internet of things (IoT) growing steadily, a wide range of application fields are being offered. These include monitoring health, weather, smart homes, autonomous vehicles, and so on. The result is the incorporation of solutions in various commercial and residential areas and the eventual emergence of them as ubiquitous objects in everyday life. Due to such circumstances, cybersecurity would be essential to mitigate risks, such as data exposure, denial of service efforts, malicious system exploitation, etc. A large majority of entry-level IoT consumer devices lack adequate protection systems, which makes them susceptible to a wide range of malicious attacks. The chapter discusses IoT architectures in depth, along with an analysis of potential applications. A detailed and thorough analysis of challenges in the IoT domain is provided, emphasizing flaws in current commercial IoT solutions and the importance of designing IoT solutions with security and privacy in mind.

Chapter 24

Swati S. Roy, SOA University (Deemed), India
Shatarupa Dash, SOA University (Deemed), India
Bharat Jyoti Ranjan Sahu, SOA University (Deemed), India

With the rapid development of technology, the internet of things (IoT) has been an integral part of human society. The expansion and usage of IoT are further being accelerated by the global rollout of 5G cellular technology. The 5G and beyond wireless communications are especially focused on IoT requirements and use cases. One hundred percent coverage and connectivity are promised by the 5G beyond cellular network. The IoT devices may have to connect to any other known or unknown devices for sharing information, which urges different connectivity quality as well as different security and privacy requirements. In this chapter, the authors have explored the usage of 5G network slicing to cater to the diverse IoT connectivity requirement such as latency, bandwidth, and reliability. Moreover, as IoT devices may need to connect to other devices for various purposes, there is a need for trust evaluation among IoT devices. This chapter also discusses the establishment of social relationship among IoT devices to maintain privacy and security requirement through trust management.

Chapter 25

L. Harish, CMR Institute of Technology, India
D. Rashmi, CMR Institute of Technology, India

Artificial intelligence is an excellent solution for handling big data streams and storage in IoT networks. The IoT is becoming more significant with the discovery of high-speed internet networks and lots of superior sensors that may be incorporated into microcontrollers. Internet information streams will now consist of sensor record and user data sent and obtained from workstations. As the range of workstations and sensors keep growing, some information may face reminiscence, latency, channel boundaries, and network congestion problems. Within the last decade, many algorithms were proposed to avoid some of these issues. Amongst all algorithms, AI stays the best solution for data mining, network control, and congestion management.

Anurag Vijay Agrawal, Indian Institute of Technology, Roorkee, India
Lakshmana Phanendra Magulur, Koneru Lakshmaiah Education Foundation, India
S. Gayathri Priya, RMD Engineering College, India
Amanpreet Kaur, Chitkara University Institute of Engineering and Technology, Chitkara
University, India
Gurpreet Singh, Chitkara University Institute of Engineering and Technology, Chitkara
University, India
Sampath Boopathi, Muthayammal Engineering College, India

In precision agriculture (PA), the internet of things (IoT) and wireless sensor networks (WSN) can be utilised to more effectively monitor crop fields and make quick choices. The sensors can be installed in crop fields to gather pertinent data, but doing so uses up some of their limited energy. The use of IoT and WSN for smart precision agriculture necessitates energy-efficient operations, location-aware sensors, and secure localization techniques. In this chapter, agricultural problems are identified using IoT and WSN technologies to rectify them. Pests, a lack of water supply, and leaf diseases can be identified for best solutions through pest identification and classification, soil and water conservation, and leaf issues. The integration of Arduino and various sensors is used in the IoT and WSN to solve the issues automatically. Securing energy conservation can be achieved through IoT and sensor systems using efficient programmes.

B. Srinivas, Kakatiya Institute of Technology and Science, India
Lakshmana Phaneendra Maguluri, Koneru Lakshmaiah Education Foundation, India
K. Venkatagurunatham Naidu, Guntur Engineering College, India
L. Chandra Sekhar Reddy, CMR College of Engineering and Technology, India
M. Deivakani, PSNA College of Engineering and Technology, India
Sampath Boopathi, Muthayammal Engineering College, India

The integration of robot activities with cloud computing and the internet of things is essential to Industry 4.0 implementation. In the chapter, the fundamental principles of cloud computing and integrated robotics are explained. Emergence, characteristics, service delivery models, and computing models of robot-cloud computing principles have been discussed. Classical principles of service-oriented architecture, service models, web services, gSOAP, robotic operating systems, and challenges of robot cloud computing fields were illustrated. The main objective of this chapter is to illustrate cloud computing architecture frameworks. The architecture, platform, setup, and implementation principles of fixed and variable-length strings for cloud robotic frameworks have been briefly illustrated.

Preface

The term "Industry 4.0" (I4.0) refers to a recent industrial revolution in which a large number of sensors, actuators, and intelligent components are connected to Internet communication technologies to provide intelligent real-time applications. Disruptive innovations are now propelling I4.0 and presenting new opportunities for value generation in all major industry segments. I4.0 Technologies' innovations in cybersecurity and data science provide smart apps and services with accurate real-time monitoring and control. Through enhanced access to real-time information, it also aims to increase overall effectiveness, lower costs, and increase the efficiency of people, processes, and technology. Industry 4.0 technologies such as Cyber Physical Systems, Cloud Computing, Internet of Things, Artificial Intelligence, Smart Factories, Smart Manufacture, and Cognitive Computing, have already made it possible for a wide range of applications across multiple industries.

This book aims to introduce readers to cybersecurity, data science and its impact on the realization of the Industry 4.0 applications. The focus of the book is to cover the technological foundations of cybersecurity and data science within the scope of the Industry 4.0 landscape and to detail the existing cybersecurity and data science innovations with Industry 4.0 applications, as well as state-of-the-art solutions with regard to both academic research and practical implementations.

Academicians, Researchers, UG/PG students, Information Technology professionals, Technology aspirants will find this book useful in furthering their research exposure to pertinent topics in Industry 4.0 Technologies in furthering their own research efforts in this field.

The book is organized into twenty-seven chapters in three sections. A brief description of each of the chapters follows:

SECTION 1: DATA SCIENCE INNOVATIONS IN INDUSTRY 4.0

Chapter 1 establishes a futuristic analysis and applications of Artificial Intelligence (AI), and Data Science (DS) which includes fields like healthcare, education, building and construction, industrial design, and agriculture.

Chapter 2 presents key features, how industrial AI distinguishes itself within the field of AI, major components in Industrial AI, Industrial AI eco-system, various tools and traits of AI, cyber physical applications, AI Technologies and Tools, Industrial IoT (IIoT) and data analytics, benefits of adopting an Industry 4.0 Model, Benefits of Deploying AI models, Significant advancements and challenges of industrial artificial intelligence.

Chapter 3 provides a brief study about the identification of factors that affect successful software development and explores various sources of requirement risks. It intends to create an intelligent framework based on Artificial Intelligence for managing risks in software requirements. The framework includes a model for volatile requirement prioritization and a model for requirement ambiguity and uncertainty management.

Chapter 4 propose a study to compare the difference on Industry Revolution 4.0 technology adoption between developed, developing countries and Brunei Darussalam and their current interest and investment level for future adoption.

Chapter 5 discusses knowledge engineering to intellectualize higher education. Also, explains how knowledge engineering (KE) can be utilized to construct intelligent learning and smart tutoring systems (STSs).

Chapter 6 discusses the analysis of Campus Recruitment Data and Career Counseling in the Engineering Sector. This research can also assist career counselors in adjusting their offerings to meet the shifting demands of the labor market and guarantee that they are offering engineering students useful and pertinent advice.

Chapter 7 describes identification of student groups for smart tutoring and collaborative learning based on online activities using Neural networks. This work proposes an intelligent solution to group learners based on their outcomes and participation in various online assessment activities. This chapter considers the online assessment results of the learners and uses Kohonen Self – Organizing Map neural network (SOM) to group the learners.

Chapter 8 focuses on Industry 4.0 and the contemporary tendencies that it has spawned. The readers would gain knowledge on what Industry 4.0 is, how it affects current manufacturing technologies, and its potential in the future. The authors improve comprehension of the effects imposed by Industry 4.0 by using a bibliometric method. Using web-scraping Python code and the YouTube Data API, this is accomplished using randomly selected 45–50 YouTube videos and 25–30 Medium blogs.

Chapter 9 presents the survey on Information Diffusion models for Social Media Text. It becomes essential to monitor the rate of flow of information and stop spreading the fake or false message. The application of suitable graph network modelling and theories would support this research issue and recommend the appropriate model for the social media data.

Chapter 10 presents an Automated Text Summarization and Machine learning based Framework for Heart disease prediction. An automated summarization of text have been implemented using Sentence Scoring approach which includes finding the frequent terms and sentence ranking method . This technique mainly focuses on summarizing the medical reports.

Chapter 11 discusses the role of NLP in Travel and Tourism along with the challenges in this field. NLP tries to provide a hassle-free experience to the tourist and thus improves the revenue generation. It helps to streamline the business opportunities and benefits all the interconnected industries.

Chapter 12 elaborates the enhancement of Automatic Speech Recognition and Speech Translation Using Google Tran. This speech recognition model not only demonstrates technological proficiency, but also offers a helpful platform for those who have hearing challenges For those who have hearing impairments, speech recognition software would offer a comprehensive long-term answer because live speech-to-text translations will improve their communication skills.

Chapter 13 discusses how to predict the occurrence of a flood using the rainfall data and recommend nearby evacuation areas away from flood hazard areas. Providing the utmost safety has been the major idea in working on this chapter. Perfect accuracy for our rainfall data was obtained using the Random

Forest Algorithm. Five algorithms were chosen and applied to the training data set. Accuracy was found precisely while using Random Forest Algorithm.

SECTION 2: CYBERSECURITY INNOVATIONS IN INDUSTRY 4.0

Chapter 14 explores the Ethereum Blockchain. Consensus Mechanisms, Smart Contracts, Gas Fees, different security protocols, Web3 Wallets, Oracles are some of the concepts and features that make blockchains immutable and secure. This chapter covers major contemporary concepts and terms profoundly.

Chapter 15 explains about the building blockchain based infrastructure tracking donations. Based on blockchain technology, the system provides a clear accounting of donor performance, foundations of giving, and recipients. The donation channel should be available from the charity platform, which allows community users and donors to follow and monitor where, when, and to whom donations are made were released.

Chapter 16 highlights the issues on traditional production sectors, evaluation blockchain application in industry 4.0, limitations of blockchain, privacy and security requirements and adoption of blockchain inside this context of Industry 4.0.

Chapter 17 discusses the viability of utilizing blockchain for advanced metering infrastructure and the security risks and threat landscape. With the deployment of Advanced Metering Infrastructure (AMI) and distributed ledgers, blockchain may aid in safeguarding and facilitating the movement of data.

Chapter 18 explores various facets of CPSs and proposes a blockchain-based framework to offer a smart tourism eco-system, catering to the dynamic preferences and needs of the tourists. The key idea is to use a novel blockchain-based data security mechanism, which uses a set of policies to enforce data security for smart tourism services.

Chapter 19 gives a clear idea of what cyber-crime, its different types and cyber terrorism cause and types and how these are done and what is the main difference between cyber-crime and cyber terrorism. What precautions can be taken which may help a user from these attacks.

Chapter 20 describes the prevention and overcoming of cyberbullying. The impact of cyberbullying, preventive measures and law support are discussed.

Chapter 21 proposes to advance Data Security in software used in the domain of Healthcare and to make use of Electronic Health Records in an efficient way; Enabling quick and safe access to patient records for more coordinated, efficient care; Ensuring data security that should tackle the vulnerability.

SECTION 3: INDUSTRY 4.0 TECHNOLOGIES

Chapter 22 covers the fundamentals, effects, applications, restrictions, and potential future developments of Augmented Reality.

Chapter 23 provides detailed and thorough analysis of challenges in the Internet of Things domain, emphasizes flaws in current commercial IoT solutions and the importance of designing IoT solutions with security and privacy in mind.

Chapter 24 discusses the establishment of social relationship among IoT devices to maintain privacy and security requirement through trust management.

Chapter 25 insists that the deployment of AI in IoT also presents significant challenges, such as data privacy and security, ethical concerns and the need for robust and scalable infrastructure. These challenges must be addressed to ensure the responsible and effective deployment of AI in IoT.

In Chapter 26, agricultural problems are identified using IoT and WSN technologies to rectify them. Pests, a lack of water supply, and leaf diseases can be identified for best solutions through pest identification and classification, soil and water conservation, and leaf issues. The integration of Arduino and various sensors is used in the IoT and WSN to solve the issues automatically. Securing energy conservation can be achieved through IoT and sensor systems using efficient programmes.

Chapter 27 illustrates the cloud computing architecture frameworks. The architecture, platform, setup, and implementation principles of fixed and variable-length strings for cloud robotic frameworks are presented.

"The future is now," a common phrase used by the technology spearheads, has now become a thing to believe in. A technology which has been in the womb for almost a decade has now started to evolve and get into a prime shape. Data Science, Cybersecurity, and Industry 4.0 are technologies that have the potential to reshape the very rules which we have been fundamentally following to live. Overall, this book provides various research experiences of data science and cybersecurity Innovations in Industry 4.0 from researchers.

Thangavel Murugan
United Arab Emirates University, Al Ain, UAE

Nirmala E.
VIT Bhopal University, India

Acknowledgment

The editors would like to acknowledge the help of all the people involved in this project and, more specifically, to the authors and reviewers that took part in the review process. Without their support, this book would not have become a reality.

First, the editors would like to thank each one of the authors for their contributions. Our sincere gratitude goes to the chapter's authors who contributed their time and expertise to this book.

Second, the editors wish to acknowledge the valuable contributions of the reviewers regarding the improvement of quality, coherence, and content presentation of chapters. Most of the authors also served as referees; we highly appreciate their double task.

Section 1
Data Science Innovations in Industry 4.0

Chapter 1
Application of Artificial Intelligence and Data Science Across Domains:
A Perspective Study

R. K. Kavitha

Kumaraguru College of Technology, India

W. Jaisingh

Presidency University, India

V. Kaarthiekheyan

Kumaraguru College of Technology, India

ABSTRACT

The advent of artificial intelligence (AI) and data sciences has disrupted our society in terms of fast and proactive technical development. The field of artificial intelligence embeds itself with multidisciplinary proficiency where the ultimate objective is to systematize all human actions and responses that currently need human intelligence. On the other hand, data science is a trending field that rationally tries to solve complicated problems. In addition, data science enables the mining of knowledge from data which includes the study of theories and techniques to collect, process and communicate with data during its life cycle once the data is obtained. This chapter establishes a futuristic analysis and applications of artificial intelligence (AI) and data science (DS), which includes fields like healthcare, education, building and construction, industrial design, and agriculture. Ironically, AI in industrial design remains unexplored in enhancing the utility, benefit, and aesthetics of manufactured goods to enhance client satisfaction.

DOI: 10.4018/978-1-6684-8145-5.ch001

Copyright © 2023, IGI Global. Copying or distributing in print or electronic forms without written permission of IGI Global is prohibited.

INTRODUCTION

The science and engineering of developing intelligent machines is what is known as artificial intelligence (AI) (McCarthy, 2007). A subfield of computer science called artificial intelligence (AI) integrates machine learning, algorithm design, and natural language processing (Akgun & Greenhow, 2021). Like the exponential expansion that database technology witnessed in the late 20th century, this technology has grown to be highly well-known in the modern era and is currently expanding at a breakneck pace. The foundational technology that powers enterprise-level software is now databases. Similarly, during the next few decades, it is anticipated that AI will account for the majority of new value added in software. In the simplest type of AI, computers are taught to "imitate" human behaviour utilizing a wealth of data from prior instances of the same behaviour. AI enables machines to operate effectively and quickly evaluate massive volumes of data, finding solutions through supervised, unsupervised, or reinforced learning. Artificial intelligence can be a very effective tool for big businesses that produce a lot of data (Cassel, Lillian & Dicheva 2016). It is now a crucial component of technology. Automating tasks that previously would have required human intelligence is one of the primary goals of AI. Gains in efficiency can be made by reducing the number of labour resources an organization has to use on a project or the amount of time a person needs to spend on repetitive chores. For instance, medical assistant AI can be used to detect diseases based on patients' symptoms, while chatbots can be used to answer customer service concerns.

Utilizing data analysis and analytics is at the heart of data science (where it uses past and present data to predict future data). Data collection, analysis, and decision-making are all part of data science. Data science is the in-depth analysis of a vast amount of data, which entails extracting some useful information from the raw, structured, and unstructured data in order to uncover patterns in the data, through analysis, and make predictions for the future. Businesses can improve their decision-making by utilising data science. Large amounts of data are structured and stored using big data analytics so that they may be quickly accessible and analysed for better decision-making (Corsi & de Souza, 2020). Processing of data, which can be done using statistical techniques and algorithms, scientific methodologies, various technologies, etc., is required in order to extract useful data from massive data sets. It extracts useful information from unstructured data using a variety of tools and methods. The Future of Artificial Intelligence refers to data science. Real-time data from online sources like social media have been extensively collected using big data. To get better outcomes, researchers commonly combine data science and artificial intelligence methods. Contrarily, numerous research studies asserted that big data has a considerable impact on the domains of decision support systems and predictive analytics. Patterns in enormous data sets can be found by AI and data science that are not visible to the human eye. In this approach, the application of AI and Data Science technologies can add value to even commonplace and superficially unimportant data. This work consolidates most of the trending and recent applications in the field of Artificial Intelligence. Also, the key issues and trends have been discussed.

STATE-OF-THE-ART REVIEW

The current period is being taken over by artificial intelligence and data science, which is transforming it into a revolutionary step. Fast-moving computing technologies and a wide range of paradigm-shifting evolutionary concepts are all around us, making the world a much better bubble in which to live and observe the countless future excursions (Shakirov & Solovyeva, 2018). Deep learning, data science, and AI together have created a wide range of options. AI will have a big impact on the future advantages that humans might experience (Abd Aziz & Adnan, 2021). The AI-powered computer can gather, assimilate, and process data considerably more quickly than humans. Without typing a single word, you may use speech recognition software to find the closest ice cream shop or place a pizza order thanks to the usage of AI and various efforts by smartphone makers. Artificial neural networks were developed to further the comprehension that computers have of your speech. Google is happy to have used improved deep learning and data science algorithms that ensure consumers see material that is judged appropriate for them. The search engine searches through more than a billion pages to rank the ones that are best for you first and utilises machine learning algorithms to gather a wealth of information about what people are searching for Rav Panchalingam and Ka C. Chan (2021). This entire process takes only a few microseconds. Spread, a lettuce-producing company, has disclosed its plans to outfit robots for managing business inside the farms. Robots will significantly improve efficiency by picking 30,000 heads of lettuce every day. These robots' processors have been provided a huge amount of data on the lettuce harvesting procedure. This AI revolution will not only boost productivity but also create new opportunities.

Relationship Between Data Science and AI

All the disciplines needed to make sense of enormous amounts of data can be thought of as falling under the umbrella of data science. Whether they are ML-based or DL-based, clever AI products are built on a foundation of data science research. Data science is a field of science that is constantly developing with the goal of comprehending data (both structured and unstructured) and looking for the insights it contains. As shown in Figure 1, data science makes use of huge data as well as a variety of research, techniques, tools, and technologies, including machine learning, artificial intelligence (AI), deep learning, and data mining (Shwartz-Ziv, Ravid, & Amitai Armon, 2022). Data analysis, statistics, mathematics, programming, as well as data visualisation and interpretation, are heavily used in this scientific subject. Everything discussed enables data scientists to draw value and useful business insights from data and make informed decisions based on it. Massive volumes of data are used by data scientists to interpret it. Data scientists may gather, process, and analyse data to draw conclusions and make predictions based on uncovered insights with the correct data analytics technologies in place.

Data Mining

Data pre-processing and actual data mining are the two steps that make up the data mining process. Data mining is concerned with identifying patterns and representing information in data in a way that is clear and understandable. It includes steps like data purification, data integration, and data transformation. The entire data mining process is shown in Figure 2. Data mining is frequently seen as a subset of the larger area of Knowledge Discovery in Databases (KDD). When working on AI projects, data mining is also frequently used (Shwartz-Ziv, Ravid, & Amitai Armon, 2022).

Figure 1. Relationship between AI, DS, DL, and ML

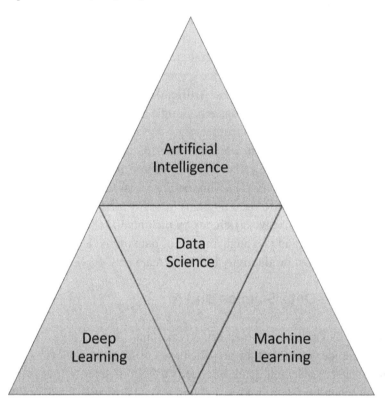

Figure 2. Data mining process

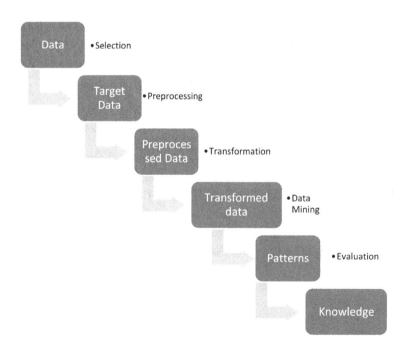

Machine Learning and Its Types

A collection of techniques, instruments, and computer algorithms known as machine learning are used to teach computers to evaluate, comprehend, spot hidden patterns in data, and make predictions (Chen et al., 2020). The ultimate goal of machine learning is to use data for self-learning, do away with explicit machine programming. Machines that have been trained on datasets can apply learned patterns to fresh data, improving predictions.

- With the aid of humans who gather and identify data and then "feed" it to systems, machines are educated to find solutions to a specific problem through the process of supervised learning. The data qualities that a machine should focus on are specified so that it may identify patterns, classify items into appropriate groups, and assess whether its prediction was accurate or not.
- With unsupervised learning, computers develop the ability to spot patterns and trends in unlabeled training data without human supervision.
- Models are trained using both supervised and unsupervised learning in semi-supervised learning, which uses a small amount of labelled data and a significantly larger amount of unlabelled data.

Deep Learning

A form of machine learning called "deep learning" uses complex neural networks that were first motivated by the organic neural networks in human brains (Preface, 2021). Nodes in neural networks are arranged in several interconnected layers and communicate with one another to process massive amounts of input data.

There are many different kinds of neural networks, including convolutional, recursive, and recurrent neural networks. The input layer, numerous hidden layers, and the output layer are all stacked on top of one another to make up a conventional neural network.

Artificial Intelligence

AI is about creating a functional data product that can solve set tasks by itself, which remotely resembles human problem-solving. In traditional terms, artificial intelligence or AI is simply an algorithm, code, or technique that enables machines to mimic, develop, and demonstrate human cognition or behavior. In the business world, AI is a real-life data product capable of carrying out set tasks and solving problems roughly the same as humans do. The functions of AI systems encompass learning, planning, reasoning, decision making, and problem-solving.

Machine learning falls within an AI system that can self-learn based on algorithms and previously learned patterns. Deep learning is a kind of machine learning, but this approach uses neural networks for making predictions based on processed data (Ahmed et al., 2021). Most AI work involves either ML or DL since the so-called "intelligent" behavior of machines requires massive knowledge, which, in turn, requires data science and data mining research.

Research in AI and Data Science

AI is about developing a useful data product that can perform certain tasks on its own and, in some ways, mirrors how people solve problems. Artificial intelligence (AI), as it is often known, is just an algorithm, code, or technique that enables machines to imitate, develop, and exhibit human cognition or behaviour. In the business world, artificial intelligence (AI) is a real-world data product capable of performing predetermined tasks and resolving issues roughly in the same way as humans do. Learning, planning, reasoning, decision-making, and problem-solving are all functions of AI systems (Ahmed et al., 2021).

An AI system that can self-learn based on algorithms and previously discovered patterns is referred to as machine learning. While deep learning is a form of machine learning, this method makes predictions based on analysed data using neural networks. Since the so-called "intelligent" behaviour of machines necessitates huge knowledge, which in turn necessitates data science and data mining research, the majority of AI work involves either ML or DL.

AI AND DATA SCIENCE IN BUILDING AND CONSTRUCTION INDUSTRY

Introduction

In order to further improve the effectiveness, productivity, accuracy, and safety of built environments, the building and construction industry is slowly but steadily evolving and embracing new technologies such as the Digital Twin (DT), Building Information Modeling (BIM), Artificial Intelligence (AI), Internet of Things (IoTs), and Smart Vision (SV) (Jimenez-Martinez & Alfaro-Ponce, 2019). The term "Industry 4.0," often known as the "fourth industrial revolution," describes how cutting-edge digital technologies are being used to transform conventional business procedures and manufacturing techniques into autonomous smart systems. In a similar vein, the "building and construction industry 4.0" can be defined as the fusion of cutting-edge industrial production systems, cyber-physical systems, and digital and computing technologies to redefine the design, construction, operation, and maintenance of buildings and infrastructure while taking circularity into consideration (Mandal, 2017). Cyber-physical systems would include IoT, robots, cobots, actuators, and blockchain. Digital and computing technologies would include BIM, AI, deep learning (DL), machine learning (ML), cloud computing, big data and data analytics, blockchain, augmented reality (AR), and digital twins. Industrial production systems would also include 3D printing and assembly, prefabrication, and offsite manufacturing. Massive amounts of data are produced as a result of this digital transformation, and systematic analysis of these data combined with predictive modelling can be used to create creative architectural and structural designs, improve operational and construction safety, lower operational and construction costs, speed up construction, shorten payback times, and increase sustainability. However, it is not practical for humans or traditional computer programmes to analyse enormous amounts of data and identify patterns using rule-based approaches. Therefore, one of the primary drivers of the building and construction sector 4.0's ability to process its digital data is AI's ability to process enormous volumes of data, spot patterns, and build large-scale statistical models (Mallela, 2016). The term "artificial intelligence" (AI) was first used in the 1940s, and it is generally understood to refer to the study of creating intelligent robots or computer programmes that resemble human intelligence. The application of artificial intelligence (AI) has significantly advanced during the past few years in a number of fields, including computer vision, robotics, autonomous cars, language translation, gaming, medical diagnosis, speech recognition, and generative designs. Machine learning and deep learning are the main technologies that underpin these developments. In the branch of AI known as machine learning, predictions are based on prior data. Using the input data, machine learning may change the data in meaningful ways and discover insightful patterns and representations. A subset of machine learning known as "deep learning" can be defined as a machine learning technique having numerous layers of easy-to-use computational components (Tan, 2017). Neural networks are a stack of layers commonly used in deep learning. Due to the increase in computing power, deep learning with a stack of Convolution Neural Networks (CNN) is a frequently utilised methodology today (Padil et al., 2017). This method is extensively employed in the fields of machine translation, speech recognition, picture synthesis, and object recognition in visual and audio formats. The areas of AI, ML, DL, and commonly utilised algorithms are listed as follows. CNN stands for Convolutional Neural Networks, RNN stands for Recurrent Neural Network, LSTM is for Long Short-Term Memory Network, and RBFN stands for Radial Basis Function Network (Zhang & Akiyama, 2021). In the building and construction sector, AI, ML, and DL have a wide range of applications. The majority of these applications only recently became a reality as a result of increased computational power provided by high-performing graphics processing units (GPU), the availability of advanced ML and DL algorithms, and the relative ease with which these algorithms can be implemented using widely used computer languages, ML and DL libraries, and software.

Structural Analysis and Design

Once the construction material has been chosen, AI algorithms can help with the structural analysis and design processes. Commonly, analytical models derived from fundamental principles, codes of practise, or computer simulations based on numerical simulations, like Finite Element Analysis, are used in structural design (FEA). The biggest obstacle to integrating AI algorithms in actual structural engineering design is their black box character. The advantages of AI in resolving these uncertainties, however, outweigh the drawback of black box nature in some ambiguous and unexpected design difficulties where designs are based on statistical analysis and probabilistic theories. The use of artificial intelligence (AI) to enhance specific facets of structural engineering is covered in this section. Among the subjects covered are seismic design, buckling and fatigue analysis, loading capacity prediction, and damage level prediction of existing structures for retrofitting. The benefits of novel elements like generative design, which offer more design options than conventional design methods, for structural design are also explored. The performance of conventional seismic load and response models for structures is impacted by the complexity of seismic events, which also hinders the development of seismology as a whole. It is challenging to effectively identify the earthquake response and extract indicative features from continuously detected seismic data (Torky & Aburawwash, 2018). Utilizing their advantages in data analysis, AI techniques can help with this and be utilised as efficient statistical tools to handle these challenges. AI assists in the discovery of undiscovered features by separating meaningful sensing information from noisy data and exposing seismic events that are below the detection threshold. The application of AI to assist in architecture design using seismology knowledge is a crucial additional factor. Failure of the structural system that was not properly taken into account during the architectural design phase results in unanticipated alterations during the project execution phase, which costs time and money (Yoo et al., 2021). An Irregularity Control Assistant (IC Assitant), which may provide architects with general information regarding the acceptability of structural system decisions, can be built using deep learning and the ImageAI Python package to get around this (Güçlüer & Ozbeyaz, 2021). AI algorithms and models can also be used to enhance the analysis of buckling and fatigue of structural components. Using a neural network technique, Jimenez-Martinez and Alfaro-Ponce (2019) investigated the fatigue of steel components. In terms of structural member instability, an artificial neural network technique was used to forecast the buckling behaviour of structural elements under axial stress for a number of geometries, including shells (Chou & Tsai, 2014), panels (Bui et al., 2018), and I-section beams (Chen et al., 2009). AI can also be used to increase the loading capacity and damage level prediction in existing structures for retrofitting. Non-probabilistic artificial neural network models based on vibration data were utilized by Tan et al. (2017) and Padil et al. to locate and quantify damage in steel beams. Atici et al. (2011) have reviewed the use of vibration-based damage detection from conventional approaches to machine learning and deep learning in more detail. Since cracks and damage sustained during assembly are hard to quantify, determining the flexural loading capability of existing RC structures is complicated. Because of the high cost involved, retrofitting is typically done to be safe. In one work, Zhang et al. (2021) employed machine learning approaches to estimating the steel weight loss distribution from the observed corrosion-induced crack distribution of RC beams, which may subsequently be utilised to forecast flexural load. AI algorithms can be used to perform automated generative design and analysis based on deep learning. Automated structural analysis and design of prestressed members can be accomplished utilizing a deep learning approach. For instance, optimal member prestressing can be predicted using deep learning and grid search-accessible hyperparameters, eliminating the need for structural engineers to do infinite analysis and design iterations.

Material Design and Optimization

Once the architectural design process is complete, choosing the right building material becomes crucial. Using AI approaches, high-performing materials and composites can be created and developed taking these factors into account. Construction materials have an impact on the speed of construction, durability, strength, energy efficiency, emission, aesthetics, and thermal comfort of the structure (2013). Current studies to construct ML-based models that predict mechanical properties were carried out by researchers in order to reduce material consumption, costs, and testing time. Currently available technologies with AI applications frequently target the microstructure and material qualities of concrete, steel, and wood. Concrete has been extensively studied and is the most common building material worldwide (Bilim, 2011). Numerous studies have been done using ANN, DL, SVM, GA, and fuzzy logic to predict concrete behaviour. In the past few years, there has been an increase in interest in ANN and DL applications for predicting the properties of fibre reinforced polymers (FRP), recycled concrete aggregate (RCA), and permeable pavements (Chen et al., 2018). Concrete's durability characteristics have also been extensively researched utilising AI systems. In this field, researchers have looked into concrete durability issues such forecasting carbonation depth, concrete property prediction under sulphate assault and chloride penetration. Optimizing the use and design of concrete, wood, and steel based on an objective purpose and numerous restrictions presents the main problem. This process of forecasting various objective functions based on historical data can be helped by ML and DL algorithms. A single objective function or several objective functions can be used for optimization. Cost, performance requirements like compressive strength and shear strength, and environmental criteria like embodied carbon and embodied emissions are typically included in these objective functions (Ahmad & Farooq, 2021). The optimization problem has a number of limitations that might be imposed by the designer, the needs of the client, or building codes. These constraints are based on various decision factors. Due to its composite composition with numerous constituents, concrete is the construction material optimised the most. The majority of optimizations are carried out primarily by means of optimization algorithms, such as linear programming, second-order conic optimization, metaheuristic optimization methods, and ML/DL is mostly used for property prediction as part of the optimization process. Applications of ML/DL in material optimization have primarily focused on improving cost, strength, and environmental performance. DL/ML can help with the microstructural, surface, and bond properties examination of building materials. Also utilised in the majority of these investigations were ANN.

Opportunities and Challenges

New technologies present a variety of opportunities for construction projects. It gives companies a competitive advantage by lowering costs and increasing efficiency. Adaptive manufacturing is a growing concept that introduces flexible machines capable of customizing part productions and enabling new cost-effective building methods. This novel strategy leads to the potential alteration of occupations by merging planning, design, and construction responsibilities. To adopt new technologies into their projects effectively, it is crucial for users to recognize the advantages and performance enhancements that AI may bring to a construction site. AI can be used for estimating and scheduling resources, site analytics, supply chain management, and health and safety. Initial costs, cultural difficulties, security, and information exchange may be obstacles.

Summary

Numerous applications of AI, ML, and DL have been made to monitoring and enhancing construction safety, and the majority of the research in this area makes use of neural networks. Similar to this, ANN was employed to analyse data from wearable sensors used by employees when manually lifting loads in order to predict the factor of safety for slope stabilization during construction. To instruct employees to wear earplugs, devised automated training. Also, ANNs were used to forecast future safety issues and to forecast the outcomes of construction-related mishaps. In addition, SVM was used to analyse complex scaffolding structures in real-time and evaluate the safety of the scaffolds, and was used it in conjunction with linear discriminant analysis (LDA), ANN, and k-nearest neighbour to analyse cloud data. These project areas included safety management and construction management. Models were developed for predicting dangerous conduct by examining the association between the cognitive components and behavioural data, using SVM in addition to other ML methods. If an incident has already occurred or there are enough signs present in a construction project to forecast an occurrence, NLP was used to analyse databases and predict the consequences of safety mishaps. In order to assess accident antecedents from injury reports and to predict an incident's result once it has already happened, NLP was employed in conjunction with CNNs. To understand data from smart construction objects (sensors), it was planned to integrate the Case-Based Reasoning (CBR) and Rule-based Reasoning (RBR) methods. The result was an OHS management system. In a similar manner, CBR was used to enhance hazard identification and management throughout a worker's routine tasks of recognizing hazards and choosing suitable mitigations. The tracking of construction equipment has also been extensively studied using AI algorithms], and the majority of these investigations utilized CNN. This can guarantee both the productivity of operations and the safety of the workforce. Commercially available cutting-edge technologies offer onsite safety monitoring, predictive analytics, and best practices recommendations for improved construction safety.

AI AND DATA SCIENCE IN HEALTH CARE

Introduction

Healthcare has traditionally been a data-driven industry. The care process within and between businesses is driven by the information flow from patients to doctors and the sharing of choices, instructions, and information among the care providers. Information and statistics have long played a significant role in decision-making and the delivery of healthcare (Raghupathi & Raghupathi, 2014). As healthcare becomes more digitised, enormous amounts of data are also produced by sectors other than hospitals and healthcare providers, such as medical insurance, medical equipment, life sciences, and medical research. There is currently a huge amount of data available, which has the potential to support numerous medical and healthcare operations. On the clinical front, advanced analytics, machine learning, and artificial intelligence techniques are opening up a variety of opportunities for turning this data into insightful knowledge that can be used to support decision-making, deliver high-quality patient care, respond to urgent situations, and save more lives; and on the operational and financial fronts, optimise resource use, enhance processes and services, and lower costs (Bates et al., 2014). Healthcare stakeholders can harness the power of data by using analytical approaches to analyse past data (descriptive analytics), forecast future results (predictive analytics), and determine the best course of action for the present situation (prescriptive analytics) (Mohammed, 2014; Wang & Hajli, 2017). In the past, clinical practitioners treated patients based on the few information that was accessible to them and their prior experiences. Today's accessibility to data from various sources provides the chance to have a comprehensive view of patient health. Utilizing cutting-edge technologies over this data also makes it possible to give the proper care by allowing access to the right information at the right time and place (Kayyali & Knott, 2013). The majority of healthcare data is unstructured, including static data from patient records, diagnostic pictures, and reports, as well as dynamic data from bedside monitors or remote patient monitoring. Big data analytics and artificial intelligence can process this data to produce insightful findings that are essential to preserving the lives of patients. On the other hand, by examining disease trends and monitoring disease outbreaks, this technology also offers a significant potential for enhancing population health management (Knowledgent, 2016). Big data analytics and artificial intelligence are used in life sciences and medical research in addition to having an effect on overall patient care. The development of new therapeutic choices is expanded by molecular data analysis. Bringing together and analysing genetic and clinical data creates another potential to develop personalised therapy. To find genetic disease markers, create new medications, and evaluate their effectiveness, predictive analytical models can be applied to omics data (Gutierrez, 2016). Big-data Clinical Trials (BCT), which provide researchers with access to a huge sample of data, will supplement and complement Randomized Controlled Trials (RCT) in the field of clinical research (Harpaz & DuMochel, 2016). Thus, using cutting-edge data analytics and machine learning techniques, researchers can now plan future clinical trials based on hypotheses derived from data analysis (Hudis, 2015), evaluate the outcomes of clinical trials, and identify potential risks and side effects of products before they are released for use (Alemayehu & Berger, 2016). These developing strategies are receiving more and more attention in healthcare research and practise because to their enormous potential to improve the standard of healthcare. The use of big data analytics and artificial intelligence in healthcare has been influenced by a number of research, but the literature is still mainly fragmented. A systematic mapping research was conducted to gain a thorough grasp of the potential applications of these technologies in healthcare. A systematic mapping research is thought to be relevant given the wealth and diversity of available material in this field (Kitchenham & Charters, 2007).

Data Mining and Big Data in Healthcare

Data mining is important in the healthcare industry since it aids in decisions regarding the treatment of various diseases as well as in areas like insurance and billing. As a result, it will ease the strain on patients and aid medical professionals in providing patients with better care. Generally speaking, data mining will assist in mining both category and numerical data (Brownlee, 2019). The use of machine learning to data mining will aid doctors and patients by improving health care performance with the highest level of accuracy in predicting illnesses. It will be difficult to diagnose diseases because medical clinic data structures are largely designed for billing goals rather than clinical ones. Again, it will be a laborious effort to transform paper data into digital data because the previous patient data is paper-based rather than digital. Unsupervised learning and supervised learning are the two main categories in data mining. Here, classification will fall under supervised learning because it can be highly useful for classifying diseases based on different symptoms in the medical field. A variety of data mining techniques, including Decision Trees (SSenthilkumar & Rai, 2018) and Support Vector Machines (SVM), can be used to more accurately estimate deaths in the healthcare industry. When identifying patients who are at danger, Support Vector Machines in particular will be essential, but it will take longer than other techniques like the Naive Bayes Classification methodology. In contrast to these methods, the ensemble approach would be considerably more successful because it can be used to compare the classification accuracy of different classifiers. If the class label is known, supervised learning algorithms can be used efficiently for categorization. However, one can no longer use categorization algorithms if the data is vast and unclassified. In that scenario, since the class label is uncertain, clustering techniques (Chen & Yixue, 2017) are used. Because clustering may be used for individual variables, it is possible to group data based on how similar and dissimilar they are, making it simpler to classify groups of data than individual ones. As there is no class label for disease, clustering algorithms can be used efficiently to analyse the symptoms of numerous known diseases. Generally, when compared to objects outside the cluster, things inside the cluster will have a high degree of resemblance. The closest resemblance between two sets of things can be determined using one of the many clustering approaches that already exist, such as hierarchical clustering algorithms, allowing one to gauge the degree of similarity between the objects. But if the data set is too big, these strategies are not practical. Given that the hierarchical clustering technique requires a significant amount of system memory to allocate space for objects, the time complexity is relatively high. Partitional clustering techniques help address the drawbacks of hierarchical clustering. Here, items can be divided into k groups based on how similar they are by determining their mean or median using the K-means and Kmedoids algorithms. The same synergy can be used in healthcare to identify commonalities among distinct disease symptoms. Finding more accurate clusters over huge data sets is the main benefit of partitioning techniques over other algorithms. The relationship between multiple items can be detected using association rule method, i.e., Apriori algorithm to extract association rules from real data bases, although outcomes were dependent on initial centroid clusters to some extent as the centroids will be generated randomly. Generally speaking, the Apriori algorithm requires two sorts of inputs, such as support and confidence, in order to uncover often occurring patterns for more accurate disease diagnosis. In the end, the main goal of all these algorithms is to forecast various diseases by gathering patient data from multiple sources (Chen & Wang, 2017). The redundant attributes must be found during the feature selection process while choosing the patient's various attributes. The relationship between dependent and independent variables may change during this process. Nevertheless, outliers must be removed, especially when clustering items because the outcome would have an impact on patient data. Data mining offers several opportunities for fraud detection in the healthcare industry because it is possible to use a wide range of classification techniques to patient data in order to forecast a variety of diseases, which ultimately results in significant cost savings. By ranking patients according to their risk of contracting certain diseases, this categorization (Wu & Cheng, 2017) will assist in providing rankings for patients. The goal of this is to locate patients who are in the early stages and who can benefit from better therapy, which lowers the overall cost of care. Because there is often limited information available regarding diseases in their early stages, clustering can frequently be used in the healthcare industry. Applying Association mining algorithms can efficiently specify the relationship between different medications and diseases. These data mining algorithms can be efficiently used in the biomedical and healthcare industries, allowing for the prediction of disease diagnoses, the detection of insurance claim fraud (Huda & Yearwood, 2017), as well as the length of hospital stays, which significantly lowers the cost of care. Data mining will enable simultaneous examination of multiple regions and reduce the amount of time needed to discover diseases in the healthcare system. In addition to this, affinity analysis will aid in understanding how future events will likely link to past ones. Affinity analysis is particularly useful in healthcare for identifying co-occurring patient indications and symptoms. By analysing previous data that has been gathered from a variety of sources, data mining can be used to forecast a patient's future health. Therefore, using historical data and effective data mining tools, clinical choices can be made. Because patients must undergo so many tests, it is very important to forecast cardiac disease, hence mining previous data will aid in doing so. In the field of healthcare, neural networks are extremely important for diagnosing various disorders. In addition to this, Bayesian networks (Huda & Yearwood, 2017) will have an effect on patient characteristics that will influence the classification of diseases. Data mining will assist in identifying high risk patients, allowing for the tracking of various diseases and a consequent decrease in the number of hospital admissions. Traditional data mining approaches will eventually become obsolete due to the exponential growth of data because performance is a key factor in extracting knowledge from massive amounts of data. In addition to the aforementioned uses, data mining can be used to obtain DNA information by testing DNA databases against different disorders. Data mining will be crucial in the fight against diseases like diabetes because it affects other serious illnesses. Big data is a solution that uses the Hadoop framework to handle all challenges as a result of the tremendous growth in data.

Hospitals are having a lot of trouble handling patients as the patient population is growing daily. Estimating the number of beds needed for patients daily is a significant problem for hospitals because both the admission and discharge of patients are uncertain. Here, daily forecasting is necessary to determine how many beds are needed for the patients who were admitted to the separate hospitals. But given the wide variations in daily hospital admissions and discharges, predicting is one of the biggest challenges. To optimise bed reservations and patient admission scheduling, which will lessen the uncertainty in allocating beds for the number of patients, time series forecasting (Xie & Schreier, 2015) can be of great assistance. One must reserve beds in forecasting for patients who are experiencing emergencies as well as for backlogged admission requests. These details will enable them to estimate the number of beds needed the next day. Effectively implementing planned discharged policy in hospitals will allow group leaders of each specialty unit to submit the discharged master plan of their patients as well as the number of beds still available for today, allowing for the estimation of the number of discharged patients for the following day. However, patients who were scheduled for discharge cannot be released for a variety of reasons, such as a change in their sickness, a failure to receive payment, etc. The overestimation of bed capacity may also cause delays in admitting patients who are experiencing emergencies and large cost overruns. Several models, including the SPARIMA model, which can be used to capture the weekday effect, and the ARIMA model, which is prepared to handle the regression surplus, were employed to forecast daily discharges. In addition, MSARIMA-Markov chain type models perform better at forecasting when there are more fluctuations.

Opportunities and Challenges

It is believed that AI will play a significant role in the future of healthcare services. In the form of machine learning, it is the driving force behind the creation of precision medicine, a much-needed advancement in medical care. Although early efforts to provide diagnosis and treatment recommendations proved difficult, we anticipate that artificial intelligence will eventually master this domain as well. Given the rapid development of AI for imaging analysis, it is likely that the majority of radiology and pathology images will be analyzed by a computer at some time. Speech and text recognition are currently used for tasks such as patient communication and the capture of clinical notes, and their application will increase. The major hurdle for AI in many healthcare sectors is not whether the technologies will be effective, but rather guaranteeing their adoption in routine clinical practice. There are also numerous ethical implications associated with the usage of AI in healthcare. In the past, almost all healthcare decisions were made by humans, and the use of intelligent machines to make or assist with such decisions raises questions of accountability, transparency, permission, and privacy.

Summary and Discussion

Every human being now needs health analysis more than ever before due to the drastic changes in global living standards. When it comes to health analysis, prediction is necessary at every level because it can be difficult to diagnose diseases in a short amount of time. Patients must also have a lot of patience because they must undergo numerous tests in order to determine the sort of disease they are experiencing. In health analysis, it is necessary to forecast a range of patient outcomes, including nonnegative, continuous, binary, and count outcomes. Since all of these possibilities are restricted to events of the same types, it is exceedingly difficult to anticipate all of them at once. Correlation must be used for all outcomes in order to provide equal results. Since predicting each result separately is substantially more expensive, multi-outcome prediction is absolutely necessary. Multi-task learning (MTL), where each outcome is considered as a separate activity, must be used in multi-outcome prediction. In addition to MTL, multivariate decision trees can be used, allowing for the application of many outcomes of any type as long as the results are identical. Since there is no method for anticipating which patients would spend how many days in the hospital, it is becoming increasingly difficult to track bogus insurance claims in the health care sector. Big data will be extremely important in identifying patients who stay at least one day by utilising different methods like decision tree algorithms. A growing portion of the health care sector, insurance is in higher demand as the population grows. However, the majority of health institutions make misleading claims since there is no adequate tracking system for identifying the right patients. Because the data sets are so huge and contain information about all patients, including historical and present information, getting patient information across departments has become a difficult undertaking. Even though it can be used for all sorts of outcomes, multiple outcome predictions cannot be managed for mixed type outcomes.

AI AND DATA SCIENCE IN EDUCATION

Introduction

The importance of AI development has been emphasised mostly in secondary and higher education, but little research has been done at the kindergarten level (Su et al., 2022). Children in their earliest years of life can engage with tablets and toys that have orders of magnitude more computational power than personal computers just a decade ago because the younger generation now has robots in their homes and intelligent agents in their wallets. The number of studies on early childhood AI education has increased recently (Williams & Park, 2019; Kewalramani & Kidman, 2021). Use PopBots, knowledge-based systems, supervised machine learning, and generative AI, for instance, to instruct kids on AI principles. The literature currently available, however, does not contain enough research on early childhood education AI programmes. AI in elementary school is considerably different from AI in secondary and higher education. AI in kindergarten mostly concentrates on fundamental ideas and easy AI exercises (e.g., drawing concept maps and AI framing). However, programming (using tools like Scratch and Google Teachable Machine) and difficult topics are where most AI in secondary and higher education is concentrated. Children in kindergarten should learn AI. Learning AI in kindergarten has a lot of advantages. Children's computational thinking and problem-solving abilities, for instance, were improved by AI activities, and AI knowledge was increased through AI curricula. Additionally, young children who played with the AI robot developed their creative, emotional, and collaborative inquiry literacy skills. We therefore strongly advise kindergarteners to learn AI. "The sum of all direct and indirect experiences, activities, and events that occur within a setting intended to support children's learning and development" is what is meant by the phrase "curriculum". Goals or objectives, material or subject matter, methods or procedures, and evaluation and assessment are the four possible divisions of a curriculum (Scott, 2008). Numerous academic studies have demonstrated the benefits of high-quality early childhood education for kids' academic success or their relationships with teachers (Muijs et al., 2004). Governments and legislators around the world have started incorporating computational thinking into the curriculum starting in the earliest grades to ensure high-quality early childhood education. Numerous studies have shown that utilising coding or programming applications can assist youngsters develop their computational thinking abilities and help them reason and communicate in an increasingly digital world (Egert et al., 2018). Research has expressed that the contemporary computational participation that includes students who code not just for the sake of coding but also to create games, stories, and animations to share; an increase in the number of young people participating in programming communities; challenges in the practises and ethical use of programming; and students moving beyond stationary screens to programmable toys, tools, and textiles (Wesley & Buysse, 2010). We found that there are no methodologies that are advised for AI teaching and learning for children, despite the fact that early AI studies are advantageous for children's cognitive, intellectual, and social development. We advise adopting problem-based learning as a teaching technique for group projects as a result. The qualities of critical thinking, problem solving, and cooperation can all be improved through problem-based learning. As a result, it is necessary to develop early AI curricula, teaching strategies, assessment ideas, and future directions.

Classification and Regression

Data scientists utilise a variety of machine learning techniques to identify patterns in huge data that result in insights that can be put into practise. Based on how they "learn" from data to create predictions, these various algorithms can be broadly divided into two groups: supervised learning and unsupervised learning. Both classification and regression are within the supervised machine learning category. Both methods use well-known datasets (also known as training datasets) to produce predictions, which is a similar idea.

A formula, $y = f$, is used in supervised learning to learn the mapping function from the input variable (x) to the output variable (y) (X).

In order to forecast the output variable (y) for the dataset whenever there is new input data (x), the goal of this task is to approximate the mapping function (f) as accurately as feasible. Regression methods in machine learning try to calculate the mapping function (f) from the input variables (x) to the discrete or continuous output variables (y). Y is a real value in this instance, which can either be an integer or a floating point value. Regression prediction issues therefore typically include quantities or sizes.

Teachers can use educational data mining to filter information and build performance models of students' work that predict achievement. A crucial idea in educational data mining is student modelling, which describes a qualitative description of students' behaviour that may be applied to decision-making regarding instruction. Models can represent a variety of things, including content knowledge, problem-solving abilities, learning styles, student emotions and attitudes, experience or self-confidence, mistakes and misunderstandings, and the outcomes of actions or intermediate results. Classes, clusters, associations, and sequential patterns are the four types of relationships between data that data mining looks for. The performance that may be obtained in a certain application area, the degree of results correctness, or the model's understandability are some examples of the elements that influence the algorithm to be utilised. Perhaps the two mining tasks that are used the most commonly when mining huge data sets are classification and clustering. Because classification is a supervised learning process, the algorithm builds a model that places new, unforeseen cases in established classes after learning from examples that are presented. Each example includes prior knowledge as a pair of input vector data traits or features and a value or label designating the class to which the example belongs. The base classifiers used to categorise brand-new, previously unexplored data include Nearest Neighbors, Decision Trees, Rule-based Classifiers, Artificial Neural Networks, Support Vector Machines, and Naive Bayes Algorithm. Contrarily, clustering is an unsupervised learning process that places data records in groups that already have components that are more similar to the incoming record than the components in the other clusters. The degree of similarity between items is determined by distance functions, such as Euclidean or cosine distance; good quality clusters have high intra-cluster and low inter-cluster similarity. The three main clustering techniques are density-based clustering, K-means clustering, and hierarchical clustering.

Prediction of Student Performance

Because student status analysis helps institutions perform better, predicting student achievement is crucial in the educational field. Educational institutions frequently have access to a variety of information sources, including traditional (demographic, academic background, and behavioural traits) and multimedia databases. These resources assist administrators in gathering data (such as entrance requirements), forecasting the timetable scale of class enrolment, and assisting students in selecting courses based on how well they would perform in those courses.

As shown in Figure 3, supervised, unsupervised, and semi-supervised learnings are the three fundamental forms of machine learning. The training dataset for supervised learning only contains labelled data. During the learning process, a supervised function is trained with the intention of forecasting the labels of upcoming unobserved data. Regression and classification are the two fundamental supervised tasks, particularly for continuous regression and discrete function classification. Without human assistance, unsupervised learning attempts to identify regular, meaningful patterns in unlabeled data. There is no instructor present to assist with identifying these patterns, and its training set is built up entirely of unlabeled data. Clustering, novelty detection, and dimensionality reduction are a few common supervised approaches. Combining supervised and unsupervised learning techniques is known as semi-supervised learning. It is used to produce improved outcomes with a limited number of labelled instances. Both labelled and unlabelled data are included in the training dataset. In various scientific domains, well-known supervised techniques with correct findings include DT, NB, Logistic Regression, SVMs, KNN, SMO, and Neural Network (Wesley & Buysse, 2010).

Figure 3. Machine learning techniques

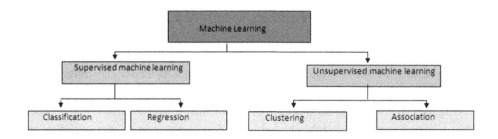

A supervised machine learning technique called DT employs branching methodology to display all potential outcomes of a choice in line with predetermined criteria. Each tree branch represents one or more results from the original dataset, and the tree structure is made up of sets of rules that are organised hierarchically, starting with root attributes and ending with leaf nodes. The root node, which is the top node in the tree without any incoming branches, represents all of the rows based on the dataset, and all of the outgoing branches represent those rows. It is possible to verify the attribute using the internal node in the tree, which is the node with incoming and outgoing branches. The downward node, also known as a leaf, has only an incoming branch. The tree's final node, which may contain several leaf nodes expressing the results of the calculations, is represented by this node.

The Bayes theory served as the foundation for the algorithm NB. Thomas Bayes is the one who came up with this theory. Large datasets are the principal use for this model, which is simple to construct. The method of the conditional probability distribution for each characteristic is calculated by NB. The probability product of each attribute of the vector in class C represents the conditional likelihood of a vector being assigned to class C. Because of its fundamental premise of conditional independence, this algorithm is referred to be "naive." We assume that each input feature operates independently of the others. An NB classifier can converge more quickly than other models, such as Logistic Regression, assuming the conditional assumption of independence genuinely holds.

Logistic regression is frequently used to analyze and explain the relationship between a set of predicted factors and a binary variable (such as "pass" or "failed"). In order to understand the link between the dependent and independent variable sets, the best model that fits the data must be found. Together with linear regression, logistic regression was created, however, their responses to binary variables and continuous variables varied.

On Vapnik's principle of theoretical learning, SVM version is based. Systemic risk minimization is embodied by SVM. SVMs have been used extensively in the disciplines of regression, classification, and outlier detection. A kernel in an SVM maps the original input space into a high-dimensional dot product space. The new space is known as the feature space, and an ideal hyperplane is defined there to maximize generalizability. The ideal hyperplane can be chosen using a small number of data points, known as support vectors. Despite not implementing problem-domain knowledge, an SVM can produce high generalization output for classification tasks.

A simple machine learning technique called KNN grades an object based on the consensus of its neighbours. The object is put into the class that its nearest neighbours share the most of. K is a positive number that's typically modest. The object is placed in the class of its nearest neighbour if k is equal to 1. In binary (two class) classification issues, picking k as an odd integer helps to break ties. This algorithm's choice of parameter k may be crucial. A new SVM training algorithm is called SMO. John Platt proposed the SMO algorithm, a straightforward and quick technique to train an SVM, in 1998. The key concept is to solve the dual quadratic optimisation issue by optimising the minimal subset with two components at each iteration. SMO breaks down the complex issue of quadratic programming into a number of smaller issues that may be resolved analytically. When SMO is controlled with a small number of training sets, the required memory is linear. SMO scales between linear and quadratic in the size of the training set because matrix computing is avoided, whereas the normal chunking SVM technique scales between linear and cubic. SMO is therefore the quickest linear SVM.

Another typical EDM technology is neural networks. Multiple units (neurons) are connected in a pattern to form a multi-layer neural network. Input, output, and hidden units are the three categories into which a network's units are separated. The neural network's ability to identify all potential interactions between variables is a benefit. Without a shadow of a doubt, it can also carry out a complete detection even when there is a nonlinear relationship between the dependent and independent variables.

Key Issues and Trends

E-learning, video-assisted learning, block chain, computerised reasoning, and learning analytics are the trends in the field of education. Because the subject of artificial intelligence in education is extremely dependent on technology and interdisciplinary, these obstacles occur. Without understanding the functions of AI in education and the operation of AI technologies, researchers may fail to execute such applications and activities successfully.

Summary and Discussion

Artificial intelligence is widely used today, and more research is being done to simplify human life as much as possible. The process of data mining can also be used in educational settings, particularly in higher education institutions. Education stakeholders are usually very concerned about student academic progress, particularly in today's quick-paced, web-enabled classrooms. High quality instructional materials, carefully crafted curricula, student-centered learning, and academic support have a significant impact on student success and help to level off variations in educational background. Although there are numerous factors that can affect academic success, research has shown that participation in activities with an educational goal lowers failure rates in introductory college courses and boosts retention. Academic performance is greatly influenced by how much time and effort students invest in activities that are connected to desired learning objectives, such as active and collaborative learning, communication with academic staff and peers, and participation in enriching educational experiences. By predicting student achievement, teachers can stop students from quitting before exams, spot those who need more assistance, and raise the standing and prestige of their institutions. The goal of machine learning techniques used in educational data mining is to create a model for identifying significant hidden trends and investigating valuable data from educational contexts.

AI AND DATA SCIENCE IN AGRICULTURE

Introduction

Agriculture is one of the key economic activities in India. The agriculture sector in India accounts for between 60 and 70 percent of all jobs. It has the second-most arable land behind the United States. This is brought on by the rich soil fertility and extensive network of irrigation water sources. The wide range of climatic conditions at various locations ensures that vegetation is abundant and productive. Despite the fact that resources are present, they do not always yield the same results. It is due to the limited supply and ineffective use of technology, the lack of knowledge and awareness among farmers, and the usage of some antiquated techniques (Abdulridha et al., 2016). Additionally, pests, insects, and illnesses harm the majority of crops, lowering output. Insect or pest attacks cause damage to numerous crops. Pesticides and insecticides are not always proven to be effective because certain birds and animals may be poisoned by them. Additionally, it harms food chains and the natural animal food web. Crop disease has a very low throughput impact. Research described the 20% to 40% yield reduction in agricultural productivity that is brought on by insects, pests, viruses, animals, and weeds (Al Bashish et al., 2010). Additionally, they have a variety of aspects, some having immediate effects and others with long-term effects on world food security. In India's semi-arid climate, crop output losses from pests and diseases are particularly significant (Behmann et al., 2014). The impact of weather on agricultural production is enormous. In general, weather-based frangible agriculture systems produce greater crops. According to surveys, if the population increases to 10 billion people, we will undoubtedly reach food catastrophe by the year 2050. It means that unless we develop and expand smart agricultural technologies, our ability to produce food will go bankrupt. Therefore, it is essential to provide a cost-effective technology for Indian farmers in order to properly manage the country's scarce resources. The method ought to assist farmers in increasing food production and quality while promptly preventing crop illnesses. In order to provide prompt prevention and treatment in mountainous regions like Jammu and Kashmir, the system must be dependable (Chaudhary et al., 2012). This is due to their ability to strategically deploy sensors remotely and monitor ambient parameters, soil parameters, and plant parameters. The agriculturalists can benefit from early illness prediction induced by numerous hazardous organisms, whether by a lack of or excess in the normal values of the monitored parameters. so that they can effectively take additional precautions against the attack of these pests and insects. This will stop the use of any chemicals and lower the number of animal ailments. Additionally, it would undoubtedly increase Aggie production, bridging the gap between rising population and rising food demand. Evidently, the overall percentage of crops that are lost would decrease. The last ten years have seen a global revolution in science and technology. The era we live in now is one of technology. Currently, remote monitoring systems are being employed to give useful information to agriculturalists. Internet of Things and wireless sensor networks are crucial in this connection. The Internet of Things (IoT) nirvana is the outcome of technology's miniaturisation. Kevin Ashton coined the phrase "Internet of Things" (IoT) for the first time in a 1999 presentation on supply chain management. The Internet of Things (IoT) is a network of computational devices with unique identifiers, such as sensors. Things refers to a broad range of items, sensors, people, smart devices, and any other entity with the capacity to connect to and share information with other entities, be aware of its context, and make anything accessible at any time and from any location. It indicates there are no time or place limitations and everything is available. Wireless technologies are crucial to the IoT's data collection and communication processes (Dhakate et al., 2015). Radio-frequency identification (RFID) and wireless sensor networks (WSN) are regarded as the two primary building blocks of sensing and communication technologies for the Internet of Things (IoT). There are many uses for wireless sensor networks, including in the military, agriculture, sports, medical, and industry. Large amounts of data are being generated as a result. The amount of data is produced through wireless sensor networks, smart devices, RFID tags, tablets, palmtops, laptops, smart metres, smart phones, smart healthcare, social media, software programmes, and digital services. They continuously produce a significant volume of organised, semi-structured, and unstructured data. Data analytics has committed to various wireless sensor networks to take advantage of the growth of data in a variety of application domains, including network operation, healthcare management, social media, intelligent traffic systems, business, marketing, resource optimization, precision agriculture, and social behaviour, among others. Data analysis is the process of gathering data, transforming it, cleaning it up, and modeling it with the intention of learning the necessary information. By making recommendations and offering help for decision-making, the outcomes and findings thus obtained are communicated. Data analytics is the act of analyzing massive data sets that include a range of data kinds to uncover hidden correlations, market trends, customer preferences, and other important business information. The most well-intentioned use of WSN, data analytics, and machine learning to increase crop yields and lessen farmers' labor-intensive tasks is agronomy consideration. Site-specific farming, often known as precision agriculture (PA), is a technological strategy that makes use of current data technology and expertise to provide high-quality agricultural produce. WSN are practical methods to increase crop output. Precision agriculture is currently in its advanced stages. Some farmers have begun implementing PA in their fields and have seen the best results while managing to recoup the investment necessary for doing so. Therefore, the operations associated with PA include: mapping and monitoring of plantings; identification and localization of crops, insects, and weeds; performance monitoring; machinery; variable dosing of fertilisers; and herbicides, insecticides, and fungicides. The agriculture sector is adopting data analytics and machine learning approaches to address the growing problems brought on by weather and climatic variations, such as temperature, rain, humidity, etc., which are seriously harming crop productivity. To support robust and widespread production, data analysis must become more accurate. An organisation can manage significant information that may have an impact on the business with the support of the ability to evaluate massive amounts of data. Such analytical tools' procedures and algorithms need to find data's hidden correlations and patterns. The field data gathered by the deployed sensors is in the form of multimedia, which aids in weed detection and smart irrigation as well as disease detection in stems, leaves, fruits, and roots as well as fruit quality and health.

Precision Agriculture

Numerous agronomic applications use wireless sensor networks, such as remotely monitoring soil and ambient factors to forecast the health of crops. By using WSN as an observer of environmental parameters such pressure, humidity, temperature, soil moisture, soil salinity, and soil conductivity, irrigation schedules for agricultural fields can be predicted. Numerous studies have been conducted, and the major contributions of numerous scholars are highlighted in the literature. The scalable network design was suggested (Grift, 2008) to monitor and manage agricultural fields in rural areas. They suggested an IoT-based control system for the advancement of farming and agriculture. All the system upgrades and parts are looked at and scrutinised from every angle. Energy efficiency, reduced delay, and high throughput were all achieved by the routing and MAC solution in the IoT. The system combines a fog computing solution with a Wi-Fi based long distance (WiLD) network to achieve this performance. The purpose of the WSN framework design was to put up a DSS for the detection of Apple Scab in Himachal Pradesh using Mills tables. IoT was used in agriculture by to increase crop yields, enhance crop quality, and cut costs. Researchers suggested and created a method that can optimally irrigate agricultural products including homegrown veggies and lemons based on wireless sensor networks. The solution that is being suggested has three primary components: a hardware component (the control box), a web application, and a mobile application as shown in Figure 4. The control box, which assisted in data collection, was actually a WSN and electronic control system. Large-scale data was gathered from the control box using a web application, and data mining association rules were used to evaluate it. The farmer was informed via the mobile application of the soil's moisture content, and if necessary, either automatic or manual watering was carried out. According to data mining, the ideal temperature and humidity for homegrown lemons and veggies is 29°–30°C. Smartnode precision agriculture system, is noted for being cost-effective. It used a platform of hardware and software that enables for the monitoring of agroclimatic factors for the best possible crop development. To boost the crop's yield, they installed the system in the field. The major goal was to use a model to notify farmers when the downy mildew disease in a vineyard context would be best treated. Following the IoT paradigm they proposed the system termed SEnviro (Sense our Environment platform) to monitor grape crops. They reduced communication between endpoints by utilising the edge computing paradigm. Unreliability and high cost of the current technologies was demonstrated and information was given on how to use IoT and machine learning in precision agriculture to anticipate crop illnesses. They suggested a system concept that included IoT and machine learning. They used environmental sensors, such as those for temperature and humidity, to gather data. The finished product was generated and then sent as an SMS to the nearby farmers. Different wireless technologies and protocol suites, including Wi-Fi, Bluetooth, GPRS/3G/4G, ZigBee, LoRa, and Sig Fox, were compared in a research work (Grinblat & Uzal, 2016). Due to their suitable communication range and low power consumption, they demonstrated that LoRa and ZigBee wireless technologies are particularly effective when used for Precision Agriculture. There is a categorization of numerous methods and algorithms pertaining to the energy effectiveness of wireless sensor networks. The methods that can be applied in PA have also been described. Also discussed are the difficulties and restrictions faced by WSN in PA. Machine learning techniques were coupled with the internet of things and demonstrated how these techniques could be used in next-generation networks. Public Safety IoT (PS-IoT) ecosystem was developed, which combines wireless powered communication and unmanned aerial vehicle technology to increase the energy efficiency of NOMA (non-orthogonal multiple access) public safety networks. A creative service process based on the Internet of Things' cloud computing platform was proposed (Islam et al., 2017). This process can be utilised to enhance the integration of the current cloud-to-physical networking and to speed up the Internet of Things' computing. This study applies cutting-edge platform technologies to the cloud agriculture platform. Farmland with limited network information resources can be connected and automated, including agricultural monitoring automation and pest control image analysis, through the application of cloud integration to vast area data collecting and analysis. A system based on the Internet of Things was used by constructing a unique Nitrogen-Phosphorus-Potassium (NPK) sensor using Light Emitting Diodes (LEDs) and Light Dependent Resistor (LDR) (LED). The colorimetric approach is employed to track and evaluate the nutrients that are present in the soil. The information gathered from fields is kept in a Google cloud database for quick retrieval. The concept of fuzzy logic has been used to determine the shortage of nutrients from sensed data. The sensed data is fuzzified and divided into five fuzzy values: very high, high, medium, low, and very low. Python is used to build both the intended hardware and software for the microcontroller on the Raspberry Pi 3. The proposed model has been tested on three different types of soil, including red, desert, and mountain soil. The devised system produced linear variation with respect to the solution soil's concentration. A sensor network scenario is created using the Qualnet simulator in order to analyse the performance of the designed NPK sensor in terms of end-to-end delay, throughput, and jitter (Jaware et al., 2012). When compared to existing alternatives, the built IoT system was proven to be the most beneficial to agrarians for high yielding crop production. Researchers have compiled a detailed survey and determined the most significant IoT applications, with precision agriculture receiving special attention. New taxonomies for Internet of Things technologies were mentioned which brings the most important technological advancements closes and have the potential to significantly improve people's lives, particularly those of the old and the disabled (Kulkarni et al., 2012). This work has thoroughly and exhaustively explored significant technologies, from sensing devices to applications, in comparison to the similar survey papers. Additionally, the fundamental unit technologies the well-accepted to meet the needs of IoT applications. A classification that shows how well-suited the suggested designs are for IoT features was mentioned. Additionally, they have emphasised the benefits of current approaches and suggested new directions based on the state of the art. They intend to develop a strategy that will be able to address the shortcomings of the IoT at each specific layer of the internet in a future study. Researchers looked at the possible uses for wireless sensor networks, as well as the difficulties and restrictions that come with deploying WSN to increase crop productivity. The use of WSN-connected smart, sensing, and communication devices in agronomy applications is heavily stressed. To investigate the current remedies suggested in the literature, they cited various case examples. In the literature review, it is highlighted how precision agriculture has been used all around the world, including in India. By presenting the future directions employing cutting-edge technologies, they have illustrated the shortcomings of these current solutions. Authors have looked into the use of IoT in precision agriculture (Lavanya et al., 2020). To achieve site-specific monitoring of the greenhouse, they deployed wireless communication technology. They suggested a wireless remote monitoring device for greenhouses. System management was taken into consideration when designing an information management system. Research has made use of the field data. This remote monitoring system accurately sensed greenhouse field data, such as temperature and humidity, and after doing the necessary research, the system produced good conditions for vegetable growth. Performance and reliability have both risen as a result of the suggested solution. The system's user interface was simple enough for regular farmers to utilise. Authors have suggested a strategy for effective crop monitoring for agricultural fields (Trilles Oliver & Torres-Sospedra, 2019). Data may be stored and retrieved from anywhere with IoT applications. The field conditions are tracked and gathered using a variety of sensors. Through GSM technology, the farmer is supplied information about the state of the farm as a whole. The sensor component of the proposed effort is restricted to crop monitoring alone. A study concentrated on data collected from agricultural fields using a variety of methods. During their research, WSN, IoT, weather stations, smartphones, drones, and cameras were found to be helpful. Additionally, the authors improved the IoT platform known as SmartFarmNet (Venkatesan & Kathrine, 2018). This was capable of processing the field data gathering for a variety of parameters, including soil, moisture, irrigation, soil fertility, humidity, and temperature. The suggested system was able to link the data that had been examined and predict crop status. Thus precision agriculture has a good impact on farmers.

Figure 4. Precision agriculture components

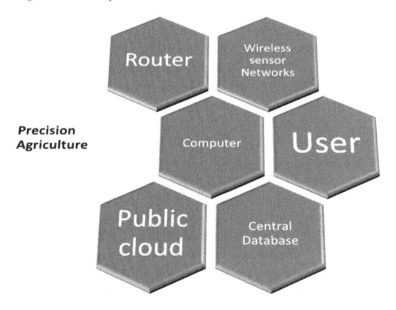

Plant Disease Detection

Infection with the disease is agriculture's biggest problem. The Quality and Quantity of agricultural products suffer because of this drawback. The AI approach can be used to identify and diagnose diseases on agricultural products. Image processing is a technique used to quantify the diseased area and identify colour changes in the affected area and the stages are depicted in Figure 5. The segmentation of the plant leaf images into surface areas like background, diseased area, and non-diseased area of the leaf is ensured by image sensing and analysis. The sick or infected area is then removed and sent to the lab for further analysis. A digital infrared thermograph can detect plant diseases since temperature measurement is directly related to a reduction in water content caused by the opening of stomata. Early detection of disease is made possible by thermal imaging of plant leaves, which lowers significant agricultural losses. A method for the diagnosis of disease in plants using silhouette registration using visible photos is proposed in the study (Zhang & Dabipi, 2018). The system first finds silhouettes in pictures taken in visible light. For the same, it also uses stationary wavelet transform for thermal pictures. This multi-scale technique employs the gradient-based methodology.

Figure 5. Classification of disease using image processing

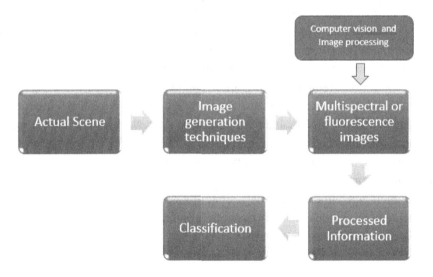

Summary

Animals and people alike use agricultural goods to meet their nutritional demands. Everyone's life has been impacted by agriculture, whether directly or indirectly. Due to building (housing, dams, factories, industries, etc.), natural shrinkage of arable land, and other factors, the amount of arable land is slowly decreasing (floods, earthquakes, landslides etc.). Therefore, it is essential to place a priority on superior and knowledgeable crop disease approaches in order to meet the rising food need of the expanding population. The sections provide information on precision agriculture utilising machine learning and IoT data analytics. The uses of these technologies in precision agriculture are also emphasised. Additionally, the part attempted to solve one of the issues with agricultural growth, namely that crop growers continue to use traditional disease prediction methods without the aid of technology like IoT or WSN. Real-time precautions against any potential sickness, such as scab, will be one strategy to address this issue if they are accurately and promptly predicted. Although there are numerous obstacles to overcome before applying agricultural techniques, such as the initial cost of implementation, deployment, training, weather conditions, and other factors. However, the gains will take on a visible and usable shape after the afore mentioned restrictions are overcome.

CONCLUSION

Artificial intelligence (AI) is the study of how the human brain functions while attempting to solve issues. AI offers fresh possibilities for enhancing human intelligence and enhancing people's lives. AI seeks to enhance computer abilities that are similar to human learning, problem-solving, reasoning, and knowledge. Numerous industries are being transformed by AI, and it is becoming more and more prevalent in various industry sectors. One of the most fruitful areas for artificial intelligence is agriculture. In Agriculture alone, spending on AI technology and solutions is expected to increase from $1 billion in 2020 to $4 billion in 2026. The increased complexity of datasets and the volume of healthcare data are the main factors propelling the market for artificial intelligence in healthcare. Automated disease diagnosis, drug discovery, robotic surgery, virtual nursing assistants, and information management for doctors and patients are all applications of artificial intelligence (AI) and machine learning. Quality checks, quicker maintenance, more reliable design, less environmental impact, exploitation of useful data, supply chain communication, waste reduction, integration, enhanced customer service, and post-production assistance are examples of how AI may be used in manufacturing. By assuring smarter planning and efficient management to improve worker and material safety, AI is working miracles in supply chain and logistics management. AI-enhanced solutions can prove to be incredibly successful in building design and construction management because of their capacity to handle large amounts of data. AI is beginning to enter the education sector; with its assistance, instructors can recognize the various student learner types and anticipate their academic achievement, enabling them to make important decisions quickly. As a result, developments in AI have made it possible for humans to improve in a wide range of fields that are not just related to applications on Earth.

REFERENCES

Abd Aziz, N., Adnan, N. A. A., Abd Wahab, D., & Azman, A. H. (2021). Component design optimization based on artificial intelligence in support of additive manufacturing repair and restoration: Current status and future outlook for remanufacturing. *Journal of Cleaner Production*, *296*, 126401. doi:10.1016/j. jclepro.2021.126401

Abdulridha, J., Ehsani, R., & Castro, A. (2016). Detection and differentiation between laurel wilt disease, phytophthora disease, and salinity damage using a hyperspectral sensing technique. *Agriculture*, *6*(4), 56. doi:10.3390/agriculture6040056

Ahmad, A., Farooq, F., Ostrowski, K. A., Sliwa-Wieczorek, K., & Czarnecki, ́. S. (2021). Application of novel machine learning techniques for predicting the surface chloride concentration in concrete containing waste material. *Materials (Basel)*, *14*(9), 2297. doi:10.3390/ma14092297 PMID:33946688

Ahmed, I., Ahmad, M., Jeon, G., & Piccialli, F. (2021). A framework for pandemic prediction using big data analytics. *Big Data Res*, *25*, 100190. doi:10.1016/j.bdr.2021.100190

Akgun, S., & Greenhow, C. (2021). Artificial intelligence in education: Addressing ethical challenges in K-12 settings. *AI and Ethics*, 1–10. doi:10.100743681-021-00096-7 PMID:34790956

Al Bashish, D., Braik, M., & Bani-Ahmad, S. 2010. A framework for detection and classification of plant leaf and stem diseases. *International Conference on Signal and Image Processing*, 113–118. 10.1109/ICSIP.2010.5697452

Alemayehu, D., & Berger, M. L. (2016). Big Data: Transforming drug development and health policy decision making. *Health Services and Outcomes Research Methodology*, *16*(3), 92–102. doi:10.100710742-016-0144-x PMID:27594803

Atici. (2011). Prediction of the strength of mineral admixture concrete using multivariable regression analysis and an artificial neural network. *Expert Systems with Applications, 38*, 9609–9618. https://doi.org/.eswa.2011.01.156 doi:10.1016/j

Bates, D. W., Saria, S., Ohno-Machado, L., Shah, A., & Escobar, G. (2014). Big data in health care: Using analytics to identify and manage high-risk and high-cost patients. *Health Affairs (Project Hope)*, *33*(7), 1123–1131. doi:10.1377/hlthaff.2014.0041 PMID:25006137

Behmann, J., Steinrücken, J., & Plümer, L. (2014). Detection of early plant stress responses in hyperspectral images. *ISPRS Journal of Photogrammetry and Remote Sensing*, *93*, 98–111. doi:10.1016/j.isprsjprs.2014.03.016

Bilim, C., Atis ̧, C. D., Tanyildizi, H., & Karahan, O. (2009). Predicting the compressive strength of ground granulated blast furnace slag concrete using artificial neural network. *Advances in Engineering Software*, *40*(5), 334–340. doi:10.1016/j.advengsoft.2008.05.005

Brownlee, J. (2013). *A tour of machine learning algorithms.* https:// machinelearningmastery.com/a-tour-of-machine-learning-algorithms/

Bui, Nguyen, Chou, Nguyen-Xuan, & Ngo. (2018). A modified firefly algorithm-artificial neural network expert system for predicting compressive and tensile strength of high-performance concrete. *Construction and Building Materials, 180*, 320–333. https://doi.org/.conbuildmat.2018.05.201 doi:10.1016/j

Cassel, L., Dicheva, D., Dichev, C., Goelman, D., & Posner, M. (2016). Artificial Intelligence in Data Science. *Lecture Notes in Computer Science*, *9883*, 343–346. doi:10.1007/978-3-319-44748-3_33

Chaudhary, P., & Chaudhari, A. K. (2012, June). Color transform based approach for disease spot detection on plant leaf. *Int. J. Comput. Sci. Telecomm*, *3*(6).

Chen, Chang, Shih, & Wang. (2009). Estimation of exposed temperature for fire-damaged concrete using support vector machine. *Computational Materials Science, 44*, 913–920. https://doi.org/.commatsci.2008.06.017 doi:10.1016/j

Chen, H., Qian, C., Liang, C., & Kang, W. (2018). An approach for predicting the compressive strength of cement-based materials exposed to sulfate attack. *PLoS One, 13*(1), e0191370. Advance online publication. doi:10.1371/journal.pone.0191370 PMID:29346451

Chen, M., & Hao, Y. (2017). *Disease Prediction by Machine Learning over Big Data from Healthcare Communities*. IEEE. doi:10.1109/ACCESS.2017.2694446

Chen, M., & Wang, L. (2017). *Disease Prediction by Machine Learning over Big Data from Healthcare Communities*. IEEE. doi:10.1109/ACCESS.2017.2694446

Chen, T. (2020). A simple framework for contrastive learning of visual representations. In *International conference on machine learning*. PMLR.

Chou, J.-S., Tsai, C.-F., Pham, A.-D., & Lu, Y.-H. (2014). Machine learning in concrete strength simulations: Multi-nation data analytics. *Construction & Building Materials, 73*, 771–780. doi:10.1016/j.conbuildmat.2014.09.054

Corsi, A., de Souza, F. F., Pagani, R. N., & Kovaleski, J. L. (2020). Big data analytics as a tool for fighting pandemics: A systematic review of literature. *Journal of Ambient Intelligence and Humanized Computing, 12*(10), 9163–9180. doi:10.100712652-020-02617-4 PMID:33144892

Dhakate, M., & Ingole, A.B. (2015). Diagnosis of Pomegranate Plant Diseases Using Neural Network. *Fifth National Conference on Computer Vision. Pattern Recognition, Image Processing and Graphics (NCVPRIPG)*.

Egert, F., Fukkink, R. G., & Eckhardt, A. G. (2018). Impact of in-service professional development programs for early childhood teachers on quality ratings and child outcomes: A meta-analysis. *Review of Educational Research, 88*(3), 401–433. doi:10.3102/0034654317751918

Grift, T. (2008). A review of automation and robotics for the bioindustry. *Journal of Biomechanical Engineering, 1*, 37–54.

Grinblat, G. L., Uzal, L. C., Larese, M. G., & Granitto, P. M. (2016). Deep learning for plant identification using vein morphological patterns. *Computers and Electronics in Agriculture, 127*, 418–424. doi:10.1016/j.compag.2016.07.003

Güçlüer, Ozbeyaz, Goymen, & Günaydın. (2021). A comparative investigation using machine learning methods for concrete compressive strength estimation. *Materials Today Communications, 27*, 102278. https://doi.org/.mtcomm.2021.102278 doi:10.1016/j

Gupta, S. (2013). Using artificial neural network to predict the compressive strength of concrete containing nano-silica. *Civil Engineering and Architecture, 1*(3), 96–102. doi:10.13189/cea.2013.010306

Gutierrez. (2016). *InsideBIGDATA Guide to Healthcare & Life Sciences*. DellEMC and INTEL.

Harpaz, R., DuMochel, W., & Shah, N. H. (2016). Big data and adverse drug reaction detection. *Clinical Pharmacology and Therapeutics, 99*(3), 268–270. doi:10.1002/cpt.302 PMID:26575203

Huda, S. (2017). *A Hybrid Feature Selection with Ensemble Classification for Imbalanced Healthcare Data: A Case Study for Brain Tumor Diagnosis*. IEEE.

Hudis, C. A. (2015). Big data: Are large prospective randomized trials obsolete in the future? *The Breast*, *24*, S15–S18. doi:10.1016/j.breast.2015.07.005 PMID:26255742

Islam, M., Dinh, A., Wahid, K., & Bhowmik, P. (2017). Detection of potato diseases using image segmentation and multiclass support vector machine. *IEEE 30th Canadian Conference on Electrical and Computer Engineering (CCECE)*. 10.1109/CCECE.2017.7946594

Jaware, T. H., Badgujar, R. D., & Patil, P. G. (2012). Crop disease detection using image segmentation. *Proceedings of Conference on Advances in Communication and Computing*.

Jimenez-Martinez, M., & Alfaro-Ponce, M. (2019). Fatigue damage effect approach by artificial neural network. *International Journal of Fatigue*, *124*, 42–47. doi:10.1016/j.ijfatigue.2019.02.043

Kayyali, B., Knott, D., & Van Kuiken, S. (2013). *The big-data revolution in US health care: accelerating value and innovation*. McKinsey Co. doi:10.1145/2537052.2537073

Kewalramani, S., Kidman, G., & Palaiologou, I. (2021). Using artificial intelligence (AI)- interfaced robotic toys in early childhood settings: A case for children's inquiry literacy. *European Early Childhood Education Research Journal*, *29*(5), 652–668. doi:10.1080/1350293X.2021.1968458

Kitchenham, B., & Charters, S. (2007). Guidelines for performing Systematic Literature reviews in Software Engineering Version 2.3. *Engineering (London)*, *45*, 1051–1052. doi:10.1145/1134285.1134500

Knowledgent. (2016). *Big data analytics in life sciences and healthcare: An overview*. Academic Press.

Kulkarni, & Patil. (2012). Applying image processing technique to detect plant diseases. *Int. J. Mod. Eng. Res.*, *2*(5), 366.

Lavanya, Rani, & GaneshKumar. (2020). An automated low cost iot based fertilizer intimation system for smart agriculture. *Sustain. Comput.: Inf. Syst.*

Mallela & Upadhyay. (2016). Buckling load prediction of laminated composite stiffened panels subjected to in-plane shear using artificial neural networks. *Thin Walled Structures, 102*, 158–164. https://doi.org/. tws.2016.01.025 doi:10.1016/j

Mandal, P. (2017). Artificial neural network prediction of buckling load of thin cylindrical shells under axial compression. *Engineering Structures*, *152*, 843–855. doi:10.1016/j.engstruct.2017.09.016

McCarthy, J. (2007). From here to human-level AI. *Artificial Intelligence*, *171*(18), 1174–1182. doi:10.1016/j.artint.2007.10.009

Mohammed, E. A., Far, B. H., & Naugler, C. (2014). Applications of the MapReduce programming framework to clinical big data analysis: Current landscape and future trends. *BioData Mining*, *7*(1), 22. doi:10.1186/1756-0381-7-22 PMID:25383096

Muijs, D., Aubrey, C., Harris, A., & Briggs, M. (2004). How do they manage? A review of the research on leadership in early childhood. *Journal of Early Childhood Research*, *2*(2), 157–169. doi:10.1177/1476718X04042974

Padil, K. H., Bakhary, N., & Hao, H. (2017). The use of a non-probabilistic artificial neural network to consider uncertainties in vibration-based-damage detection. *Mechanical Systems and Signal Processing, 83*, 194–209. doi:10.1016/j.ymssp.2016.06.007

Panchalingam, R., & Chan, K. C. (2021). A state-of-the-art review on artificial intelligence for Smart Buildings. *Intelligent Buildings International, 13*(4), 203–226. doi:10.1080/17508975.2019.1613219

Preface. (2021). *The ultimate guide for artificial intelligence (AI) for kids.* https://www.pr eface.ai/blog/kids-learning/ai-for-kids

Raghupathi, W., & Raghupathi, V. (2014). Big data analytics in healthcare: Promise and potential. *Health Information Science and Systems, 2*(1), 3. doi:10.1186/2047-2501-2-3 PMID:25825667

Senthilkumar, S. A., & Bharatendara, K. (2018). Big data in healthcare management: A review of literature. *Am. J. Theor. Appl. Bus., 4*(2), 57–69. doi:10.11648/j.ajtab.20180402.14

Shakirov, V., Solovyeva, K. P., & Dunin-Barkowski, W. L. (2018). Review of State-of-the-Art in Deep Learning Artificial Intelligence. *Optical Memory and Neural Networks (Information Optics), 27*(2), 65–80. doi:10.3103/S1060992X18020066

Shwartz-Ziv, R., & Armon, A. (2022). Tabular data: Deep learning is not all you need. *Information Fusion, 81*, 84–90. doi:10.1016/j.inffus.2021.11.011

Su, J., Yu, C., & Ng, D. T. K. (2022). A meta-review of literature on educational approaches for teaching AI at the K-12 levels in the Asia-Pacific region. *Computers and Education: Artificial Intelligence*, Article 100065.

Tan, Z. X., Thambiratnam, D. P., Chan, T. H. T., & Razak, H. A. (2017). Detecting damage in steel beams using modal strain energy based damage index and artificial neural network. *Engineering Failure Analysis, 79*, 253–262. doi:10.1016/j.engfailanal.2017.04.035

Torky, A. A., & Aburawwash, A. A. (2018). A deep learning approach to automated structural engineering of prestressed members. *International Journal of Structural and Civil Engineering Research, 7*, 347–352. doi:10.18178/ijscer.7.4.347-352

Trilles Oliver, S., Torres-Sospedra, J., Belmonte, O., Zarazaga-Soria, F.J., González Pérez, A., & Huerta, J. (2019). *Development of an open sensorized platform in a smart agriculture context: A vineyard support system for monitoring mildew disease.* Academic Press.

Venkatesan, R., Kathrine, G. J. W., & Ramalakshmi, K. (2018). Internet of things based pest management using natural pesticides for small scale organic gardens. *Journal of Computational and Theoretical Nanoscience, 15*(9–10), 2742–2747. doi:10.1166/jctn.2018.7533

Wang, Y., & Hajli, N. (2017). Exploring the path to big data analytics success in healthcare. *Journal of Business Research, 70*, 287–299. doi:10.1016/j.jbusres.2016.08.002

Wesley, P. W., & Buysse, V. (2010). *The quest for quality: Promising innovations for early childhood programs.* Paul H. Brookes Publishing Company.

Williams, R., Park, H. W., Oh, L., & Breazeal, C. (2019a). Popbots: Designing an artificial intelligence curriculum for early childhood education. *Proceedings of the AAAI Conference on Artificial Intelligence, 33*, 9729–9736. 10.1609/aaai.v33i01.33019729

Wu & Cheng. (2017). Omic and electronic health record big data analytics for precision medicine. *IEEE Transactions, 64*(2).

Xie, Y. (2015). *Predicting Days in Hospital Using Health Insurance Claims*. IEEE.

Yoo, S., Lee, S., Kim, S., Hwang, K. H., Park, J. H., & Kang, N. (2021). Integrating deep learning into CAD/CAE system: Generative design and evaluation of 3D conceptual wheel. *Structural and Multidisciplinary Optimization, 64*(4), 1–23. doi:10.100700158-021-02953-9

Zhang, L., Dabipi, I.K., & Brown Jr, W.L. (2018). Internet of things applications for agriculture. IoT A to Z. *Technol. Appl.,* 507–528.

Zhang, M., Akiyama, M., Shintani, M., Xin, J., & Frangopol, D. M. (2021). Probabilistic estimation of flexural loading capacity of existing RC structures based on observational corrosion-induced crack width distribution using machine learning. *Structural Safety, 91*, 102098. Advance online publication. doi:10.1016/j.strusafe.2021.102098

Chapter 2
Artificial Intelligence Impacts on Industry 4.0:
A Literature-Based Study

Shyam Sunder Gupta

Amity University, Gwalior, India

Rajeev Goyal

Amity University, Gwalior, India

Deepak Gupta

ITM University, Gwalior, India

ABSTRACT

Artificial intelligence (AI) provides appropriate information for decision-making and alerting people of possible malfunctions. Industries will use AI to process data transmitted from the internet of things (IoT) devices and connected machines based on their desire to integrate them into their equipment. It provides companies with the ability to track their entire end-to-end activities and processes fully. Accordingly, the research objectives are crafted to facilitate researchers, practitioners, students, and industry professionals. It includes key features, how industrial AI distinguishes itself within the field of AI, major components in Industrial AI, Industrial AI eco-system, various tools and traits of AI, cyber physical applications, AI technologies and tools, Industrial IoT (IIoT) and data analytics, benefits of adopting an Industry 4.0 model, benefits of deploying AI models, significant advancements, and challenges of industrial artificial intelligence. Furthermore, this technology seeks correlations to avoid errors and eventually to anticipate them.

DOI: 10.4018/978-1-6684-8145-5.ch002

Copyright © 2023, IGI Global. Copying or distributing in print or electronic forms without written permission of IGI Global is prohibited.

INTRODUCTION

In today's world of revolutionized technology everything is become more and more intelligent and advanced. This leads to a great advancement in the field of innovation where it majorly impacted by revolution of Industry 4.0 which has recently undergone major improvement in the area of Artificial Intelligence.

Industry 4.0 has recently undergone major improvements thanks to artificial intelligence. Industries are concentrating on enhancing product uniformity, productivity, and lowering operational costs, and they hope to do this by collaborating with humans and robotics. Hyper-connected production processes in smart industries are dependent on many devices that communicate via AI automation systems by gathering and processing all data kinds. Modern manufacturing may be transformed in significant ways by the use of intelligent automation technologies. AI delivers relevant information to aid in decision-making and warn users of potential errors. Based on their aim to incorporate internet of things (IoT) devices and linked machines into their equipment, industries will utilise AI to process data supplied from those devices. So these companies are able to track their entire end-to-end activities and processes fully.

The concept "Industry 4.0" originally appeared in 2011 at the Hannover Fair in Germany. According to a report written by Henning Kagermann, Wolfgang Wahlster, and Wolf-Dieter Lukas, a new era known as Industry 4.0 has begun in the world (Rozario & Zhang, 2022). The world today is undergoing a tremendous technological shift. Operations in commercial organisations are becoming unstable due to the Fourth Industrial Revolution (4IR). In order to create an intelligent product, 4IR involves digitising the actual world and traditional production methods. The goal is to completely integrate suppliers and customers. Digital transformation is a revolution in how people use digital technology to produce value. Implementing and merging a variety of cutting-edge information and communication technologies in order to create a more resilient and adaptable solution is part of the notion of digital transformation. By modifying company processes, procedures, and capacities through digital transformation (DT), society has benefited from disruptive innovations. Due to the ubiquity and growth of contemporary digital technology, DT has gained recognition in many service companies throughout the globe (Okunlaya et al., 2022).

This book chapter offers a concise summary of the impact of cutting-edge technologies like artificial intelligence, how they are altering the industrial industry, and how robots are beginning to become much smarter as a result. The emphasis is on examining Industry 4.0, how it altered the whole industrial sector, and what potential it has for a better, more productive future. The advantages and difficulties of artificial intelligences in industry 4.0 are the main topics of this examination.

KEY FEATURES: INDUSTRY 4.0 (UNIDO, 2016)

1. Increasing awareness of Industry 4.0's effects on inclusive and sustainable industrial development (ISID) and facilitating access to knowledge, skill, education, and technology are important.
2. The huge potential for developing economies and transitioning economies to use innovation management principles to progress quicker into Industry 4.0.

The potential for UNIDO to support the creation of multi-stakeholder knowledge-sharing platforms to increase awareness of Industry 4.0 opportunities and challenges for pursuing ISID in developing nations; for sharing available tools and methods for innovation management; designing training curricula for new workforce skill requirements; researching techniques and best processes to support SMEs digital transformation and bridging the gender digital divide; raising awareness.

The development of artificial intelligence (AI) during the years is shown in Figure 1.

Figure 1. History of AI development
Source: Sharabov and Tsochev (2020)

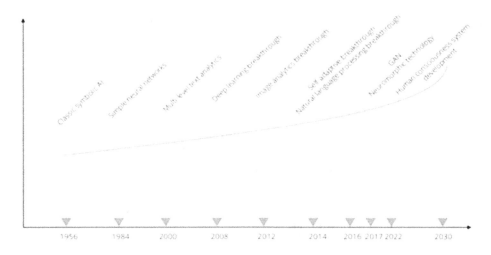

The major focus areas that utilize AI are mentioned in Figure 2.

Figure 2. Major focus areas
Source: Sharabov and Tsochev (2020)

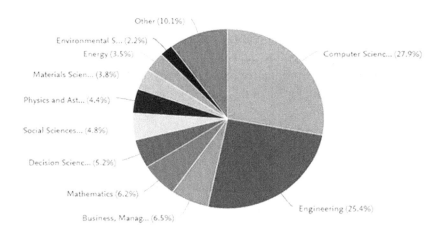

Education, lodging and food services, construction, wholesale & retail, healthcare, and social services are a few of the top industries benefiting from AI (Sharabov & Tsochev, 2020).

By offering an automated system, smart factories' primary goals are to lower production mistake rates, speed up production, and lower production costs. Additionally, a variety of elements, including autonomous robots, simulation technologies, augmented reality, block-chain technology, and sensor technologies, might be considered crucial dynamics for Industry 4.0. These components are becoming more prevalent as technology advances (Rozario & Zhang, 2022).

AI has created a massive in analyzing the capabilities of AI in area of information technology, this shows in industrial sector is soon going to experience a drastic game-changing effect at various levels of production. For utilizing advantage of Industry 4.0's tremendous potential and capabilities, businesses must begin focusing on where AI can offer more value and increase efficiency and productivity. This study analyzes the manufacturing capabilities of Industries powered by Artificial Intelligence. The role of GDP in AI for manufacturing industries globally by 2030. This is somehow show the impact of AI in Manufacturing on the economy and scaling of the same (Chopra et al., 2021).

AI's effects on manufacturing every region of the world is expected to see an increase in GDP. By 2030, it is expected that AI will contribute around 25% of China's GDP to the industrial sector. North America ranks in second with a 10% contribution from AI in the industrial sector. The automotive industry now holds the top spot for AI deployment in production. The automotive industry has nevertheless emerged as the largest centre for smart manufacturing employing AI models in quality control, product development, and production, despite being a sector with a poor growth rate in many regions of the world. GM has employed machine learning to create products that are more quickly and inexpensively thanks to its "Dreamcatcher system," which was inspired by the success of their initial AI system (Chopra et al., 2021).

Artificial intelligence (AI) is a branch of cognitive science that has many research activities in a variety of fields, including robotics, machine learning, natural language processing, and image processing. Machine learning and artificial intelligence (AI) have historically been seen as black-art approaches, and there is sometimes a dearth of strong data to persuade business that these techniques will deliver a return-on-investment time and time again. At the same time, a developer's choices and expertise have a big impact on how well machine learning algorithm's function. As a result, AI has had mixed success in industrial applications. Industrial AI, focuses on creating, testing, and implementing various AI and machine learning (ML) algorithms for uses in the industrial sector include long-term effective performance (Lee et al., 2018).

Figure 3. GDP impact of AI by 2030 around various regions of the world in the manufacturing industry
Source: Chopra et al. (2021)

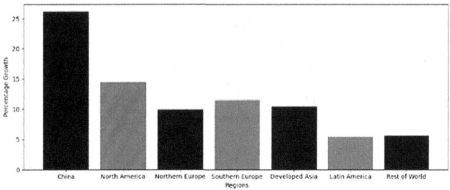

Through its data-driven predictive analytics and ability to support decision-making in extremely complex, non-linear, and frequently multistage environments, artificial intelligence has demonstrated its potential to help manufacturers address the challenges associated with this digital transformation of Cyber-Physical Systems (Peres et al., 2020).

INDUSTRIAL AI DISTINGUISHES ITSELF WITHIN THE FIELD OF AI IN FIVE PARTICULAR DIMENSIONS (PERES ET AL., 2020)

1. **Infrastructures:** Real-time processing capabilities for hardware and software are highly prioritised, enabling industrial-grade dependability with strict security standards and interconnection;
2. **Data:** Data that are plentiful, moving quickly, varied, and coming from different units, goods, regimes, etc.
3. **Algorithms:** This calls for the fusion of heuristic, digital, and physical knowledge. high complexity caused by model deployment, governance, and administration.
4. **Decision-Making:** Given the industrial environment, there is typically very little tolerance for error, making the management of ambiguity crucial. Efficiency is especially crucial for complex optimization issues.
5. **Goals:** Industrial AI seeks to create value primarily through the reduction of scrap, enhancement of quality, augmentation of operator performance, or quick ramp-up times.

The following three queries provide the information you seek (Peres et al., 2020):

1. For the first question, "What is the current status of industrial AI in manufacturing?" the following information was taken from the eligible publications: (1) The application domain, (2) references to the authors' software or hardware, (3) a rating of the proposed application's Technology Readiness Level (TRL), and (4) the degree of autonomy.
2. In response to the second query, "What are the basic design tenets of Industrial AI?" (1) text descriptions (sentences in the publication's entire text showcasing the writers' design choices) (e.g., service orientation, continuous engineering).
3. "What are the primary difficulties and future research directions?" Each article addresses two study objectives (e.g., predictive maintenance, energy optimization, or ergonomics) as well as one or more research objects (e.g., production data, logistics, or personnel).

Industrial AI is still in its infancy, hence a framework for its adoption in industry must explicitly specify its structure, methodology, and problems. In order to do this, the author created an industrial AI ecosystem, which covers all of the crucial components and offers instructions for better comprehending and utilising it. The enabling technologies that may be used to build an Industrial AI system are also outlined. A schematic comparison of Industrial AI's intended system performance over time with other learning systems is shown in Figure 4a (Lee et al., 2018).

KEY ELEMENTS IN INDUSTRIAL AI

The major components in Industrial AI can be represented by 'ABCDE'.

These major components are:

1. Analytics technology
2. Big data technology
3. Cyber technology
4. Domain knowhow
5. Evidence

AI's main component is analytics, but it can only be useful if other components are also present. Big data technology and the cloud are both crucial components that give Industrial AI a platform and a supply of information (data). In addition to these crucial components, domain expertise and evidence are equally significant but sometimes disregarded features in this situation.

From the following perspectives, domain knowledge is the crucial component:

1. Take the issue into account and direct industrial AI's power toward finding a solution.
2. Consider the method to gather accurate data of high quality.
3. Consider the parameters' physical meanings and how they relate to the physical properties of a system or process.
4. Consider the fact that these factors vary from machine to machine.

Incorporating cumulative learning capacity into Industrial AI models and evaluating them requires evidence as a key component. The only way to improve the AI model's precision, scope, and resilience is to gather more data patterns and the supporting evidence (or labels) for each pattern. Figure 4b illustrates how AI may enable us to travel from the visible world into the unseen and from resolving problems to averting them altogether (Lee et al., 2018).

INDUSTRIAL AI ECO-SYSTEM

Refer to Figure 5. It shows the Industrial AI ecosystem, It outlines a sequential thinking approach for the requirements, difficulties, technology, and development processes of industry-relevant revolutionary AI systems. This graphic may be used by practitioners as a methodical roadmap for creating a plan for the development and implementation of industrial AI. Within the targeted industry, this ecosystem defines the common unmet needs such as Self-aware, Self-compare, Self-predict, and Self-optimize and Resilience.

Figure 6 also covers four implementable technologies containing Data Technology (DT), Analytic Technology (AT), Platform Technology (PT) and Operations Technology (OT). These play better role to understood when placed in the circumstance of the Cyber-Physical Systems (CPS) (Lee et al., 2018).

Figure 4. (a) Comparison of Industrial AI with other learning systems; (b) the influence of Industrial AI: from solving noticeable problems to avoiding invisible
Source: Lee et al. (2018)

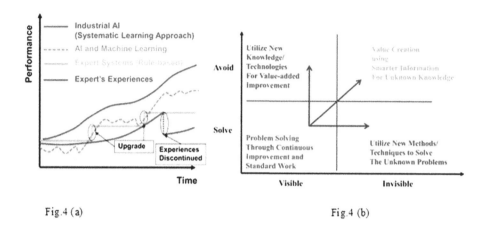

Fig.4 (a)　　　　　　　　　　　Fig.4 (b)

Figure 5. Industrial AI eco-system
Source: Lee et al. (2018)

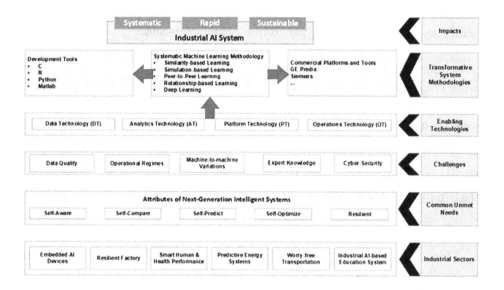

Data Technologies

Data Technologies which enable successful acquisition of valuable data with important performance metrics across dimensions (Lee et al., 2018).

Figure 6. Various tools and traits of AI for Industry 4.0

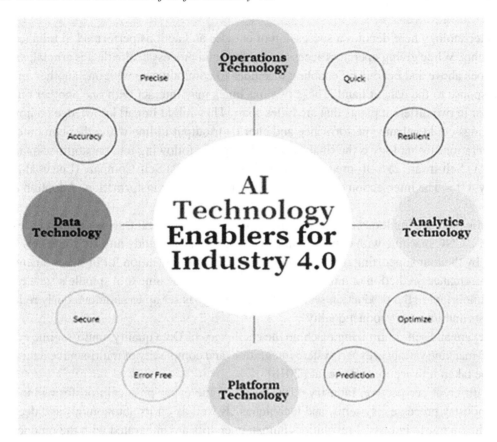

Analytics Technology

Transforms the sensory data from important modules into useful data. Hidden patterns, unknown connections, and other valuable information from industrial processes are revealed via data-driven modelling. Use as an illustration to produce a health value. For increased efficiency and creativity, analytical technologies combine this data with other technologies (Lee et al., 2018).

Platform Technologies

H/w architecture for industrial data storage, research, and feedback is included. One of the key determining factors in achieving smart industrial features like agility and complex-event processing is a platform architecture that is compatible for data analysis. Stand-alone, embedded, and cloud platform configurations are the three main types that are typically encountered. Regarding computational, storage, and servitization capacities, cloud computing represents a tremendous leap in information and communication technologies. Rapid service deployment, a high degree of customisation, knowledge integration, efficient and effective visualisation, and considerable scalability may all be provided by the cloud platform (Lee et al., 2018).

Operation Technology

Operation technology here denotes a succession of choices and actions performed in reliance on data-driven insights. While giving operators access to machine and process health data is crucial, an Industry 4.0 plant goes above and beyond by enabling machines to communicate with one another and take actions in response to the data at hand. These two machines may interact with one another on the same shop floor or in two different plants that are miles apart. They might impart knowledge on how altering certain settings could enhance performance and alter their output in line with other computers' accessibility. Operations technology is the final stage leading to the following four capabilities in an industry 4.0 factory:1) Self-aware 2) Self- predict, 3) Self-Configure and 4) Self-Compare (Lee et al., 2018).

Industry 4.0 = The Intersection of Manufacturing and Digital Transformation (Adoption & Report, 2021).

The application and implementation of the Industrial AI architectural framework as it is described to a spindle of a CNC machine with computer numerical control. This study aims to show how Industrial AI, backed by the four supporting technologies, can provide a full solution for in-the-moment monitoring and performance prediction of a machine tool spindle. The machine tool spindle's state of health is extremely important in the production sector. The technology is set up to simultaneously reduce maintenance costs and improve product quality.

A self-aware and self- optimizing machine the challenges of Data quality, multi-regime complexity, machine-to-machine variance, expert system integration, and complexity of multi-source data are factors that must be taken into account (Lee et al., 2018).

From a different perspective, Industry 4.0 is based on the cyber-physical transformation of manufacturing industry processes, systems, and techniques, as well as on its autonomous and decentralised operation. In the fourth industrial revolution, human operators are integrated with the production environment, including the supply chain, marketplaces, other intelligent factories, and logistical systems. Information management is one of the key foundations for a successful implementation of Industry 4.0, from data generation through decision-making. In this sense, artificial intelligence and data analytics are the driving forces behind the next wave of smart factories.(Deep & Sood, 2023).

By digitizing and interconnecting the industrial environment, it is possible to create virtual clones of the factory and its processes for the improvement of production and operational efficiency. Research and development of the techniques and methods associated with cyber-physical systems are based on the modelling and processing data collected by connected sensors and actuators. The data is integrated by software, artificial intelligence and big data-based algorithms for the development of advanced monitoring and control applications. The data is used to develop optimum decision-making, control, predictive maintenance and management algorithms for both industrial processes and assets (Osornio & Prieto, 2020).

CYBER PHYSICAL APPLICATIONS

1. Trends of Digital Transformation in the Ship Building Sector
2. Energy Infrastructure of the Factory as a Virtual Power Plant: Smart Energy Management
3. Novel Methods Based on Deep Learning Applied to Condition Monitoring in Smart Manufacturing Processes

4. Smart Monitoring Based on Novelty Detection and Artificial Intelligence Applied to the Condition Assessment of Rotating Machinery in the Industry 4.0 (Osornio & Prieto, 2020)

AI TECHNOLOGIES AND TOOLS

1. AI for Improving the Overall Equipment Efficiency in Manufacturing Industry
2. Decision Support Models for the Selection of Production Strategies in the Paradigm of Digital Manufacturing, Based on Technologies, Costs and Productivity Levels
3. Developing Cognitive Advisor Agents for Operators in Industry 4.0 (Osornio & Prieto, 2020)

INDUSTRIAL IOT (IIoT) AND DATA ANALYTICS

1. Current Transducer for IoT Applications
2. How the Data Provided by IIoT Are Utilized in Enterprise Resource Planning
3. Big Data Analytics and Its Applications in Supply Chain Management (Osornio & Prieto, 2020)

Demand planning is crucial to manufacturing since it helps to guarantee that there is always enough production going on. AI helps companies increase product availability by lowering waste and stock outs. AI can be utilised to help us understand sales patterns better (Chopra et al., 2021).

BENEFITS OF ADOPTING AN INDUSTRY 4.0 MODEL

Design, sales, inventories, scheduling, quality, engineering, customer, and field service are all included in the scope of Industry 4.0, as well as the complete product life cycle and supply chain. Everyone provides accurate, current, and pertinent perspectives on business and production processes—as well as significantly more thorough and timely analytics.

1. It increases your competitiveness, particularly vs market disruptors like Amazon: You should be making investments in technology and solutions that will help you enhance and optimise your own operation as businesses like Amazon continue to improve supply chain management and logistics. You must have the systems and procedures in place to give your consumers and clients the same quality of service (or better) as they may receive from a business like Amazon if you want to remain competitive.
2. You become more appealing to the younger workforce: Businesses that make investments in cutting-edge Industry 4.0 technology are better positioned to draw in and keep new employees (e.g., in India Govt Initiative schemes (National Skill Development Corporation (NSDC) etc. in the field of employment generating, Digital India program).
3. It strengthens your team and fosters collaboration: Organizations that invest in Industry 4.0 solutions can boost departmental collaboration, increase efficiency, enable predictive and prescriptive analytics, and give operators, managers, and executives more access to real-time data and intel-

ligence to help them make better decisions as they carry out their daily tasks (latest innovation in the science field – i.e. Sophia (a human robot), Alexa, Google assistant).

4. It enables you to handle prospective issues before they turn into major difficulties. Automation, real-time data, internet-connected gear, and predictive analytics may all help you be more proactive in identifying and resolving possible supply chain management and maintenance concerns (emerging topologies which help in better connectivity).

5. Industry 4.0 technology lets you oversee and optimise every part of your manufacturing processes and supply chain, which enables you to save costs, increase profits, and spur development. It provides you with the real-time data and insights you require to make quicker, more informed business choices that will eventually increase the productivity and profitability of your whole enterprise. Now a day AI also helps in creating a Scalable and profitable business model.

ADVANTAGES

Benefits of Deploying AI Models

1. In order to meet the growing demand of customers throughout the world, businesses have been seen extending their manufacturing capacity. Even though introducing AI to the industrial sector will need a substantial financial outlay, the return on investment will be fantastic (Chopra et al., 2021) (Example – Digital nurturing concept came into existence).

2. As duties are handled by intelligent devices on a daily basis, businesses might experience much lower operating expenses. As a result, the human resource, which previously performed all labor-intensive tasks, is now better used and can concentrate on complex and creative tasks as AI takes over the production facility and automates routine and dull human labour. Humans can concentrate on advancing innovation and elevating their company while AI handles routine tasks (Chopra et al., 2021) (Example- like Alexa, Google assistant, mini robots working in house hold, smart home automation, smart health monitoring system, smart irrigation system, smart cart).

3. Although introducing AI to the industrial sector will need a substantial financial outlay, the payoff will be enormous. As intelligent gadgets handle routine activities, businesses can see substantially lower operating expenses (Chopra et al., 2021).

Scaling AI in Manufacturing Operations

Machine learning and AI models will be used to integrate greater automation into the Industry 4.0. However, the integration and implementation of digital platforms and technologies is still a problem for manufacturers. Only 14% of automobile manufacturers have implemented AI on a large basis. A smart place to start when deploying an AI system is with a successful prototype's introduction into real-world industrial settings. In a sandbox or other controlled environment, prototypes have implemented. The system's exposure to real-time data sets and challenges is thus constrained. A model must be educated to an accuracy level appropriate for real-time manufacturing operations before being introduced into a production-ready environment. Testing on real-time data will not only improve development accuracy but will also confirm that the solution meets industrial requirements (Chopra et al., 2021) (dealing with the real life problem helps in terms of better services in minimum efforts which result in a good amount of employment generation as well). Involvement in the tertiary sector of country leads to the GDP growth as well.

Significant Advancements in Industry 4.0 Through Artificial Intelligence

The combination of AI and ML is demonstrated by the successful introduction of autonomous cars and robotics. The outcome of each development step may be continuously analysed with the aid of sensors and ML. One of the frequent issues in the sector is the ability to match supply and demand. Machine learning (ML) integration makes it possible to fulfil energy needs as efficiently as possible. Additionally, user service is improved by using AI technology. For instance, a lot of chat bots on e-commerce websites are AI-driven and set up to instantly respond to numerous common inquiries from customers. Intelligent plucking devices and advanced tractors have become more prevalent in the agriculture industry. Another important use of AI in the financial sector is fraud detection (Javaid et al., 2022).

Industrial firms spend in automated AI vehicles to automate logistic processes to help manage the delivery hubs. Self-driving cars thus eliminate need on human drivers. The demand for products can also be effectively predicted by AI systems using predictive analytics. AI manufacturing applications gather data from different sources. Later on, it can forecast product demand correctly based on evidence. The AI app can handle order records and uninstall/install new stocks. It is one of the premium technologies for production management, market management and inventory management. Through analyzing historical product–price data, algorithms for ML will predict the price of a product. It can use neural networks and in-depth modeling to recognize images and supervise predictive model learning (Javaid et al., 2022).

AI assists the robot in precisely capturing minute air bubbles and determining the location of the gas leak. Along with data retrieved from the whole production chain, it promptly identifies problem regions and production lines, considerably lowers personnel costs, and detects mistakes. In the Industry 4.0 environment, sensors are included into every piece of hardware to facilitate machine-to-machine communication. Additionally, ML offered by data-physical systems and cloud computing facilitates seamless resource linkage between people, equipment, and machines. As a consequence, all elements of the production process, including cars, production lines, factories, and buildings, may be intimately integrated (Javaid et al., 2022).

CHALLENGES OF INDUSTRIAL ARTIFICIAL INTELLIGENCE

1. Machine-to-machine interactions
2. Cybersecurity
3. Increase in job displacements and transformation of work
4. Lack of Specialized Workforce for AI Systems
5. Lack of Trust and Explainability
6. Unreal Expectations From AI Enabled the utilized Systems
7. The Need for Accuracy in Data for AI Systems

FUTURE OF ARTIFICIAL INTELLIGENCE IN INDUSTRY 4.0

AI will offer useful data that helps company executives create unique and reliable business models. When it comes to seeing patterns and occurrences that a normal person cannot notice clearly, this technique will prove to be quite helpful. AI will generate the data needed to support fact-based, data-driven business choices. It will in many ways give a more thorough assessment and assist in removing personal preconceptions from the calculation. In order to uncover growth, extension, and even new market prospects, AI and ML technologies may gather data from a variety of sources. As a result, new goods and services will be created. In addition to the IoT, other breakthroughs like edge computing and blockchain have grown in popularity and opened up new possibilities. AI will soon take off with new benefits that will contribute to the development of a connected, intelligent, and smart society. For instance, production practices, which are often continually improved and adjusted, may be quite ineffective. Future robotics as a service might replicate particular human abilities like voice and image recognition with the aid of AI. It can monitor, examine production quotas, and add to models of preventive maintenance.

CONCLUSION

Artificial intelligence has a major impact on Industry 4.0. In this respect, this book chapter reviews some applications that benefit and challenges from AI. From the examined sources is could be concluded that the heart of nowadays industry is the AI & ML, every aspect is connected to it and they all share that.

There is an urgent need for methodical AI development and application in order to observe its true influence in the next generation of industrial systems, namely Industry 4.0. AI is emerging from science fiction to become the frontier of world-changing technologies.

Industry 4.0, with the help of AI, completely automates the control of the different stages of the production processes. Based on the product specifications, any stage of the manufacturing procedure will be refined in real time. It can integrate the complete development chain, and the job load involved in data processes can be extended to many divisions.

With proper research and vision, AI models can be integrated into a stepwise process involving the integration of AI models with the old manufacturing methods and then slowly eliminating the loopholes of the current model and moving on to a newer and better version until the whole manufacturing unit becomes AI friendly with better efficiency and greater profits.

Also there is nothing more perfect than the human way of interaction, authors try to build that, just on bigger scale, that's industry 4.0.

REFERENCES

Adoption, T., & Report, S. (2021). *The First Signpost on the Road from Early Adoption to Widespread Application of Industry 4.0 Technologies 2021 Industry 4.0 Technology Adoption Survey Report*. Academic Press.

Becker, F. G., Cleary, M., Team, R. M., Holtermann, H., The, D., Agenda, N., Science, P., Sk, S. K., Hinnebusch, R., Hinnebusch, A. R., Rabinovich, I., Olmert, Y., Uld, D. Q. G. L. Q., Ri, W. K. H. U., Lq, V., Frxqwu, W. K. H., Zklfk, E., Edvhg, L. V., … Wkh, R. Q. (2015).主観的健康感を中心とした在宅高齢者における 健康関連指標に関する共分散構造分析. *Syria Studies, 7*(1). https://www.researchgate.net/publication/269107473_What_is_governance/link/548173090cf22525dcb61443/download%0Ahttp://www.econ.upf.edu/~reynal/Civilwars_12December2010.pdf%0Ahttps://think-asia.org/handle/11540/8282%0Ahttps://www.jstor.org/stable/41857625

Chopra, M., Singh, S. K., Sharma, S., & Mahto, D. (2021). Impact and Usability of Artificial Intelligence in Manufacturing workflow to empower Industry 4.0. *CEUR Workshop Proceedings, 3080.*

Deep, A., & Sood, M. (2023). Effective Detection of DDoS Attack in IoT-Based Networks Using Machine Learning with Different Feature Selection Techniques. *Proceedings of Data Analytics and Management ICDAM, 2022*, 527–540.

Ding, H., & Yuan, Y. (2020). Preface: Industrial Artificial Intelligence. *Zhongguo Kexue Jishu Kexue/ Scientia Sinica Technologica, 50*(11), 1413. https://doi.org/ doi:10.1360/SST-2020-0383

Gartner, Inc. (2020). *Gartner survey reveals 66% of organizations increased or did not change AI investments since the onset of COVID-19.* https://www.gartner.com/en/newsroom/press-releases/2020-10-01-gartner-survey-revels-66-percent-of-orgnizations-increased-or-did-not-change-ai-investments-since-the-onset-of-covid-19

Ing Tay, S., Te Chuan, L., Nor Aziati, A. H., Nur Aizat Ahmad, A., Tay, S., Lee, T., Hamid, N. A., & Ahmad, A. (2018). An Overview of Industry 4.0: Definition, Components, and Government Initiatives Microencapsulation of self-healing agent for corrosion applications View project Biomedical Technology and IR 4.0: Management, Applications & Challenges View project An Overview of Industry 4.0: Definition, Components, and Government Initiatives. *Journal of Advanced Research in Dynamical and Control Systems, 12*. https://www.researchgate.net/publication/332440369

Javaid, Haleem, Singh, & Suman. (2022). Artificial Intelligence Applications for Industry4.0: A Literature-Based Study. *Journal of Industrial Integration and Management, 7*(1), 83–111. DOI: doi:10.1142/S242486222130004083

Kinkel, S., Baumgartner, M., & Cherubini, E. (2021). Prerequisites for the adoption of AI technologies in manufacturing – Evidence from a worldwide sample of manufacturing companies. *Technovation, 102375*. doi:10.1016/j.technovation.2021.102375

Lee, J., Davari, H., Singh, J., & Pandhare, V. (2018). Industrial Artificial Intelligence for industry 4.0-based manufacturing systems. *Manufacturing Letters, 18*(September), 20–23. doi:10.1016/j.mfglet.2018.09.002

Mhlanga, D. (2021). Artificial intelligence in the industry 4.0, and its impact on poverty, innovation, infrastructure development, and the sustainable development goals: Lessons from emerging economies? *Sustainability (Basel), 13*(11), 5788. Advance online publication. doi:10.3390u13115788

Okunlaya, R. O., Syed Abdullah, N., & Alias, R. A. (2022). Artificial intelligence (AI) library services innovative conceptual framework for the digital transformation of university education. *Library Hi Tech, 40*(6), 1869–1892. Advance online publication. doi:10.1108/LHT-07-2021-0242

Osornio, R. A., & Prieto, M. D. (2020). New Trends in the Use of Artificial Intelligence for the Industry 4.0. New Trends in the Use of Artificial Intelligence for the Industry 4.0. doi:10.5772/intechopen.86015

Peres, R. S., Jia, X., Lee, J., Sun, K., Colombo, A. W., & Barata, J. (2020). Industrial Artificial Intelligence in Industry 4.0 -Systematic Review, Challenges and Outlook. *IEEE Access : Practical Innovations, Open Solutions, 8*, 220121–220139. doi:10.1109/ACCESS.2020.3042874

Rozario, A., & Zhang, C. (2022). The Effects of Artificial Intelligence on Firms' Internal Information Quality. SSRN *Electronic Journal*. doi:10.2139/ssrn.3850823

Sharabov, M., & Tsochev, G. (2020). The Use of Artificial Intelligence in Industry 4.0. *Problems of Engineering Cybernetics and Robotics, 73*, 17–29. doi:10.7546/PECR.73.20.02

UNIDO. (2016). Opportunities and Challenges of the New Industrial Revolution for Developing Countries and Economies in Transition. *Department of Trade, Investment and Innovation*, 6–7. https://www.unido.org/sites/default/files/2017-01/Unido_industry-4_NEW_0.pdf

Chapter 3
Solutions for Software Requirement Risks Using Artificial Intelligence Techniques

Vijaya Kumar Reddy R.

Koneru Lakshmaiah Education Foundation, India

U. Rahamathunnisa

Vellore Institute of Technology, India

P. Subhashini

Vel Tech Multi Tech Dr. Rangarajan Dr. Sakunthala Engineering College, India

H. Mickle Aancy

Panimalar Engineering College, India

S. Meenakshi

RMK Engineering College, India

S. Boopathi

Muthayammal Engineering College, India

ABSTRACT

Software projects have a very high probability of failure, and a major reason for this is a poor requirement engineering process. Requirement elicitation and documentation are the primary and most vital steps in the software development life cycle. There is a lack of a model or framework that deals with these risks in parallel, and a lot of work is needed to manage them holistically. This chapter includes the identification of factors that affect successful software development and explores various sources of requirement risks. It intends to create an intelligent framework for managing VUCA risks in software requirements. The relationship between VUCA and terrorism risks identification at an early stage using fuzzy logic, ANFIS, and intelligent Bayesian network models. The framework includes a model for volatile requirement prioritization and a model for requirement ambiguity and uncertainty management.

DOI: 10.4018/978-1-6684-8145-5.ch003

Copyright © 2023, IGI Global. Copying or distributing in print or electronic forms without written permission of IGI Global is prohibited.

INTRODUCTION

The software business has radically altered our way of life by affecting practically every aspect of it. The growth of the software industry is a result of users' rising needs for customization and convenience. The tech industry has a significant positive impact on employment, exports, economic growth, and global trade. More "intelligent" products and apps will be created in the next few years, including watches, cars, home appliances, and even eyewear. As a result, Forrester Research predicts that the market for software products will keep expanding and improving. The software industry generates more than a trillion dollars annually in the US alone. The annual salaries of software developers are more than twice as high as those of all other US employees. According to IBEF figures, the predicted costs for packaged applications are visible in the BRIC countries of Brazil, Russia, India, and China. About 8% of India's GDP comes from the country's software sector (Naseem et al., 2021; Shaukat et al., 2018). Around 200 billion USD in revenue is generated by the sector, of which 150 USD comes from exports. The software sector has generated 12 million prospects for indirect employment in addition to 4 million direct positions.

Software development is a dynamic process that advances continuously to address the various business needs of its clients and end users. Many SMEs (small and medium enterprises) in India have benefited from the inclusion of the software industry, which also supports the formal economy. It has helped to digitise a number of industries, including banking and rail. The list of features that every system must have in order to meet client expectations is a well-defined requirement. The successful completion of software projects depends heavily on the effective management of these requirements. A proactive methodology is a better strategy for risk assessments. Early on in the software development process, it can be challenging to identify these risk-related requirements. To analyse and evaluate these requirements, a team of software domain specialists is needed. These hazards must be foreseen in advance for software development to be successful. For the prediction of risks in the requirements, a method comprising software requirement risks is necessary. These requirement-based hazards are currently predicted, classified, and prioritised using methods that are not based on formal modelling methodologies (Letier et al., 2014).

Risk management in software development includes risk assessments as a crucial component. They are informal, highly subjective assessments made by a risk group or team. The benefit of having a team of requirement specialists conduct this analysis is not available for all software projects. As they are labour-intensive and extremely subjective, the risk assessment techniques that are now available have a significant likelihood of being inaccurate. The popular abbreviation VUCA stands for volatility, uncertainty, complexity, and ambiguity. The literature demonstrates that VUCA elements have been repeatedly found and are acknowledged to have had the greatest impact on the software sector. The study's objectives are to pinpoint the variables that influence software development, investigate different risk factors, and examine how VUCA risks are related to one another. Additionally, it intends to provide a framework with artificial intelligence that can control VVCA risks early on and successfully utilise a number of methods (Haribalaji et al., 2021; Sampath et al., 2022).

The requirement engineering phase is the cornerstone of all software initiatives. Any software is developed based on the analysis of the requirements and the agreement between the businesses. One of the key elements affecting the project's time, money, and quality is successfully completing the requirement elicitation process. Requirement risk is defined as the degree of uncertainty between the users' expectations and the system's perceived requirements. A technique for examination that is primarily anticipated to identify writing that is relevant to a certain research area is the review or survey of the literature. A number of studies and comparisons of alternative methodologies have been conducted in recent years, with various performance factors related to software requirement risks being considered. A significant portion of the GDP of many nations, including India, is contributed by the software industry. The complexity of the programme is also increased by the density of its products. In India's software industry, a significant number of projects have encountered difficulties or failed during the past few years (Demirel and Das, 2018; Marasco, 2007).

Software development initiatives are known for having a relatively high failure rate. A systematic technique must be chosen at an early stage of development in order to create a successful software project. A cleaner agent module with a tuple of coordinates in a room representing seven objectives enables autonomous agent testing. Cost, coverage, similarity, and feasibility are the four objectives considered by the extended finite state machine in order to determine the appropriate test path sequence. The authors' work has influenced NSGA-II to create an algorithm that links the SBST to other recurrent testing tasks and is based on individual preferences (Myilsamy & Boopathi, 2017; Saravanan et al., 2022; Vanitha et al., 2023).

Combining test programme units in both aspect-oriented and object-oriented using a multi-objective algorithm with a generic approach. Four coupling measures are minimised, automatically chosen genetic operators are used, and an ideal graph partition is used to represent software package or module dependencies. New methods and formulations could be investigated by maintaining a trade-off between minimal coupling and high cohesion using the MQ measure of SBSE. Reduced execution time and more sophisticated module clustering arise from the replacement of metric and discarding MQ with EVM (Domakonda et al., 2022; Samikannu et al., 2022; Sampath et al., 2021; Sampath & Myilsamy, 2021).

Software engineering heavily relies on testing, hence it's critical to create fitness functions for each goal. The SBST field maturity has been added to this. Three key maintenance procedures are utilised to raise system quality: software modularization, software rectification, and software reworking. Because projects vary in size, multi-objective optimization algorithms used in software analysis and design stages can produce erroneous findings.

Through increased precision, recall, F-measure, and decreased error rate, soft computing-based evolutionary algorithms can enhance software project performance. The accuracy of the optimal solutions for the decision-making criterion has risen when using conventional multi-objective algorithms. Evolutionary methods based on soft computing can be used to address the complexity of mistake faults that appear during intermediate stages of software project development. This method can aid in the evaluation of actual case studies involving various projects inside a company (Boopathi, 2019; Boopathi & Sivakumar, 2016; Myilsamy & Sampath, 2021).

REQUIREMENT ENGINEERING

The following are some ways in which Requirement Engineering helps manage software risks (Hoodat & Rashidi, 2009):

- **Identifying Risks Early:** Requirement Engineering helps identify potential risks before they occur, allowing project teams to take proactive steps to mitigate them.
- **Defining Requirements Clearly:** Clear and concise requirements reduce the risk of misunderstandings and errors, which can lead to defects, delays, and cost overruns.

- **Prioritizing Requirements:** Requirement Engineering helps prioritize requirements based on importance, complexity, and risk, reducing the risk of project failure.
- **Verifying Requirements:** Requirement Engineering reviews and validates requirements to ensure they are complete, correct, and consistent, helping to identify and resolve potential issues before they become problems.
- **Managing Changes:** Requirement Engineering helps manage changes to requirements throughout the software development lifecycle, reducing the risk of defects or delays.

VUCA OUTLOOK

Project managers can determine the group that poses the most risk by classifying hazards based on their potential impact and underlying causes. It is possible to define risk attributes and categorise risks according to these attributes. As a result of grouping related criteria, a risk category will be created. In requirements engineering, there are many different kinds of risks. VUCA risk, or a necessity. Volatility, uncertainty, complexity, and requirement ambiguity are the primary causes of hazards for other risks, but no formal model exists for these risks.

Requirement Volatility: According to the software industry, the impact of requirement changes during the software development process can be managed in a number of ways. The fluctuation of requirements is one of the key elements that makes a project difficult. Many researchers have contributed their expertise in the areas of requirement volatility and novel management techniques. It is described as the quantity of a requirement changing over a predetermined period of time. Demonstrated volatility is the term for changes to requirements made after the initial agreed-upon set of criteria. Change management is an important aspect of software development that can increase production costs, labour requirements, and software product quality if not handled properly. It involves eliciting criteria that have changed or are unstable (Boopathi et al., 2023; Giudici, 2018; Vanitha et al., 2023).

The inclusion of new needs, the modification of existing ones, and/or the deletion of others are all considered changes in requirements. Some needs may change even after they have been finalised and included in the software requirement specification document. Requirement volatility refers to changes made after the basic set has been determined. A variety of people, including stakeholders, operators, and other interface groups, may submit change requests. The produced software product's quality, price, and delivery schedule will be impacted by this. New priorities are established during the requirements assessment, design, and development phases of software release planning. Volatility may have detrimental consequences for the software development process. Previous investigations have shown that requirement fluctuation poses serious difficulties for the development process. The impact of requirement volatility on the software project schedule, maintenance, and defect density has been investigated through ongoing experimental studies and literature analyses. It is well understood that requirements volatility is a critical factor in the development and maintenance of a good software system. Characterization and evaluation of issues related to the change in requirements are the most crucial things that may be done for this goal. This will make it easier to clearly identify the requirements and volatility (Giudici, 2018; Hoodat & Rashidi, 2009; Kumara et al., 2023; S. et al., 2022).

Requirement volatility is a major reason why many software projects fail. It is the frequency of changes in requirements during a specific time period, which cannot always be prevented. Customers will reject a product if it does not meet their needs, and if changes in specifications are not managed appropriately, the project's cost could increase and the final product's quality could suffer.

Requirement Uncertainty: One of the main problems in the software development industry is uncertainty. It may lead to complicated obligations and additional risks. Tools and methods to help developers manage their software needs more successfully have been developed as a consequence of ongoing field research. All stakeholder needs must be successfully gathered, assessed, and prioritised before software development can begin. Any stage of requirement engineering can experience requirement uncertainty. It could be the result of a lack of knowledge about numerous things, like the goals and priorities of investors in terms of their needs, financial restrictions, and so on. It's crucial to address this weakness if you want to construct a software system successfully. It might be described as the separation between information held by developers and information needed to assess user needs (Marasco, 2007; Sampath et al., 2022).

Requirement Complexity: The most important details in this text are the ways in which requirement complexity can impact software risk. These include development time and cost, defects, quality, communication and collaboration, and scope creep. Complex requirements can require more development time and resources, leading to increased costs and potentially delayed project schedules. Defects may not be discovered until later in the development lifecycle, leading to rework and increased costs. Quality may not meet stakeholder needs and expectations, leading to lower quality software and potential project failure. Communication and collaboration between stakeholders, developers, and testers can be difficult, leading to misunderstandings and errors. Scope creep can lead to potential scope creep and increased risk of project failure (Domakonda et al., 2022; Giudici, 2018; Samikannu et al., 2022; Vennila et al., 2022).

Requirement Ambiguity: The most important details in this text are the ways in which ambiguous requirements can impact software risk. Misinterpretation: These requirements can be interpreted differently by different stakeholders, leading to misunderstandings and potential misalignment between stakeholders' needs and expectations. Design and development: These requirements can make it difficult for developers to design and develop software that meets stakeholder needs and expectations, leading to rework, cost overruns, and delays. Testing: These requirements can lead to incomplete or ineffective testing, leading to defects and decreased software quality. Communication and collaboration: These requirements can make communication and collaboration between stakeholders, developers, and testers more challenging, leading to misunderstandings and increased project risk (Hu et al., 2013).

Syntactic Ambiguity: A sentence that can have many meanings in English depending on the grammatical arrangement and structural alterations that have been made to it is said to have primary ambiguity. It is also known as grammatical ambiguity, structural ambiguity, and ambiguity based on structure. The nouns, adverbs, and adjectives that can be perplexing are usually to blame for this ambiguity.

Referential Ambiguity: Referential ambiguity is predicated on the relationship between the sentence's context and intended meaning. It depends on the reader and the requirements. Two readers from different disciplines who are interpreting the requirements differently are an example of this kind of ambiguity (Kumara et al., 2023; Saher et al., 2018a).

Optimization: The new internet of things, wireless networks, communication between the sectors, and optimization of processes could be done to provide a solution to the software-related risk problems (Babu et al., 2022; Boopathi et al., 2022; Boopathi et al., 2023; Jeevanantham et al., 2022; Palaniappan et al., 2023; S. et al., 2022; Sampath et al., 2022; Senthil et al., 2023; Trojovský et al., 2023). The TOPSIS, ANN, and machine learning techniques can also be utilised to minimise the risks (Boopathi et al., 2021; Boopathi & Sivakumar, 2013; Kavitha et al., 2022; Myilsamy & Sampath, 2021; Sampath & Myilsamy, 2021; Yupapin et al., 2022).

This research demonstrates that VUCA risks in requirements have a significant impact on the outcome of software development projects. It provides a framework to address these risks to aid in the development of risk-free products. This review aids in the effective management of all necessary risks.

INTELLIGENT FRAMEWORK FOR REQUIREMENT RISK MANAGEMENT

An efficient framework is required to effectively control requirement risks in software development. An effective framework for requirement risk management at an early level of the SDLC is presented in this article. In addition to using machine learning to help identify and manage VUCA risks, it suggests using artificial intelligence to prevent software project failures. It entails a series of actions where volatility is identified using a few criteria and their relationships. Volatile requirements are identified and moved on to the next level for prioritising. The next steps are to assess and manage requirement ambiguity and uncertainty. By examining how requirements are interdependent, uncertainty is assessed. The complexity of requirements is predicted using Bayesian analysis. Finally, a number of reports are created, and management plans are offered to address the issue of VUCA risks.

This article offers a methodology for identifying and categorising the major concerns and difficulties associated with VUCA risks and their effects on software projects. It includes employing requirement inspection to identify volatility, detecting ambiguous requirements, fuzzy inference system (FIS) prioritisation, Adaptive Neuro-Fuzzy Inference System (Adaptive Neuro-Fuzzy Inference System) to perform the requirement ambiguity examination, and Bayesian networks to predict requirement complexity early on (Abdelazim et al., 2020; Devadas & Cholli, 2022; Sadia et al., 2019).

VUCA-Free Requirements

Due to the fluctuating needs of the software business, educational groups assist the sector by creating better tools and procedures. The proposed framework's three phases are shown in Figure: requirement ambiguity and uncertainty assessment, requirement ambiguity identification and prioritization, and requirement complexity prediction. Prior to the framework's implementation, it is essential to understand all the contributing variables and root causes of demand risks. The requirement management process may be improved and maintained with a clearer understanding of these causes and their effects. The following subsections provide a brief explanation of each of the proposed framework's phases (Sadiq and Jain, 2013).

Workflow of the Framework

This section presents the process by which the Intelligent Framework was developed. It is made up of three blocks that stand in for the three major stages of the suggested framework. Each block is in charge of carrying out the task assigned to it. Each of the three parts is interconnected and has a different purpose.

Requirement Volatility Identification and Prioritization: The most important phase in this framework is the identification of volatile requirements (Figure 1). Volatile needs cannot be disregarded because it is occasionally important to take stakeholder-requested changes into account. It is suggested to prioritise the changing requirements using a fuzzy-based method. Initial requirements are used as an input, and several interconnected characteristics are used to determine the level of volatility (Devadas & Cholli, 2022).

Requirement Ambiguity and Uncertainty: A programme called Ambiguity Finder has been created to help users of specification documents identify ambiguities of four different types: lexical, syntax, syntactic, and referential (Figure 2). An adaptive fuzzy neural network implementation has been used to assess ambiguity. In this article, we examine the creation of a data dictionary for ambiguity analysis and requirement detection. The University of Bristol is now conducting research in the fields of data mining and data analysis, and one of its current projects examines the relationship between uncertainty and ambiguity (Saher et al., 2018b).

Requirement Complexity Prediction: At the beginning of the SDLC, a requirement tree is produced, and the complexity of the requirement definition is predicted. The forecast of requirement complexity is prepared using a Bayesian network-based model (Figure 3). The framework's final stage is to make sure all requirements are met. Identification of the complexity type, the construction of relationships between types, and Bayesian analysis for complexity prediction are important tasks in this stage (Malik & Singh, 2020).

INSPECTION TECHNIQUE FOR IDENTIFYING REQUIREMENTS

One of the most efficient and widely acknowledged methods for finding and fixing flaws is inspection. For source code, Software Inspection was initially developed. The use of it for different software life cycle products, such as design and requirements specifications, was further expanded. Scenario-based reading is a subcategory of perspective-based reading (PBR). PBR offers numerous distinct audits, each from the perspective of a particular customer requirement. According to studies, there are five different angles from which a requirement can be examined to find areas of volatility (Ejnioui et al., 2012; Saher et al., 2018b).

Security Perspective: Security restrictions are typically added as needed later in the life cycle, changing other requirements as a result, which either causes a delay in the project's schedule or increases the budget.

Stakeholders' Perspective: "A requirement must be viewed from the viewpoint of the stakeholders, since doing so can help identify a stakeholder's degree of expertise, which can be used to decide what training is required to prevent volatile requirements." Experience has demonstrated that partners or stakeholders are frequently ill-suited to express their needs.

Elicitation Perspective: The British Industry argued that unwanted and undocumented requests should be combined with more aware and archived requirements.

Technological Perspective: The likelihood of requirement revisions will be reduced by reading the requirement document from a variety of technological perspectives. The best method for spotting variable requirements so that preventative measures can be taken is perspective-based reading (PBR). The research's next step is to create a fuzzy based prediction algorithm.

Environmental Perspective: The requirements must be examined while taking the environment's factors into account. Any project's requirements can alter as a result of shifting governmental policies.

Figure 1. Requirement volatility identification and prioritization

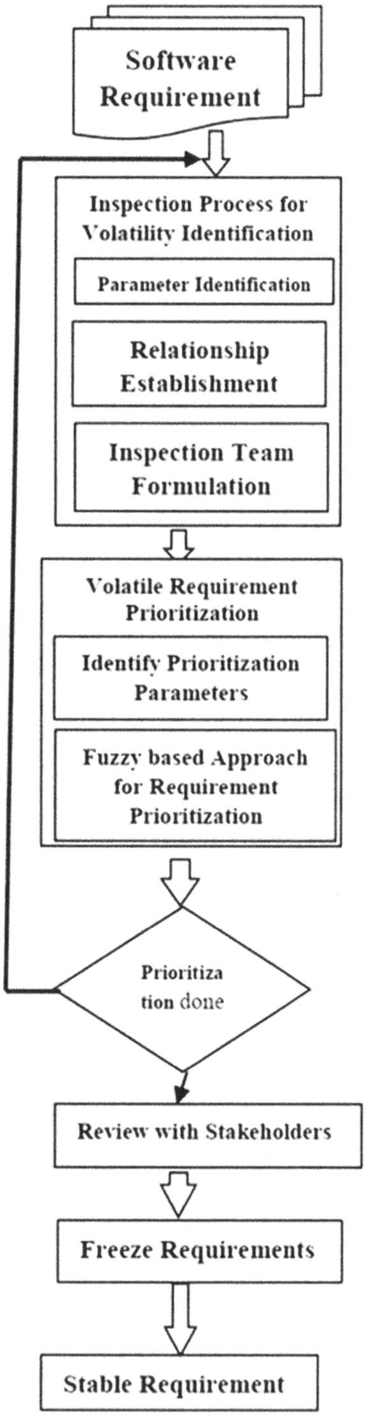

Figure 2. Requirement ambiguity and uncertainty assess

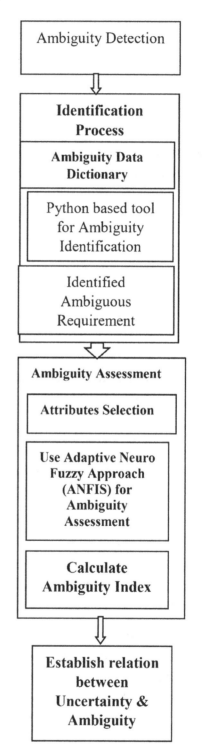

Figure 3. Requirement complexity prediction

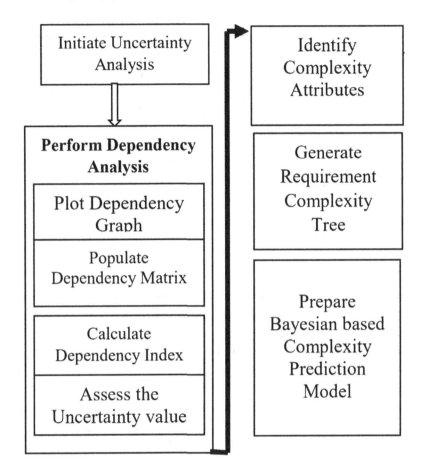

VOLATILE REQUIREMENT PRIORITIZATION TECHNIQUES

The goal of requirement prioritisation is to identify the key criteria that can be fulfilled while still retaining customer loyalty. To improve the chances of a software product developing successfully, each modification to the specifications should be focused on. When requirements are volatile, there is no one method that can help with requirement prioritisation. Generally speaking, cost and benefit considerations are considered when using need-prioritizing strategies. In order to rank the needs according to their relevance, information is employed in a variety of ways. There aren't many methods that combine logic and quantitative data collection to determine priorities. Some plans use informal groupings and generalisations to indicate priorities (Demirel & Das, 2018; Hoodat & Rashidi, 2009; Letier et al., 2014).

Cost-Value Approach: The value-cost ratio measures how much a good or service costs in relation to how much it is worth. This ratio is further illustrated graphically and used as a factor in choosing which component of the system to purchase.

Analytical Hierarchy Process (AHP): The Analytic Hierarchy Process (AHP) is a statistical method used to prioritize requirements based on risk, urgency, and priority. The process performs $n \, x \, (n-1) \, / \, 2$ comparisons for „n" number of requirements.

B-Tree Prioritize: The dynamic nature of requirements can be integrated into this prioritisation technique. Requirements never stop coming and never stop flowing. It employs a binary tree technique with a mapping function that compares the set of all previously prioritised requirements with the set of requirements based on the priority value.

Numerical Assessments: This approach is built on an ordinal scale, which organises needs into various groups that stakeholders can connect to. Despite having a wide range of applications, the approach has many drawbacks. How to define the groups precisely is one of the main problems. The final priorities are determined using the average ranking that the stakeholders gave to the requirements. The stakeholders' task of grouping their requirements into a few categories is quite simple.

Voting Test: Every purchase demand made on behalf of a stakeholder is considered. The textual values are then added together to get a total value, which is then displayed on a chart. The criteria with the highest score are considered to be the most crucial. The stakeholders can simply use this strategy because of how simple it is.

Ranking: This method ranks requirements based on an ordinal scale, with the highest and least important needs listed as 1 and n respectively. Sorting methods such as bubble sort, fast sort, and binary search tree are used to obtain rankings.

Planning Game: Instead of providing a single list of tasks or objects to be completed, customers are required to break down their requirements into a collection of tales.

Top Ten Requirements: From a predetermined list of needs, stakeholders are asked to select the top 10. This avoids an unwelcome conflict between the priorities. With regard to sophistication, the technique is simple but incredibly helpful when dealing with various stakeholders. Contrarily, the granularity of it is unusually coarse.

Theory W: The scheme's fundamental premise is to engage in negotiations with various stakeholders to settle any differences of opinion also known as the win-win model. The technique's guiding philosophy is the monitoring of product development based on the suggested plan, risk assessment, and handling.

REQUIREMENT PRIORITIZATION USING FUZZY BASED APPROACH

This paper suggests a method for ranking requirements according to their volatility. Each method of prioritising needs has advantages and disadvantages. It is acknowledged that there is no method currently in use that can effectively prioritise the volatile requirements (Abdelazim et al., 2020; Devadas & Cholli, 2022; Sadia et al., 2019).

Volatile Requirement Prioritization Factors

Volatile requirements can be ranked using three criteria: detectability, dependability, and changeability. These criteria have a significant effect on how volatile requirements are prioritized.

Prioritization of Volatile Requirement Through Fuzzy Inference System

When dealing with the elusiveness and granularity of information, fuzzy logic is a potent problem-solving method. A fuzzy model is typically employed when traditional analytical techniques are ineffective or when there are erroneous, uncertain, or ambiguous data sets (Ejnioui et al., 2012; Salais-Fierro et al., 2020).

Fuzzy logic is a powerful tool for problem-solving when traditional analytical techniques are ineffective or data sets are incomplete, ambiguous, or erroneous. It involves fuzzifying inputs, applying fuzzy operators, applying implication methods, aggregating outputs, and defuzzing results.

The outcome of each aggregated fuzzy set is used as the input for the defuzzification technique, which then outputs a single crisp value. Using membership functions, fuzzification determines the level to which information sources fit into appropriate fuzzy sets. A fuzzy-based model for prioritising variable requirements is represented in this study. Almost all sorts of software projects can be supported by the prioritising factors detectability, dependability, and changeability. These variables serve as the fuzzy system's linguistic inputs. The rules are developed using a fuzzy inference method. The three linguistic variables/factors indicated in the following sections are inputs into the system. The three input variables are mapped to a single linguistic variable termed Volatile Requirement Priority Ranking (VRPR), which is produced as an output.

Volatile Requirement Prioritization Using Fuzzy Logic Method

- The Mamdani approach is used to prioritise volatile requirements using a fuzzy inference system, which is based on a set without a new and clearly defined limit. It is an effective way to collect expert information.
- Fuzzification and FIS variables are added to the Java programming language, allowing for the definition of input variables through membership function editor.
- Rules for Volatile Requirement Prioritization using a Rule Editor for Fuzzy Deduction Framework.
- Rule Assessment Combining the rule's output and De-fuzzing the output value obtained.
- The issue of volatile requirement prioritisation from the outside.

In requirements engineering, prioritisation is a significant and frequent occurrence. Setting priorities aids in resolving the tension between competing demands and finite resources. Deploying the most beneficial product features is crucial, especially when deadlines are short and customer expectations are high. By weighing each requirement's relative relevance, project managers can structure development plans to maximise value and minimise cost. There has been a lot of effort put into requirement prioritisation, and there are many strategies available that are effective for this particular purpose (Okwu & Tartibu, 2020; Sadia et al., 2019; Salais-Fierro et al., 2020).

The static nature of needs like cost, benefit, risk, and time has been the subject of earlier studies. This study examines other factors, such as the investigation of how several factors interact with one another. The requirement engineering process is not complete without the prioritisation of requirements. A fuzzy logic-based technique in MATLAB is used to construct a volatile need prioritisation model. Since requirements vary continuously during the course of software development, the idea of prioritising these altering requirements would undoubtedly be helpful to the project managers.

REQUIREMENT AMBIGUITY ASSESSMENT USING ANFIS

It is important to evaluate requirement ambiguity from the start of the software development process to accurately estimate the ambiguity. This paper explores many aspects of requirement ambiguity to spot potential issues. Uncertainty in software development can be brought on by ambiguity in requirements in later stages. The software's quality may potentially be impacted. Utilizing an adaptive neuro-fuzzy approach, a Requirement Ambiguity Assessment Algorithm (RAAA) has been suggested (Okwu & Tartibu, 2020; Sadia et al., 2019; Salais-Fierro et al., 2020).

Dealing with and measuring ambiguity is a difficult problem. This issue is resolved by requirement ambiguity assessment, which uses a fuzzy based approach to provide a quantitative analysis using the aforementioned attributes. ANFIS is a hybrid strategy that combines the benefits of fuzzy logic and artificial neural networks, and has been used to address forecasting and modelling issues. Through a dataset of 60 different inputs leading to a single output, the ANFIS system is trained. It is a five-layer network that trains using two separate passes and a few epochs. Once properly trained, the system performs flawlessly in its role as a fuzzy expert system. It is common practise to use the Sugeno fuzzy inference system (SFIS) to determine the link between a number of input and output sets. First-order Sugeno FIS, a linear equation, can be used to describe the relationship. Errors are returned through the layers in SFIS in order to obtain the assertion parameter (Okwu & Tartibu, 2020; Salais-Fierro et al., 2020; Sremac et al., 2018).

The network is trained using a hybrid learning technique that combines least mean square and back-propagation algorithms. The steps include loading training information, building an ANFIS model, training an ANFI model, studying for requirement ambiguity, rules formation, and generating a FIS Surface.

Analysis of Ambiguity and Uncertainty

The following meaning groups emerged when the literal meaning of "ambiguity" was compiled across different dictionaries: Ambiguity is the potential for more than one different interpretation of a given utterance Second-order uncertainty is a situation or statement that is ambiguous and can be interpreted in different ways. It is when there is doubt about the definitions of uncertain states or outcomes. The term "second order uncertainty" refers to conceptions and definitions used by humans rather than an immutable law of nature. Statistical distributions associated with uncertainty are mathematically defined as having ambiguity. These are circumstances in which it is impossible to foresee the roles that the involved parties will play. Any software project's success is closely correlated with how well its functional requirements were written. The amount of requirement definition is significantly impacted by ambiguities in requirements throughout the development life cycle. The needs are interrelated and have compound effects; thus, they cannot be handled separately. Analysing the interdependencies between the requirements is necessary to assess the uncertainty brought on by ambiguous requirements. Determining dependencies between needs is essential to understand how they behave when there are ambiguities. This study identifies any potential ambiguities in the requirements document and provides advice to remove any doubts.

Requirement Uncertainty by Analysing Requirement Dependency

The requirements that the method described above identified as being unclear are gathered into a requirement repository. The requirement, along with its definition, characteristics, and dependency details, are all present in the repository. The relationship between needs is described by the dependency information, which is helpful in determining how one demand influences and probably affects other requirements. Software failure, excessive development costs, and schedule delays as a result of requirements rework are always consequences of ambiguity and uncertainty in the requirement definition. A model is developed to manage ambiguity and uncertainty in software requirement specifications.

A BAYESIAN NETWORK FOR COMPLEXITY PREDICTION MODEL

This study develops a method for reducing requirement complexity and establishing a link between VUCA hazards. It is useful for determining the development and testing requirements for a potential software product during the requirement analysis stage of the software development life cycle (SDLC). VUCA is the main cause of project failure in software development (Luo et al., 2005; Sadia et al., 2023; Vassileva et al., 2017).

To forecast the required complexity of software products, a Bayesian approach is suggested. In the requirement engineering phase, the many elements influencing requirement complexity are recognised. If the requirements are not accurately elicited at the elicitation phase, the entire development process will fail, costing time and money. Many requirements in large software products have confusing or complicated descriptions. The requirements that developers start with are typically unclear, uncertain, incomplete, insufficient, and variable in nature. The software design process depends on having clear requirements, yet getting the desired level of understanding ability can be challenging. As the requirements change over time, functionalities may be added, removed, or modified. The goal of this study is to create an efficient method for predicting requirement complexity at an early stage.

Complexity

Software complexity is the degree of difficulty in analysing, maintaining, testing, designing, and altering software. It affects every phase of the software lifecycle and permeates the entire software development process. The degree to which a requirement is challenging to comprehend and verify is referred to as its complexity. Each need is either more or less complex depending on a variety of factors (Sadia et al., 2023; Sremac et al., 2018).

Prediction Model

A methodology for gauging the complexity of needs based on the characteristics that help define software requirements is created. It has been discovered that the requirements become complex due to their fundamental elements, such as the quantity of requirements, the variety of stakeholders, etc. These qualities have been derived from both a thorough analysis of the literature and suggestions for software requirements.

Requirements and Expectations: The most important details in the requirement engineering process are the quantity of needs and their interdependencies, which determine the quality and complexity of the requirements. These properties include ambiguity, constantly changing, and uncertainty.

Parties Involved: Various stakeholders are defining what is required of a software product. These stakeholders can differ in a variety of ways, including their culture and technical subject knowledge. These elements influence a requirement's difficulty; hence consideration must be given to them when calculating the complexity of the need. User involvement is a key factor in successful project development, including number of stakeholders, categories of stakeholders, cultural variety, geographic distance, and ignorance of technology.

Development Characteristics: The software product being developed is significantly impacted by the development environment. As a result, the requirements must be modified appropriately, which occasionally increases their complexity. several supporting variables. Extreme new technology use, numerous infrastructure limitations, restrictions on communications, iterative or incremental methodology, many different techniques and tools used.

Development Team: Successful software initiatives depend heavily and significantly on the development team. If not handled correctly, it may have a negative impact on a project's success. One of the most important tasks for software project managers is overseeing the various stakeholders and parties engaged in the development of software projects. Due to his technical expertise and cultural variety, a team member's perception of a specific demand may differ from person to person.

Requirement Complexity Tree: A complexity tree is a graphical representation of various combinations of complexity traits. To assess complexity, it is necessary to identify a system in an undesirable condition. Each difficulty trait's potential occurrences are investigated separately. The required complexity tree is produced by combining all of the separate subtrees developed for each complexity attribute. Then, a list of every scenario in which these occurrences might occur is made. The analysis of the connections between various complexity categories led to the creation of the required complexity tree. For the same reason, AND and OR logic gates have been employed. The primary inputs for developing the model are the subtrees from 1–4. These branches work together to form the tree as a whole.

BAYESIAN NETWORKS

A Bayesian network is a probability-based model that illustrates conditional interdependence between random variables. It is a directed acyclic graph with arcs representing causal influences and nodes representing the random variables themselves. The prior probability distributions and conditional probability distributions of nodes are used to define them. The minimal probability dispersion of variables is stored in the NPT. For example, a node addressing variable A is the likelihood that variable A will still be present at state xi if all of An's defenders are in one of its authorised states (Luo et al., 2005; Sadia et al., 2023; Vassileva et al., 2017).

The Bayesian network is a useful tool for probabilistic derivation, with each node having its default probability at the beginning. Dynamic Bayesian networks are extensions of the network that provide a transient measurement. A requirement complexity prediction model based on requirement complexity attributes has been created using a Bayesian network. Data specifying the complexity features that previously had an impact on the system must be used to train the network.

RCPM Model

GeNIe modeller creates a Bayesian network model for RCPM by combining various qualities for requirement complexity through the interaction between attributes in the requirement complexity tree.

These steps are briefly explained below:

- The Bayesian model proposed in this work is built by fusing different subtrees. The probability distribution values used to forecast the complexity of a software product are defined by the SRS. The probability distribution scored between 0 and 10 is considered extremely complexity-deteriorating for the BN model.

- Based on the relationship between each node and its parent, it trains the agents using conditional probability tables (CPTs). Before creating a network, GeNIe turns all equations into tables. The dependent nodes' CPTs are constructed using the following built-in function as an equation.
- The tool is pre-programmed with the opinions of practitioners and subject-matter experts, gathered through a structured survey. Case studies and social media and direct communication were used to validate the model.

Survey Design

An expert opinion survey was conducted to identify the key complexity factors that influence software project success.

- Years of experience, industry sector, professional profile, and firm profile are all included in the profiles of experts. The questions have been created to reveal the profiles of experts and to give you a better understanding of what it takes to be an authority in a certain field of business, finance, technology, or sport.
- What do you believe is the aspect that experts examine most strongly when determining whether or not to approve a project?
- Inquiries on each component's own complexity factors in order to do a more thorough analysis have been asked of the experts about the components where new complexity elements have been added as an expansion.
- The survey's results were combined to create a Bayesian network, which is covered in the next section.

The GeNIe modeller now uses the RCPM model, which can be used by the requirement analyst to discuss complexity values and further explore requirements with stakeholders (Sadia et al., 2023).

SUMMARY

VUCA risks, which stand for volatility, uncertainty, complexity, and ambiguity, are becoming increasingly relevant in the software development industry. Requirement ambiguity is a significant risk, as it can lead to misunderstandings, misinterpretation, and potential project failure. To manage requirement ambiguity and mitigate associated risks, it is essential to prioritize clarity and precision in requirement definition and involve stakeholders in the process.

Fuzzy logic and ANFIS (Adaptive Neuro-Fuzzy Inference System) are two techniques used to manage requirement ambiguity and uncertainty. Fuzzy logic is a mathematical approach that allows for the handling of imprecise or uncertain information, while ANFIS is a hybrid technique that combines fuzzy logic and neural networks to provide a more precise and accurate approach to managing uncertainty and risk.

Software requirement risk management is essential for software development, particularly in the face of VUCA risks. Techniques such as involving stakeholders, using fuzzy logic and ANFIS, and prioritizing clarity and precision in requirement definition can help manage these risks and ensure the success of software development projects.

REFERENCES

Abdelazim, K., Moawad, R., & Elfakharany, E. (2020). A Framework for Requirements Prioritization Process in Agile Software Development. *Journal of Physics: Conference Series, 1454*(1), 12001. doi:10.1088/1742-6596/1454/1/012001

Babu, B. S., Kamalakannan, J., Meenatchi, N., Karthik, S., & Boopathi, S. (2022). Economic impacts and reliability evaluation of battery by adopting Electric Vehicle. *IEEE Explore*, 1–6.

Boopathi, S. (2019). Experimental investigation and parameter analysis of LPG refrigeration system using Taguchi method. *SN Applied Sciences, 1*(8), 892. doi:10.100742452-019-0925-2

Boopathi, S., Arigela, S. H., Raman, R., Indhumathi, C., Kavitha, V., & Bhatt, B. C. (2022). Prominent Rule Control-based Internet of Things: Poultry Farm Management System. *IEEE Explore*, 1–6.

Boopathi, S., Khare, R., KG, J. C., Muni, T. V., & Khare, S. (2023). Additive Manufacturing Developments in the Medical Engineering Field. In Development, Properties, and Industrial Applications of 3D Printed Polymer Composites (pp. 86–106). IGI Global.

BoopathiS.MyilsamyS.SukkasamyS. (2021). Experimental Investigation and Multi-Objective Optimization of Cryogenically Cooled Near-Dry Wire-Cut EDM Using TOPSIS Technique. *IJAMT*. doi:10.21203/rs.3.rs-254117/v1

Boopathi, S., Siva Kumar, P. K., & Meena, R. S. J., S. I., P., S. K., and Sudhakar, M. (2023). Sustainable Developments of Modern Soil-Less Agro-Cultivation Systems. In Human Agro-Energy Optimization for Business and Industry (pp. 69–87). IGI Global. doi:10.4018/978-1-6684-4118-3.ch004

Boopathi, S., & Sivakumar, K. (2013). Experimental investigation and parameter optimization of near-dry wire-cut electrical discharge machining using multi-objective evolutionary algorithm. *International Journal of Advanced Manufacturing Technology, 67*(9–12), 2639–2655. doi:10.100700170-012-4680-4

Boopathi, S., & Sivakumar, K. (2016). Optimal parameter prediction of oxygen-mist near-dry Wire-cut EDM. *International Journal of Manufacturing Technology and Management, 30*(3–4), 164–178. doi:10.1504/IJMTM.2016.077812

Demirel, S. T., & Das, R. (2018). Software requirement analysis: Research challenges and technical approaches. *6th International Symposium on Digital Forensic and Security, ISDFS 2018 - Proceeding*, 1–6. 10.1109/ISDFS.2018.8355322

Devadas, R., & Cholli, N. G. (2022). Interdependency Aware Qubit and Brownboost Rank Requirement Learning for Large Scale Software Requirement Prioritization. *International Journal of Computing and Digital Systems, 11*(1), 625–634. doi:10.12785/ijcds/110150

Domakonda, V. K., Farooq, S., Chinthamreddy, S., Puviarasi, R., Sudhakar, M., & Boopathi, S. (2022). Sustainable Developments of Hybrid Floating Solar Power Plants: Photovoltaic System. In Human Agro-Energy Optimization for Business and Industry (pp. 148–167). IGI Global.

Ejnioui, A., Otero, C. E., & Qureshi, A. A. (2012). Software requirement prioritization using fuzzy multi-attribute decision making. *2012 IEEE Conference on Open Systems, ICOS 2012*, 1–6. 10.1109/ICOS.2012.6417646

Giudici, P. (2018). Fintech Risk Management: A Research Challenge for Artificial Intelligence in Finance. *Frontiers in Artificial Intelligence*, *1*, 1. doi:10.3389/frai.2018.00001 PMID:33733089

Haribalaji, V., Boopathi, S., & Asif, M. M. (2021). Optimization of friction stir welding process to join dissimilar AA2014 and AA7075 aluminum alloys. *Materials Today: Proceedings, 50*, 2227–2234. doi:10.1016/j.matpr.2021.09.499

Hoodat, H., & Rashidi, H. (2009). Classification and analysis of risks in software engineering. *World Academy of Science, Engineering and Technology*, *56*(8), 446–452.

Hu, Y., Du, J., Zhang, X., Hao, X., Ngai, E. W. T., Fan, M., & Liu, M. (2013). An integrative framework for intelligent software project risk planning. *Decision Support Systems*, *55*(4), 927–937. doi:10.1016/j.dss.2012.12.029

Jeevanantham, Y. A., Saravanan, A., Vanitha, V., Boopathi, S., & Kumar, D. P. (2022). Implementation of Internet-of Things (IoT) in Soil Irrigation System. *IEEE Explore*, 1–5.

Kavitha, C., Malini, P. S. G., Charan, V., Manoj, N., Verma, A., & Boopathi, S. (2022). (in press). An experimental study on the hardness and wear rate of carbonitride coated stainless steel. *Materials Today: Proceedings*. Advance online publication. doi:10.1016/j.matpr.2022.09.524

Kumara, V., Mohanaprakash, T. A., Fairooz, S., Jamal, K., Babu, T., and B., S. (2023). Experimental Study on a Reliable Smart Hydroponics System. In *Human Agro-Energy Optimization for Business and Industry* (pp. 27–45). IGI Global. doi:10.4018/978-1-6684-4118-3.ch002

Letier, E., Stefan, D., & Barr, E. T. (2014). Uncertainty, risk, and information value in software requirements and architecture. *Proceedings - International Conference on Software Engineering. International Conference on Software Engineering*, *1*, 883–894. doi:10.1145/2568225.2568239

Luo, J., Savakis, A. E., & Singhal, A. (2005). A Bayesian network-based framework for semantic image understanding. *Pattern Recognition*, *38*(6), 919–934. doi:10.1016/j.patcog.2004.11.001

Malik, V., & Singh, S. (2020). Artificial intelligent environments: Risk management and quality assurance implementation. *Journal of Discrete Mathematical Sciences and Cryptography*, *23*(1), 187–195. doi:10.1080/09720529.2020.1721883

Marasco, J. (2007). Software requirements. In Dr. Dobb's Journal (Vol. 32, Issue 9). Pearson Education. doi:10.1201/b12149-5

Myilsamy, S., & Boopathi, S. (2017). Grey Relational Optimization of Powder Mixed Near-Dry Wire Cut Electrical Discharge Machining of Inconel 718 Alloy. *Asian Journal of Research in Social Sciences and Humanities*, *7*(3), 18. doi:10.5958/2249-7315.2017.00157.5

Myilsamy, S., & Sampath, B. (2021). Experimental comparison of near-dry and cryogenically cooled near-dry machining in wire-cut electrical discharge machining processes. *Surface Topography : Metrology and Properties*, *9*(3), 035015. doi:10.1088/2051-672X/ac15e0

Naseem, R., Shaukat, Z., Irfan, M., Shah, M. A., Ahmad, A., Muhammad, F., Glowacz, A., Dunai, L., Antonino-Daviu, J., & Sulaiman, A. (2021). Empirical assessment of machine learning techniques for software requirements risk prediction. *Electronics (Basel)*, *10*(2), 1–19. doi:10.3390/electronics10020168

Okwu, M. O., & Tartibu, L. K. (2020). Sustainable supplier selection in the retail industry: A TOPSIS- and ANFIS-based evaluating methodology. *International Journal of Engineering Business Management*, *12*, 1847979019899542. doi:10.1177/1847979019899542

Palaniappan, M., Tirlangi, S., Mohamed, M. J. S., Moorthy, R. M. S., Valeti, S. V., & Boopathi, S. (2023). Fused Deposition Modelling of Polylactic Acid (PLA)-Based Polymer Composites: A Case Study. In Development, Properties, and Industrial Applications of 3D Printed Polymer Composites (pp. 66–85). IGI Global.

S., P. K., Sampath, B., R., S. K., Babu, B. H., & N., A. (2022). Hydroponics, Aeroponics, and Aquaponics Technologies in Modern Agricultural Cultivation. In *Trends, Paradigms, and Advances in Mechatronics Engineering* (pp. 223–241). IGI Global. doi:10.4018/978-1-6684-5887-7.ch012

Sadia, H., Abbas, S. Q., & Faisal, M. (2019). Volatile requirement prioritization: A fuzzy based approach. *International Journal of Engineering and Advanced Technology*, *8*(5), 2467–2472.

Sadia, H., Abbas, S. Q., & Faisal, M. (2023). A Bayesian Network-Based Software Requirement Complexity Prediction Model. In *Lecture Notes on Data Engineering and Communications Technologies* (Vol. 139, pp. 197–213). Springer. doi:10.1007/978-981-19-3015-7_15

Sadiq, M., & Jain, S. K. (2013). A fuzzy based approach for requirements prioritization in goal oriented requirements elicitation process. *Proceedings of the International Conference on Software Engineering and Knowledge Engineering, SEKE,* 54–58.

Saher, N., Baharom, F., Romli, R., Bikki, S., Saher, N., Baharom, F., Romli, R., & Bikki, S. (2018a). A Review of Requirement Prioritization Techniques in Agile Software Development. *Knowledge Management International Conference (KMICe)*, 25–27. http://www.kmice.cms.net.my/ProcKMICe/ KMICe2018/pdf/CR63.pdf

Saher, N., Baharom, F., Romli, R., Bikki, S., Saher, N., Baharom, F., Romli, R., & Bikki, S. (2018b). A Review of Requirement Prioritization Techniques in Agile Software Development. *Knowledge Management International Conference (KMICe)*, 25–27.

Salais-Fierro, T. E., Saucedo Martínez, J. A., & Pérez-Pérez, B. I. (2020). A decision making approach using fuzzy logic and anfis: A retail study case. *EAI/Springer Innovations in Communication and Computing*, 155–172. doi:10.1007/978-3-030-48149-0_12

Samikannu, R., Koshariya, A. K., Poornima, E., Ramesh, S., Kumar, A., & Boopathi, S. (2022). Sustainable Development in Modern Aquaponics Cultivation Systems Using IoT Technologies. In *Human Agro-Energy Optimization for Business and Industry* (pp. 105–127). IGI Global.

Sampath, B., & Myilsamy, S. (2021). Experimental investigation of a cryogenically cooled oxygen-mist near-dry wire-cut electrical discharge machining process. *Strojniski Vestnik. Jixie Gongcheng Xuebao*, *67*(6), 322–330. doi:10.5545v-jme.2021.7161

Sampath, B., Sureshkumar, M., Yuvaraj, T., & Velmurugan, D. (2021). Experimental investigations on eco-friendly helium-mist near-dry wire-cut edm of m2-hss material. *Materials Research Proceedings*, *19*, 175–180. doi:10.21741/9781644901618-22

Sampath, B. C. S., & Myilsamy, S. (2022). Application of TOPSIS Optimization Technique in the Micro-Machining Process. In Trends, Paradigms, and Advances in Mechatronics Engineering (pp. 162–187). IGI Global. doi:10.4018/978-1-6684-5887-7.ch009

Saravanan, M., Vasanth, M., Boopathi, S., Sureshkumar, M., & Haribalaji, V. (2022). Optimization of Quench Polish Quench (QPQ) Coating Process Using Taguchi Method. *Key Engineering Materials*, *935*, 83–91. doi:10.4028/p-z569vy

Senthil, T. S., Puviyarasan, M., Babu, S. R., Surakasi, R., & Sampath, B. (2023). Industrial Robot-Integrated Fused Deposition Modelling for the 3D Printing Process. In Development, Properties, and Industrial Applications of 3D Printed Polymer Composites (pp. 188–210). IGI Global.

Shaukat, Z. S., Naseem, R., & Zubair, M. (2018). A dataset for software requirements risk prediction. *Proceedings - 21st IEEE International Conference on Computational Science and Engineering, CSE 2018*, 112–118. 10.1109/CSE.2018.00022

Sremac, S., Tanackov, I., Kopic, M., & Radovic, D. (2018). Anfis model for determining the economic order quantity. *Decision Making: Applications in Management and Engineering*, *1*(2), 81–92. doi:10.31181/dmame1802079s

Trojovský, P., Dhasarathan, V., & Boopathi, S. (2023). Experimental investigations on cryogenic friction-stir welding of similar ZE42 magnesium alloys. *Alexandria Engineering Journal*, *66*(1), 1–14. doi:10.1016/j.aej.2022.12.007

Vanitha, S. K. R., & Boopathi, S. (2023). Artificial Intelligence Techniques in Water Purification and Utilization. In *Human Agro-Energy Optimization for Business and Industry* (pp. 202–218). IGI Global., doi:10.4018/978-1-6684-4118-3.ch010

Vassileva, J., Wang, Y., & Vassileva, J. (2017). Bayesian Network-Based Trust Model Bayesian Network-Based Trust Model. *Proceedings IEEE/WIC International Conference on Web Intelligence (WI 2003)*, 372–378.

Vennila, T., Karuna, M. S., Srivastava, B. K., Venugopal, J., Surakasi, R., & Sampath, B. (2022). New Strategies in Treatment and Enzymatic Processes: Ethanol Production From Sugarcane Bagasse. In Human Agro-Energy Optimization for Business and Industry (pp. 219–240). IGI Global.

Yupapin, P., Trabelsi, Y., Nattappan, A., & Boopathi, S. (2022). Performance Improvement of Wire-Cut Electrical Discharge Machining Process Using Cryogenically Treated Super-Conductive State of Monel-K500 Alloy. *Iranian Journal of Science and Technology - Transactions of Mechanical Engineering*, 1–17.

APPENDIX

Abbreviations

AHP: Analytic Hierarchy Process
ANFIS: Adaptive-Network-Based Fuzzy Inference System
ANN: Artificial Neural Networks
BRIC: Brazil, Russia, India, China Countries
CBI: Confederation of British Industry
CIO: Chief Information Officer
CPTs: Conditional Probability Tables
FIS: Fuzzy Inference System
GDP: Gross Domestic Product
GeNIe: Graphical User Interface Modular
IBEF: India Brand Equity Foundation
NL: Natural Language
RE: Requirement Engineering
SDLC: Software Development Life Cycle
SFIS: Sugeno Fuzzy Inference System
SMEs: Small and Medium Enterprises
SRS: Software Requirements Specification
VUCA: Volatility, Uncertainty, Complexity, and Ambiguity

Chapter 4
Identifying the Different Categories of IR4.0 Technology Usage Clusters Amongst Brunei Darussalam's MSMEs Using K–Means Approach

Izzati Zaidi
Universiti Teknologi Brunei, Brunei

Mohamed Saleem Haja Nazmudeen
Universiti Teknologi Brunei, Brunei

Fadzliwati Mohiddin
Universiti Teknologi Brunei, Brunei

ABSTRACT

Technologies for the Fourth Industrial Revolution (IR 4.0) are widespread due to their significant advantages for various industries, including productivity performance, efficiency, and adaptability. Brunei Darussalam is a developing country that has recently considered the significance of IR 4.0. The maturity level on technology adoption for IR4.0 technologies are crucial to determine its operation performance and effectiveness. Data is collected from 40 micro, small, medium enterprises (MSMEs) from different industries of Brunei Darussalam. The model is from K-means clustering that can show the level of technology adoption in different sectors and sizes of businesses which in turn will help to determine the impact of technology on the performance of the firm. This study is to compare the difference on IR4.0 technology adoption between developed, developing countries, and Brunei Darussalam and their current interest and investment level for future adoption.

DOI: 10.4018/978-1-6684-8145-5.ch004

Copyright © 2023, IGI Global. Copying or distributing in print or electronic forms without written permission of IGI Global is prohibited.

INTRODUCTION

The recent technological revolution known as the Fourth Industrial Revolution has compelled businesses in a different industry to prioritize technological advancement in order to achieve global competitiveness and increase market opportunities. Different countries have varying degrees of adoption for IR 4.0 technologies. Industry 4.0 was started in Germany in 2011 to increase their manufacturing industries competitiveness (Hermann et al., 2015; Issa et al., 2018; Stentoft et al., 2019). Industry 4.0 is where systematic technologies are integrated with the internet of things (Kagermann et al., 2013; Kersten et al., 2017; Lasi et al., 2014; Xu, 2012).

Industry 4.0 is a systematic high-tech strategy that incorporates robotics, the internet of things, big data analytics, digitisation and advanced manufacturing technologies such as additive manufacturing/3D printing (Kagermann et al., 2013). IR4.0 is set to enhance production, operation, service, design, and manufacturing processes. With the integration and networking of technologies and systems, there will be a significant rise in manufacturing efficiency and customisation, resulting in a tremendous competitive advantage (Ganzarain & Errasti, 2016).

By using digital technologies like sensors, Artificial Intelligence (AI), and automation, businesses can be more flexible and quick to meet customer needs. Jones and Pimdee (2017) said that this can be done by making changes to technology (Jones & Pimdee, 2017). They also mentioned that agility can increase the competitiveness of an organisation (Gligor and Holcomb, 2011).

BACKGROUND

At this present, Brunei Darussalam is moving towards IR4.0, the nation is focusing on few important aspects in order to reach the goal to be adapted with IR4.0 which are by identifying the real and local needs, having a strategic planning, more involvement of stakeholders, initiating government drive, more operators and industry players, build infrastructure and spectrum readiness, plan deployment in phases (James Kon, 2019). At this point, there have been different models to assess maturity levels and industry readiness in adopting IR4.0 technologies. Models such as IMPULS, Industry 4.0 Readiness Assesment Tools, Singapore Smart Industry Readiness Index, Industry 4.0 Maturity Model, Industry 4.0-MM, RAMI 4.0, Schumacher et al., Rojko, Kichtblau et al. and Agca et.al and Singapore Economic Development Board model are mainly used to assess the readiness of manufacturing companies. But however, there is limitation to those models that focuses on manufacturing businesses only. Study on IR4.0 on business models remains a least explored topic (Arnold, Kiel, and Voigt 2016). Especially when empirical research on the business models in the context of the Industrial Internet of Things have mostly unnoticed what is needed for the MSMEs (Arnold et al. 2016; Müller et al. 2018; Müller, Buliga, and Voigt 2021).

industry 4.0

Understanding Industry 4.0 readiness is important to businesses nowadays (Schaupp, Abele, and Metternich 2017). By understanding the readiness models, it can help businesses to identify the important factors in digital transformation that can assist in the innovation of an organisation. According to Almamalik, 2020, by identifying the maturity models it can help to understand their current situation and reflect on their strategy for IR4.0 technology adoption (Almamalik, 2020). Hence, in this research study it is mostly focused on most adopted Industry 4.0 technologies rather than on particular type of technology to encourage the researchers to increase the standpoint in the technology adoption area. This paper aims to present another method on identifying different levels of IR4.0 technology adoption that focuses on MSMEs and types of IR4.0 technologies are based on the fundamental of 9 Pillars of IR4.0 technologies by Mendes et al., 2017 (Mendes et al., 2017).

Type of IR4.0 Technologies

In this study, there were a few types of IR4.0 technologies covered for further research. In the models, there were three main categories of IR4.0 technologies based on each technology's level of advancement. First were the basic technologies in IR4.0 such as business management systems, mobile communication systems, e-commerce platforms, e-payment systems, smart devices, internet networks and wireless devices. Such technologies have been proven to have made significant contributions to businesses nowadays, especially for efficiency and an increase in competitive advantage.

According to a previous study, technologies such as social media help to promote SMEs in getting sustainability in competitive environments, they are also less expensive to be implemented by SMEs to operate which is a huge advantage as SMEs have always been related to limited funds to implement technologies (Qalati et al., 2021). Moreover, according to Tajudeen, et al. (2018), they found that social media has a positive impact on the use of new technologies (Tajudeen et al., 2018). As relates to Mahakittun, et al. (2021), innovation and mobile payment expertise in an organisation can help it to increase processes and achieve better results on firm performance, have more knowledge support in a dynamic environment, have faster innovation and result in a better upskilling rate and outcome (Mahakittikun et al., 2021).

The second category was intermediate IR4.0 technologies where these technologies are slightly advanced compared to IR4.0 fundamental technologies. Listed technologies in this category are big data analytic, cloud systems and cybersecurity systems. Advantages of Big data analysis include the ability to manage large amounts of data and conduct well-defined analyses in order to run the manufacturing system in accordance with its objectives. By analysing large amounts of data, adaptability and flexibility enhance the interoperability and responsiveness of a system (Oztemel & Gursev, 2020). To fully utilise the potential of big data, businesses are beginning to pursue technologies and solutions that can process and analyse these various sources of information and types of data (Davenport, 2014).

According to a study by Ahmad Salleh, et al. (2016), the organisation that adopts big data can contribute significantly towards top management support, compatibility, information security culture and learning culture, but it is not adopted by other organisations because of its complexity and the risk of outsourcing the system (Ahmad Salleh et al., 2016). Another previous study mentioned that big data in the cloud facilitates are easier access to better and more efficient data manipulation and this is also beneficial for developing data analysis and interpretation systems for IR4.0 adoption. They also mentioned that 5G broadband, IoT, Big Data Analytics, Cloud Computing and Software Defined Networks are important in Industry 4.0 (Chang et al., 2016).

Supported with an earlier study by Oliveira, et al. (2014), adopting technologies in cloud computing helps to boost a firm's operation efficiency and productivity which can give better business opportunities (Oliveira et al., 2014). Parra, et al. (2019), mentioned that using diagnostic tools for descriptive, predictive and prescriptive applications has helped, significantly, companies all over the world in terms of decision making (Parra et al., 2019). With the use of real-time data, simulation technologies can help for testing and optimising machine settings in a virtual world before the real implementation, which helps to save time and increase the quality of the machines (Aiman et al., 2016). Cybersecurity is another important technology in IR4.0. According to Hussain, et al. (Hussain et al., 2020), there are some factors needed to be considered in cybersecurity such as access control and authorisation, data management security, secure data sharing and handling identity. These are important factors that can have effects on the level of implementing the technologies.

Advanced technologies like Artificial Intelligence, Robotics, and Augmented Reality are complex and expensive to implement. They require skilled experts to operate and use complex algorithms to improve business performance. Companies in the manufacturing or assembly industries, usually medium to large, are the main users of these technologies.

MSME AND IR4.0

The Micro, Small and Medium Enterprises' (MSMEs) sector contributes significantly to the manufacturing output, employment and exports of a country. The global community has come to realise the crucial role that small and medium-sized enterprises play on economic growth, including job creation, output growth and exportation (International Labour Organization, 2013). The globalisation of the economy requires many BUSINESSES to adapt in order to survive. To compete in these global marketplaces, SMEs must develop and implement innovative business strategies and technologies (Caldeira & Ward, 2002).

SMEs are the largest contributors to industries and nations; therefore, their market competence must be sustainable (Moeuf et al., 2018). They must optimise their planning, resource allocations, productions, and operational performances, amongst other business operations. Diversification enables businesses to be more active and strategically organised in their new economic operations. Organisations must implement Industry 4.0 technology to become more competitive and dynamic.

In developing countries, small and medium-sized enterprises (SMEs) encounter unique obstacles, such as inadequate funds, a lack of expert knowledge management, and limited resources. They also deal with economical shifts government rules and regulations, the rise of globalization, changing consumer demands, increasing competition, and shorter product life cycles.

MSMES IN BRUNEI DARUSSALAM

Brunei Darussalam has recently encouraged the diversification of the economy by promoting more MSMEs as the motivation for growth (Azlan Othman, 2020). According to the number of employees, all firms in Brunei Darussalam fall into one of four business size categories, mainly micro, small, medium and large. Micro businesses are those with less than 5 employees, small businesses with 5 to 19 employees, and medium-sized businesses with 20 to 99 employees. Companies having 100 or more employees are regarded as large (Department of Economic Planning and Development, 2018).

Brunei Darussalam has its own initiatives to improve businesses in the country. Two organisations were established, namely the FDI Action and Support Centre (FAST) and Darussalam Enterprise (DARe) and both are responsible to facilitate FDI and develop domestic businesses. In early 2019, Brunei Darussalam's government began to emphasise the adoption of IR4.0 technologies in order to increase the digital economy and be globally competitive. Since year 2000 to 2015, there has been increased of more than 80% of internet broadband subscription in Brunei Darussalam and Singapore, this shows the capability of the people in Brunei Darussalam and Singapore to adopt internet technologies (Box & Lopez-Gonzalez, n.d.). Now, the use of the 5G network and becoming a smart nation is one of Brunei's goals to achieve success with Industry 4.0 (James Kon, 2019). Hence, this research has identified the levels of IR4.0 adoption amongst the MSMEs in Brunei Darussalam and what the possible factors are that are influencing the success of the implementation of such technologies.

COMPARISON FOR IR4.0 A IN DEVELOPED AND DEVELOPING COUNTRIES

Table 1. Level of adoption on IR4.0 in developed countries

Country	Size	Type of Industries	Organization and Strategy		Level of Adoption Overall
Germany	Small	Heavy Manufacturing	High	N/A	Modernized
	Medium	Heavy Manufacturing	Low	N/A	Moderate
	Large	Heavy Manufacturing	Low	N/A	Modernized
Sweden	Small	Heavy Manufacturing	N/A	N/A	Moderate
	Medium	Heavy Manufacturing	N/A	N/A	Moderate
	Large	Heavy Manufacturing	N/A	N/A	Modernized
South Korea	SME	Manufacturing	Mid	N/A	Moderate
New Zealand	SME	Manufacturing	Mid	Positive	Modernized

Source: Zaidi et al. (2021a)

Referring to the Table 1 above for developed countries, Germany's small businesses are on Modernized category, medium-sized businesses are in Moderate category and large businesses are in Modernized category. For Sweden's SMEs that are in heavy manufacturing industries are mostly in Moderate and Modernized categories. South Korea's SMEs in manufacturing are mostly in the Moderate category. New Zealand 's SMEs in manufacturing industries are mostly in Modernized category.

According to the Table 2, Brazil and Indonesia SMEs are mostly in Moderate category, Malaysia SME's are in the Moderate category and Taiwan's ICT manufacturing SMEs are mostly in Modernized category, SME in traditional industry are in Moderate category, from ICT & Manufacturing are mostly Modernized and SME for producing ICT peripherals and components are mostly in Modest category.

To compare both developed and developing countries, the developed countries were only slightly advanced in comparison to developing countries, possibly reason is because the availability of worker skills in use of technologies (Zaidi et al., 2019).

Hence in this study, the research aim is to identify what level of IR4.0 technology adoption do Brunei Darussalam as a developing country. Further explanation on the research methodology will be in the next section.

Table 2. Level of adoption on IR4.0 in developing countries

Country	Size	Type of Industries	Organization and Strategy		Level of Adoption Overall
Brazil	SME	Manufacturing	N/A	N/A	Moderate
Malaysia	SME	Various Industries	Low	Positive	Modernized
Indonesia	SME	Various Industries	N/A	N/A	Moderate
Taiwan	Large & SME	ICT Manufacturing	N/A	N/A	Modernized
	SME, EMS (Environmental Management System)	Traditional Industry	N/A	N/A	Moderate
	EMS	ICT & Manufacturing	N/A	N/A	Modernized
	SME, EMS	ICT Peripherals, Components And Software Firm	N/A	N/A	Modest
New Zealand	SME	Manufacturing	Mid	Positive	Modernized

Source: Zaidi et al. (2021a)

RESEARCH METHODOLOGY

Using a random sampling technique, this study surveyed Micro, Small, and Medium-sized enterprises from various industries in Brunei Darussalam. The researchers contacted the participants directly and provided an online questionnaire. Table 3 provides details on the sample's company size, respondent profile, and primary market, based on responses from forty participants.

Data were collected from questionnaires and coded to ease the process. The information is then subgrouped to different area of findings. After that, the data numbers are computed before further analysing in K-Means Clustering analysis.

K-means clustering algorithms help to capitalize within similarity and heterogeneousness among different sets. Hence in this research, this is an applicable method to identify different sizes of businesses relating to the type of technologies they are implementing (Unterberger & Müller, 2021).

Table 3. Demographic respondents

Categories	Description	(%)	Category	Description	(%)
Main Industry	Agricultures	5%	Company Size's	Micro	75%
	Manufacturing	3%		Small	18%
	Constructions	3%		Medium	8%
	Transport and Storage	5%	Respondent's profile	Owner	85%
	Wholesale and retail	43%		Manager	10%
	Real estate and ownership of dwelling	3%		Supervisor	3%
	Other services in private sector	40%		Others	3%

Source: Zaidi et al. (2021)

According to Table 4, the MSMEs surveyed were classified into three clusters: Cluster 0, Cluster 1, and Cluster 2. Cluster 0, which consists of approximately 25 MSMEs, falls under the "Modest" category and primarily utilizes fundamental and intermediate technologies. In contrast, the "Modernized" category includes four MSMEs that primarily use basic, intermediate, and advanced technologies, while the "Moderate" category consists of 11 MSMEs using an acceptable middle level of basic, intermediate, and advanced technologies (Zaidi et al., 2021).

Table 4. Clusters of IR4.0 technology adoption

Cluster	Categories	No. of Companies	Basic	Intermediate	Advanced
Cluster 0	Modest	25	6.080	1.040	0.240
Cluster 1	Modernized	4	8.500	5.500	12.750
Cluster 2	Moderate	11	7.909	5.273	1.909

Source: Zaidi et al. (2021b)

Populations Study and Sample Size

Out of 100 distributed surveys, only 40 were received back. This gives a response rate of 50% for the duration of one month. However, breaking down the analysis into three categorical values, i.e., the Modest category (n= 25) and the Moderate category (n=4) and the Modernized (n=11).

DISCUSSION

From the previous paper (Zaidi et al. 2019), the finding shows the developed countries such as Germany, Sweden, South Korea and New Zealand are mostly in the Moderate and Modernized categories when it comes to the adoption of IR4.0 technologies. These developed countries share one similar characteristic which is they have positive level of interest in investing towards IR4.0 technologies in their future. This can be shown through their government's initiatives and economic strengths resulting strong MSMEs foundation in the countries.

As for the developing countries such as Brazil, Malaysia, Indonesia and Taiwan, most of their SMEs fall under Moderate and Modernized too. However, out of these four countries, only Malaysia has the initiatives to invest for technologies in the future and the SMEs are looking into strategies on how to implement IR4.0 technologies.

However, Brunei Darussalam is also categorized as one of the developing countries. Compared with Brazil, Malaysia, Indonesia and Taiwan, Brunei Darussalam are still on the Modest category in technology adoption while the other four are mostly towards Moderate and Modernized category. Moreover, to the developed countries where their technologies are mostly towards Modernized and Moderate category. According to the finding, 25 out of 40 MSMEs are in the Modest categories. There are few explanations for why technologies are still in their earliest stages. According to the respondents, most of the MSMEs from the Modest category agreed that primary challenges in the use of technologies are policies from the government and international transaction payment issue. They also concurred that there is inadequate encouragement for and limited use of e-payment. Whether it involves domestic or foreign currency transactions, Brunei Darussalam's e-payment regulations are stringent. Some are using personal accounts for business purposes, which violates the rules and regulation of the bank institutions. One of the banks in Brunei was strict about following the rule that companies could only conduct business transactions using business accounts. This has been a problem for MSMEs because the majority of them operate on a very small scale, often as a secondary source of income, and they are still required to utilize personal bank accounts because they are unable to register yet.

The businesses also concur that another element is how policy of the government has impacted the trading of technologies in Brunei Darussalam. For instance, Brunei has a rule requiring that all imported radio and communications goods be approved by AITI. Businesses believe that technology is critical to their operations and that to remain competitive, their present services must add more value and be more innovative. Fast internet can help businesses function and interact with foreign enterprises more effectively because businesses also need resources from other regions.

However, the majority of the firms in this category believed that the country's internet remains mediocre, which has an impact on how technologies are used in the businesses. The 5G network has only recently begun, in the year 2023, and is currently in the introduction stage. Imagine Sdn Bhd Unified National Network (formerly known as TelBru), Progresif Sdn Berhad, and Data Stream Digital (DST) all shared one primary network provider under Unified National Network (UNN). Since then, network structure are finding better stability, making it difficult for firms to rely on good internet to function effectively. MSMEs agree that implementing high standards of safety and protocol for technology adoption is also difficult.

Next, around 11 firms are in the Moderate category, similar to the reason that government regulation and international transaction payment issues have been a huge barrier why they are lacking in implementing E-Payment services. They also believe that government regulation is also negative influencing the trading in and out for technologies in Brunei Darussalam. Nevertheless, most of the business in this category anticipated on the cost to adopt technologies and they believe it is hard to get a suitable technology for their business. They also agree that adopting technologies will be hassle and require high standard of procedures. The fact that businesses need advanced technologies to get better resources from international countries, it should be on par with fast internet to conduct business efficiently.

Finally, around 4 out of 40 MSMEs in Brunei Darussalam are in Modernized category. Although they are using advanced technologies, but there are few challenges that hinders them from adopting further technologies. One of the reasons is that the lack of suitable technologies and software for their nature of business. They also agree the level of internet speed in Brunei Darussalam is inadequate at the moment.

Nevertheless, these MSMEs believe that they less need the technologies for operating and communicating efficiently with regional business, which is a possible reason why they might not need further advance technologies. Modern technologies typically entail a sophisticated system that relies for more experienced personnel and may involve safety precautions. Additionally, these companies believe that they have private and confidential information that is risky for to be used on technologies.

From the finding in Brunei Darussalam, the Modest category have interest to invest a little bit in technology IR4.0 for basic technologies. While the Moderate category is prepared to invest more on technologies than the basic techs, they will not spend more than the Moderate category. While the Modernized category, the majority of MSMES are prepared to invest more than the standard cost of technology on their operations. Similar to the developed countries, most of them are interested to invest in IR4.0 technologies for their future while for developing counties most of them are not interested to invest for future technologies. Most of the countries from developed and developing countries do not have strategies yet, but New Zealand and Malaysia are looking forward to better strategize and plan their future technologies adoption for IR 4.0. This shows that most of the countries whether from developed or developing countries are looking forward to adopt more technologies for IR4.0 in the future.

CONCLUSION

In conclusion, developed countries show that majority of them are focusing on IR4.0 earlier than the developing countries. The developing countries are also pushing their capacity in implementing IR4.0 technologies adoption. Looking into the perspective of Brunei Darussalam, despite of the challenges in IR4.0 technology adoption, MSMEs are still keen to adopt better technologies and are willing to learn new knowledge.

FUTURE RESEARCH DIRECTION

For future research, it is recommended to further analyse factors that could influence the level of IR4.0 technology adoption. There is a need to research on the precise often used type of IR4.0 technologies based on the nature of businesses in the countries. It is suggested for the studies to be more detailed in specific regional area and do further comparison studies.

REFERENCES

Ahmad Salleh, K., Janczewski, L., & Ahmad, K. (2016). Association for Information Systems AIS Electronic Library (AISeL) Adoption of Big Data Solutions: A study on its security determinants using Sec-TOE Framework Recommended Citation "Adoption of Big Data Solutions: A study on its security determinants usin. *International Conference on Information Resources Management (CONF-IRM)*, 66.

Aiman, M., Bahrin, K., Othman, F., Hayati, N., Azli, N., & Talib, F. (2016). Industry 4.0: A review on industrial automation and robotic. *Jurnal Teknologi, 78*.

Almamalik, L. (2020). *The Development of the Maturity Model to Assess the Smart Indonesia Manufacturing Companies 4.0 Readiness.* doi:10.2991/aebmr.k.200305.026

Arnold, C., Kiel, D., & Voigt, K.-I. (2016). How the industrial internet of things changes business models in different manufacturing industries. *International Journal of Innovation Management, 20*(8), 1–25. doi:10.1142/S1363919616400156

Box, S., & Lopez-Gonzalez, J. (n.d.). *The Future of Technology: Opportunities for ASEAN in the Digital Economy.* Academic Press.

Caldeira, M. M., & Ward, J. M. (2002). Understanding the successful adoption and use of IS/IT in SMEs: An explanation from Portuguese manufacturing industries. *Information Systems Journal, 12*(2), 121–152. doi:10.1046/j.1365-2575.2002.00119.x

Chang, V., Ramachandran, M., Wills, G., Walters, R. J., Li, C.-S., & Watters, P. (2016). Editorial for FGCS special issue: Big Data in the cloud. *Future Generation Computer Systems*, *65*, 73–75. doi:10.1016/j. future.2016.04.007

Davenport, T. (2014). *Big data at work: dispelling the myths, uncovering the opportunities*. Harvard Business Review Press. doi:10.15358/9783800648153

Department of Economic Planning and Development. (2018). *Report of Summary Findings*. Author.

Ganzarain, J., & Errasti, N. (2016). Three stage maturity model in SME's towards industry 4.0. *Journal of Industrial Engineering and Management*, *9*(5), 1119–1128. doi:10.3926/jiem.2073

Gligor, D. M., & Holcomb, M. C. (2012). Understanding the role of logistics capabilities in achieving supply chain agility: A systematic literature review. *Supply Chain Management*, *17*(4), 438–453. doi:10.1108/13598541211246594

HermannM.PentekT.OttoB. (2015). Design Principles for Industrie 4.0 Scenarios: A Literature Review. *Technische Universitat Dortmund*, *1*(1), 4–16. doi:10.13140/RG.2.2.29269.22248

Hussain, F., Hussain, R., Hassan, S. A., & Hossain, E. (2020). Machine Learning in IoT Security: Current Solutions and Future Challenges. *IEEE Communications Surveys and Tutorials*, *22*(3), 1686–1721. doi:10.1109/COMST.2020.2986444

International Labour Organization. (2013). Global employment trends 2013. In Global Employment Trends. ILO.

Issa, A., Hatiboglu, B., Bildstein, A., & Bauernhansl, T. (2018). Industrie 4.0 roadmap: Framework for digital transformation based on the concepts of capability maturity and alignment. *Procedia CIRP*, *72*, 973–978. doi:10.1016/j.procir.2018.03.151

Jones, C., & Pimdee, P. (2017). Innovative ideas: Thailand 4.0 and the fourth industrial revolution. *Asian International Journal of Social Sciences*, *17*(1), 4–35. doi:10.29139/aijss.20170101

Kagermann, W., & Helbig, J. (2013). *Recommendations for implementing the strategic initiative IN-DUSTRIE 4.0*. Final Report of the Industrie 4.0 WG.

Kersten, W., Blecker, T., Ringle, C. M., Gallay, O., Korpela, K., Tapio, N., & Nurminen, J. K. (2017). Published in: Digitalization in Supply Chain Management and Logistics A Peer-To-Peer Platform for Decentralized Logistics. *Tubdok.Tub.Tuhh.De*, 301–318.

Kon, J. (2019, March 10). Industry 4.0 initiatives to help develop Brunei Digital Economy. *Borneo Bulletin*. https://borneobulletin.com.bn/industry-4-0-initiatives-to-help-develop-brunei-digital-economy/

Lasi, H., Fettke, P., Kemper, H. G., Feld, T., & Hoffmann, M. (2014). Industry 4.0. *Business & Information Systems Engineering*, *6*(4), 239–242. doi:10.100712599-014-0334-4

Mahakittikun, T., Suntrayuth, S., & Bhatiasevi, V. (2021). The impact of technological-organizational-environmental (TOE) factors on firm performance: Merchant's perspective of mobile payment from Thailand's retail and service firms. *Journal of Asia Business Studies*, *15*(2), 359–383. doi:10.1108/JABS-01-2020-0012

Mendes, C., Osaki, R., & Da Costa, C. (2017). Internet of Things in Automated Production. *European Journal of Engineering Research and Science*, 2(10), 13. doi:10.24018/ejers.2017.2.10.499

Moeuf, A., Pellerin, R., Lamouri, S., Tamayo-Giraldo, S., & Barbaray, R. (2018). The industrial management of SMEs in the era of Industry 4.0. *International Journal of Production Research*, 56(3), 1118–1136. doi:10.1080/00207543.2017.1372647

Müller, J. M., Buliga, O., & Voigt, K. I. (2018). Fortune favors the prepared: How SMEs approach business model innovations in Industry 4.0. *Technological Forecasting and Social Change, 132*, 2–17. doi:10.1016/j.techfore.2017.12.019

Müller, J. M., Buliga, O., & Voigt, K. I. (2021). The role of absorptive capacity and innovation strategy in the design of industry 4.0 business Models - A comparison between SMEs and large enterprises. European Management Journal, 39(3), 333–343. doi:10.1016/j.emj.2020.01.002

Oliveira, T., Thomas, M., & Espadanal, M. (2014). Assessing the determinants of cloud computing adoption: An analysis of the manufacturing and services sectors. *Information & Management*, 51(5), 497–510. doi:10.1016/j.im.2014.03.006

Othman, A. (2020, October 31). MSMEs drive Brunei's economy. *Borneo Bulletin*. https://borneobulletin.com.bn/msmes-drive-bruneis-economy/

Oztemel, E., & Gursev, S. (2020). Literature review of Industry 4.0 and related technologies. *Journal of Intelligent Manufacturing*, 31(1), 127–182. doi:10.100710845-018-1433-8

Parra, X., Tort-Martorell, X., Ruiz-Viñals, C., & Álvarez-Gómez, F. (2019). A maturity model for the information-driven SME. *Journal of Industrial Engineering and Management*, 12(1), 154–175. doi:10.3926/jiem.2780

Qalati, S. A., Yuan, L. W., Khan, M. A. S., & Anwar, F. (2021). A mediated model on the adoption of social media and SMEs' performance in developing countries. *Technology in Society*, 64(January), 101513. doi:10.1016/j.techsoc.2020.101513

Schaupp, E., Abele, E., & Metternich, J. (2017). Potentials of Digitalization in Tool Management. *Procedia CIRP*, 63, 144–149. doi:10.1016/j.procir.2017.03.172

Stentoft, J., Jensen, K. W., Philipsen, K., & Haug, A. (2019). Drivers and Barriers for Industry 4.0 Readiness and Practice: A SME Perspective with Empirical Evidence. *Proceedings of the 52nd Hawaii International Conference on System Sciences, 6*, 5155–5164. 10.24251/HICSS.2019.619

Tajudeen, F. P., Jaafar, N. I., & Ainin, S. (2018). Understanding the impact of social media usage among organizations. *Information & Management*, 55(3), 308–321. doi:10.1016/j.im.2017.08.004

Unterberger, P., & Müller, J. M. (2021). Clustering and Classification of Manufacturing Enterprises Regarding Their Industry 4.0 Reshoring Incentives. *Procedia Computer Science, 180*, 696–705. doi:10.1016/j.procs.2021.01.292

Xu, X. (2012). From cloud computing to cloud manufacturing. *Robotics and Computer-integrated Manufacturing*, 28(1), 75–86. doi:10.1016/j.rcim.2011.07.002

Zaidi, I., Nazmudeen, M. S., & Mohiddin, F. (2019). Identifying Factors Contributing to the Level of Industry 4. 0 Technologies Adoption among SMEs in Different Countries. Academic Press.

Zaidi, I., Nazmudeen, M. S., & Mohiddin, F. (2021a). A Comparative Study on IR4. 0 Technologies and its Maturity Level on Small, Medium Enterprises in Developed and Developing Countries. *ICBIM*, 1–16.

Zaidi, I., Nazmudeen, M. S., & Mohiddin, F. (2021b). K-Means Clustering Approach to Categorize the Maturity Level of Industry 4.0 Technology Adoption of MSMEs in Brunei Darussalam. *3rd International Conference on Business, Economics and Finance (ICBEF) Proceedings*, 76. https://doi.org/https://doi.org/10.36924/20220

Chapter 5
Smart Education System Initiatives to Support Data Science and Industry 4.0

V. Saranya

Hindusthan College of Engineering and Technology, India

S. Uma

HIndusthan College of Engineering and Technology, India

ABSTRACT

Internet of things, data science, deep learning, augmented reality, edge computing, and digital twins present new opportunities, challenges, and solutions for agriculture, plant sciences, animal sciences, food sciences, and social sciences. These disruptive technologies are at the centre of the fourth industrial revolution. The chapter discusses knowledge engineering to intellectualize higher education. Also, it explains how knowledge engineering (KE) can be utilized to construct intelligent learning and smart tutoring systems (STSs). The intersection of AI, web science, and data science enables a new generation of online-based educational and training tools to determine and examine the benefits of such computational paradigms for smart tutoring systems. Built on this architecture, data science courses should be user-, tool-, and application-based.

INTRODUCTION

In the last decades, technological advances in Information Technology (IT) have made computing devices more economical and widespread than ever. From households to industrial plants, a variety of devices allow a quick and effortless access to information. In an industrial environment a series of sensors gather process data which can be posterior analyzed with the main goal of productivity increase and preventive maintenance. To take advantage of the increasing role of IT on the factory floor, a set of design practices were identified and proposed under the common concept of a fourth industrial revolution. In Europe this concept is commonly designated as Industry 4.0(I4.0) after the German industrial development program

DOI: 10.4018/978-1-6684-8145-5.ch005

Copyright © 2023, IGI Global. Copying or distributing in print or electronic forms without written permission of IGI Global is prohibited.

with the same name. This new concept makes use of cyber-physical systems, the Cloud and the Internet of Things to aid in the management of the complete product life cycle (Pacheco & Reis, 2019). Industry 4.0 is a shift from the previous industry shape. Automation is as a result of technology involving electrical energy. Changes occur and lead to paperless and humanless, but these changes require preparation both in the industrial world and in other supporting worlds. Data is a different side of technology. Data involves many different concepts from the industrial world, even though either data of the industrial world involve the same technology. Specifically, data management is different than industry management. The realization of Industry 4.0 model requires theoretical knowledge and practical skills in industrial automation and networking (Yakimov & Iovey, 2019). Universities have a relevant and essential key role to ensure knowledge and development of competencies in the current fourth industrial revolution called Industry 4.0. The Industry 4.0 promotes a set of digital technologies to allow the convergence between the information technology and the operation technology towards smarter factories. Under such new framework, multiple initiatives are being carried out worldwide as response of such evolution, particularly, from the engineering education point of view (Prieto et al., 2019). One of the primary indices to determine the economic progress of a country is its gross domestic product (GDP). The higher the percentage of GDP, the better will be the country's performance in terms of economic production and growth (Mian et al., 2020).

Figure 1. Digital skills in education

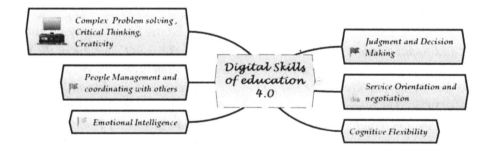

ACTIVE LEARNING BY PRACTICAL

Inter-disciplinarily and creativity are recognized by several institutions as two key skills that need to be enhanced in engineering courses in higher education. Current research concludes that future industrial engineering work will be characterized by increased networking, flexibility, and control over innovative technologies. The student team aims to cover the automation and digitization of industrial processes through his horizontal and vertical network of relevant OT and IT elements. Students thus lead to the development of features and services such as flexible automation, IIoT devices, development of CPS based on artificial intelligence, and augmented reality based on interfaces. All these elements interact to facilitate an enhanced, connected environment of human-machine collaboration. In this context, the proposed content for the promotion of Engineering 4.0 programs at the Bachelor and Masters level lies in the design of challenging environments in which students are involved in complete industrial processes as a real learning framework. This approach offers a combination of active learning techniques such as problem-based learning and problem-oriented learning, where the educational process is linked to experimental solutions to proposed tasks. In this way, students should experience participation in a collaborative laboratory where interdisciplinary projects are carried out in real industrial cells.

Figure 2. Five stage teaching-learning model

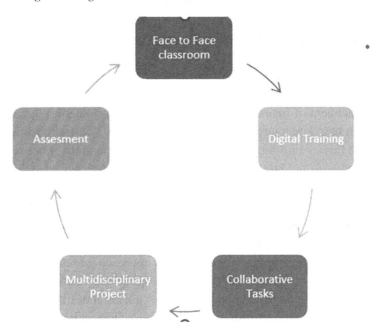

The first phase will consist of a series of face-to-face sessions to present the lab architecture, technology, objectives and procedures. The global objective proposed to students is therefore the design and development of information-based services related to the production, maintenance, and energy aspects of industrial cell management and supervision. At the second level, students begin problem solving by accessing available information and teaching materials related to each technology being considered (flexible automation, IIoT devices, cyber-physical system development, augmented reality). increase. All students work with a series of partially solved problems related to each of the four related technologies as hands-on training. (ii) her IIoT devices in operation, including signal acquisition, digital processing, and communications; (iii) models of databases under cloud computing architectures for energy monitoring, predictive maintenance, and production monitoring; (iv) augmented reality projects involving surveillance and educational scenes; The figure shows a five-step teaching-learning model. In a third stage, the students are distributed in four different groups, each one focused on one of the considered technologies. For each station and technology, the input and output information as well as details about expected functionalities are specified. In this stage, the students organize themselves to discuss, define and check their solutions over safe environments for code simulation and debugging. This stage finalizes with the validation of the integrated solution at station level with the teacher supervision. In a fourth stage, the connectivity among stations is faced. The students' teams, each one specialized in one considered technology by this time, face a common problem from a multidisciplinary approach. A set of additional aspects about the expected services related with the management and supervision of production, maintenance and energy are defined in this stage in order to focus the exercises to specific functionalities. This stage finalizes with the experimentation of the solution over the industrial cell from the functional and operation point of view. Finally, in a fifth stage, the assessment of the acquired competencies are assessed. All students are evaluated by means of a test exam including questions about the studied technologies, functionalities, services and industrial cell operation. In order to promote the active learning approach from the beginning to the finalization of the sessions, a presentation of the developed solution by each group to the rest of groups is also considered. In this way, the students learn the rest of works done over the industrial cell and received assessment from their pairs (Prieto et al., 2019). This reshaping of higher education in consonance with the vision of Industry 4.0 possesses its opportunities and challenges. There are, of course, a multitude of factors involved and they need a reasonable assessment to strategically plan this metamorphosis. Therefore, this work aims to explore and analyze the different factors that influence the progression and enactment of Industry 4.0 in universities for sustainable education. For this purpose, a systematic approach based on a questionnaire as well as a SWOT (strengths (S), weaknesses (W), opportunities (O), and threats (T)) integrated with the analytic hierarchy process (AHP) is adopted. The questionnaires are administered to university employees and students (or stakeholders) to assess their viewpoint, as well as to estimate the priority values for individual factors to be included in SWOT. The AHP is implemented to quantify the different factors in terms of weights using a pair-wise comparison matrix. Finally, the SWOT matrix is established depending on the questionnaire assessment and the AHP weights to figure out stakeholders' perspectives, in addition to the needed strategic scheme. The SWOT implementation of this research proposes an aggressive approach for universities, where they must make full use of their strengths to take advantage of the emerging opportunities in Industry 4.0. The results also indicate that there are fundamental requirements for universities in Industry 4.0, including effective financial planning, skilled staff, increased industrial partnerships, advanced infrastructure, revised curricula, and insightful workshops. This investigation undoubtedly underlines the importance of practical expertise and the implementation of digital technologies at the university level to empower novices with the requisite skills and a competitive advantage for Industry 4.0 (Mian et al., 2020).

SUSTAINABILITY EDUCATION IN INDUSTRY 4.0

The massive and ubiquitous changes occurring in the political, economic, social, technological and environmental spheres, the fourth wave of development is characterised by several intertwined factors, including diversity, equity, inclusion, complexity, uncertainty, risk and hyper-connectivity. As such, creative learning, lifelong learning, inter- or transdisciplinary learning and personalised student-centred learning based on humanistic values lie at the heart of Education 4.0. Because these spheres are interconnected and interdependent due to globalisation, what happens in one sphere usually impacts on the other spheres. As such, education at all levels, as with anything else, must be contextualised and adapted to the environment in which it operates. For instance, UNESCO believes that higher education should reorient its mission, vision and values along three interrelated themes: 1) the need to develop interdisciplinary and trans-disciplinary teaching, learning and research; 2) the need to become fully open institutions by focusing on diversity, equity, inclusion and humanistic values; and 3) the need to take a more active role in society by partnering with other institutions to serve the interests of the common good.

Figure 3. Sustainability levels of Industry 4.0

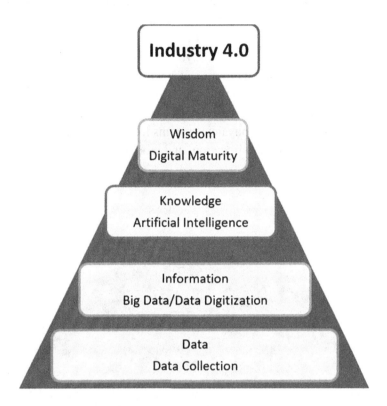

Education 4.0 cannot be isolated from changes occurring around the world. In the fourth wave, education at all levels must be more flexible and dynamic in response to emergencies (such as the COVID-19 pandemic) where distance learning was a "forced choice" rather than an educational option. it won't work. The technical skills of educators, teachers and students are evolving around distance learning and online learning communities. In the fourth wave, educational policies, curricula, teaching and assessment practices must reflect contemporary demands, opportunities and realities.

EFFECTIVE ANALYSIS IN SMART LEARNING

Considering all these cases, the use of Industry 4.0 in higher education is of great importance for training qualified personnel. Teaching the concepts of Industry 4.0 principles in courses for students helps form the background. Therefore, the curriculum should be designed with Industry 4.0 design principles in mind. Therefore, this concept needs to be learned theoretically and students are oriented to the design principles of Industry 4.0. Additionally, laboratory practice should be supported in this matter. It should really provide a rationale for acquiring and processing real-time data using sensor applications in the laboratory. Also, teaching effectiveness should improve with changes in course content, processed with information technology concepts and supported by visual elements. There are basically six different design principles for implementing Industry 4.0. These are interoperability, information transparency, technical support, real-time data collection and processing, modularity, and decentralized decision-making respectively. The most important features of Industry 4.0. To enable machines, devices, sensors and people, especially the Internet of Things-IOT, to connect and communicate with each other. In this case, production moves to cyber-physical systems. Cyber-physical systems basically mean that the entire process from production to consumption communicates with each other (Schlick, 2012). Therefore, in addition to current production conditions, consumers are also included in the production process. Research on cyber-physical systems points to the difficulties of theory and application of these systems. We begin by examining the characteristics of cyber-physical systems from various perspectives, including power control, security control, system resource allocation, and model-based software design.

Figure 4. Analysis of smart learning

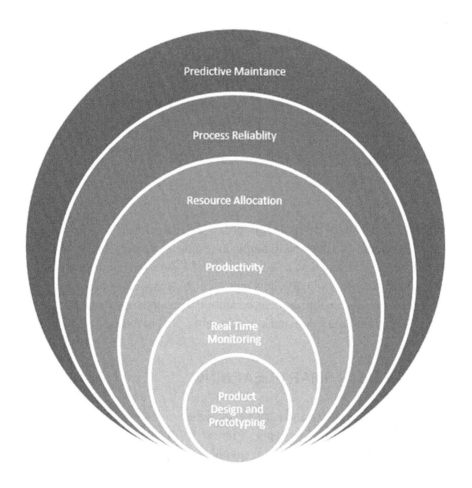

HIGHER EDUCATION SYSTEM

Modern students work in "Industry 4.0" and create Russia's digital economy. The digital economy is based on an infrastructure organization of production based on the networked interaction of production and technology. The world infrastructure of transport, trade and finance provides technical organizations of producers and consumers. Industry 4.0 begins with the creation of redundant infrastructure networks - the Industrial Internet of Things (IIoT). Today's university education corresponds to a processed form of technical organization. An infrastructure form of organization of the educational process is required. No information technology exists to support the entire training process and deliver it over the Internet. A new methodology of educational process is proposed. The training process training, lectures, seminars and laboratory work are organized according to the logical achievement of the intended work. The teacher's job is to design the subject work and analyze the results. The increases research productivity and quality, reduces operating costs, and implements remote access to devices on your local network or the Internet. These current technologies enable you to realize the benefits of the Industrial Internet (IoT). Students who apply these techniques are able to solve radio system design and computational problems. They must be able to work in teams to achieve their goals in a timely manner within design constraints. They must also be able to apply the concepts they have acquired during their teaching career in new and innovative ways. To ensure student preparation, concepts must be understood in the context they appear in the real world. Then you should be challenged with projects that promote teamwork or encourage effective use of tools and engineering stimulus methods. Today's university education corresponds to a processed form of technical organization. Educational Process Infrastructure Form Organization required. No information technology exists to support the entire training process and deliver it over the Internet. A new methodology for the educational process has been proposed.

LEARNING IN THE DIGITAL ERA

Today, imagination, innovation, inspiration, interaction, connection, and improvement are the new paradigms emanating from the pillars of education. New types of learning in the digital age include social, personal, blended, interactive, immersive, adaptive, and continuous (Netexplo, n.d.).

- **Adaptive Learning:** Adaptive learning, in its basic form, is learning that adapts to the learner. The digital ecosystem is tasked with creating training programs and presenting them to the right people at the right time. It enables tailor-made lessons tailored to each learner. It is based on several principles of collecting data in real time, analyzing learner behavior, analyzing results, and adjusting the difficulty of training sequences as needed.
- **Blended Learning:** Blended learning concepts meet user experience requirements. It has the advantage of being able to mobilize different approaches and types of materials.
- **Continuous Learning:** Technology can monitor digital learning activity. They can always suggest appropriate training and learning new skills. This seems obvious, but relatively few people aspire to continue exercising throughout their lives.
- **Tailor Made Learning:** In this study, digital technology enables profiling and content delivery on a personalized and localized basis.

Figure 5. Step-by-step problem solving

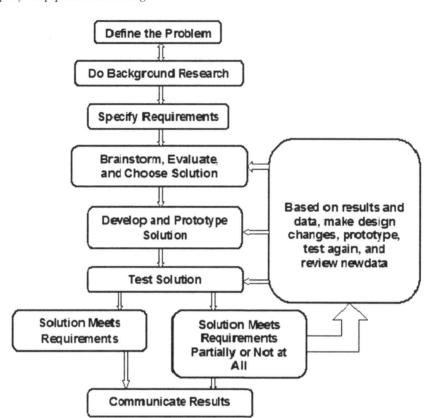

- **Immersive Learning:** Digital innovation puts learners in real-world situations so that they can practice specific skills and techniques and perform them in multiple environments. Of course, this immersion is more engaging for learners.
- **Interactive Learning:** Interaction is central to more engaging teaching and learning. This means greater flexibility and responsiveness on the teacher's part, and more adaptability to real-time situations. In the digital age, teachers and their digital tools are agile.
- **Social Learning:** Social Learning allows learners to create fun educational games and quizzes to help them review. Learners are grouped around a shared screen and can participate simultaneously.

Figure 6. Smart learning system

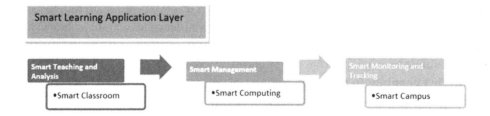

The smart classroom component can use AR, VR (or both), and hologram technology to deliver an interactive, personalized, and immersive classroom learning experience. Intelligent classrooms provide an interactive classroom environment that allows interaction between teachers and students. Hologram technology provides an intuitive, 3D and immense experience. An intelligent teaching solution that supports real-time multi-point interactions.

- The intelligent analytics component analyzes teacher and student behavior in the classroom. Data is collected and analyzed. Use AI and ML technology to analyze student behavior and emotions based on the behavioral model. Analytics can be used by teachers to optimize lesson design and guide students to improve their learning skills. In addition, teacher behavior is analyzed to assess the quality of teaching in the classroom.

Analysis includes classroom, homework, exams, and exercises. Collecting statistics on student attendance can help identify anomalous behavior. This also allows immediate diagnosis and treatment of mental and physical problems.

- Intelligent management enables effective use of educational resources, administration, spaces and development archives for teachers, students and parents. Intelligent management allows you to audit student internet usage and avoid overuse.
- Intelligent monitoring and tracking integrate student monitoring systems and automation technology. Monitor students and their activities in a more convenient, secure and cost-effective way. You can integrate radio frequency identification (RFID) technology with intelligent attendance systems to create automated systems. This integration process improves the performance and efficiency of intelligent education systems compared to traditional methods. With intelligent monitoring and tracking, RFID tags allow university administrators to monitor and monitor student movements on campus.
- The Smart Analytics component performs regression analysis on collected data to derive values. Smartanalytics can apply regression or ML in addition to collected data.
- A domain expert in the education industry adds much-needed value by providing insights and sharing their experience with data scientists or analysts. A data scientist or analyst can create educational software models.
- In intellectual education, end-users or consumers are administrators of educational institutions/ businesses/athletic associations, students, teachers, administrators, coaches, parents, academics, coaches, and so on.

Smart Computing Layer. The smart computing layer is a key layer for intelligent education solutions. These include smart computing, education cloud, smart education network, and social computing. The smart computing layer transforms the data received from the smart learning layer and sends it to the smart campus layer. Leverage cloud computing and ubiquitous computing to support distributed processing and improves the performance of Smart education Smart Campus Tier The Smart Campus Layer supports teaching and research, optimizes service quality, and enables unified decision-making. Smart campus components are set up in both wired and wireless networks. It used Internet, wireless, RFID and IoT technologies to provide integrated transmission for multiple devices. Intelligent technology keeps students, teachers and employees safe on campus. Intelligent technology facilitates property, student, staff and teacher attendance, transport or vehicle movement, and location management. A smart campus can also support mobile learning and teaching. Technology Architecture, Data Architecture and Application Architecture are the main pillars of Smart education. All services can run on a centralized service, making it easier to access, monitor and maintain intelligent education solutions.

ENVIRONMENT FOR EDUCATION

A new industrial production model based on digitalization, system interconnection, virtualization and data exploitation, has emerged. Upgrade of production processes towards this Industry 4.0 model is one of the critical challenges for the industrial sector and, consequently, the training of students and professionals has to address these new demands. To carry out this task, it is essential to develop educational tools that allow students to interact with real equipment that implements, in an integrated way, new enabling technologies, such as connectivity with standard protocols, storage and data processing in the cloud, machine learning, digital twins and industrial cyber security measures. For that reason, in this work, we present an educational environment on Industry 4.0 that incorporates these technologies reproducing realistic industrial conditions. This environment includes cutting-edge industrial control system technologies, such as an industrial recall and a virtual private network (VPN) to strengthen cyber security, an Industrial Internet of Things (IIoT) gateway to transfer process information to the cloud, where it can be stored and analyzed, and a digital twin that virtually reproduces the system.

The proposed environment is based on an educational industrial pilot plant (PROFINET, 2014), but the industrial instrumentation consists of three separate circuits. The main process loop is designed to control her four variables (level, flow, temperature and pressure) in the recirculation line. This includes two tanks or reservoirs connected at different levels, a centrifugal pump, various valves for moving the liquid and regulating the flow rate, and a control circuit for the above volumes to be able to be implemented. It contains several sensors. Two other circuits are related to temperature. The heating circuit consists of a tank for storing hot water, heated by electrical resistance and releasing heat to the process via a plate heat exchanger. Finally, another plate heat exchanger is used to re-circulate the refrigerant from an external source through the refrigeration cycle. The physical system can be seen in the comments. The process is controlled by a Siemens Programmable Logic Controller (PLC) that provides PROFINET communication (*IBM Watson IoT Platform,* n.d.) and uses distributed I/O for signal acquisition. These elements are organized by engineering stations. The process is monitored by her SCADA system on another workstation. Since the industrial plant and distributed I/O are installed in one lab and the rest of the equipment is installed in another lab, PROFINET communication between these labs is over a private network isolated from the rest of the university network. is done. The network architecture is divided into four different zones. The industrial zone includes all the aforementioned elements of the facility, plus an IoT gateway, an edge device responsible for communicating between the and cloud services. Communication in and out of this zone is filtered by industrial routers/firewalls. This device enforces zone isolation, but is also the endpoint of a VPN connection, allowing secure remote access, management and configuration. This access is provided by a Remote Connect server within the demilitarized zone (DMZ) that exposes the environment's outgoing services. Various clients, such as remote engineering stations and digital twins, can connect to the system externally via his VPN. Finally, the cloud platform uses data storage, analytics, and visualization services provided by the *IBM Cloud* (n.d.) and its IoT platform *IBM Watson IoT Platform* (n.d.). The digital twin contained in the environment provides physics-based modeling of the industrial pilot plant, its virtual reality display, and data transfer from the cloud platform. Equations describing the behavior of the process circuit were used for the simulation. The goal is not to simulate physical entities with high precision and multiple scales, but to give students an understanding of the key features of physical behavior. The virtual representation uses his 3D model of the pilot plant. Visual features such as conduit color and numbers representing liquid temperature have been added to support this representation framework for implementing virtual reality (VR) simulations that can run on mobile devices. Alternatively, you can use specific applications currently offered by industrial manufacturers. These tools are well suited for developing highly accurate simulations that are tightly integrated with automation technology. The 3D engine provides the necessary functionality to enable simple graphical representation of dynamic motion simulated by scripts programmed in C#. The digital twin has been developed for Windows and Android, and includes a virtual reality version of the latter that can be used immersive with VR goggles, but can be easily ported to other his platforms such as Linux and iOS. . A 3D representation of the digital twin of the desktop and mobile VR versions. In the development environment, various communication flows are generated as shown in the activity diagram. First, the PLC cyclically reads the desktop version of the digital twin (top) and the virtual reality glasses version (bottom) in the control loop. Analog and digital inputs from distributed peripherals compute control actions and write to outputs again via distributed peripherals. As needed, configuration and management tasks can be performed on the controller either locally from the engineering station of the industrial plant or from a remote engineering station via a VPN connection. Parameters, setpoints and/or manual values can be changed at any time required by the operation via the Node-RED dashboard of the SCADA or IoT gateway. System monitoring is also done via the SCADA or Node-RED dashboard of the IoT Gateway. Both platforms communicate with the PLC via the PROFINET protocol. IoT gateways also transfer variables to the cloud via the MQTT protocol, which is suitable for communicating over public networks. In the cloud, data is stored, processed and visualized in appropriate databases. The digital twin gets the inputs required for the simulation from the cloud.

ICT TOOLS AND PLATFORMS POWERED BY IOT

The recommendations of ICT tools in the smart education system play a vital role in the development of smart education environment (Chauhan, 2021). The educational landscape is evolving as a result of the Internet of Things (IoT). Not only is education becoming more pervasive because to the adaption of digital tools, but traditional educational systems are also becoming more effective and inclusive. Nearly all age groups of students utilise smartphones and tablets in digital classrooms. To facilitate a better comprehension, complex processes are being explained via graphics and augmented reality. On their websites, schools and other educational institutions keep a real-time online log of their students' progress. Live classrooms, recorded lectures, and problem-solving tools are all connected to a unique server and software that is tailored for educational usage as learning platforms change.

When it comes to deploying IoT devices for use, the education sector is one of the most flexible and effective. This will increase education's collaborative, interactive, and open nature for all students. IoT devices give students dependable access to everything they need to learn, including communication channels and clear understanding. They also enable professors to track students' academic progress in real-time. Speaking of education, the COVID-19 epidemic has done a good job of emphasising the necessity of educational resources. IoT merely facilitates the switch from traditional to digital education methodologies with a number of extra advantages and greater effectiveness.

With the use of graphics and animation, this may be utilised to teach various disciplines, from languages to math to teaching practical skills like medical sciences, in order to improve student comprehension. Not only can everything migrate automatically from the physical world to the central system-based control world, including these smart attendance devices, boards, integrated alarm systems in schools, assessment checking tools, cameras, and school locks, but also the physical world itself.

EVOLVING METHODOLOGIES

When we talk about IoT in education, we're talking about the incorporation of digital and internet-based smart devices for students and teachers in educational institutions. Modern education platforms are adopting devices such as e-books that can be downloaded and have zooming and saving features, smart boards instead of blackboards that can be used as a whiteboard to write with a marker and can also display topic-related images and graphics to students. These devices are linked to a central server, which can control and monitor the students' syllabus and topic categorization. Not only that, but voice command systems for teachers, speech-to-text note-taking systems for students, smart security cameras, GPS tracker equipped school buses, disaster alarms, and tablets, as well as smartphones with educational applications, are changing the way traditional schools and educational systems have always operated.

These features make it safer, more convenient, and easier for students, teachers, and parents to use. It is a well-known fact that immediate changes in teaching methods and methodologies cannot be implemented; however, such devices are gradually being personalised and updated with the necessary software. In this case, students can read traditional books while also benefiting from IoT in the form of smart boards in the classroom that display animated and 3D versions of the topics discussed.

AUTOMATED ATTENDANCE RECORDING

Student attendance is a concern for teachers, and in schools, it is a daily task with no alternative. IoT can assist in providing a solution to the difficult task of recording and calculating attendance for various purposes. Almost every class can benefit from IoT in reducing this task. Biometric attendance or barcode-based attendance with the student's identity card number can be used to automatically record attendance as they enter the classroom. This will not allow teachers to devote more time to their primary concern, which is teaching the students, but such systems can be made more effective by sending a direct message to the pupil's parents informing them of their absence in the classroom.

SAFETY IN PREMISES

Most schools lack the infrastructure to detect red flags for theft, abuse, sexual assault, and other crimes that can occur within the institution, and they also lack a proper disaster or emergency plan. IoT can assist in resolving such issues on a large scale; for example, if any unacceptable activity is detected on the camera, it can be immediately addressed thanks to a network system that allows the camera recording to be displayed on various screens throughout the premises. In the event of a fire or a short circuit, IoT-based sensors can activate alarms pinpointing the exact location of the problem, resulting in less hassle and risk in resolving the problem.

DISTANCE LEARNING

IoT-based systems have the capability of storing and forming data in the form of an application form with special software and in the form of a sign-in feature of websites that allows anyone from anywhere to access that with a user id and a password that the institution can provide to their distance learning learners. This can benefit anyone who is unable to attend a legitimate educational institution but wishes to pursue its educational programme. Live classes, pre-recorded classes, online timer-based assessment questions, and time tracking on the portal can all contribute to the development of a comprehensive approach for distance learners.

ENHANCED INTERACTION AND PRODUCTIVITY

Students become more interactive in smartphone-based virtual application-based classes. As previously stated, when students are able to understand more and more clearly, they are also able to think beyond the confines of the classroom and communicate and voice their learning and doubts. This interaction-based learning can make students more interested in participating in assessments, activities, and even self-learning by scanning the codes on the books to see the digital version of the same. They can even review the taught topic at their leisure using their educator's web portal and access the material provided by them. This entire process is ideal for increasing student productivity while also improving their abilities.

AR-EQUIPPED SYSTEMS

Augmented Reality can be defined as an enhanced version of the real world that is presented in a more understandable manner using computerised tools. The use of AR can make IoT-based devices and systems even more efficient; proper markings and details can be presented to students simply by scanning a barcode against the topic they are studying. AR, with its graphics and sounds combined with a software system, can provide enhanced details and 3D visions of the topic being taught, for example, the anatomy of a human ear can be better understood in an animated way than theoretical explanations read aloud in the classroom.

SPECIAL EDUCATION

It was once nearly impossible and comparatively difficult for specially-abled students to receive a regular and detailed education. The educational curriculum is being specially modified and classroom environments are being made sound and light-sensitive with the incorporation of IoT tools and smart devices to cater to the special needs of students with sensory disabilities.

CLOSE MONITORING

Whether the website portal is accessed from within the school grounds or from elsewhere, there is always the option to track a student's activities and time spent on a specific topic. The Internet of Things sensors in education collect data and automatically recommend academic topics of interest to students for further learning processes. Also, who was a part of which assessment can be easily identified, and even scoring and progress can be tracked. In so far as students' smartphones connected to school Wi-Fi systems can get internet usage for a specific usage application made for the specific purpose, this helps to prevent misuse and unnecessary activities.

TEACH IN THE 4TH INDUSTRIAL REVOLUTION

In order to facilitate individualised learning for creativity, innovation, and problem solving and have more time for individualised instruction, teachers are being pushed by the 4th Industrial Revolution to improve their instructional approaches.

Educating Students About Industry 4.0

The Fourth Industrial Revolution has given educators what may be the greatest duty of our time: to develop lesson plans that can help students reach their full potential and equip them with the knowledge and skills they need to change the future through technological innovation.

It's crucial to consider the relationship between employment requirements and education while considering previous industrial revolutions. During the First Industrial Revolution, physical work was required in order to produce things using the power of water and steam. Electricity and assembly lines were used during the Second Industrial Revolution to facilitate mass production by skilled labourers who had received higher education. Through the emergence of intelligent machines and the development of those who could programme them, the Third Industrial Revolution automated production using computers, data, and information technology (IT).

Technology and the Fourth Industrial Revolution

The Fourth Industrial Revolution is currently fusing the physical and digital worlds by utilising smart factories, the Internet of Things (IoT), artificial intelligence (AI), and other technologies to generate things. Nowadays, repetitive, boring, dangerous, or regular work are delegated to computers and robots. This enables employees to concentrate on management, communication, and strategic decision-making tasks. As a result, workers on both sides of the technology divide collaborate. Technology and creativity are creating new jobs. It will be more crucial than ever for humans to be certified for and skilled at using technological systems as machines help human jobs.

These changes are not just having an influence on production, manufacturing, or the industrial sector; they are also having an impact on every other industry. Numerous other professions, including those in medicine, finance, research, technology, marketing, healthcare, and education, are also adapting to incorporate new technologies. In addition to being able to adapt to these changes, today's students also need to be in a position to influence them through innovative problem-solving and open-mindedness.

Open thinking entails being constantly creative, coming to decisions, and acting creatively, inspiring the next generation of creative thinking. Simply put, mistakes are opportunities to grow. Students will be able to provide professional value to society while also being able to do so through open thinking, especially when combined with technology that applies exponential thinking.

Participating in the 4IR requires teaching methods to change. Teaching needs to evolve so that students learn how to apply, evaluate, and create utilising the material they learn in the classroom rather than just remembering and understanding it. Not as a means to these ends, but rather as a means to them, is personalised learning. Using the technology tools at their disposal, which enable them to solve problems in ways they had never imagined before, the objective is to develop students' talents and problem-solving abilities. One hierarchical classification system that educators use to specify and distinguish between various stages of thinking, learning, and understanding is Bloom's taxonomy. Different learning levels correspond to different levels of intellect. By building on lower-level reasoning, Bloom's taxonomy aims to promote higher-order thinking in students.

In order to foster the greatest amount of creativity, innovation, and convergent thinking while assuring more time for individualised instruction, teachers can employ Bloom's taxonomy and other technology-supported approaches. It is now more important to provide kids the freedom to think for themselves and create their own futures in the workplace than it is to prepare them to perform tasks as future employees.

The pandemic has had a significant impact on education, among other societal variables, to the point where goals need to be reevaluated in order to maximise continuity, relevance, and resilience in education. To create and influence future work, a combination of technology and more advanced creative thinking abilities is required.

FACILITATORS ARE NOW TEACHERS

Teachers must become facilitators of learning outside of their areas of specialisation in order to prepare students for the Fourth Industrial Revolution. They ought to let technology assist students' freedom in developing skills and following interests. It is no longer an effective teaching strategy to lecture to a class of students and expect them to learn something from a thorough presentation. Instead, educators must shift their focus to supporting learning that meets students where they are in their engagement and thought processes.

The teaching methods used in the classrooms that function in hybrid, online, and in-person settings have changed to fit the new criteria. Among these instructional techniques are:

- Students in a flipped classroom work on assignments at home and engage in practical exercises in class.
- A teaching approach called "active learning" encourages pupils to actively participate and learn by "doing."
- Collaboration in the classroom refers to shared, student-centered spaces that are appealing to tech-savvy, visually inclined learners who take an active part in their education.

One student might be watching a video lecture, another might be in a virtual learning lab, and a group might be working together on a project related to the same subject, as an illustration of the new learning environment. No matter where each student is physically, a variety of activities are going on at once. A variety of modalities ensure that students receive individualised instruction and time with the teacher as needed. Leveraging technology for effectiveness and performance is necessary to support this level of diverse learning.

While instructors and their students should always be at the heart of any learning environment, school administrators also need to be aware of the state of education technology in order to offer the assistance, materials, and financial commitment needed to facilitate individualised learning. Delaying student preparation for potential work prospects until they attend higher education, community colleges, or trade institutions can be simple. However, even in K–12 school contexts, students must become self-learners since workplace demands and technology are evolving so quickly.

INTELLIGENCE AND EDUCATION STRATEGIES

Education is changing to help teachers maximise each student's potential and get them ready to learn on their own so they can change the world tomorrow. Modern classrooms and the globe are being shaped by Intel® technologies.

For the past 50 years, Intel has led the way in technology during both the Third and current Fourth Industrial Revolutions. As a result, Intel not only pioneers core technology innovation but also observes new emerging technology applications as they develop across a range of sectors and workplaces. Focusing on kids and their education to prepare for our collective future workforce makes sense, especially with education technology at our disposal (EdTech).

Students can access the appropriate technology for possibilities to learn new skills thanks to EdTech. Since technological advancements are occurring quickly, students must pace their learning appropriately. EdTech exists to encourage greater student collaboration, engagement, and learning outcomes that matter. Effective use of EdTech ultimately leads to the development of student competencies that close the talent gap in the labour market of the future.

In order to run their classes, teachers also need greater technology, better connectivity, and simplicity of use. With the right technology and sufficient processing power, teachers may spend more time with their pupils and have more teaching options. The most important resource in the classroom—the teacher—can concentrate more on instruction thanks to technology. Several instances include:

- **Interactive Whiteboards:** Interactive flat panel displays that assist in ensuring that all students have access to high-quality instruction.
- **Artificial Intelligence (AI):** Identifies learning patterns, solves incredibly difficult educational problems, and more accurately forecasts student behaviour and outcomes.
- Supports existing hardware and software in schools for more immersive learning environments with the Intel Unite® solution.

Beyond technology, Intel also assists educators in driving change in the classroom through a number of initiatives, one of which is the Intel® Skills for Innovation (Intel® SFI) programme. When creating and implementing active, engaging learning experiences to achieve skill-building objectives, educators and decision-makers are guided by the Intel® SFI framework. With Intel® SFI, decision-makers and educators can confidently incorporate technology into the curriculum and aid kids in gaining the skills necessary to succeed in today's technologically advanced society.

To assist educators in learning about and integrating Intel® SFI, Intel provides a substantial library of resources. With the help of the Intel® SFI Starter Pack, educators and administrators may implement brand-new, technologically enhanced learning opportunities that can help kids in classrooms develop higher-order cognitive skills. With practical activities that can be used for online or in-person instruction, this pack encourages students to get involved and interested in the subjects covered in their curriculum.

Educators can also access the Intel® SFI Professional Development Suite as part of the Intel® SFI effort to find resources for their own professional growth as well as lesson plans that can assist turn current instructors into 4IR-ready educators. To keep teachers up to date with trends affecting students' futures and resources that maximise learning outcomes, there are more than 80 hours of online learning and in-person workshops. Technology adaptation to encouraging innovative thinking are some of the topics covered. The step-up strategy has been thoughtfully designed to meet the needs of educators regardless of their individual level of experience using technology to enhance learning.

Students can study STEM (science, technology, engineering, and math) problem-solving and exploration skills through another Intel programme called Intel® Future Skills. Students are given practical, real-world innovation tasks to complete that push their thinking, let them fail quickly, and help them cultivate a growth attitude.

BEST PRACTICES IN STUDENT LEARNING

For instructors and students, teaching in the fourth industrial revolution brings new opportunities and problems. In education, technologies are combining to support:

- Expanded access
- Engagement
- Skill development
- Individualized instruction

To assist in the development of a comprehensive ecosystem, Intel collaborates with academics, supervisors, and decision-makers. Today's students, who will influence our collective future through their labour, innovation, and creativity, require support for effective learning.

Additionally, Intel is dedicated to bridging the technological gap that stops children from having access to the tools they require to succeed in the classroom and beyond. The Intel Online Learning Initiative was established to assist commercial partners and nonprofits with an emphasis on education in their efforts to supply devices and online learning resources to students who do not have access to technology. The plan will enable PC donations, online virtual resources, study-at-home tutorials, and device connectivity support in close collaboration with public school systems. The Intel Online Learning Initiative expands on Intel's long-standing dedication to educational technology, especially in underprivileged areas. The objective of Intel is to support school systems, teachers, and administrators in providing effective, exciting, and dynamic learning opportunities for students.

CONCLUSION

Thus, introducing ICT (Information and Communication Technologies) into everyday practice and create a process-based "smart education" system. The chapter discusses using knowledge engineering to intellectualize higher education. Also, explains how knowledge engineering (KE) can be utilized to construct intelligent learning and smart tutoring systems (STSs). The intersection of AI, web science, and data science enables for a new generation of online-based educational and training tools. To determine and examine the benefits of such computational paradigms for smart tutoring systems. A layered Data Science Education Framework (DSEF) containing building blocks that include people, technology, and data, computational thinking, and data-driven paradigms. Built on this architecture, data science courses should be user-, tool-, and application-based. This framework will help students think about data science problems from a big picture perspective and build problem-solving abilities and wide data science life-cycle perspectives. The latest research and teaching on control and decision methods, control structures, information and communication technologies, and their applications in varied industrial processes, with an emphasis on Industry 4.0 trends and problems.

REFERENCES

Chauhan, M. (2021, June 8). 8 Applications of IoT in Education. Analytics Steps. In *Smart Education in Industry 4.0: A Systematic Literature Review*. Academic Press.

IBM Cloud. (n.d.). IBM. Retrieved from https://www.ibm.com/cloud

IBM Watson IoT Platform. (n.d.). IBM. Retrieved from https://internetofthings.ibmcloud.com

Mian, S. H., Salah, B., Ameen, W., Moiduddin, K., & Alkhalefah, H. (2020). Adapting universities for sustainability education in industry 4.0: Channel of challenges and opportunities. *Sustainability (Basel)*, *12*(15), 6100. doi:10.3390u12156100

Netexplo. (n.d.). A Brief Review of New Ways of Learning in the Digital Era, Human Learning in the Digital Era, UNESCO Publishing. PROFINET system description: Technology and application, ''PROFIBUS Nutzerorganisation e. V. (PNO) PROFIBUS & PROFINETInternational (PI), Karlsruhe, Germany. *Tech. Rep.*, *4*, 132.

Pacheco, A., & Reis, J. C. (2019, October). A small-scale educational workbench for Industry 4.0. In *IECON 2019-45th annual conference of the IEEE industrial electronics society* (Vol. 1, pp. 3127-3132). IEEE.

Prieto, M. D., Sobrino, Á. F., Soto, L. R., Romero, D., Biosca, P. F., & Martínez, L. R. (2019, September). Active learning based laboratory towards engineering education 4.0. In *2019 24th IEEE international conference on emerging technologies and factory automation (ETFA)* (pp. 776-783). IEEE.

Schlick, J. (2012, May). Cyber-physical systems in factory automation-Towards the 4th industrial revolution. In *2012 9th IEEE International Workshop on Factory Communication Systems* (pp. 55-55). IEEE.

Yakimov, P., & Iovev, A. (2019). *Towards Industry 44.0 Oriented Education.*. doi:10.1109/ET.2019.8878609

ADDITIONAL READING

Bangor, A., Kortum, P. T., & Miller, J. T. (2008). An empirical evaluation of the system usability scale. *International Journal of Human-Computer Interaction*, 24(6), 574–594. doi:10.1080/10447310802205776

Jazdi, N. (2014, May). *Cyber physical systems in the context of Industry 4.0. In 2014 IEEE international conference on automation, quality and testing, robotics*. IEEE.

Lee, J., Bagheri, B., & Kao, H. A. (2015). A cyber-physical systems architecture for industry 4.0-based manufacturing systems. *Manufacturing Letters*, *3*, 18–23. doi:10.1016/j.mfglet.2014.12.001

Pahlavan, K., Geng, Y., Cave, D. R., Bao, G., Mi, L., Agu, E., Karellas, A., Sayrafian, K., & Tarokh, V. (2015). A novel cyber physical system for 3-D imaging of the small intestine in vivo. *IEEE Access : Practical Innovations, Open Solutions*, *3*, 2730–2742. doi:10.1109/ACCESS.2015.2508003

Chapter 6
Analysis of Campus Recruitment Data and Career Counseling in the Engineering Sector:
Engineering Career Guidance by Data Exploration

M M. Nirmala Devi

🆔 https://orcid.org/0000-0003-1262-9933

Department of Computer Science and Engineering, Thiagarajar College of Engineering, India

B. Subbulakshmi

Department of Computer Science and Engineering, Thiagarajar College of Engineering, India

G. Naga Nivedithaa

Department of Computer Science and Engineering, Thiagarajar College of Engineering, India

R. Swathi

Department of Computer Science and Engineering, Thiagarajar College of Engineering, India

ABSTRACT

Analysis of campus recruitment data and career counseling in the engineering sector can offer insights about the job market trends, company preferences, and student preferences. These insights will improve career counseling services for students. The effectiveness and impact of career counseling services in the engineering sector can be significantly improved by a thorough analysis of college recruitment data. This research can also assist career counselors in adjusting their offerings to meet the shifting demands of the labor market and guarantee that they are offering engineering students useful and pertinent advice. In this study, an online service application is developed to provide all the information needed by the students about internships industry recruitment, higher education, and government employment. In order to provide career counseling services in the engineering field, it is vital to build a model for campus recruitment data. Linear regression outperforms other traditional models and produces an accuracy of 95.7%.

DOI: 10.4018/978-1-6684-8145-5.ch006

Copyright © 2023, IGI Global. Copying or distributing in print or electronic forms without written permission of IGI Global is prohibited.

INTRODUCTION

In every person's life, selecting the appropriate career path is quite important. To obtain Career Guidance Support, a significant amount of effort must be put into analysis. Career guidance is the Student support system that will guide the students to choose the appropriate career path depending on their educational and professional choices and skillset. In India, every year only 10-15% of over 3 million regular graduates and post-graduates are considered "Employable". India's population is around 67% of persons between the ages of 15 and 64. Most of this group is in the 15–30 age range. This indicates that many people require assistance in choosing a suitable career path for them and they are struggling and spending more time selecting the appropriate Career path.

Over 71 percent of students think critically about their potential employers, according to the results of the most current 2021 IC3 Institute Student Quest Survey. The Careers Services Unit for Higher Education which is a research charity and division of Universities UK and Guild HE, conducts research on all facets of graduate employability in collaboration with careers and employability professionals and their institutions. Prospects, a website with information on graduate careers, is also operated by Careers Services Unit for Higher Education. A career guidance system enables students to view a wide range of employment options. The system displays a range of fields that are open to applicants for graduation and even after their graduation. The survey also found that students benefited from career guidance because they perceived them as useful career guidance resources, priceless career counseling toolkits, user-friendly tools, and helpful for outlining potential career choices.

Overall, an analysis of campus recruitment data and career counseling in the engineering domain will provide valuable patterns that can help improve career counseling services for engineering students. By understanding job market trends, employer preferences, student preferences, skill gaps, and feedback, career counselors can guide students in a better way to opt for their career choices and develop the cognitive, behavioral, and attitude skill set to succeed in their chosen field of engineering. Some key aspects of this analysis are explained below:

Job Market Trends: Analyzing college recruitment data can give insights into the market's demand for engineering graduates. Data on the number of job openings, wage trends, job profiles, and industry preferences are some examples. Career counselors can use this knowledge to better understand the dynamics of the job market and assist students in making educated career decisions. For instance, career counselors can concentrate on directing students toward developing skills in that field if the data shows that there is a high demand for software engineers in the IT industry.

Employer Preferences: Campus recruitment data can also reveal information about an employer's preferences, such as the engineering fields, credentials, and skills they prefer. With the aid of this knowledge, career counselors can assist students in matching their educational and professional development to the needs of prospective employers. For instance, career counselors can advise students interested in that industry to concentrate on acquiring pertinent knowledge and skills in that field if data indicates that businesses in the automotive industry are hiring more mechanical engineers.

Student Preferences: Examining college recruitment data can also assist career advisors in learning about the preferences of engineering students, including their top-choice sectors, job functions, and workplaces. Career counselors can use this information to better tailor their counseling services to the needs and goals of students. For instance, career counselors can create specific programs or workshops related to that industry to help students if the data shows that a sizable number of students are interested in pursuing careers in it.

Skill Gap Analysis: Employers may have discovered skill gaps or deficiencies among engineering graduates during the recruitment process, and campus recruitment data can disclose these. This data can be used by career counselors to pinpoint the knowledge and skill gaps that students have that need to be filled in order to increase their usefulness. For instance, career counselors can emphasize the value of developing communication skills during counseling sessions and suggest pertinent training programs or workshops if data indicates that employers are looking for engineers with strong communication skills.

Analysis of Feedback: Analyzing feedback regarding the efficiency of job counseling services from both employers and students can shed light on areas that require improvement. Employers can provide feedback on the caliber of applicants they find through campus recruitment, and students can provide feedback on the value of the counseling services they receive. In order to better meet the requirements of both employers and students, career counselors can use this feedback to assess the strengths and weaknesses of their counseling methodology.

A detailed study was conducted and the results are analyzed for the above-mentioned key factors of campus recruitment data and career counseling in the engineering domain.

Background

Lodders and Meijers (2017) proposed an article that mainly concentrates on careers in post-industrial civilizations that are largely unexpected. People are therefore expected to become increasingly more self-directed. Universities often support the idea of helping their students become more self-directed, but they frequently fail to provide the kind of learning environment that can support this. The underlying inventive processes in three university departments that successfully implemented a careers advice program based on innovative and novel methods are examined and qualitatively analyzed in this study. They claim that teachers' collaborative learning is essential for successful implementation and that managers' transformational leadership is necessary to support teachers' collaborative learning. First, there is research on the connections between transformative leadership and group learning. Second, by combining the information from all three scenarios, they look at the regular actions that constitute collaborative learning and transformative leadership. By highlighting the breadth and complexity of the concepts of communal learning and transformative leadership as they relate to developing great collaborative career-learning environments in higher education, the study seeks to provide a descriptive and exploratory contribution to the body of literature. But they have provided a completely functional online application for informing students about their job offers from product-based organizations, etc. They have not offered prospective alternatives to obtain professional prospects.

The goals of counseling and advice, the traits of career counseling, and the underlying presumptions of the career counseling process can all be used to better appreciate the value of career guidance and student counseling. All educational institutions now place more importance on career counseling. People who are scared, upset, or concerned about their career prospects or future can go to a dedicated counseling facility in higher education institutions for support and assistance. By obtaining this assistance, their concerns can be assuaged, and they can locate employment or start a satisfying career.

Alkaabi et al. (2022) discussed one of the difficulties that students frequently have is choosing appropriate professional objectives, particularly when they are undergraduate students and must choose a specialization path to follow. In this work, they introduce Takhasosi, their proposed specialization advice app. It is an online application platform designed to assist students in choosing an appropriate specialty based on their academic history and other relevant data that is maintained within a request-based blockchain for distributed data storage and access of data. The majority of students struggle to decide on a major and keep working toward their professional objectives. Even with today's cutting-edge technology and enhanced learning options, this is a significant problem that many students encounter. The distributed application that is being offered gives many entities access to and evaluation of student academic achievement and the capacity to analyze those students' interests in a Special Interest Group based on their academic success. The proposed web-based career guidance chapter was more effective among college students as there is a durable increase in the statistical graphs for the past years.

Supriyanto et al. (2019) proposed a study with the objective of creating ESGuichar-web, as an Online Career Guidance system with mentoring modules for aspirants who were attending vocational high schools. Creating a web-based system requires both software and hardware; a database management system is the software and laptops, PCs, or notebooks are the hardware. The study focused on the potential readiness and success of vocational graduates in terms of their ability to find employment, pursue post-graduate education, or develop entrepreneurship using the expert system. Students can use this technique to help them decide what they want to pursue after finishing vocational high school. They replied to career items as they moved through the system. These items were created to assist them in reaching certain judgments and career-related advice that the experts later confirmed. The ESGuichar-web has undergone testing and has been shown to function as intended. The outcomes of ESGuichar-career web's advice services can be used as support when speaking with school career teachers and parents.

The research done in 2013 by TimesJobs.com found that between 70 and 80 percent of graduates are hired through university recruitment. Students now use the internet for a variety of tasks, including booking, academic research, blogging, job applications, etc. In India, parents think that one of the most important elements in investigating the background of a specific school is whether that school ensures their child's campus recruiting. To attract top personnel for admissions or research, an educational institution needs to build a reputation within the industry. To attract MNC1 companies for domestic and international recruiting as well as academic alliances, the universities participate in a number of branding strategies. The industrial contacts that a professional educational institution maintains with regard to recruiting, research, and educational institutes and their partnerships can be used to assess the university's standing in the country. The placement recruitment process takes place in the last year of the course for both undergraduate and graduate students enrolled in a programme. Campus hiring is the main way of hiring new engineering talent in India.

Ujakpa et al. (2021) explained the fact that the nation also has other sciences and professional programmers, but engineering students are considered the focal point of and main target of university recruitment. Predicting student success is crucial to the educational process. Exam questions are a crucial tool for measuring pupils' progress and separating proficient from amateur students. Exams are a crucial component of the educational system, which has a few goals. It is helpful since it gauges how well a pupil is doing in relation to predetermined goals. One of the most often used methods to evaluate students' performance is data mining. Recently, data mining algorithms and techniques have been used extensively in the field of education. It is referred to as educational data mining, and it offers helpful data and patterns that may be utilized to forecast student success. It would aid educators in developing a successful teaching strategy.

Alimam et al. (2017) discussed An automated system that uses the science process skill model to link scientific students with the right job path. Campus recruitment is a crucial component for both Industries and academic organizations. According to the study literature, there is a disconnect between student competencies and what employers look for. There are several reasons why a student would be interested in a job that a company is offering. Soft skills are prioritized during the university employment process above technical prowess and topic knowledge. If the industry is willing to hire top talent from an academic institute, it should work with the academic institute campuses through internships, Course Content- Syllabus Design, student training programs, etc. The findings show more focus has to be given to the steps of the college hiring process when engineering students select their journey of the professional path. It is found that the more internal factors supersede external factors in the recruitment process and the largest campus recruiters in India are IT services firms.

Zhang (2021) mentioned that they hire from various engineering areas because they think a student with logical and problem-solving skills may succeed in the IT field. The visualization of surveys demonstrates that companies need to improve their reputation on college campuses in order to draw top-level cognitive, skilled, and attitude-oriented students. The company's popularity is recognized as a major deciding factor when non-Circuit students have the opportunity to choose their career path from a variety of organizations. The process of university recruitment shouldn't be thought of as a one-time employment exercise, it is concluded. It should be seen as a continuous process. Instead of going to every college, the company might pick a few prestigious institutes where it could establish its fame and brand.

According to Healy et al. (2022) universities are being given more attention than ever on how they assist their graduates in achieving their career goals and it was discussed as a critical effect of significant corporate and public investment. Researchers in the disciplines of graduate employability and career development have looked at the traits and factors that support or hinder graduates' employment success. The findings show that, despite a strong alignment of research interests and educational goals, there hasn't been any theoretical or practical communication between the two fields. On deliberation between the two fields of research and Industry which will be advantageous to both and, when put into practice, might direct the creation of an evidence-based, integrative pedagogy for careers and employability learning in higher education.

Reid and Kelestyn (2022) examined a recent multidisciplinary design thinking jobs intervention that looked at how employability is depicted at one UK university. A critical discourse analysis was conducted using a framework for policy analysis and found four trending problem representations. These heightened silences regarding the opportunity frameworks exposed covert presumptions regarding the lack of employability skills among students and the responsibility-based definition of "employability." They also emphasized the neoliberal paradigm's unchallenged employment assumptions. The importance of group interaction and the requirement for critical discourse in altering these narratives are also emphasized. Design Thinking has the potential to assist practitioners and individuals in beginning to co-create a new critical consciousness as a creative intervention for career education practice.

Jackson and Lambert (2023) discussed that being the major professional influences in adults' life, parents must help adolescent kids navigate the shifting and more challenging career environments. Parents' perceptions of opportunities by sector and industry were generally in line with what was believed, but many lacked knowledge of contemporary trends that affected how young people's careers developed, did not use outside career resources, and lacked confidence in their understanding of young people's labor markets. Some participants saw the importance of social and cultural capital for landing and holding a job, but it devalued components of human capital such as work experience and connections. Variations in parent attitudes by education level and their own point to the need for focused efforts to better support parents in providing informed career counseling for the success of upcoming adolescents' career experiences.

In qualitative research, it was examined how engineering students who were involved in a student organization used their emergent resistance capital to advance in their academic careers. developing resilient capital was characterized by a change in the type of resistance from conformist to creative, as shown by three major themes. This study shows that emergent resistant capital enabled students to become engineering resistors by serving as role models, engaging in community outreach, and organizing collective resistance. The scientific and policy implications of this study can help engineering programmes that want to serve students. The corporation should involve the selected campuses in branding initiatives like guest lectures, student workshops, sponsorships, etc. if there aren't many hiring choices available year-round. The goal of the study is to examine how students and HR managers see two critical aspects of the college recruiting process: (a) the hiring season and (b) the wage offered to new hires. The aforementioned parameters were examined using the following hypotheses: H1: With regard to university recruitment season, HR managers and students have the same opinions. H2: Students and HR managers share similar perceptions about what to expect from university hiring salaries.

Students who are trying to decide what they want to study or what career they would like to follow may find it helpful to conduct research on career paths. The following actions can be done for career path data exploration:

Identify the Data Sources: There are a number of data sources that can be used to examine job options. As well as official databases like the Bureau of Labor Statistics, these may include job-related websites like LinkedIn, Glassdoor, or Indeed. (BLS). To guarantee accuracy, it's critical to rely on trustworthy sources of information.

Determine the Relevant Variables: When looking into career options, relevant variables might include job titles, job descriptions, pay ranges, educational requirements, and job growth forecasts.

Data Collection and Cleaning: The data can be collected and cleaned once the factors of interest have been determined. This could entail eliminating duplicates, fixing mistakes, and making sure the data is formatted regularly.

Identify Trends and Patterns: Linked to various career paths by analyzing the data that has been cleaned and organized. In order to visualize the data, it may be necessary to create charts or graphs. Additionally, statistical analyses to find correlations between various factors may need to be performed.

Draw Inferences and Give Suggestions: Inferences about various career paths can be made based on the analysis of the data, including which ones are most likely to be in demand in the future, which ones pay the highest salaries, and which ones demand the most education or training. Students can then receive recommendations based on their unique hobbies and abilities.

By taking these actions, students can develop insightful perspectives on various career paths and make well-informed decisions regarding their educational pursuits and potential career choices.

MAIN FOCUS OF THE CHAPTER

This Chapter has two main modules i) Selection of Career Path in Engineering Education and (ii)On-Campus Recruitment. Exploratory Data analysis is done and results are explained through Visualization. Data Mining and Machine Learning Algorithms are employed to strengthen the analysis Outcomes.

A. Selection of Career Path in Engineering Education: In-House Web Application

There are many different career paths within the field of engineering education.

- **Teaching at a University or College:** This can involve both performing research in a particular field of engineering as well as instructing undergraduate or graduate-level courses.
- **Industry Training:** Engineers are frequently hired by businesses to instruct staff members on particular technology or procedures.
- **Curriculum Development:** Engineering curricula schools and universities can be created and updated by engineers with a background in education.
- **Consulting:** Engineers with specialized knowledge in a given field might provide consulting services to businesses and organizations that want engineering guidance.
- **Research:** Engineers can carry out research in a wide range of areas, including civil, computer, electrical, mechanical, biological, aerospace, and more.

Consideration must be given to a variety of variables when choosing a career path in engineering education, including individual preferences, abilities, skills, and job market trends. The following are some important steps to consider when choosing a career route in engineering education:

1. **Self-Assessment:** Students can start by evaluating their own aptitude, hobbies, and skills. Students have to think about their passions, weaknesses, and strong and vulnerable points. Self-Assessment will help the students to determine the areas in which the students can excel and take pleasure in working, taking into account their academic performance and accomplishments in subjects connected to engineering. In this way, students can find a potential job path that fits their interests and skills using this self-assessment.

2. **Complete Research on Different Engineering Fields**: Students can thoroughly research the various engineering career choices that are available on the job market. Students can investigate different engineering specialties, such as computer, mechanical, electrical, and civil engineering. Students can discover the job requirements, employment outlook, and market trends for each field. Students can take into account the potential for long-term career growth, market demand, and compatibility with their individual interests and objectives.

3. **Seeking Advice:** Getting guidance from knowledgeable individuals, educators, or job counselors who can offer perceptions and counsel on various engineering career pathways. They can provide information about the skills, credentials, and certifications necessary for various engineering roles as well as assist the students in understanding the advantages and disadvantages of various choices.

4. **Acquire Practical Experience:** Students can gain practical experience by participating in co-curricular activities like participation in coding contests, hackathon, seminars/paper presentations and Design contests and internships in various engineering areas. Students can gain leadership and communication skills by taking part and volunteering in professional SocSocietylub activities and organizing events.

5. **Keep Up With Industry Trends:** Following the most recent developments in engineering disciplines and industry trends will help more. Self-learning, upskilling of upcoming technologies and recent trends by completing reputed certification courses like Coursera, udemy, NPTEL etc. Also

participating in hands-on workshops and technical seminars, and keeping up with industry news. This can assist the students in keeping up with changes in the engineering field and spotting new career possibilities,

6. **Think About Long-Term Goals:** Students can think about their long-term professional objectives. Students have to find their future and how their job path fits with those aspirations. Students can examine elements like career security, expansion possibilities, work-life balance, and advancement potential in the chosen engineering profession.

7. **Make an Informed Decision:** The students have to choose the engineering job path that most closely fits their interests, skills, and ambitions based on their self-evaluation, research, advice, practical experience, and long-term goals. Students should keep in their mind that career paths can change over time, and it's acceptable to change course as they acquire more experience and investigate new opportunities.

A Career path system is proposed as Website in this Chapter and the Students can view the following details on the career guidance website. The detailed design is given in the Overall Website Design for Career Guidance in Engineering Domain Figure 1.

Facilities:

*   Placements
*   Higher Education
*   Government jobs

The following facilities are given for the below-mentioned departments:

*   Department of Computer science and Engineering
*   Department of Information Technology
*   Department of Computer Science and Business System
*   Department of Electronics & Communication Engineering
*   Department of Electrical and Electronics Engineering
*   Department of Civil Engineering
*   Department of Mechanical Engineering
*   Department of Data Science
*   Department of Mechatronics

Initially. the user has to sign in to the web application. If the user doesn't have an account, then he/she should log in to the page using their Mail-Id. The web page opens and the students can select one of the options (i.e They can choose higher studies, placements, or government jobs). They can view various information regarding On-campus placements, higher studies that can be pursued after they complete their Graduation, and various government jobs. Students can also view the details of how their alumni and seniors got placed through campus- Recruitment. Students are able to view their seniors and super-seniors' placement experience from the placement portal. Students are also able to view the procedure of the placement rounds.

Figure 1. Proposed model for career path selection and campus recruitment data analysis

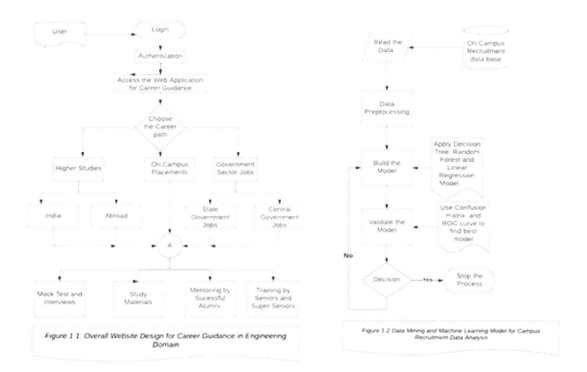

Figure 1 1: Overall Website Design for Career Guidance in Engineering Domain

Figure 1 2 Data Mining and Machine Learning Model for Campus Recruitment Data Analysis

The students can refer to study materials which will be available in the placement portal in this proposed web application. Details of various government exams like the commencement of examinations, results, etc. are mentioned. This portal consists of two sections, one about the details of state government exams like TNPSC and the second about the details of central government exams like UPSC, Public Sector Banks, Defense service exams, SSC exams, etc. This portal consists of details of exam eligibility criteria such as age limit, educational qualification, no of attempts, etc. The admission process of all colleges and universities in India as well as in and abroad are also published. Students who are looking to pursue higher education abroad can also use this proposed web application. It contains all the details of the exams such as the IELTS, PTE, and TOEFL and general exams such as SAT, GMAT, GRE, and ACT, etc. The comments section is also available. So that the Students can ask doubts and it will help other users to clarify their doubts. Users can attend a separate session with career experts where they can receive recommendations for the best careers out of all the available and pertinent possibilities.

On-Campus Recruitment Data Analysis Using Data Mining and Machine Learning Model

A Descriptive Analytics approach is used to examine the purpose of the survey and evaluate the stated hypotheses. Transformation is the process of changing the format of data from one form to another. For this analysis VIT University which is a Deemed University in Tamil Nadu, India is taken for building the model. The main beneficiaries in a campus recruitment process, students and human resources managers were chosen as the sampling units.

Stratified Random Selection-Sampling Technique and Modeling of the Data

Using earlier research and the advice of experts (from the business and academic worlds), an instrument was developed and scientifically evaluated. The population of the study consisted of 172 HR managers from different companies who had visiting history of VIT for campus recruitment. Using the stratified random selection technique, the HR managers were split into two groups, representing the (i) core engineering and (ii) software industries. A fixed sample size of 86 HRs was used. Using the random number-generating approach of the basic random sample method, 43 HR managers from each industry were selected. Up until the sample size reached 30% of the population, respondents received repeated phone calls and emails to remind them to respond. After Cleaned data-filled questionnaires were removed, 65 sample respondents were chosen for the study, of whom 39 were from the IT sector and the analysis is presented for the 65 HR sample rather than industry. Final-year VIT University students who were considered to be extended stakeholders in the hiring process for the institution made up the study's participants. A predetermined sample size of 1299 pupils from the last year's 2598 students was selected. The basic random number-generating procedure was used to determine the 1299 respondents. Out of a total of 760 responses, 697 legitimate questionnaires were discovered after data cleaning. Out of a total of 760 replies, 697 valid questionnaires were found after data cleaning.

SOLUTIONS AND RECOMMENDATIONS

Selection of Career Path in Engineering Education: In-House Web Application

For this analysis, Thiagarajar College of Engineering Data is taken for exploration. During their freshman and sophomore years, the designed web-based tool aids students in selecting a major and/or career route. Additionally, it is beneficial to support students in finding opportunities to obtain experience in the career domains where they will be placed. It also reinforces students in learning about government job opportunities in their intended career path. It also helps hand students in learning about opportunities in the field of higher studies. The proposed web-based career guidance chapter application also helps students to build healthy relationships between the current seniors and super seniors. Students have the option to attend a separate session with career specialists where they can get advice on the best possible careers out of all the available and relevant options. The last three years' data are given below in *Table* 1 and the following discussions are made.

When a variable is measured on a nominal scale, the relative frequencies for the various values can be displayed on a bar chart. In both on-campus and off-campus environments, the Origin variable can take one of three potential values. Table of placement: "Total Students Participated," "On-Campus," and "Off-Campus." It is necessary to first determine how many observations in the data table correspond to each of these numbers. The height of each bar in the bar chart in Figure 2 corresponds to the frequency

Table 1. Placement statistics

Year	Total no of Students	On Campus	Off Campus
2020-21	877	592	17
2019-20	856	603	19
2018-19	845	627	15

of the values each bar represents. All UG and PG programmes make use of outcome-oriented education, a flexible choice-based credit system, and an evaluation process based on Bloom's Taxonomy.

Active learning and ICT tools are included in the instructional learning methodologies. Capstone programmes, guided learning, engineering design courses, and project evaluations using rubrics are a few of the ideas being implemented. The best practices applied in academic settings include curriculum design, new courses, new types of courses, content delivery, and evaluation. Curriculum design includes elements like competency-based instruction, outcome-based learning, a choice-based credit system, and the incorporation of innovation. Among the newly added courses are those in engineering design, capstone programmes, general electives, foundation electives, guided study programmes, flexible elective programmes, and workshop techniques (such as Circuit branches).

Of course, the new kind also includes theory and practice-based courses, courses entirely based on internal assessments, courses funded by business, Conceive Design Implement Operate (CDIO Initiatives), and courses that incorporate engineering best practices into community services. The curriculum used at colleges is uniform and standardized. As a result, campus interviews are conducted with the majority of college students. Content delivery includes using active and collaborative learning strategies such as

Figure 2. On-campus and off-campus placement details

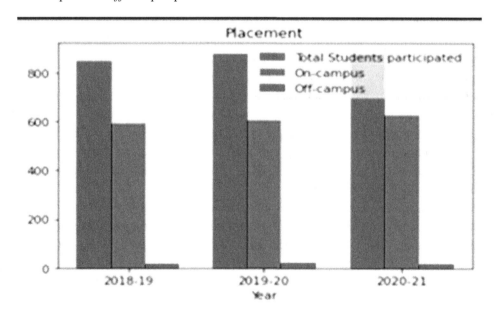

Think Pair Share (TPS), Think Aloud Pair Problem Solving, Group Grid, Jigsaw, Flipped Classroom, use of ICT Tools, Quality Enhancement in Engineering Education (QEEE), and IUCEE - International Engineering Certified Faculty Members.

Introduction of Bloom Taxonomy, flexible assessment pattern based on the nature of the course, rubrics for project review and presentation, and adapting modern tools for intern assessment are the practices of assessment. The above-mentioned curriculum is standard and consistent so that most of the students are placed in on-campus interviews when compared to that off-campus interviews. In the proposed, web-based career guidance chapter was more effective among college students as there is a

Figure 3. Exams qualified by engineering students over the last three years

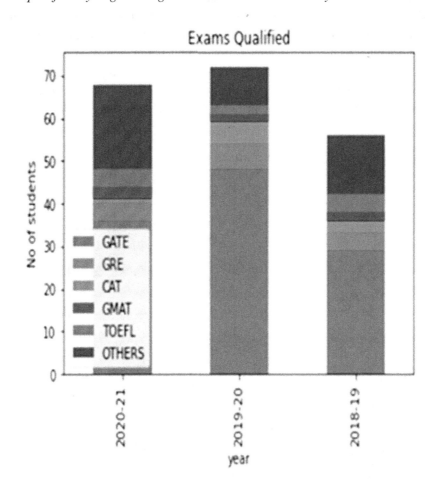

durable increase in the statistical graphs for the past years.

Exams qualified by the Engineering Students for the past three years are represented in *Figure* 3 and the graph in Figure 3 follows the Normal distribution which is in bell shape. GATE, GRE, CAT, GMAT, and TOEFL exams are written by students to pursue their higher education in India or abroad. Government exams including civil service exams, and state or central government exams are also written in order to get a good post in the government sector. The clubs functioning under the career guidance cell are (i)Higher Studies Club, (ii)Civil Service Exam Club, and (iii) Language Studies Club. The civil services Exams Club provides learning resources for the aspirants of IAS, IES, IRS, etc.

The Career Guidance and higher studies club invites distinguished speakers to speak with the students on (i)exam preparation, (ii)planning study sessions, (iii)attending exams, and (iv)interviews. Additionally, it offers time slots for knowledge exchange among potential learners in order to facilitate peer learning. The details of engineering students who pursue further education both in India and abroad. The college offers a higher studies club, which arranges for top external organizations and internal resource people to conduct GATE, GMAT, CAT, GRE, TOEFL and IELTS coaching inside the college's walls. To encourage higher education in India and abroad, the Higher Studies club administers practice exams for various competitive exams and higher education. To aid those aspiring to higher education, study materials are also made available. The proposed web-based career guidance chapter application will assist the students in finding the best college and course in their chosen field, whether it be in India or Abroad.

There are several different methods for determining how strong a link is between two variables. These measurements are often based on the categories of variables being evaluated, such as a comparison of categorical and continuous data. A correlation coefficient (r) can be computed for two variables recorded on an interval or ratio scale. By producing values between 1.0 and +1.0, this value quantifies the linear connection between the variables. The value of r represents how near the points are to the ideal straight

Figure 4. No of students selected for higher studies

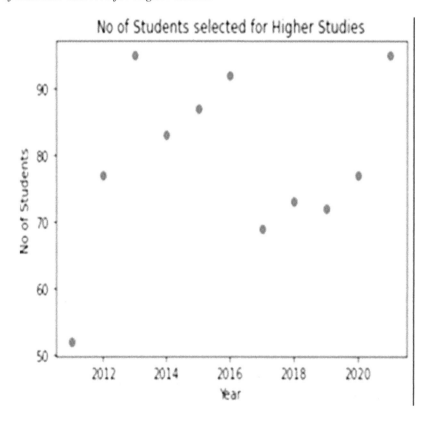

line when it is drawn through the points on a scatter plot. R values that are positive or negative represent a positive or negative correlation between the two variables, respectively. When r is near to 0, there is little to no correlation between the variables. The formula used to determine r is shown here in equation (1),

$$r = \frac{\sum_{i=1}^{n}\left(x_i - \bar{x}\right)\left(y_i - \bar{y}\right)}{\left(n - 1\right)s_x s_y} \tag{1}$$

where x and y are variables, x_i is a set of values of x, y_i is a set of values of y, $\bar{x}$ is the mean of the variable 'x', $\bar{y}$ is the mean of the variable 'y', s_x and s_y are the *standard deviations* of the variables x and y, respectively, and n is the number of observations.

Given that the points are very close to an idealized line with an upward slope through their centers, one can infer from the scatter plot's graph that there is a positive correlation between the variables.

Kendall Tau is yet another technique for identifying relationships between two variables. It was created based on a scoring of the observations for two variables. This rating is obtained by sorting the values and then replacing the actual values with a rank between 1 and n. A Kendall Tau measure is

Figure 5. Positive correlation graph

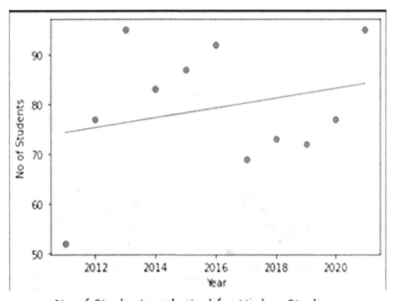

No of Students selected for Higher Studies

computed using these computed sums. Kendall Tau measures relationships between variables, with a value of 1 signifying a perfect ranking and a value of 1 signifying a perfect disagreement of the rankings. When there is a tie in the rankings, a zero number is used to indicate that there is no correlation or independent relationship between the two variables. The Kendall Tau computation's simplest form, or the Tau A formula, is equation (2):

$$\tau_A = \frac{n_c - n_d}{n\left(n-1\right)_{/2}} \tag{2}$$

where n_c and n_d are the numbers of concordant and discordant pairs, respectively, and n is the number of observations.

In many situations, there are ties based on either variable. In these situations, the formula Tau B is often used. It takes the ties in the 1st variable (t_x) and the ties in the 2nd variable (t_y) and is computed using the forthcoming formulas w.r.t equation (3):

$$\tau_B = \frac{n_c - n_d}{\sqrt{\left(n_c + n_d + t_x\right)\left(n_c + n_d + t_y\right)}} \tag{3}$$

Utilizing the heat map, it is visualized the density of the students placed, higher studies, and the exam qualified by the students. The higher and lower values are represented by each column and the gradient causes the color to fade values in between centered upon the average. The correlation is determined

Figure 6. Heat map for various categories of outcomes

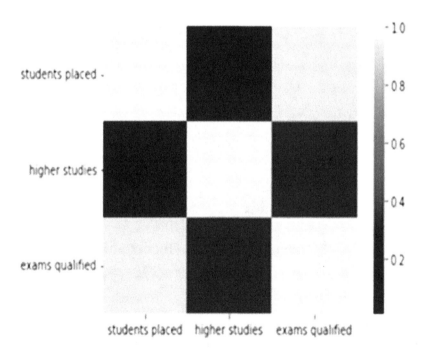

between different variables including the predictor and response variables. The variable exams qualified & students placed has a strong positive correlation. The higher education and students placed have correlation values near 0. From this Map, it can be assumed that pupils who are placed won't continue their studies after high school. Students who pass the exam will either study overseas or in India for their higher education. From all these graphs, it's inferred that the Career Guidance Cell has made the student's life easier by getting all the details about the placements, higher studies, and even information about the government exams and other exams to pursue higher education.

On-Campus Recruitment Data Analysis Using Data Mining and Machine Learning Model

Data Source

The dataset from the UCI Machine Learning repository was used for this study. It includes an actual dataset of 299 samples of data with 13 different features (12 predictors; 1 class), including SSLC, HSS, college CGPA, and other grades. In this study, four algorithms are utilized to gather the causes of heart disease and build the most accurate model possible. The Student Performance in Exam data collection comprises results from three exams as well as a range of interacting personal, societal, and economic variables. The dataset consists of 1000 occurrences and 8 columns of student grades across several topics. Gender, race/ethnicity, parental education level, lunch, test preparation course, math, writing, and reading scores are all listed in these reports. Both categorical and numerical features are present.

Data Preprocessing

There is a lot of missing and noisy data in real-world information. These data are preprocessed to get around these problems, make predictions forcefully, and explain the suggested model's sequential chart. Data cleaning typically includes noise and missing values. These data must be cleaned of noise and any missing values must be provided in order to obtain an accurate and efficient output. another to clear up the meaning. It involves aggregation, normalization, and smoothing operations.

Data Distribution, Descriptive, and Inferential Statistics

To visualize the features of the data set, Bar Chart, histograms and other visualization methods are used.

A Histogram of the degree percentage, in Figure 7, it shows that most students are getting a salary of 20-25 Thousand Rupees per month. Its know Average salary of the Sample and Population.

According to the bar diagram in Figure 8, men get paid more than women in companies.

In Figure 9, it shows that most of the student's parents went to some college or have an associate's degree with the Children and few have a bachelor's or a master's degree.

In the Figure 10, it shows that most student didn't prepare for the Internal tests.

Relationship

Scatter Plot which is given in Figure 11, is mainly used for finding the dependency between various attributes of a data set. Based on the analysis the reading and writing scores are depending on each other. It

Table 2. Parameters to be considered in data preprocessing

S. No	Attributes	Details
1.	Gender	Male or Female
2.	SSC score	Certification at the end of secondary schooling in India, after the successful completion of an exam
3.	SSC board	State Secondary Education Examination Board is a state education board in the Indian state
4.	HSC score	The Higher Secondary Certificate is a public examination used for university admissions in India
5.	HSC Board	In India, which is conducted at the state level by the state boards of education.
6.	Degree percentage	It is a grading system followed by many colleges in order to evaluate the overall performance of an individual.
7.	Degree of Department	An academic department is a division of a university faculty devoted to a particular academic discipline.
8.	Work	Fresher or Experience
9.	Specialization	Doing projects and improving skillset in a particular subject or research area/domain
10.	Status	Placed or Not placed
11.	MBA	Plan for MBA
12.	E-test	Small puzzles, aptitude, coding marks
13.	Salary	Placed student's salary per month.

Figure 7. Degree vs. salary

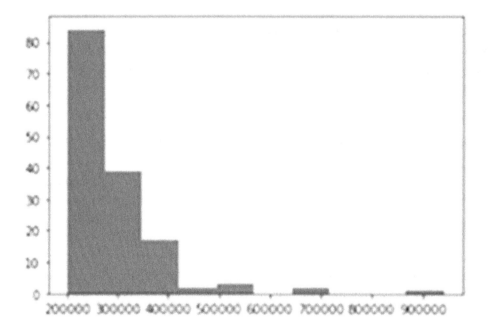

Figure 8. Comparison of salary and gender

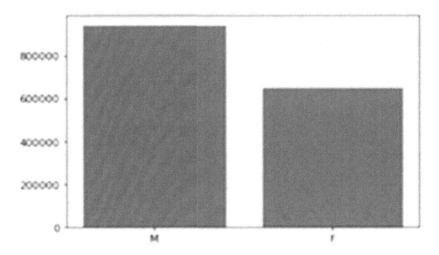

Figure 9. Bar graph for attribute parental level of education

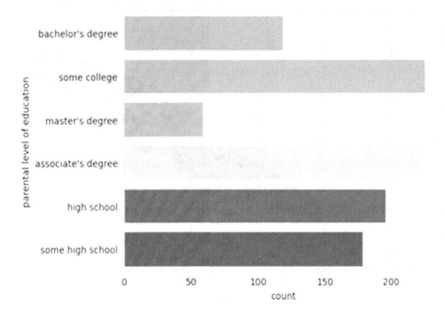

is common practice to assess correlations between categorical data using the Chi-Square statistic. Figure 12., its is shown that the final score of the students are depending on their parent's education levels. The Chi-Square test's null hypothesis(H_0) states that there is a null association between the categorical variables in a population and it is assumed that the variables are independent. It is implemented by using the scipy library in Python. Scipy is imported and the Chi-Square method is called Predicting the dependent variable if the value is less than the alpha value of its dependent variable.

Figure 10. Bar graph for attribute test preparation course

Figure 11. Scatter plot for reading score and writing score

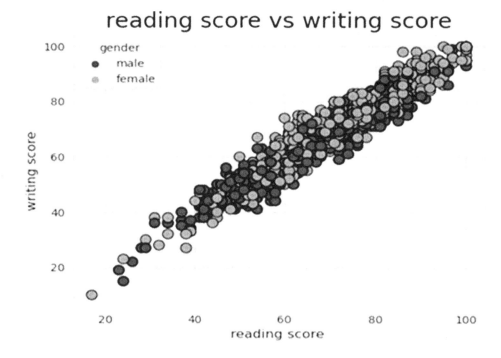

Inferential Statistics

Conditional Probability

The likelihood that an event will occur given its link to one or more other events is known as conditional probability.

Figure 12. Cat plot for total marks and parental level of education

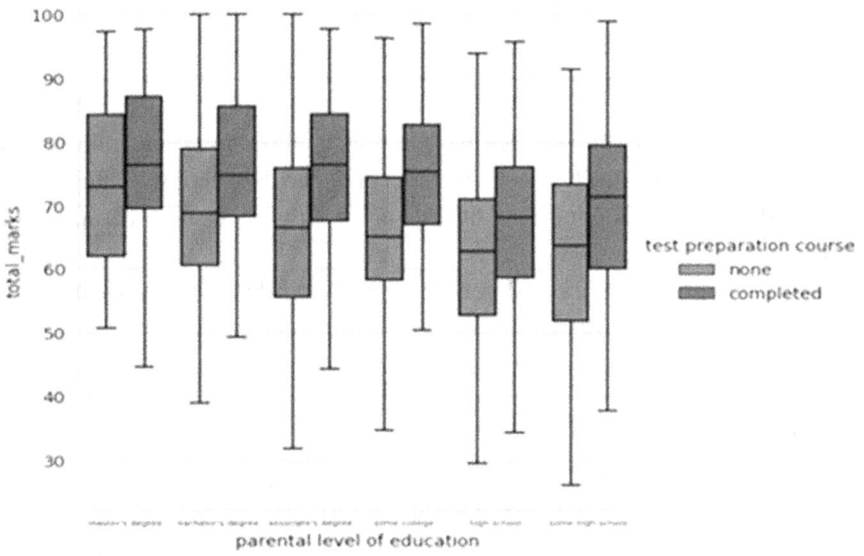

Probability Distribution Function

- The normal distribution or Gaussian distribution, is a probability distribution that is symmetric about the mean. It shows that data close to the mean occur more frequently than data far from the mean. On a graph, a normal distribution is visualized using a bell curve.
- Skewness is a distributional condition in which there is a strong bias toward the right or left side of the plot.

The Sample Mean and Population and Confidence Interval

- Sample data is the subset of the population
- Calculate the sample and population mean values.
- The mean of both would be near or a little far.
- Z-critical value is calculated which has been used to calculate the margin of error.
- Margin of error is used to calculate the confidence interval.
- Make necessary tests using sample data itself and using sample data
- Analyze the whole population.

Hypothesis Testing

- The probability of receiving test results that are at least as extreme as the outcomes actually seen during the test, assuming that the null hypothesis(H_0) is true, is known as the p-value or probability value in statistical hypothesis testing.

- For the given attribute in a given condition the mean of that attribute and the mean of the target attribute is compared and The p-value is determined.
- H_0 is accepted when the p-value is greater than 0.05; else, rejected.

Chi-Square Test

- A series of significance tests known as chi-square tests allow us to evaluate hypotheses on the distributions of categorical data. The tests for independence between two categorical variables are also covered in this article. Goodness-of-fit tests are used to determine if sample data matches a proposed distribution.
- Chi-square test is applied to salary and gender to test their dependencies whether Dependent or Independent.

Figure 13. Comparison of regression algorithms

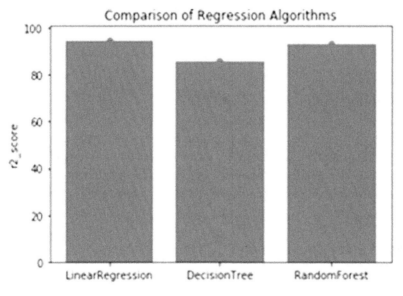

Decision trees, random forests, and linear regression models are employed to model sample student documents. The Decision variable has the floating point - Continuous valued output. So the existing best regression techniques of the Decision tree, Random Forest, and a Linear regression model are taken for model building. The best model for student performance prediction data is Linear Regression >Random forest > Decision Tree. Linear regression outperforms other regression models and produces an accuracy of 95.7.%.

FUTURE RESEARCH DIRECTIONS

The system could be improved in the future by connecting more career counselors who might assist students in an effective way and keep track of their progress and workflow. The proposed work can be extended by offering a Mobile application for students and career advisors. The entrepreneurship details can be added along with the one-to-one mentoring in which one person can give advice, guidance, encouragement, and support to the younger entrepreneurs. The career advisor can be assigned to one student and they guide them on the right path.

The Proposed Campus Recruitment Data Analysis model will be useful before choosing a company in a college Placement Selection process, students should explore on several aspects. The entry-level pay provided by the software services companies was generally criticized for being on the low side. According to the HR managers' input, it is advised that students temper their expectations for entry-level pay because the salaries currently quoted by software services firms are based on industry norms and take both the need and supply of fresher-level graduates into account. Even schools and universities should evaluate each of their students individually based on their academic records and assist them in getting the training they need to be hired through campus hiring. Therefore, performing this type of study on their campus recruiting increases their campus recruitment and also aids in the development of the students.

CONCLUSION

The developed web application helps students select a major and/or career choice. Many students were placed in software companies, there is little student interest in pursuing higher education. College placement offices assist with college recruitment for multinational and national organizations. The career guidance cell helps the students by assisting them by creating clubs for higher studies so that they can prepare for their exam to pursue their higher studies. Several events have been held in collaboration with the Institution of Engineers (IE) to improve the student's technical and professional abilities. Students take the GATE, GRE, CAT, GMAT, and TOEFL tests to prepare for higher education in India or abroad.

To obtain a good position in the government sector, candidates must pass government tests, such as civil service exams and state or central government exams. To pursue higher education in a good reputed college or university in India, one has to write exams like GATE, CAT, GMAT, etc. The proposed web-based career guidance chapter is thought to be or develop into truly the all-in-one tool for assisting students in selecting the best career path, enhancing their job prospects, and ultimately assisting them in climbing the corporate ladder.

June and July at the start of the academic year would be far too early because they wouldn't be anticipated for the interviews. These months are less well-liked because October and November are exam months and because students are involved in their Final Semester Course of Projects in January. HR professionals believe that the period following July is ideal for hiring because the majority of businesses reserve their cash for on-campus hiring by June or July. August and September were regarded as the greatest hiring months by both hiring managers and students. Based on the aforementioned findings, the firms should develop a recruitment schedule that is convenient for the students.

Additionally, the career guidance system will make hiring managers, a chance to engage in College branding initiatives to increase student awareness. With the help of well-planned recruiting schedules, the recruitment managers would be better able to arrange for the joining of the recruited students and give them internships or project work throughout their IV years- last semester. The previous studies highlighted the ongoing gap between entry-level graduates' expected and actual salary levels. The appeal of a career in IT has not lessened despite the fact that the pay scales for campus hiring in the Indian IT services sector have not changed in more than 7 years. Despite lower pay at the beginning, as workers accumulate more experience, their salaries increase. Entry-level salary has not increased despite the fact that there are now much more graduates employed in the IT industry than there were previously. Students now have higher expectations for entry-level salaries due to the rising cost of education.

REFERENCES

Alimam, M. A., Seghiouer, H., Alimam, M. A., & Cherkaoui, M. (2017, April). Automated system for matching scientific students to their appropriate career pathway based on science process skill model. In *2017 IEEE Global Engineering Education Conference (EDUCON)* (pp. 1591-1599). IEEE. 10.1109/EDUCON.2017.7943061

Alkaabi, S. H. A. S., Almulla, H. A. R., Ahli, S. K. A., & Amin, A. H. M. (2022, May). Takhasosi: Career Specialization Guidance System on Permissioned Blockchain Infrastructure for Undergraduate Students. In *2022 8th International Conference on Information Technology Trends (ITT)* (pp. 183-188). IEEE.

Healy, M., Hammer, S., & McIlveen, P. (2022). Mapping graduate employability and career development in higher education research: A citation network analysis. *Studies in Higher Education*, *47*(4), 799–811. doi:10.1080/03075079.2020.1804851

Jackson, D., & Lambert, C. (2023). Adolescent parent perceptions on sustainable career opportunities and building employability capitals for future work. *Educational Review*, *0*(0), 1–23. doi:10.1080/00131911.2023.2182763

Lodders, N., & Meijers, F. (2017). Collective learning, transformational leadership and new forms of careers guidance in universities. *British Journal of Guidance & Counselling*, *45*(5), 532–546. doi:10.1080/03069885.2016.1271864

Myatt, G. J. (1969). Making sense of data I: a practical guide to exploratory data analysis and data mining (2nd ed.). Academic Press.

Nirmala Devi & Priya. (2016). *Invoicing and analytics for small and micro manufacturing enterprises 2016*. Academic Press.

Reid, E. R., & Kelestyn, B. (2022). Problem representations of employability in higher education: Using design thinking and critical analysis as tools for social justice in careers education. *British Journal of Guidance & Counselling*, *50*(4), 631–646. doi:10.1080/03069885.2022.2054943

Revelo, R. A., & Baber, L. D. (2018). Engineering Resistors: Engineering Latina/o Students and Emerging Resistant Capital. *Journal of Hispanic Higher Education*, *17*(3), 249–269. doi:10.1177/1538192717719132

Supriyanto, G., Abdullah, A. G., Widiaty, I., & Mupita, J. (2019). Career guidance web-based expert system for vocational students. *J. Eng. Sci. Technol*, *14*(4), 1865–1877.

Ujakpa, M. M., Nghipundjwa, O., Hashiyana, V., Mutalya, A. N., André, P., & Ndevahoma, I. (2021, May). An Investigation of the Use of Career Guidance App by Undergraduate Students: Case Study of Namibia. In 2021 IST-Africa Conference (IST-Africa) (pp. 1-9). IEEE.

Zhang, J. (2021). The Application and Thinking of Big Data in the Career Planning Education of College Students. *2nd International Conference on Information Science and Education (ICISE-IE),* 868-871. 10.1109/ICISE-IE53922.2021.00198

Chapter 7
Identification of Student Groups for Smart Tutoring and Collaborative Learning Based on Online Activities Using Neural Networks

D. Kavitha
Thiagarajar College of Engineering, India

D. Anitha
Thiagarajar College of Engineering, India

C. Jeyamala
ⓘD https://orcid.org/0000-0001-5233-4393
Thiagarajar College of Engineering, India

ABSTRACT

As the current education scenario has transformed itself to online mode, all learning and assessment activities including quizzes, report submissions, problem solving, peer assessment are done online. Identification of students' characteristics in terms of their academic performance and attitude is the need of the hour for personal tutoring. Also, collaborative learning, which forms an integral part of learning, has group formation as an influential activity for the success of learning. This work proposes an intelligent solution to group learners based on their outcomes and participation in various online assessment activities. This chapter considers the online assessment results of the learners and uses Kohonen self-organizing map neural network (SOM) to group the learners. The proposed method is experimented with a student set in the course "Digital Systems" (n=84). MATLAB is used for implementing SOM and the results obtained from simulations confirm the efficacy of the proposed network with 93.33% performance metric.

DOI: 10.4018/978-1-6684-8145-5.ch007

Copyright © 2023, IGI Global. Copying or distributing in print or electronic forms without written permission of IGI Global is prohibited.

INTRODUCTION

Smart education requires smart tutoring and peer learning. Facilitating good learning opportunities among the students is a major role of a teacher. Active learning and collaborative learning are always considered appreciable in improving student engagement. The entire world suffers from pandemic for years. The situation transforms the education sector from physical classes to virtual classes. Due to the sudden transformation of learning from face-to-face classes to online classes, the inclusion of these activities such as active learning and collaborative learning got disrupted a while. A wide range of online tools for implementing active learning and collaborative learning has been identified then and introduced in the teaching community. The pedagogical training has been given to the faculty to handle the new change. Lots and lots of challenges are faced by teaching community to adapt to this massive change. The online tools have increased the opportunities to provide better learning amidst the challenges faced during online classes. Online quiz tools and feedback tools are identified and used for formative and summative assessments. Conventionally, the group formation shall be done by the students based on their preference or by the instructor based on the students' academic performance, attitude or random methods. There are lot of online activities and results which makes the team formation task of the instructor to be tedious. With a rich set of online activities available now, the group formation can be done without much effort from the instructor with intelligent automatic techniques.

Collaborative learning refers to doing certain tasks as a group and the same needs intellectual efforts among the group of students jointly (Chu & Kennedy, 2011). The major activities of Collaborative learning include group formation, conduct of collaborative tasks and assessment of the tasks. Group formation is a crucial factor for the success of any collaborative activity. There are many methods of group formation including random formation, any specific order of number or name, specific methods based on academic performance and voluntary. Groups may be composed as heterogeneous or homogeneous with respect to few parameters such as students' cognitive ability, culture, attitude and gender. Grouping the students according to their cognitive ability shall help the teachers to understand the potential of the students for further measures like assigning challenging problems, counselling and peer assistance. The group composition may have its impact on the performance and comfort level of the individual and the whole team as well. It becomes a tough job for the teacher to identify the characteristics of the students in a large classroom for appropriate grouping of students. Especially with lot of online activities, the identification of cognitive ability tends to be tougher. There is a need of looking into suitable strategies for group formation in a learning environment which comprises of many online activities. As every online activity of a learner is now available in the online environments, intelligent techniques shall be used for group formation with the learner data. Clusters of students can be identified with their performance and collaborative groups shall be framed based on the intended learning outcomes.

Clustering is an unsupervised artificial intelligence technique that groups any data without labels. Clustering helps to group data based on the similarity between them. The clusters so formed have many applications which are dealt in literatures vastly. A SOM is an artificial neural network(ANN) and it is basically an unsupervised technique used in machine learning and uses competitive learning for clustering data. Kohonen, T. conducted many simulation experiments and explained the self-organized map clearly and also suggested that architecture for artificial neural networks along with practical applications. It is also stated that these SOMs have the property of creating internal representations of various features of input data and their concepts and are spatially organized, thereby discovering sematic relationships effectively.

Normally, Student academic counselling is done based on performance of the students. It requires interest of the students to provide additional learning materials, one-to-one discussions and learning opportunities for the students.

This research work uses this clustering technique with appropriate learner data and attempts to use the results for the group formation in collaborative activities and special counselling of students.

LITERATURE REVIEW

Importance of collaborative learning and team formation in engineering education to improve learning and graduate attributes are well established in engineering education literatures.

A research study (Gratton & Erickson, 2007) explains different methods to create collaborative teams. A creative environment shall be formed through the proper selection of individual members for a collaborative group. This type of environment will improve the meaningful interactions among the members and lead to robust learning and Through the adequate selection of individuals to a group, it is possible to create surroundings that adopts the occurrence of expressive interactions and hence, healthy learning and knowledgeable growth can be increased (Cruz & Isotani, 2014). It is also identified that the poor formulation of groups can demotivate the students and may delay the learning process (Odo et al., 2019). This may reduce the required outcome in spite of collaborative exercises developed by the teacher or facilitator. Computer-Supported Collaborative Learning (CSCL) is now fast growing. CSCL has reached its peak in the pandemic situation and lots of improvement happened in the digital learning during the pandemic phase. The field is also focusing on testing the groups in collaborative learning with methods of formulation with contexts using different pedagogical approaches and many other best practices. Collaborative groups formed with students of different cognitive abilities and attitude shall help them to learn from each other. Farhangian et al. (2015) has explored collaborative project group formulation for small, short-term projects and explored the challenges in modelling collaborative learning teams. An agent-based modelling approach have been proposed and the method has a capability of assisting the collaborative learning group formation of such project teams. Priorly, most literatures emphasis the need of categorization of students according to different learning components (Inyang et al., 2019). With more online features such as students motivation in taking online assignments, discussions, assessments, performance, it is mentioned that difficulty arises in categorizing the students into various groups (Purbasari et al., 2020). More interesting works have been done using academic data. Three-dimensional Dense-Net self-attention neural network is used for automatic detection of student's engagement (Mehta et al., 2022). Emotions of learners and engagement in online learning are classified based on facial expression recognition neural network (Savchenko et al., 2022).

Kohonen map or network is a computationally expedient notion building on different models of neural systems. In a research work (Wendel & Buttenfield, 2010), the authors used Kohonen's MatLab toolbox and anlyzed the various characteristics of SOMs using different booting parameters, training methods, network nodes. They have compared the outputs, uncertainty measures and provided interpretations. From this exhaustive research study. certain guidelines for the creation of purposeful SOMs, was established. A research work (Setiadi et al., 2019) has created a recommender system which considers the lecturer's workload and applicable for thesis examiners and preceptors. Another work categorizes consumers' load profiles (Dragomir et al., 2014) using unsupervised neural network. One more study calculates the similarity between reports on selected topics with thesis proposal. In a study (Hartono & Ogawa, 2014) the authors have proposed an unique visualization algorithm called as Context-Relevant Self Organizing Map. The map conserves the topographical characteristics of high dimensional data along with their context. The map is applied for visualizing LMS data. A research work has classified the students with different interests using SOM and three distinct clusters which represents Life Sciences, Social Sciences, and Linguistics study areas are obtained (Purbasari et al., 2020). Another study has clustered bright students based on their daily routines with Kohenen SOM (Bhanuprakash et al., 2018). An intelligent tutoring system has been developed to create the teaching strategies based on SOM neural networks and on knowledge of the expert teacher (de Carvalho et al., 2020). An exploratory research work finds that the grouping technique employing self-organizing map neural networks and hierarchical unsupervised algorithms can be used MOOC instructors for the purpose of identifying similar students based on many input variables and analyze their traits from several viewpoints (Lee, 2019). Though there are many clustering methods, it can be observed from the literature study that SOM neural network is one of the most widespread networks for extracting information and is done by grouping the high dimensional data that characterize the information. A research paper explores k-means and self-organizing map (SOM) in clustering the students' dataset with features like selected demographic, pre-admission and first year performance and has recommended SOM for clustering (Inyang et al., 2019). There are few research works that combine both the SOM and k-means algorithm for their intended research (Carter & Farquharson, 2020). This research study proposes to apply Self Organizing Map (SOM) neural network to group the student data and also focusses to reduce the number of features in input data to make grouping process more forthright.

There are several studies which have measured the effectiveness of active and collaborative learning strategies in terms of students' academic performance (Hosain & Aydin, 2011; Liang & McQueen, 2000; Strijbos et al, 2004; Zhan et al., 2015). It is often required to classify the students according to their learning characteristics. Some students shows great interest only in assessments which will be considered for end semester marks and they ignore basic discussions and online formative assessments. Some attempts everything and excel in all. Some students will score good in certain assessments. With these variety of students responses in various online activities, it is tougher for a teacher to classify them manually and there is a need of special methods to cluster them according to certain characteristic traits. (Kavitha & Anitha, 2016, 2018, 2020, 2021; Lee, 2019; Purbasri et al., 2020). Learning from peers through teaching and evaluation is another important factor of student group formation (Carvalho & Santos, 2021). A report from a Peer Learning Summit (Larson et al., 2020) has stated that score-based peer review leads to peer learning in collaborative learning activities. A research study (Goh et al., 2019) has indicated that there is indirect effect on learning outcomes is visualized by providing feedback from peers. A reasonable strength of connotation is present between peer review and the motivation of students. (Thuraisingam et al., 2019). From the discussed literature, it is observed that the outcome of any innovative pedagogical activity is measured in terms of the academic performance and the learner participation in learning activities. The participation of students in the learning activities (submission and peer review) and the resultant scores of the assessment can be effectively used in grouping the students. Hence, this research study suggests Kohonen Self Organizing Maps (SOM) for clustering the students based on their online activities including their participation and results in assessment activities. This research work uses SOM in identifying the similar response characteristics among the students in online assessments.

RESEARCH QUESTIONS

With the learning from interesting literatures, certain observations are made. The need of suitable software support for the instructors to categorize students is understood. Also, the features and number of online activities to be input to the system needs to be studied. With this wide understanding, the following research questions have been formulated for the research.

RQ1. How can the students of a class be grouped with online assessment activities as features?
RQ2. How can we reduce the number of features without change in the result of grouping?

MATERIALS AND METHODS

This research is proposed as a quantitative analysis that considers various online assessment marks as major elements in data collection. The research is conducted with second year Electrical and Electronics Engineering students of an Engineering Institution in a course "Digital Systems" (N=84). Initially the online class room has 70 regular students who have taken all the assessments provided in the learner management system (LMS). The learner management system used is Moodle and all the data sets are obtained from this platform as a downloadable file. Later, 14 lateral entry students who completed diploma course and joined directly in the second year of engineering are added to the online class. Hence, the class room when taken for analysis consists of 84 students data. Among 84 students, 14 lateral entry students didn't take any of the assessments on time due to the delay in their admission process. The students are informed that their academic data shall be used for research purpose and the student acceptance is obtained concurrently. In the literatures, the optimal team size for the collaborative learning activities is recommended as 4 (Kavitha & Anitha, 2021). Hence, the students are grouped into 4 clusters so that any team in collaborative learning shall be framed with one member from each cluster. Also, mentoring or counselling shall be facilitated to students in clusters having the characteristics of less performance. However, with SOM, the number of clusters is always customizable. If number of clusters is increased, the distance between the clusters may get reduced indicating the closeness of clusters with each other.

For this study, different online assessment elements which are commonly employed in virtual classes are taken as feature elements. Table 1 lists the various online assessment elements for different concepts which are given as inputs to the SOM. Thus, each sample consists of seven different features which are identified as per Table 1 and provided into the classification neural network. The assessments include quizzes, online assignments including file submission evaluated by peers and facilitator. The various important concepts of the courses such as logic gates, Boolean algebra, combinational circuit design, sequential circuit design are assessed online and are used as the training data. The data is trained in MATLAB for clustering.

Each data set have certain topological structure. Kohonen SOM finds a two-dimensional representation of a data set which originally have more than two dimensions and also conserve the topological structure of the data. A data set with many input features measured using different experimentations are characterized as groups of observations with similar values of the input variables. These groups then could be drawn as a two-dimensional "map". It can be observed that proximal groups data have more like values than observations in distal groups. This transformation is helpful for analysing and visualizing the high dimensional data. Figure 1 represents the architecture of SOM layer. All the inputs are presented to all the clusters and categorized to a specific cluster based on the weights. Self-Organizing Feature Maps (SOM) use algorithms that learn and classify input data vectors based on the input space. They show their difference from other competitive and learn to recognize neighbouring sections of the input space. Hence, it is evident that SOM neural networks are capable of learning the distribution like a competitive layers as well as topology of the training input vectors.

Table 1. Online assessment elements

Element ID	Online Assessment Elements	Concepts Assessed	Input to SOM
E1	Pre requisite Quiz marks	Logic gates and Boolean algebra	Input1 (I1)
E2	Assignment 1	Combinational circuit design and solution	Input2 (I2)
E3	Peer evaluation assignment 1	Evaluating the E2 activity of peers	Input3 (I3)
E4	Summative Quiz 1	Summative test on combinational circuit	Input4 (I4)
E5	Assignment 2	Sequential circuit design and solution	Input5 (I5)
E6	Peer evaluation assignment 2	Evaluating the E5 activity of peers	Input6 (I6)
E7	Summative Quiz 2	Summative test on sequential circuit	Input7 (I7)

Figure 1. Architecture of SOM layer

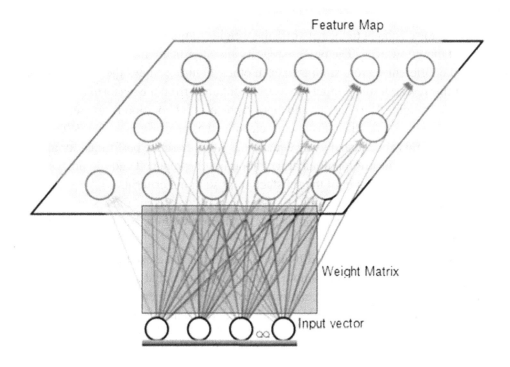

Initially the neurons in the layer of an SOM are organized in physical positions based on a topology function. Feature mapping is a process of transforming the patterns of higher dimensionality into a one-dimensional array or two-dimensional arrays of neurons. It converts a uninhabited pattern space into characteristic feature space. Let the number of input neurons be n, number of output clusters be m, xi is the current input instance and wij is the weight vector of the neural network node. The clustering process in Kohenen SOM uses Euclidean distance as given in Equation 1.

$$E(j) = \sum_{i=1}^{m} \sum_{j=1}^{n} (x_i - w_{ij})^2 \tag{1}$$

A SOM neural network finds neuron i* with minimum distance (d) and states it as a winner. Then, all neurons residing in the neighbourhood NDi* (d) of the neuron that wins are also updated. The updation is done using Equation 2 as per the Kohonen rule.

$$w_{ij\,new} = (1 - \alpha) w_{ij\,old} + \alpha x_i \tag{2}$$

Where α is the learning rate. Here the neighborhood NDi* (d) contains the indices for all of the neurons that lie within a radius d of the winning neuron i* as provided in equation 3.

$$NDi(d) = \{j, \text{ if } dij \leq d\} \tag{3}$$

Thus, when a vector x_i is input to the network, the weights of the winning neuron and the neurons in its neighbourhood move toward x_i. The process repeats and after many iterations, neighboring neurons will learn about the different vectors similar to each other. Figure 2 shows the flow chart of Kohonen SOM training for this research study. Input j to SOM is obtained from the performance of the student in assessment j (E_j). The weights, learning rate and topographical neighbourhood parameters are initialized. Then, for each input sample, Euclidean distance is calculated as per the equation 1. Winning unit index is obtained and the weights are updated using equation 2. After these are performed for all the samples, learning rate is updated. Radius of topological neighbourhood is reduced and the process is continued for all the samples again and again until the satisfaction of stopping criteria.

Once the network is trained, the weights from the network are taken. Each similar input data of a student is presented to the network. The inputs along with these weights are used to fix the appropriate cluster for each student.

The labelling for the cluster is provided by the inspection of the clustered data. The clustered data is compared with the ability of selected sample students and their input assessment features. Then the labelling such as Top performers, average performers doing all assessments, average performers missing some assessments, below average performers etc are fixed for each cluster.

Figure 2. Kohonen self-organizing map learning flow

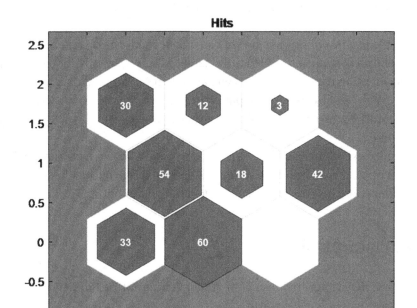

In this study, the total number of samples are 84 including the lateral entry students data. As the number of students is limited 84, the concept of elitism shall be used to improve the results. Elitism strategy is introduced in Genetic Algorithm which is the first evolved optimization algorithm. Elitism introduces a genetic drift in the data and ensures the copying of the characteristics of the fittest chromosome string to the following generations. Elites means copying the best traits in GA and thus it will improve the convergence speed of the algorithm by adding selective pressure to the chromosomes in Genetic Algorithm. Similar strategy is applied here with the assumption that all the input entities are fitting ones and allowed to copy their characteristics in the input space with certain elitism factor. Here the results of the original samples without elitism are taken and the average value of all the features in each cluster is determined. Every sample in each cluster is compared against the average value and the normalized deviation is measured for each feature. Then the sample with more deviation is copied back to the pool of samples with a small variation of about 1% in the random feature. Certain samples with more deviation is taken as a duplicate copy and mixed up with the available samples. The sample with less deviation is copied back with comparably more variation of about 8% in random feature. For example, the sample in cluster 1 is taken and its difference from its cluster average is found. After finding the differences of all samples with respect to the average cluster value, the values are normalized. Then, more deviated and less deviated samples are taken and variation is applied accordingly to the random feature. The elitism factor is determined by trial-and-error method until the distance between neuron clusters increases. These interesting trials are made as a simulation is performed in MATLAB Toolbox. The analysis is done for the two different cases with and without elitism. The research study attempts to group students into 4 clusters as the optimal team size for the collaborative learning activities is recommended as 4 (Kavitha & Anitha, 2021).

Case 1: Clustering the students with original samples without elitism into four clusters.
Case 2: Clustering the students with elitism into four clusters.

Thus, in Case 1, the features of original 84 data are taken and formed as a cluster. In Case 2, elitism is applied. Though elitism is applied to increase the samples, it is used only for calculating the weights. The weights calculated using the algorithm is then applied on the original data to obtain its cluster.

Apart from these case studies, effect of input parameters in SOM is also studied for the Research Question 2 and performance metric is calculated further to understand the possibility of reduction in input number of features.

If it is wished to increase the cluster size to "n" for a particular data which may not have "n" number of different characteristics, the analysis may result in empty or sparse cluster. This argument is analysed by increasing the number of clusters for the same data as an additional study.

RESULTS AND DISCUSSIONS

This section of the chapter depicts the results of simulation performed in MATLAB software for the two different cases.

Case 1: Clustering the students with original samples without elitism into four clusters.
Case 2: Clustering the students with elitism into four clusters

A.   **Case 1:** Clustering the students without elitism into four clusters.

For each of the 84 students, 7 inputs from 7 assessment activities are fed into SOM neural network for clustering the students into four distinct clusters. The neural network configuration for this case is given in Figure 3. The network consists of one input layer and an output layer with self-organizing layering weights.

The results obtained from SOM can be visualized in Figure 4. From Figure 4, distance between the nearest neuron clusters is found to be very minimum in three neurons (N1, N2, and N3).

In Figure 4 the small hexagons having labels N1, N2, N3 and N4 indicate output neurons that corresponds to number of clusters. The other hexagons containing inner lines show the connecting weights from a neuron to another. The colour shades of these hexagons indicate the weight of the connectivity. A hexagon of light shade means a minimum distance between the neurons where dark colour indicates that the distance is larger between the respective neurons. From Figure 4, it is understood that the samples clustered under 3 neurons N1, N2 and N3 are having very minimum distance and there is a huge possibility of similar characteristics among those clusters. As one neuron(N4) shows maximum distance from all other three neurons, it indicates that grouping of students under that cluster(N4) is proper. As the clusters are not formed effectively with a sample size of 84, the need of a greater number of samples for proper training and clustering is realized. From this preliminary analysis, the need of elitism is highlighted.

Figure 3. Architecture of Kohonen SOM

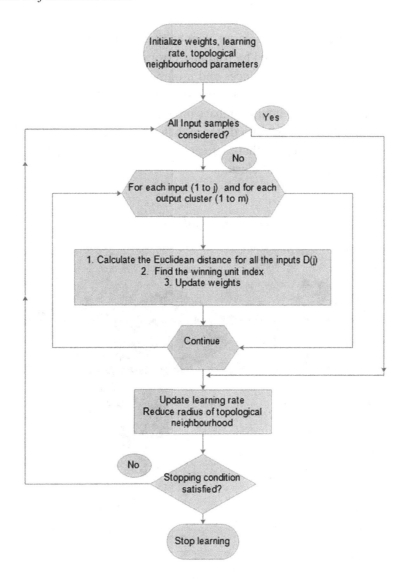

Figure 4. SOM neighbour weight distance for samples = 84

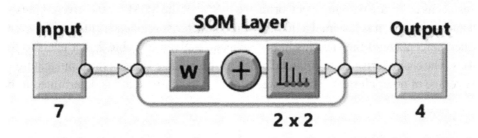

B.   **Case 2:** Clustering the students with elitism into four clusters.

In this case, number of samples is increased from 84 to 252 by elitism process with the elitism factor of three. The elitism factor is selected by trial-and-error method. The trial is based on the trade-off between maximum neighbor weight distances and minimum elitism factor. The number of epochs is fixed as 200 and after learning, the SOM neighbor weight distances are obtained. Figure 5 shows SOM neighbor weight distance from the sample that have undergone elitism. From Figure 5, it is clearly seen that the neuron N1 and N2 has a minimum distance than other connections. The distance between all other combinations is higher. It implies that there are definitely three distinct clusters are possible out of four and subsequently leading to four clusters.

Figure 5. SOM neighbour weight distance with samples = 252 and 7 inputs

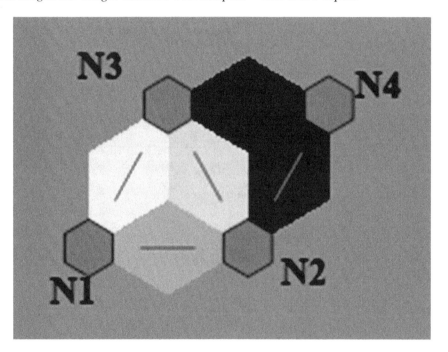

After training the data with SOM, the samples are grouped under four clusters. The number of hits of samples under each cluster is given in Figure 6 as N1 = 177, N2=18, N3=15 and N4 = 42. The training is repeated for 30 runs. In each run, 200 epochs are used for training. In 30 runs, 28 runs give the same clustering results as in Figure 6 giving a performance metric of the SOM for the given inputs as 93.33%.

As the data is clustered, it is essential to identify the characteristics of each cluster. The average scores and attendance percentage of the samples in each cluster is given in Table 2 that leads to four neuron characteristics. The characteristics are obtained based on the average value of the input features compared against the average of other clusters. The average score for the entire class is determined to be 60.65%.

Figure 6. SOM hits of samples with elitism in 4 different clusters

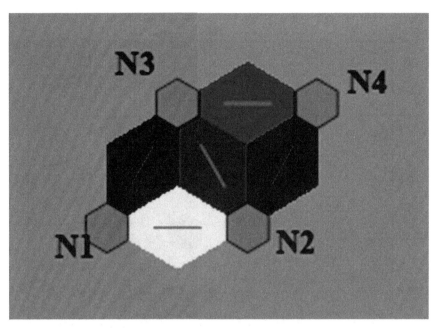

Table 2. Characteristics of each cluster in the sample

Neuron	Number of Actual Students (Without Elitism)	Number of Samples (With Elitism)	Group Name Assigned	Average Score in %	Activities Performed	Characteristics of Students
N1	59	177	Group A	78.25	100%	Above average students who did all the activities
N2	6	18	Group B	72.90	82%	Above average students who missed some activities
N3	5	42	Group C	58.23	85%	Below Average students who missed some activities
N4	14	15	Group D	0	0%	Students who missed all the activities (**Lateral entry students**)

The formation of groups is thus facilitated by an intelligent technique. The number of clusters shall be increased or decreased based on the plan of the instructor.

C.   Feature space reduction of input parametersin SOM

This section studies the effect of 7 different input parameters of SOM (Result of 7 assessment elements) on the 4 clusters and groups the assessment elements considered for this research study. Understanding the effects of the inputs, the feature space shall be reduced, thereby resulting in a lesser time for clustering. The observed inference is visualized in Figure 7.

Figure 7. Weights from various inputs: SOM input plane

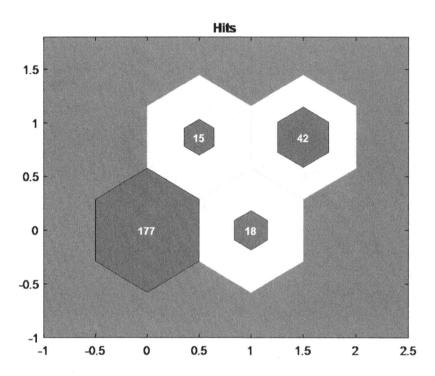

Lighter and darker colours in SOM input plane indicates higher and lesser weights, respectively. If the linking patterns of two inputs are very alike, it characterizes the high correlation between inputs. In Figure 7, the inputs 1 and 3 show same hit pattern and hence, are highly correlated. This enables to reduce the feature space to any one of these inputs. Similarly, by observing the picture, inputs 6 and 7 are highly correlated. In case of large set of inputs, this correlation can be used to reduce the size of input vector used.

The hit pattern found in Figure 8 is similar to Figure 5 after clustering the data with the elimination of two of the highly correlated inputs 3 and 7. This logic can be applied to cluster larger number of students who have undergone the same activities in a minimum time as clustering time is reduced if the size of input vector reduces. This research, thus, has explored the possibility of reducing the feature space or inputs to the clustering techniques to identify different student groups.

D.   Performance metric of self-organizing map

It is required to study the consistency and precision of clustering done. Hence, the learning is repeated for 30 runs. In each run, 200 epochs are used for training. In 30 runs, 28 runs give the clustering as in Figure 6 and during the intermediate 2 runs alternate SOM hit pattern shown in Figure 9 is obtained. This implies that the performance metric of the SOM for the given inputs is 93.33%. The index may be improved by providing more relevant data and also by varying SOM parameters which will be explored in further research. Table 3 shows the comparison of different cases done with respect to cluster accuracy in 30 runs and time taken for each case. It is clear from these simulations that though introducing elitism

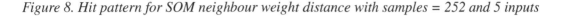

Figure 8. Hit pattern for SOM neighbour weight distance with samples = 252 and 5 inputs

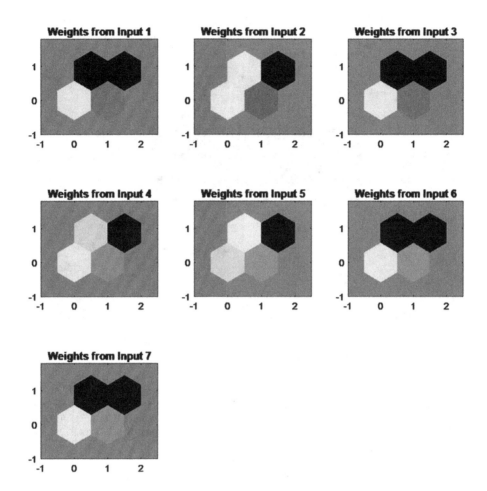

in SOM increases training time, the clusters can be obtained with decent distance between each other. Also, feature space reduction has no much impact on distance between clusters but it reduces the training time. It is also worth noted that if the original input set is applied without elitism, the same clusters are formed for many numbers of runs.

E.   Effect of increase in clusters

The effect of increasing the number of clusters is studied. The number of clusters in fixed as 9 in this analysis. It is assumed that 9 clusters are very big baskets to hold this minimum students data. Hence, the data is elitised with the elitism number 3 and given as input for clustering. The clustering formed is given in Figure 10. Figure 10 gives the information of SOM hit pattern of samples in 9 different clusters. The weights obtained are applied to the original data and the Table 4 shows the number of students in each clusters.

Figure 9. Alternate SOM hit pattern of samples in 4 different clusters

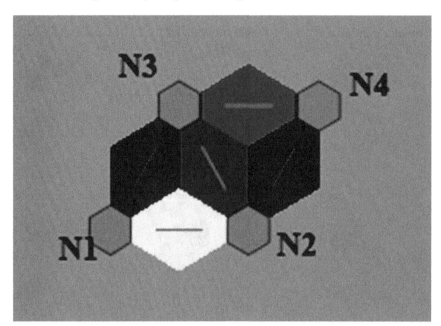

Table 3. Characteristics of each cluster in the sample

S. No	Cases	Cluster Accuracy for 30 Runs (Average %)	Number of Clusters With Very Minimum Distance With Neighbouring Clusters	Approximate Time Taken for Training (S)
1	Clustering the students with original samples without elitism	86.67	3	2.25
2	Clustering the students with elitism factor =3	93.33	1	6.5
3	Clustering the students with original samples without elitism and with feature space reduction	86.67	3	1.5
4	Clustering the students with original samples with elitism factor = 3 and with feature space reduction	93.33	1	5

The characteristics of each cluster are notified as follows:

A. Top performing students group without missing the online activities
B. Top performing students group without missing the online activities
C. No group
D. Above average performance without any miss
E. Above average performance with some miss
F. Missed all assessments
G. The characteristics of D and E combined.
H. Below average

Figure 10. SOM hit pattern of samples in 9 different clusters

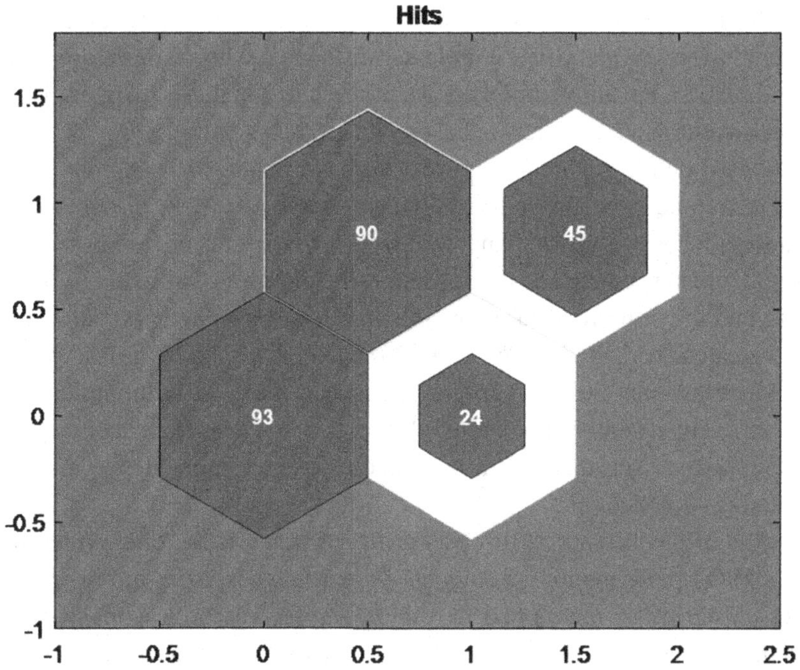

Table 4.

Cluster No.	1	2	3	4	5	6	7	8	9
Cluster name	A	B	C	D	E	F	G	H	I
No. of students in the cluster	11	20	0	18	6	14	10	4	1

I.   50% of missed assessments

From the analysis, it is noted that the data provided cannot be clustered effectively to 9 groups as there is a complete empty group. When compared to the cluster of 4 results, it is observed that single cluster in previous case is split into 3 different clusters here with minimum distance. Lateral entry group is separated as a single group as there is much distance.

ADDRESSING THE RESEARCH QUESTIONS

This section discusses the results of the proposed work in the perspective of the research questions proposed earlier.

Research Question 1

In the first step of clustering the 84 students with SOM clustering, one dominant cluster has been identified and three other clusters are identified with lesser distance as shown in Figure 4. In a research work (Bhanuprakash et al., 2018), the number of students participated in the experiment is 200 and the results of SOM is compared with manual clustering based on the grades. Another research work has used 275 students to cluster based on only academic scores (Purbasri et al. 2019) and has got the similar result of one dominant cluster and two other clusters with lesser distance. In the presented research work, the number of students whose results are analysed is 84 and the clusters are not well formed with few clusters having smaller distance between them. Hence, the concept of elitism has been used to increase the population size and to get more accurate results in clustering. The application of elitism has been followed in many research works (Khan & Jaffar, 2015; Neme et al., 2015, E. Alfaro-Cid et al., 2009, Thirumoorthy & Muneeswaran, 2021). Applying elitism in the existing population has increased the population size to 252. The result obtained after elitism is assured with an accuracy of 93.3% with 200 iterations and has no comparison made with manual clustering results. Hence, the results obtained by the proposed method is objective.

Next phase of this research work is to observe the characteristics of the identified clusters. The assessment score and the participation of students in learning activities are used, as these have been the parameters for clustering as mentioned in Table 3. In the research work of Purbasri (2019), the characteristics of the clusters are studied only through manual observation and presumption where in our research study, a statistically supported data is used to identify the characteristics. In the identified characteristics of the present work, it is noted that there is no category such as "Below average students with all activities done" leading to important observation as the students get above average scores if they attempt all the activities. Also, our clustering technique has identified lateral entry students as separate cluster as there have no activities and no scores for them. As four different clusters have been identified based on the similarity, collaborative learning groups of different team size shall be easily formed by picking out suitable students from each group. Also, the students who belong to least performing groups shall be personally counselled for their academic needs. The high performing students shall be given challenging tasks for engaging them in tasks of higher cognitive ability. This clustering framework is customizable to any number of clusters.

Research Question 2

The third phase of this research work answers to the Research Question 2 by attempting to reduce the feature space involved. This research works considers only 7 inputs to the SOM, but the number of online activities may not be restricted to a limited number. Many research works have identified the need for future space reduction in SOM networks to reduce the computational complexity (Van Gassen et al., 2015; Li et al., 2018; Qu et al., 2021). Hence, this research work attempts to reduce the feature space and identifies whether the same clusters are identified with integrated activities.

Also it is fount that If the number of clusters increases, based on the data input, the neighbor weight distances decreases for certain clusters. The inference is more output neurons results in clusters with similar characteristics or very low variance clusters for minimal set of sample input data. Similar results are obtained with and without elitism and with and without feature reduction.

CONCLUSION

In the current scenario of online learning, there is a presence of vast data of assessments in online classes. As it is tough for the instructor to use this data manually to identify groups of students for collaborative learning and personal counselling, this research proposed a clustering technique to identify students with similar characteristics. The study will help the teachers to plan for their future collaborative activity, tutoring and counselling. The work is also useful to understand the different category of students and the number of students in each category. A good strategic planning for tutoring and grouping can be done by the help of this proposed work. Also, this research work extends its applicability of the same technique to the reduction of feature space if the number of online activities is greater in number.

As of the scope of the present work, the groups of students are identified with SOM only once and the output cluster information is given to the instructors for further processing. The research study identifies its limitation as the smaller data size that shall be improved with elitism. However, the clustering may bring best results for larger classes. These clusters shall be used in team formation for collaborative learning activities and the impact of the clustering shall be presented in the next research work of the authors. The future directions of this research work will be expanding the same with other clustering methods and providing appropriate recommendations at periodical intervals to the instructors with the data obtained during the intervals. This may enable the instructors to adjust their level of teaching and individual tutoring according to the student group. This periodical recommendation shall be customized to students, enabling the students to understand their level of learning and improve themselves. Though this work used the data of a single class room, the same algorithm and methodology shall be extended for a large class rooms and with larger data sets.

FUTURE WORK

The extension of the work is being done to fix the standard labelling for each cluster by suitable algorithm. The rank of each cluster may be automatically done and the ranking mechanism may be extended for many courses studies by the same student set. From the ranks obtained by each student in different courses, the preference of electives, personal tutoring etc may be done. This smart tutoring methodology and continuing education processes implementation is the future scope of this work.

REFERENCES

Alfaro-Cid, E., Mora, A. M., Merelo, J. J., Esparcia-Alcázar, A. I., & Sharman, K. (2009). Finding relevant variables in a financial distress prediction problem using genetic programming and self-organizing maps. In *Natural computing in computational finance* (pp. 31–49). Springer. doi:10.1007/978-3-540-95974-8_3

Anitha, D., Kavitha, D., Prakash, R. R., & Raja, S. C. (2020). Identification of Opinion Difference in Teaching Learning Methods and Recommendation to Faculty. *Journal of Engineering Education Transformations*, *33*(0), 421–424. doi:10.16920/jeet/2020/v33i0/150197

Bhanuprakash, C., Nijagunarya, Y. S., & Jayaram, M. A. (2018). An Informal Approach to Identify Bright Graduate Students by Evaluating their Classroom Behavioral Patterns by Using Kohonen Self Organizing Feature Map. *International Journal of Modern Education & Computer Science, 10*(8), 22–32. doi:10.5815/ijmecs.2018.08.03

Carter-McAuslan, A., & Farquharson, C. (2020). Application of SOMs and k-means clustering to geophysical mapping: Lessons learned. *SEG Technical Program Expanded Abstracts, 2020*, 3843–3846. doi:10.1190egam2020-w10-01.1

Carvalho, A. R., & Santos, C. (2021). Developing peer mentors' collaborative and metacognitive skills with a technology-enhanced peer learning program. *Computers and Education Open*, 100070.

Cruz, W. M., & Isotani, S. (2014, September). Group formation algorithms in collaborative learning contexts: A systematic mapping of the literature. In *CYTED-RITOS International Workshop on Groupware* (pp. 199-214). Springer. 10.1007/978-3-319-10166-8_18

de Carvalho, S. D., de Melo, F. R., Flôres, E. L., Pires, S. R., & Loja, L. F. B. (2020). Intelligent tutoring system using expert knowledge and Kohonen maps with automated training. *Neural Computing & Applications, 32*(17), 13577–13589. doi:10.100700521-020-04767-0

Dhanasekaran, S., Devi, V. A., Narayanan, S. S., Vijayakarthik, P., Hariharasitaraman, S., & Rajasekaran, S. (2022). A smart digital attendance monitoring system for academic institution using machine learning techniques. *Webology, 19*(1).

Dragomir, O. E., Dragomir, F., & Radulescu, M. (2014). Matlab application of Kohonen Self-Organizing Map to classify consumers' load profiles. *Procedia Computer Science, 31*, 474–479. doi:10.1016/j.procs.2014.05.292

Farhangian, M., Purvis, M., Purvis, M., & Savarimuthu, T. B. R. (2015, May). The effects of temperament and team formation mechanism on collaborative learning of knowledge and skill in short-term projects. In *International Workshop on Multiagent Foundations of Social Computing* (pp. 48-65). Springer. 10.1007/978-3-319-24804-2_4

Gallén, R. C., & Caro, E. T. (2018). A benchmarking study of K-Means and Kohonen self-organizing maps applied to features of mooc participants. *European Journal of Open, Distance and E-learning, 21*(1).

Goh, C. F., Tan, O. K., Rasli, A., & Choi, S. L. (2019). Engagement in peer review, learner-content interaction and learning outcomes. *The International Journal of Information and Learning Technology*.

Gratton, L., & Erickson, T. J. (2007). Eight ways to build collaborative teams. *Harvard Business Review, 85*(11), 100. PMID:18159790

Hartono, P., & Ogawa, K. (2014, October). Visualizing Learning Management System Data using Context-Relevant Self-Organizing Map. In *IEEE International Conference on Systems, Man, and Cybernetics (SMC)* (pp. 3487-3491). IEEE. 10.1109/SMC.2014.6974469

Hossain, M., & Aydin, H. (2011). A Web 2.0-based collaborative model for multicultural education. *Multicultural Education & Technology Journal, 5*(2), 116–128. doi:10.1108/17504971111142655

Hsu, C. M. (2011). A hybrid procedure for stock price prediction by integrating self-organizing map and genetic programming. *Expert Systems with Applications*, *38*(11), 14026–14036. doi:10.1016/j. eswa.2011.04.210

Inyang, U. G., Umoh, U. A., Nnaemeka, I. C., & Robinson, S. A. (2019). Unsupervised Characterization and Visualization of Students' Academic Performance Features. *Comput. Inf. Sci.*, *12*(2), 103–116. doi:10.5539/cis.v12n2p103

Kavitha, D., & Anitha, D. (2016, December). Project Based Learning Using ICT Tools to Achieve Outcomes for the Course'Microcontrollers Based System Design': A Case Study. In *IEEE 4th International Conference on MOOCs, Innovation and Technology in Education (MITE)* (pp. 223-228). IEEE.

Kavitha, D., & Anitha, D. (2018). Flipped Classroom Using ICT Tools to Improve Outcome for the Course'Soft Computing'-A Case Study. *Journal of Engineering Education Transformations*, *32*(2), 39–45.

Kavitha, D., & Anitha, D. (2021). Measuring the effectiveness of Individual assessment methods in Collaborative/Cooperative activity in online teaching. *Journal of Engineering Education Transformations*, *34*(0), 637–641. doi:10.16920/jeet/2021/v34i0/157235

Kavitha, D., Zobaa, A. F., Kumar, V. S., & Renuga, P. (2011). NSGA-II Optimized Neural Network Controlled Active Power Line Conditioner under Non-sinusoidal Conditions. *International Review of Electrical Engineering*, *6*(5).

Khan, A., & Jaffar, M. A. (2015). Genetic algorithm and self organizing map based fuzzy hybrid intelligent method for color image segmentation. *Applied Soft Computing*, *32*, 300–310. doi:10.1016/j. asoc.2015.03.029

Kohonen, T. (1990). The self-organizing map. *Proceedings of the IEEE*, *78*(9), 1464–1480. doi:10.1109/5.58325

Larson, D. B., Broder, J. C., Bhargavan-Chatfield, M., Donnelly, L. F., Kadom, N., Khorasani, R., Sharpe, R. E. Jr, Pahade, J. K., Moriarity, A. K., Tan, N., Siewert, B., & Kruskal, J. B. (2020). Transitioning from peer review to peer learning: Report of the 2020 Peer Learning Summit. *Journal of the American College of Radiology*, *17*(11), 1499–1508. doi:10.1016/j.jacr.2020.07.016 PMID:32771491

Lee, Y. (2019). Using self-organizing map and clustering to investigate problem-solving patterns in the massive open online course: An exploratory study. *Journal of Educational Computing Research*, *57*(2), 471–490. doi:10.1177/0735633117753364

Li, T., Sun, G., Yang, C., Liang, K., Ma, S., & Huang, L. (2018). Using self-organizing map for coastal water quality classification: Towards a better understanding of patterns and processes. *The Science of the Total Environment*, *628*, 1446–1459. doi:10.1016/j.scitotenv.2018.02.163 PMID:30045564

Liang, A., & McQueen, R. J. (2000). Computer assisted adult interactive learning in a multicultural environment. *Adult Learning*, *11*(1), 26–29. doi:10.1177/104515959901100108

Mehta, N. K., Prasad, S. S., Saurav, S., Saini, R., & Singh, S. (2022). Three-dimensional DenseNet self-attention neural network for automatic detection of student's engagement. *Applied Intelligence*, *52*(12), 13803–13823. doi:10.100710489-022-03200-4 PMID:35340984

Neme, A., Pulido, J. R. G., Muñoz, A., Hernández, S., & Dey, T. (2015). Stylistics analysis and authorship attribution algorithms based on self-organizing maps. *Neurocomputing*, *147*, 147–159. doi:10.1016/j.neucom.2014.03.064

Odo, C., Masthoff, J., & Beacham, N. (2019, June). Group formation for collaborative learning. In *International Conference on Artificial Intelligence in Education* (pp. 206-212). Springer.

Purbasari, I. Y., Puspaningrum, E. Y., & Putra, A. B. S. (2020, July). Using Self-Organizing Map (SOM) for Clustering and Visualization of New Students based on Grades. *Journal of Physics: Conference Series*, *1569*(2), 022037. doi:10.1088/1742-6596/1569/2/022037

Qu, X., Yang, L., Guo, K., Ma, L., Sun, M., Ke, M., & Li, M. (2021). A survey on the development of self-organizing maps for unsupervised intrusion detection. *Mobile Networks and Applications*, *26*(2), 808–829. doi:10.100711036-019-01353-0

Savchenko, A. V., Savchenko, L. V., & Makarov, I. (2022). Classifying emotions and engagement in online learning based on a single facial expression recognition neural network. *IEEE Transactions on Affective Computing*, *13*(4), 2132–2143. doi:10.1109/TAFFC.2022.3188390

Setiadi, H., Saptono, R., Suryani, E., & Agnestya, N. R. (2019, December). Recommendation System Using Self Organizing Map (SOM) for Thesis Examiners and Preceptors of Universitas Sebelas Maret-Department of Informatics. In *IEEE 6th International Conference on Engineering Technologies and Applied Sciences (ICETAS)* (pp. 1-7). IEEE.

Strijbos, J. W., Martens, R. L., Jochems, W. M. G., & Broers, N. J. (2004). The Effects of Functional Roles on Group Efðciency: Using multilevel modeling and content analysis to investigate computer-supported collaboration in small groups. *Small Group Research*, *35*(2), 195–229. doi:10.1177/1046496403260843

Thirumoorthy, K., & Muneeswaran, K. (2021). An elitism based self-adaptive multi-population Poor and Rich optimization algorithm for grouping similar documents. *Journal of Ambient Intelligence and Humanized Computing*, 1–15.

Thuraisingam, T., Ean, T. C. G., & Singh, P. K. H. (2019). Impact of Peer Assessment Intervention on Student Motivation and Learning in Composition Classes. *International Journal of Education, Psychology and Counseling*, *4*(30), 225–236.

Van Gassen, S., Callebaut, B., Van Helden, M. J., Lambrecht, B. N., Demeester, P., Dhaene, T., & Saeys, Y. (2015). FlowSOM: Using self-organizing maps for visualization and interpretation of cytometry data. *Cytometry. Part A*, *87*(7), 636–645. doi:10.1002/cyto.a.22625 PMID:25573116

Wendel, J., & Buttenfield, B. P. (2010). *Formalizing guidelines for building meaningful self-organizing maps. GIScience*. Short Paper Proceedings.

Zhan, Z., Fong, P. S., Mei, H., & Liang, T. (2015). Effects of gender grouping on students' group performance, individual achievements and attitudes in computer-supported collaborative learning. *Computers in Human Behavior*, *48*, 587–596. doi:10.1016/j.chb.2015.02.038

Chapter 8
Bibliometric Review on Industry 4.0 in Various Sites:
Online Blogs and YouTube

P. Karthikeyan
https://orcid.org/0000-0003-2703-4051
Thiagarajar College of Engineering, India

Vivek A. R.
Thiagarajar College of Engineering, India

ABSTRACT

This work focuses on Industry 4.0 and the contemporary tendencies that it has spawned. The readers gain knowledge on what Industry 4.0 is, how it affects current manufacturing technologies, and its potential in the future. The authors improve comprehension of the effects imposed by Industry 4.0 by using a bibliometric method. Using web-scraping Python code and the YouTube Data API, this is accomplished using randomly selected 45–50 YouTube videos and 25–30 Medium blogs. Spreadsheets are used to organize the information that the web scraping programme has obtained. Following data organization, it is divided with the parameters serving as the key based on how well they coincide with the outcomes. To improve visualization, the results can be shown in a variety of graphs. The knowledge linked to Industry 4.0 that is provided in blogs and videos will provide readers with a better understanding of its impact.

INTRODUCTION

Technology is used in Industry 4.0 to provide real-time data for a variety of applications. The manner that many industries run their operations and carry out their responsibilities has changed as a result of this technology, which is mostly employed in industrial communication. The majority of industries have now begun to employ Industry 4.0 technological implementations, from small and medium-sized businesses (SMEs) to multinational corporations (MNCs). Using the data tools covered in this chapter, the writers would describe Industry 4.0 and related terminology. Industry 4.0 was first started in Germany and has

DOI: 10.4018/978-1-6684-8145-5.ch008

Copyright © 2023, IGI Global. Copying or distributing in print or electronic forms without written permission of IGI Global is prohibited.

received a lot of attention in recent literature. The economy has incorporated modern industrial growth for several hundred years. The notion of industrial manufacturing underwent a significant upheaval with the advent of Industry 4.0. The invention of mechanical production facilities using steam and water power in the 18th century marks the beginning of industry. The second industrial revolution, which began at the turn of the 20th century, was built over the course of a century. It entailed massive labor output that was based on labor production. The third industrial revolution got its start in the 1970s, and its hallmark was automatic production based on electronics and internet technology. The fourth industrial revolution, often known as Industry 4.0, is the most recent one. The main objectives of Industry 4.0 are to increase operational productivity and efficiency. It also strives to achieve a fully automated environment in an industry by automating at a higher degree than what is currently being done in the sector. These objectives and characteristics of Industry 4.0 are frequently closely tied to cutting-edge algorithms and internet technologies. These also contribute to the idea that Industry 4.0 is an industrial process of knowledge management and value addition. In order to demonstrate how Industry 4.0-related technology is used in contemporary manufacturing processes and industrial practices, the authors emphasize an analysis-based study using the data gathered from YouTube and Medium. Additionally, a number of analogies and visualizations are provided so that readers may quickly grasp the description's context. In this chapter, numerous methods of data interpretation and visualization are used. The offered illustrations and images can be used by the readers to gain rapid understanding. The structure of this chapter ensures that the procedures for data collection, organization, classification, analysis, and result extraction are carried out in a systematic manner. The authors have only focused on sporadic blogs and videos to check the quality of the content offered by the platforms, as the readers can see. Another crucial component of this study is the classification of users according to their level of skill. However, the authors are limited to the feedback, keywords, and comments made in the blogs and videos. This chapter focuses on explaining to the readers the terminology and ideologies associated with Industry 4.0. Using YouTube and Medium as the main data sources, a variety of data is gathered and examined to determine how Industry 4.0 will affect the industrial revolution. This chapter's major goal is to demonstrate how industries using Industry 4.0 technologies have evolved and to assure current trends, impacts, and tendencies.

BACKGROUND

The phrase "Industry 4.0" is now being used often in the software industry. Concerns have been raised about the realization of digital transformation and its effects on many industries. Many businesses are implementing methods and plans created with Industry 4.0. These businesses can now deliver a real-time decision-making system without increasing their labor costs. The case of Renault in the automotive industry is offered in the further reading area for readers to examine in order to learn more about digital transformation in industry (Aminul Islam, 2022). Even while the most recent technological advances can offer an expansive, scalable system for Industry 4.0, the system nevertheless has a number of drawbacks. Cyber security and data privacy concerns are two examples of this. For those who are adopting Industry 4.0, these two difficulties may present a barrier. Industry 4.0's full potential won't be realized until these difficulties are resolved using the right recovery techniques. Information on the impact of Industry 4.0 technology on transforming manufacturing can be found in Additional Reading (Biba, 2018). For instance, according to a research based on a poll of senior manufacturing experts conducted in 2020 by The Manufacturer on IBM's behalf, cyber security was voted as the most extensively used technology by manufacturers by 88% of Industries. The source was gathered from a wide range of industrial respondents, including those in the fields of aerospace, chemicals and pharmaceuticals, defense, electronics and electrical equipment, food and beverage, and machinery. Industry 4.0 can improve the industrial company's efficiency, agility, and adaptability with a good adoption. These actions also encourage the business to commit to socially responsible actions, ensuring that the UN Sustainable Development Goals (SDGs) are consistently followed. Industries today must manage cyber security-related concerns with the help of the organization's stakeholders. Therefore, it is important for the organization's stakeholders to be aware of and comprehend the wider picture in order for the business to grow. As a result, Industry 4.0 requirements might be met with a minimum degree of security by integrating systems across all dimensions. Although Industry 4.0 technologies offer practical benefits and save time, each of these technologies and initiatives has an economic viability. A possible risk for SMEs implementing Industry 4.0 approaches in their manufacturing processes is also sufficiently demonstrated by the facts. As was already said, the main cause of this is because the SMEs' economic standards have been lowered or restricted to meet Industry 4.0 standards. However, when these SMEs develop over time, they use this technology on a smaller scale and with less money invested. As a result, the majority of industries adapt their operations to Industry 4.0 methods, which has a significant impact on the world economy.

Literature Review

Manufacturing industries have witnessed an impact on their economic and societal advancement as a result of recent trends in Industry 4.0. Industry 4.0 has made great strides in both the commercial and scientific communities. Industry 4.0 is a widely used phrase that has long been a topic of academic study (Oztemel & Gursev, 2018). In terms of academic study, it outlines the idea and offers pertinent case studies for creating an associated system. The key to using Industry 4.0 paradigms is to comprehend the concepts and put them into practice. Therefore, in order to prepare for a future shift from production that is dominated by machines to digital manufacturing, the industries must concentrate on comprehending the features and substance of Industry 4.0 (Oztemel & Gursev, 2018). Even if businesses use these tactics, they should have a clear understanding of their respective situations and potentials in order to succeed. Industries need to decide on their fundamental requirements for the Industry 4.0 standard in order to develop a well-planned road map. For the majority of real-world applications, Industry 4.0 is still in an unstable state. Only the research community will be able to translate this into a solid implementation (Oztemel & Gursev, 2018). According to experts, Industry 4.0 and related technologies will have a significant impact on people's social lives. This is due to the fact that producing, implementing technology, cooperating, making decisions, and solving problems are all areas where robots will likely show to be more powerful and dominant than humans. The production process could be dominated by this (Oztemel & Gursev, 2018). In order to maintain a competitive advantage over the manufacturing community, the natural manufacturing society may be impacted by this social revolution, forcing them to adapt their manufacturing processes and meet customer demands (Oztemel & Gursev, 2018). Implementing such manufacturing methods can also encourage industries to develop novel business strategies in order to dominate the industrial sphere. The other manufacturers are under pressure, as was previously mentioned, to study, comprehend, plan, and carry out the transformation process. The following details aid in fully comprehending the aforementioned (Oztemel & Gursev, 2018).

1. **Industry 4.0 And Green Supply Chain Management:** The majority of researchers and industry professionals are more interested in this crucial portion. This is due to the company's increased level of digitization in this particular region. By using green fuels during the production and product-making processes, industries can reduce their emissions levels (Ghadge et al., 2022).

2. **Struggle of SMEs:** In larger businesses, the deployment of extensive digitization projects is incorporated into the main corporate plan. However, it is challenging to integrate these Industry 4.0 principles in small and medium-sized businesses (SMEs). These SMEs have a huge leveraging effect because they are the foundation of the economy. Consequently, a unique set of initiatives must be created for smaller businesses (Matt & Rauch, 2020). Refer additional reading Ghadge et al. (2022) and Oztemel and Gursev (2018) for further information.

3. **Rise in Technological Implementation:** The most often employed technologies in the area of Industry 4.0 are the usage of robots and the adoption of cyber security. The scale of its adoption varies depending on the geography. African businesses embrace technologies at the slowest rate, while Asian businesses do so most frequently. A tiny percentage of businesses in Europe and North America are using these implementations to promote an environmentally friendly approach to using the Industry 4.0 ideas. Additionally, there are widespread adoptions being made to improve operational effectiveness and realize environmental benefits. Eastern businesses adopt the former, whereas western businesses adopt the latter (Oztemel & Gursev, 2018). The readers might refer to the recommended reading section (Javaid et al., 2022) to acquire a sense of environmental benefits and efficiency.

4. **Smart Factories:** Industry 4.0's provision of digital transformation has converted conventional factories into smart factories. The need for more competent engineers has changed as a result of how rapidly industries are developing thanks to technology. Additionally, for the establishment of a better smart factory, coordination between Internet of Things and Cyber-Physical systems is needed in addition to these engineers. Industries would be able to survive longer than their typical competition as a result (Oztemel & Gursev, 2018).

The design guidelines that must be adhered to for the implementation of the Industry 4.0 plan are outlined in Table 1. Other scholars and business people claim that if a new industry developing standards adheres to these six design principles, it will be essential to the success of their operations. The ethical and human considerations that would be necessary for an industry that is implementing Industry 4.0 policies and processes for the first time are stated in these six design principles. The foundational prerequisites for establishing Industry 4.0 in an industry are the six design concepts listed in Table 2. These can be successfully put into practice thanks to industrial professionals' abilities and researchers' knowledge of the relevant fields. Employees need to have a particular set of skill sets in order to boost their prospects for employment in the sector. The skills are classified into two types:

1. **Business Skills:** These skills involve Critical Thinking, Cognitive Flexibility, Adaptive Training Ability, Qualitative Skills, Communication Skills, Complex Problem – Solving Skills (Aminul Islam, 2022).

2. **Technical Skills:** These skills involve Programming skills, Data Interpretation skills, Data Visualization skills, Virtual Collaboration Skills (Aminul Islam, 2022).

Table 1. Six design principles of Industry 4.0 and their required standards (Oztemel & Gursev, 2018)

Serial Number	Design Principle	Definition	Required Standards
1	Interoperability	It is regarded as the ability of computer systems or computer software to exchange and use information.	Industrial machines are supposed to have higher interoperability to mark a better-quality standard.
2	Virtualization	A technology which makes available a computer system to simulate and run hardware functionality in a virtual environment.	Usage of multiple virtual system enables a single system to run multiple OS and applications without additional resources
3	Decentralization	It is defined as transferring and splitting the workload to local systems rather than a group processing towards a single organizational goal.	Smart factories with facilities that can make a decision individually and independently without deviating from the goal.
4	Real – time Capability	A systematic solution to collection and analysis of real – time data and then applying the concepts of decentralization.	Large amounts of real – time data availability makes accuracy and decisions of the systems to be improved.
5	Service Orientation	A system which helps in enabling the services of companies, cyber – physical systems and humans so that they can be used efficiently.	Every Industry needs to implement service orientation in its central corporate strategy in order to be successful according to Industry 4.0 standards.
6	Modularity	Establishment of design boundaries to facilities at both manufacturing and assembly in case of hardware equipment.	Modular production units and smart factories to make easier flow of communication in the industry.

Source: Literature review of Industry 4.0 and related technologies (2018)

These skill sets are a list of the abilities that it takes to accomplish a certain job well. The modern company market doesn't seem to be steady and fluctuates in the twenty-first century. Only by effectively using human influence in the sector can this be resolved. As a result, workers in the commercial and industrial sectors need a certain set of abilities (Aminul Islam, 2022).

To comprehend the specifics of how industrial robots are employed in accordance with Industry 4.0 guidelines, refer to Table 2. When compared to a human labor, these robots are quicker, more economical, and more efficient. Industrial robots also show to have an advantage in terms of security and safety. Take a look to the supplemental reading (SAP, n.d.) supplied to learn more about industrial robots and their various varieties.

Table 2. Industrial robots being used in various industries

Serial Number	Robot Name	Manufacturer	Function
1	Kuka LBR iiwa	Kuka	Lightweight robot for sensitive tasks
2	Baxter	Rethink Robotics	Interactive production robot for packaging purpose
3	BioRob Arm	Bionic Robotics	Usage in close proximity with humans
4	SCARA	Fanuc	Usage in assembly of products
5	BX200L	Kawasaki Robotics	Housing construction industry with the capability of constructing individual housing units
6	SCARA	Mitsubishi Electric Automation Ltd	Usage in assembly as well as pick and place

Source: SAP (n.d.)

1. **Current Industrial Practices:** The shift from mass production to customized production is the current trend in the manufacturing sector. Humans are strictly integrated into the production process in order to provide a continuous improvement and focus on value-adding activities. This is done in order to increase productivity and provide a new level of organization. Another benefit is that situations where wastes could be avoided could arise if human-based integration is given priority in industries (Vaidya et al., 2018).

2. **Growth of Cyber Physical Systems:** If an environment provides real-time data collection, transparency, and analysis throughout all phases of manufacturing processes, it is referred to be a cyber-physical system. The promotion of sustainability in their operations has seen a huge increase in the use of cyber-physical systems. Only the expanding use of sensor technology has made these systems conceivable (Standards for Industry 4.0, 2019).

3. **Automation:** Automated control is the use of a variety of control methods to operate machinery in a field with little or no human involvement. Less energy is used, fewer people are employed, higher-quality products are produced, and accuracy and precision are all advantages of automation (Mamodiya & Sharma, 2014).

Industry 4.0 Standards

A business that adheres to a set of standards is more likely to provide manufactured goods with the right values. Industries may set up innovations and incorporate them into their machinery, but without a standard operating procedure (SOP), resources may be used inefficiently. This could result in a decline in the profit margin that the sector must achieve (Standards for Industry 4.0, 2019). Therefore, standards are crucial for an industry to create automated smart technology that can be used effectively and securely. A measure termed the "Smart Industry Readiness Index (SIRI)" is used to verify estimates of an industry's readiness to adopt Industry 4.0 strategies and technology. This index includes a number of frameworks and tools to assist manufacturers in beginning, accelerating, and maintaining their digital transformation. Regardless of their size or line of business, all of these frameworks and technologies are applicable to industries (Singapore Economic Development Board, 2019). SIRI was developed in Singapore in collaboration with a network of top tech firms. Additionally, it is a part of the Global SIRI initiative of the World Economic Forum. International use of SIRI by MNCs and SMEs spans 30 distinct countries and 600 manufacturing nations.

Process, technology, and organization are the three main components that form the basis of SIRI. The full potential of Industry 4.0 can only be realized by an industry if all three are combined. The sixteen dimensions and eight pillars that the companies must concentrate on are shown in Figure 1. Operations, Supply Chain, Product Lifecycle, Automation, Connectivity, Intelligence, Talent Readiness, Structure, and Management make up the SIRI's eight pillars. These agreements promote the company's growth while directing it towards the important areas on which businesses and industries should concentrate. Vertical and horizontal integration, integrated product lifecycle, shopfloor, enterprise, facility, workforce learning and development, leadership competency, inter- and intra-company collaboration, strategy, and governance are the SIRI's dimensions. These words aid an industry in outlining its life cycle and establishing goals for raising awareness. This is being done as a global measure to track the evolution of Industry 4.0.

Figure 1. Overview of smart industry readiness index (SIRI)
Source: International Centre for Industrial Transformation

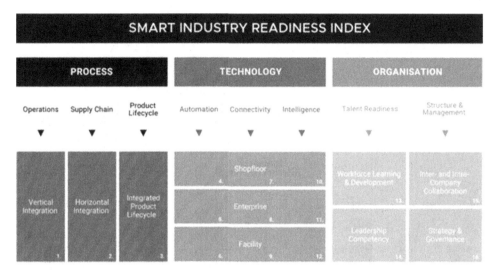

Industry 4.0 Technologies

Industrial Internet of Things (IIoT) and cyber-physical systems that are intelligent, automated, and monitor and control physical systems using computerized algorithms are collectively referred to as "Industry 4.0 technologies" in basic terms. Nine technologies provide as a link between advances in physical and digital systems. These innovations continue to power Industry 4.0. They are:

1. **Big Data and AI Analytics:** Collection of big data is available from a large range of sources from equipment to IIoT devices. AI powered analytics and ML are utilized to process the real-time data. The results are used to improve the decision-making and automation in the various areas of supply chain management.
2. **Horizontal and Vertical Integration:** It was also considered under the SIRI dimensions as it is an backbone to Industry 4.0. Using horizontal integration, tight field level integration of processes is possible. Using vertical integration, all the layers of an organization are brought together. There is a close integration of production and business process in this category.
3. **Cloud Computing:** Promotes the digital transformation of industries. Cloud technology utilized by industries is faster, scalable, more storage and cost efficient as compared to the local datastore process. AI and ML technologies are faster and more effective in combination with a cloud system. Hence, they provide an opportunity to industries an ideology to bring up new ideas. All the data for the Industry 4.0 technologies are being stored using this cloud computing technology. This further enables cyber-physical systems to communicate between one system to another system.
4. **Augmented Reality:** Provides an interactive experience by overlaying digital content on a real-world environment. Employees can use smart glasses or any other AR tool to visualize the IIoT data in real time, validation in manufacturing and assembling without actually making the change. It also has several other utilities in training the employees for skills and safety programs.

Figure 2. Technologies being used in Industry 4.0
Source: SAP Insights

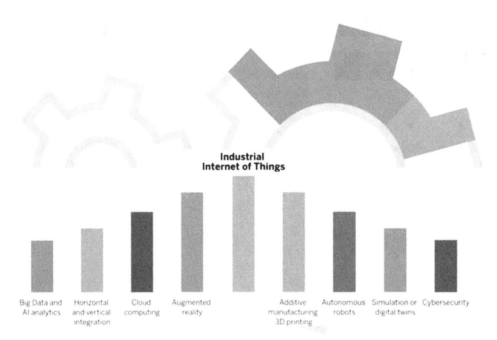

5. **Industrial Internet of Things:** Most of the industrial equipment used by organizations implementing Industry 4.0 strategies would use sensors and RFID tags for communication purpose. They provide continuously real-time data with the parameters being geography, condition of the equipment, performance. The advantage of using IIoT is that downtime of equipment can be significantly reduced to minimum and product tracking can be easily done.

6. **3D Printing:** Also referred to as additive manufacturing method, it was at first being used as a rapid prototyping tool. After Industry 4.0, it found more applications from mass customization to distributed manufacturing. Using this technology, products can be saved and kept as design files in virtual inventories. The major advantage of this technology is that there could be maximum savings in terms of transportation costs. These design products can be shared easily over long distances as files. Then they are printed at the destination region to complete the manufacturing process.

7. **Autonomous Robots:** An autonomous robot is a man-made machine that performs the task assigned to it without any human interference. These robots are of different types – separated widely by means of the task they would be performing. Integration with AI could enable these machines to think themselves, improve their decision-making ability and perform difficult and delicate tasks.

8. **Simulation:** Virtually representing a computer object and functionalities using a real-world machine is referred to be a digital twin of the real-world machine. The objective of using a simulator is to make the organization to understand, analyze and improve the maintenance and performance of the industrial systems. Employees can simulate an environment similar to the one prevalent in the

industry using a simulator and provide solution to a damaged machine accessory, make predictions of the problems in the machine. This ideally improves the uptime of the system.

9. **Cyber Security:** Usage of big data and connectivity brings in another important aspect of Industry 4.0 that is safety of these utilities. Cyber security is an essential to protect these data from being stolen from other harmful users of the internet. Blockchain and ML technologies are together used by companies to automate detection of threats in as system or network, provide minimum risk of data breaches and involve in delays in production over the networks.

Figure 3. Diagram that showcases a brief of literature review section
Source: Authors

PROBLEM DESCRIPTION

Industries must find solutions to a wide range of issues in order to survive and make money. Threats, issues, and inaccurate maintenance may be the most frequent concerns that sectors encounter from a commercial standpoint. Scalability is difficult for SMEs. They only make a small amount of money, which they use to reinvest in their services and products; therefore they are unable to expand their firm. Additionally, a poor regard for upkeep and rising overheads would result from a shortage of competent people for running machines. Industry 4.0 strategies and associated cooperative methods are the most evident and widely used solutions to these issues. They empower industries to run businesses by providing:

1. **Real-Time Data:**
    a. It is a form of information that is delivered immediately after the collection process is over. The time delay between collection and delivery of data is practically assumed to be zero.
    b. Using these data, a company can resolve the errors possibly immediately even after their detection. Thus, this helps in providing the industry with a secure way in protecting their resources and enhances their business outcomes.

2. **Predictive Analytics:**
    a. A statistical modeling technique that helps in making future predictions of outcomes and performance.
    b. It can be applicable to every industry as they can be implemented in forecasting risks and management of assets and equipment's in an industry.
3. **Automation:**
    a. Minimizing involvement of human interactions and reduction of input provided.
    b. Automation involves many types like Business Process Automation (BPA), IT Automation in industries.
4. **Internet-Enabled Machinery:**
    a. A machine that can communicate via a wireless network through the internet.
    b. These machineries are highly capable and help in information interchange by providing performance, efficiency reports and also mitigate the faults even before they are manually diagnosed.

SMEs are the focal point in shaping an enterprise policy. As these companies contribute more to the economic improvement, it is a right choice for SMEs to introduce IIoT system that can be used to communicate and help in tracking and tracing SME logistics.

PROPOSED WORK

The authors have used the data source as YouTube videos and Medium web-blogs. The duration of the collected data for YouTube videos is 5 Years (2017 – 2022). The duration of the collected data for Medium Blogs is 4 Years (2018 – 2022). The essential parameters were collected using web-scraping Python scripts and the YouTube Data API (only for Comments).

The parameters for YouTube videos include:

1. **Video Comments:** These Comments are the immediate public reviews for any video that are posted after the video is viewed by the users. These data are useful as it states the thoughts of the public regarding to the content posted by the YouTube Channel.
2. **Like Count:** Likes can be treated as the degree of approval which the general public is concerned with. It represents the interests of the user.
3. **Date Published for Comments:** The date in which the comments are published on is used for validating the recent trends in the Industry 4.0 technologies.
4. **Reply Count:** The number of feedbacks received for each comment.
5. **Reply to Comment:** It is used for getting further information about the comment.

The parameters for Web Blogs from Medium include:

1. **Article Name:** From the name of the articles, it can be verified that the correct articles are being chosen.
2. **Published Date:** The date in which the comments are published on is used for validating the recent trends in the Industry 4.0 technologies.

3. **Author Details:** These details include author's name, author's biography provided in his/her profile page, Followers count.

4. **Published In:** Publication of Industry 4.0 articles is also considered to verify whether they are published in a journal or any other blogging site.

5. **Read Duration:** This represents the time for which the article can be read in a single go-through and it is denoted in minutes.

6. **Claps:** They refer to the number of upvotes received by the article done by the particular author. It is similar to the likes count in YouTube videos.

7. **Keywords:** The most used terms in the article are also taken into consideration for making a conclusive statement on Industry 4.0 technologies. It is based on each article and their count is used for generating visualization of keywords.

8. **Comment Count:** The number of feedbacks received by the author from other blog users is referred as comments in blogging sites. More number of comments represents a better response from the blog users and also by the other industry using the vlog as medium of communication.

9. **Comments:** These are generally related to additional information about the content posted by the author or any further improvements to the article that can be further improved by the author from the reviewer's point of view. Comments are sometimes used in deriving the growth of a industry 4.0 related technology.

SOLUTIONS AND RECOMMENDATIONS

The authors have proposed a bibliometric analysis-based study to address the issues raised earlier in the problems section. This study will provide insights into how Industry 4.0 technologies are currently being used, current trends in the technology, and the potential for future advancement in the relevant field. The information from the previously stated YouTube videos and Medium Web blogs would be discussed. According to the search results for the keywords "Industry 4.0," "Industry 4.0 Paradigms," "Industry 4.0 and related technologies," "Industry 4.0 Implementation," and "Current trends in Industry 4.0," the comments and keywords from YouTube videos and Medium Web blogs used in this study were selected at random. The information on Industry 4.0 and its present implementation in the industry supplied in the references section can be useful to readers. To gain additional insight on a stage's overall context, the data utilized to generate Figures 4 and 5 using the VOSViewer tool is based on the total number of comments and replies. A total of 45 to 50 YouTube videos are taken into consideration, and 650 comments are used for the same. Similar to the comments, the authors have taken into account 150 or so responses to the comments. The authors utilize the VOSViewer visualization tool with these data so that readers can see the most commonly used phrases clearly. To obtain better clarity on a broad scale, the data utilized to generate Figures 6 and 7 using the VOSViewer tool is based on the total number of comments and keywords used in the blogs. A total of 25 to 30 Medium blogs are taken into consideration, and 100 comments are used for the same. Similar to this, the writers took into account roughly 25 frequently used terms in the blogs when choosing their keywords. The authors utilize the VOSViewer visualization tool with these data so that readers can see the most commonly used phrases clearly.

YouTube Videos and Related Observations

A connective relationship between the important terms used in the YouTube video comments is shown in Figure 4. By looking at the graph, readers can deduce that Industry 4.0 represents the Fourth Industrial Revolution because it is given the most weight in the graph relative to other trends. The readers can see a country, Japan, that is being introduced in this forum by looking at the figure. This is due to the fact that Japanese businesses and industries are far ahead in adopting Industry 4.0 concepts and methods. Consider Toyota Manufacturers as an example. They are one of the top automakers in the entire world, and they also control the Japanese auto industry. In Toyota's production facilities, Industry 4.0 technology is being used. They use automation-based strategies and excel in their own industry. The use of robots for both the production of auto parts and the assembly of those parts has shown to be cost-effective for both organization and the nation. The Japanese work ethic of Kaizen is another excellent example that was mentioned in the Comments. Kaizen is a Japanese word that means "change for the better" and "produce an improvement." According to this philosophy, little, gradual adjustments have an effect over time. Additionally, it is said in various places that Kaizen improves particular areas in an organization by including both top management and rank-and-file workers in daily adjustments.

Figure 4. A graph generated using the comments of YouTube videos and abstracting the key words
Source: Authors

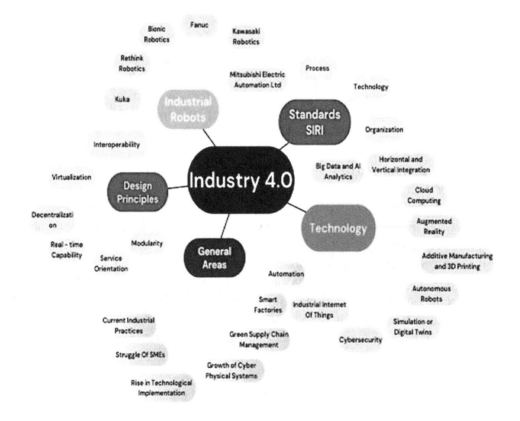

Similarly, it can be seen that another term, poverty, is also a crucial term. The readers may question how poverty fits into this element. The response to this query will be provided shortly. As Industry 4.0 is put into practice on a bigger scale, it also has some drawbacks. MNCs carry out these implementations at a set rate, but for SMEs, as was already mentioned in the difficulties section, this turns out to be an issue. The automation of equipment operating systems and the transmission of real-time data for filing bring about the problem of poverty. However, because access to these devices is their main source of income, this proportionally has an impact on the lives of low-skilled workers. As a result, it invariably has an impact on their life-dependent occupancy, which causes poverty in the nation. Automation is often used in business since it can produce economically sound results, but on the other hand, it affects these workers who are paid a daily pay. The industries have also developed additional concepts to help the lives of the unemployed people as a result of the automation of the machines in order to deal with this transition. By offering some training bootcamps, it entails turning low-skilled or unskilled people into skilled workers. Instead of being unemployed, these skill development programmes could aid these workers in a better rehabilitation. Additionally, it should be emphasized that reputable institutions and organisations are starting graduate degree programmes that incorporate Industry 4.0 ideals, ethics, technology, and a fundamental grasp of these methods and tactics. This can aid in the understanding of Industry 4.0 by new learners, leaders, and working professionals.

Table 3. Top 7 key words that are used mostly in Youtube comments prioritized by the greatest number of occurrences

Serial Number	Key Word	Description
1	Revolution	In context of Industry 4.0, a revolution in an industry is a change in the manufacturing process of an organization.
2	Poverty	Access to primary income source blocked or removed leads to poverty. But several MNCs have also start up a few initiatives to bring this poverty by unemployment down.
3	Internet	It helps in the communication between the smart devices used in the industries using the IIoT technology.
4	Resource	Utilization of resources in the industry is optimized and efficient. This could make the manufacturing process move towards the likelihood of the organizational goal.
5	Graduate Degree	Many graduate degrees exclusive for industry 4.0 is organized by industries and educational institutions to promote the growth of Industry 4.0 technologies and in development of more skilled entrepreneurs.
6	Change	Industry 4.0 has brought up a huge impact in the industrial manufacturing process. It has changed the way in which the manufactured products are produced with maximum efficiency.
7	Japan	Japan has demonstrated the Industry 4.0 principles and have succeeded with them. They also follow a few other ethics different from others.

Source: YouTube

The term "internet" is another that is used more frequently and is associated with a revolution. An established and widely utilized worldwide communication system is the internet. It facilitates data processing, and numerous other applications rely on the Internet for communication. One of the comments claims that the smart factory market is anticipated to be worth 153.7 billion USD in 2019 and will experience a CAGR of 9.76% from 2019 to 2024. The Internet of Things is the key Industry 4.0 technology that underpins it. It promotes a speedier market transition to digitization and direct connection. Figure 4 connects the phrases that were commonly used in the response to the video comments. A minimum of three to four comments received an average of answers at the time the data was collected. But using these responses was also helpful for summarizing the outcomes. The diagram makes it simpler to grasp how Industry 4.0 techniques and strategies, which have a bright future and may be used in many different industries, are used. There are a few responses as well detailing how Industry 4.0 is now being used in various nations. The two countries with the most users at the moment are Germany and Japan. The US industrial sectors are likewise attempting to establish them as the following successor to the aforementioned nations. After the beginnings of the Industry 4.0 revolution in 2011, FANUC, a Japanese company, was once again established. In 2013, it applied the guidelines and tactics recommended by Industry 4.0. For further reading refer the additional reading section (Matt & Rauch, 2020).

Figure 5. A graph generated using the reply related data of the YouTube videos
Source: Authors

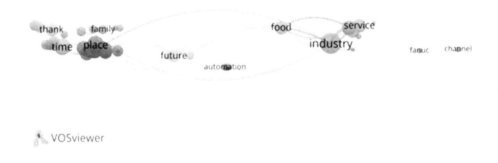

In some of the responses, it is also said that industrialization is harmful to social well-being and that traditional ways should be used instead in the areas of farming, food processing, etc. This is due to the possibility that using AI in these fields could lower output product quality and constrict product availability. Due to the need for a fair ratio between input and output to obtain the requisite profit from the raw materials, this may not be practical. It was proposed in the provocative responses section that these reforms and industrialization might result in a service-based economy for the use of the goods produced by the industry. Some of the most vital system that help towards this economy are:

1. Supply Chain Management System
2. Safety Monitoring System
3. Production Quality Control System

Figure 5 shows that the keyword family also contributes significantly to the creation of Industry 4.0 standards. Although there was a lessened response to these technologies in the food industry, it has been noted that industries backed by Industry 4.0 go above and above to help the workers' families. This is another admirable step the industries have taken in the direction of societal development.

Table 4. Top 7 key words that are used more frequently in the replies to the comments prioritized by the greatest number of occurrences

Serial Number	Key Word	Description
1	Future	The possibilities for Industry 5.0 which focusses more on the people and their stabilization. The main objective of Industry 5.0 is to manufacture products by the principles and strategies of Industry 4.0 such that these products can be customized according to the need of the customer.
2	Automation	A network of inter-connected IIoT devices that make necessary operations to perform the actions involved in manufacturing process by means of real – time data as the key source through cloud computing as the source.
3	Family	It better represents the society that needs some attention regarding the standard of living. In countries like India the availability of unskilled laborers is quite high as compared to the skilled people. Thus, this marks an imbalance between the weaker sections of the society.
4	Service	By the growth of Industry 4.0, there is a new term emerging called Product-as-a-Service (PaaS) which involves the concept of providing the services and outcomes that a product offers rather than the product itself.
5	Food	Industry 4.0 supports the food industry too. But the according to food revolution, it highlights the negative effects of modern farming methods and emphasizes the population to adopt a vegetarian lifestyle from natural resources.
6	Fanuc	Fanuc is the worldwide leader in providing factory automation technologies. These Japanese group of companies have involved actively in contribution towards Industry 4.0 standards and to the evolution of automation in machinery and equipment for factories.
7	Time	In context of Industry 4.0, time refers to a sub term in the real-time data is produced by IIoT devices which is used for decision making. In context to the YouTube comment replies, it symbolizes the right time that the videos prove to be a great source of information to know about Industry 4.0.

Source: YouTube

Medium Web Blogs and Related Observations

The interconnected graph in Figure 6 illustrates the main phrases and key words that are most commonly used in blog comments. This statistic makes sure that comments are made using terms relating to Industry 4.0.

This can be viewed as a good example of how Industry 4.0 is a term that comprises of many interconnected sub-terms. An Industry implementing Industry 4.0 technologies and standards must implement the required stack of implementations as a single investment. The readers can infer from the Figure 3 that most of the terms are inter-related to each other, which means that Industry 4.0 technologies are grouped together and cannot function individually as a single unit. Figure 6 shows that for an improved and sustained use of Industry 4.0 technology, computer machines, robots, communication systems, and dealing with a real-time data processing system are required. Automation, manufacturing, enterprise, digitization, and a few other key words also support this. Numerous blogs also claim that the use of AI, ML, DL, and CPS is suitable for a wide range of jobs needed by the organization. These technologies are still developing and changing with the passage of time. As a result of this discovery, it is critical that businesses concentrate on regularly updating and improving their systems and strategies in order to keep up with customer demand.

Table 5. Top 7 key words that are used more frequently in the blog comments prioritized by the greatest number of occurrences

Serial Number	Key Word	Description
1	Manufacturing	Industry 4.0 improves the process of producing more efficient products with higher quality. Enabling better results and upgrades to current process being followed. This results in a lower downtime and less capital expenditure.
2	Industrial Automation	A manufacturing system that supports augmentation and wireless connectivity with the use of electronic devices that communicate with each other to provide a seamless integration with software.
3	Smart City	A city utilizing the leading technological advancements like information and communication technologies to improve efficiency in operations and share information. This is done in order to improve the quality of services provided.
4	Enterprise	It is defined as the unit of an economic organization or an activity that has a purpose. Industry 4.0 can be implemented in an enterprise to advance their manufacturing process and improve their economy.
5	IIoT	Usage of smart devices that transfer real-time data for enhancing the manufacturing and industrial process.
6	Digital Transformation	Business organizations evolving from traditional methods involving paper to a complete change which involves the storage of files in a digital form.
7	Industry	Often synonymous to organization and enterprise an industry serves to be an economic activity that processes raw materials to finished products by the process of manufacturing.

Source: Medium

Figure 6. A graph generated using the keywords used in comments
Source: Authors

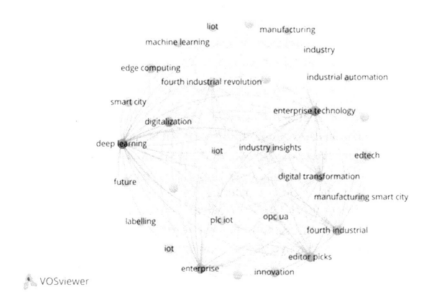

Table 6. Top 7 key words that are used more frequently in the replies to the blog comments prioritized by the greatest number of occurrences

Serial Number	Key Word	Description
1	Industry	Already discussed in Table 5 keyword 7.
2	Accelerator	Improvement in Industry 4.0 strategies has accelerated the growth of the industries.
3	Cyber Article	An article which involves a detailed explanation of computers and related technologies like cybersecurity, cyber-physical systems etc.
4	Experience	The AR technology provides an immersive visualization for making real world objects by superimposing information or real-time data generated by IIoT devices.
5	Path	Industry 4.0 leads the organization to newer dimensions by exploring and experimenting newer research in the research and development (R&D) department of the organization.
6	Primary Understanding	Articles, videos and blogs are helpful in providing a primary understanding of the Industry 4.0 terms and technologies.
7	Requirement	Industry 4.0 will prove to be the main requirement for organizations as it provides the basic fundamentals for an organization to be successful.

Source: Medium

Also, when taking into consideration about the type of comments being posted for the blogs it can segregated into 2 categories:

1. **Suggestive Comments:** These comments include add – on to the content posted by the blogger on medium. A suggestion for improvement in the blog or a suggestion for what the content would refer to are being posted.
2. **Appreciative Comments:** These comments involve a blogger providing greetings or encouraging the post blogger to post similar kind of blogs and informative contents on other communication mediums like github, social media platforms etc. Appreciation posts usually involve a few complements and a request for taking on the project from there on. This could be useful for first time bloggers or new researchers in their respective field.

Figure 7 shows a list of the phrases that other bloggers who comment on the article use the most frequently. This statistic is meant to provide a content enhancement type that bloggers can evaluate in terms of the technology being employed. Readers may tell that this graph isn't completely interconnected. This is due to the use of comment classification and the seeming independence of the comments. The remarks that are derived from the web blogs are unique and do not repeat themselves. It also demonstrated the fact that many of the articles lacked comments. This is due to the fact that Industry 4.0 is still evolving and needs development.

We can see from the figure that the most frequently recurring terms are industry, acceleration, primary understanding, requirement, cyber article, experience, and path. These phrases stand for the fundamental background knowledge required to implement Industry 4.0 tactics. The articles, according to the comments, serve as a primary source of information on the requirements of Industry 4.0 and can also be posted on other platforms for a wider audience. Industry 4.0 technologies have the potential to speed up the process of industrial improvement while also enhancing an organization's financial performance. Additionally, only a few others claim that AI, which already serves as an aid in Industry 4.0

approaches, will be applied as a whole in a system to fully depend on itself and lessen the impact of human meddling in many industries.

Figure 7. A graph generated using the most frequently used terms in blog comments
Source: Authors

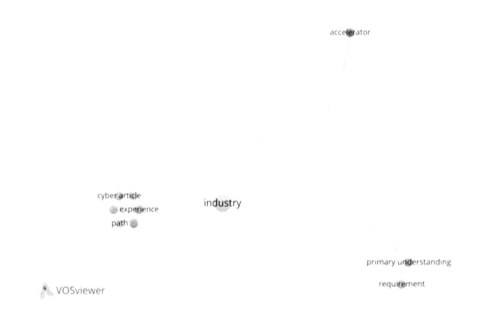

CONCLUSION

Readers can gain a good knowledge of Industry 4.0 technologies from the observations, as well as how they are currently influencing how industries use their manufacturing equipment in accordance with Industry 4.0 strategies and practices. The future scope of Industry 4.0 technologies is currently transitioning from Industry 4.0 standards to Industry 5.0 standards. According to data from YouTube, there are advantages and disadvantages to Industry 4.0 technologies. On the plus side, it promotes the technological development of an industry, albeit MNCs occasionally face obstacles in putting these advances into practice. Japanese companies who adopt Industry 4.0 see considerable advantages for their industrial sector. The dimensions indicated in SIRI are supported by the data from Medium. The conclusions drawn from the observations suggest that the cutting-edge technologies stated must be integrated into the Industry 4.0 technologies. These technologies still need to be updated to the most recent versions despite being in use. The organization's production may increase as a result, and the outcome would be superior to the conventional ones. The advantages of using Industry 4.0 are numerous, but the compatibility with industry-standard equipment, the room for improvement that encourages better research and development teams and the positive effects on a company's business performance include increased business yield, profitability, sales growth, and production speed. Together, these factors enable the business to industrialise with much higher quality and efficiency. With the use of Industry 4.0 and its supporting technologies, the industry's scalability is more durable. Industry 4.0 and the Sustainable

Development Goals can be mapped together to gain a general picture of the chapter. (SDGs). The kind of industry that uses the technology also plays a role. In general, it has an impact on productivity, industry growth, and affordable and clean energy use (SDG target 3), as well as industry, innovation, and infrastructure development (SDG goal 9) and Ensure Sustainable Consumption and Production Patterns (SDG goal 12). To get more idea on sustainable operations and performances, the readers can refer to additional reading section (Thomas & Schaefer, 2017). Overall Industry 4.0 can improve the economy of the country and also help the organization to gain more profit margins, sustainable manufacturing processes and technological advancement.

FUTURE RESEARCH DIRECTIONS

In Industry 4.0, in the majority of sectors, technologies are being used, and they show to be more beneficial than businesses that apply traditional methodologies. This is due to less human participation and more practical methods of functioning. Using the information from more online sources, this study can be expanded. This can broaden the range of data sources available and enhance both the quantity and quality of data being used. The data obtained from the sources indicated above can also be subjected to a quantitative and qualitative study. Industry 4.0 and the future Industry 5.0 technologies will be necessary for the next step in economic growth and global development. This may also prove to be a new subject of study for further scientists and researchers. To find out how the general population is responding to these Industry 4.0 technologies, research can also be done on various social media platforms, such as Facebook, LinkedIn, Instagram, etc. However, study can allow the researchers to quickly gain insights into how these social media platforms contribute to Industry 4.0 solutions, approaches, and strategies. The inclusion of this example may also have detrimental effects. The current study discusses the remarks and responses to YouTube videos as well as the remarks and keywords utilized in Medium Web Blogs. This study project can be expanded further by separating the different user types who respond to the videos and blogs. The platforms YouTube and Medium kept user information private and did not make it available to the public at the time the essay was written. Therefore, there may be potential for user-related data to become available in the future so that novice to expert comment/feedback analysis can continue. The numerous Industry 4.0 frameworks and technologies might also be the focus of research. It is possible to analyze existing frameworks and make recommendations for new ones. It is also possible to study the inclusion of more recent technologies like quantum computing, which have not yet been widely adopted. These topics can serve as a suitable place for newly registered researchers to begin since they are thought to be the direction of computing.

REFERENCES

Aminul Islam, M. (2022). Industry 4.0: Skill set for employability. *Social Sciences & Humanities Open*, 6(1), 100280. doi:10.1016/j.ssaho.2022.100280

Aravindaraj, K., & Rajan Chinna, P. (2022). A systematic literature review of integration of industry 4.0 and warehouse management to achieve Sustainable Development Goals (SDGs). In Cleaner Logistics and Supply Chain (vol. 5). Elsevier Ltd. Publishing

Biba, J. (2018). *20 Top Industrial Robot Companies to Know*. https://builtin.com/robotics/industrial-robot

Ghadge, Mogale, Bourlakis, Maiyar, & Moradlou. (2022). Link between Industry 4.0 and green supply chain management: Evidence from the automotive industry. Computers and Industrial Engineering, 169.

IBM. (2021). *2021 Digital Transformation Assessment COVID – 19: A Catalyst for change*. https://www.ibm.com/downloads/cas/MPQGMEN9

Javaid, M., Haleem, A., Singh, R. P., & Suman, R. (2022). An integrated outlook of Cyber–Physical Systems for Industry 4.0: Topical practices, architecture, and applications. In *Green Technologies and Sustainability*. KeAi Publishing.

Lu, Y. (2017). Industry 4.0: A survey on technologies, applications and open research issues. *Journal of Industrial Information Integration*, *6*, 1–10. doi:10.1016/j.jii.2017.04.005

Mamodiya, U., & Sharma, P. (2014). Article. *Journal of Electrical and Electronics Engineering*, *9*, 33–38.

Matt & Rauch. (2020). SME 4.0: The Role of Small - and Medium - Sized Enterprises in the Digital Transformation. In Industry 4.0 for SMEs (pp. 3-36). Palgrave Macmillan.

Oztemel & Gursev. (2018). Literature review of Industry 4.0 and related technologies. Journal of Intelligent Manufacturing, 31, 127-182.

SAP. (n.d.). *What is Industry 4.0?* https://www.sap.com/india/insights/what-is-industry-4-0.html

Singapore Economic Development Board. (2019). *The Smart Industry Readiness Index*. https://www.edb.gov.sg/en/about-edb/media-releases-publications/advanced-manufacturing-release.html

Standards for Industry 4.0. (2019). http://standardsi40.sg/

Thomas & Schaefer. (2017). Industry 4.0: An Overview of Key Benefits, Technologies, and Challenges. In Cybersecurity for Industry 4.0: Analysis for Design and Manufacturing (pp. 1-33). Springer Publishing.

Vaidya, S., Ambad, P., & Bhosle, S. (2018). Industry 4.0 - A Glimpse. In Procedia Manufacturing (pp. 233 - 238). Elsevier B.V. Publishing.

ADDITIONAL READING

Tortora, A. M. R., Maria, A., Valentina, D. P., Iannone, R., & Pianese, C. (2021). A survey study on Industry 4.0 readiness level of Italian small and medium enterprises. *Procedia Computer Science*, *180*, 744–753. doi:10.1016/j.procs.2021.01.321

KEY TERMS AND DEFINITIONS

Augmentation: Addition and expansion of current dimensions to another dimension for better visualization.

Digitalization: Proper usage of digital technologies to invoke a change in an organization to provide a better revenue and more opportunities for improvement.

Downtime: Time during which an operation is not carried out in a machine due to some failure or maintenance repairs.

Economy: A production area in which manufacturing process and production along with supply chain work inter-dependently to provide finished products to the society.

Quantum Computing: Computation technique that implements the quantum mechanics phenomena.

Supply Chain: From the product manufacturing stage to product delivery stage the sequence of activities and individuals involved makes a supply chain.

Uptime: Time during which the machine provides maximum output by proper operative procedures.

Chapter 9
A Comprehensive Survey on Information Diffusion Models for Social Media Text:
Social Media Analytics

A. M. Abirami

 https://orcid.org/0000-0002-7957-5143

Thiagarjar College of Engineering, India

S. Sumitra

 https://orcid.org/0000-0002-0461-9789

Indian Institute of Space Science and Technology, India

ABSTRACT

People use social media platforms like Facebook, Twitter, and blog sites for expressing their views and criticising the products purchased and movies watched. They use these platforms for getting information like blood donation requirements and job opportunities. During the disastrous situations like floods and earthquakes, these platforms act as powerful media for passing messages to all people. During this COVID-19 pandemic period, all social media platforms are effectively used by all businesses for the instant communication and interactions between the groups of people. In all these scenarios, the information gets diffused and reaches different levels of people. Sometimes this diffusion gives positive aspects to the readers; sometimes it creates negative impacts to them, which has its own cascading effects. It becomes essential to monitor the rate of flow of information and stop spreading the fake or false messages. The application of suitable graph network modelling and theories would support this research issue and recommend the appropriate model for the social media data.

DOI: 10.4018/978-1-6684-8145-5.ch009

Copyright © 2023, IGI Global. Copying or distributing in print or electronic forms without written permission of IGI Global is prohibited.

INTRODUCTION

The COVID-19 pandemic increased the number of social media users worldwide in recent days. Data science has a significant role in social media data analytics. Social media becomes the prominent forum for most of the business wherein they adopt digital marketing strategies to attract the new customers and retain the old customers (Darwiesh, 2022). Social media accumulates a large amount of data both in structured or unstructured formats. It becomes the data source for big data analytics like trend analysis, market analysis, sentiment analysis and so on. Data science techniques like data mining, machine learning, deep learning, Artificial Intelligence (AI) and Natural Language Processing (NLP) are widely used in social media analytics. For example, if a company wants to study its consumer behavior to predict its market, then clustering and regression techniques play a crucial role in this forecasting analysis. Social media companies use AI and NLP techniques to analyze users' profile and their behavior. They develop intelligent algorithms to recognize people in pictures and for content development.

Social media analytics is the process of gathering data from social media platforms like twitter, Facebook, LinkedIn, Reddit and infer information from them. This analytics is highly helpful for businesses in their decision making processes and tracking their performance (Trifiro, 2022). It is not only the count of likes and dislikes, tweets and retweets, and so on. It requires the support of web crawlers which collect data from different channels based on the search queries, then pre-processed, modeled and analyzed for further interpretation.

The success or failure of a new product launch, movie release and others depends on how people react on social media platforms. The bad experience of customer service spread very fast whereas the good messages spread slowly. Organizations have to continuously monitor their brand values and public perception in social media in order to sustain in the market (Chaudhary, 2021). Governments start monitoring the wellbeing of their people and their emotions for the launch of new policies or regulations through social media text and its dashboard (Ismail, 2022). Sometimes, fake news or rumors which spread in internet or social media badly hit the business (Gao, 2022). Machine learning techniques can be used for detection of fake news and the business may take corrective and preventive measures at the right time to protect their customers (Kausar, 2022).

Cyberbullying becomes a serious issue now-a-days in social media platforms. People send abusive or harmful messages or attachments to other users through these digital platforms, which in turn creates psychological impact to the receivers. Social media analytics specific to these type of harassments, comments or tweets along with Natural Language Processing (NLP) algorithms and machine learning techniques like Bayesian analysis help them to trace those senders and it is possible to do further investigations (Perez, 2023; Kausar, 2022).

Social media becomes more active during elections, final matches in sports, new movie release, and so on. During these days, the users may express their own views and opinions in these platforms. Either it may trigger the reactions of followers in the positive way or in the negative way. This cascading effect or information diffusion in the social network depends on the network topology and who spreads the information. It becomes inevitable to perform social media analytics in these data and inform the appropriate stakeholder at the right time, which helps to take suitable preventive measures.

Benefits of Social Media Analytics

Social media text and its analytics can be better utilized in the productive way for the following reasons:

- To understand the present trend among the buyers
- To ensure whether the selling point is reached the public correctly
- To perform sentiment analysis on the products and services and predict market
- To perform market study and identify the product values and the gaps in features w.r.t competitors
- To understand whether any external factor impact the product performance

Product insights obtained by social media analytics are used by businesses in changing their strategies in product development, customer experience, operational efficiency and competitor analysis.

Figure 1. Impact of social media in global market
Source: www.alltheresearch.com/report/5/social-media-analytics-market

As per the AllTheResearch report on the global social media analytics market for the period 2016-2023, Northern America dominated this market from the beginning whereas Asia-Pacific region started showing progress since 2021, as shown in Figure 1. The growth of social media analytics is used for brand promotion among the competitors.

Types of Social Media Analytics

Businesses have to select the right social network for promoting their products and services. Facebook is used by all age groups whereas Instagram is used only by teenagers; LinkedIn and Twitter are professionally used by many people. Organizations collect and analyze users' data from different social networks to improve their business strategies and decisions. They make use of this information to understand the present trends and the influential factors of business. The different types of social media analytics are discussed as follows:

Performance: Social media analytics support business by tracking the data and the interactions between the users. By counting the number of likes, retweets or shares, the companies can estimate their Return On Investment (ROI) of their marketing efforts through social media. They can analyze their marketing strategies which worked effectively and change their style for strategies not working for them. The performance of marketing teams can be assessed as well by this social media analytics.

Customer Engagement: It's very important for the business to understand its target customers rightly irrespective of small, medium or large scale business (Trifiro, 2022). It helps to place the products or services in the right place where they are looking for, which in turn get favorable customer experiences. The companies make use of user interactions over time in different platforms and measure themselves whether their customers are engaged properly, whether there is an increase in the number of customers and so on. If the content is posted to the right targeted audience in social networks, then the companies can save money in their business promotional activities.

Market Analysis: The companies can compare their performance with their competitors and measure their sustainability in the market. Artificial Intelligence (AI) based tools and techniques shall be used in their sites for performing benchmarking, automated decision making and for increasing the business performance. The teams can measure their performance by analyzing the number of clicks, cost generated by advertisements, etc.

Sentiment Analysis: It analyzes the review comments given by the customers. It helps to retain the customers and attract the potential customers. There are possibilities that the fake or spam messages may defame the product or services. The companies have to take necessary precautionary measures to alleviate these serious issues, inform the customers timely and improve the perception of people.

Social Media Analytics Tools

There are many free and commercial tools available for performing social media analytics, especially social media marketing. They help the companies to create performance reports and dashboards which can be used by the business to revisit their strategies and improve decision making process. These tools help the business by giving information like the best product in the year, whether the particular social media is useful for their business, and so on.

Google Analytics is a free tool useful for business depending on the websites. Businesses can set up to receive reports like the most influential social media platform, the favorable content, market segments with demographics of customer, and ROI of business through social media marketing. Top social media platforms provide in-built tools; Facebook Insights provide competitor intelligence and customer behavior analysis but lack in sentiment analysis. Twitter Analytics tells about the most successful tweets, breakdown of user details and the trending tweets; however, twitter does not allow to contact the particular user through messages. Pinterest Analytics and Instagram Insights gives key insights about followers and traffic that the websites get. YouTube Analytics provides video analytics and helps to support business earnings. LinkedIn Analytics gives basic information with demographic details of users. Hootsuite Analytics is one of the prominent commercial tools used by business managers to learn more about audience growth rate, profile reach, analysis on followers, and so on.

Generic Processes in Social Media Analytics

Social media analytics include various processes like goal setting, data collection, text analytics using suitable algorithmic techniques and visualizations, as shown in Figure 2.

Figure 2. Social media analytics processes

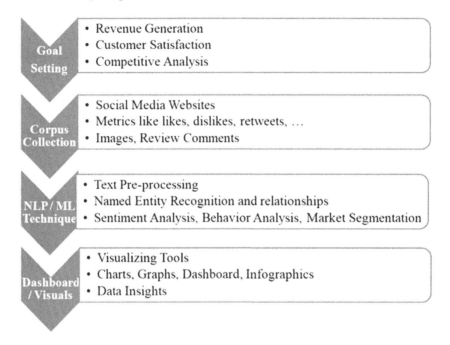

Goals can range from improving the revenue of the company to addressing the customer issues. Corpus collection has to be focused in the relevant social media sites like YouTube video comments, Facebook chats, Amazon/Google reviews, blogs, etc., based on the objectives set using the suitable search terms. Natural Language Processing (NLP) and Machine Learning (ML) techniques are used in text pre-processing, in extracting the entities involved in the discussions and their relationships. Different analytics like behavior analysis, sentiment analysis on the products, etc., are performed on the extracted data. The inferred data is visualized in dashboards or as infographics, which provide information in a more precise way (Andrayani, 2019). These techniques play a vital role in bringing out the insights. Graph and network analysis along with NLP/ML algorithms are widely used in social media analytics, which are detailed in the subsequent sections.

MOTIVATION

Large amount and variety of data is available in social media. Big data analytics in this data is possible with the use of graph and machine learning algorithms. The social networks analysis makes the researchers focus on the type of social interactions that the users have, the amount of information propagating in the network, the time needed to reach all nodes in the network, how well that it provides entertainment to the users and so on. Suitable model has to be selected for the research purpose among the different social network analysis models. This chapter explored a variety of research issues from different research articles and summarized the social network models, use of application of machine learning or deep learning algorithms and the metrics adopted in them.

BACKGROUND

Social media becomes very dynamic now-a-days. It helps the users to create content as well as to interact with other users. People use internet forums, blogs, wikis, podcasts and other medias to express their views. These web resources capture the pulse of human kind directly, which in turn can be analyzed to get more insights. Social media data is rich and very big by having text, images and videos of billions of users. This big data analytics supports in predicting the user behavior, their preferences, and present trends from the large voluminous social media data.

Social media analytics involves graph theory and network analysis. This section details the basic concepts of graph theory, metrics and information diffusion models. Entities in the dataset usually form the Nodes in the graph and the relationship between the entities form the Edges. In a Facebook network structure, if user A gives comments for user B's post, then A and B form the nodes connected by a directed edge from A to B. Figure 3 shows the simple social network structure where each node represents the user and edge represents that two users have some common attributes or relationships. Information gets propagated or diffused in the network starting from the node A. All grey colored nodes in Figure 3 received the information from their neighbors. Among 14 nodes in the network, 10 nodes received information. It means that information is diffused deep into the network.

Figure 3. Information diffusion in social network

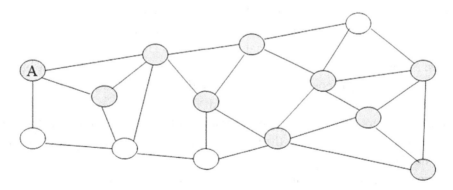

Nodes have certain properties like weight, size, degree (number of followers), etc. Similarly, edges have attributes like strength, direction, etc. These two basic elements nodes and edges describe various phenomenon like viral marketing, topmost post, trending topic, etc.

Centrality Measures

Centrality measures are very important for understanding the networks. Each metric works differently and specifies the importance of nodes present in the graph. They are:

Degree Centrality: The number of links that each node has. It tells how many neighbor nodes present with direct connections. It is useful when there is a need to identify the most popular node which can spread information widely and quickly to all other nodes. Further, this metric can be used to get a few more additional information like number of incoming and outgoing links.

Betweenness Centrality: Number of times a node lies in the shortest path between the nodes. The node which has this measure higher acts as a bridge between other nodes. The shortest paths for all nodes are computed and then the count of occurrences of each node in all paths is determined. This metric is useful to identify the influential nodes in the network. If it is high, it tells that there exists one powerful node which dominates the entire network or an intermediate node between two or more groups.

Closeness Centrality: It is the number which tells how close the nodes are to each other, based on the shortest path values. This measure is also used to determine the influential node which assists in passing the information to the remaining nodes quickly. It helps to identify the good broadcaster nodes in the network.

EigenCentrality: It measures the node's influence based on the number of links it has with other nodes in the network. It considers how well its neighbors are connected to each other. This metric helps to determine how quickly the influential node can pass the information to other nodes.

PageRank: It is similar to the EigenCentrality measure. It determines how wide the information can be reached in a larger network. It assigns a score to each node based on its links, its neighbor's links, direction and weight. Links pass information in one direction with different amounts of influence, by which number of citations and authoritativeness can be measured.

Social Media Metrics

Social media metrics help the business to keep them on the right track and advise them to make decisions. This allows them to change their business strategy according to the target audience and keep their brand value positively. Some of the recent social media metrics are:

Impressions: Number of times the content is seen by the users. For example, if the business has 100 followers, and each user sees the content two times, then the business has 200 impressions. It is a very important measure to create awareness about the brand.

Reach: Number of users who have seen the content. For example, if the business has 100 followers, and each user sees the content two times, then the reach is 500 only. If the business wants to reach the new users, they need to focus on this metric.

Audience Growth Rate: Refers to the time in which the number of followers grows. Businesses can set the time-bounded goal like to reach 20% users in the next two months. It is an important metric as it gives the information whether the content is reaching the audience. If not, the content may be changed for advertisement.

Engagement Rate: Ratio of number of engagements and impressions or reach. Number of engagements is determined by the number of likes, comments, and shares on the content. This metric gives the quality of content and tells how the audience is actively involved in it. These engaged users can easily be converted into customers. This metric plays the role of business growth as it will increase the impressions and reach.

Click-Through Rate: Ratio of number of clicks on links and number of impressions. Higher the click-through rate, better the quality of content is and the users are interested in the content.

Bounce Rate: Refers to the percent of users who visit the business website and do not click the links for navigation. Lower bounce rate is preferred. If it is high, it may result in lower engagements which in turn result in losing customers.

Average Time on Page: Refers to the time spent by each user on the web page. It is another means of checking for the quality of content. If the site has highly engaging content, the users remain in the website for a longer period of time. Google analytics is more helpful in tracking these metrics.

Referrals: These are the sources from where the users come to this website. This metric gives an idea to the business which social media platform is more helpful in directing the users to the product website. If more users access the website from their Facebook account, then the business has to take more efforts in using this platform instead of other media.

Cost per Click: The amount of money spent on the media advertisements. If it is very high but the referrals are low, then the marketing strategy has to be adjusted. Return on Investment (ROI) is better, when the amount spent is lesser than the sales revenue generated. The business has to focus on their campaigns in order to improve their ROI.

Response Rate and Response Time: Response rate refers to the percent of users that the business responds to. If the business responds to 25 comments or messages out of 50, then the response rate of the business is 50%. Response time refers to the time taken for responding to the users. These two metrics are the most significant metrics, as they build and sustain the customer relationships. The business may set the time bounded goal like 100% response rate and 8 hours response time.

The metrics such as impressions, reach, and audience growth rate says about the quantum of awareness that the public has about the products or services given by the business. The other set of metrics like engagement rate, click-through rate, bounce rate, and average time on page talk about the user engagement in the business. The metrics like referrals and cost-per-click give information about conversions. Finally, the metrics like response rate and response time talks about the care and concern that the business gives it to their customers.

LITERATURE SURVEY

Social media analytics involve network analysis models which analyze the interactions between the actors involved in the process. The information diffusion model describes how the information is spread in the network and how the information is exchanged between the nodes in the network. The network topology and its parameters decide the rate and intensity of the diffusion process. The amount of information passing in the network paves the way for application of machine learning algorithms for knowledge extraction. These algorithms are used in network analysis such as spam detection, link prediction, user profile classification, trend analysis, cluster detection, sentiment analysis and so on. This section describes the various research work carried out in social media platforms and how the analytics is useful for the social and business purposes.

Taxidou et al. (2013) explored real time data analysis methods for twitter data. They used twitter datasets like Olympics 2012 in London, US elections 2012 and Super bowl 2013. All these have more than

8 lakh retweets and have large complex network structures. They concluded that the lifetime of cascades differ and they might last for days or upto years. Davis et al. (2013) explored Partial Differential Equation for developing information diffusion model for twitter data set. Chae et al. (2014) developed interactive visual tool using the spatiotemporal data received from social media platforms during the disaster events like hurricanes and tornadoes and supported for evacuation planning and other investigations.

Farasat et al. (2015) used various probabilistic graphical models like Bayesian networks, Markov models and Exponential Random Graph models and their applications in social network analysis. They suggested that conditional independence and probabilistic models could be used for social network applications. Chen et al. (2016) used geo-tagged social media data and analyzed the patterns in user movements using the transportation methods. Al-Taei et al. (2017) used different information diffusion models like two-step flow model and deterministic compartment models (SIS, SIR, SI, SIRS) for analyzing the better model for propagating the information in the social networks. They used different scenarios and explained metrics adopter rate, amount of exposure, and critical mass for the information diffusion models. Li et al. (2017) analyzed the amount of information diffusion in social networks.

Chang et al. (2018) detailed the different information diffusion models using the three practical problems like authority and influence evaluation, influence maximization, and information source detection. They used different graph algorithms to improve the efficiency of influence spread evaluation in the diffusion models for various social network datasets. They concluded that influence maximization is much needed for viral marketing and source detection is needed for rumor source tracing. They also listed future research directions in social media analytics. Qiang et al. (2019) proposed Linear Threshold (LT) learning model and Random Walk (RW) learning model for synthetic data for different network topologies and for different cascaded generations, where random walk learning model outperformed well for the dataset considered. They built a large network using the Lerman Digg 2009 dataset and applied the same two learning models and mixed learning models using the approximate Neural Network (NN) methods, where the speed of computation becomes faster in the later approach. However, Linear Threshold Neural Network (LTNN) converges earlier than Random Walk Neural Network (RWNN) and also needs less memory space for computation.

Li et al. (2019) explored different information diffusion models like basic epidemic models and influence models for online social networks. They listed the challenges as follows: identification of weak nodes, competitive influence maximization, using sentiments/emotions for influence, etc. They concluded that Independent Cascade (IC), Linear Threshold (LT) and Game Theory (GT) diffusion models are more appropriate for research applications in social media analytics. Ansari et al. (2020) used social media platforms and mobile devices for collaborative learning and concluded that it has great impact in building the relationship with peers. Li et al. (2021) reviewed research work done in social network structures. They explored the use of different graph models like exponential random graph model, small-world network model, and scale-free network model in simple, medium and complex network structures. They presented their observations that more research focused on single and static network structures and there are lots of research scope available for dynamic and complex network structures.

Sinha et al. (2021) proposed information diffusion methodology for predicting the rate of information spread in the temporal domain of social media structures. They used large complex network datasets like Florentine marriages, Facebook ego network and email network structures. They experimented their idea in three different states like healthy, susceptible and infected with three different centrality measurements like minimum, average and maximum. They concluded that the nodes with higher degree of centrality communicate the information faster than the other types of nodes. This epidemic model is useful and it predicts how the information is diffused among the nodes in the social network over the period of time. Kostygina et al. (2021) studied Instagram messages given for the topic electronic cigarettes by different account types like commercial, vape community and organic users and developed semantic network for the content.

Kumar et al. (2021) developed a forest fire-based information diffusion model for predicting the information spread in social media platforms. They used six different twitter datasets like Corona Virus, FIFA World Cup, NBA Finals, Game of Thrones S8, MeToo movement and Coachella Festival for the analysis of different diffusion models. They tried identifying the non-spreader nodes in the network by separating the nodes into different categories like empty, tree, fire and burst. They concluded that the modified forest fire model is the suitable network model for determining the spread of information in complex network data structures like twitter. Madilla et al. (2021) explored 44 different research articles on social media analytics. They identified different analytics tools, techniques and research domains that are suitable for social media analytics. They concluded that sentiment analysis and twitter platform are the most widely used among the researchers. Chaudhary et al. (2021) developed a linear predictor model for predicting the consumer behavior using their perception and attitude in social media platforms. Zakaria et. al. (2021) captured the dynamics of social process using the agent-based Action Network (AN).

Machine Learning Techniques for Social Media Analytics

Tan et al. (2019) studied the social network representation techniques and classified them into three groups like look-up tables, autoencoders and graph convolutional networks. They also discussed various research issues like dynamics, heterogeneity and scalability in networks and the application of machine learning techniques for these issues. Shi et al. (2019) developed RNN model for the detection of bursty topics which have the more capability of spreading fast in the sparse and high dimensional bigger social networks; thereby distinguished these topics from the common topics.

Ganguli et al. (2020) used different machine learning algorithms and compared their performance for social network analysis applications like detection of fake user profiles, depressed users and users' personality traits. Nurek et al. (2020) applied social network features to classification algorithms like Decision Tree, Random Forest, Neural Network and SVM for studying the organizational hierarchical structure using the manufacturing company dataset and Enron dataset. They concluded that the decision tree algorithm outperformed in the collective classification algorithm with interpretable results. Molokwu et al. (2020) developed a representation learning framework for embedded knowledge graph using Convolutional Neural Network and studied applications like node classification, link prediction and community detection.

Balaji et al. (2021) explored different machine learning algorithms for the applications like anomaly/crime/event detection, epidemics, and business intelligence and summarized their advantages and shortcomings. Abbas et al. (2021) compared the features of different machine learning algorithms while studying different applications like sentiment analysis, text classification, and fake news detection.

Fake news or rumors easily spread in the social media platforms and quickly change the mindset of readers. Kausar et al. (2022) used deep learning models like Recurrent Neural Network (RNN), Long Short-Term Memory (LSTM) and Bidirectional Encoder Representations from Transformers (BERT) to handle the sequencing of data and for setting the context in the fake news detection. Gao et al. (2022) used SIR model and fractional differential equation technique to determine the rumor propagation effect in social media. They concluded that if people are educated about rumors, then there would be less effect in the propagation. Wanda (2022) used special non-linear activation function namely RunMax in CNN architecture for the identification of fake user profile detection.

Ismail et al. (2022) developed an analytic framework for measuring the wellbeing of the public using the social media data. They used word embedding models like BERT and predicted whether the public supported the government decisions on policies by visualizing the analyzed results in the dashboard. Perez et al. (2023) studied the hateful and bullying messages in the Twitter for the time period 2019-2021. They built the Bayesian time series model using the NLP techniques and the pre-trained model, and concluded that the bullying message count was reduced during the covid-19 pandemic period.

INFORMATION DIFFUSION MODELS

Social media analytics is performed in two different ways: how the information is diffused in the network and what are the rich interactions. Information in social networks flow across the nodes like viral disease spread among the people. It is contagious and dynamic by absorbing the state and behavior of neighbors. This spread of information makes the interactions between some nodes higher. These rich interactions help in the study of user behavior and market analytics. Many social media analytics models have been developed to understand the information diffusion and the strength of interactions in the social network. Classification of information diffusion models in social networks is shown in Figure 4.

Figure 4. Types of information diffusion models
Source: Kumar et al. (2021)

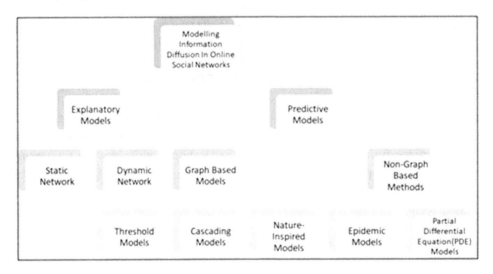

Explanatory and predictive models are widely used by social media analysts. Information in the network spreads like an epidemic spread among the people. It is more common that information can easily spread from the infected users to non-infected users, making the spread wide. Users of epidemic models are of two types: (1) infected users - users infected by disease, (2) susceptible users – users may get the disease in near future.

Epidemic Models

Epidemic models are evolved considering the different types of users in the network (Li et al., 2017). These models are inherited from the mathematical models developed for epidemiology by A.G. McKendrick in 1927. These deterministic compartment models assume the closed population with three classes like Susceptible (S), Infected (I) and Recovered or Removed (R). Birth, death and migration of people do not change the total population of the model. S(t) is the number of healthy people at time t, they are not yet infected but susceptible to infection. I(t) is the number of infected people at time t and capable of spreading the disease. R(t) is the number of recovered people from the infection at time t.

1. Susceptible-Infected (SI) model is the simplest model in which the infected persons spread the disease to other persons (Pastorsatorras, 2001). The SI model is explained as follows:

$S \rightarrow I$

$S(t) + I(t) = N$

where N is the total population. β refers to the transmission rate of infection per person in unit time. Tc = 1/ β is the average time for getting infected. βS(t) people would get infection at any instant t. The total number of infected persons in population after δt time is given by

$$I(t + \delta t) = I(t) + \beta \frac{S(t)}{N} I(t) \delta t \tag{1}$$

The increase in infected persons is given by:

$$\frac{dI(t)}{dt} = \beta \frac{S(t)}{N} I(t) \tag{2}$$

Similarly, the total number of susceptible persons in population after δt time is given by

$$S(t + \delta t) = S(t) - \beta \frac{S(t)}{N} I(t) \delta t \tag{3}$$

The change in susceptible persons is given by:

$$\frac{dS(t)}{dt} = -\beta \frac{S(t)}{N} I(t) \tag{4}$$

The SI models is represented in fraction of population as follows:

$$s(t) = \frac{S(t)}{N}, \ i(t) = \frac{I(t)}{N}, \text{ and s(t)+i(t)=1}$$

Rewriting the equations (2) and (4) in fraction forms as,

$$\frac{di(t)}{dt} = \beta s(t) i(t) \tag{5}$$

$$\frac{ds(t)}{dt} = -\beta s(t) i(t) \tag{6}$$

Substituting s(t)=1–i(t) in the equation (5),

$$\frac{di(t)}{dt} = \beta (1 - i(t)) i(t) \tag{7}$$

Initial infected population i(t=0) is given as i_0. Solving the differential equation (7) gives the logistic growth function, as shown in equation (8)

$$i(t) = \frac{i_0}{i_0 + (1 - i_0) e^{-\beta t}} \tag{8}$$

Figure 5. Behavior of SI model
Source: www.researchgate.net/profile/Mikayel-Poghosyanpublication:320508832

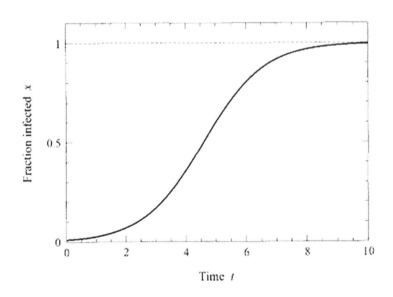

The behavior of SI model is well explained in Figure 5. As t→∞, $i(t)$→1 and $s(t)$→0; because the term $(1-i_0)e^{-\beta t}$ in the equation (8) is zero. It means that whole population is infected. When t is small, there is an exponential growth which is dictated by the term $e^{-\beta t}$ and i_0 is very small. As time passes, there is less number of s(t) in that compartment and hence the growth is less or it is stopped.

2. Susceptible-Infected-Susceptible (SIS) is the second compartment model in which nodes not having immunity have the more chance to get infected again (Newman et al., 2005).

S→I→S

S(t) + I(t) = N

β refers to the transmission rate of infection and γ is the recovery rate. $T_r = 1/\gamma$ is the average time for recovery. $\beta S(t)$ people would get infected and $\gamma I(t)$ would get recovered at any instant t. SIS model is expressed as:

$$\frac{di(t)}{dt} = \beta s(t)i(t) - \gamma i(t) \tag{9}$$

$$\frac{ds(t)}{dt} = -\beta s(t)i(t) + \gamma i(t) \tag{10}$$

Substituting s(t)=1−i(t) in the equation (9),

$$\frac{di(t)}{dt} = \beta(1-i(t))i(t) - \gamma i(t) \tag{11}$$

The equation (11) is simplified to

$$\frac{di}{dt} = (\beta - \gamma - i)i \tag{12}$$

Initial infected population i(t=0) is given as i_0. Solving the differential equation (12) gives the infection function, as shown in equation (13)

$$i(t) = \left(1 - \frac{\gamma}{\beta}\right)\frac{C}{C + e^{-(\beta-\gamma)t}} \tag{13}$$

where $C = \dfrac{\beta i_0}{\beta - \gamma - \beta i_0}$

The SIS model depends on the ratio of β and γ. When t is small, there is an exponential growth in infection where the recovery is very meager. As time passes and t→∞, when $\beta > \gamma$, $i(t) \to \left(1 - \dfrac{\gamma}{\beta}\right)$. It means that some constant fraction of population remains infected. The disease may persist for a longer time or few persons would remain infected. When $\beta < \gamma$, $i(t) \to i_0 e^{(\beta - \gamma)t} \to 0$. It means more and more population get recovered and results in the end of epidemic after certain time.

3.   Susceptible-Infected-Recovered (SIR) is the third compartment model in which an infected node which gets recovered from the disease, is removed from the model (Liu et al., 2014).

S→I→R

S(t) + I(t) + R(t) = N

β refers to the transmission rate of infection and γ is the recovery rate. $T_r = 1/\gamma$ is the average time for recovery. $\beta S(t)$ people would get infected and $\gamma I(t)$ would get recovered at any instant t. SIR model is expressed as:

$$\frac{di(t)}{dt} = \beta s(t) i(t) - \gamma i(t) \tag{14}$$

$$\frac{ds(t)}{dt} = -\beta s(t) i(t) \tag{15}$$

$$\frac{dr(t)}{dt} = \gamma i(t) \tag{16}$$

Number of people recovered are reduced from the infectious compartment, as shown in the equation (14). The negative sign in the equation (15) shows that the number of susceptible people is getting reduced as some amount of population is getting recovered. In SIR model,

s(t) + i(t) +r(t) = 1   (17)

This SIR model is complicated than other two models SI and SIS. It cannot be solved by analytical methods whereas it can be solved by numerical methods, that is by identifying the parameters which impact the model the most and by changing their values. This can be tried by representing the susceptible people in terms of recovered people and then solving for the time taken for recovery. SIR model is represented as follows:

Using the equation (16), the equation (15) is rewritten as

$$\frac{ds(t)}{dt} = -\beta s(t)\frac{dr(t)}{dt}\frac{1}{\gamma} \tag{18}$$

$$s = s_0 e^{\frac{-\beta r}{\gamma}} \tag{19}$$

Substituting (17) and (19) in (16), we get

$$\frac{dr(t)}{dt} = \gamma\left(1 - r - s_0 e^{\frac{-\beta r}{\gamma}}\right) \tag{20}$$

Solving for t, we get,

$$t = \frac{1}{\gamma}\int_0^r \frac{dr}{1 - r - s_0 e^{\frac{-\beta r}{\gamma}}} \tag{21}$$

In equation (20), as t→∞, the rate of recovery r_∞ becomes constant. Hence, $\dfrac{dr(t)}{dt}$ becomes 0. So,

$$1 - r_\infty - s_0 e^{\frac{-\beta r_\infty}{\gamma}} = 0$$

Rewriting this, we have, $r_\infty = 1 - s_0 e^{\frac{-\beta r_\infty}{\gamma}}$. Substituting the initial parameters like r_0=0, i_0=c/N *(some constant value)*, then s_0=1- c/N, which can be approximated to 1.

$$r_\infty = 1 - e^{\frac{-\beta r_\infty}{\gamma}} \tag{22}$$

The model completely depends on the ratio β/γ, which is further explained by the Figure 6.

Figure 6 explains the scenario when ratio of infection to recovery (β/γ) is greater than 1 and initial infected people (i_0) is minimum. For example, if β/γ is 4, it means that recovery rate is much smaller; on an average, a single infected person infects 4 new people. In Figure 6, the green curve depicts the rate of infection. It increases exponentially, it reaches the maximum point and drops down slowly. The red line represents the status of healthy people. As time passes, more people get infected and the curve declines. The blue curve denotes the recovered or removed people from the population. Figure 6 shows that almost all people recovered which means that the entire population got infected. After the saddle point in the green curve, the rate of infection declines very fast. At the same time, the rate of recovery is

Figure 6. Behavior of SIR Model
Source: www.en.wikipedia.org/wiki/SIR_trajectory.png

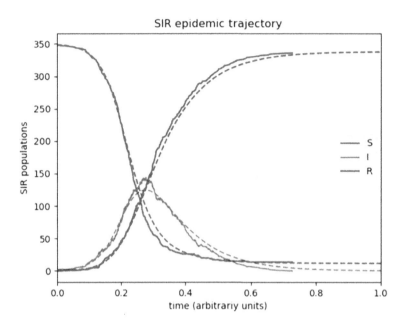

faster. On the other hand, if β/γ is maintained less than 1 (by taking special measures to avoid contacts), on an average, a single infected person infects less than 1 person; the recovery rate can be increased. The diseases can be brought under control and the epidemics may come to an end earlier.

Information diffusion in social network is mapped to epidemic models. However, the factors like time, relationship between the nodes, content and the network structure impact the model. More research is happening in this field by evolving more models. Susceptible-Infected-Recovered-Susceptible (SIRS) model was evolved assuming that a cured user may get infection again after a certain time period. Susceptible-Infected-Recovered-Deceased (SIRD) model was developed to differentiate the recovered people from the deceased people. Susceptible-Infected-Recovered-Vaccinated (SIRV) model was developed in order to consider the vaccinated people in the recovered population.

Epidemic social network models explain the behavior of networks and support to get insights out of them. Based on the information in hand and the objectives of the task, the data can be modeled into a network structure and inferences like how deep the information is diffused, the rate of transmission and the like can be brought out.

Predictive Models

This type of social network models shall be used for prediction. For example, after releasing the movie trailer in social media, the production team can decide whether the movie will be a hit or flop by analyzing the rate of information passed among the followers. Predictive social network models forecast the expected outcomes by performing information extraction from the existing datasets and determine the patterns using the probability distributions. These are determined by various measures like strength of ties between the nodes and number of connected components. Three different models like Independent Cascade (IC), Linear Threshold (LT) and Game Theory (GT) models fall under this category.

1. Independent Cascade (IC) model is a stochastic information diffusion model. It means that the model depends on the probability distribution of information received by the nodes from the random nodes. The information cascades in the network. Each node has two states: the node is *active*, if it received information already; the node is *inactive* if it has to receive information from others. Each of the neighbor in the network has a separate chance to activate the node or not. This process is run in discrete steps. Initially, few nodes are identified (say seed nodes) and are given information. These nodes become active now and try to influence their neighbors who are inactive in different iterations. If a node fails to activate another node, then it will not be given another chance. The success of making other node active depends on the strength of relationship with their neighbors. The inactive node v is activated by the active node u with the probability $P_{u,v}$, then the node v becomes active node. The process terminates when all the nodes become active or no active nodes exist to influence remaining inactive nodes. For example, the Covid-19 infection among the people is independent and probable; it has cascading effect by spreading the disease to others by chance. This model is used to study the influence behavior of social networks and is mostly influenced by the senders.

2. Linear Threshold (LT) model defines the behavior such that the node gets activated only if the cumulative influence from its neighbors is greater than the threshold value. In this model, each node has activation threshold at time t. Assume the node v is inactive at time t. If neighbor nodes of v influence node v and if its cumulative influence is greater than its original activation threshold, then v becomes active at time $t+1$. For buying a new mobile phone, the user may read multiple reviews and comments to make a decision to buy or not. Like IC model, this model is used to explore the influential node in the social networks and mostly the influential nodes are of type receiver nodes.

3. Game Theory (GT) model is the strategy based model to maximize the profit. The information is either spread or not in the network based on the factors like cost, benefit and the like. Human strategies while playing and the cooperative gaming theories are widely explored and studied in directed social networks (Pagan, 2019; Molinero 2021).

In all these models, the behavior of the node is studied either individually or combined with its neighbors. The dynamic behavior of nodes are studied by building the robust social network model.

Influence Models

Information diffusion social network models are used predominantly to perform the influence analysis. It is done in three different ways – (1) individual influence, (2) community influence, and (3) influence maximization (Li et al., 2015).

Individual influence refers to opinion-leader research. One node in the network, designated as *leader*, is the sole responsible for information diffusion. In this model, the diffusion is based on the factors like network structure, attributes and behavior of neighbor nodes, content, and others. It uses centrality measures and ranks by PageRank algorithm. It gives better results for smaller networks.

Community influence refers to the influential behavior of group of nodes in the network. Community in the social network is referred by the group of nodes with common attributes and behavior. Detecting the existence of community in the network is the key research issue, and it influences the information diffusion to the densely connected nodes.

Influence maximization research focused on finding the seed node which influences the information diffusion to other nodes in the network. Many researchers use different existing models to determine the most influential node in the network, so that the social media marketing is performed comfortably.

RESULT SUMMARY

Social media analytics become inevitable in this 21st century. It becomes necessary to include automated analytics tools in the company's website. It periodically does the search and analyzes the comments and updates the business dashboard. Some of the challenges existing in social media analytics are as follows:

1. People use freehand writing for expressing their views. Sometimes, the automated tools may find it difficult to identify the real sentiment along with the context used by the user.
2. The number of likes or dislikes do not capture the accurate information about customer engagement or conversions. This lack of information impacts the business to a greater extent.
3. Mostly, younger generations are active in social media. The inactive or dormant users of social media, aged people who neglect social media and other similar users miss the campaigns and other branding information posted in the social media. This incomplete picture impacts the business as it is much harder for them to reach this kind of audience.
4. Access restrictions to user profiles, fake data add irrelevance to analysis and lower the quality in social media analytics. In spite of these issues and challenges, most of the companies use the power of social media analytics aptly to reach the target audience at the right time with the right amount of information.

Researchers used different social network datasets and explored different network topology and suitable network models for analysis. Table 1 summarizes the social media analytics research along with the dataset and metrics used in their research.

Table 1. Research summary of social media analytics

Author(s)	Purpose	Dataset	Network Model	Metric	Remarks
Taxidou et al. (2013)	Proposes real time analysis methods for information diffusion in social media networks	Olympics 2012 in London, US elections 2012, Super bowl 2013	Cascade Model	Size, Shape and temporal measures, influence factors	Rate of interactions indicates the rate of diffusion, hence the prediction.
Farasat et al. (2015)	Explores the possibilities of using probabilistic graph models in social network analysis	TREC twitter dataset 2011	Probabilistic Graph Model	Suitability of Graph models for applications like link prediction, viral marketing, etc	Conditional independence and probabilistic models can be used for social network applications
Al-Taei et al. (2017)	Identifies the suitable diffusion model for the propagation of information	Social media text	Two-step Flow model, Epidemic model	Adoption rate, Amount of exposure Critical mass,	Epidemic model is suitable for information diffusion in social networks

continues on following page

Table 1. Continued

Author(s)	Purpose	Dataset	Network Model	Metric	Remarks
Li, et al. (2017)	Compares explanatory and predictive information diffusion models	Social Networks Dataset	Epidemic model, Influence Model, Predictive model	Influence factors, Strong/Weak nodes	Independent Cascade (IC), Linear Threshold (LT) and Game Theory (GT) can be used for research applications
Chang et al. (2018)	Proposes authority and influence evaluation, influence maximization, and information source detection	Stanford large network dataset, Aminer, Social computing data repository, KONECT	Independent Cascade, Linear Threshold, Epidemic models	Influence factors	Influence maximization is much needed for viral marketing and source detection is for rumor source tracing.
Qiang et al. (2019)	Learns diffusion influence between the pair of users	Lerman Digg 2009 dataset	Linear Threshold Learning model, Random walk Learning model	Accuracy	Approximate approaches in random walk learning model gives better performance
Li et al. (2021)	Reviews research work done on simple, medium, complex network structures	No data used	exponential random graph model, small-world network model, and scale-free network model	Type of network structures Type of network models,	Many researches done on single network structure and there exists more research scope in complex network structures.
Sinha, et al. (2021)	Predicts the rate of information diffusion in the network for the given time with the set of initial parameters	Fifteenth-century Florentine marriages, Facebook Ego Network, Email networks	Bass and SIS	average path length, average degree, betweenness centrality, diameter, sub-graphs and cluster coefficient	Diffusion depends on the degree of centrality value
Kumar et al. (2021)	Modeled information diffusion in social network as forest fire	Corona Virus, FIFA World Cup, NBA Finals, Game of Thrones S8, MeToo movement, Coachella Festival	Independent cascades (IC) model, susceptible-infected-recovered (SIR) model, modified forest-fire (MFF) model	User-follower relationship, Topic significance	Differentiated the users who spread the information from those who are not involving in the diffusion process
Madilla et al. (2021)	Reviews research articles for the use of social media analytics	No data used	Graph models	Tools usage, Platform usage	Identified different analytics tools, techniques and research domains for social media analytics
Kostygina (2021)	Active account types detection	Electronic Cigarette messages in Instagram	Graph model with community detection	Number of followers, Use of hash tags, Number of Clusters	Community exists in the network depending on the messages being discussed
Wanda (2022)	Fake user profile detection	User profile data	Graph with CNN	Precision and Recall	Non-linear activation function RunMax improves accuracy in the model

Emerging Research Issues and Challenges

The scope for using big data technologies for social media analytics can be explored to make the life of social media users easier and comfortable. Some of the research issues are highlighted in this section:

1. Big data analytics in healthcare domain can be amalgamated with social media analytics. Multimodal data obtained from different social media platforms can be analyzed on daily basis and news feed can be generated and reported to Governments, hospitals or other forums for the public vicinity. These type of analytics is helpful for the epidemics like Covid-19 to control the spread and to cas-

cade the preventive information to the users. In the year 2019, China used these type of analytics and brought the diseases spread under control (Chew, 2021).

2. Big data available in social media is like a double edged sword. Differentiating the truth and false information and identifying the reliable source are much challenging tasks. Both social media platforms and the Governments have to jointly address this issue by including authenticity when the information is communicated in the network.

3. Quality and data relevance are the key challenges. Fake user profile and the spread of false information is inevitable in social media. Detection of rumors and spam messages in digital platforms are the recent research focus area.

4. Social media environment is dynamically changing. Sometimes, the privacy and anonymity of users may be disclosed to the public which will then become a serious ethical issue (Hunter, 2020).

5. Finding the right platform for branding the product and setting the goals and indicators are another challenging tasks for the company. Apart from these, the creating content which makes the audience engaged for the longer period of time is crucial issue for digital marketing and advertising. Levels of engagement differ between the high profile active users and low profile normal users. Businesses need to have different strategies to attract different types of users.

6. Users use free text for expressing their views and comments. Understanding the context and identifying the sentiments become more complex in these scenarios.

7. Game theory can be applied to understand the human behavior and their gaming strategies using small world social networks.

In spite of all these issues and challenges, social media is still an active platform for most of the users. Companies use these media as their brand ambassadors. Platforms like Facebook, WhatsApp and other payments apps linked together and perform the complete the supply chain management. Users of these platforms need to be very cautious while uploading the content, images or performing any payments.

CONCLUSION

Social media is fast growing in recent years so that people are always connected. The users of social media share information and pass on to other friends. This sharing of information creates a huge network on the internet. Various social network models can be built based on the type of network structure, the type of users and their behavior, the shared content, time that it is shared, type of relationship between the users of the network, the information may diffuse deeper or wider in the network. These characteristics of the social network creates a huge impact to the business which predominantly uses social media for their marketing and sales.

This chapter discussed importance of social media analytics, processes involved in the analytics, different types of social network analysis models along with the mathematical concepts behind them. It summarized the research work carried out in this domain and tabulated them. Various research issues and open challenges are also discussed. Social media analytics can be merged with Artificial Intelligence tools and techniques to make automated decision making and for improving business intelligence in social marketing.

ACKNOWLEDGMENT

This research work is supported by SERB Teachers Associateship For Research Excellence (TARE) fellowship (TAR/2022/000425).

REFERENCES

Abbas, A. M. (2021). Social network analysis using deep learning: Applications and schemes. *Social Network Analysis and Mining*, *11*(106), 106. Advance online publication. doi:10.100713278-021-00799-z

Al-Taie, M. Z., & Kadry, S. (2017). *Information Diffusion in Social Networks. In Python for Graph and Network Analysis*. Springer. doi:10.1007/978-3-319-53004-8

Andrayani, R., & Negara, E. S. (2019). Social Media Analytics: Data Utilization of Social Media for Research. *Journal of Information Systems and Informatics*, *1*(2), 193–205. doi:10.33557/journalisi.v1i2.23

Ansari, J. A. N., & Khan, N. A. (2020). Exploring the role of social media in collaborative learning the new domain of learning. *Smart Learning Environment*, *7*(9), 9. Advance online publication. doi:10.118640561-020-00118-7

Balaji, T. K., Annavarapu, C. S. R., & Bablani, A. (2021). Machine learning algorithms for social media analysis: A survey. *Computer Science Review*, *40*, 6–32.

Chae, J., Thom, D., Jang, Y., Kim, S., Ertl, T., & David, S. (2014). Public behavior response analysis in disaster events utilizing visual analytics of microblog data. *Computers & Graphics*, *38*, 51–60. doi:10.1016/j.cag.2013.10.008

Chang, B., Tong, X., Qi, L., & Chen, E. (2018). Study on Information Diffusion Analysis in Social Networks and Its Applications. *International Journal of Automation and Computing*, *15*(4), 377–401. doi:10.100711633-018-1124-0

Chaudhary, K., Alam, M., Al-Rakhami, M. S., & Gumaei, A. (2021). Machine learning-based mathematical modelling for prediction of social media consumer behavior using big data analytics. *Journal of Big Data*, *8*(1), 73. doi:10.118640537-021-00466-2

Chen, S., Yuan, X., Wang, Z., Guo, C., Liang, J., Wang, Z., Zhang, X., & Zhang, J. (2016). Interactive Visual Discovering of Movement Patterns from Sparsely Sampled Geo-tagged Social Media Data. *IEEE Transactions on Visualization and Computer Graphics*, *22*(1), 270–279. doi:10.1109/TVCG.2015.2467619 PMID:26340781

Chew, A. M. K., & Gunasekeran, D. V. (2021). *Social Media Big Data: The Good, The Bad, and the Ugly (Un)truths*. https://www.frontiersin.org/articles/10.3389/fdata.2021.623794/

Darwiesh, A., Alghamdi, M. I., El-Baz, A. H., & Elhoseny, M. (2022). Social Media Big Data Analysis: Towards Enhancing Competitiveness of Firms in a Post-Pandemic World. *Journal of Healthcare Engineering*, *2022*, 1–14. Advance online publication. doi:10.1155/2022/6967158 PMID:35281539

Davis, C., Ramirez, S., & Whitmore, D. (2013). *How Does News Diffuse Through Twitter? Predicting spread of information through social media using a Mathematical Model.* https://www.public.asu.edu/~fwang25/poster/Davis2013.pdf

Farasat, A., Nikolaey, A., Srihari, S. N., & Blair, R. H. (2015). Probabilistic Graphical Models in Modern Social Network Analysis. *Social Network Analysis and Mining, 5*(1), 1–28. doi:10.100713278-015-0289-6

Ganguli, R., Mehta, A., & Sen, S. (2020). A Survey on Machine Learning Methodologies in Social Network Analysis. *Proceedings of 8th International Conference on Reliability, Infocom Technologies and Optimization (Trends and Future Directions) (ICRITO)*, 484-489. 10.1109/ICRITO48877.2020.9197984

Gao, X., Liu, F., & Liu, C. (2022). Fractional-order rumor propagation model with memory effect. *Social Network Analysis and Mining, 12*(1), 159. doi:10.100713278-022-00988-4 PMID:36321165

Hunter, R. F., Gough, A., O'Kane, N., McKeown, G., Fitzpatrick, A., Walker, T., McKinley, M., Lee, M., & Kee, F. (2018). Ethical Issues in Social Media Research for Public Health. *American Journal of Public Health, 108*(3), 343–348. doi:10.2105/AJPH.2017.304249 PMID:29346005

Ismail, H., Serhani, M., Hussien, N., Elabyad, R., & Navaz, A. (2022). Public wellbeing analytics framework using social media chatter data. *Social Network Analysis and Mining, 12*(1), 163. doi:10.100713278-022-00987-5 PMID:36345490

Kausar, N., AliKhan, A., & Sattar, M. (2022). Towards better representation learning using hybrid deep learning model for fake news detection. *Social Network Analysis and Mining, 12*(1), 165. doi:10.100713278-022-00986-6

Kostygina, G., Feng, M., Czaplicki, L., Tran, H., Tulsiani, S., Perks, S. N., Emery, S., & Schillo, B. (2021). Exploring the Discursive Function of Hashtags: A Semantic Network Analysis of JUUL-Related Instagram Messages. *Social Media + Society, 7*(4). doi:10.1177/20563051211055442

Kumar, S., Saini, M., Goel, M., & Panda, B. S. (2021). Modeling information diffusion in online social networks using a modified forest-fire model. *Journal of Intelligent Information Systems, 56*(2), 355–377. doi:10.100710844-020-00623-8 PMID:33071464

Li, H., Cui, J., & Ma, J. (2015). Social influence study in online networks: A three-level review. *Journal of Computer Science and Technology, 30*(1), 184–199. doi:10.100711390-015-1512-7

Li, M., Wang, X., Gao, K., & Zhang, S. (2017). A Survey on Information Diffusion in Online Social Networks: Models and Methods. *Information (Basel), 8*(4), 118. Advance online publication. doi:10.3390/info8040118

Li, N., Huang, Q., Ge, X., He, M., Cui, S., Huang, P., Li, S., & Fung, S.-F. (2021). A Review of the Research Progress of Social Network Structure. *Complexity, 6692210*, 1–14. Advance online publication. doi:10.1155/2021/6692210

Liu, D., Yan, E. W., & Song, M. (2014). Microblog information diffusion: Simulation based on SIR model. *Journal of Beijing University of Posts and Telecommunications, 16*, 28–33.

Madilla, S. S., Dida, M. A., & Kaijage, S. (2021). A Review of Usage and Applications of Social Media Analytics. *Journal of Information Systems Engineering & Management, 6*(3), 1–10. doi:10.21601/jisem/10958

Molinero, X., & Riquelme, F. (2021). Influence decision models: From cooperative game theory to social network analysis. *Computer Science Review, 39*(1), 100343. Advance online publication. doi:10.1016/j.cosrev.2020.100343

Molokwu, B. C., & Kobti, Z. (2020). Social Network Analysis using RLVECN: Representation Learning via Knowledge-Graph Embeddings and Convolutional Neural-Network, *Proceedings of the Twenty-Ninth International Joint Conference on Artificial Intelligence (IJCAI-20)*, 5198-5199. 10.24963/ijcai.2020/739

Newman, M. E. (2005). Threshold effects for two pathogens spreading on a network. *Physical Review Letters, 95*(10), 108701. doi:10.1103/PhysRevLett.95.108701 PMID:16196976

Nurek, M., & Michalski, R. (2020). Combining Machine Learning and Social Network Analysis to Reveal the Organizational Structures. *Applied Sciences, 10*(1699), 1-43.

Pagan, N., & Dörfler, F. (2019). Game theoretical inference of human behavior in social networks. *Nature Communications, 10*(1), 5507. doi:10.103841467-019-13148-8 PMID:31796729

Pastorsatorras, R., & Vespignani, A. (2001). Epidemic spreading in scale-free networks. *Physical Review Letters, 86*(14), 3200–3203. doi:10.1103/PhysRevLett.86.3200 PMID:11290142

Perez, C., & Karmakar, S. (2023). An NLP-assisted Bayesian time-series analysis for prevalence of Twitter Cyberbullying during the COVID-19 pandemic. *Social Network Analysis and Mining, 13*(1), 51. doi:10.100713278-023-01053-4 PMID:36937491

Qiang, Z., Pasiliao, E. L., & Zheng, Q. P. (2019). Model-based learning of information diffusion in social media networks. *Applied Network Science, 4*(1), 111. doi:10.100741109-019-0215-3

Shi, L., Du, J., Liang, M., & Kosrtm, F. (2019). A Sparse RNN-Topic Model for Discovering Bursty Topics in Big Data of Social Networks. *Journal of Information Science and Engineering, 35*(4), 749–767.

Sinha, A., & Kumar, P. (2021). Information diffusion modeling and analysis for socially interacting networks. *Social Network Analysis and Mining, 11*(1), 11. doi:10.100713278-020-00719-7 PMID:33456625

Tan, Q., Liu, N., & Hu, X. (2019). Deep Representation Learning for Social Network Analysis. *Frontiers in Big Data. Frontiers in Big Data, 2*(2), 2. Advance online publication. doi:10.3389/fdata.2019.00002 PMID:33693325

Taxidou, I., & Fischer, P. (2013). Realtime Analysis of Information Diffusion in Social Media. *Proceedings of the VLDB Endowment International Conference on Very Large Data Bases, 6*(12), 1416–1421. doi:10.14778/2536274.2536328

Trifiro, B., Clarke, M., Huang, S., Mills, B., Ye, Y., Zhang, S., Zhou, M., & Su, C. C. (2022). Media moments: How media events and business incentives drive twitter engagement within the small business community. *Social Network Analysis and Mining, 12*(1), 174. doi:10.100713278-022-01003-6 PMID:36505398

Wanda, P. (2022). RunMax: Fake profile classification using novel nonlinear activation in CNN. *Social Network Analysis and Mining*, *12*(1), 158. doi:10.100713278-022-00983-9

Zakaria, N. (2021). Action network: A probabilistic graphical model for social simulation. *Simulation*, *98*(4), 335–346. doi:10.1177/00375497211038759

Chapter 10
An Automated Text Summarization and Machine Learning–Based Framework for Heart Disease Prediction

Sandeep Kumar Hegde

NMAM Institute of Technology, Nitte University (Deemed), India

Rajalaxmi Hegde

NMAM Institute of Technology, Nitte University (Deemed), India

ABSTRACT

Heart disease is the primary cause of death of humankind nowadays. Text summarization is currently a major research topic in natural language processing, and it is an important activity in the analysis of high-volume text documents. In the chapter, an automated summarization of text has been implemented using sentence scoring approach, which includes finding the frequent terms and sentence ranking method. This technique mainly focuses on summarizing medical reports. The proposed approach also uses three algorithms, namely SVM (support vector machine), KNN (k-nearest neighbor), and random forest algorithm, for disease prediction. Experimental results are carried out on several data sets, and they show that the proposed approach provides best accuracy compared to traditional techniques.

INTRODUCTION

Heart disease is currently the leading cause of death worldwide. In the US, cardiovascular disease is responsible for about one-third of all fatalities. Another study discovered that cardiovascular disease(CVD) accounts for 35% of deaths in Europe . Similar circumstances exist in low- and middle-income nations, where CVD causes about 28% of fatalities. With 0.36 doctors per 1000 residents, the nation experiences a physician shortage similar to that experienced by Indonesia. As a result, many studies and innovations in healthcare service improvement are flourishing. Every day, thousands of people lose their lives to

DOI: 10.4018/978-1-6684-8145-5.ch010

Copyright © 2023, IGI Global. Copying or distributing in print or electronic forms without written permission of IGI Global is prohibited.

CVD, which is on the rise among India's younger population and around the world. According to cardiac doctors, a lack of physical activity and sedentary lifestyle are the key reasons for the development of the condition. In India, at least one out of every five deaths is caused by CVD and other cardiac illnesses. In the year 2022, alone, 9,80,000 persons died as a result of a heart attack that did not manifest any symptoms.In the proposed chapter, text summarization in combination with machine learning algorithms are used to predict the CVD in preliminary stage. A computer program shortens a text by the technique of text summarization, also known as automatic summarization. This procedure produces a product that retains the most important points of the original text and is commonly referred to as an abstract or a summary. This method is employed to condense patient medical inquiries. This method primarily focuses on simplifying medical records so that physicians can quickly and easily continue to analyze them. Extraction and abstraction are the two main methods used for text summarization.

While abstraction entails paraphrasing portions of the source content, extraction strategies replicate the most crucial data from the original document to the summary. In general, abstraction can produce more condensed summaries than extraction, but these programs are considered much more difficult to develop. For generating summaries, both techniques make use of natural language processing and/ or statistical methods. With high success rates, text summarization is widely employed in the business world, including word processing, data mining, and telecommunications. Emerging uses of text summarization for businesses include the health industry, where it can help doctors by summarizing reports. Text summarization is implemented using an extractive approach. This method predicts heart disease by combining distilled BERT (Bidirectional Encoder Representations from Transformers) with instant measurement parameters. DistilBERT is a BERT-based Transformer model that is small, fast, cheap, and light. Expertise extraction is used to shrink a BERT model by 40% during the pre-training phase. Following summarization, prediction techniques are applied to forecast the likelihood of heart disease. There are various prediction techniques, such as text mining, data mining, image processing, and so on. A text-mining technique was used in this paper to attempt to predict diseases. A high-accuracy prediction algorithm is required to analyze and mitigate the effects of various diseases.

One sort of illness that can be fatal is heart disease. Heart disease is responsible for far too many fatalities each year. Weak cardiac muscles can lead to heart disease. Heart failure can also be defined as the heart's inability to pump blood. Another name for heart disease is coronary artery disease (CAD). Due to the recent increase in the prevalence of heart disease, a model is created that can assist a user in determining the possibility of heart disease without having to visit a doctor and in the comfort of their own home. This paper used DistilBert Methods, a distilled version of BERT, to create an automated text summarization tool. A process for condensing a huge model—the teacher—into a smaller model—called Student. The likelihood of heart disease was then predicted using a text mining technique. Let's say a patient wishes to text a doctor a paragraph to let him or her know they are sick, but the doctor does not have the time to read all those lengthy messages. So, using our model, we summarise that message to make the task of the doctor easier. By summarising medical reports and utilising sophisticated machine learning (ML) algorithms to forecast the likelihood of cardiac illness, this model aims to simplify medical reports.

BACKGROUND

Table 1 summarises all of the research studies that the researcher has published in the field of CVD prediction using various machine learning algorithms.

Table 1. Literature review on ML algorithms for CVD prediction

Author Name	Purpose	Techniques Used	Accuracy
Mohan et al. (2019) Gavhane et al. (2018)	ML Algorithms to Predict the CVD	1) Decision tree 2) Naïve Bayes Classifier	Decision tree obtained good result of 86.9% where as Naïve Bayes obtained 84.86% accuracy
Kishore et al. (2018)	ML Algorithms to Predict the CVD	1) Multi-layer perceptron algorithm	The MLP Obtained accuracy of 90.1%
Lakshmanarao et al. (2019) Krishnan et al. (2019) Yadav et al. (2021)	Machine learning techniques for predicting heart disease	1) Decision Tree 2) Support Vector Machine 3) Naïve Bayes	SVM has obtained accuracy of 88.54% where Decision Tree obtained 86.9%, Naïve bayes generated 84.3% .
Senthilkumar et al. (2021)	Deep Learning Technique for Predicting Heart Attacks	1) RNN	RNN obtained accuracy of 82%
Manikantan et al. (2013) Amin et al. (2019)	ML Algorithms to Predict the CVD	1) Decision Tree 2) Naïve Bayes	Naïve Bayes obtained 81% accuracy and 79.05% accuracy achieved using Decision Tree
Shah et al. (2017)	ML Algorithms to Predict the CVD	1) KNN 2) K-mean clustering 3) Adaboost 4) Decision Tree	Adaboost achieved 86.60% Accuracy where as Decision Tree recorded 83.5%, KNN obtained 87.94% and Kmeans clustering obtained 84.2% Accuracy
Xiao et al. (2011) Vindhya et al. (2020)	Effective Heart Disease Prediction Using Hybrid Machine Learning Technique	1) Decision tree 2) Language Model 3) Support Vector Machine 4) HRFLM 5) Neural Networks 6) Naïve Bayes 7) KNN 8) Random Forest	HRFLM obtained 85.4% Accuracy where as Decision tree recorded 76.4%, Language Model obtained 81.2%, Support Vector Machine generated 79.03%, Random Forest obtained 83.4%, Naïve Bayes recorded 82.5%, Neural Networks obtained 84.2%, and KNN obtained 82.7% accuracy
Abdullah et al. (2012)	ML Algorithms to Predict the CVD	Random and Synthetic over sampling using ML algorithm	,Support Vector Machine obtained accuracy of 82.30% with Random Over Sampling. Random Forest obtained 86.3% accuracy with Synthetic Minority Oversampling. For Adaptive synthetic sampling, Random Forest obtained 87.04% accuracy
Almalis et al. (2022)	Sentiment Analysis on Clinical Data	NLP with Deep Learning	Obtained an accuracy of 79.29%
Palenzuela et al. (2022)	Text Analysis on Clinical Data	Neural Network in combination with DistilBert	Obtained an accuracy of 85.04%
Kabir et al. (2023)	Depression data analysis from social media text	DistilBert Architecture	Obtained an accuracy of 86.6%
Rodrawangpai et al. (2022)	Consumer Product related data analysis using NLP and Machine Learning	Default language models in combination with DistilBert Architecture	Obtained an accuracy of 92%
Ameer et al. (2023)	Emotion classification using LSTM and Transfer Learning	LSTMs and Transfer Learning along with attention network	Obtained an accuracy of 91.4%
Lauriola et al. (2022)	Deep Learning in combination with NLP for Biomedical data analysis	CNN using BERT architecture	Obtained an accuracy of 92.8%

PROPOSED METHODOLOGY

The summarizer in the proposed approach is designed using the DistilBert algorithm. It works by filtering out words that are only about heart disease. Large pre-trained models are increasingly used in transfer natural language processing (NLP) for learning, but it is still difficult to run these large models on the edge or with constrained CPU resources for inference or training. The DistilBERT methodology, which is a way to pre-train a simpler general cognitive representational structure that can subsequently be adapted to accomplish well on a wide range of tasks more like relatively broad equivalents, is detailed in this study. It is also demonstrated that information distillation even during pre-training step allows us to minimize the size of a model BERT by 40% while retaining 97% from its vocabulary comprehension ability and being 60% faster.

The Clinical Test results and prescriptions are just a couple of the patient-specific details that are included in clinical notes. The utilisation of clinical notes has lagged behind that of organised data despite their high dimensionality and sparseness. The DistilBERT methodology is an adaptation of BERT that focuses on clinical notes. It clearly illustrates how medical concepts are connected in the eyes of the public. The learning process is more faster with DistilBERT than with LSTM or CNN models for this purpose as we are dealing with pre-trained models that just need tweaks. In contrast to past approaches, the iterations of these models benefit from a biological domain understanding. While DistilBERT versions use the idea of sequence classification to foresee relationships, relationship extraction (RE) was used for token classification in the named entity identification challenge.

In contrast, the majority of earlier studies concentrated on employing distillation to create task-oriented models. A triple loss strategy is one that incorporates language modelling, distillation, and cosine-distance losses to capitalize inductive biases that bigger ones pick up during pre-training. A proof-of-concept experiment demonstrates the capabilities of this more compact, quicker, and lighter approach for on-device calculations. The architecture of the summerizer is shown in Figure 1. The distilled form of BERT is called DistilBERT, and it is lighter, smaller, quicker, and less expensive. Because of its size, BERT is challenging to manufacture. The lighter, more effective Distil-BERT model is what we'll need if we wish to use these versions on mobile phones. Distil-BERT performs 97% better than BERT despite using only 50% of BERT's training data.

Both BERT-base and BERT-large have 340 parameters each, which are challenging to handle. In order to address this issue, the distillation process is used to scale down the size of these enormous models. The several Distil-BERT modules are covered in further detail below.

Student Architecture Created With DistilBERT: Generic Architecture and BERT are identical, with the exception of the elimination of token-type embeddings, the pooler, and a factor of 2 reduction in the number of layers. The impact of this on computing effectiveness is enormous.

DistilBERT Initialization: The best time to initialise the sub-network must be determined in order to guarantee that it converges throughout model training. Take one layer out of two and initialise the pupil from the teacher as a consequence.

Distillation: The model was developed in extremely large batches and combined dynamic masking and sentence prediction. It was known as masking and Used to convert a word to the Hidden Word embedding and train the entire sequence to anticipate that specific word.

Data and Computational Power: On eight 16GB V100 GPUs, the model was trained for about 90 hours using the combined dataset of the English Wikipedia and Toronto Book Corpus. The building plans for DistilBert are shown in Figure 3. The NLP modules of DistilBert are covered in more detail below.

Figure 1. Summarizer architecture

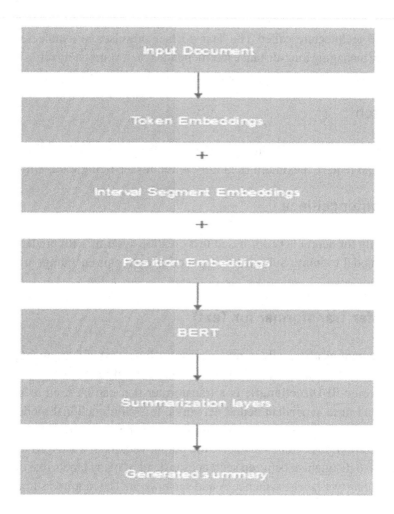

Figure 2. DistilBert architecture

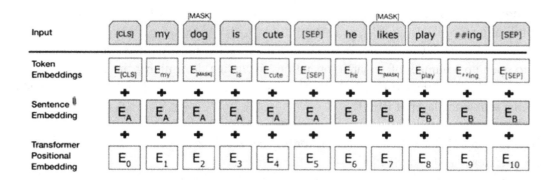

NLP Transformer

A revolutionary NLP architecture called The Transformer promises to handle sequence-to-sequence problems while deftly managing long-distance interdependence. It completely relies on self-attention and does not compute representations of its input and output using sequence-aligned RNNs or convolution.

Lightning PyTorch

PyTorch Lightning is a deep learning framework designed for professional AI researchers and machine learning engineers who require maximum flexibility without sacrificing scalability.

Tokenizer for SentencePiece

It is intended primarily for neural network-based text creation systems with predetermined vocabulary sizes before neural model training. Subword units, such as byte-pair encoding, are supported by SentencePiece (BPE).

Model T5 (Transfer Transformer for Text)

By considering all operations identically as receiving some input text and producing some text with job descriptors encoded in the input, the very same framework is used for a variety of activities.

BERT (Transformer-Bi-Directional): Is a transformer that can be used to solve the drawbacks of RNN and other long-term dependent neural networks. It is a bidirectional model that has been pre-trained. This pre-trained model is quickly optimised to perform the specified NLP tasks, in this particular instance of Summarization. Instead of sentences, the output vectors of a masked model are tokened. It employs embeddings to distinguish between sentences instead of many labels like other extractive summarizers do and only has two labels: sentence A and sentence B. The required summaries are produced by altering these embeddings.

The entire process can be broken down into the following stages:

Encoding Multiple Sentences: During this phase, sentences from the incoming document are encoded so that they may be preprocessed. Before and after each sentence the SEP and CLS tags are inserted. The components of one or more sentences are grouped using the CLS tag.

Embeddings: In essence, it alludes to the vector representation of words. It enhances the flexibility of their utilisation.

As shown in Figure 2, Google also makes use of the BERT feature for better query understanding. It helps to open up a number of semantic operations, including determining the document's aim and building a model of how the terms are related. Our text undergoes three different types of embeddings before being sent to the layer of BERT:

1. **Token Embeddings:** The conversion of words in the vector form with a predetermined dimension. The prefixes [CLS] and [SEP] are used to finish sentences.
2. **Segment Embeddings:** These employ binary coding to differentiate or categorise various inputs.
3. **Position Embeddings:** Up to 512 character input sequences can be processed by BERT.

Words shouldn't be represented similarly to vectors since their placement in a sentence can alter the context in which they are understood. For instance, "We were there to observe, but we didn't play. The proposed framework predicts diseases using five ML algorithms: SVM, Random Forest, KNN, Logistic Regression and Nave Bayes. The outcome of these frameworks is discussed in section 4 below.

EXPERIMENTAL RESULTS

The screen shot of the dataset is shown in Figure 3. The dataset is gathered from the Kaggle website which has description about 550 patients who were suffering from heart disease.

Figure 3. Screen shot of the CVD dataset

A1 f_x Age

	A	B	C	D	E	F	G	H	I	J	K	L	M	N
1	Age	Sex	Chest pair	BP	Cholester	FBS over 1	EKG result	Max HR	Exercise a	ST depres	Slope of S	Number o	Thallium	Heart Disease
2	70	1	4	130	322	0	2	109	0	2.4	2	3	3	Presence
3	67	0	3	115	564	0	2	160	0	1.6	2	0	7	Absence
4	57	1	2	124	261	0	0	141	0	0.3	1	0	7	Presence
5	64	1	4	128	263	0	0	105	1	0.2	2	1	7	Absence
6	74	0	2	120	269	0	2	121	1	0.2	1	1	3	Absence
7	65	1	4	120	177	0	0	140	0	0.4	1	0	7	Absence
8	56	1	3	130	256	1	2	142	1	0.6	2	1	6	Presence
9	59	1	4	110	239	0	2	142	1	1.2	2	1	7	Presence
10	60	1	4	140	293	0	2	170	0	1.2	2	2	7	Presence
11	63	0	4	150	407	0	2	154	0	4	2	3	7	Presence
12	59	1	4	135	234	0	0	161	0	0.5	2	0	7	Absence
13	53	1	4	142	226	0	2	111	1	0	1	0	7	Absence
14	44	1	3	140	235	0	2	180	0	0	1	0	3	Absence
15	61	1	1	134	234	0	0	145	0	2.6	2	2	3	Presence
16	57	0	4	128	303	0	2	159	0	0	1	1	3	Absence
17	71	0	4	112	149	0	0	125	0	1.6	2	0	3	Absence
18	46	1	4	140	311	0	0	120	1	1.8	2	2	7	Presence
19	53	1	4	140	203	1	2	155	1	3.1	3	0	7	Presence
20	64	1	1	110	211	0	2	144	1	1.8	2	0	3	Absence
21	40	1	1	140	199	0	0	178	1	1.4	1	0	7	Absence
22	67	1	4	120	229	0	2	129	1	2.6	2	2	7	Presence
23	48	1	2	130	245	0	2	180	0	0.2	2	0	3	Absence
24	43	1	4	115	303	0	0	181	0	1.2	2	0	3	Absence
25	47	1	4	112	204	0	0	143	0	0.1	1	0	3	Absence
26	54	0	2	132	288	1	2	159	1	0	1	1	3	Absence
27	48	0	3	130	275	0	0	139	0	0.2	1	0	3	Absence
28	46	0	4	138	243	0	2	152	1	0	2	0	3	Absence
29	51	0	3	120	295	0	2	157	0	0.6	1	0	3	Absence
30	58	1	3	112	230	0	2	165	0	2.5	2	1	7	Presence
31	71	0	3	110	265	1	2	130	0	0	1	1	3	Absence
32	57	1	3	128	229	0	2	150	0	0.4	2	1	7	Presence
33	66	1	4	160	228	0	2	138	0	2.3	1	0	6	Absence
34	37	0	3	120	215	0	0	170	0	0	1	0	3	Absence
35	59	1	4	170	326	0	2	140	1	3.4	3	0	7	Presence
36	50	1	4	144	200	0	2	126	1	0.9	2	0	7	Presence

Heart_Disease_Prediction

Ready Accessibility: Unavailable

The CVD dataset contained descriptions about the following features where each of these feature resulted in two outcomes, i.e., absence and presence of the disease.

- Age
- Sex
- Chest pain type (1 - 4 intensity)
- BP (90/60mmHg – 120/80mmHg)

- Cholesterol
- FBS (Fasting Blood Sugar levels) over 120
- EKG (ECG) result (60-100 bpm)
- Max HR (170-190 bpm)
- Exercise Angina
- ST Depression
- Slope of ST (1-3)
- Number of vessels fluro (0-3)
- Thallium

Figure 4. Screenshot of implemented framework

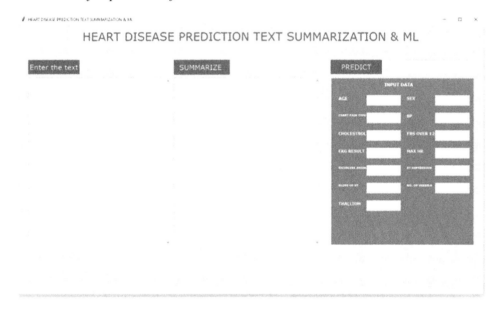

Figure 4 depicts the screenshots of the implemented framework. Tkinter is used to create the model's user interface. The first text field accepts text input, which is then summarised when the summarise button is clicked. The scenario below is provided as input to the proposed framework. "The patient was 60 years old and had a history of hypertension and diabetes." His both feet had been swollen for two months, and he had seen an orthopaedic one month before. And for the past three days, he has been experiencing mild chest pain that is transferring from right to left. He has a family history of heart disease and diabetes mellitus. Patient is known to consume alcohol, possibly in excess on occasion. He is not a smoker. He has been taking BP and diabetic tablets for four years. He is slightly overweight and has a high cholesterol level. He has had several episodes of mild lightheadedness in the last two weeks and is being treated with Antivert 25 mg t.i.d. Physical examination revealed that he is a well-developed, well-nourished male who appears to be in good health.

His blood pressure is 140/94, his pulse is 88, his respiratory rate is 18, and his temperature is 99.6. He is alert and focused, with normal pupils. There isn't any ataxia. The neck is not sensitive. The lungs are clear, and the heart has an irregular sinus rhythm with slight murmurs. As shown in Figure 4, initially entire dataset containing text message is passed as input to the the dataset.As discussed in the section above the DistilBert technique have been applied to summarize the text .Once text is summarized, to predict the occurrence of the disease, the patient data need to be filled in the blocks provided .On clicking the predict button, the proposed framework will apply the machine learning algorithms to decide whether the patient has CVD disease or not .

Figure 5. Screenshot of GUI with sample input

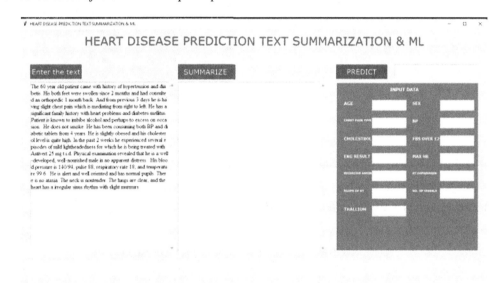

Figure 5 shows a screenshot of the GUI with sample input. The user should click the summarise button after entering the sample input in the first text field to obtain the summarised output. When the user clicks the summarise button, the model selects heart disease-related terms and displays the desired output in the second text field, as illustrated in Figure 6. After obtaining the summarised result, the user must enter the necessary values for prediction. After entering the prediction values, the user must click the predict button. The proposed model will then display whether or not the patient has heart disease by applying the machine learning algorithms. In the proposed approach five machine learning algorithms namely SVM, KNN, Random Forest, Nave Bayes, and Logistic Regression algorithms are applied to make prediction out of the data.

Various parameters, including precision, accuracy, ROC rate and recall are used to validate the proposed approach's performance. The performance of the suggested framework in relation to various machine learning models versus the presence or absence of the CVD disease is shown in Figure 7. The graphical representation states that the SVM algorithm in combination with DistilBert has achieved the highest accuracy rate of 94.03% when compared to other approaches .

Figure 6. Screenshot of summarized output

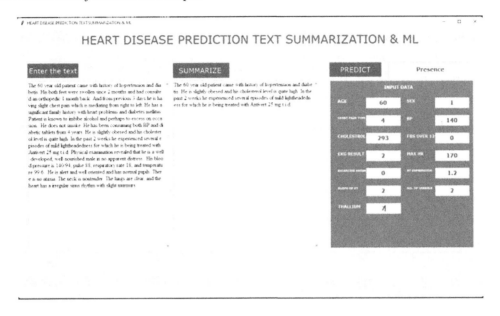

Figure 7. Accuracy comparison of different ML algorithm

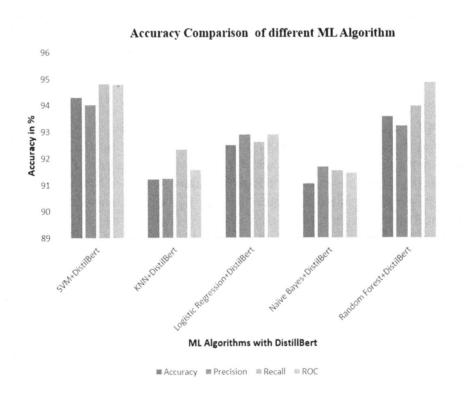

CONCLUSION AND FUTURE WORK

In this study, a novel framework for predicting the existence of heart disease is proposed using text summarization and several machine learning methods. Text summarization is accomplished using the Distil-Bert framework, while disease prediction is accomplished using a variety of machine learning methods, including KNN, Random Forest, SVM, Logistic Regression, and Nave Bayes. The dataset is fed into multiple machine learning algorithms, and the accuracy of the machine learning methods is compared, in order to validate the proposed method. The experimental findings demonstrate that the suggested the combination of SVM and DistilBert framework outperformed conventional methods with an accuracy of 94.03%. As part of future work the combination of DistilBert framework and machine learning can be applied on a few more chronic disease datasets for early prediction of disease.

REFERENCES

Abdullah, A. S., & Rajalaxmi, R. (2012, April). A data mining model for predicting the coronary heart disease using random forest classifier. In *International Conference in Recent Trends in Computational Methods, Communication and Controls* (pp. 22-25). Academic Press.

Almalis, I., Kouloumpris, E., & Vlahavas, I. (2022). Sector-level sentiment analysis with deep learning. *Knowledge-Based Systems*, *258*, 109954. doi:10.1016/j.knosys.2022.109954

Ameer, I., Bölücü, N., Siddiqui, M. H. F., Can, B., Sidorov, G., & Gelbukh, A. (2023). Multi-label emotion classification in texts using transfer learning. *Expert Systems with Applications*, *213*, 118534. doi:10.1016/j.eswa.2022.118534

Amin, M. S., Chiam, Y. K., & Varathan, K. D. (2019). Identification of significant features and data mining techniques in predicting heart disease. *Telematics and Informatics*, *36*, 82–93. doi:10.1016/j.tele.2018.11.007

Fischbach, J., Frattini, J., Vogelsang, A., Mendez, D., Unterkalmsteiner, M., Wehrle, A., Henao, P. R., Yousefi, P., Juricic, T., Radduenz, J., & Wiecher, C. (2023). Automatic creation of acceptance tests by extracting conditionals from requirements: Nlp approach and case study. *Journal of Systems and Software*, *197*, 111549. doi:10.1016/j.jss.2022.111549

Gavhane, A., Kokkula, G., Pandya, I., & Devadkar, K. (2018, March). Prediction of heart disease using machine learning. In *2018 second international conference on electronics, communication and aerospace technology (ICECA)* (pp. 1275-1278). IEEE. 10.1109/ICECA.2018.8474922

Greco, C. M., Simeri, A., Tagarelli, A., & Zumpano, E. (2023). Transformer-based language models for mental health issues: A survey. *Pattern Recognition Letters*, *167*, 204–211. doi:10.1016/j.patrec.2023.02.016

Kabir, M., Ahmed, T., Hasan, M. B., Laskar, M. T. R., Joarder, T. K., Mahmud, H., & Hasan, K. (2023). DEPTWEET: A typology for social media texts to detect depression severities. *Computers in Human Behavior*, *139*, 107503. doi:10.1016/j.chb.2022.107503

Kishore, A., Kumar, A., Singh, K., Punia, M., & Hambir, Y. (2018). Heart attack prediction using deep learning. *International Research Journal of Engineering and Technology*, *5*(04), 2395–0072.

Krishnan, S., & Geetha, S. (2019, April). Prediction of Heart Disease Using Machine Learning Algorithms. In *2019 1st international conference on innovations in information and communication technology (ICIICT)* (pp. 1-5). IEEE.

Lakshmanarao, A., Swathi, Y., & Sundareswar, P. S. S. (2019). Machine learning techniques for heart disease prediction. *Forest*, *95*(99), 97.

Lauriola, I., Lavelli, A., & Aiolli, F. (2022). An introduction to deep learning in natural language processing: Models, techniques, and tools. *Neurocomputing*, *470*, 443–456. doi:10.1016/j.neucom.2021.05.103

Liang, S., Zuo, W., Shi, Z., Wang, S., Wang, J., & Zuo, X. (2022). A multi-level neural network for implicit causality detection in web texts. *Neurocomputing*, *481*, 121–132. doi:10.1016/j.neucom.2022.01.076

Manikantan, V., & Latha, S. (2013). Predicting the analysis of heart disease symptoms using medicinal data mining methods. *International Journal of Advanced Computer Theory and Engineering*, *2*, 46–51.

Mohan, S., Thirumalai, C., & Srivastava, G. (2019). Effective heart disease prediction using hybrid machine learning techniques. *IEEE Access : Practical Innovations, Open Solutions*, *7*, 81542–81554. doi:10.1109/ACCESS.2019.2923707

Nikhar, S., & Karandikar, A. M. (2016). Prediction of heart disease using machine learning algorithms. *International Journal of Advanced Engineering. Management Science*, *2*(6), 239484.

Palenzuela, Á. J. J., Frasincar, F., & Truşcă, M. M. (2022). Modeling Second Language Acquisition with pre-trained neural language models. *Expert Systems with Applications*, *207*, 117871. doi:10.1016/j.eswa.2022.117871

Rodrawangpai, B., & Daungjaiboon, W. (2022). Improving text classification with transformers and layer normalization. *Machine Learning with Applications*, *10*, 100403. doi:10.1016/j.mlwa.2022.100403

Senthilkumar, R. (2021). Prognostic System for Heart Disease using Machine Learning: A Review. *Journal of Science Technology and Research*, *2*(1).

Shah, S. M. S., Batool, S., Khan, I., Ashraf, M. U., Abbas, S. H., & Hussain, S. A. (2017). Feature extraction through parallel probabilistic principal component analysis for heart disease diagnosis. *Physica A*, *482*, 796–807. doi:10.1016/j.physa.2017.04.113

Vindhya, L., Beliray, P. A., Sravani, C. R., & Divya, D. R. (2020). Prediction of Heart Disease Using Machine Learning Techniques. *International Journal of Research in Engineering, Science and Management*, *3*(8), 325–326.

Xiao, X., Wu, Z. C., & Chou, K. C. (2011). A multi-label classifier for predicting the subcellular localization of gram-negative bacterial proteins with both single and multiple sites. *PLoS One*, *6*(6), e20592. doi:10.1371/journal.pone.0020592 PMID:21698097

Yadav, K. K., Sharma, A., & Badholia, A. (2021). Heart disease prediction using machine learning techniques. *Information Technology in Industry, 9*(1), 207-214.

Chapter 11
Innovative Applications of Data Science:
NLP in Travel and Tourism Industries

Poorani Marimuthu
CMR Institute of Technology, India

Santhanalakshmi S. T.
https://orcid.org/0000-0002-1377-1408
Panimalar Engineering College, India

C. Christlin Shanuja
CMR Institute of Technology, India

ABSTRACT

The travel and tourism sector is one among the important sectors that contribute or generate income to a country, which in turn raise the economy. More than one billion tourists travel to their desired international destinations as normal tourist, for their business, medical, study purpose, etc. every year contributes 9.8% of global GDP. This value represents 7% of the world total exports. Today with the natural language processing (NLP), most of the major challenges in these sectors have been addressed, which results in the increased revenue generation to the country. Moreover, NLP tries to provide a hassle-free experience to the tourist and thus improves the revenue generation. It helps to streamline the business opportunities and benefits all the interconnected industries. This chapter tries to provide the role of NLP in travel and tourism along with the challenges in this field.

INTRODUCTION

Travel and tourism (TT) (Darbellay & Stock, 2012; Schuckert et al., 2015) is one of the world's largest service industries which drive the economics of many nations by their tourist trade. It is an extended sector, comprising many other small sectors within it, including hotel, transport, industry, aviation, hospitality,

DOI: 10.4018/978-1-6684-8145-5.ch011

Copyright © 2023, IGI Global. Copying or distributing in print or electronic forms without written permission of IGI Global is prohibited.

culture and heritage of the visited nation. All the industries are interdependent to each other and contribute to the growth of travel and tourism sector. In travel and tourism, the contributing each industry or sector has its own challenges and the deviation in one sector will be reflected in another. Among different tourism business and medical tourism plays a vital role in the growth of the visited nation. The purpose of travel may be for heritage and cultural exchange, business, medical emergency, sports, international events, general tourist to see their desired places, etc. Every nation has its own tourist sector that focus on the growth of their heritage locations, pilgrims, and its related industry sectors like hotels. The main objective of the tourist sector of any nation is to promote and develop tourism, to maintain tourist places, to enhance tourist products with respect to the travellers need, to make the tourist or travellers happy in terms of their visit, stay, purchase etc. and through this to increase the employability in nation which intern increases the economy of the nation. The entire nation's travel and tourism sector has been monitored and taken care by the World Tourism Organization (WTO), which is the United Nations agency that is responsible for promoting a sustainable, responsible, and universally accessible travels. It leads to economic growth through directly and indirectly. Revenue generation by foreign exchange, aviation, lodging, and purchase on the tourist dependent country leads to direct growth of economy, whereas creating business opportunities through tourism thrives for indirect economy growth. Figure 1 shows the number of international tourist arrivals worldwide from 2005 to 2022.

Figure 1. International tourist arrivals worldwide: 2005 to 2022

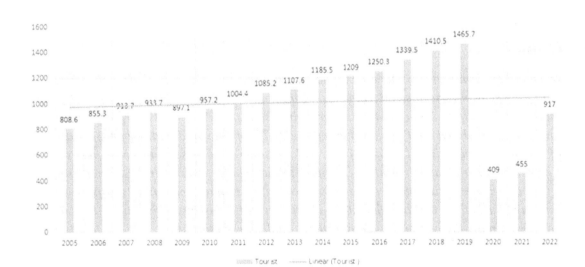

Tourism can be divided into 5 major types that include domestic tourism, national tourism, international tourism, inbound tourism, and outbound tourism. The visitors may be same day visitors, international visitors, and domestic visitors. International visitors are the visitors from other countries and are usually overnight visitors i.e., they will stay for more days (3 days to 30 days) usually. Same day visitors are usually from the same nation or businessperson. The tourist sector maintains the data of both international and domestic visitors. Various services to the travellers were provided by tourist sector that includes information on travel destinations through web portal, mobile applications, information about holiday homes, tourist stay, products, registration for important places etc. It always follows up the visitors travel, and the international visitors are always kept in track. This paves the way for more automated language processing and textual data manipulation that involves natural language processing. Through proper integration of NLP and tourist sector we can improve the revenue of the country, more jobs can be created, develop the infrastructure of the country and proper cultural exchange between citizens and foreigners. Moreover, today four more tourism has been evolved that includes food tourism, sustainable tourism, experimental tourism and well tourism. Figure 2 shows the tourist visit to India for the years 2019, 2020 and 2021.

Generally, tourism can impact the economy of a nation by three ways, that includes (1) direct effect, (2) indirect effect, and (3) induced effect. Both the impact and the structure of the tourist sector impacts the economy of nation. As per Seyidov et al. (Seyidov & Adomaitienė, 2016), three elements determine the number of visitors to a country, and they are amenities, accessibility, and attractions towards the desired destination. Tourism can aid the development of low-income country when this sector is properly governed and managed.

Apart from this general tourist, medical tourist became the one of the main sources of income and it involves life of a person. Today people started to travel beyond their nation for their medication or for their loved ones. The search of experienced, expertise and well qualified doctors, nurses, along with infrastructure support with less cost drive the patients to travel for the other countries. Many foreigners coming to countries like India where the cost for similar healthcare services is comparatively cheaper than their own countries with well qualified doctors. Usually, they came for surgeries, dental, liver transplants and nowadays for cosmetic surgery also. Thus, medical tourist is nowadays become common and natural language processing plays a vital role in medical tourist to sort them the best medical centres all over the world as per their requirements. The people who travelled to other countries for treatment says that they were able to save nearly 30% to 80% of their savings that would have incurred in their own countries if they did the same medications there. The increase in more medical tourist results in higher profits for the medical community and the medical professionals will be recognized worldwide and get a global exposure.

The remaining part of the chapter is organized as Section 2 briefly discusses the various techniques implemented in travel and tourism using NLP, Section 3 elaborates the challenges in travel and tourism, Section 4 discusses the benefits of tours and travels, Section 5 elaborates about Natural Language Processing, NLP in tours and travels has been discussed in Section 6, Section 7 briefly explains the need of NLP in tours and travels, NLP based chatbot has been discussed in Section 8; Challenges in tours and travel while adopting NLP is discussed in Section 9; Research challenges in NLP while adopting for tours and travel and finally conclusion / future scope has been elaborated in Section 11.

Figure 2. Tourist visit during the period of 2019, 2020, and 2021

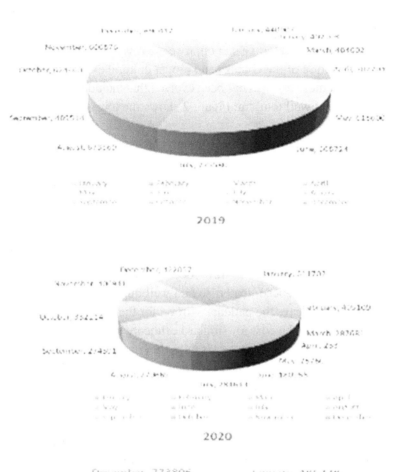

2019

2020

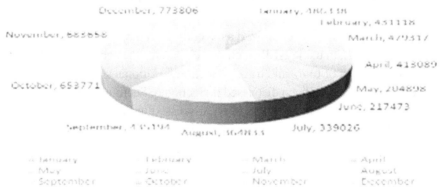

2021

BACKGROUND

Xu et al. (2022) proposed a work based on comprehensive evaluation method after the implementation of analysing the validity of online review text, performing comprehensive evaluation based on text classification, then finding out the hot words in text mining and finally combining the gained information to obtain unknown information. From the obtained new words trying to find good scenic spots with respect to their search. A recommender system for health tourism has been proposed by Halkiopoulos et al. (2021) in which the needs of patients are analyzed, and the proposed intelligent model will suggest them with a good medical tourism information. This system has been designed in such a way that it provides good information of medical sector along with their holiday packages. The scope of improving tourism with machine learning has been discussed in Egger and Gokce (2022). This paper reveals the text preprocessing for the unused data available on the internet that can be effectively used in tourism sector. Mich (2022) discussed about the various innovative methods that can be applied in tourist sector with the help of AI and machine learning techniques. This work elaborately explains every stage of processing from text retrieval to decision making. The various digital marketing approaches in tourism have been proposed by Egger (2022), using machine learning. This paper reveals the importance of machine learning techniques along with NLP in the field of tourism.

Hotel ratings (Yan & Subramanian, 2019) have been done using machine learning and these ratings are helps the tourist with the pros and cons of the hotel. Many tools with crawling websites are discussed in the work. Online travel Reviews (OTR) analyzation (Guerrero-Rodriguez et al., 2021) has been done for Guanajuato, Mexico and the authors used NLP for the text analytics. The work proceeds with positive and negative experience of the travellers. These two polarities have been evaluated with the main aspects of cleanliness and price. Tripathi et al. (2022) proposed a work that tries to identify the gap in implementing the AI based model for hospitality organizations. The work covers how small hotels can be gained advantage of machine learning models. A study on dark tourism has been done by Kleshcheva (2021) to find the factors that attract the people to travel to the places like Chernobyl. The work proposes a data analytics method that investigates the data in the social media with respect to dark tourism. This also provides the scope to understand the needs and wishes of the tourist as per the tourist location. A review on tourism has been provided by Li et al. (2019) in which detailed study about the tourist profile, his / her interest, their views, various recommendation system with machine learning has been studied. This work provides a good guideline for the researchers. García-Pablos et al. (2016) proposed a work on hotel reviews based on OpeNER platform. Here the training and testing has been performed with hotel reviews obtained from websites like Holidaycheck, HolidayInn, Zoover etc. Bandara et al. (2018) proposed a study on tourist guidance and proposed a work based artificial conversational agent. The proposed model is customizable with respect to language and statistical survey has been done for data set generation with respect to locations, accommodations, intentions, destinations as per the traveller requirements. An optimized trip plan will be forwarded to the traveller based on his / her query.

Based on OpeNER accommodation reviews has been done by García-Pablos et al. (2015) and the work also includes the geo spatial information. Bulchand-Gidumal (2022) proposed a work that states about the impact of artificial intelligence in travel. The work further discusses about the research scope and the how far it should be carried out without artificial intelligence dominates human mankind. Malaka and Zipf (2000) proposed a research work that deals with developing a prototype for geo spatial information system, DeepMap. DeepMap was a tourist guide and allows the user for prior planning of their travel. It is a user interactive system and provides a 3D view for the traveller in online mode. Based on Theory of Lodging, Roy (2023) proposed a paper on tourism that reflects experience of luxury, mid-tier, and low-tier hotels. The work has been carried out on both objective and subjective manner. From the study it is noted that luxury people go with subjective preferences whereas others go with objective factors.

CHALLENGES IN TOURS AND TRAVELS

The common challenges faced by tourism department are improper communication among the travellers and the guides, native persons, language, etc. In earlier times, the tourist will hire a guide who knows both the tourist language and the local language, or else the guide will be able to speak the world common language i.e., English. The traveller will be narrated with the information regarding the tourist spot by the hired guide. There is no surety for the information provided by the guide. Language barrier is one of the main issues in tourist sector which can be resolved through NLP. The other challenges faced by tourism are travel promotions, safety, cross border set of laws, tax etc.

These challenges can also be resolved through natural language processing. To afford a good travelling experience to a traveller, NLP based application can be implemented with any one of the personal assistive devices. Today travellers need timely information when they are on the move and the technology is also supporting. Many small countries all over the world with high natural ambience are attracting tourist by properly utilizing the upcoming technologies such as artificial intelligence, virtual reality, natural language processing etc. For proper income, tourism requires good management or else it became unsustainable.

The main challenges in medical tourism faced all over the world includes proper follow up, language, lack of infrastructure and professionalism, legal problems etc. Today, the Marketing Development Assistance Scheme (MDA) provides the required financial assistance for the approved tours and travel agents. This helps them to improvise the expected facilities of the visitors and thus MDA tries to promote the tourism in each country. With the help of publicity materials or marketing strategies like brochures, expo etc the promotion of medical tourism and other normal tourism have been done in target markets. It is expected that the medical field will grow nearly 20% CAGR during 2022 – 2032. Figure 3 shows the tourist arrival to India from 2019 – 2021 and Table 1. shows its equivalent count.

Figure 3. Tourist arrival to India (2019-2021)

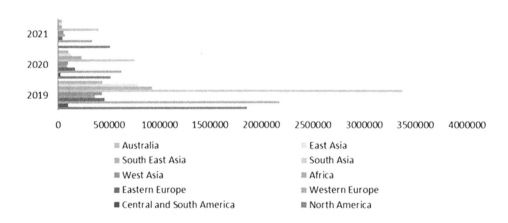

Table 1. Tourist visitor to India

Country of Nationality	2019	2020	2021
North America	1863892	516960	510299
Central and South America	98926	26968	6798
Western Europe	2178441	624615	334850
Eastern Europe	456481	168145	43114
Africa	362308	90296	68914
West Asia	431943	97651	52174
South Asia	3375819	750061	398722
South East Asia	930540	231622	38474
East Asia	782225	130383	33762
Australia	438939	105047	38865

Figure 4 and Table 2 shows the medical travelers around the world for various medical issues. Medical tourism has been taken care of by Economic Cooperation among all over the world. Some of the major reasons for medical tourism are as follows,

1. **Shorter Waiting Time:** Patients are provided with immediate medication once they arrived which will not happen in developed countries.
2. **Quality Healthcare:** Good healthcare is assured by Medical Tourism Association (MTA) which is operating all over the world.
3. **Cost Effective:** MTA tries to provide a cost-effective medical treatment to the needy.
4. **Access to Specialist:** Best doctors can be fixed through proper information retrieval of NLP.
5. **Availability of Alternate Treatments:** Alternate treatment suggestions are provided by MTA.
6. **Freedom of Movement From One Country to Another:** This allows the patients to move from one nation to other.

According to market research, it is estimated that the medical tourism market worldwide has been increased from $62 approximately in 2016 to $ 166 by 2023. NLP plays a major role in searching of hospitals, specialist through proper information retrieval system. The tourism sector can utilize NLP for good search engines with prompt data. It is mandatory to provide the best destination in the search engines. As far as the tourism sector, a high growth is expected with utilizing the benefits of natural language processing, since all the available information are now scattered. If the information has been provided in an organized and authenticated manner, then definitely a high income can be achieved through the tourism sector.

NLP based mobile application tries to map the languages and it can be used as a personal assistant like Siri, Alexa, etc. for our own native languages. WTTC (World Travel & Tourism Council) has forecasted the Tourist sector economy contribution to be reach by Rs. 1.9 trillion and through which employment levels will grow by almost 35 million jobs. The total contribution of TT sector is shown in Table 3.

Figure 4. Medical travellers 2022

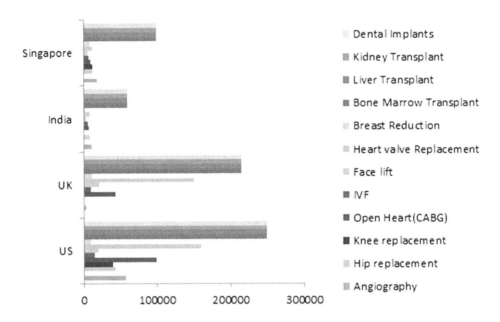

Table 2. Medical travellers count 2022

Procedure	US	UK	India	Singapore
Angioplasty	57000	21000-27000	11000	18500
Angiography	2500 – 3000	3000	600	1000
Hip replacement	43000	43000-46000	9000	12000
Knee replacement	40000	36000-38000	6000-9000	12000
Open Heart (CABG)	100000	43000	7500	9600
IVF	15000	10000	6000	7000
Face lift	20000	21000	3100	6250
Heart valve Replacement	160000	150000	9000	12500
Breast Reduction	10000	11000	2200	8000
Bone Marrow Transplant	250000	215000	60000	100000
Liver Transplant	250000	215000	60000	100000
Kidney Transplant	250000	215000	60000	100000
Dental Implants	250000	215000	60000	100000

Table 3. Contribution of travel and tourism (worldwide) towards economy

2021 Rank	USD bn
United States	1,271.2
China	814.3
Germany	251.0
Japan	206.3
Italy	179.0
India	178.0
France	177.9
Mexico	168.8
United Kingdom	157.5
Spain	113.1
Brazil	103.5
Canada	88.0
Australia	76.5
Netherlands	76.3
Russia	66.0
Turkey	59.3
Saudi Arabia	51.5
South Korea	48.8
Iran	48.1
Switzerland	44.5

BENEFITS OF TOURS AND TRAVELS

Moreover, other than economy growth, tourism creates the opportunity to preserve local culture and heritage, community strengthening, regenerate customs and art forms, cultural exchange between foreigner's and citizens, infrastructure development, employment generation, also it improves the country's brand image. Also, the educational sector has also been improved with more other nation students and this implies a good exchange of knowledge transfer among student community that provides the opportunity of global recognition of local colleges. This in turn improves the international job opportunities. Hence, in recent years the focus towards the improvement of travels and tourism sector has been undertaken by many countries. The percentage of students opting for abroad studies in states of India during 2022 is shown in Figure 5 and 6, and its corresponding data is provided in Table 4.

Figure 5. Student travellers abroad

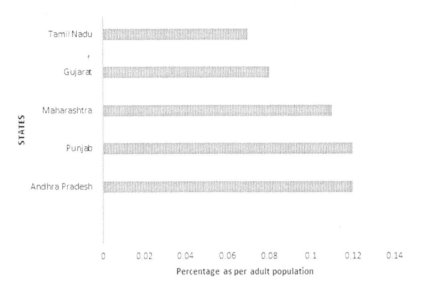

Table 4. Student travellers from India abroad (2018-2022)

Year	Number of Students
2018	517998
2019	586337
2020	259655
2021	444553
2022	750365

Figure 6. Student travellers from India abroad (2018-2022)

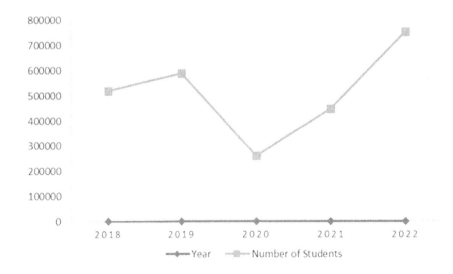

NATURAL LANGUAGE PROCESSING

Natural Language Processing (NLP) (Cambria & White, 2014) is based on two main aspects, that includes, Natural Language Understanding (NLU) or Natural Language Interpretation (NLI) and Natural Language Generation (NLG). Natural Language Processing depends on search, logic, and knowledge representation, in which search, and logic depends on Machine Learning (ML). NLP deals with both speech processing and written language processing. The two primary task of NLP are syntactic analysis and sematic analysis. Syntactic analysis involves in the correct formation of text, speech with respect to the corresponding grammar of the referred language. It does the parsing and grammar rules are applied to group of words. It includes many inner functional steps like parsing, sentence breaking (Tokenization), part of speech tagging, morphological segmentation, word segmentation, lemmatization and stemming. Each step has its own functionality that includes,

1. **Parsing:** Grammatical analysis for the given sentence.
2. **Sentence Braking:** Identifying the sentence boundaries or stop words on a large phrase.
3. **Word Segmentation:** Large phrase is cut down into individual units.
4. **Part of Speech Tagging:** Identifying the part of speech for each word in the given phrase.
5. **Lemmatization:** Finding the inflected forms of a word in the given sentence.
6. **Stemming:** Inflected words are cut down to their root form.

All these functional components are very important for syntactic analysis, whereas semantic analysis refers to the meaning of the sentence. It is the main tasks of the language processing because a sentence which is syntactically correct does not mean to be semantically correct. Semantic analysis is the process of understanding and interpreting the words, tone, sign, and structure of the provided sentence. Here, usually in real time, humans understand or intuited the spoken or written language based on their language proficiency. The main task of semantic analysis includes Named Entity Recognition (NER) and Word Sense Disambiguation (WSD). The named entity recognition is one of the subtasks of NLP that identifies the part of the word, and it classifies the named entities in an unstructured text into predefined categories like name of a person, locations, time expressions, organizations, quantities, percentage, monetary values etc. The ambiguity in the words is solved using word sense disambiguation technique that tries to find the actual context of the word in the given phrase. It is mainly used in information extraction, lexicography, text mining, information retrieval etc. The next, high-end task is the natural language generation that involves the word database, tries to identify the semantic intentions and converting the same into human language.

Natural Language Processing is concerned with the development of computational models of aspects of human language processing. Two main reasons for NLP development includes, In this field of research, computers perform useful and interesting tasks with human languages, taking as input one natural language such as English Language and output its translation in another Target Language (TL), pronounce the source language (SL), or give semantic knowledge of the source language (SL).

Today, Natural Language Processing (NLP) plays a vital role in improvising the TT sector. NLP enables a customized experience from the initial stage to the final stage of a travel. NLP, as its name implies, is one among the driving force of Artificial Intelligence (AI) that helps the machines to understand, learn, in turn respond to any given text or speech in any language. Thus, NLP influence AI and AI in turn influence NLP. The application of NLP includes Information Retrieval (IR), Information Extraction (IE),

Machine Translation (MT), Speech Recognition, Spam detection, Grammar Checking (GC), NLP based Personal Assistance devices, Question Answering (QA), text simplification, Predictive Typing (PT), Sentiment Analysis (SA), Behavioral Analysis (BA), Autocomplete, Document Summarization (DS) etc.

Thus, NLP can be effectively used in any process, application, or computation in unstructured data (Zong, 2013) that involves language modelling. Now, the chapter moves with how NLP can be applied to Travel and Tourism sector that improves the sector value and tourist satisfaction.

NLP IN TRAVEL AND TOURISM

Today, artificial intelligence has put up its footprints in almost all the sectors that include technology, health, management, business, education, construction, language modelling, translation, information processing, extraction, retrieval, etc. As with other field, AI is also playing its role in travel and tourism sector. Here, the data is text, language in either spoken or written form that requires the NLP engine (Yan & Subramanian, 2019). NLP is applied in almost all the areas of travel and tourism, that appears as various applications such as conversational system or chatbots (Siri, Alexa, Google Assistant, Cortana, etc.) (García-Pablos, Cuadros, & Linaza, 2016; Miah et al., 2017), personalization or recommender system (Irwan et al., 2020; Zheng et al., 2018) for Travel assist (provide support to both travel agents and traveller regarding the accommodation, knowledge of tourist sites, digital guided tours, educating travellers about the places of interest, etc. – smart travel agents [Yuan et al., 2016]), prediction forecasting systems, language translation applications (Google translate, iTranslate, Linguee, Microsoft Translator, PONS translate, SayHi Translate, DeepL etc) and voice recognition / natural language processing systems that includes simplified ticket bookings, hotel reservations, navigation etc.

There is enormous opportunity in the global travel sector where AI can be contributed further to improve the global GDP with the utilization of NLP (Marrese-Taylor et al., 2013) in this concern. Each process has its own NLP mechanism and thus supports the travelers with utmost comfortability. All the NLP applications for travel and tourism work round the clock unlike humans and provides respond to the queries any time of the day. Some of the opportunist where travel brands can be leveraged by adopting NLP that involves AI is shown in Figure 7.

Figure 7. NLP cum AI in travel and tourism

NEED OF NLP IN TRAVEL AND TOURISM

It is always noted that all the industry are either in one way interconnected with each other. The shortcomings of one sector will has its impact on other. Now, many travel agents are providing a on hand support to the travellers by using Market Basket Analysis (MBA) in searching hotels, places to visit, restaurant, booking flight tickets, taxis, etc. (Ricci, 2022). A hassle-free experience to the traveller and businessperson/medical tourist in their operations can be provided through NLP application as it understands their language and intelligently act upon it as per the context and language. Travel brands also faces many challenges while adopting NLP that includes No Clear Insights on Return on Investment, Lack of Privacy and Defined Responsibility, AI Still Holds Some Unsolved Bugs, Data availability etc. Some of the ways through which NLP can help the travel industry are as follows:

The NLP can be effectively used in the major processes involving in travel:

1. Improved Booking experience
2. Drafting Personalized tours
3. Improving maintaining procedures
4. Rejuvenating the hotel experience
5. Reinventing the hotel experience
6. Redefining the sightseeing experience
7. Sightseeing experience is redefined with NLP based applications

Improved Booking Experience

In travel, booking or reserving plays a vital role and it becomes the foremost job of any traveller. The booking includes all sorts of (i) commutes such as train, flight, bus, cab based on duration differs); (ii) accommodations that includes hotel rooms for stay (long term or short term) resorts, paying guest, apartments; (iii) reserving the visiting place; (iv) booking for physician appointment for medical tourist (v) to make appointments for any celebrity, VIP visit etc. Booking again is an hectic process, which has to satisfy many criteria as per the requirements such as finding the shortest duration in travel (airline, train, trans commute etc), low price with basic needs (flight ticket, rooms etc), for rich persons high comfort one environment, like this the option goes on changes as per their economy levels. Hence, it is mandatory to know all the information, to do comparative data analytics so that the chatbot can be able to do the recommendation properly. The NLP chatbot is trained to perform with good recommendations and immediate response for queries. The NLP chatbot may be fully automatic or partially. Nowadays, fully automatic chatbot has got more attention. In semi-automatic chatbot, the chatbot collects information from the customer and provide the same to the human agent of the company. By this way, the chatbot helps the businessperson and the traveller with proper early information exchange. The key parameters of the travel are well identified, and this information are kept for future answering, so that the customer real time grievances are solved seamlessly without any delay. The NLP chatbot can be easily respond in any language as per the user interest. The key points during the conversation are marked for future use.

Drafting Personalized Travel

The chatbot and NLP tools allows the traveller to plan their travel in a personalized way that includes where to stay, the option to choose their resorts or hotels as their needs or expected way, the suggestion of the length of stay in a particular place, the priority of places to visit, etc. The NLP chatbots helps in providing suggestion and to curate the travel packages for each individual. Today's chatbot are designed in such a way that recommends the options as per the preferences of the traveller. It collects all the information from the traveller and try to recollect the history of travel and based on past, present selection's, the analytics on the data has been performed to provide a good service on demand basis.

Improving Maintenance Procedures

On the other side, chatbots help the service provider with authentic, reliable data of the customer, which helps to provide a better service and to maintain the same. It helps the businesspeople to know about the interest of the traveller, through which the service provider and the traveller be a good partner. It acts as a bridge between the two, i.e., the service provider and the customer, and thus improves the business. There is vast growth in both financial and reputational status of the travel service provider because of chatbots. By using NLP tools, the Airlines and other commute services are improving their maintenance.

Rejuvenating the Hotel Experience

Today, due to digital change, it is possible to view all data, maintain it reflecting in big data. This big data allows us to analyse the information and provide the recommendations, suggestions, high visionary on anything that we deal with. Moreover, the social platform provides the huge data from which more information has been shared to many people at same time. Today's many mobile based applications have been evolved that includes, Airbnb, Booking.com, Hostelworld, Hotels.com, HotelTonight, etc., which serves effectively for all kinds of customer. NLP along with big data analytics play a major role here to segregate the hotels as per their ratings in social media, individuals blog etc.

Reinventing the Hotel Experience

The maintenance of hotels also be improved with many NLP tools like, voice assisted caller, like Alexa or Siri to help the traveller. These robots try to help the customer with their needs. They help in cleaning the rooms, washing, which are all done through simple voice recognition, which is possible only by NLP. For any traveller, here there is no language barrier, and the traveller will be quite comfortable for his / her local needs. Moreover, a good security has been provided by facial and voice recognition robots.

Sightseeing Experience Is Redefined With NLP-Based Applications

As per eMarketer study, it is noted that, travel based mobile applications are in high download category (7th most downloadable mobile applications) and around 60% of travellers prefer using these apps for planning their tours. Hence, today many travel guide based mobile applications are being developed with better user interface and graphic designing. For foreign tourist, it is very difficult to understand the local language, traffic signs, the real environment etc. NLP applications are highly useful these situations where, the language translation happens within a fraction of time, without change in context of the meaning. Many geolocation apps have been developed to indicate the local changes in traffic that provides a good commute to the destination. Many local tour apps, route apps, restaurant finder, are being developed daily. Real time data driven applications helps the traveller or businessperson to know about the current situation and all rating are mostly near real time only. Today in all over the world, all display units in any commute junctions including Airport terminals, train terminals, bus, or any display in tourist spots are not just shows the content, those display units are all changed into smart displays, that shows the current relevant data as per the viewer's requirement. Intelligence has been imported into all the devices that have been embedded with NLP enabled software.

All the above tasks can be achieved using Market basket Analysis (MBA), where the retailers use the data analytics to improve the sales and bookings by understanding the tourist expectations, the pattern of stay from each nation, people, their culture etc. It involves in big data analytics of huge data comprising of booking history of rooms, flights, brand, purchase, product groupings, associated thing or bookings where the products to be purchased or booked together. The MBA involves in surveys, gathering group information, customer likes / observation and their expectation in social media.

NLP-BASED CHATBOT (VIRTUAL TOURIST GUIDE)

Majority of tourist queries are satisfied by chatbot which is one among the contribution of NLP. A chatbot is referred to intelligent Virtual Agent (IVA), which can play the role of a guide and provide the information as per the customer's request. Here the customers are the travellers. Implementing NLP in TT sector provides an end-to-end solution the tourist. The rise of digital technology paves the way for artificial intelligence, machine learning, and language processing field to boom up. The nature of learning from the environment made the NLP to grow faster than expected. The precision of NLP based applications can be improved by the real time data provided by the customers and an efficient self-learning algorithm. With this a seamless travel experience to the travellers has been provided continuously.

A chatbot not only plays the role of virtual agent, it also provides the recommendations as per the needs of tourist. Today's chatbots are more sophisticated than earlier versions as it is responded smartly, recommendations are provided as per recent review, more accurate answers, good recall in information retrieval etc. Hence, whatever be the agency as hotel, airline, shopping, tourist destinations, restaurant a chatbot act like a virtual intelligent agent. A chatbot's NLP will be usually designed with the following keys, Intent – the semantic of the words of the query; utterances – the perception of the user for the query; entity – information that includes place, date, time, person, etc.; context – the actual requirement of the query that maps intent with utterances and finally the session – the whole conversation from start to end, with the inclusion of interrupts. Thus, the artificial intelligence enabled NLP chatbot's provides a better friendly experience to the user, without human intervention. Chatbots are of different kinds that includes, Keyword recognition based chatbots, Menu / button based chatbots, Linguistic based chatbots, and Machine learning based chatbots, Hybrid model, Voice bots, Appointment scheduling (Booking) chatbots, Customer support chatbots. All these chatbots are widely used in travel and tourism sector.

Nowadays, the chatbots become smarter as they are learning from their conversation and try to respond with accurate answers for the queries. Some of the major contributions of NLP enabled chatbots are as follows,

1. **Business Logic Integration:** The companies business logic has been enabled in the chatbot.
2. **Dialogue Management:** Both syntactic and semantic analyses of the conversation have been done by the AI enabled chatbot.
3. **Rapid Iteration:** The chatbots are easily programmable and provides good accuracy in information retrieval.
4. **Human Handoff:** It refers to the seamless handoff between the human and AI chatbot.

While designing a chatbot two things must be taken care, proper training, and user friendly.

Training

To generate a smart chatbots the designer has to ensure an NLP based chatbot, which has to be trained with more real time corpus and feedback has to be given, so that the learning process will be very high and when implemented the chatbot will be able to act smart as a human being.

User Friendly

The chatbot must be user friendly and it should provide good suggestions as per the query and it should be easily upgradeable. Too much delay should be avoided.

All the available chatbots are nowadays, associated with social networks, which enables them for suggestions, recommendations, etc. This shows that today's chatbot are highly intervened with latest technologies that include AI for self-learning, NLP for language understanding and generation, Data Analytics for suggestions and recommendations, Computer vision for human perception, GPS for location information etc.

Advantages of Chatbots include:

1. **24/7 Availability of Customer Service:** A tourist chatbot can be available round the clock which enables the tourist to take last minute changes in the travel log or any last-minute changes in plan.
2. Chatbots are multilingual and support all languages queries with ease. No need of information search on browser by the traveller, chatbots will provide accurate needed information.
3. Pre, ongoing and post booking is available all the time. (Anywhere and anytime)
4. Most of the AI chatbots are available in mobile phones today and it is developed with platform independent, or able to map with available platform.
5. Chatbots provide a good customer relationship management, avoiding the need of sales agent.
6. Personalized messages are sent to the tourist, during the travel and maintain a good relationship with the person after the travel also.
7. Recommendations are done automatically, and valuable suggestions are provided.
8. All the chatbot conversation has been maintained and database has been generated for enquired customer and regular targeted communication is done as they are the potential future customers. They are finetuned over a period.
9. If the chatbot was not able to find the answer or if the traveller is not satisfied with answer provided by the chatbot, then it eventually connects the traveller to a live person instead of closing the website or moving with other customer. – It is stated as per Econsultancy statistics that when

a traveller is provided with personalized experience, then nearly 44% the person would become a repeat customer.

Apart from these benefits, nowadays the expectation of tourist or businessperson are high that includes with more personalized recommendations, more demanding, expecting more detailed accurate information, satisfying their budget or business plan, to provide good profit with their travel and immediate response to their queries for their travel. Many companies, government in tourist sector use the method of recommendations to attract more people. The working of AI chatbots (Virtual Agents) includes five levels, and they are, tokenization, normalization, entity recognition, dependency parsing and language generation that corresponds to read, interpret, understand, formulate and to send the response.

1. **Tokenization of the Query:** Removal of stop words and chopping the query or sentence into tokens.
2. **Normalizing:** Irrelevant information are removed, and the query has been put up in normal case.
3. **Entity Recognition:** Ability to identify the entities i.e., the thing being referred, such as name, place, time, organisation, etc. Syntactic analysis has been done here.
4. **Dependency Parsing:** The role of each word with respect to the other, the interdependence of each word along with its parts of speech. By doing this semantic analysis has been done.
5. **Language Generation:** After understanding the context of the query, the bot now tries to respond the tourist with appropriate answer.

Any automatic systems when implemented in the real environment, initially does many flaws, but through effective learning mechanism with real time data, they able to make themselves smarter with continuous interaction with them. Hence, in general, initial monitoring has to be done for all kinds of automatic systems, Likewise, NLP chatbots also turns into smarter with every interaction and initial monitoring.

CHALLENGES IN ADOPTING NLP BASED TOOLS IN TRAVEL BRANDS

All technology is having its own positive and negative towards its applications. Similarly, applications based on AI / NLP has its own challenges which are faced by travel brands while implementing the NLP based tools.

Security Issues, Defined Responsibility, Privacy Lagging

In online booking of travel, rooms etc. there is no guarantee of privacy and in most of the apps many personal information has been enquired. Proper security has to be enabled using high end crypto algorithms. Software and hardware malfunction has to be identified earlier that left to data theft. To identify the malfunctioned, data thieve is itself a high-end task due to automatic learning environment.

Lack of Clear Insights on ROI (Return on Investment)

Even though artificial intelligence has many pros, it is not easy to understand the hidden factors in it and it became challenge to calculate the benefits for the travel companies. To predict the return on investment and understanding the timeline of AI for non-technical person is hard. Earlier, without AI the identification to figure out where the problem has been occurred, i.e., with respect to customer, developer is easy. More chances of data theft, as it involves full data driven application.

Unsolved Bugs in AI

Implementing AI / NLP based application is still in its developing phase and has many bugs to resolve. Combining NLP along with AI is a huge task and involves high computations, training with real time data which is not afford by small service providers. It involves a lot of research in AI/NLP based applications.

Change in Perspective for AI/NLP-Based Applications

As these approaches are all data driven, the output is entirely based on the provided input. Hence a good knowledge in AI along with data handling mechanism is required for proper application development and maintenance.

RESEARCH CHALLENGES IN NLP FOR TOURIST AND TRAVEL APPLICATIONS

Through digitization tourist and travel industry has gained many advantages with the help of NLP. In spite of these advancements, the industry has many challenges that has to be sorted which includes language translation as per region, updating the information in portal, miscommunication, legal partnership with government sector etc, apart from the general challenges, data security, privacy, mislead information, truth in the provided data etc plays avital role in selecting the online booking websites. Apart from these understanding the tourist wish, motivating them, set the priorities, strengthen profit, to identify the trend in market, are also major challenges in online tourism.

This research received no specific grant from any funding agency in the public, commercial, or not-for-profit sectors.

REFERENCES

Bandara, S. B. G. J. S., Jayasundera, J. M. K. H., Udayanga, U. H. N., Iloshini, P. A. A., & Pathirana, K. P. P. S. (2018). *Artificial Conversational Agent Based Tour Guide System*. Academic Press.

Bulchand-Gidumal, J. (2022). Impact of artificial intelligence in travel, tourism, and hospitality. In *Handbook of e-Tourism* (pp. 1943–1962). Springer International Publishing. doi:10.1007/978-3-030-48652-5_110

Cambria, E., & White, B. (2014). Jumping NLP curves: A review of natural language processing research. *IEEE Computational Intelligence Magazine*, *9*(2), 48–57. doi:10.1109/MCI.2014.2307227

Darbellay, F., & Stock, M. (2012). Tourism as complex interdisciplinary research object. *Annals of Tourism Research*, *39*(1), 441–458. doi:10.1016/j.annals.2011.07.002

Egger, R. (2022). *Machine Learning in Tourism: A Brief Overview Applied Data Science in Tourism. Tourism on the Verge*. Springer. doi:10.1007/978-3-030-88389-8_6

Egger, R., & Gokce, E. (2022). Natural Language Processing (NLP): An Introduction: Making Sense of Textual Data. In *Applied Data Science in Tourism: Interdisciplinary Approaches, Methodologies, and Applications* (pp. 307–334). Springer International Publishing. doi:10.1007/978-3-030-88389-8_15

García-Pablos, A., Cuadros, M., & Linaza, M. T. (2015). OpeNER: open tools to perform natural language processing on accommodation reviews. In *Information and Communication Technologies in Tourism 2015: Proceedings of the International Conference in Lugano, Switzerland, February 3-6, 2015* (pp. 125-137). Springer International Publishing. 10.1007/978-3-319-14343-9_10

García-Pablos, A., Cuadros, M., & Linaza, M. T. (2016). Automatic analysis of textual hotel reviews. *Information Technology & Tourism*, *16*(1), 45–69. doi:10.100740558-015-0047-7

Guerrero-Rodriguez, R., Álvarez-Carmona, M. Á., Aranda, R., & López-Monroy, A. P. (2021). Studying online travel reviews related to tourist attractions using nlp methods: The case of Guanajuato, Mexico. *Current Issues in Tourism*, 1–16.

Halkiopoulos, C., Dimou, E., Kompothrekas, A., Telonis, G., & Boutsinas, B. (2021, June). The E-tour facilitator platform supporting an innovative health tourism marketing strategy. In *Culture and Tourism in a Smart, Globalized, and Sustainable World: 7th International Conference of IACuDiT, Hydra, Greece, 2020* (pp. 609-623). Springer International Publishing.

Irwan, Sukaesih, & Alamsyah. (2020). *Opinion mining using analytics to understand global tourism attraction*. Academic Press.

Kleshcheva, A. (2021). Perception of Dark Tourism. *Zeitschrift für Tourismuswissenschaft*, *13*(2), 191–208. doi:10.1515/tw-2021-0014

Li, Q., Li, S., Zhang, S., Hu, J., & Hu, J. (2019). A review of text corpus-based tourism big data mining. *Applied Sciences (Basel, Switzerland)*, *9*(16), 3300. doi:10.3390/app9163300

Malaka, R., & Zipf, A. (2000). Deep Map: Challenging IT research in the framework of a tourist information system. In *Information and Communication Technologies in Tourism 2000: Proceedings of the International Conference in Barcelona, Spain, 2000* (pp. 15-27). Springer Vienna.

Marrese-Taylor, E., Velásquez, J. D., Bravo-Marquez, F., & Matsuo, Y. (2013). Identifying customer preferences about tourism products using an aspect-based opinion mining approach. *Procedia Computer Science*, *22*, 182–191. doi:10.1016/j.procs.2013.09.094

Miah, S. J., Vu, H. Q., Gammack, J., & McGrath, M. (2017). A big data analytics method for tourist behaviour analysis. *Information & Management*, *54*(6), 771–785. doi:10.1016/j.im.2016.11.011

Mich, L. (2022). AI and Big Data in Tourism: Definitions, Areas, and Approaches. In *Applied Data Science in Tourism: Interdisciplinary Approaches, Methodologies, and Applications* (pp. 3–15). Springer International Publishing. doi:10.1007/978-3-030-88389-8_1

Ricci, F. (2022). Recommender systems in tourism. In *Handbook of e-Tourism* (pp. 457–474). Springer International Publishing. doi:10.1007/978-3-030-48652-5_26

Roy, G. (2023). Travelers' online review on hotel performance–Analyzing facts with the Theory of Lodging and sentiment analysis. *International Journal of Hospitality Management, 111*, 103459. doi:10.1016/j.ijhm.2023.103459

Schuckert, M., Liu, X., & Law, R. (2015). Hospitality and tourism online reviews: Recent trends and future directions. *Journal of Travel & Tourism Marketing, 32*(5), 608–621. doi:10.1080/10548408.20 14.933154

Seyidov, J., & Adomaitienė, R. (2016). Factors influencing local tourists' decision-making on choosing a destination: A case of Azerbaijan. *Ekonomika (Nis), 95*(3), 112–127. doi:10.15388/Ekon.2016.3.10332

Tripathi, P., Kumar, S., & Rawat, P. (2022). Paradigm Shift in the Functioning of the Tourism and Hotel Industry Using NLP, Digital Assistant, and AI Models. In Artificial Intelligence for Societal Development and Global Well-Being (pp. 196-210). IGI Global.

Xu, H., & Lv, Y. (2022). Mining and Application of Tourism Online Review Text Based on Natural Language Processing and Text Classification Technology. *Wireless Communications and Mobile Computing, 2022*, 2022. doi:10.1155/2022/9905114

Yan, L. X., & Subramanian, P. (2019). A review on exploiting social media analytics for the growth of tourism. In *Recent Trends in Data Science and Soft Computing: Proceedings of the 3rd International Conference of Reliable Information and Communication Technology (IRICT 2018)* (pp. 331-342). Springer International Publishing. 10.1007/978-3-319-99007-1_32

Yuan, H., Xu, H., Qian, Y., & Li, Y. (2016). Make your travel smarter: Summarizing urban tourism information from massive blog data. *International Journal of Information Management, 36*(6), 1306–1319. doi:10.1016/j.ijinfomgt.2016.02.009

Zheng, X., Luo, Y., Sun, L., Zhang, J., & Chen, F. (2018). A tourism destination recommender system using users' sentiment and temporal dynamics. *Journal of Intelligent Information Systems, 51*(3), 557–578. doi:10.100710844-018-0496-5

Zong, C. (2013). *Statistical Natural Language Processing*. Tsinghua University Press.

KEY TERMS AND DEFINITIONS

Artificial Intelligence (AI): Making intelligent machines, particularly intelligent computer programmes, is a scientific and engineering endeavour.

Chatbot: Chatbots mimic human receptionist or a helper for the new person which provides the required information to the enquired person through chats.

Hospitality: Relationship that exists between a host and a guest in which the host accords the guest some measure of goodwill.

Natural Language Processing (NLP): NLP is the processing of natural languages (English, Tamil, Chinese, etc.) in order to make understand and generate these languages by the computers.

Return on Investment (RoI): A ratio between net income and investment is known as return on investment or return on costs.

Travel and Tourism: Travel and tourism involves information about various tourist places around the world. It deals with products, sites, airlines, hotels information for the travellers.

Travel Guide (TG): A person who discusses the interesting facts about a place as they pass through it.

Virtual Tourist Guide (VTG): VTG is an electronic travel guide that provides information about travel information in any of the electronic gadgets that use internet.

Chapter 12
Enhancing Automatic Speech Recognition and Speech Translation Using Google Translate

S. Arun Kamaraj
Thiagarajar College of Engineering, India

M. Gautham
Thiagarajar College of Engineering, India

S. Karthikeyan
Thiagarajar College of Engineering, India

R. Parkavi
Thiagarajar College of Engineering, India

ABSTRACT

Communication between speakers of many languages is made possible by cutting-edge technologies like spoken language translation. The process of automatically recognizing, translating speech in real life is still a particularly challenging part of spoken language translation. Because it necessitates a fundamental modification of both linguistic and non-linguistic attributes, interpreting spoken words directly from one language to another is difficult. Numerous basic modules, like Google Translate and Text-to-Speech, are capable of achieving this. This speech recognition model not only demonstrates technological proficiency, but also offers a helpful platform for those who have hearing challenges. The majority of hearing-impaired people find it difficult to communicate because they rely on lipreading or other specialized treatments and struggle to understand broad information in this modern era. For those who have hearing impairments, speech recognition software would offer a comprehensive long-term answer because live speech-to-text translations will improve their communication skills.

DOI: 10.4018/978-1-6684-8145-5.ch012

Copyright © 2023, IGI Global. Copying or distributing in print or electronic forms without written permission of IGI Global is prohibited.

INTRODUCTION

Speech-to-text software can understand spoken language and translate it into text by using computational linguistics. Other names for it include voice recognition and computer speech recognition. Speech-to-speech translation is an essential phenomenon that enables intercommunication between speakers of various languages. One of the most important issues with globalization is the language barrier, which must be overcome with the help of multilingual speech-to-speech translation tools. Language boundaries continue to be infamous barriers to open communication as globalization grows. One cutting-edge tool that makes it possible to converse with people who speak different languages is spoken language translation. To translate spoken language, which requires identifying and mechanically translating speech in real-time, is still an extremely challenging task. Transcribing audio streams into text in real-time so that it can be displayed and used by particular tools, gadgets, and software. We can improve speech recognition using automatic voice recognition and a full-speech translation model. This paradigm usually employs a cascading of an automatic speech detection module and a specific language processing module to build speaking language processing systems. The results of Automatic Speech Recognition affect the performance of each of the natural language processing modules. To improve speech translation performance, it is required to either eliminate experimental errors in grouped and verified systems or guarantee that there is enough data to train the models. We discovered that Google's text translation services could handle both mistake correction and voice translation between languages.

HISTORY AND CURRENT SCENARIO

The idea of voice recognition emerged in the 1940s, and the first successful speech recognition programme was developed in 1952 at Bell Labs. This programme is now working on recognising a simple number in a sound environment. Early voice recognition technology focused on the fundamentals of speech recognition, which were mostly concerned with information theoretic models, in the 1940s and 1950s. Recognition of tiny vocabularies (about 10 to 100 words) of distinct words in the 1960s was based on their basic speech sound characteristics. Time normalising techniques were among the emerging technologies at this time. The vocabulary (about 100–1000 words) was discovered using pattern recognition techniques in the 1970s. Large vocabularies (thousands of words) were employed in the 1980s, and the main focus was on speech recognition issues with vast networks for language structures. The Hidden Markov model and the stochastic language model were two significant advancements during this time period that allowed for new, strong solutions to continuous voice recognition problems. The methodologies for stochastic language understanding, the statistical construction of big vocabulary speech understanding systems, and the learning of acoustic and linguistic models were among the advancements developed in the 1990s. Speech recognition technology has finally entered the market after over 50 years of study, and it is beneficial to consumers in a variety of ways. Let's examine the most current advancements in these technologies.

RECENT DEVELOPMENTS IN SPEECH RECOGNITION

Ximera Model

XIMERA is made up of four main modules, including a text processing module, a prosodic parameter generation module, a selection module, a waveform module, and a development module. Chinese and Japanese are the languages XIMERA is designed to support. The text processing module, speech corpora, acoustic models for parameter generation, and function of cost for segments finding method are examples of language-dependent modules. The cost function of the segment selection finds method is also connected to the target language. At the moment, XIMERA is concentrating on a reading voice pattern appropriate for news reading and emotionless conversations between humans and machines. The following are XIMERA's salient characteristics:

1. It's an extensive corpus with nearly 110 hours of the corpus of a Japanese male, 60 hours of the corpus of a Japanese woman, and 20 hours of the corpus of a Chinese woman.
2. The production of prosodic parameters using HMM.
3. A segment selection cost function that has been improved using perceptual studies.

pyttsx3 Module

Python's pyttsx3 module converts text to speech. It works offline and is appropriate for Python versions 2 and 3, in contrast to competing libraries. The pyttsx3 initiation factory method is used by an application to obtain its function from the pyttsx3 Engine instance. This tool turns the required text into speech and it is fairly simple to use. The "sapi5" for Windows programs provides the first voice, which is a female voice, and the second voice, which is a male voice. There are three TTS engines it supports: SAPI5 on Windows, and Mac OS X uses NS Speech Synthesizer and eSpeak on other platforms.

Shazam Application

An excellent illustration of the functions of speech recognition technology is Shazam. This software, for which Apple paid $400 million in 2018, uses the device's microphone to recognize songs, ads, movies, and TV series based on a brief audio sample. So, when you start the recognizing process inside the application, the audio recording starts around your surroundings. It can easily distinguish between background noise and the required source content, recognize the pattern of the music, and verifies the presence of the audio recording in the application's database. Following that, it will find the exact song that's playing and inform the end-user.

CURRENT SCENARIO

The basic idea behind this project is to create an effective and user-friendly model for people communicating in different languages and who have hearing disabilities. The model breaks the barriers and increases fluency of communication for people with hearing difficulties.

Nowadays there are very less effective models for fluent speech translation and recognition. We think it is necessary to create a model that responds to an individual with the language of his own, when he is communicated with an unknown language. In this era, there are many models that respond to a person both text based and speech based, But very limited models that take input in one language and respond in another language of our choice. Also there is a need for a model that helps the hearing disabled people to understand speech in a more efficient way and to act as a replacement for sign language usage.

LITERATURE REVIEW

A complete assessment of the literature revealed that the majority of solutions in use lacked a dependable module for the accurate and seamless translation of recognized speech into textual characters. The works of authors Alexander, Wei Sung, Lee, and Chuang on enhancing speech translation and automatic speech recognition by word embedding. According to prediction, an existing Speech translation model may be readily separated into original language recognition parts and a target translation portion, but performance worsens when the input speech differs from that used during training. The technical and theoretical works and journals that authors have produced to design a better module for voice and language recognition are listed below:

Table 1. Related works

Author	Objective	Algorithm/Method	Merits/Demerits
Furui et al. (2004)	Summarization of Speech to Text conversion and Speech to Speech conversion methodologies.	Displaying of straightforward concatenated speech fragments that were taken from the original speech and utilization of speech synthesizer to synthesize the text of a summary.	MERITS: 1. It is simple to browse the documents. 2. It is simple to extract the portions of papers that are useful to users. 3. It is simple to use information extraction and retrieval techniques on the papers. DEFICIENCIES: The main issue with employing extracted speech segments is the concatenation's unnatural and noisy sound.
Nakamura et al. (2005)	To create a Multilingual Speech to Speech System that makes accurate translation	Corpus based techniques are limited to used to make narrow domains because of a lack of a sufficient size dual spoken languages in language databases.	MERITS: Compared to rule based systems generally, corpus-based systems are easier to construct and of superior quality. DEFICIENCIES: If they have any drawbacks, it is that storing corpus data requires a lot of memory. Rule-based systems are frequently employed in embedded applications as a result.
Chuang et al. (2021)	Improving of ASR and translation of speech through embedding of words.	In this Speech to Text translation system. The sequence to sequence dynamic Automatic Speech Recognition models are thought about, what is automatic decoder is typically used to and a transcription prediction which corresponds to enter the speech systems. In the Speech Translation, end to end model, the system learns how to transform the Source language speaking to language of the destination.	MERITS: Due to the absence of paired data, multitasked learning offers a method for utilising a single language content to enhance an end to end Speech Translation model. It is simple to divide an existing multitasking Speech Translation model into a language recognition structure and a destination language translation structure. DEFICIENCIES: Performance deteriorates when speech input is not the same as that used during training.

continues on following page

Table 1. Continued

Author	Objective	Algorithm/Method	Merits/Demerits
Alharbi et al. (2021)	Enhancement of automatic speech recognition.	DNN-HMM-based sound modelling sound of the background. They apply two strategies. The is based on first multi conditional exercise regarding the acoustic models. The following is auto-denoising encoders then carry out sound model instruction based on preprocessed data.	MERITS: 1. To improve speech clarity based on signal-to-noise ratio (SNR). 2. For noise reduction, independent components such as analysis and subspace speech enhancement are used in the model. DEFICIENCIES: The ability to discern human emotion is quite tough.
Stolcke et al. (2006)	To study the innovations at SRI-ICSI-UW on Speech to Text Transcription ideologies and methodologies.	It was acoustic modeling enhanced with many front ends. working at different frame speeds and by modifying the conventional techniques for discriminative Gaussian estimation.	MERITS: It is correct in other languages as well, including Arabic and Mandarin. DEFICIENCIES: The main issue with employing extracted speech segments is figuring out how to prevent the concatenation's unnaturally noisy sound.
Jorge et al. (2021)	Recognition of speech Using Acoustic Models and Language Models through live streaming of speech.	Using long, bidirectional speech recognition can be effectively combined with short-term memory acoustic models, general interpolated language models, and little performance degradation.	MERITS: It is an offline system that can be modified to function in a streaming environment. DEFICIENCIES: Performance deteriorates when speech input is different from that used during training.
Kano, Sakti, & Nakamura (2020).	Transcoding of End to End translation of Speech with the help of language pairs and learning by multi-tasking.	Direct translation from speech to text and beginning to end using a single model that combines ASR and MT.	MERITS: It offers notable gains over traditional cascade of the models and the direct translation of speech, which employs without transcoding a single model and other CL techniques. DEFICIENCIES: In most cases, speech acoustics include information on language and paralinguistic parameters which are rhythms, emotions, etc. Unfortunately, much cannot be said in writing since this information is not taken into account in the written part of the communication.
Kaur & Singh (2015).	Indian Sign Language Generation System.	A hearing impairment is used by those who use sign language. A system was created for real-time translation to Indian Sign Language from the natural language in order to close the communication gap between people who use it and those who do not.	MERITS: The suggested system is an automatic Sign Language generating system which translates spoken or written texts into its corresponding Sign Language animations. DEFICIENCIES: The present systems are only available in some domains, and there are no publicly available online systems for producing Indian Sign Language from Hindi or English sentences.
Naveen & Ponraj (2020)	Speech Recognition with Gender Identification and Speaker Diarization	Employing the microphone to record the voice in all directions. An angle of 360 degrees is used to record the direction of arrival. The technique of transforming an unknown speech waveform into the corresponding orthographic transcription is the speech recognition without manual control (ASR). Utilizing analytical methods, the voice signal was synced with the pitch frequency.	MERITS: Speaker Diarization lets you know who says what during an audio recording of a conversation. The model has a 92% accuracy rate in speech recognition. DEFICIENCIES: It's a little challenging to determine the gender.
Park et al. (2021)	Implementation of a processor that functions as Speech to Text Converter in back transcription using Text to speech to Text ideology.	Using Back Transcription (BTS), a de noising-based technique, such corpora can be produced automatically. Using Text-to-Speech, BTS corrupts the text from the raw corpus (TTS) and STT (Speech to Text) systems. The original text can then be rebuilt using a post-processing model that has been trained using the wrong input.	MERITS: Both the quantitative and qualitative assessments reveal that a processor that is trained using this method is quite successful in resolving the difficult speech recognition problems such as improper handling of words of unknown words. DEFICIENCIES: The out-of-vocabulary (OOV) problem causes terms that are not in the dictionary to be incorrectly identified.

PATENT REVIEWS

Table 2. Related works with respect to patent

S. No	Patent Number/ File	Inventor	Applications
1.	US 10,388,274 B1	Bjorn Hoffmeister	Answering questions the relevant question is one typical application for a voice processing system. To locate and get an unstructured text that might be relevant to the question, the text might be used to do a web search.
2.	US 10,600,413 B2	Dazhao Zhang et al.	A voice control method was revealed, and it consists of a device and a terminal. When a terminal enters voice control mode, it receives voice input and generates the speech text that corresponds to it. In response to the determination of the speech-to-text matches an interface list effectively, comparing the speech text to an interface list of words relating to an existing operational interface, where the interface list of words contains text information of the current required to operate interface; locating an operation link in the current interface operations that relate to the speech text; and having to perform the operation that relates to the interface.
3.	US 11,062,726 B2	Sasha P. Caskey et al.	A method for giving a user real-time speech analysis involves recording a speech input, trying to perform real-time voice recognition of the input, which could include turning the speech input into text, trying to analyze the recognized speech input to spot a mistake in the user's voice, which may involve comparing the voice of a correct text produced by an automated speech generation system with the collected speech input, and processing the text to produce the desired output audio message.
4.	US 2020/0035231 A1	Sree Hari Krishnan Parthasarathi et al.	Incoming audio can be categorized as desired speech, unwanted speech, or non-speech by a system set up to handle spoken commands. Desired speech is speech that comes from the same speaker as the reference speech. A trained neural network classifier may compare the reference feature vector and the input audio data frame by frame to assess if each frame of the input audio data was produced from the same person as the reference speech. The labels may be provided to an automatic speech recognition (ASR) component so that it may focus its processing on the necessary speech.
5.	WO 2005/098817 A2	Ashwin Rao	This invention primarily relates to a system and method for converting speech to text utilizing a limited dictation approach. It also generally refers to the user interface for speech recognition systems.

COMPARATIVE STUDY WITH THE EXISTING MODEL

As we all know Alexa works on speech recognition where the speaker will be able to communicate with it but the speaker will only be able to get the reply in the same language as the speaker speaks whereas the model we are coming up with has a great advantage where there will be option to switch between languages depending on their convenience. Not only Alexa, Google home, Homepod all these work on the same basis where the input and output languages are the same.

Our model has n number of features like it will convert 108 languages depend upon user, it will listen to the data from the user for at least 5 minutes without any interruption,, it will automatically recognize the data after user data that is listened to by the model. In Alexa works on speech recognition only but our model works on both speech recognition and speech translation. Our model has an additional feature that is converting speech to text format for understanding for disabled people.

PROPOSED METHODOLOGIES

Attribute Description

Automatic Speech Recognition (ASR)

Automatic speech recognition, or ASR, is a method that enables users to use their voices to communicate with computers in a manner that, in its most sophisticated forms, closely resembles natural human speech. The most advanced ASR solutions currently being developed are built on natural language processing, or NLP for short. We are already seeing some impressive outcomes in the shape of intelligent smartphone interfaces like the Siri programme on the iPhone and other systems used in business and sophisticated technological contexts, even though there is still a long way to go before it achieves its pinnacle of development. This type of ASR comes the closest to making it possible for humans and artificial intelligence to have a meaningful conversation.

Even though these NLP programmes have an "accuracy" of between 96 and 99%, they can only produce results of this calibre under the ideal conditions in which the questions that humans ask them are either of the straightforward yes-or-no variety or have a limited number of viable response alternatives based on selected keywords. Similar principles apply to voice recognition technology. The voice recognition software turns the speech into a digital format, decodes the input speech to be taken as bits so it can understand, and then analyses the content of the bits. Then, based on prior information and typical speech patterns, it concludes and formulates hypotheses about what the user is saying. The smart device can respond with the most appropriate statement after determining what the user most likely stated. The best practices for AI are still being developed, but humans have improved their methods. They have been educated the same way our parents and instructors educated us, which requires a lot of labor, study, and creativity.

The Basic Functioning of Automatic Speech Recognition (ASR)

The following is the basic series of actions that causes any Automatic Speech Recognition program, regardless of sophistication, to pick up and break down your speech for analysis and response:

1. You communicate with the software via an audio feed.
2. The device to which you are speaking generates a wave file of your words.
3. By the reduction of the noise in the background and the normalization of the volume, the wave file is cleaned.
4. The filtered waveform that results is then broken down into phonemes. (Phonemes are the fundamental building blocks of language and words. English has 44 of them, which are made up of sound blocks. Each phoneme is built like a chain, and the Automatic Speech recognition program employs the probability in the deduction of the whole words and complete sentences by the evaluation of them in succession, beginning with the initial phoneme.
5. Your Automatic Speech Recognizer can respond in a more meaningful way because it has integrated your words throughout.

The Capacity to Recognize a Voice Signal in a Speech Recognition System May Be Classified as Follows

1. **Separate Words:** The algorithm only accepts one of these utterances at a time. And it frequently requires a speaker to pause between each phrase, as well as silence on both sides of the sample window. When only one word is entered, it responds more favorably, whereas multiple words generate inferior results.
2. **Connected Words:** A system is provided with several words that act independently and with little time between them in this way.
3. **Continuous Voice:** This type is used by the user, and the system recognizes their genuine speech. Continuous voice recognition is difficult to design since it necessitates a one-of-a-kind implementation technique.

GTTS

The Google Text-to-Speech (gTTS) library converts spoken mp3 data to a file with corresponding textual transcription of (byte string), or stdout, for interaction with the Google Translate API. As an alternative, external software is provided with Google Translate TTS's request URLs in advance. Text-to-speech conversion is the process of converting text into an audio format. The software processes text input provided by the user using natural language processing techniques, takes into account the linguistic characteristics of the language selected, and draws conclusions from the text. The next block receives this processed text and applies digital signal processing to it before sending it on. The final step involves applying a variety of algorithms and transformations to convert this processed text into a speech format. The process is conducted with speech synthesisers the entire time. To help you understand below is a simple block diagram.

Figure 1. Working of the speech synthesizer

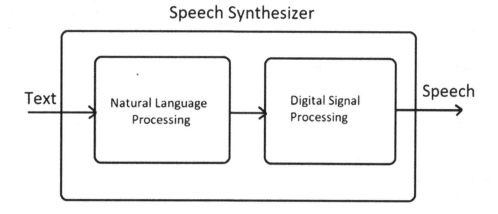

This appears to be a difficult operation, but due to Python and the gTTS module, it can be reduced to a few lines of code. The block diagram shows that the text being given is first pre-processed using natural language processing and then translated to speech using digital signal processing. The act of translating is a communicative activity as well as a linguistic one (Vermeer, 1992). the process of producing a document in the target language that fulfils the same purpose as the target document published in the source language Translators take into account the function of each textual element, such as running text, titles, list items, and other captions, as well as other non-linguistic elements like figures and equations that are incorporated into the document's structure when translating a document to the target language.

Google Trans Module

You may translate words, documents, and website material from one language to another with Google Translate, a powerful and cost-free tool created by Google. Google Translate supports 109 languages as of April 2021 and performs daily word translations in excess of one trillion. Contrary to popular belief, Google Translate does not provide straight translations between languages. The original is typically translated into English before being translated into the target language. The process is made simpler by the fact that the majority of the material is readily available online in English. Languages cannot be translated with Google Translate (Language 1 to Language 2). Instead, it frequently translates from one language to another in this order: Language 1 -> ENGLISH -> Language 2, for example. Like all human languages, English is more ambiguous and dependent on linguistic situations, therefore translation errors may happen. For instance, you would get т OR в/в if you translated from French to Russian. If Google were to utilize an unambiguous artificial language as the intermediary, it would be Vous -> you в/в OR tu -> thou т. The many meanings of nouns are clarified by this suffixing. Because of this, publishing in English, using clear language, providing context, and using terms like "you all" may or may not lead to a better one-step translation, depending on the target language.

Some languages continue to employ the conventional translation method known as statistical machine translation, despite Google's introduction of a new technique called neural machine translation to enhance translation quality. This translation system is entirely rule-based and makes educated assumptions about how to translate documents into foreign languages using predictive algorithms. Instead of translating individual words, the intent is to interpret the entire phrase before gathering any overlapped phrases. Additionally, it examines bilingual text corpora to develop statistical models for translating texts between languages.

Human translation is more reliable than Google Translate. When text is well built and written in formal language, with the help of simple sentences, relates to formal issues, and has a large amount of training data, it typically yields conversions that are similar to manual translations done between English and a variety of well-built languages. Accuracy for those languages drops as fewer of those characteristics are met, such as sentence length growing, if the text contains similar or literary languages.

Hidden Markov's Model

Speech temporal patterns can be recognised and enhanced using hidden Markov models. A simple and effective framework for modelling time-varying spectral sequences is the hidden markov model. As a result, Hidden Markov's Models are the foundation of almost all contemporary large vocabulary continuous voice recognition systems. Although the core concepts underlying the Hidden Markov's Model continuous speech recognition system for large vocabulary are straightforward, the approximations and simplifications of the assumptions required for direct implementation would lead to a system with the lowest accuracy and the least sensitivity to changes in the operating environment. As a result, applying Hidden Markov models in real-world systems calls for a high degree of sophistication.

Continuous Speech Recognition has many potential uses, including commands, control, dictation, transcription of speech, searching of audio documents, and interactions such as spoken conversations. All voice recognition systems are built around a set of models that reflect the sounds of the language to be recognized. The Hidden Markov model gives a framework for the creation of models since speech has only a temporal structure and is recorded as a sequence in spectral vectors across the frequency range. The goal is to illustrate an entire system architecture using extremely simple acoustic models. Google translate was identified as the best and most basic module for speech recognition processes. It proved to be effective in the detection of the language of input speech by itself.

Description of Methodology

In Python, Speech recognition works with the performance of algorithms that mainly focuses on linguistic and acoustic modeling. Acoustic models are mainly used in the identification of the phonemes/phonetics in the speech so that we can easily reach an effective and significant part of the speech, such as words and sentences, which is the most needed step to be done.

Figure 2. Working of speech recognition

Speech   Electrical   Digital data   Text
                energy

Speech recognition begins by translating the voice given by the person speaking into a microphone. This electrical energy is then converted from the analog signal to the digital signal, and then further into the text. It divides the total audio data into separated sounds and analyzes the sounds using algorithms to identify the most likely word that matches the audio. Natural Language Processing is used throughout the process. Our contribution to this application is the ability to execute direct voice translation without the need for massive amounts of parallel speech data. The necessity for parallel speech (speech-to-text or speech-to-speech translation) data, which uses a lot of data in identifying the same actual text throughout the modules, is a major challenge in designing a direct Speech to text system. We wish to employ the fundamental voice recognition modules available to reduce large-size speech data and boost the translator's live caption capacity so that the end user can translate the user's spoken language to his destination language in real-time. Auto voice recognition and Speech translation models can help us improve speech recognition. This paradigm typically implements spoken language processing systems as a group of an automatic speech recognition module and a specialized natural language processing module both combined. ASR recognition gives an impact on the performance of every natural language processing module. To achieve higher performance in Speech Translation, it is necessary to prevent error propagation in the systems and collect enough data to train the end-to-end models. We discovered that Google text translation services were effective in both error correction and spoken translation from one language to another.

Advantages of Using Speech-to-Text

Like many other technologies, speech-to-text technology has a lot of applications that can help us enhance our daily tasks. Some of the key benefits of employing speech-to-text are these:

- **Time-Saving:** Automatic speech recognition technology dynamically delivers correct textual transcripts, which saves a lot of time.
- **Cost-Effective:** Very few speech-to-text systems are free; the majority of them require a monthly membership. The cost of the subscription, however, is far lower than using a human transcribing service.
- **Enhancing Audio and Video Content:** Real-time audio and video data conversion is possible using speech-to-text software, resulting in fast video transcription and the provision of subtitles.
- **Simplifying the Customer Experience:** By focusing on natural language processing, the customer experience is improved in terms of simplicity, accessibility, and convenience.

Limitations in Existing Solution

- **Is Not Flawless:** Although dictation technology is an essential tool, it has not yet reached its full potential and is still in its early stages, which leaves some performance gaps. It only produces verbatim text, thus you can get a transcript that is clunky or wrong or lacks important quotations.
- **Requires Human Input:** Due to voice-to-limitations text's accuracy, some human editing of the speech data is necessary for best performance.
- **Requires Clear Recordings:** We must make sure that recorded audio is crystal clear and clearly heard in order to acquire a better transcript from speech recognition. In other words, there shouldn't be any background noise, the pronunciation should be clear, there shouldn't be any accents, and only one person should be speaking at a time.

NATURAL LANGUAGE PROCESSING AND MACHINE TRANSLATION

Machines can learn and comprehend human language and speech, thanks to natural language processing. AI (Artificial Intelligence) includes NLP (natural language processing) and ML (machine learning). Both subfields share methods, formulas, and information. Natural language processing (NLP) uses machine learning to extract the structure and meaning of the text. For a better understanding of consumer interactions and sentiment on social media, businesses may utilize natural language processing software to analyze text and extract information about specific people, places, and events. The foundation of Google Translate is enormous amounts of statistically processed material from both languages. It is superior to MT (machine translation) systems that rely on manually supplied grammatical rules.

Even though NLP greatly improved language translation, AI translations are still far from flawless. Machine translation frequently struggles to comprehend cultural nuances or the context of a translation like human readers can. Because of this, accurate translation of text from one language to another still requires human review. NLP transforms unprocessed text into a form that computers can comprehend and process. Modern NLP can quickly evaluate huge amounts of text to produce insights and finish many tasks. For instance, you can use Google Translate, a translation service powered by NLP, to automatically draft a translation rather than manually translate an entire page into a foreign language. To improve the fluency and accuracy of Google Translate, Google developed and released Google Neural Machine Translation (GNMT), a neural machine translation (NMT) system that uses an artificial neural network. By employing a machine translation technique called example-based machine translation (EBMT), or "learns from millions of instances," GNMT improves the quality of translations. The GNMT-recommended system learning architecture was originally tested on the more than a hundred languages that Google Translate offers. Because of the broad end-to-end structure, the system learns over time to offer better, more accurate translations. Instead of only translating words individually, GNMT tries to translate entire phrases at once. Instead of learning translations phrase by phrase, the GNMT network may do interlingual machine translation by encoding the semantics of the sentence. The translation procedure is now simpler than ever thanks to AI tools. Machine translation's blazing-fast processing speed is a key advantage. A whole book, website, or product database can now be translated by computers in a matter of seconds. Cost is also another important benefit. For businesses who want to localize their websites, several top AI translation technologies have affordable corporate versions.

PERFECT REPLACEMENT FOR A HUMAN TRANSLATOR

The person who translates from one language into another is known as a translator. Translators can interact with persons who speak different languages since they are fluent in at least two of them. A translator will be able to translate either by oral or in a written format to improve communication for those who don't speak many languages.

- Knowledge of different languages
- Knowledge of various cultures
- Communication skills
- Writing of transcripts
- Research on various attributes
- Computer-assisted translation
- Active listening in current changes
- Organizational needs

The model consists of all these skills and can act effectively as a good replacement for a language translator. It can further be error-free as well as less time-consuming.

Choosing and Installing a Voice Recognition Software Package

To do voice recognition in Python, we must first install a Python library. Python has several packages available for speech-related activities. Table 3 summarizes the basic functions and applications of the packages.

Package Name: Apiai

Functionality: Natural language processing is used in the model for the study of the speaker's voice.

Installation: Pip install apiai

Package name: Google cloud speech module

Functionality: In-person speech-to-text conversion

Installation: $ pip install virtualenv

Package Name: Speech Recognition

Functionality: Processing of audio and accessibility to the microphone.

Installation: $ pip install Speech Recognition

Package Name: Watson's developer cloud

Functionality: Watson programmer cloud is an Application Platform Interface that facilitates the design, debugging, operating, and deployment of APIs. It may be used to conduct simple voice recognition tasks.

Installation: $pip-upgrade watson-developer-cloud

1. 6.2 Supported languages in Google trans library:Creole
2. Hausa
3. Hawaiian
4. Hebrew
5. Hindi
6. Hmong
7. Hungarian
8. Icelandic
9. Igbo
10. Indonesian
11. Irish
12. Italian
13. Japanese
14. Javanese
15. Kannada
16. Kazakh
17. Khmer
18. Kinyarwanda
19. Korean
20. Kurdish (Kurmanji)
21. Odia
22. Pashto
23. Persian
24. Polish

25. Portuguese
26. Punjabi (Gurmukhi)
27. Serbian
28. Shona
29. Sindhi
30. Sinhala
31. Slovak
32. Slovenian
33. Somali
34. Sotho
35. Spanish
36. Sundanese
37. Swahili
38. Swedish
39. Tajik
40. Tamil
41. Tatar
42. Telugu
43. Thai
44. Turkish
45. Turkmen
46. Ukrainian
47. Romanian
48. Russian
49. Samoan
50. Scottish Gaelic
51. Czech
52. Danish
53. Dutch
54. English
55. Esperanto
56. Estonian
57. Filipino
(Tagalog)
58. Chinese (Simplified)
59. Finnish
60. French
61. Galician
62. Georgian
63. German
64. Greek
65. Gujarati
66. Haitian
67. Kyrgyz

68. Albanian
69. Amharic
70. Arabic
71. Armenian
72. Azerbaijani
73. Basque
74. Belarusian
75. Bengali
76. Bosnian
77. Bulgarian
78. Burmese
79. Catalan
80. Cebuano
81. Chewa
82. Lao
83. Latin
84. Latvian
85. Lithuanian
86. Luxembourgis
87. Yiddish
88. West Frisian
89. Yoruba
90. Afrikaans
91. Zulu
92. Welsh
93. Uzbek
94. Uyghur
95. Urdu
96. Chinese (Traditional)
97. Norwegian (Bokmål)
98. Vietnamese
99. Croatian
100. Xhosa
101. Urdu
102. Nepali
103. Mongolian
104. Marathi
105. Maori
106. Maltese
107. Malayalam
108. Malagasy
109. Macedonian

IDEOLOGY AND IMPLEMENTATION

The basic idea behind this project is to create an effective and user-friendly model for people communicating in different languages and who have hearing disabilities. The model breaks the barriers and increases fluency of communication for people with hearing difficulties. The process begins with the digitizing of a speech sample with Automatic Speech Recognition. The voice template is broken up into several segments made up of several tones. These are further divided into time steps in the spectrograms using the short-time Fourier transform. Analysis of the spectrogram and the transcription based on the Natural Language Processing algorithm predicts the probability of all words in a language's vocabulary. To avoid any potential mistakes in the model, a contextual layer is added.

These people can speak the required content to the model and the model recognizes the speech from the language library and also identifies the source language from the speech, conversely when the source language is out of the library, the recognition of the speech fails and the user is requested to input the content again. The ASR works for nearly 5 to 6 seconds continuously even in a low frequency until the voice is processed, the recognition ends only if there is nothing recognized by the speech recognizer for a short period, Once the content is recognized successfully by the model's speech recognizer, it requests the user for the destination language(The language of the content to be converted), Once the language has been recognized and processed by the google trans model, the voice input is further trimmed into chunks for easy verbal searching in the destination language library. The Google trans module in python language supports the translation of nearly 108 languages that are grammatically verified by google. The chunks of voice inputs are converted into text for translation by the google trans module. The translated texts are then integrated by the google text-to-speech library and voice content is created for the integrated sentence. Hidden Markov's model provides a broad platform for the continuous speech recognition of the large vocabulary in the model. English acts as an intermediary language for the conversion of the context between any two languages. Google translate functions in such a way that the context of any language is first of all translated into English, irrespective of the grammatical correctness and verbal spelling. The translated words are further processed in the model for their conversion to the destination language. The languages in the Google trans library are well constructed in such a way that the words can be found easily. When the chunks of text have been arranged and translated perfectly according to the voice input given, these chunks are processed by the text-to-speech synthesizer to give the textual sequence a vocal form. The model can give the output in both textual form and voice form. The continuous textual captions are easily readable by the users. This conversion process occurs in increments such that both inputs and outputs are given simultaneously to the model for increased fluency.

Computer Code

Importing modules like play sound, speech_recognition, google trans, gtts, os, pyttsx3.

```
# Voice recording
# uses the microphone to issue commands.
Using Function  command():
 1. start
2. Using e= speech recognizer.Recognizer()  with help of speech recognizer.
Microphone() as src
```

```
•           print "listening to the audio"
•        e.pause__threshold = 1
•           audio1=e.listento(src)
3. Using  try block
•        print "recording …."
•          q = e.recognize_google() with argument audio, lang=en-in
•        print("The audio recorded was{q}")
4. Exception block
•          Printing "please say that again"
•          Return None
5. return q
6. end
Function  des_language():
          1. start
          2. print Enter the language for the content to be converted: Ex. Tam-
il, English, etc.,
          3. print
          # Enter in the destination language.
             # the user wants to translate
          4.language = command()
          5.loop (language == "None")
                language = command()
          6.language = language.lower()
          7. return language
             8. end
```

Table 3.

Modules Used	Importing Packages
play sound	play sound
Speech recognition module	sr
Google trans module	translator
Google TTS module	gTTS
	os,pyttsx3

BASIC PROCEDURE

Here below is the procedure required for a simple language translator for speech-to-text as well as speech-to-speech conversion

```
1. start
#All languages are included in a tuple, and language codes will be recognized.
2.dic1=('UK,' Afrikaans,' Belarusian', 'danish', 'Filipino', 'Luxembourgish',
'maori', 'ky' (Kurmanji)'
        'ku', 'tg', 'ne', 'gu'
        'Haitian, 'Xhosa', ' th', ' Samoan, 'fr', 'Yi', 'hausa', 'cy', 'fa'
        'polish', 'Maltese',
        'mt', 'English', 'lv', 'Portuguese', 'lo',
        'Latin', 'Zulu', 'Gujarati', 'Hindi',
        'hi', 'Mongolian',
        'mn', 'sr', 'ko', 'he', 'el', 'my',
        'Nepali', 'Kazakh', 'ht' (traditional)',
        'zh-tw' (simplified)',
        'zh-cn', 'Malagasy', 'et',' Gaelic creole', 'Spanish', 'so', 'Punjabi,
        'pa', 'hy', 'hr',
        'Czech', 'ml', 'mk', 'es', 'Bosnian', 'Latvian', 'Hebrew', 'Lithu-
anian',
        'lt', 'or',
        'Pashto', 'ro', 'Khmer'
        'km', 'hmn', 'sinhala', 'arabic', 'swahili', 'jw'
        'Kannada', 'sm', 'french', 'Indonesian',
        'id', ' Malayalam, 'odia', 'ka', 'Croatian', ' Persian, 'Catalan',
'fy', 'Finnish',
        'fi', 'welsh', 'Italian',
        'it'. 'Igbo', 'Sundanese',
        'su', 'german',
        'de', 'Chinese ', Tajik, 'Korean', 'en', ' Irish, 'xh',
        'Yiddish', 'Turkish',
        'tr', 'kk', 'urdu', 'esperanto', 'lao', 'ca', 'yoruba',
        'yo', 'mg', 'Frisian', 'Uyghur',
        'ug', 'ps', 'slovenian', 'gd',
        'serbian', 'bs', 'da', 'corsican', 'mi', 'haw', 'thai', 'cs', 'ga',
'zu', 'ar',
        'Armenian', ' is' (Burmese)', 'Azerbaijani', 'Hungarian',
        'hu', 'Kyrgyz', 'ny', 'sq',
        'Amharic', 'ig', 'Norwegian', 'la', 'tl', 'vi', 'Galician',
        'gl', 'be',
        'Bengali', 'kn', 'eo',
        'Estonian', 'Ukrainian', 'Swedish',
        'sv', 'ur', 'ha',
        'Hawaiian', 'Chinese ', 'dutch'
        'nl', 'no', 'cebuano',
        'ceb', 'Uzbek', 'Bulgarian',
        'bg', 'sw', 'af' ','am', ' Russian,
```

```
        'ru', 'ta', 'Myanmar 'Javanese', 'Icelandic', 'bn', 'Sesotho', 'uz',
        'Vietnamese', 'Japanese', 'scots', 'pl', 'eu', 'ja', dic, 'sk', 'Alba-
nian', 'lb'
        'Macedonian', 'Kurdish 'greek', 'co', 'si'
        'Slovak', 'st',
        'Shona', 'Malay',
        'ms', 'Tamil', 'Chichewa', 'Sindhi', ' Telugu,
        'te', 'sd', 'mr', 'Hmong', 'az',
        'basque', 'pt', ' Marathi, 'Georgian', 'sl',
        'Somali', 'Romanian')
3.flag = 0
# receive the input from the user
# Make all input lowercase.
4 . q= command()
5 . Loop (q=="None")
        q= command()
6 .language = des_language()
# Using the code to map it
7 .loop (language not in dic1):
•       Print  "Language in which you are trying to convert is unavailable,
please try some other destination language"
•       language = des_language()
8.lang = dic1[dic1.index(language)+1]
# usage of the Translator
9. t = translator()
10. print q
11. Print  lang
# Translating from source  to distinction language
12. text_to_trans = translator.translate(q, dest=language)
13. text1 = text_to_tran.text
14. Print  text1
15. engine1 = pyttsx3.init()
16. engine1.say(text1)
17. invoke the engine1.run and wait()
# Using the gTTS() function for Google-Text-to-Speech
# to read aloud the translation of the text into
# Thelang variable stores the destination language.
# Additionally, we deemed the third argument to be false because
# It talks quite slowly by default.
18.speak1 = gTTS(text1=text1, lang=lang, slow=False)
# Save the captured voice using the save() function.
19.speak1.save("c_voice.mp3")
# Running the converted speech to use an Os module.
20.playsound('capture_voice.mp3')
```

```
21. os.remove('capture_voice.mp3')
# print the  output
22. End
```

APPLICATION AND USE CASES

This model is mainly devised for people with limited knowledge about other languages and to introduce effective communication between two individuals of unknown language. Most of the time, communication between unknown people occurs only with the help of a linguistic person who is well-versed in the grammar of many languages. When this model is used as a tool between those two individuals, it eliminates the requirement of the linguistic guide. The model recognizes the speech, that is to be converted into another language and does it according to the user's choice whether it's speech to speech or speech to text between languages. Considering speech to text conversion, it helps a hearing disabled person to interact with people as the speech from the people will be converted into textual transcription. The hearing disabled people can easily identify the speech from a person that is now in the textual form of their preferred language.

LIMITATIONS

The model we have come up with needs adequate internet connectivity to work properly without any hindrance as the language libraries are accessed through the internet. Emotions from the speaker at one end will be recognised only partially and this model is an AI model that receives and works according to the dataset provided to it, but this model lacks recognising emotions and feelings between individuals which is a major drawback. The major limitation is that the model lacks fluency, as conversation between a normal talk and the conversation through this model varies completely.

CONCLUSION AND FUTURE WORK

We are glad that we have worked on an idea that benefits everyone irrespective of their country, language, society as well as culture. It is always essential for ideas to flow throughout the minds of every person in the world. Our work isn't over yet, our main motto is to enhance the automatic speech-recognizing tool and translation of speech in a more powerful and standardized manner. A live streaming speech-to-speech translation software needs to be worked on with more care and technology to increase the fluency between people communicating with each other in unknown languages. This above said model also offers a helpful platform for those who have hearing challenges. The majority of hearing-impaired people find it difficult to communicate with others and also with each other, this model introduces an eye on text principle which suggests these people keep an eye on the translated live streaming scripts offered by the model so that they can understand more easily and eliminate their dependency on lip reading.

It is difficult to directly translate spoken utterances from one language to another since this implies a fundamental change to both linguistic and para/nonlinguistic elements. Traditional speech-to-speech translation approaches include machine translation (text-to-text), automated voice recognition, and text-to-speech synthesizers. Numerous free basic modules, like Google Translate and Text-to-Speech (GTTS), have accomplished this. It's better to keep a model as simple as possible. NLP employs machine learning algorithms to learn new things every day and get wiser. And it's included in many of the products that we use daily, including spell checks and smart speakers.

The future work from this idea is to build reliable software that is well-versed and trained in natural language processing to recognize speech from an audio input device and give the translated audio from the google trans module to another audio output device that is manually operated by the user. This model can be the best replacement for the speech translation headphones that are used in international conferences and expos which are expensive and cannot be used by everyone as well. Mobile phones and other related devices have become an integral part of our life and this model would be more successful and user-friendly if we implement it as software. Implementation of this requires two audio devices (The device speaker is a must and another pluggable or wireless audio device). This is our planned future work and would be doing the required real-time implementations soon.

REFERENCES

Alharbi, S., Alrazgan, M., Alrashed, A., Alnomasi, T., Almojel, R., Alharbi, R., Alharbi, S., Alturki, S., Alshehri, F., & Almojil, M. (2021). Automatic Speech Recognition: Systematic Literature Review. *IEEE Access: Practical Innovations, Open Solutions, 9*, 131858–131876. doi:10.1109/ACCESS.2021.3112535

Chuang, S.-P., Liu, A. H., Sung, T.-W., & Lee, H. (2021). Improving Automatic Speech Recognition and Speech Translation via Word Embedding Prediction. *IEEE/ACM Transactions on Audio, Speech, and Language Processing, 29*, 93–105. doi:10.1109/TASLP.2020.3037543

Furui, S., Kikuchi, T., Shinnaka, Y., & Hori, C. (2004). Speech-to-Text and Speech-to-Speech Summarization of Spontaneous Speech. *IEEE Transactions on Speech and Audio Processing, 12*(4), 401–408. doi:10.1109/TSA.2004.828699

Jorge, J., Gimenez, A., Silvestre-Cerda, J. A., Civera, J., Sanchis, A., & Juan, A. (2022). Live Streaming Speech Recognition Using Deep Bidirectional LSTM Acoustic Models and Interpolated Language Models. *IEEE/ACM Transactions on Audio, Speech, and Language Processing, 30*, 148–161. doi:10.1109/TASLP.2021.3133216

Kano, T., Sakti, S., & Nakamura, S. (2020). End-to-End Speech Translation With Transcoding by Multi-Task Learning for Distant Language Pairs. *IEEE/ACM Transactions on Audio, Speech, and Language Processing, 28*, 1342–1355. doi:10.1109/TASLP.2020.2986886

Kaur, S., & Singh, M. (2015). Indian Sign Language animation generation system. *2015 1st International Conference on Next Generation Computing Technologies (NGCT)*. 10.1109/NGCT.2015.7375251

Nakamura, S., Markov, K., Nakaiwa, H., Kikui, G., Kawai, H., Jitsuhiro, T., Zhang, J.-S., Yamamoto, H., Sumita, E., & Yamamoto, S. (2006). The ATR Multilingual Speech-to-Speech Translation System. *IEEE Transactions on Audio, Speech, and Language Processing, 14*(2), 365–376. doi:10.1109/TSA.2005.860774

Naveen, M., & Ponraj, A. S. (2020). Speech Recognition with Gender Identification and Speaker Diarization. *2020 IEEE International Conference for Innovation in Technology (INOCON).* 10.1109/INOCON50539.2020.9298241

Park, C., Seo, J., Lee, S., Lee, C., Moon, H., Eo, S., & Lim, H. (2021). BTS: Back TranScription for Speech-to-Text Post-Processor using Text-to-Speech-to-Text. *Proceedings of the 8th Workshop on Asian Translation (WAT2021).* 10.18653/v1/2021.wat-1.10

Stolcke, A., Chen, B., Franco, H., Gadde, V. R. R., Graciarena, M., Hwang, M. Y., ... Zhu, Q. (2006). Recent innovations in speech-to-text transcription at SRI-ICSI-UW. *IEEE Transactions on Audio, Speech, and Language Processing, 14*(5), 1729–1744. doi:10.1109/TASL.2006.879807

KEY TERMS AND DEFINITIONS

Automatic Speech Recognition: With the use of automated speech recognition (ASR), users of information systems can enter data by speaking it rather than typing numbers into a keypad. The main purposes of ASR are informational purposes and call forwarding.

Google Trans: Google trans, a free and infinite Python module, makes use of Machine Translation (API). This uses the Google Translate Ajax API to call methods like detect and translate.

Gtts: Gtts is a user-friendly tool that will convert the text entered into audio and save it as an mp3 file. The saved mp3 file can be played using two audio speeds fast and slow.

Hidden Markov's Model: The hidden Markov model is a statistical model that is mainly used for the observation of the evolution of events based on internal factors that are not directly observable. It is the foundation of many other modern-day algorithms.

Machine Translation: This is a process in which humans are not involved and artificial intelligence plays an important role. They help in converting text from one language to another language.

Natural Language Processing: Natural language processing NLP's major purpose is to allow computer systems to interpret natural human language.

Speech Translation: Conversational spoken sentences are quickly translated and spoken aloud in a second language through the technique of speech translation. The system only translates a fixed and finite set of phrases that have been manually placed into the system in phrase translation, which is different from this.

Chapter 13
Flood Prediction and Recommendation System

S. Riddhi
Thiagarajar College of Engineering, India

G. Kanishta
Thiagarajar College of Engineering, India

R. Parkavi
Thiagarajar College of Engineering, India

A. M. Abirami
ⓘ https://orcid.org/0000-0002-7957-5143
Thiagarajar College of Engineering, India

ABSTRACT

Floods are one of the most common natural disasters that occur, destroying human life and the environment. Flash floods can cause catastrophic damage to society. The impacts of the flood on society include loss of human life, worsening of health conditions due to waterborne diseases, loss of livestock, and many other factors. It could be difficult to set things back after a huge flood. The main aim of this work is to develop a flood prediction system by reading the rainfall that occurs and to predict the possibilities of floods as well as to recommend the nearby evacuation area for the people to move immediately. Thus, the idea of this chapter is to predict the occurrence of a flood using the rainfall data and recommend nearby evacuation areas away from flood hazard areas. Providing the utmost safety has been the major idea in working on this chapter. Perfect accuracy for rainfall data was obtained using the random forest algorithm. Five algorithms were chosen and applied to the training data set. Accuracy was found precisely while using random forest algorithm.

DOI: 10.4018/978-1-6684-8145-5.ch013

Copyright © 2023, IGI Global. Copying or distributing in print or electronic forms without written permission of IGI Global is prohibited.

INTRODUCTION

Disasters are serious disruptions to society caused by either man-made or natural. They are those who need to be keenly noticed and be made aware of at early stages for society. Prevention is better than cure but to prevent predicting at earlier stages is the most important aspect. Nature is always unpredictable. Nobody or any system can predict nature. Predictions can never be accurate. It's that we can't stop natural disasters but we can arm ourselves with prior knowledge. Creating awareness among every kind of person in society would be the first step to work with. Making even the commoners knowledgeable about the change in climatic conditions that would lead to disasters and the catastrophic damage that they could cause.

There are different types of disasters: wildfires, earthquakes, droughts, hurricanes, floods, and many others shall join the list. These create terrifying catastrophic damage to society. It is said that people who face or live through a disaster can handle emotional distress. This makes people strong mentally. All these days there would have been millions of loss of lives due to sudden natural disasters. Mishaps occur most of the time leading to unrecoverable damage. The effect that it leaves back on society is unimaginable. Fatality or physical injury is the main effect that a flash flood or sudden natural disaster can cause in society. People could lose their homes, possessions, food, and community. Food would be a major problem for the people. The availability of food grains would be scarce and in such conditions, people would face or die of hunger due to the unavailability of food. Therefore, Disasters are a great threat to society that needs to have a discussion.

Predicting their arrival to take preventive measures and protect society from the effects disasters imprint on society is the immediate action that the society needs. Natural disasters are of different types but looking into the particular fact of rains and floods, proper predictionsand preventive actions are needed. Pouring rain is completely unpredictable. But with the historic rainfall data, prediction can be made easy to an extent. In such a way, creating a model with accurate predictions is the utmost need for society.

With the irregular change in climate patterns, it's been difficult to predict the occurrence of floods using traditional methods leading to massive destruction. Thus to cope with flash floods and to handle critical situations new methodologies are invented to overcome such difficulties. Technology has to be more aware to reduce the loss that a flash flood would make. In the modernizing era, it's made even easier to predict the occurrence of floods and recommend nearby evacuation areas. Hazard areas that are prone to destruction and devastating loss are monitored regularly and the rainfall readings are collected, integrated from multiple resources, curated, mined, analyzed and prediction is done over patterns. With the prediction, recommendation areas are listed for the society.

Safety needs to be the utmost goal for any societal issue. Providing safety measures is one of the main aspects for an Engineer and one of the major issues faced by natural disasters. Landslides, earthquakes, floods, droughts, forest fires, and many such factors occur continuously throughout the globe. Natural calamities are unpredictable. People can never judge climate. They leave an ever-recoverable impact on society. They can't be prevented but the effects can be controlled. Going against nature backfires most of the time. Hence agreeing with nature's conditions prevention and protection methods can be taken. Thus, to reduce the effect or impact they cause on the environment, human life, and livestock, predicting the occurrence of natural calamities is one effective way to prepare to fight against them. One such natural calamity is flooding. The main aspect of this work is to create a recommendation system by predicting the arrival of floods using rainfall data. The rainfall data is collected and by analyzing the data, prediction is made using the machine learning algorithm. With the help of the result evacuation areas are recommended in the hazard areas.

The early warning system can be considered an adaptive measure for climate change. It is a major component of disaster risk reduction. The main aim of the system is to integrate communication between different communities as a preventative measure to prepare for hazardous climate-related events. The objective of this system is to successfully save lives and reduce the economic effect that the disaster can leave on the environment and society when they flood back. A disaster could cause loss of lives, cattle, livestock, plants, and also on fields. The effect on fields could be major destruction. It is very useful for the society to predict the occurrence of flood with the available rainfall data accurately beforehand and to take preventive measures accordingly to reduce the catastrophic destruction that a flash flood could cause.

The early warning system can help the communities to plan accordingly the steps to be taken, the financial and economic stability that the government should handle, and the evacuation areas nearby for a longer period. Based on the early warning system awareness programs and technologies have been developed in recent times. UNDP's Signature Programme "Strengthening Climate Information and Early warning systems For Climate Resilient Development and adaptation to climatic change" is successfully implemented across Africa, Asia, and the Pacific. Systems at sub-regional and regional levels ensure preparedness and rapid response to natural disasters using a model that integrates components of risk knowledge, monitoring and forecasting, information dissemination, and warning response. Under the seven global targets set by The Sendai Framework for Disaster Risk Reduction 2015-2030, increasing the availability of multi-hazard early warning systems and disaster risk reduction is one among them. Effective early warning systems have to be developed for different hazards such as tsunamis, volcanoes, earthquakes, floods, landslides, and droughts.

The early warning system has to analyze the data acquired from previous occurrences and predict accurate results in such a way that provides meaningful warning information to the communities, individuals, and organizations who are threatened by the occurrence of flash floods to act and prepare appropriately in sufficient time to reduce the possibility of harm or loss. This would be helpful for them to set the capacities, evacuation areas, required food, and places for shelter beforehand to reduce the risk of fatality in human life as well as livestock. This would also be helpful for farmers to sow their crops by looking after the climatic conditions earlier on to prevent the loss of plants and agriculture.

Agriculture lies on annual rainfall for its growth and well-being. Rainfed Agriculture depends heavily on the annual and seasonal rainfall patterns and any changes in the regular flow may cause droughts or waterlog. Rainfed farming constitutes the world's 80% of cropland whereas 60% of them are cereals. Rainfed agriculture provides the majority of food production and will continue to do so. The main important challenge in rainfed agriculture is coping with climatic variability. Climatic conditions are never reliable. They can never be predicted accurately to the fullest extent. So the main challenge in rainfed agriculture is the unpredictability and unreliability of climatic conditions. This can be a great barrier for crops that completely depend on the annual and seasonal rainfall. So any changes in the rainfall can affect directly or indirectly the growth of crops and agriculture.

India's economy majorly depends on agriculture. It's not only the economy; it's agriculture that's the most important factor for livelihood. Without the occurrence of proper rainfall can lead to either droughts or flash floods. Too much of anything is good for nothing. In the same way, heavy rainfall can lead to waterlogging which could cause illness to the plants. Lack of rainfall is also a factor in the improper growth of crops leading to droughts. Sophisticated technological models can be used to predict floods caused by natural causes such as rainfall and storms. Technologists can interpret the growing amount of data with the help of the Artificial Intelligence (AI) field. The creation of flood forecasting models by technologists can help to alert the authorities automatically in an instant. In the region of Patna, a city located on the south bank of the river Ganges in northeast India, Google announced that it had begun the flood forecasting model in September 2019. Google built the inundation model to monitor the water level rise and analyzed it to provide a list of areas that will be affected by flash flooding. The inundation model estimates what areas will be flooded and how deep the water will be. The company stated that 200 million people in India can receive alerts from the flood forecasting system developed by them. This system uses Machine Learning (ML) to identify the areas prone to flooding by assessing the "water behavior". Google gets real-time data by partnering with many institutions.

The proposed recommendation system's main objectives are: (i) to use the best available data to identify the exact evacuation areas near the hazard areas (ii) to improve the system of warning to be quick and accurate with its predictions. A wrong prediction can have an effect and impact on society. This recommender system will provide the needed support for the public authorities in setting up government institutions and other recommended places for the needy people. Also, they can use this system to create awareness among the public of the risks and impact that the flood would leave on. Figure 1 explains the conceptual framework of flood prediction system.

Figure 1. Conceptual flood prediction system

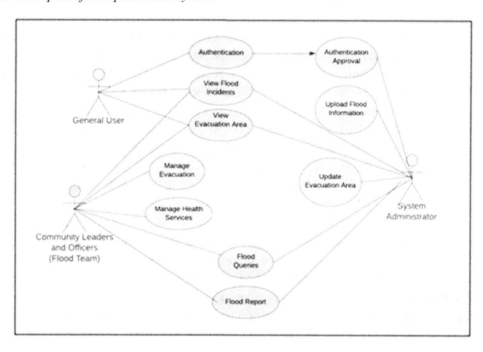

The flood sensor data is collected and pre-processing is done for the obtained data using specialized pre-processing tools to eliminate missing values or any null values to enhance the performance of the prediction system. The prepared data has undergone dimensionality reduction, feature selection, and feature extraction. The final pre-processed and prepared dataset is split into training validation and testing datasets. To train the data set, models are built and the model with the highest accuracy is taken for further prediction and testing of the dataset. Iterating the model continuously can yield better results.

BACKGROUND

Linear models and non-linear models are the two main classifications for the machine learning algorithm. The machine learning classification algorithm can be used in a variety of industries, including biometric identification, cancer tumour cell identification, speech recognition, email spam detection, and drug categorization. Support vector machines and logistic regression are additional categories for linear models (SVM).

A model is referred to as a linear model if it is defined as a linear collection of features. The weights for each feature are calculated in order to forecast the target value based on the training data. A supervised machine learning technique for binary classification is logistic regression. It applies a nonlinear sigmoidal function on a linear combination of features. The term "logit model" also applies to the logistic model. Logistic Regression does not demand a linear relationship between the input and output variables because it applies a non-linear log transformation to the odds ratio. Logistic regression is a helpful analytical method since cyber security involves classification difficulties, such as attack detection.

A supervised machine learning technique called the support vector machine (SVM) is utilised for both classification and regression. The SVM algorithm's objective is to produce the ideal decision boundary, or hyperplane, that can divide n-dimensional space into classes so that new data can be classified. When the classes merge and it becomes difficult to separate the data using a linear border, the non-linear data tends to form a circle when plotted on a graph. The activation functions used in non-linear models include exponential, reLU, sigmoid, and others. Deep learning is the principal application of nonlinear algorithms.

A supervised data categorization technique is the k-nearest neighbours (KNN) algorithm. It is employed to categorise fresh data points according to similarities that are determined using close-proximity measurements like Euclidean distance, Manhattan distance, Hamming distance, and Minkowski distance. Using a kernel function like the Radial Basis Function (RBF), the Support Vector Machine Kernel (SVM Kernel) converts a set of non-linear data into a linear equation. The term "kernel" is employed because the window for manipulating the data in a Support Vector Machine is provided by a set of mathematical operations. The Kernel trick, used by machine learning, uses Kernel to handle the dataset's nonlinearity. A group of algorithms used for pattern analysis are referred to as kernel functions.

Naive Bayes is a supervised classification algorithm. It is best suited for binary and multiclass classification. It uses conditional probability by assigning class labels to objects which are used to make future predictions. The naive bayes algorithm can be used in applications such as Weather Forecasting and Fraud Analysis. It assumes independence among predictors called class conditional independence.

A supervised machine learning algorithm is a decision tree. Using a rule-based methodology, it is useful for classification and regression. The decision trees use multiple calibrated factors to anticipate the outcomes while using a top-down approach to the dataset. Decision Tree classification algorithms can be successfully used in content marketing and offer management advice.

The Random Forest Classifier is an ensemble learning-based supervised machine learning method. A method called ensemble learning mixes multiple models to enhance prediction performance. Regression and classification issues are handled by the Random Forest Classifier. With the use of this technique, several decision trees can be combined to avoid overfitting. Healthcare, finance, banking, the stock market, and e-commerce can all use this algorithm.

LITERATURE REVIEW

To lessen the harm caused by a flood, an early warning system is constructed that forecasts the flow rate and water level. Early warning could help flood disasters have fewer fatalities. This system uses a 2-class neural network as its algorithm. Water level and flow sensors are included into this system. The information obtained from the sensors is recorded in the database and shown in real time using Thingspeak. The Azure Machine learning service from Microsoft includes a 2-class neural network module (Abdullahi et al., 2018).

Improvements in the existing and outdated models can still provide better results. Predicting the real occurrence of floods is mandatory even though nature is still unpredictable most of the time. Not only affects human society but also causes great trouble to livestock, cattle, and other living species. Predicting at early stages can protect the habitat and sufficient time for preparing against the flood. There have been a lot of Artificial Intelligence models and Machine learning-based systems in society. But making them efficient and much more useful by improving their performance should be done. The main concept is to create using the Apache SystemML machine learning software. With the emergence of python programming to a greater extent collecting and analyzing large amounts of rainfall data from different sources has been optimized. Making the code writable, reduced in error and readable can be the main efficient features that python provides in optimizing the system. With the help of advancements in the technology fields, languages such as python provide an upper hand in dealing with data and optimizing solutions (Akshay et al., 2019).

In this paper, the concept of flood prediction utilizing artificial neural networks (ANN) and the Internet of Things is discussed. This system monitors the river water level, humidity, temperature, pressure, and rainfall on a regular basis to provide temporal correlative data for flood prediction analysis. The nature of flood data is dynamic and non-linear. The system is informed by the sensors, which read the data. With such figures, the working is complete, and a choice is made regarding the likelihood of a flood (Bande & Shete, 2017).

The flood prediction can be done using two models. They are mathematical modelling and stochastic modelling. Examples of statistical modelling include the Markov Method and Autoregressive Moving Average Model (ARMA). Using these two models, we can predict the event in hydrological forecasting. However, the data required for model building is very dynamic in nature as it depends upon the varying water level. Thus, it is very important to integrate the data before we use it for modelling. Artificial Neural Networks (ANN) provide the data integration and development of the model. This paper analyses the region of the River Nile and provides a solution to forecast the flood event around that region which can be used as an early warning system in terms of the flood. The Artificial Neural Network (ANN) has a simple feed-forward network that consists of one input layer, several hidden layers, and one output layer. A neuron is modeled by taking the input from the input level and providing the activation level (output). This model is trained using the values of maximum water level as the dataset. Then the gauge and the water surface level are predicted which in turn predicts the occurrence of the flood by analyzing the past threshold level. The maximum and predicted food plain of the same year is also displayed as a satellite image. The output is accurate due to the involvement of only one input variable. Artificial Neural Network is advantageous in these types of problems because it reduces the amount of time spent on analyzing the data. It provides good information about the topographical situation of the particular region. It also gives detailed information about the hydrological information of a certain region. It also would be a better choice when compared to other models as it is simple and when the required data is lacking and difficult to collect (Elsafi, 2014).

Using wireless sensor networks data is collected from rivers located in urban areas. With these measurements flash floods nowcasting can be investigated. Different Machine learning techniques are used and different kinds of data are given as input to get accurate results (Furquim et al., 2014).

The damages caused by a devastating flood are unimaginable. It leaves back lots of debris and waste. Scouring and cleaning them is a difficult task. This waste could cause damage to human life. To rectify these issues a flood management system was built on conventional artificial intelligence that has a low false alarm rate. Thus identifying the most accurate and precise Conventional Artificial Intelligence. Ensemble Conventional Artificial Intelligence seems to have highly efficient and accurate flood prediction (Fotovatikhah et al., 2018).

Floods are considered the most dangerous and destructive natural disasters to mankind and the environment, also affecting the economic situation of the country. In the fast-moving era, there have been a lot of novel modi operandi flood forecasting technologies. The historic rainfall data are used for the analysis and forecasting of floods. This depicts the recent trends in the prediction of a flood using the efficient machine learning algorithms and techniques used in making the system for accurate prediction (Ghorpade et al., 2021).

A flood prediction system is developed based on the information provided by the gas leveling station in Goslar. Existing models of Artificial Neural Networks (ANN) for flood prediction are extended by using Tensorflow. The measuring station provides the precipitation and gauge levels. The dataset further includes the weather data provided by the Institute of Electrical Information Technology (IEI). The dimensionality of the data is reduced by using the Principal Component Analysis (PCA) which reduces the training time of the model. This model predicts the water gauge level in the Goslar region. The use of an Artificial Neural Network (ANN) increases the accuracy of the prediction (Goymann et al., 2019).

Because nature is erratic, the amount of rain falls fluctuates depending on the weather and the force of the wind. Urban flooding can be a major calamity for society in such circumstances. The real-time flood prediction model discussed in this research is classification-based, and it is supported by a numerical analysis model based on hydraulic theory and the necessary machine learning models. The Environmental Protection Agency's Storm Water Management model and a two-dimensional inundation model were used to generate the Flood database in advance. The classification of the flood depth data into five categories using Latin hypercube sampling and probabilistic neural networks. If the observed rainfall data is supplied, this machine learning model is built to identify the appropriate cumulative volume. Consequently, a system that can produce a real-time flood map by comparing the cumulative volume of each grid to the cumulative volume using both linear and nonlinear regression is needed. The created method can forecast the likelihood of floods caused by rainfall in a way that lowers the danger of disaster and limits harm to people's health and property. As a result, an effective method for managing disasters has been created in order to reduce catastrophic losses (Keum et al., 2020).

Floods being the most lethal cataclysmic events in the recent era, a proper accurate flood prediction system are the most needed technology for society at the moment. The absence of a proper accurate prediction system has brought a great loss to mankind and infrastructure. Using Artificial intelligence calculations precisely and productively, the framework has been constructed. For the development of this system, the machine learning algorithm Decision tree has been used to implement. This system would provide the required information and assist the residents of the area with flash floods. Using the android application, it provides an alert message to the local bodies and government to prepare, protect and prevent catastrophic destruction. Accurate prediction and alerting or warning about the situation are all the system aims for. The technology's objective is to generate accurate predictions from the given rainfall data and instruct or recommend the resident about the situation and the respective measures that are needed to be taken. Comparing the three machine learning algorithms Decision Tree, Random Forest, and Gradient Boost gives recommendations, for which algorithm produces the best outcome with the given rainfall training data. The best among them can be chosen for further development of the system and it will evaluate the testing data for providing accurate predictions and recommendations. Therefore, it provides the most meticulous prediction results with intricate information and high-level algorithms (Kunverji et al., 2021).

Flooding has been a major affecting factor over recent years. Complete stoppage against flooding is impossible. But proper preparation against flood and preventing catastrophic damage can be an efficient way to reduce loss of lives. Thus a model with an accurate and earlier prediction rate can be useful for preparation against floods. Certain parameters play a crucial role in the prediction of floods. Identifying and analyzing them would be an important factor. Those parameters add value to the prediction of the flood. This paper is a study about the existing machine learning models and algorithms that are effective in predicting the occurrence of floods and about the parameters playing a major role in predicting them. Thus, a clear overview of the recent machine learning techniques and notable parameters in the prediction of the occurrence of the flood is shown. This can be used as a guideline for researchers to have a better understanding of the machine learning algorithms and the role of significant parameters in prediction (Maspo et al., 2020).

As floods are the most destructive and devastating natural disasters, proper attention and care have to be laid. In such a way prediction has been made on the data in the recent two decades to get accurate results beforehand in such a way that it could be useful for prevention, preparation, and creating awareness within the society. A lot of novel research and hybridizing existing methodologies have been undertaken in recent years using different machine learning algorithms and machine learning techniques. This paper completely gives an overview of the various machine learning techniques and models that are implemented in creating robust different models. Comparison has been made based on the robustness, accuracy, effectiveness, and speed investigated on the different machine learning models. In such a way a vast and in-depth understanding has been acquired of the various machine learning techniques and methodologies that are used in implementing the novel models or hybridizing the existing features. This paper results in the effective, efficient, and most promising machine learning algorithms and machine learning techniques for the long-term as well as short-term run. This paper gives an exact view to the hydrologists as well as climatic scientists about the best suitable machine learning model required for the respective predictions. It acts as a guideline for the future predictions that are to be made, helping the researchers have a clear view of the models with their performance, efficiency, and capacity of them. A complete insight into the suitable machine learning models and techniques that are implemented using each algorithm is depicted in the paper (Mosavi et al., 2018).

The operational framework is followed to lower the risk and damage caused by flooding. This framework contains four layers such as data management; Stage forecast modelling, Inundation modelling, and the early warning system which can also be called an alert system. Ingestion, quality control, and correction of data are carried out in the data management layer of the framework. The stage forecast modelling stage includes two types: the model as a multiple linear regression model (LR) and the long-short-term memory model (LSTM). The Inundation modelling stage applies thresholding and manifold to the model. Finally, the alert system which serves as the early warning system sends alerts or warnings to the responsible authorities, people, and emergency units (Nevo et al., 2022).

The major goal of this work is to make predictions about the likelihood of dangerous and deadly pluvial floods. Using accessible data, machine learning algorithms are utilised to forecast when pluvial floods may occur in the Pattani basin. There is a time limit for data collecting. The upstream and downstream flood models have undergone analysis and testing. In the Pattani basin, the Bayesian Linear model was suggested as a potential remedy for pluvial flood prediction (Noymanee et al., 2017).

Thailand faces its main issues regarding urban flooding in most of its densely populated areas which fall under the high rainfall region. Urban flooding is caused by rainfall in densely populated areas with high rainfall areas that overwhelms the power of drainage systems and conservative steps. As an idea of a solution for overriding this hindrance and for proper management of floods: A flood forecasting system using machine learning techniques on hydrological modelling. This paper stands out from other various papers on the basis that those existing early warning systems known as EWS do not provide accurate forecasting of rainfall results. Miscalculations of the existing rainfall forecasting models lead to the need for the development of a promising early warning prediction or forecasting system with accurate results. Hydrological modelling using machine learning algorithms helps in achieving the desired results. Real-time data is generated and calculated using the hydrological model. The model augments different machine learning algorithms known as linear regression, boosted decision tree algorithm, Bayesian linear regression, and neural network regression. In the testing phase, the model known as MIKE-11 hydrological forecasting model has been developed by the Danish Hydraulic Institute situated in Denmark. As the training data set the rainfall data between the years 2012 to 2016 is considered for training the model. The trained model is applied to the 2017 rainfall data and is tested which produces accurate results and can be completely trustable for future predictive measures. Though nature is unpredictable in its ways still having a dependable forecasting or prediction system is the utmost need for society. Thailand has this hydrological modelling for prediction of the flood beforehand in such a way that it makes it easy for the society and environment from hazardous natural disasters and prevents urban flooding in the densely populated areas (Noymanee et al., 2019).

Flooding can be predicted by hydrologists by analyzing the data provided. But the results become dynamic due to the change in water levels of the watershed. To overcome this problem, technologies such as Artificial Neural Networks (ANN), Fuzzy logic, and neuro-fuzzy are used in predictions with increased accuracy. These technologies can give an optimized output by getting uncertain datasets. Water level fluctuation is one of the major difficulties in flood prediction and makes the problem nonlinear. To tackle this nonlinearity, Artificial Neural Networks (ANN) are used. The dataset taken is the real-time data obtained from Flood Forecasting and Warning Centre, Bangladesh Water Development Board. This dataset is then set to undergo statistical fit functions and finally simulated to compare the predicted and actual water levels. The weights are applied to decrease the error between the output of the Artificial Neural Network (ANN) and the real-time data. The model is then trained and tested against various hours and the hour with the best accuracy is selected for the comparison of the actual and predicted water level (Paul & Das, 2014).

Based on the design, planning, and management of water resources, flood prediction is one significant element of importance. Effective water conservation is required. Given that water is essential to life, water bodies must be preserved. Effectively managing them requires careful consideration. By using ANNs as its algorithm, the study broadens the scope of research in the field of artificial neural networks. Along with multiple linear regressions and multiple non-linear regressions, it also incorporates an adaptive neuro-fuzzy inference system called ANFIS. This can introduce the idea of predicting the highest daily flow of rainfall at the watershed's exit, which is in Iran's Fars province. They acquired sensory data from four various meteorological stations in order to create a multi-layer perceptron topology model. The perceptual data gathered from the various meteorological stations was subjected to the adaptive neuro-fuzzy inference system and multiple linear regressions. RMSE and R^2 are used to assess the effectiveness of the models created using various techniques. Non-linear regression has an advantage over other algorithms and can be used to apply the perception data for predicting the maximum daily flow of floods, according to further rigorous calculations using various methods on the perception data (Rezaeianzadeh et al., 2013).

On a high note, research has been continuously carried out on achieving efficient and accurate prediction technology or systems. With the help of machine learning techniques and algorithms, prediction can be made easy to obtain accurate and earlier results such as making the required arrangements and evacuating people from the hazard areas. Over the two decades, neural networks have shown an extraordinary outcome in predicting the occurrence of floods with the given rainfall data providing better results and cost-effective solutions. This paper is novel in the way of analyzing databases by Multi-layer perceptron classifier to read data such as dynamic identification, deficit treatment, data validation, and data cleaning to be carried across the database. Advancements in every note can provide better results based on the pre-processing of data (Sivamoorthy et al., 2022).

The management and careful monitoring of reservoirs are equally as vital as averting floods. At the moment, they need to be maintained. Medium- and long-term runoff time series are forecasted using artificial neural networks in conjunction with ensemble empirical mode decomposition (Wang et al., 2015).

Flash floods are a result of the climate trends altering. It examines how changes in water levels in the river basin can have disastrous effects on society when people are unprepared and unprepared for them. The level of the river basin directly affects how much water floods a certain area. Flooding in the area can be reduced if the river basin can store more water than it needs to. Forecasts for the occurrence of floods in a particular area can be formed by determining the change in water level in the river basin. Therefore, non-linear regression and support vector machine methods are utilised to detect changes in water levels in the river basin. Calculating the change in river water level is made easier by the machine learning algorithms. The algorithms are used to estimate the rate of flow of water in the river basin, thereby identifying the possibility of flooding. Variables included in the algorithms include precipitation amount, river inflow, peak gust, seasonal flow, frequency of floods, and many more. The straightforward classification of the available data into flood and non-flood groups has made machine learning prediction simple. The effectiveness of support vector machines and non-linear regression has been fully illustrated (Zehra, 2022).

Flood prediction being an important need for centuries to centuries the Mayan prediction using the planetary motions in the old period weren't accurate. Therefore with time and evolution of technology people were more focused with accurate prediction results. With the evolution of machine learning and Artificial intelligence people started to expect accurate results. Bayesian network model, Radical Basis Function based on Internet of things, K- Nearest Neighbour are considered and evaluated. This paper emphasis that Random Forest algorithm can provide better results. The random forest model can consider larger datasets for classification, regression and other tasks, building a set of decision pressures and performing average classification or prediction at the time of training, where the sample data set is relatively small and the accuracy rate is higher, the accuracy does not improve with more samples, but when most of the sample data is missing, can maintain the Relative Accuracy The training computational cost is relatively low compared to other models (Shruthi et al., 2020).

Flood forecasting technology can provide early warning of impending flooding. These alerts can help people evacuate affected areas, move belongings to safety, and take other necessary precautions to protect themselves and their belongings. Flood forecasting technology can also help mitigate flood damage. This helps identify areas at high risk of flooding and take action to prevent or mitigate the impacts of flooding, such as building dams and flood barriers and implementing best practices for flood control. land use. Flood forecasting technology is essential to protecting life, property and the economy. This allows people to better prepare for potential flood hazards, reduce the impact of flooding, and allocate resources more efficiently in emergencies. Random forests do not require assumptions about the relationship between the independent and response variables. It is a suitable method for analyzing hierarchical and nonlinear interactions in large data sets. Random forests can be more efficient when used to predict the capacity of new data instances (Esfandiari et al., 2020).

PROPOSED METHODOLOGY

This section discusses the proposed methodology. This work proposes to predict test data and place recommendations in the Web Application framework. The monthly rainfall Index and flood Prediction dataset was used with the application of different ML algorithms. In a Boolean value, it includes the monthly and annual rainfall as well as the likelihood of a flood. Test and train subsets of the dataset are created. The detailed processes in this recommendation system are explained in Figure 2.

Figure 2. The process involved in the prediction phase

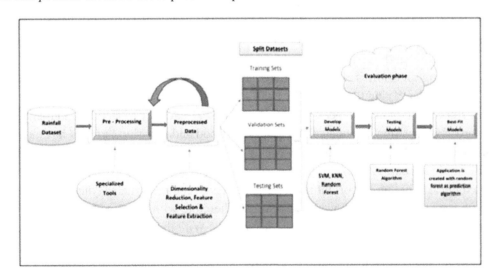

DATASET

Primarily, the dataset used as a base is the Rainfall in India dataset which contains Sub-division wise monthly data for 115 years from 1901-2015. This dataset is customized according to our problem. The selected dataset contains attributes such as Year, Monthly Rainfall Index for the months from January through December, Annual Rainfall and Occurrence of flood. The likelihood of a flood is indicated in Boolean value. The value '1' represents the occurrence of flood and '0' represents no occurrence of flood. Test and train subsets of the dataset are created.

Table 1.

	YEAR	JAN	FEB	MAR	APR	MAY	JUN	JUL	AUG	SEP	OCT	NOV	DEC	ANNUAL RAINFALL	FLOODS
0	1901	28.7	44.7	51.6	160.0	174.7	824.6	743.0	357.5	197.7	266.9	350.8	48.4	3248.6	1
1	1902	6.7	2.6	57.3	83.9	134.5	390.9	1205.0	315.8	491.6	358.4	158.3	121.5	3326.6	1
2	1903	3.2	18.6	3.1	83.6	249.7	558.6	1022.5	420.2	341.8	354.1	157.0	59.0	3271.2	1
3	1904	23.7	3.0	32.2	71.5	235.7	1098.2	725.5	351.8	222.7	328.1	33.9	3.3	3129.7	1
4	1905	1.2	22.3	9.4	105.9	263.3	850.2	520.5	293.6	217.2	383.5	74.4	0.2	2741.6	0

Using the Random Forest Classifier technique, the model is trained. It is an algorithm for supervised machine learning that categorises the unlabelled data after learning from the labelled data. The simplified proposed framework is shown in Figure 3.

Figure 3. Overview of the flood prediction system

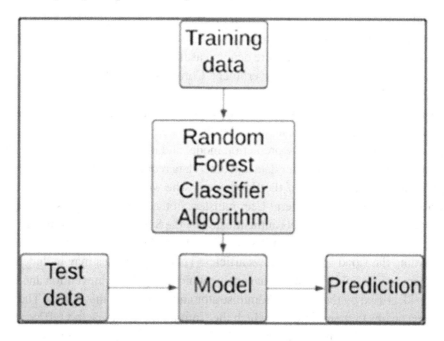

The following equations define the mathematics underlying the Random Forest classifier. The Random Classifier determines which branch is the better choice for the Regression issue by computing the distance between each node and the predicted actual value. The Mean Squared Error (MSE) is determined using the following formula if there are N data points, *fi* is the value the model returned, and *yi* is the actual value for datapointi, as shown.

$$MSE = \frac{1}{N}\sum_{i=1}^{N}(fi - yi)^2 \tag{1}$$

For classification problems, Gini Index is used to decide the branch. If *c* represents the number of classes and *pi* represents the relative frequency of the class that are observed, then the Gini Index is calculated using the following formula, as shown in the Equation 2.

$$Gini = 1 - \sum_{i=1}^{c}(pi)^2 \tag{2}$$

Entropy can also be used to decide on the branch of the forest, as shown in Equation 3.

$$Entropy = \sum_{i=1}^{c} - p_i * log_2(p_i) \tag{3}$$

The system can be further extended to a large number of stakeholders spanning a wider area. The system can involve General User, System Administrator, Community leaders, and Officers. The general user may include the common people and the farmers. The common people can use this system to predict the amount of rainfall priorly and can schedule their events based on the outcome. They can also use this system to predict the flood event and can take necessary actions such as evacuating their current living place. The community leaders and Officers are denoted as the Flood Team and they may be a team of a particular organization or a group from the government. Community Leaders and Officers (Flood Team) acts as a stakeholder in this system by helping the farmers and casuals to evacuate to a safer place. Community Leaders and Officers (Flood Team) are responsible for the safer transportation of people from flood-prone areas. The third stakeholder identified is the System Administrator. The System Administrator is the one who trains and builds the prediction model and updates the system in the backend. The System Administrator collects the weather data and other data required for the accurate prediction of the amount of rainfall and the occurrence of the flood event. The workflow of the system depicted in the picture is described as follows. The General User registers in the system using a signup page. Then he/she uses the registered credentials and gets authenticated by the System Administrator. Thus, the System Administrator acts as an approver of authentication. Once logged into the system, the user can view the information regarding the flood and other news articles. The news articles may include the latest technology developments in the field of disaster management including flood prevention and occurring. The evacuation area is identified by the System Administrator and updated in the system. The User can view the evacuation area nearer to their region to which the Community Leaders and Officers (Flood Team) can transfer the people. Community Leaders and Officers (Flood Team) and the System Administrator both can be able to answer queries related to Flood prediction, evacuation, and the available areas. The Flood report consists of the past, present, and future flood events along with the recorded rainfall. The details of the evacuation centre must be listed along with addresses and facilities. The facilities in the evacuation areas such as the health services are managed by the Community Leaders and Officers (Flood Team). It includes first aid medicines for casualties and people, medicines to treat water-borne diseases and a medical care unit for those who are injured severely. Apart from medical services, food should also be provided, and it should be enough for day-to-day supply. Thus, the Community Leaders and Officers (Flood Team) should need a sub-team to take care of various necessities at the evacuation centre and the management of the evacuation centre must be taken care of in an efficient manner.

EXPERIMENTAL RESULTS

The machine learning algorithm is deployed to a webpage using python flask. Flask is a micro web framework used for developing web applications. The model is saved and imported as a .pkl file. The flood prediction system web page consists of several pages with a pleasant User Interface. The webpage is also designed such that it is easy to operate for everyone. In the dashboard, the user can look for his required features on the pages namely Predictor, News, Contact, and About. The predictor page predicts the probability of flood when the amount of rainfall is entered. Users can enter the amount of rainfall value. If the rate of rainfall is high, the user is redirected to a recommendation site. In addition, the user can mention his place to find a nearby evacuation site. The ultimate goal of this system is to find a safer place for people during a disaster time. The news page contains articles about the new advancements in technology related to disaster management that create awareness among people. The contact page has the contact details of the System Administrator and the flood team. Also, the user can ask queries to which the System Administrator replies. The About page has a brief description of the mission and objective of the System.

The model is trained using K-Nearest Neighbors Classifier (KNN), Logistic Regression (LR), Decision Tree (DT), Ensemble Learning (EL), and Random Forest Classifier (RF). Accuracy of all algorithms are determined and shown in Figure 4. Among the algorithms used, the model with the highest accuracy is selected for prediction. The Random Forest Classifier outperformed the other models with an accuracy of 87.5000%. Recall is useful when we want to ensure we capture all the True Positives even if that means increasing our False Positives (false alarms). This model records a Recall score of 90.909091. The Receiver operating characteristic (ROC) score which is the capability of distinguishing between classes is 87.762238, which is shown in Figure 5.

Figure 4. Comparison of accuracy of algorithms

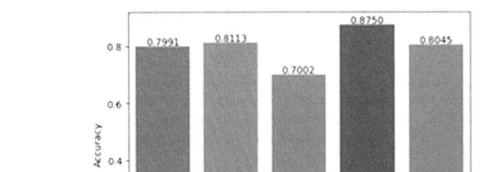

Figure 5. ROC curve for RF classifier

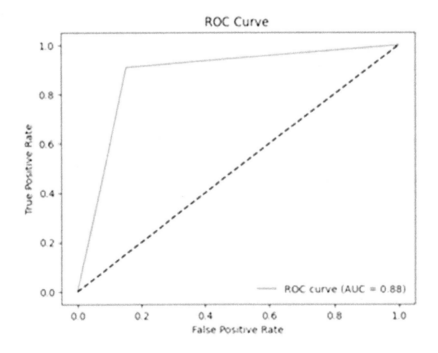

CONCLUSION

Floods are considered one of the destructive disasters causing loss of human life and property losses. It is also a complex problem to predict accurately because of the occurrence of flash floods. Flood forecasting is very much important for managing the environment and the water resource system. Machine Learning algorithms contributed to the prediction system advancement. A web page with a smooth User Interface is designed by deploying the model. The webpage is designed in such a way that it should be available both online and offline. It should be accessible to all types of users irrespective of the knowledge they possess. The user can enter the amount of rainfall and can predict the rainfall and the occurrence of the flood event. The System Administrator takes care of the testing and training of the prediction algorithm. The system uses this prediction algorithm to predict the occurrence of the flood event in a binary format. The outcome of the prediction should also be simple and informative. The directions and facilities of the evacuation area are made clear, and a team is assigned to clarify any of the queries regarding the aforementioned details of the evacuation centre. The articles related to flood prediction advancements and the early warning system are posted by the System Administrator and will be utilized by the user. Thus, a better performance algorithm and cost-effective solution are proposed in this paper to predict the occurrence of floods. These forecasts should provide enough lead time for the people to prepare and evacuate to a particular region. The constraints of the system include that the people might not be able to reach the evacuation areas as soon as possible. Flash floods may happen too quickly for a warning to be effective and before they reach the people. These algorithmic predictions do not stop the land from flooding - they just warn people that a flood is likely to happen. Nature is unpredictable. Nothing can challenge nature. Under such circumstances, there might not be floods even though it's predicted or there may be flash floods. Thus, for the mitigation of flood damage, flood prediction modelling and monitoring play a powerful role.

The prediction of flood events including flash floods can be made accurate by analysing the sensor data using satellites, lightning observing systems, radar, and rain gauges. A recommendation system that recommends an evacuation area can be made wider by monitoring the flooding on different rivers. Recent technologies such as Machine Learning (ML), Artificial Intelligence (AI), Artificial Neural Networks (ANN), and Deep Learning can be used in predicting upcoming flood events using flood risk mapping. This method can estimate the water level of a particular region and can serve as an early warning system. The water levels can be predicted by the specialized deep neural network architecture called HydroNets. It considers the structure of the river and allows for fine-tuning the performance of the algorithm for each location. The severity and immediacy of the flood event can also be recorded and mentioned in flood reports. The evacuation of people from flood hazard areas can be made more effective by undergoing wider research on the available areas that are safe and can accommodate more people. The system can be improved by adding Google maps through API, which is a web service that provides detailed geographical information of the sites globally. It can be used to show directions using real-time traffic information and can be used to propose the best route to the evacuation area. With voice recognition, it makes navigation less complex for the user. More detailed articles on treatments of waterborne and vector-borne diseases can be provided which are transmitted by floods.

In future, this research work could also include a recommendation system with a map view for easy mobility from hazard areas to evacuation areas. The directions and the paths that are blocked are mentioned in the maps instructing people to not choose them and guide them in a different direction.

Including the map view for the recommendation system can enhance the quality of the flood prediction and recommendation model. This helps them in the easy evacuation during the time of disasters.

REFERENCES

Abdullahi, S. I., Habaebi, M. H., & Malik, N. A. (2018). Flood Disaster Warning System on the go. In *Proceedings of the 7th International Conference on Computer and Communication Engineering (ICCCE)*. 10.1109/ICCCE.2018.8539253

Bande, S., & Shete, V. V. (2017). Smart flood disaster prediction system using IoT & neural networks. *Proceedings of 2017 International Conference On Smart Technologies For Smart Nation (Smart-TechCon)*. 10.1109/SmartTechCon.2017.8358367

Elsafi, S. H. (2014). Artificial Neural Networks (ANNs) for flood forecasting at Dongola Station in the River Nile, Sudan. *Alexandria Engineering Journal*, *53*(3), 655–662. doi:10.1016/j.aej.2014.06.010

Esfandiari, M., Jabari, S., McGrath, H., & Coleman, D. (2020). Flood mapping using random forest and identifying the essential conditioning factors; a case study in fredericton, new brunswick, canada. *ISPRS Annals of the Photogrammetry, Remote Sensing and Spatial Information Sciences*, *V-3-2020*, 609–615. doi:10.5194/isprs-annals-V-3-2020-609-2020

Fan, R.-E. (2008). LIBLINEAR: A library for largelinear classification. *Journal of Machine Learning Research*, *9*, 1871–1874.

Fotovatikhah, F., Herrera, M., Shamshirband, S., Chau, K., Faizollahzadeh Ardabili, S., & Piran, M. J. (2018). Survey of computational intelligence as basis to big flood management: Challenges, Research directions and future work. *Engineering Applications of Computational Fluid Mechanics*, *12*(1), 411–437. doi:10.1080/19942060.2018.1448896

Furquim, G., Neto, F., Pessin, G., Ueyama, J., de Albuquerque, J. P., Clara, M., Mendiondo, E. M., de Souza, V. C. B., de Souza, P., Dimitrova, D., & Braun, T. (2014). Combining Wireless Sensor Networks and Machine Learning for Flash Flood Nowcasting. *Proceedings of 28th International Conference on Advanced Information Networking and Applications Workshops*. 10.1109/WAINA.2014.21

Ghorpade, P., Gadge, A., Lende, A., Chordiya, H., Gosavi, G., Mishra, A., Hooli, B., Ingle, Y. S., & Shaikh, N. (2021). Flood Forecasting Using Machine Learning: A Review. *Proceedings of 8th International Conference on Smart Computing and Communications (ICSCC)*. 10.1109/ICSCC51209.2021.9528099

Goymann, P., Herrling, D., & Rausch, A. (2019). Flood Prediction through Artificial Neural Networks: A case study in Goslar. Academic Press.

Keum, H. J., Han, K. Y., & Kim, H. I. (2020). Real-Time Flood Disaster Prediction System by Applying Machine Learning Technique. *KSCE Journal of Civil Engineering*, *24*(9), 2835–2848. doi:10.100712205-020-1677-7

Kharche, Bhagat, & Ibrahim. (2019). A Review On Flood Prediction Using Machine Learning based Apache System ML Python Platform. *Journal of Emerging Technologies and Innovative Research*, *6*(1).

Kunverji, K., Shah, K., & Shah, N. (2021). A Flood Prediction System Developed Using Various Machine Learning Algorithms. SSRN *Electronic Journal*. doi:10.2139/ssrn.3866524

Maspo, N.-A., & Bin, H. (2020). Evaluation of Machine Learning approach in flood prediction scenarios and its input parameters: A systematic review. *IOP Conference Series. Earth and Environmental Science*, *479*(1), 012038. doi:10.1088/1755-1315/479/1/012038

Mosavi, A., Ozturk, P., & Chau, K. (2018). Flood Prediction Using Machine Learning Models: Literature Review. *Water (Basel)*, *10*(11), 1536. doi:10.3390/w10111536

Nevo, S., Morin, E., Gerzi Rosenthal, A., Metzger, A., Barshai, C., Weitzner, D., Voloshin, D., Kratzert, F., Elidan, G., Dror, G., Begelman, G., Nearing, G., Shalev, G., Noga, H., Shavitt, I., Yuklea, L., Royz, M., Giladi, N., Peled Levi, N., ... Matias, Y. (2022). Flood forecasting with machine learning models in an operational framework. *Hydrology and Earth System Sciences*, *26*(15), 4013–4032. doi:10.5194/hess-26-4013-2022

Noymanee, J., Nikitin, N. O., & Kalyuzhnaya, A. V. (2017). Urban Pluvial Flood Forecasting using Open Data with Machine Learning Techniques in Pattani Basin. *Procedia Computer Science*, *119*, 288–297. doi:10.1016/j.procs.2017.11.187

Noymanee, J., & Theeramunkong, T. (2019). Flood Forecasting with Machine Learning Technique on Hydrological Modeling. *Procedia Computer Science*, *156*, 377–386. doi:10.1016/j.procs.2019.08.214

Paul, A., & Das, P. (2014). Flood Prediction Model using Artificial Neural Network. International. *Journal of Computer Applications Technology and Research*, *3*(7), 473–478. doi:10.7753/IJCATR0307.1016

Rezaeianzadeh, M., Tabari, H., Arabi Yazdi, A., Isik, S., & Kalin, L. (2013). Flood flow forecasting using ANN, ANFIS and regression models. *Neural Computing & Applications*, *25*(1), 25–37. doi:10.100700521-013-1443-6

Shruthi, J, Sumathi, M S, Srivatsa Raju, S, & Vidya, R Pai. (2020). Forecasting & Detection Of Flood Using Random Forest Learning Method. *European Journal of Molecular and Clinical Medicine*.

Sivamoorthy, T., Ansari, A. M., Sivakumar, D. B., & Nallarasan, V. (2022). Flood Prediction Using ML Classification Methods on Rainfall Data. *International Journal for Research in Applied Science and Engineering Technology*, *10*(4), 499–502. doi:10.22214/ijraset.2022.41297

Wang, W., Chau, K., Qiu, L., & Chen, Y. (2015). Improving forecasting accuracy of medium and long-term runoff using artificial neural network based on EEMD decomposition. *Environmental Research*, *139*, 46–54. doi:10.1016/j.envres.2015.02.002 PMID:25684671

Wu, Lin, & Weng. (2004). Probability estimates for multi-classclassification by pairwise coupling. *JMLR*, *5*, 975–1005.

Zchra, N. (2020). Prediction Analysis of Floods Using Machine Learning Algorithms (NARX & SVM). *International Journal of Sciences, Basic and Applied Research*, *49*(2), 24–34. https://www.gssrr.org/index.php/JournalOfBasicAndApplied/article/view/10719

Section 2
Cybersecurity Innovations in Industry 4.0

Chapter 14
Exploring the Ethereum Blockchain:
An Introduction to Blockchain Technology

Gautham C. P. Krishna

School of Computer Science and Engineering, Vellore Institute of Technology, Chennai, India

Praveen Joe I. R.

School of Computer Science and Engineering, Vellore Institute of Technology, Chennai, India

ABSTRACT

Blockchain technology binds the idea of distributed ledgers and decentralization of assets into providing secure and fully ensured transparency of the data history. This technology consists of a P2P or peer-to-peer architecture of nodes that keeps a copy of the blockchain thereby enabling them to validate every transaction that is taking place in the network and has influenced developers and enthusiasts alike to adopt a decentralised mechanism. It is a robust architecture and makes hacking impossible. Consensus mechanisms, smart contracts, gas fees, different security protocols, Web3 wallets, oracles are some of the concepts and features that make blockchains immutable and secure. This chapter covers major contemporary concepts and terms profoundly. Ethereum blockchain network is dealt as the basic and foundational example that can be explained comfortably with it. Content and examples are related to solidity programming language so that even a novice can write his or her first smart contract on the Ethereum blockchain.

INTRODUCTION

The general perspective of this chapter is to provide a brief insight towards the blockchain technology and, in this chapter most of the concepts are illustrated by taking the example of the Ethereum Blockchain network. Through this approach, the reader can have a practical thinking side towards every concept which is being explained in this chapter. By the end of this chapter, the reader would be equipped with

DOI: 10.4018/978-1-6684-8145-5.ch014

Copyright © 2023, IGI Global. Copying or distributing in print or electronic forms without written permission of IGI Global is prohibited.

all the beginner tools towards blockchain development if he/she is willing to pursue the field. The reader can acquire knowledge regarding the modern technological facts and resources related to the concepts in this chapter. Topics like how to code your first smart contract is explained in detail and with layman terms so that it's easier for the reader to grasp the technical concepts present in it.

An Introduction to Blockchain Technology

Decentralization refers to the process of removing central control over sub-authorities and transferring management potential to all members of a network or community. This concept has gained popularity, particularly in the field of data transactions through the use of distributed networks composed of "nodes" - the individuals who participate in the network. This approach is made possible through internet and computing technologies, which have led to the development of blockchain technology. Blockchain technology has replaced many centralized institutions and organizations by allowing for decentralized networks. It is possible that in future, web frontends will be integrated with decentralized backends instead of the traditional Web 2.0 backends controlled by various companies and organizations. As a result, browsing the internet will involve the use of blockchain-powered decentralized backends, giving rise to Web 3.0 technologies (Cui et al., 2020). The emergence of decentralization has profound implications for the internet and society as a whole. Decentralized networks remove the need for intermediaries, making it easier to manage data transactions, and reduce the risks associated with centralization. In addition, decentralized networks offer increased security, transparency, and efficiency, making them a promising alternative to traditional databases (Li et al., 2018). Overall, decentralization and blockchain technology offer a unique approach to managing data transactions and network governance. As more organizations and individuals adopt this approach, it is possible that the internet and society as a whole will shift towards a more decentralized future, offering a range of benefits and opportunities (Polyzos et al., 2017).

Traditional Databases and Blockchain Technology

The traditional databases are the ones which stores data and information, managed through database management systems like MySQL, PostgreSQL, MongoDB and more. Most of these databases are hosted within centralized authorities and they can have control over the data. Coming to Blockchain Technology, it is based on distributed ledger systems meaning that every node (computer) in the network will contain the details of a particular transaction that had happened in the network. Blockchain offers transparency of the transaction details which can be later used for data verifications (Praveen Joe et al., 2019). Once a piece of information is mined or stored in the block; it cannot be updated later as blockchains are immutable, i.e., it cannot be used for updating the existing information on the chain.

Some Popular Blockchain Networks/ Platforms

Ethereum Blockchain Network or the Ethereum Virtual Machine (EVM) is one of the top operational decentralized networks that exist in the Web3 space. Most of the decentralized applications are powered by the Ethereum Blockchain (Chen et al., 2018). Even most of the popular De-Fi (Decentralized Finance) Applications are built on Ethereum chain. EVM executes the smart contract bytecodes produced by the solidity compiler to the network. Other than the Ethereum Blockchain, there exists other blockchains as well which powers all other sorts of cryptocurrencies and applications (Dai et al., 2019). Naming a few are Binance Smart Chain, Solana Blockchain which is known for its low gas fee transactions, Polygon Chain which is built on Ethereum. Most of the technical concepts in this chapter will be explained on the basis of Ethereum Blockchain. Binance Smart Chain is a blockchain network that runs in parallel with Binance Chain and is built to support smart contract functionality (Li et al., 2018). Solana is a high-performance blockchain network that aims to provide fast and low-cost transactions. Polygon (formerly Matic Network) is a Layer 2 scaling solution that is built on top of the Ethereum network and aims to provide faster and cheaper transactions (Huberman et al., 2017).

Basic Blockchain Architecture

In this chapter, the architecture and functioning of blockchain is explained step by step in a simplified approach.

SHA256

Secure Hash Algorithm (256 bit) is an algorithm which generates a unique signature for a given text data. For example, the text "hello" generates the hash "2cf24dba5fb0a30e26e83b2ac5b9e29e1b161e5c-1fa7425e73043362938b9824", and on further changes on the previous text data can produce a new SHA256 hash for it.

Every block has a SHA256 generator which generates these unique hashes for the data stored in it.

Block

The individual nodes that store transaction details and data and contains the hashes for next and previous nodes of the blockchain is called a block of the blockchain network. Every block also has the "nonce" number which keeps a reference track of the hashes generated after every "mining" activity of the block. To give a bit more depth towards understanding this concept, we can take an example: Suppose there is a block having a hash value that starts with "0000..." and initially it has no data in it and we can call this as a signed block. Now when we add some data into that block and mine it (which means to create that block), the SHA256 generates a new hash for that block and also a nonce value. The nonce value is, suppose say 21689, this value infers to the number of times the SHA256 algorithm took to generate that hash value that was starting with "0000...", basically to make it a signed block again. In this case, the algorithm generated the hash at the 21689th trial.

Mining

In simple terms, it basically means to add some data into the blockchain and generate a secure hash for it. The process of mining involves the use very high computational energy as the task of mining is to solve a complex computational problem which draws a lot of GPU and memory power from the system (Martin et al., 2018).

Blockchain

As the name suggests, it's a chain of blocks with each block having previous and its own hash values. You can relate this to a linked list with each node having addresses of forward and previous nodes. Since each block has the hash of the previous block and its own hash, changing the data of one particular node can break the chain (Joe et al., 2016). Take a look at the diagram given below.

Figure 1. A visual demo of blockchain

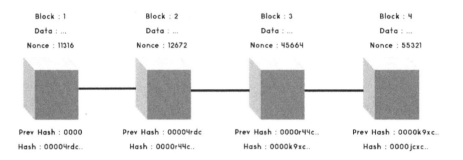

It shows a chain of four blocks, with each block containing the block number, data, nonce value, current hash value and the previous hash value and all of the blocks contain some transactional data present in it. Consider altering the data in the 3rd block, now the current hash value of the block is changed which when compared to the previous hash value of the 4th block gets invalid. Now the 3rd and 4th blocks are invalid, to make them valid again we'll have to re-mine both these blocks to get a new nonce value for both of these blocks (Novo et al., 2018). As we saw earlier, picking a new nonce value will make the block signed again.

Blockchain technology is a complex and multifaceted field, and it's important to have a clear understanding of key concepts and terminologies. One such concept is a transaction, which is a fundamental component of any blockchain-based system, including Ethereum.

In the Ethereum blockchain network, a transaction is initiated every time a user sends ether (the cryptocurrency used on the Ethereum network) to another user or node within the network. This process involves creating a digital signature that confirms the sender's identity and authorization to transfer the funds. This digital signature is then broadcast to the network and validated by the nodes in the network, which ensure that the transaction is legitimate and that the sender has sufficient funds to complete the transfer. To interact with the Ethereum network and access information about transactions, developers can use various frontend tools within the Web3 ecosystem (Kanhera et al., 2016). Two important tools in this context are Web3 Wallet and Block Explorer. A Web3 Wallet allows users to manage their blockchain accounts and perform transactions, while a Block Explorer is a web-based tool that provides a visual representation of the blockchain, including transaction history, block data, and other relevant information.

In addition to these frontend tools, developers can use Web3.js and Ethers.js libraries to interact with smart contracts deployed on the Ethereum network. Smart contracts are self-executing contracts with the terms of the agreement between buyer and seller being directly written into lines of code (Srilakshmi et al., 2023). These libraries provide a range of functions and methods that allow developers to read and write data to the blockchain, interact with smart contracts, and perform other blockchain-related tasks.

Web3 Wallets

Web3 Wallets provide an interface to interact with the web3 backend and also to monitor the funds in our account. Metamask is one of the popular web3 wallets that is used for connecting to the web3 ecosystem by both consumers and developers.

Figure 2. Metamask wallet

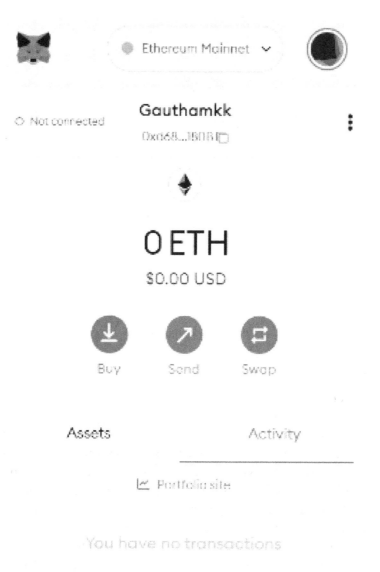

Figure 3. Metamask network selection

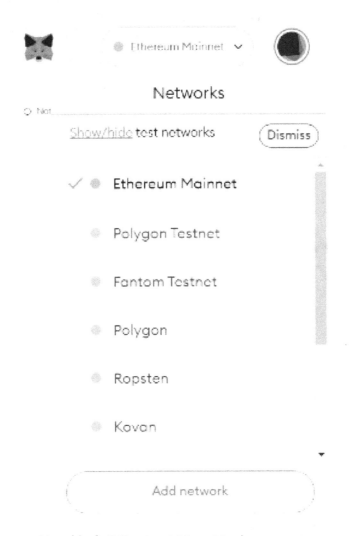

So, in Metamask you can create accounts in any of the already available networks like Ethereum Mainnet, Goerli testnet which is also built on Ethereum for testing purposes, similarly we have Polygon Network and its Mumbai Testnet. Every account that is made by Metamask comprises of three distinct elements of information that can be used for transactional purposes in the network – Public Key, Private Key and the Address of the wallet. So, when someone creates their Metamask account they will be asked to save a 12-word seed phrase and this has to be saved somewhere safe and secure because it contains the private key of your wallet associated with it (Dhanasekar et al., 2021). With the help of a private key, we can unlock all the funds in the wallet as private keys are some sort of identity verifier to prove that you are the actual owner of crypto in your wallet. On the other hand, public keys can be used to transferring funds or assets like NFTs and tokens. Difference between Main Network and Test Networks is that the mainnet requires 'gas' (that involves spending real money on it) for every transaction and the testnets are used by developers for testing their smart contract applications through any blockchain development environments like *Remix IDE*, Hardhat or Truffle (Malathy et al., 2021). Testnets also require gas but those can be satisfied with fake ether or testing ether. Test ether will be required because all transaction in the network requires gas fees to process, so to obtain test ethers you can always visit a 'faucet' website where when you paste in your wallet address, the faucet will deposit some amount of test ether. Keep in mind that these web3 wallets are acting like external accounts where with the help of your keys and account address, can be used to connect to any network that you want.

Gas

For every transaction that are happening on the network requires gas fees whether it may be a test network or main network. This gas fee is taken into stake that will be used for rewarding the miners who verify the transactions for us by using their computational power. So, there are some factors on which the gas of a particular transaction depends on, primarily it depends on how the structure of the smart contract is, some functionalities or operations in the code might require higher gas fees while some don't demand much. The gas in the Ethereum world can be divided into gas price and gas limit. The gas price is basically the amount of ether that the user is willing to pay for the gas of the transaction and the gas limit is maximum units of gas that particular transaction can consume (Agoramoorthy et al., 2021). While working with smart contracts, online tools like Remix IDE has options to set the gas limit for a transaction. For these gas dependencies to be clear for the developers, the "Yellow Paper" (which is a formal and official documentation of the Ethereum Blockchain Network), contains the gas costs chart where the gas price for different operations is assigned to their respective OPCODES or Operation Codes.

Figure 4. Smart contract opcodes and gas units from the yellow paper

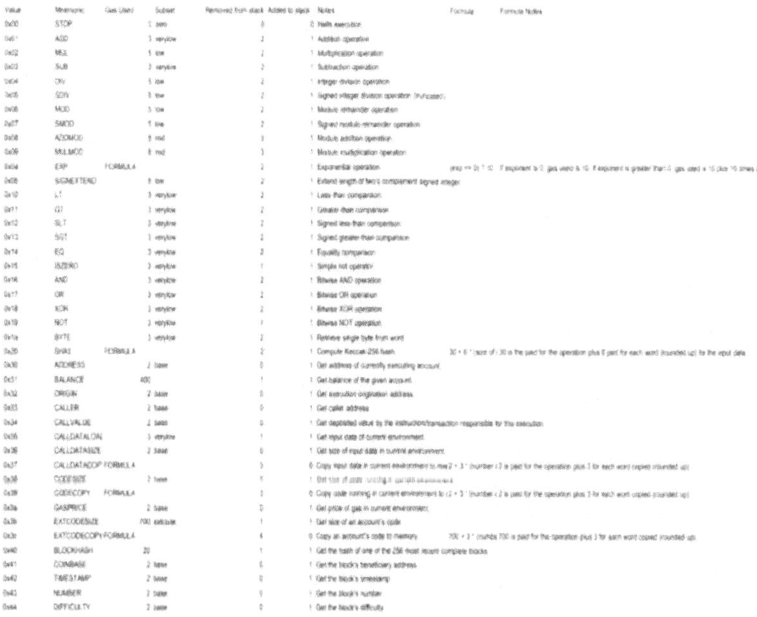

Block Explorers

A block explorer is a web-based tool that provides users with a visual representation of the blockchain network, including information about transactions, blocks, and other network activity. Think of it as an administrative portal for everyone in the network that allows users to monitor every single activity happening on the network. Etherscan is one of the most popular block explorers for the Ethereum network and its testnets. It provides a range of features and functionalities that allow users to explore and interact with the Ethereum blockchain in real-time. Some of these features include the ability to view transaction history, monitor block data, and access information about smart contracts and token transfers.

To better understand how block explorers work, consider an example of a transaction that occurred on the Ethereum Mainnet while this line was being written. A user initiates a transaction by sending ether to another user or node within the network. This transaction is then broadcasted to the network and validated by the nodes in the network. The transaction information is then added to a block and added to the blockchain, which can be viewed and tracked in real-time using a block explorer such as the Etherscan. Users can view details about the transaction, such as the sender and receiver addresses, transaction value, gas fees, and other relevant information, providing transparency and accountability within the network..

Figure 5. Transaction details from Etherscan block explorer

Every transaction consists of a transaction hash which is its unique identifier, status (success or failed), block or block number, timestamp of the transaction, from address, to address, value of ether transacted and gas used for the transaction. Block Explorers can be also used to interact with verified smart contracts and access the functions present inside it. Just note that you can only interact with smart contracts that are verified. Etherscan also provides with their own API, through which we can have access to blockchain data through different endpoints. It provides with community endpoints which is free to use and API PRO which is paid and can fetch additional blockchain derived data.

Figure 6. Verified contract options in Etherscan

Ether and Its Denominations

Since we all know that Ether or ETH is the accepted cryptocurrency of the Ethereum Blockchain, there exists its denominations like any other currency. They are as follows:

1 Ether = 1000000000000000000 Wei (Smallest)

1 Ether = 1000000000000000 Kwei

1 Ether = 1000000000000 Mwei

1 Ether = 1000000000 Gwei

1 Ether = 1000000 Szabo

1 Ether = 1000 Finney

1 Ether = 0.001 Kether

1 Ether = 0.000001 Mether

1 Ether = 0.000000001 Gether

1 Ether = 0.000000000001 Tether

There are certain protocols or rules that is followed by all nodes that are present and are contributing to the network of blockchain. These protocols are called as the Consensus Mechanism of the network.

Consensus Mechanisms or Consensus Algorithms

Blockchain algorithms establish the protocols for validating and creating blocks, securing the network, and managing energy consumption during mining. These protocols and algorithms require the consensus of a significant portion of the network's active nodes, typically 66% or more. Various blockchain networks employ different consensus algorithms. After "The Merge," the Ethereum Network transitioned to the Proof of Stake (PoS) consensus mechanism, which prioritizes creating an environmentally sustainable and economically viable ecosystem. This replaces the Proof of Work (PoW) consensus that relied on competitive mining practices and excessive computational power usage.

Proof of Work (PoW)

Proof of Work was one of the first consensus algorithms to be followed on a blockchain network. Even one of the first blockchain powered cryptocurrency – The Bitcoin Network still uses Proof of Work algorithm for validating blocks. In this mechanism, anyone can participate in the process of validation of the blocks and the validation of a block is only successful if the node is able to solve a complex computational task. The PoW algorithm has proved to be one of the most secure and robust protocol algorithms used in a blockchain network but the only problem that limits its architecture's capabilities is the high usage of electrical usage by the mining farms. Mining farms are places especially focused to mine blocks under the PoW algorithm, these mining farms use large number computers equipped with powerful GPU (Graphical Processing Unit) and more memory. Overall, the PoW algorithm has played a significant role in the development and growth of blockchain technology, and it remains an important part of several blockchain networks. However, efforts are underway to develop more energy-efficient and sustainable consensus algorithms that can address the environmental concerns associated with PoW.

Proof of Stake (PoS):

As discussed earlier, PoS eliminates the competitive ecosystem of the block validation process. In PoS, the validator is selected randomly from a list and to be a part of this list, the validator will have to stake or deposit a minimum of 32 ETH and lock it for a certain period of time. After the block is verified by randomly selected validators then they are rewarded with tokens or coins from the network. Most of these coins come from the gas price that was used during the transaction. Since, in this consensus mechanism, we only involve a certain number of validators rather than having everyone competing for validation and rewards, we can reduce the enormous energy consumption of the Proof of Work (PoW) consensus algorithm. Well, PoS hasn't been completely accepted by the network, there has been arguments and discussions regarding its potential for decentralization. To participate in the PoS validation process, the node will have to stake 32 ETH (minimum) and this value cannot be afforded by an average individual so there can be scenarios where the validator might have to borrow the funds from centralized exchanges and use it for the block mining process. This could end up making the network centralized.

Other than these two algorithms, there exists others as well like Proof of History which is being used in the Solana Blockchain, Proof of Authority, Proof of Burn, also a hybrid PoW/PoS algorithm and more.

Token Standards of the Ethereum Blockchain

So, we all know about smart contracts or if you didn't know, the protocols and functionalities of every transaction that is being occurring in the blockchain are governed and powered by scripts of code called Smart Contracts, or you can consider this as the backend of a Web3 based application. If you have been exploring the Web3 ecosystem, you might have come across NFTs, tokens, and other assets and all of these have a smart contract functioning behind them. These contracts that function in the back follow some certain standards and that will be common across in contract code of its types. For example, we all know what are NFTs and might have sold or bought one from NFT Marketplaces like OpenSea or Rarible, so these NFTs are powered by smart contracts and all of these smart contract's code follow the ERC-721 or ERC-1155 token standards (ERC – Ethereum Request for Comment). ERC-1155 are mostly for semi-fungible tokens or for "efficient trading of tokens" which is mentioned in the Ethereum Documentation for Token Standards. NFT Collections like the CryptoPunks make use of the ERC-1155 token standard in their NFT items. These token standards contain certain functions that satisfies the requirements of that decentralized asset and is considering this to be a standard, it is advised to write smart contracts that follow this standard. ERC-20 standard is used for creating tokens in the chain, this token standard will contain function like the total supply of these tokens to be minted, transfer functions and even a burn function to burn all the minted tokens.

The below image shows the list of functions that is used inside of an ERC-20 token standard. Anyone can create their own ERC-20 token and mint the total supply according to their wish. "Minting" basically means to declare that number of tokens and maintain the metadata logs of those values.

Figure 7. ERC20 token contract interface

```
contract ERC20 {
    function totalSupply() constant returns (uint theTotalSupply);
    function balanceOf(address _owner) constant returns (uint balance);
    function transfer(address _to, uint _value) returns (bool success);
    function transferFrom(address _from, address _to, uint _value) returns (bool success);
    function approve(address _spender, uint _value) returns (bool success);
    function allowance(address _owner, address _spender) constant returns (uint remaining);
    event Transfer(address indexed _from, address indexed _to, uint _value);
    event Approval(address indexed _owner, address indexed _spender, uint _value);
```

The next image shows the structure of an ERC-721 standard contract that is used for NFTs.

Figure 8. ERC721 token contract interface

```
contract ERC721 {
    // ERC20 compatible functions
    function name() constant returns (string name);
    function symbol() constant returns (string symbol);
    function totalSupply() constant returns (uint256 totalSupply);
    function balanceOf(address _owner) constant returns (uint balance);
    // Functions that define ownership
    function ownerOf(uint256 _tokenId) constant returns (address owner);
    function approve(address _to, uint256 _tokenId);
    function takeOwnership(uint256 _tokenId);
    function transfer(address _to, uint256 _tokenId);
    function tokenOfOwnerByIndex(address _owner, uint256 _index) constant returns (uint
tokenId);
    // Token metadata
    function tokenMetadata(uint256 _tokenId) constant returns (string infoUrl);
    // Events
    event Transfer(address indexed _from, address indexed _to, uint256 _tokenId);
    event Approval(address indexed _owner, address indexed _approved, uint256 _tokenId);
}
```

There are other token standards like the ERC-777 and ERC-4626 where the ERC-777 helps the user to build additional functionalities on top of tokens like an emergency recover protocol function that gets executed if you lose your private key and ERC-4626 is mostly used inside of De-Fi related apps where this standard can help in finding the best yield on their crypto tokens or coins by making use of various strategies. There also exist certain security token standards like ERC-1400 and ERC-3643, these standards enable the enforcement of compliance rules and the control of transfers to eligible investors.

To give more practical knowledge towards the Ethereum Token Standards, we'll be creating our own ERC-20 token in the upcoming sections of this chapter.

Ethereum Merge: From Proof of Work to Proof of Stake Consensus Layer

Implementing Proof of Stake (PoS) consensus protocol reduced energy consumption by 99.95% which was being used by on-chain mining activities when the Ethereum blockchain was governed by Proof of Work consensus mechanism. The Merge was basically the joining of the previous functioning layer of Ethereum with its new layer termed as the Beacon Chain which operated in the PoS mechanism. Therefore, the Merge represents the formal adoption of the Beacon Chain as the new consensus layer to the original Mainnet execution layer.

Difference Between Coins and Tokens

People sometimes get confused between these two terminologies that whether coins and tokens are the same thing but they are not. Coins represent the accepted currency of that particular blockchain network and there can be hundreds and thousands of tokens which are built on top of that blockchain. In the Ethereum blockchain, ether or ETH is the coin and assets like DAI, USDC, MATIC by Polygon Network, USDT (Tether), LINK which is the token introduced by Chainlink Labs are the examples of tokens in the network. DAI, USDC and USDT are also called as "stablecoins" whose value (~1$) will not shift much like other coins. Ether – which is the cryptocurrency of the Ethereum network governs the transaction fees and secures the network, bitcoin is the cryptocurrency for the Bitcoin blockchain network, SOL is the coin for the Solana chain. The tokens can be understood as those which operates as utility functions in the network. Other assets like the NFTs and stable coins fall under the category of tokens. Tokens can be always created using the ERC-20 token standard protocol in your token smart contract.

Smart Contracts

In the blockchain, smart contracts serve as the governing factor for every transaction or process that occurs. They can be thought of as protocols that facilitate various functionalities and store information on the chain. Solidity is the programming language used for writing smart contracts in the Ethereum blockchain, while Rust is used for writing smart contracts in the Solana blockchain. Other languages like Vyper and Yul are also used to build smart contracts for various other chains. A smart contract is essentially an account that is powered by code and has three different properties or fields: the storage of the smart contract, the balance of the contract account, and the low-level machine code of the smart contract. Each smart contract is specific to the network it is deployed to, and all deployed contracts have different addresses and are not dependent on other smart contracts of the same ABI (Application Binary Interface).

When writing a smart contract, the solidity compiler produces two outputs: the ABI and the bytecode. The bytecode is used for deploying the contract into the network with the help of the Ethereum Virtual Machine, while the ABI can be used to interact with the methods and public variables present inside the smart contract. For decentralized web application development, JavaScript libraries like Ethers.js or Web3.js make use of this ABI to serve information to the frontend code. In the following sections of this chapter, we will explain how to write smart contracts using solidity and the steps involved in deploying a smart contract.

Solidity

About the Programming Language

The smart contract language – solidity was created by developers at the Ethereum community for writing smart contracts that when compiled can be executed by the Ethereum Virtual Machine (EVM). EVM is basically a runtime ecosystem for compiling the smart contracts in the Ethereum blockchain network. This language was developed using existing languages like C++, Python and Java. So, if you have decent knowledge of these languages, it won't be much hard for you to go through Solidity.

Getting Started

For writing solidity code, we need a code editor or an IDE which stands for Integrated Development Environment, where in this case we can make use of the Remix IDE and it can be accessed by surfing into remix.ethereum.org.

Figure 9. Remix IDE interface

In the Remix IDE, to give a basic idea about its frontend interface – the above image is the one that appears when you load the website. You can close that home tab if you don't want it. There are five icons below the Remix logo at the top left corner – first one is the File Explorer tab; it gives you the structure of your current default workspace consisting a contracts folder which contains your smart contract files and its artifacts folder (ABI and other metadata files), scripts folder containing the deploy scripts and tests folder which contains code for performing tests on the contract. It's always good to write tests for a contract as it helps in resolving possible bugs in the code and this contract can be ready for production builds. Second Icon is a common search icon that you come across in most of the online and offline code editor IDEs, it's used for searching for any keyword or code line that you wrote in some file or the other. The third icon is the compile icon, you arrive here after writing your contract and by clicking on the compile <yourfilename.sol> will start compiling the code and returns a green tick mark next to the compile icon if there are no errors in your code. If errors are there, red warning circles will light up next to the line of code in the editor window. Also in the compile tab, you can get the ABI and bytecode of the contract after successfully compiling the code. The next icon is for the deploy tools, you arrive here only after the compilation of your smart contract is success. The environment dropdown selector allows you to select the environment provider that you'll be using for deploying your smart contract. By default, it is set to the Remix VM (London). There are also other providers like the Hardhat Provider, Ganache or Truffle Provider and the Injected Web3 Provider that can be used work with Metamask accounts and test networks. For beginners, it's suggested to start with the Remix Provider which is a blockchain that runs in your browser and has testing accounts containing fake or test ether to work with. Next field is the account selector which contains the list of available accounts for you to choose and deploy your smart contract. If you had selected the injected web3 provider in the environment selection, then it loads up the accounts that are present in your Metamask Wallet. Gas Limit field allows you to set the gas boundary based on which the transaction occurs. For example, if you had set the gas limit to 300000 units and the gas price per unit is, suppose, 150 per unit, then the total cost of gas would be (300000*150) Gwei (smaller denomination of ether) which gets added with the transacting amount. The next field is the "value" field that is used for low-level interaction feature. This feature enables using Remix for testing the fallback and receive methods in the smart contract. The fallback functions are those functions that gets executed when the smart contract receives Ether. After this there is a field to select the compiled contracts, this is used when you have multiple contracts defined or are getting inherited in your main contract, you can select the contract to be deployed there. You can also load a previously deployed smart contract which has been deployed to a test network or main network (by injected web3 provider), by pasting in the address of that contract into the "at address" box that comes after the deploy button. By this you can interact with an already deployed smart contract through Remix IDE. So, this is basically all of it about Remix that a beginner needs to know about and he/she can now start writing contracts, test it with the Remix IDE's interfacing and finally deploy it to an actual blockchain. Next option that you find is the debugging tools which you can also explore. To give a more practical understanding of writing and working with smart contracts in solidity using Remix IDE, let's take a look at 2 examples of how it's done.

Example 1: Storage Smart Contract (Basic Smart Contracts to Begin With!)

First go to Remix IDE and under the default workspace, create a new file named StorageContract.sol inside the contracts folder. By default, Remix already has 3 contract files inside the contracts folder, just ignore them or delete them as we don't need them for now. Code for the storage contract is given below. Now to start with the structure of the contract, the first line contains the License Identifier comment line which when not used inside of the contract will cause warning to pop up every time you compile your solidity code. It's written to ensure that our smart contract code is available for open source and by default the solidity compiler encourages that fact. If you do not want to specify a license or if the source code is not open-source, please use the special value UNLICENSED. After specifying the license standards, next thing we do is declare the solidity compiler version by using the syntax "pragma solidity ^0.8.9". Specifying the version is important as improvements and developments are being made to this language by the community regularly. Also, by doing this, you can make use of the older syntaxes for the language, you just need to specify that particular version of solidity in which that syntax was used. To give an example, the use of "constructor" keyword wasn't used in the older versions, like you just write "function name_of_the_contract" to initialize a constructor inside your contract. Constructors are executed once when the contract is deployed or created in the blockchain. Back to the storage contract, to declare and define the contract, you start with writing the keyword "contract {...}", open curly brackets after that and inside it you can start writing the main codes of your smart contract. You can declare and define multiple contracts in the same file itself. Next, we start coding the storage contract, first we create storage variable "number" and declare it to be of unsigned integer or uint256 type, "uint" by default can store numbers ranging from 0 to $2^{256} - 1$. Now to store some value into this variable, we define

Figure 10. Deploy and run transactions of remix IDE

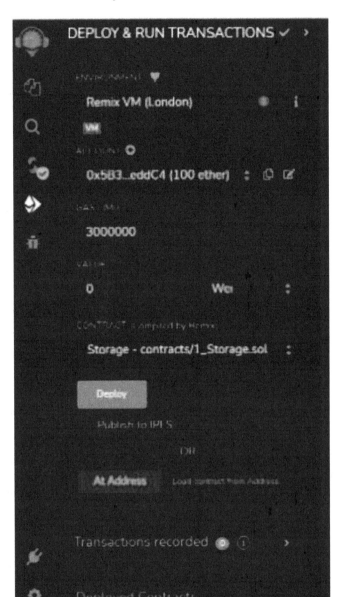

a function "store" which takes in an uint value as an argument and assigns it to the number variable we created before. Note that we have declared the scope of the store function which is set to public, means that the function is accessible from inside and outside the contract after its deployment. After storing the value by the user, to retrieve that value we can create another method to perform that too, say function "retrieve" which takes in no arguments and is declared as a "view" and a public function. Using the "view" keyword makes sure that the function is allowed to read from the state variables (in this case, the number variable) and it also restricts the modification of that state variable. There is also a "pure" keyword which restricts the function from both reading and modifying the state variables. After this, we need to specify what does that function return by using the "returns(type)", for this function to return a uint type we use "returns(uint256)". Inside the function we use "return number;" to return the stored value. This is the end of this smart contract and now we compile it and check for errors if there are any. If we see the green check mark next to the compile tab button then we are good to go.

Figure 11. Storage contract

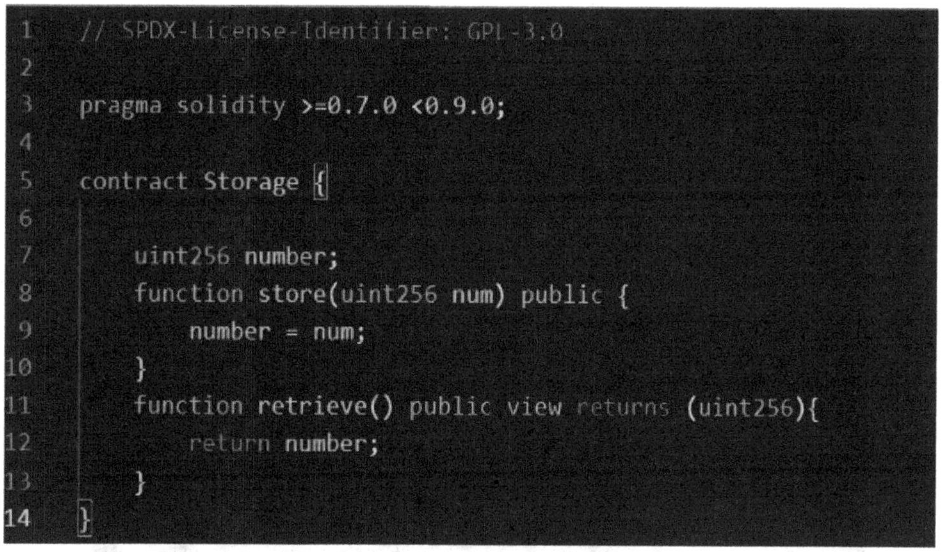

```
1    // SPDX-License-Identifier: GPL-3.0
2
3    pragma solidity >=0.7.0 <0.9.0;
4
5    contract Storage {
6
7        uint256 number;
8        function store(uint256 num) public {
9            number = num;
10       }
11       function retrieve() public view returns (uint256){
12           return number;
13       }
14   }
```

Figure 12. Deployment settings showing green tick mark as the contract compiled successfully

This contract is now set to be deployed and then we can interface with its functionalities. Remix makes use of the contract's ABI to access the functions and public variables present inside contract. For deploying this contract click on the deploy tab and select your contract from the contract selection dropdown. For now, leave the environment to be on Remix VM (London), in the next contract we can make use of the Injected Web3 Provider and deploy the smart contract into an actual test network or a blockchain. Now, inside of remix, click the blue deploy button to deploy your smart contract.

Figure 13. Deployed contract interfacing on remix

The image above shows what remix returns to you after you have deployed your smart contract. You can clearly see the store and retrieve functions presented as these coloured buttons, since the store function takes in an argument there is a field left for that. Enter some random value and click on the store button to store the value in the storage variable "number" that we created inside the contract. To get the stored value, you just simply click on the retrieve button which basically calls the retrieve function from the contract's ABI and returns the stored value.

So, this was a basic introduction to working with a smart contract using Remix IDE, let's go through one more smart contract through which you can get some extra knowledge in the solidity programming language and could help you to explore more of it. Next contract will be a registration form smart contract that can take in registrations for some event or a competition and store the data in a decentralized manner.

Example-2: Registrations Form Contract

To start with coding the contract, first create a new file and name it "registrations.sol" or any other name you like. Inside the contract, specify the license identifier and solidity compiler to be of 0.8.4 version. Declare the contract by the "contract" keyword and open the curly brackets. For the registrations to be done, we need to have a structure of the form and for this we'll be using structs in solidity.

Figure 14. Storing value in the contract and retrieving it

Figure 15. Struct of the form contract

```
pragma solidity ^0.8.4;

contract myForm {
    struct formdetails {
        string name;
        uint256 age;
        string dept;
        string year;
        uint256 timeOfRegis;

    }
```

Here the "formdetails" struct will have the structure of the registrations form. Structs are also found in other programming languages like C, C++, Java and JavaScript and these are basically used keep record of attributes, say for example: book records. Our form details struct will contain 5 attributes – name, age, department, year and time of registration which is a uint256 type for now. To maintain the list of registered members, we create an array of the form details struct type so that this array will only contain records of the form structure type, basically meaning the list of all registrations. Now in solidity there is this something called "mapping" which is used to map from one data type to another type. This mapping in solidity is somewhat like dictionaries that you find like Python. In this contract, we'll be making use mappings to map the address of a form user to map it to a boolean value, which when a user submits a registration will make map the address of that user to a "true" value. This comes in handy for keeping track of duplicate or multiple entries of the same user.

Figure 16. Declaring array of struct formList and mapping isRegistered

```
formdetails[] formList;

mapping(address => bool) private isRegistered;
```

The visibility this mapping is set to be private so that it won't be visible to the frontend user and won't be able to access its values. Before every registration entry, we need to verify few conditions, one condition is to check whether the user is 18 or above in age and the second condition is to ensure that the user is not doing multiple entries. For this we can create a function modifier that will verify these parameters and then only execute the code for registration of the user.

Figure 17. Declaration of modifier registerVerification

```
modifier registerVerification(address _add, uint256 _age) {
    require(
        !isRegistered[_add],
        "You have a already registered with this wallet, please try another with another account"
    );
    require(
        _age > 18,
        "Should be older than 18 inorder to register for this course"
    );
    _;
}
```

To declare a modifier, we can do it by writing "modifier name_of_the_modifier (any args ...)" and then inside of the modifier we define the two require statements for our two conditions. In solidity, the require statement works like some sort of a conditional tool, where in it takes two arguments, that is the condition and the second argument gets executed only when the first condition fails to get satisfied. The require tool makes sure that the codes after the require statement gets executed only after the condition given is satisfied. First require statement checks for duplicate entries and the second require statement checks for the age bar of 18. And after these two require statements, it is necessary to add an underscore so that the modifier knows to execute the main function's codes after the modifier runs. The function modifier runs every time when the function is called. Now after this, we code the function for registration of the member. The registerMember function takes in arguments for the _name, _age, _dept, _year and this is marked as a public function and the function modifier for verification is also added to it which takes in the arguments – msg.sender which is the address of the user who's calling the function and the _age argument passed to the original function is also passed to the modifier. Calldata is used in the function string arguments so that the values passed to those arguments are stored temporarily as a memory or something. Inside this function, first thing we do is set the registration mapping into "true" for that user's address so that we can prevent duplicate entries after this. Next, we push the details to the formList array that the user passed into the function. Now, we have the function to perform registrations and the registered members to a list. We can also create a function to search for members from the list.

Figure 18. Declaring and defining registerMember function

```
function registerMember(
    string calldata _name,
    uint256 _age,
    string calldata _dept,
    string calldata _year
) public registerVerification(msg.sender, _age) {
    isRegistered[msg.sender] = true;
    formList.push(formdetails(_name, _age, _dept, _year, block.timestamp));
}
```

Figure 19. Declaration and definition of search member function

```
function callMember(string memory _name)
    public
    view
    returns (formdetails memory s)
{
    for (uint256 i = 0; i < formList.length; i++) {
        if (
            keccak256(abi.encodePacked(formList[i].name)) ==
            keccak256(abi.encodePacked(_name))
        ) {
            return formList[i];
        }
    }
}
```

The function callMember takes in one argument which is the name of the registered user and the function is marked public and view since we are reading from the state variable data. Inside the function we run a for loop to go over the list of the registered users and compare every name to the name that was passed to the function. For comparing, first we encode the name into bytes data and then by using keccak256, we can hash the bytes data. After hashing the string data, we can now use it for comparing and finding the entry of the user with the name that we passed into the function. So, this was the last functionality that'll be there in our contract. To compile this contract, press Ctrl+S or go to the compile tab and click on "Compile ContractName". After compiling your contract, go to the deploy settings and under the Environment selection, select the Injected Provider – Metamask option from there. Make sure you have Metamask extension installed in your browser before you continue. Click on the deploy contract button and this will pop Metamask on the top and asks you for your confirmation. We can make use of Polygon Testing Network also known as Polygon Mumbai Testnet for this deployment. To set up Polygon Mumbai testnet in your wallet, you'll first need to add the network to your Metamask Wallet. Follow the instructions from the images below to setup the Polygon testnet.

Figure 20. Network selection in metamask

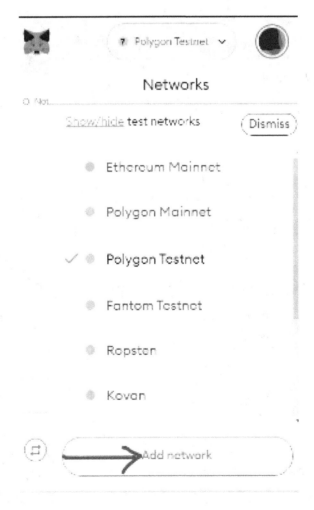

Figure 21. Network configuration in metamask

Figure 22. Custom RPC configuration in metamask

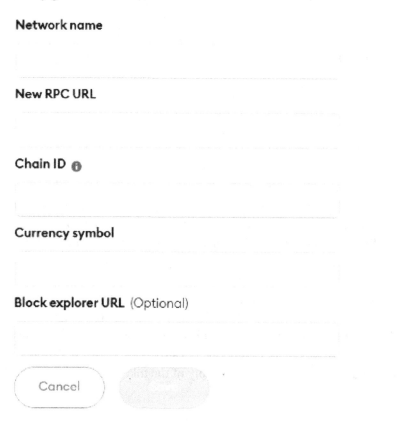

Paste in these details into the RPC settings for the Mumbai Testnet and after saving you'll have your Polygon Testnet up in your Metamask and select it in the network selection of Metamask while deploying your contract.

Network Name: Mumbai Testnet
New RPC URL: https://rpc-mumbai.maticvigil.com/
Chain ID: 80001
Currency Symbol: MATIC
Block Explorer URL: https://polygonscan.com/

For the deployment of the contract and also when you call certain functions in your contract, Metamask would ask you for your signature and confirmation in the wallet for approving the transaction. It will also show the gas estimation information for confirming your transaction (contract creation or deployment) to happen. Even when you work in the frontend apps of the decentralized apps, when it comes to integrating the smart contract using Ether.js or Web3.js you'll have to get the signature approval from the Metamask before calling any methods from the smart contract or else the code will throw an error. After signing the deployment, wait for few seconds and you'll see the message in the Remix terminal that your contract has successfully deployed.

The Remix terminal message you see above is what you get after successfully deploying your smart contract. Now you can go to the deployed contracts section in Remix and interact with the contract's functions and try playing around with it. The frontend interface that Remix generates for you to interact with the contract can be also done from a block explorer. What you'll need to do, for you to interact using the block explorers (PolygonScan in this case as we deployed our contract to the Mumbai Testnet) is that, first get your contract verified on PolygonScan and after that you'll be having access to do read and write operations on the smart contract.

Creating Your Own ERC-20 Token

Creating your own token in the Ethereum Blockchain takes less than 5 minutes of your time and doesn't involve a lot of code to get started with. Nowadays there exist blockchain services which provide auditing and security services for our smart contracts and also boilerplates for different smart contract applications. Openzeppelin is one great example of such a service, and provides readymade smart contracts for ERC-20 Token standards. We'll be making use of their ERC-20 smart contract to create and mint our tokens into the network. Below mentioned image is the example of a contract "GLDToken" which inherits from ERC20 contract from the openzeppelin contracts library. Openzeppelin is an opensource company which provides resources and boilerplate codes for smart contracts and even provides security and contract auditing related services. This is the size of the code that we'll require now to create our own ERC-20 token. So, just plug in the name and the symbol of your token and compile the code. When you deploy it, near to that button you'll be able see the field for the initial supply, put a value there, say 50000 and click on deploy. When the contract is created, the constructor of this contract and the ERC-20 token contract gets triggered and inside the constructor, it calls the "_mint" function which takes in the address of the deployer and the initial supply of the tokens and finally our tokens get minted in the network.

Figure 23. Transaction confirmation in metamask

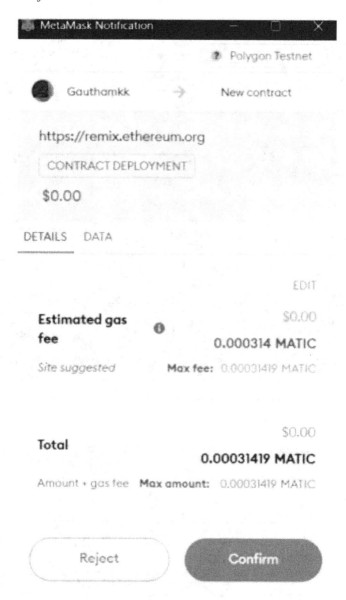

Figure 24. Successful transaction message in remix terminal

Figure 25. Deployed contract of the registration form smart contract

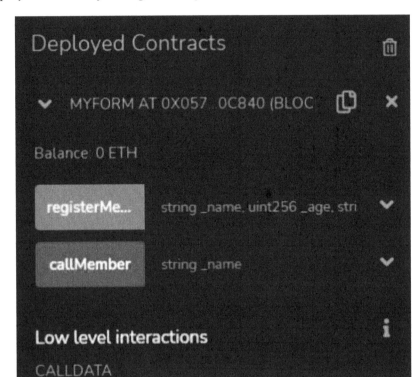

Figure 26. Example of a contract "GLDToken"

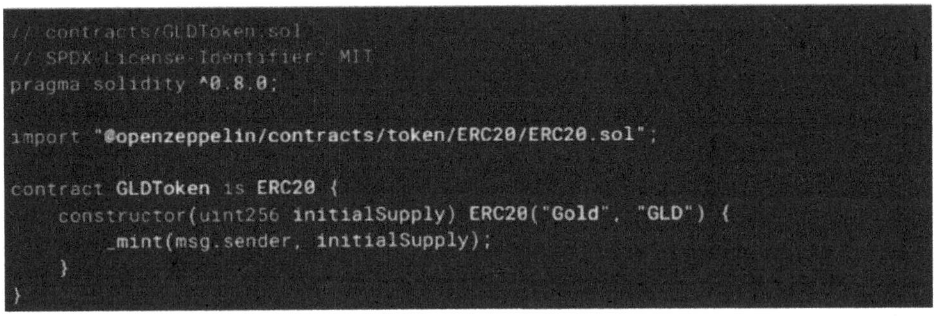

```
// contracts/GLDToken.sol
// SPDX-License-Identifier: MIT
pragma solidity ^0.8.0;

import "@openzeppelin/contracts/token/ERC20/ERC20.sol";

contract GLDToken is ERC20 {
    constructor(uint256 initialSupply) ERC20("Gold", "GLD") {
        _mint(msg.sender, initialSupply);
    }
}
```

Other than Remix, there are JavaScript frameworks that can be used to work with smart contracts locally in your system by making use of IDEs like the Visual Studio Code. Most developers prefer using Visual Studio Code or VS Code for writing, testing and developing smart contracts as it provides the best ecosystem for performing all these procedures. Frameworks or tools like Hardhat and Truffle Suite can be used for developing and testing smart contracts in your local system which is connected to the internet. Truffle suite comes with a local testing blockchain called Ganache and Hardhat has its own local testing networks with testing accounts loaded in it. The local hardhat network can be also connected to the Metamask wallet through Metamask's custom RPC integration settings.

Now you might have got a decent understanding towards the solidity programming language and how you can use Remix IDE to work with it.

Let's now take a look into the different applications of the blockchain and the web3 technologies in the real-life scenarios. First and the most important use case of this tech comes in the finance sector. Web3 technology is booming in the finance industry through the hype of using decentralized finance to tackle a lot of problems that's being faced in the centralized finance systems. Primary reason is that it removes the involvement of banks who control your funds and other assets.

Decentralized Finance

Decentralized Finance, or De-Fi, aims to eliminate the control of centralized authorities such as banks over our assets. The overall architecture of cryptocurrency is based on both Ce-Fi and De-Fi models. Blockchain Oracles act as a middleware that fetches data from the Ce-Fi world and feeds it into on-chain processes. In De-Fi, anonymity is maintained, whereas in Ce-Fi, a lot of personal information is collected. Automated Market Makers (AMMs) are algorithms that keep the De-Fi ecosystem robust and running smoothly. One of the significant advantages of De-Fi is that users do not need to go through Ce-Fi processes like KYC (Know-Your-Customer). Even if some developers are developing decentralized KYC platforms, it won't be as much of a hassle as the ones that banks and other authorities require for completing KYC procedures. The De-Fi community is constantly pushing new solutions and experimenting with methodologies to solve current problems faced in the Ce-Fi world and to test its capabilities. De-Fi is also addressing issues within its own ecosystem, such as using BTC or Bitcoin for coin swaps, which was not possible until the idea of "Wrapped Coins" emerged, like WETH and WBTC. Wrapped tokens make use of the ERC-20 token standard to wrap the coins, like Bitcoin or Ether. This involves sending these coins to a smart contract, where they are placed on hold, and the user receives WETH or WBTC tokens in their wallet. Coin swap is another critical feature that comes with the De-Fi world. D-Apps like Uniswap, Pancake Swap, Sushi Swap, and AAVE allow users to swap tokens just by having an Ethereum wallet or any other crypto wallet. These D-Apps fall under the category of Decentralized Exchanges (DEXs), and they have significantly risen over the years, allowing more people to invest and make use of their services.

Decentralized Exchanges

Decentralized Exchanges (DEXs) have revolutionized the way people trade cryptocurrencies by removing the need for intermediaries and central authorities. Uniswap, an open-source DEX, has played a crucial role in popularizing DEXs and inspiring the creation of other token swapping services like Pancake Swap and Sushi Swap.

Liquidity is a crucial component of DEXs, referring to their ability to generate the demanded tokens from the DEX's pool. Without adequate liquidity, users may not be able to perform trades involving certain tokens. Liquidity Pools are used to ensure that the DEXs function smoothly, where users who deposit their assets into the pool are known as the Liquidity Providers. These Liquidity Providers earn LP tokens after they have provided token assets into the pool, making them eligible for earning interest from the trading activities in the exchange. Automated Market Makers (AMMs) are a vital part of these DEXs, and they rely on liquidity pools to function correctly. For instance, if a liquidity pool holds ten million dollars of USDT and ten million dollars of USDC, a trader could swap 500k dollars' worth of their own

USDC for USDT, which would raise the price of USDT on the AMM. Another exciting development in the DEXs space is the concept of Flash Loan Arbitrage, which allows users to borrow millions of dollars from an exchange like AAVE for a short period, perform some arbitrage, and then return the loan amount in the same transaction back to the exchange. Unlike traditional loans, no collateral is required for flash loans, making them an attractive option for those looking to perform arbitrage. Arbitrage is an investment strategy where investors simultaneously buy and sell an asset in different markets, taking advantage of price differences to make a profit. In summary, the world of DeFi and DEXs has opened up new possibilities for trading cryptocurrencies, providing users with more autonomy, privacy, and control over their assets. The liquidity pools and Flash Loan Arbitrage are examples of innovative solutions that have emerged to address the challenges of trading in decentralized markets. As the DeFi ecosystem continues to evolve, we can expect more exciting developments and advancements that will redefine the way we trade and invest in cryptocurrencies.

Blockchain in NFTs, Metaverse, and Gaming

Gaming and virtual reality has taken a ton of inspiration from the idea of entralization and using blockchain for web3 gaming. The web3 gaming originates from users owning NFTs and then using it inside the game as a collectible to be eligible for certain levels and game points. Take the example of a really popular NFT collection like the "Bored Ape Yacht Club" or the BAYC has unveiled their metaverse platform and only the persons holding their NFTs get access to their metaverse. These NFT holders get "airdrops" into their crypto wallet every month or so, it could be crypto tokens or maybe souvenirs and goodies which are exclusive to their collection. There's this really popular NFT game which is based on the Polygon network, it's called the "The Zedd Run" and it is a digital horse racing game. The horses that are used in the game can be purchased from NFT platforms like Opensea and Rarible. Go to the Zedd Run website and connect your wallet, the dApp checks whether you possess any Zedd Run NFTs in your wallet and based on that only you will be redirected to the game. The NFT gaming also brings us the concept of breed able NFTs and their collections, basically allowing the collector or the holder to breed two NFTs and produce an offspring NFT and its metadata will depend on the parent NFT's metadata and the code that the developers wrote to generate such offspring values for different combinations of properties while breeding.

CONCLUSION

Foundational topics about decentralization and the basic architecture of blockchains has been discussed with insightful examples. After going through them, concepts and terminologies regarding the blockchain powered applications like the web3 wallets, block explorers and gas fees were covered. Blockchain governing factors like the consensus mechanisms and token standards has been also briefed in the next sections. Primary part of this chapter comes to the solidity programming language as the author approached the delivery of the programming concepts through examples that can help even a novice to understand the logic and the language. The information regarding deployment of smart contracts has been discussed thoroughly in this chapter. The final sections include the application of blockchain and web3 technologies and topics like decentralized finance, decentralized exchanges, NFTs and metaverse are discussed in that section. As a review, you might enjoy reading about the smart contract section to see how formerly difficult to decipher concepts starts making sense.

REFERENCES

Agoramoorthy, M., & Joe, I. P. (2021). Hybrid cuckoo–red deer algorithm for multi-objective localization strategy in wireless sensor network. *International Journal of Communication Systems*. Advance online publication. doi:10.1002/dac.5042

Chen, M., Li, Y., Xu, Z., Huang, X., & Wang, W. (2018). A Blockchain Based Data Management System for Energy Trade. *First International Conference Smart Block 20*, 44-54. 10.1007/978-3-030-05764-0_5

Cui, L., Yang, S., Chen, Z., Pan, Y., Xu, M., & Xu, K. (2020). An Efficient and Compacted DAG-Based Blockchain Protocol for Industrial Internet of Things. *IEEE Transactions on Industrial Informatics*, *16*(6), 4134–4145. doi:10.1109/TII.2019.2931157

Dai, H.-N., Zheng, Z., & Zhang, Y. (2019). Blockchain for internet of things: A survey. *IEEE Internet of Things Journal*, *6*(5), 1–19. doi:10.1109/JIOT.2019.2920987

Dhanasekar, V., & Preethi, Y. (2021). A Chatbot to promote Students Mental Health through Emotion Recognition. *2021 Third International Conference on Inventive Research in Computing Applications (ICIRCA)*, 1412-1416. 10.1109/ICIRCA51532.2021.9544838

Dorri, Kanhere, & Jurdak. (2016). *Blockchain in internet of things: Challenges and solutions*. arXiv:1608.05187.

Huberman, G., Leshno, J., & Moallemi, C. (2017). Monopoly Without a Monopolist: An Economic Analysis of the Bitcoin Payment System. SSRN *Electronic Journal*, 1-56.

Joe, I. R. P., & Varalakshmi, P. (2016). A Two Phase Approach for Efficient Clustering of Web Services. In M. Senthilkumar, V. Ramasamy, S. Sheen, C. Veeramani, A. Bonato, & L. Batten (Eds.), *Computational Intelligence, Cyber Security and Computational Models. Advances in Intelligent Systems and Computing* (Vol. 412). Springer. doi:10.1007/978-981-10-0251-9_17

Joe & Washington. (2018). Art network—A solution for effective warranty management. *Curie J.*

Joe, P. (2015). A Survey on Neural Network Models for Data Analysis. *Journal of Engineering and Applied Sciences (Asian Research Publishing Network)*, *10*(11), 4872–4876.

Li, J., Yuan, Y., Wang, S., & Wang, F. (2018). Transaction Queuing Game in Bitcoin Blockchain. *IEEE Intelligent Vehicles Symposium*, 1–6.

Li, R., Song, T., Mei, B., Li, H., Cheng, X., & Sun, L. (2018). Block chain for Large-Scale Internet of Things Data Storage and Protection. *IEEE Transactions on Services Computing*, 1–11. doi:10.1109/TSC.2018.2789893

Malathy, E. M., Praveen Joe, I. R., & Ajitha, P. (2021). Miniaturized Dual-Band Metamaterial-Loaded Antenna for Heterogeneous Vehicular Communication Networks. *Journal of the Institution of Electronics and Telecommunication Engineers*, 1–10. doi:10.1080/03772063.2021.1892539

Novo, O. (2018). Blockchain Meets IoT: An Architecture for Scalable Access Management in IoT. *IEEE Internet of Things Journal*, 5(2), 1184–1195. doi:10.1109/JIOT.2018.2812239

Polyzos, G. C., & Fotiou, N. (2017). Blockchain-assisted information distribu- tion for the Internet of Things. *2017 IEEE International Conference on Information Reuse and Integration (IRI),* 75–78. 10.1109/IRI.2017.83

Praveen Joe, I. R., & Varalakshmi, P. (2019a). An Analysis on Web-Service-Generated Data to Facilitate Service Retrieval. *Applied Mathematics & Information Sciences*, 13(1), 47–55. doi:10.18576/amis/130107

Praveen Joe, I. R., & Varalakshmi, P. (2019b). A Multilayered Clustering Framework to build a Service Portfolio using Swarm-based algorithms. *Automatika (Zagreb)*, 60(3), 294–304. doi:10.1080/0005114 4.2019.1590951

Praveen Joe, Malathy, Aishwarya, Akila, & Akshaya. (2022). A Hybrid PSO-ACO Algorithm to Facilitate Software Project Scheduling. *International Journal of e-Collaboration*. doi:10.4018/IJeC.304039

Reyna, C., Martín, C., Chen, J., Soler, E., & Díaz, M. (2018). On Blockchain and its integration with IoT Challenges and opportunities. *Future Generation Computer Systems*, 88, 173–190. doi:10.1016/j. future.2018.05.046

Srilakshmi, G., & Praveen Joe, I. R. (2023). A-DQRBRL: Attention based deep Q reinforcement battle royale learning model for sports video classification. *Imaging Science Journal*, 1–20. Advance online publication. doi:10.1080/13682199.2023.2180022

KEY TERMS AND DEFINITIONS

Automated Market Makers: Automated market makers (AMMs) are decentralized exchanges that use algorithmic "money robots" to provide liquidity for traders buying and selling crypto assets.

Ether: The native cryptocurrency of the Ethereum Blockchain.

Liquidity Pool: Basically a storage or collection containing different asset pairs that can be used for trading/swapping purposes in the DEX platform.

Liquidity Providers: People or institutions who are ready to invest their share into the Liquidity Pools and later earn interest or tokens from it.

NFT: Non-Fungible Tokens are digital assets where its information or metadata and other transactional details are stored inside of smart contracts and are based on blockchain technology.

Remix IDE: An online GUI tool for developing Ethereum smart contracts.

RPC or Remote Procedure Call: This term is found mostly in the web3 wallets like the Metamask wallet, these enable and provide the client the tools required for interacting with a blockchain from the browser frontend.

Chapter 15
Charity Management Using Blockchain Technology

R. Parkavi

Thiagarajar College of Engineering, India

S. Vigneshwaran

Thiagarajar College of Engineering, India

N. Sambath

Thiagarajar College of Engineering, India

P. Sanjai

Thiagarajar College of Engineering, India

ABSTRACT

Beneficiaries have no confidence in the way donated money is spent. Humanitarian organizations are at a similar risk to the forms of fraud that plague businesses, such as money laundering. Recently, blockchain technology has been implemented in various fields. The use of blockchain technology allows you to perform the process of giving and receiving money openly. It is necessary to build a single donation tracking platform that will track all information about gifts, transactions, and sponsors. The purpose of this work is to explain building blockchain-based infrastructure tracking donations. Based on blockchain technology, the system provides a clear accounting of donor performance, foundations of giving, and recipients. The donation channel should be available from the charity platform, which allows community users and donors to follow and monitor where, when, and to whom donations are made. This work summarizes the activities carried out in the design and implementation of the web-based blockchain management system.

DOI: 10.4018/978-1-6684-8145-5.ch015

Copyright © 2023, IGI Global. Copying or distributing in print or electronic forms without written permission of IGI Global is prohibited.

INTRODUCTION

Technology like blockchain is not new. Digital signatures, often regarded as the basis of blockchain, were first used to guarantee the integrity of documents in 1991. With the launch of his Bitcoin in 2008, Satoshi Nakamoto presented one of the most significant blockchain applications. After researching its advantages, the government and its industry have been using blockchain in several industries recently, including supply chain, identity management, record keeping, and education (Berentsen, 2019). Datasets can be accessed and replicated by several parties thanks to blockchain technology's decentralised nature. Only by following a specific rule can the database be changed, and any changes are immediately communicated with all parties. A chain connecting each transaction on the blockchain guarantees that everyone has access to the most recent version of the register. A distributed ledger is a mechanism to duplicate and store transaction data on a blockchain network. This concept is expanded by distributed ledgers, which replicate data across numerous nodes. Blockchain is a peer-to-peer network that provides timestamps and eliminates the need for third parties to verify transactions. As a result of the fact that every peer has a copy of the full ledger and that new transactions can only be added with the consent of a majority of peers or in accordance with present regulations, this sort of record is impervious to tampering. A basic blockchain is made up of three parts: a block, a chain, and a network. Tracking goods or assets, sensitive medical information, or significant data generated by IoT devices. Blocks comprise transactions that store information about these key activities. For a fresh blockchain, some rules are established as the network is constructed. These guidelines establish how your network functions and control specifics like the number of transactions and their sizes in each block, among other things. An algorithm known as a hash produces a constant value unique to the transactions utilising one direction in a block. The block can only provide the same hash if it also includes the same transactions. The hash value would modify if any peer or during transmission altered the block of data. The data in the original block has been altered and is no longer trustworthy, thus if the hash value changes. One can get a single hash or Merkle root by mixing and hashing several hash values. By adding more hashes to the base, a Merkle tree is formed. Blockchain platforms make it possible for developers to create blockchain applications. Numerous blockchain platforms are available, each with its own set of capabilities. Bitcoin, Ethereum, Hyperledger, R3, Ripple, and the Electro-Optical System are some popular blockchain platforms (EOS) many factors influence the choice of a blockchain platform, including the most popular blockchain technology, Bitcoin. Since there is no implied trust in Bitcoin, there can be many decentralised nodes, ensuring that the blockchain is impenetrable.

Hackers have manipulated active users and miners oversee scattered nodes. Cryptocurrency platforms assert that the answers that miners provide to cryptographic riddles serve as proof of work, which is subsequently confirmed by other miners or nodes. It rewards problem solvers and puzzle verifiers with cryptocurrency. Unlike Bitcoin platforms, other blockchain platforms do not demand miners. In this charity management system, donors can donate money using cryptocurrency (Ethereum), which will boost security, instead of, say, donating money to a charity using Indian rupees (INR), which does not ensure payment security. When foreigners donate to charities, banks are involved, transactions take time, and there are transaction fees; however, with this sort of donation, foreigners can donate the money quickly and conveniently thanks to technology. This is distributed decentralized technology which stores data in the form of blocks. By design, these blocks are immutable but publicly readable. When a donor wants to send some funds to a destination address, instead of sending them directly to that address, they will use this method. It's so helpful and can be used anywhere.

LITERATURE REVIEW

Transparent and Genuine Charity Tracking System Powered by Blockchain

People's willingness to donate to charities is diminishing day by day because the transactions used in charities are opaque and challenging to adequately monitor. Strictly speaking, the blockchain that underpins the Bitcoin network has added additional choices to the charity system. This is a proposed blockchain-based charity scheme detailing the platform's design patterns, architecture, and operational procedures. On Ethereum, some of the basic functions of the philanthropic platform have been achieved and confirmed. We want to improve the transparency of philanthropic organisations, increase public trust in them, and promote the growth of humanitarian endeavours through a blockchain-based charity system.

To give contributors, charities, and beneficiaries a precise accounting of their acts, the system leverages blockchain technology. Build four levels on the platform: Public, Private, Consortium and Hybrid blockchains. The application service layer directly provides platform services to users and includes various app things including creating an account, donating, disclosing charity information, and sending inquiry messages. Scripts and smart contracts make up the layer of smart contracts; it contains details on transaction processing, query techniques, and other subjects. Decentralized accounting tasks for charity platform services such as packet blocking, transaction consensus obtaining, broadcast blocking, and data synchronization with the local database are performed by the blockchain services layer. They built an Ethereum-based charity fundraising DApp to test their system and demonstrate some basic charity platform functionality. To test their strategy, they have employed the Metamask Browser Extension, and Solidity was used to build smart contracts. The usage of DAppfor processes including work development, funding approval, and fund transfer has been approved (Naiknavare,2022).

Blockchain-Based Transparent and Genuine Charity Application

Donors are worried that their money won't get to the people who need it. According to an HSE poll from 2017, around68% of citizens, said that they would be willing to donate more if they had proof of where and what they were doing. The Foundation is required by law to keep public records (specifically, to post reports on its website), and all reports are currently prepared manually by Foundation staff. It will increase problems such as donor distrust and fund outflow can be addressed by maintaining an external database that records on the blockchain. As a result, the development of a social platform based on blockchain technology is essential that supports the work of nonprofits, foundations, volunteers, and social entrepreneurs making the donation process clear and understandable to all parties involved. The blockchain enables all platform users to view their accounts as well as a description of each payment made by the organizations that support them. Distributed ledger technology also ensures that donations will reach their intended recipients without the use of intermediaries. According to Rosstat, he had over 9,600 charities and approximately 1,700 nonprofits in 2017.

The application divides users into four categories based on their roles: donors, organizations, retailers, and public servants. Charity, non-governmental organizations (NGOs), and other social enterprises are examples of organizations (beneficiaries) that need funding (financial or otherwise).They can post their requests in the charity chain system in a predefined format. It is also very important in mining. Retailers are businesses that create offers and quote prices. Government officials choose the retailers with the best pitches. Donor: A body that reviews the requirements issued by various organizations and selects approved bids to donate to the cause based on their abilities and preferences. Government Officials: This agency validates smart contracts and authenticates requirements published by organizations. Donors can only donate once they have received official verification (Naiknavare et al., 2022).

D-Donation: Charity Fraud Prevention Using Blockchain

Charity is an act of goodwill in which a person who has more than enough of what he needs donates a portion of his surplus earnings to those who are considerably less capable. Charity organisations are opaque and difficult to supervise, which has a negative impact on them people's readiness to donate. Blockchain, as an underlying technology, provides a new answer for the charitable system. This project presented a blockchain-based donation system (D-Donation) and expounded on the platform's design pattern, architecture, and operational process. Some essential functionalities of the D-Donation app have been realised and verified on Polygon Blockchain. This is what they intended to achieve. This is what we intend to achieve. We expect that by utilising a blockchain-based charity system, we would be able to boost charity transparency, increase public trust in charities, and support the development of philanthropy (Kumar et al., 2022).

Crowdfunding Charity Platform Using Blockchain

When many governments throughout the world began collecting income taxes, no one is sure what is being done with the money. Most of us would like to donate those sums to charity/donations/sponsorships. At the same time, no one knows who or which organisation to trust with their tax returns. To alleviate these fears and uncertainties, a crowdfunding portal/community/non-profit organization/peer-to-peer automatic helping programme was established, where anyone can donate/sponsor money to people/startups that need/deserve it. This CF application employs blockchain technology to ensure secure funding transactions. Every transaction will take place solely through Ethereum. Users/employees from all over the world come together in this portal to help each other and demonstrate humanity. It is a completely transparent, trustworthy, and open-source platform that focuses not only on the cause but also on how to make it as simple and smooth as possible for people to fundraise (Saranya et al., 2022).

Decentralized Charity Organization Crowdfunding Application Using Smart Contracts and Blockchain

Online crowdfunding sites have evolved into locations where people donate dollars to support lasting missions, such as promoting local art sales or assisting underprivileged people in obtaining an education. However, as cybercrime and data breaches have increased, crucial information and transaction records in crowdfunding have become targets for hackers. In this work, Blockchain technology is used to protect the information in crowdfunding, such as donation transactions. This research shows how Blockchain can be used to store data on the Ethereum network. Following that, a decentralised Blockchain web application, FunddApp, is proposed, with the goal of designing a decentralised crowdfunding web application with peer-to-peer transfers, developing a Blockchain website for crowdfunding purposes, and testing the application on Ethereum. This application is built with an Object-Oriented Software Development Model, and the major functions are built with the Python Flask framework and the Web3.js library. The results, on the other hand, reveal that the web application may initiate point-to-point communication between two participants using the smart contract mechanism. The findings of this study are predicted to have a substantial impact on and boost the use of cryptocurrencies in our everyday lives, as well as the use of blockchain technology in corporate privacy.

This work employs the object-oriented analysis and design work development approach (OOAD). This technique for both donors and organisations includes object-oriented requirements analysis, object-oriented design, and object-oriented implementation and testing procedures. It describes the primary functions that both users can do using the proposed technology. The donor can register and spend the cryptocurrency on OTP's smart contract before submitting the hash to her PBKDF2 Ethereum blockchain login module by entering the relevant user details. Donors can also leave comments, give money, update their profiles, examine transaction records, and obtain refunds if the task is completed but the desired objective is not met (Shakila & Sultana, 2021).

Transparent Charity System Using Smart Contracts on Ethereum Using Blockchain

The article analyses the viability of employing blockchain technology to benefit charities. To ensure data safety, fund integrity, and contribution control, problems in this field demand the adoption of cutting-edge storage tools, as well as the transfer of knowledge between donors, foundations, donation recipients, and other charity players. Donors are worried about how their money is handled. Blockchain technology is now being employed in a wide range of sectors. You can use blockchain technology to make the process of donation and financial transactions transparent. A single platform for tracking donations that tracks all information about gifts, transactions, and donors must be built. This article suggests a blockchain-based charity system and outlines the platform's planning pattern, design, and operational process. Some of the charity platform's fundamental capabilities are realised and proven on Ethereum in this article. This blockchain system provides transparent accounts of donor operations; charitable foundations and donors have supported blockchain technology; charitable platforms should provide transparent donation routes; and public users and donors should be able to trace and cover where, when, and to whom charity funds were distributed (Patil, 2022).

A Survey of Blockchain-Based Strategies for Healthcare

Blockchain, a distributed digital ledger system, has evolved into a technology that supports the verification, execution, and recording of transactions between parties by combining encryption, data management, networking, and incentive mechanisms. Blockchain technology was primarily developed to safeguard transactions involving digital currencies, but it is now understood that it has enormous potential in all kinds of transactions. Companies that accept and offer can benefit from providing donors with a transparent and secure trading mechanism using a smart contract system. This allows users to track their donations and know how their donations are being used, making it a very clear and transparent mechanism.

The existing problems in the charity management system are:

- No proper record of funds and tracking transparency
- Payers do not know what their money is being used for
- Corruption by unscrupulous authorities
- Corruption by intermediaries who control funds and services.

However, healthcare records containing personal patient data complicate this approach due to the danger of a privacy breach. This project attempts to address research into blockchain healthcare applications. It begins by examining medical information management, as well as the sharing of medical records, image sharing, and log management. We also address articles that overlap with other topics, such as the Internet of Things, information management, medicine monitoring along the supply chain, and security and privacy issues. Because we are aware of other blockchain in healthcare studies, we study and compare both the positive and negative parts of their papers. Finally, we hope to investigate blockchain principles in the medical field, rating their merits and downsides and providing assistance to other researchers in the field. Furthermore, we describe the strategies employed in healthcare by application area and highlight their benefits and drawbacks (De Aguiar et al., 2020).

Blockchain-Based System for Tracking Donations, Aid, and Charities

Blockchain is a promising technology that is gaining popularity for tackling a variety of security issues in both the public and private sectors. Blockchain technology is popular in the world of charity. Donors are unable to determine if their contributions are being utilized responsibly due to the opaque nature of the transactions that precede donations, which undermines public confidence in non-profit organizations. This study suggests a decentralized contribution shadowing system based on the Ethereum blockchain that offers complete accountability, full transparency, and direct access to targeted donors.

Government realities are defined as the donors/beneficiaries, NGOs, and users who play significant roles in the system. These users turn into account holders on the blockchain network, and a 160-bit account address serves as a unique link between each one of them. With bit private keys, they may subscribe, do transactions, and access their accounts. Non-Governmental Organizations, Section (NGOs), these stand for groups that support social concerns, via the system dashboard, the system enables raising conditions in a specific format. Governmental Body NGOs submit terms for approval to this agency. The conditions won't be shown on the patron's dashboard until after this benediction, at which point they will be available for donation. Donors have the right to view the conditions decided by the NGO and accepted by the government. Based on their skills and inclinations, they can contribute to various states (Singh et al., 2020).

Proposed Blockchain Solution for Trackable Donations

People no longer trust charities due to a lack of transparency; causing social funding to stagnate not corruption exacerbates donor mistrust. The study suggests a decentralized network based on the Ethereum blockchain named Charity Chain. It uses smart contract-based incentives to help social groups carry out their work in a transparent, accessible, and impactful way. Funders (charities, powerful investors, and small donors) will find it easier to monitor transactions and, as a result, rebuild donor trust in such social groups.

Donors, organizations, retailers, and public servants are among the application's role-based categories. Companies (Beneficiaries): These are non-profit organizations, social enterprises, or charities that require funding (monetary or otherwise). They can use a predefined format to submit requests to the charity chain system. It is also important in mining. Retailers are companies that create products and provide price quotes. The retailers with the most compelling pitches are chosen by government representatives. Donor: A person or organization that evaluates the specifications provided by various organizations and selects accepted bids to support the cause based on their preferences and capabilities. Representatives of the government: This body verifies smart contracts and authenticates organizational requirements made public. Only donors are eligible (Sirisha et al., 2019).

Blockchain-Based Charity System Research

People are less eager to give to Chinese organizations because they are opaque and hard to administer. Blockchain, which powers the Bitcoin system, offers fresh technical approaches to the charitable system. This article discusses the platform design pattern, architecture, and operational procedure of a blockchain-based charity system. In this article, certain fundamental aspects of the platform for charitable giving are realized and confirmed on his Ethereum. They want to boost charity transparency through our blockchain-based charity system in order to raise public trust in charities and encourage the growth of giving.

They developed a charity fundraising dApp on the Ethereum platform to test the system and show some key capabilities of the platform. They developed smart contracts in Solidity using the Metamask Browser Extension to test the system. They tested the dApp's capabilities for initiating works, making donations, approving transfers of money, and more. A beneficiary will start a charitable initiative using a smart contract, and it will be implemented on the blockchain after that. Donors use their browsers to browse charitable works and make donations to the ones they like. The dApp administrator will get the funds in their account. Smart contract's are used to start investment requests when a beneficiary needs money. If the work's participants as a whole consent to the By You can ask for the workdonation to be moved from the dApp administrator account to the recipient account by casting a vote (Hu & Li, 2020).

During the COVID-19 Outbreak, Creating a Reliable Service System for Charity Donation

In response to the difficult service demands faced by philanthropists due to the Covid-19 pandemic, this work explores the possibilities of building a blockchain-based charitable donation service system according to the functional characteristics of blockchain technology by considering practicality and reliability. Using blockchain technology as the underlying data ledger, this work focuses on the practicalities of charitable donation funds and stock allocation, as well as information sharing and sharing charitable giving, and organizational autonomy. Therefore, in this work the authors discuss the general structural design, functional design, and key techniques related to specific performance areas of donor service systems. It also provides an overview of the working mechanisms of the system in relation to the needs of users seeking, receiving and managing help. All of the above ideas are claimed to have the ability to alleviate the crisis of confidence in Chinese philanthropy due to its lack of openness. This work is intended to serve as a useful resource for innovation in blockchain-based philanthropy.

The system requirements for blockchain are the management tools for material donations and initial coin offerings. The fund's donation is carried by Ethereum virtual tokens in the system for charitable donations, and information management is utilised to coordinate the logistical delivery of donation items, began to raise money for charity. The blockchain-based system for charity donation services develops charitable works that are in line with charitable donations, work money and logistics data which are precisely recorded with work querying capability. Beneficiaries or donors to charities can use the blockchain to trace the movement of resources and finances, as well as to confirm plans, distribution of donations to charities. The system may track logistical details for charitable gift materials as well as designate donations made to charities to particular works or beneficiary accounts, role of performance evaluation (Wu & Zhu, 2020).

A System for Employing Blockchain Technology to Make Charity Collection Transparent and Auditable

Around the world, giving to charity is seen as a moral obligation, and enormous sums of money are donated in its name. The majority of the time, organisation faces difficulty gaining the confidence and attention of contributors since their donation gathering procedures are opaque. This article introduces a blockchain-based platform for managing charities that seek to offer a clear, safe, reliable, and effective approach. The proposed platform introduces Charity Coin (CC) as a digital currency and thoroughly covers the process of collecting donations for charities using cryptocurrency wallets, initial coin offerings (ICOs), and economic models. Additionally, smart contracts have been implemented for associated use cases like converting cryptocurrency into fiat money, purchasing and selling cryptocurrency, and transferring cryptocurrency.

This work presents a secure, transparent and efficient framework for managing donations to the underprivileged using cutting-edge blockchain technology. The technology makes the system more transparent by allowing donors to use blockchain traceability properties to verify the whereabouts of their donations and be notified when their donations reach beneficiaries. As donors donate, they are blocked by a smart contract that provides secure transactions using proof of work (Farooq et al., 2020).

Blockchain-Based Proposed Solution and Concepts and Applications

Donor mistrust is exacerbated by corruption. In the work, a decentralised network dubbed Charity Chain that is based on the Ethereum blockchain is proposed. This makes it easier for social groups to manage their programmes openly, and Martha makes use of contract-based incentives to guarantee that their effect is openly and independently verifiable. Funders (charities, powerful investors, and small contributors) will find it simpler to monitor transactions and rebuild donor confidence in such social groups as a result. Role-based categories for application users include donors, organisations, retailers, and public servants. Charity, NGOs, and other social businesses are examples of organisations (beneficiaries) that need funding (financial or otherwise). They can post their requests in the charity chain system using a specified format. It is significant in mining as well. Retailers are businesses that develop offerings and provide price quotes. Government representatives choose the retailers with the most compelling pitches. Donor: An entity that evaluates bids submitted in response to specifications provided by various organisations, and selected bidders choose to support the cause in accordance with their capacities and preferences. Government representatives: This body verifies smart contracts and authenticates requirements made public by organisations. Only after getting formal confirmation may donors make a donation (Saini, 2021).

Platform for Charitable Foundations to Track Donations Using Blockchain Technology

Donors have reservations about how their contributions will be used. Several sectors are presently using blockchain technology. Blockchain technology creates transparency in the donation and financial transaction processes. To track all data regarding donations, transactions, and donors, a single platform for donation tracking should be created. This article outlines the development of a blockchain-based network for tracking donations. Based on blockchain technology, the system offers transparent accounting for contributors, charities, and recipients. Platforms for non-profits must provide clear pathways for donations. This will make it possible for contributors and members of the public to keep tabs on how charity funds are being used and to follow their progress. They worked with neighbourhood foundations and non-profit companies (NPOs) to evaluate ideas in order to better understand ecosystem requirements, and they shared this experience in their work. All platform users have access to their accounts and a description of each payment made by the organisations that assist them thanks to the blockchain. Distributed ledger technology also provides contributors with the assurance that their contributions will be used directly to achieve their objectives. Transparency in transactions is made possible by the fact that each device linked to the network houses information about every operation, rather than having it saved on a separate server. It is thought that a social blockchain approach to the charity system can assist boost donor confidence, improve charity transparency, and substantially simplify the operation of reports and works. Information about charities is categorized and arranged in a decentralised database, increasing public transparency (Saleh et al., 2019).

Blockchain for Charities: Platform for Donation Tracking

This work explores the potential uses of blockchain technology in charitable endeavours. Issues in donation tracking area include the introduction of new storage solutions and the assistance of donors, foundations, grantees, and other non-profit organisations to preserve data security, financial integrity, and gift management. Sharing of information between parties is necessary using blockchain can attract more prospective donors for charitable organisations thanks to features like guaranteed data security, the ability to track the movement of money and transactions, and other benefits. In this work, the author investigates the need for blockchain-based philanthropic platforms in Russia and other countries. They provide an example of how to build a platform for making and tracking monetary donations to charities using decentralised registration technologies. Donors want their money to go to the appropriate people when they donate to organizations. They must be assured that their contribution will aid the people they actually wish to assist. We want to make sure the non-profit is legitimate and not a scam. In charitable ventures, blockchain technologies seek to link donors and recipients. Moments when people exchange money or personal data are frequently objectively insecure, which increases the likelihood of misuse and fraud. People therefore act extremely cautiously under these circumstances (especially when both money and personal data are displayed at the same time (Avdoshin & Pesotskaya, 2020).

Blockchain-Based Donations Traceability Framework

The fast growth of cutting-edge technologies has led non-profit companies (NPOs) to apply those technologies to higher serve the philanthropic area, specifically in terms of the charitable giving system. Non-profit groups rely usually on fundraising, which may be followed with the aid of opaque operations, fuelling worries that donations are being used for illicit functions or not reaching the folks who deserve them. The need for a charitable donation traceability system is essential to deal with concerns that negatively impact donor confidence in the donation technique. This look describes a blockchain-primarily based donation traceability framework that aims to enable all parties to music the evolution of charitable donations from the instant a donor donates to the instant it reaches the supposed recipient. The machine is based totally on a publicly accredited blockchain on the Ethereum platform, with every transaction recorded as a block at the chain. These blocks of records are immutable, seen to all events, and also permit a well-timed and traceable transaction. The trustee, the needy, and the donor are the three people involved. In this case, a trustee may be thought of as a company operating inside the Blockchain-based Donation Traceability (BBDT) system and keeping track of all the necessary parties. The chain of charity giving starts with contributors and concludes with people in need under the suggested paradigm and creating a new blockchain-based platform for monitoring donations to charities. Additionally, a system of authority, responsibility, and immutability are made possible because of the assurance of the participant's identification (Almaghrabi & Alhogail, 2022).

Blockchain Technology for Decentralized Autonomous Organizations

Decentralized Autonomous Organizations (DAOs) are the current need of organizations as their operational and business needs are constantly changing. Centralized Autonomous Organizations (CAOs) are opaque and controlled by a small number of efficient administrators, while DAOs are controlled by smart contracts and automate critical operations. A new scalable and self-organizing coordination on the blockchain agrees to the rules and principles laid down by the Code of Conduct without human involvement. DAOs are necessary, and this chapter discusses the key initiatives in this field. The Ethereum blockchain, which supports the complete Turing programming language and smart contract computing, is then used to provide a potential resolution. The creation of an organisation with codified, automated, and software-enforced governance standards will enable members to see their contributed collections in real-time. A DAO is built using the fundamental smart contract programming on the Ethereum blockchain. It also describes the operation of the DAO code, emphasising fundamental setup and governance procedures including formation, incorporation, and voting rights. The DAO is deemed to have agreed to the expectations of doing business in the future. However, the blockchain community does not yet have an operational foundation for DAOs (Sriman et al., 2022).

Charity Donation System Based on Blockchain Technology

The potential of blockchain technology for charity endeavours is examined in this work. In order to maintain data privacy, fund integrity, and contribution management, issues in this field include the development of new storage technologies and the flow of information between donors, foundations, beneficiaries, and other charities. Potential contributors to charitable organizations will be drawn in because of the blockchain's capacity to guarantee data security and trace the flow of money and transactions. The authors of this work concentrate on the requirements of global blockchain-based charity networks. They demonstrate how to create a platform for charity donations and follow-up using a decentralized registration system. As part of their work, the authors worked with regional organizations and foundations to verify solutions, understand ecosystem requirements, and publish their findings. Donors are concerned with how their money is used. Several sectors presently employ blockchain technology. Utilizing blockchain technology, payments are made. The contribution and payment processes are open and clear. You should create a single database for monitoring donations that includes information on donors, transactions, and donations. The goal of this work is to outline the implementation process for a blockchain-based framework for monitoring donations. The system, which is based on blockchain technology, enables donors, charities, and receivers to do business in a safe and transparent manner. User transparency and privacy are pain points of current centralized posting methods. For transparency, they have developed a blockchain-based donation system. This step makes donations more transparent. The anonymity of users of the donation system is preserved by not documenting contributions from specific donors to specific recipients, etc. Organizations: Organizations receive donation requests and send them to sponsors. They also verify the authenticity of requests and resend donations received from sponsors. Sponsor: The sponsor receives the request from the organization and transfers the amount to the organization if they wish to donate (Abhijeet et al., 2022).

Decentralized E-Voting System Based on Smart Contract by Using Blockchain Technology

Currently, the use of the Internet is increasing; E-voting systems have been employed by various countries since they lower the cost and time that traditional voting consumes. A web browser and a server are required when a voter wants to access the E-voting system via the web application. The voter accesses a centralised database via a web browser. The use of a centralised database for the voting system has various security risks, such as data alteration by a third party in the network as a result of the usage of the central database system, and the voting results are not displayed in real-time.But, the purpose of this work is to use blockchain to build a secure E-voting system. Blockchain provides a decentralised approach that allows the network to be dependable, reliable, versatile, and capable of supporting real-time services (Al-madani et al., 2020).

Bitcoin: A Peer-to-Peer Electronic Cash System

A peer-to-peer electronic cash system would allow internet payments to be transmitted directly from one party to another without going through a banking institution. Although digital signatures contribute to the solution, the main advantages are lost if a trusted third party is still necessary to prevent double-spending. We suggest a peer-to-peer network-based solution to the double-spending problem. Transactions are timestamps by the network by hashing them into an ongoing chain of hash-based proof-of-work, resulting in a record that cannot be modified without redoing the proof-of-work. The longest chain not only proves the sequence of events witnessed, but it also proves it came from the largest pool of CPU power. As long as nodes that are not cooperating to attack the network hold the bulk of CPU power, they will produce the longest chain and overtake attackers. The network itself demands very little organisation. Messages are broadcast using best efforts, and nodes are free to quit and rejoin the network at any time, accepting the longest proof-of-work chain as verification of what transpired while they were gone (Berentsen, 2019).

MAIN FOCUS OF THE CHAPTER

Charity Management System Using Blockchain

The manner in which money is contributed is not trusted by the recipients. Humanitarian groups are susceptible to the same types of fraud that affect businesses, like money laundering and fraud. Blockchain technology has recently been used in many different industries. You are able to give and receive money in an open manner when using blockchain technology. In order to maintain track of all donations, transactions, and sponsors, a centralized platform for monitoring donations is needed. Our proposed work describes how to set up a blockchain-based infrastructure for tracking donations. The blockchain-based approach allows for a transparent accounting of donor performance, giving foundations, and recipients. The donation route should be accessible via the charity platform, which allows donors and community members to track the locations, times, and recipients of donations. This work summarises the efforts involved in designing and implementing the web-based blockchain management system. Although the charity management system allows users to send money using cryptocurrency, the security of your donations made using INR is not guaranteed (Ethereum). Assume that when foreigners donate to charities, banks are involved, transactions take some time, and there are transaction fees. However, with this form of gift, foreigners can send money quickly and easily thanks to technology. This technology is decentralized and distributed, and it saves data as blocks by intention, these Blocks are publicly viewable but immutable. Instead of sending money straight to the recipient's address, a donor will employ this technique to send money; it is really useful and portable.

The creation of a social network powered by blockchain will benefit a non-profit organization. The implementation of distributed ledger technology will also guarantee that donations are sent without the use of any middlemen to the intended recipient. The charity's information will be provided and the organizations are crucial. Due to the blockchain, all platform users will be able to see their own accounts and a description of each gift made by a charity they support.

Figure 1. Overview of charity management system

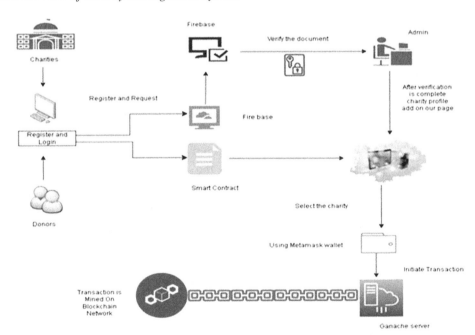

Need

The charity management system will make it simple for NGOs to locate donations. Three modules make up this system: Admin, NGO, and Donor. Admin can oversee the request made by the NGO by approving or denying it by logging in with their credentials. It is demonstrated by two types of actors (donors and support base).The performance of the supplier includes: Acquiring knowledge about making a donation online. It is possible to find information on donor gifts using a unique identifier. The provider will receive data on numerous companies' financial flows. Actually, the most crucial aspect of starting a charity is that you associate it with a goal and a person who has a big impact on your life since you have a tendency to care for the people.

Problem Statement

There are no systems that non profit organisations can utilise to guarantee security while maximising accessibility. Transparency is the main issue, as anyone can legitimately use their right to information by requesting a record of charity expenditures. Even if such tools exist, smaller organisations without a strong user interface for accessibility cannot use them.

Requirements

1. **Solidity Web3**
2. **Metamask:** The platform automatically connects to users' Metamask to provide an easy-to-use and secure wallet service.
3. **Node.js:** Node.js is used as the application's backend. It keeps track of transactions, communicates between applications, and integrates the front end.
4. **Ganache:** Ganache provides a GUI-based local Ethereum blockchain development environment for contract deployment and testing.

Working Model

The platform instantly connects to users' Metamask accounts to provide a user-friendly and secure wallet solution. For our application's backend, Node.js is utilised. It keeps track of communications across the Applications, integrates the front end, and records transactions. The locally accessible GUI-based Ethereum blockchain is provided by the Ganache environment for developing and testing contracts. The programme cannot be used for any transaction without a metamask connection. Using the node.js interface, a ganache RPC (Remote Procedure Call) server is run with metamask as the wallet. Information about the organisation and the charity is saved in the application, and a hash value is produced. Between an organisation and a charity, a transaction is made, and a transaction hash is generated for each transaction. When a user mines all the updated transactions, a block is formed. To use this work first make sure you have npm installed. These are dependency managers that will download everything you need for the work. You must add a file named mnemonic.txt in the root directory containing your 12-word seed phrase. This file must be one line.

Prerequisites

npm must be installed on the machine you wish to test on. Oasis is built with:

- React
- Truffle
- Ganache

Using the Platform Procedure

1. **Donor:** The provider should explore the charity's initiatives after successfully logging in, and then select one. The donor account's balance will be checked. The user will be advised about the deposit if the balance is not enough. Only when I have enough money in my account can I terminate the contribution.
2. **Persons in Need:** Before submitting the redemption to a charity for testing, he must fill out the information. Authorized initiatives that are listed in the charity court must give these specifics. The beneficiary can check the account balance to see the current state of the work and spend tokens to make purchases at other cooperative businesses.
3. **Cooperative Stores:** By collecting tokens, stores offer the beneficiaries the appropriate services or products, such as guidelines or recipients appropriately get goods or services like mail or instructions. Charitable organizations may trade tokens for actual money.
4. **Charitable Organization:** This organisation has access to platform donations for charitable purposes as well as the ability to utilise those funds to trade tokens for items in cooperative stores.

Constraints

1. For accessing the web application, the donor needs a laptop or a smartphone with a pre-installed browser.
2. The user must have access to the Internet.
3. The donor must be fluent in either Tamil or English to use the web application.
4. Requires fundamental understanding of topics related to the Ethereum blockchain
5. Donors must set up an account on the Ethereum blockchain using Metamask.

PROPOSED METHODOLOGY

Users of apps are categorised into four groups based on their purposes: donors, organisations, suppliers, and public servants.

1. **Beneficiary Organization:** These are nonprofits, NGOs, or other small businesses in need of financial support (money or something). They can use a specific format to post their needs in the Charity-Chain system. They will make a substantial contribution to mining.
2. **Vendors:** These are the businesses that release their bids and offer pricing estimates. The representatives of the government choose the best voiced seller.

3. **Donors:** These are the businesses that will examine the public requests made by different organizations and choose the best gift based on their qualifications and preferences for the task.

4. **Governmental Official:** This team will confirm the public requests made by organizations and recognise the knowledgeable contracts. After the formal confirmation, the donor will be permitted to make a donation.

IMPLEMENTATION

Front End

When creating a web application, basic HTML is utilised for the front end, and CSS is used to add specific styling. The majority of sites use Angular.js to make them more interactive. Bootstrap is used to make applying styles simpler and to cut down on the number of lines of code.

Backend

To connect to the application's backend, we utilise Node.js is an unrestricted, a back-end, and cross-platform runtime environment for JavaScript that uses the V8 engine to execute JavaScript code outside of a web browser. By running scripts server-side to create dynamic web page content before the page is sent to the user's web browser, Node.js developers can create command-line tools and server-side scripts.

Metamask

With MetaMask, users may send and receive Ethereum-based cryptocurrencies and tokens, broadcast transactions, store and manage account keys, and securely connect to decentralized applications using a suitable web browser or the built-in browser of the mobile app.

Ganache

The most recent iteration of TestRPC, a quick and adaptable blockchain emulator, is Ganache CLI. Without the costs associated with maintaining an actual Ethereum node, it enables you to make calls to the blockchain.For testing your decentralized application, you can connect to a local blockchain using the Ethereum client Ganache-CLI. Choosing an Ethereum Client you'll learn more about Ethereum clients, but for now, just be aware that they enable us to connect to a local Ethereum blockchain (localhost:8545).

Firebase

For any kind of application (Android, iOS, Javascript, Node.js, Java, Unity, PHP, C++, etc.), Firebase provides hosting services. It provides real-time and NoSQL hosting for databases, content, notifications, and social authentication (including Google, Facebook, Twitter, and GitHub). It also provides services like a real-time communication server.

Languages Used

Frontend

HTML, CSS, J Query, and Angular are the front-end technologies/tools used. Content is displayed using HTML. CSS is used to arrange the content and apply styling. Prior to sending the forms to the backend, JavaScript is utilised to validate them. Additionally, Angular is used to streamline features like content sorting and filtering.

Backup Documents

Node.js and Firebase are the technologies/tools used as the backend. NodeJS is used to process data and redirect users to the appropriate webpage as needed. Data is kept in Firebase, a relational structured database, in the form of rows and columns.

- NodeJS
- Express
- Firebase

DEPLOYMENT

Module 1: User Registration and Verification

Prior to using the system, the user must register as a provider or beneficiary. As a result, he will enter his information into the Charity Chain system. The organization's name, contact information, and website link will all be part of the beneficiary information. On the user's website, these particulars and verification information will be saved.

Module 2: Generating Bids

Beneficiaries submit their requests in the form of a tender, following the structure established by the Poor Care Program. This section contains information on the requirements and expected costs for each component. These bids will be accessible to sponsors in this manner. Government officials, too, have applied for a permission and verification module. Bids are certified by government officials using a mechanism based on the dependability of the organisations and their individual applications.

Module 3: Tracking and Donations Module

Donors may donate any amount of money to the organization in accordance with their talents and interests once the donation has received official approval. At this point, the genesis node will be formed. Donors will be able to view all transactions pertaining to the organization on its profile page. The donor will be better able to choose wisely and donate appropriately as a result of this. Additionally, the donor will be able to follow the worker's journey till they arrive at their destination.

Business Aspects

USP

The term "unique selling point" refers to the uniqueness of a business product. It refers to the feature of promoting charity management using blockchain in this application. There are numerous apps (web/ mobile) for connecting donors, but none for promoting charity management using blockchain by raising awareness about training sessions. This is the product's distinguishing feature.

Marketing

Because it is obvious that marketing is done for charity management using blockchain, marketing is considered a business aspect. The use of blockchain techniques for charity management is being broadcasted and promoted. The webapp aims to raise awareness by reminding registered users about charity management training sessions using blockchain. Marketing charity management through the app is an important business aspect, and it is obvious to promote them.

Customer Service

The service includes connecting Donors and charities without the involvement of middlemen. This reduces the intermediate cost between both ends and benefits by an increase in contacts. Moreover, the service also includes notifying the training sessions of many charity management using blockchain techniques and it helps in promoting charity management using blockchain to a greater extent.

Customer Loyalty

The donor loyalty aspect should be also considered since the app should not leak any information about the users who have registered in this webapp and no functionality under any circumstances must be available at a cost. All the functionalities must be available at free of cost so that donor loyalty is achieved. The necessary steps for the security of the users' information must be implemented to meet this business aspect.

FUTURE SCOPE

The future scope of this project is to migrate all data from local database to firebase and shift all operations to cloud. Adding more features to meet the societal need, improving UI so that is more users friendly and easy to use, document storage using IPFS and Hosting application in AWS.

CONCLUSION

The current centralised contribution methods have problems with user privacy and transparency. In this study, we built a Blockchain-based donation mechanism to promote transparency. This process results in the transparency of donations. Donations made from a particular donor to a certain recipient are encrypted to safeguard the privacy of donation system users. In order to promote transparency, we've presented a decentralised strategy for charitable activity that takes use of blockchain. However, some people are interested in earning money illegally in the process. This system will take care of the requirements for greater security and authenticity. Additionally, it will provide a dependable system and improve process transparency. As a result, there is no longer a need for middlemen to connect donations with philanthropic organisations. As a result, there is no longer a need for middlemen to connect donations with philanthropic organisations. The strategy reduces both the speed and cost of processing help because payments are not transferred through a middleman. The potential of Blockchain technology is constrained since the value of cryptocurrencies is not widely understood. The only feasible alternative in the event that the banking system crashes is cryptocurrencies. Expanding the system is conceivable.

OUTPUT SCREENSHOTS

Figure 2. Login page

Figure 3. Login and register page

Figure 4. Donate and request option

Figure 5. This page shows request form the users have to enter details for asking help of donors

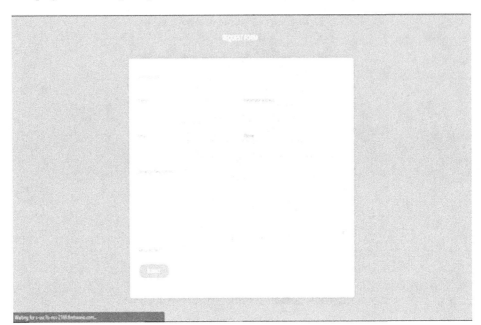

Figure 6. This page shows donate option. It displays no of charity details

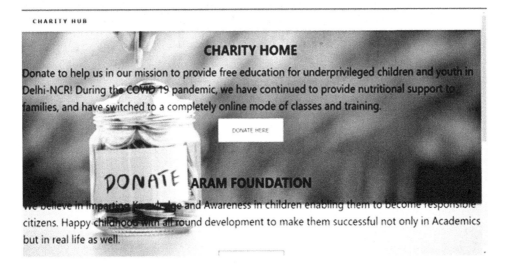

Figure 7. This page shows donate option. It displays charity details the user has to enter details for performing crypto transaction

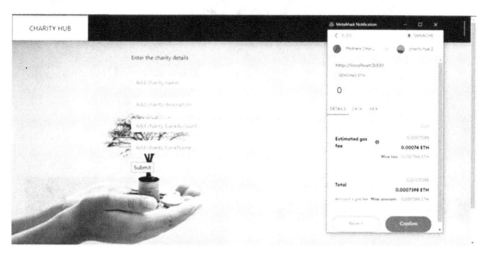

Figure 8. This page shows donate option after entering the details. It will redirect to metamask account and send the crypto to particular metamask address

Figure 9. This page shows donate page after performing the transaction it confirms the transaction

Figure 10. Ganache platform here the block will mine

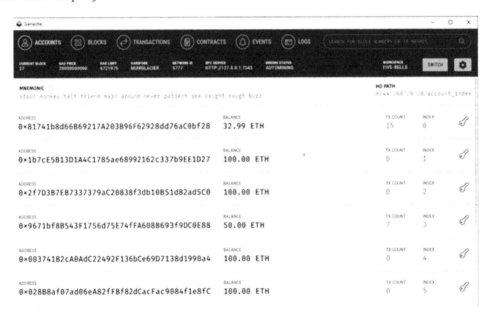

Figure 11. This page shows transaction details and blocks address

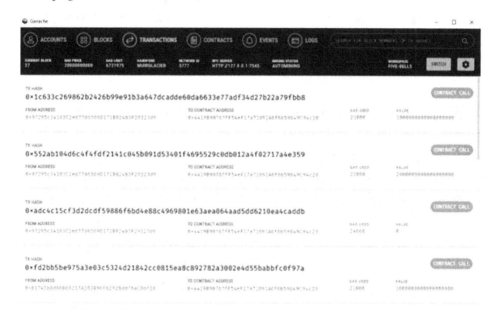

REFERENCES

Al-madani, A. M., Gaikwad, A. T., Mahale, V., & Ahmed, Z. A. T. (2020). Decentralized E-voting system based on Smart Contract by using Blockchain Technology. *2020 International Conference on Smart Innovations in Design, Environment, Management, Planning and Computing (ICSIDEMPC).* 10.1109/ICSIDEMPC49020.2020.9299581

Almaghrabi, A., &Alhogail, A. (2022). Blockchain-based donations traceability framework. *Journal of King Saud University - Computer and Information Sciences, 34*(10), 9442–9454. doi:10.1016/j.jksuci.2022.09.021

Avdoshin, S., & Pesotskaya, E. (2020). Blockchain in Charity: Platform for Tracking Donations. *Proceedings of the Future Technologies Conference (FTC) 2020, 2,* 689–701. 10.1007/978-3-030-63089-8_45

B, S., Sh, A. S., E, S. K., K, S. N., & S, N. (2022). Blockchain Industry 5.0: Next Generation Smart Contract and Decentralized Application Platform. *2022 International Conference on Innovative Computing, Intelligent Communication and Smart Electrical Systems (ICSES).* doi:10.1109/ICSES55317.2022.9914151

Berentsen, A. (2019). Aleksander Berentsen Recommends "Bitcoin: A Peer-to-Peer Electronic Cash System" by Satoshi Nakamoto. *21st Century Economics,* 7–8. doi:10.1007/978-3-030-17740-9_3

De Aguiar, E. J., Faiçal, B. S., Krishnamachari, B., & Ueyama, J. (2020). A Survey of Blockchain-Based Strategies for Healthcare. *ACM Computing Surveys, 53*(2), 1–27. doi:10.1145/3376915

Farooq, M. S., Khan, M., & Abid, A. (2020). A framework to make charity collection transparent and auditable using blockchain technology. *Computers & Electrical Engineering, 83,* 106588. doi:10.1016/j.compeleceng.2020.106588

Hu, B., & Li, H. (2020). Research on Charity System Based on Blockchain. *IOP Conference Series. Materials Science and Engineering, 768*(7), 072020. doi:10.1088/1757-899X/768/7/072020

Khamkar, Kotwal, & Khatri. (2022). CharityChain - A Charity App Built on Blockchain. *International Journal of Scientific Research in Science, Engineering and Technology*, 73–77. doi:10.32628/IJSR-SET122933

Kumar, N., Gusain, R., Kumar, S., & Sharma, R. (2022). D-Donation: Charity Fraud Prevention using Blockchain. *International Journal for Research in Applied Science and Engineering Technology, 10*(5), 3775–3778. doi:10.22214/ijraset.2022.43222

Naiknavare, M. (2022). Blockchain based Transparent and Genuine Charity Application. *International Journal for Research in Applied Science and Engineering Technology, 10*(5), 4232–4248. doi:10.22214/ijraset.2022.42839

Naiknavare, O. S., Patil, M., Chawate, M. R. C., Borana, M. A. B., & Sonawane, P. S. (2022). Blockchain based Transparent and Genuine Charity Application. *International Journal for Research in Applied Science and Engineering Technology, 10*(3), 1909–1915. doi:10.22214/ijraset.2022.41021

Patil, P. D., Mhatre, D. J., Gharat, N. H., & Tinsu, J. (2022). Transparent Charity System using Smart Contracts on Ethereum using Blockchain. *International Journal for Research in Applied Science and Engineering Technology, 10*(4), 743–748. doi:10.22214/ijraset.2022.41339

Saini, K. (2021). Blockchain Foundation. *Essential Enterprise Blockchain Concepts and Applications*, 1–14. https://doi.org/1 doi:10.1201/9781003097990-

Saleh, H., Avdoshin, S., & Dzhonov, A. (2019). *Platform for Tracking Donations of Charitable Foundations Based on Blockchain Technology. In 2019 Actual Problems of Systems and Software Engineering.* APSSE. doi:10.1109/APSSE47353.2019.00031

Saranya, S., Muvvala, S. P., Chauhan, V., & Satwik, R. (2022). Crowdfunding Charity Platform Using Blockchain. *2022 International Conference on Inventive Computation Technologies (ICICT)*. 10.1109/ICICT54344.2022.9850562

Shakila, U. K., & Sultana, S. (2021). A Decentralized Marketplace Application based on Ethereum Smart Contract. *2021 24th International Conference on Computer and Information Technology (ICCIT)*. 10.1109/ICCIT54785.2021.9689879

Singh, A., Rajak, R., Mistry, H., & Raut, P. (2020). Aid, Charity and Donation Tracking System Using Blockchain. *2020 4th International Conference on Trends in Electronics and Informatics (ICOEI)*, (48184). 10.1109/ICOEI48184.2020.9143001

Sirisha, N. S., Agarwal, T., Monde, R., Yadav, R., & Hande, R. (2019). Proposed Solution for Trackable Donations using Blockchain. *2019 International Conference on Nascent Technologies in Engineering (ICNTE)*. 10.1109/ICNTE44896.2019.8946019

Wu, H., & Zhu, X. (2020). Developing a Reliable Service System of Charity Donation During the Covid-19 Outbreak. *IEEE Access : Practical Innovations, Open Solutions, 8*, 154848–154860. doi:10.1109/ACCESS.2020.3017654 PMID:34812351

Chapter 16
Privacy and Security Through Blockchain in Industry 4.0:
An Industrial Cybersecurity Perspective

R. Sasikumar
K. Ramakrishnan College of Engineering, India

P. Karthikeyan
Thiagarajar College of Engineering, India

Thangavel Murugan
United Arab Emirates University, Al Ain, UAE

ABSTRACT

The name Industry 4.0 describes a synthesis of modern manufacturing techniques that help producers to hit targets more quickly. The manufacturing sector's trend is changing significantly because of digitalization and technological improvements. Technology that aids in comprehensive integration, such as IoT, cybersecurity, blockchain, big data, etc. Due to the internet's open nature as a means of data transmission, security and privacy must be given top priority. The integration of blockchain is currently taking place as part of Industry 4.0. Blockchain enables Industry 4.0 through bringing a variety of processing activities in a protected environment. The inherent characteristics of decentralization, blockchain technology is a promising platform for cybersecurity. This chapter's purpose is to highlight the issues on traditional production sectors, evaluation blockchain application in Industry 4.0, limitations of blockchain, privacy and security requirements, and adoption of blockchain inside this context of Industry 4.0.

INTRODUCTION

The principle of "Industry 4.0" has been getting a lot of attention recent time. Many emerging concepts have recently evolved because of the expanding developments in manufacturing processes and technology. Due to ongoing technical advancements and improvements in manufacturing systems, the global

DOI: 10.4018/978-1-6684-8145-5.ch016

Copyright © 2023, IGI Global. Copying or distributing in print or electronic forms without written permission of IGI Global is prohibited.

industrial environment has gone through significant transformation in recent time. The "First Industrial Revolution" supported in the progress of mass production by using water and steam power rather than just both human and animal power. The usage of oil, gas, and electricity were both exhibited at "Second Industrial Revolution", as well as assembly lines. The "Third Industrial Revolution" improved its efficiency with the aid of the following three technologies: computers, cutting-edge telecommunications networks, and data analytics. Mechanization, electricity, and information technology (IT) were all introduced to support workers during the first three industrial developments. People are currently living through the "Fourth Industrial Revolution" might abbreviated as Industry 4.0. By utilizing industrial automation and intelligent equipment, the production of goods and services could become more productive and efficient. Because manufacturing procedures have evolved to be more automated, complex, and sustainable, individuals can now operate machinery with ease, effectiveness, and consistency. In the European Union, industry contributes about 17% of the GDP and supports 32 million jobs, in addition to many other occupations. But in recent years, issues including an ageing population and competition from developing countries have harmed European countries' industries. These issues motivate the development of industrial technologies, two of which are the Cyber-Physical System (CPS) and Internet of Things (IoT), two cutting-edge technologies developed within the past ten years (Aoun et al., 2021). These technologies reduce Labouré force requirements, speed up product development, use resources more effectively, and other objectives.

Germans came up with the term Industry 4.0 because of the emergence of these technologies. The phrase "Industry 4.0" known as fourth industrial revolution, which is a new degree of degree of organization and control over the whole value chain of products. In contrast to computer integrated manufacturing, industry 4.0 places a high value on the contribution of human workers to the production process. To increase productivity and promote development, the Fourth Industrial Revolution aims to make our robots more autonomous, able to "speak" to one another, and capable of analyzing vast amounts of data in ways that humans just cannot. Manufacturers are infusing superior technology into their industrial processes, including the IoT devices, cloud computing, analytics, Artificial Intelligence (AI), and Machine Learning (ML). Such "smart" companies have been designed and equipped by advanced sensors, embedded software, and robotics which collect information, analyze them, and support decision-making. With the use of these digital technologies, processes can be improved through self-optimization, proactive maintenance, and greater mechanization. A variety of technological advancements, including CPS, IoT, Robotics, Big Data, Cloud Computing, and Augmented Reality, are included in such emerging industrial perspective will have a consequence on both products and processes.

Industry 4.0 concepts and technology are advantageous to all industrial companies, including those in the manufacturing, oil and gas, and mining sectors. The key components of a smart manufacturer are IoT sensors and devices. When emerging equipment's like IoT devices are deployed in smart factories, both quality and productivity are maximized. Manufacturing businesses can benefit fully from AI and machine learning. The replacement of mechanical handling operating models via AI-powered visual intelligence and insight minimizes manufacturing errors with improved performance in terms of time and cost. By applying machine learning algorithms, manufacturers can spot errors before they become costly to fix. Cloud computing seems to be a crucial part of Industry 4.0 plan. Utilizing the cloud, a smartphone simplifies the work of a quality control employee easier. An employee could remotely monitor and control the manufacturing process. Business organizations really haven't considered the importance of information security or cyber-physical systems. However, the factory's operating equipment's connectivity opens new entry points for hostile attacks and malware.

Characteristics of Smart Industry

For manufacturing organizations, embedded sensors and networked equipment generate a significant percentage of big data. Analyzing previous trends, seeing patterns, and improving judgments are all made possible by data analytics for manufacturing. Smart factories can more efficiently generate things that are personalized to each customer's needs. More streamlined and transparent supply chain is fundamental for industrial operations, as well as a solid Industry 4.0 philosophy needs link this chain with production activities (Bianco et al., 2022). This changes how suppliers get raw materials and how businesses distribute final goods. Interconnectivity is crucial to the network architecture of the smart factory. Real-time data generated by sensors, equipment, and devices on the production line becomes immediately accessible to it and usable by other manufacturing assets.

Components of Industry 4.0 and the Key Enabling Technologies

Industry 4.0 technology has a challenging technical structure that emphasizes the opportunities for connecting, integrating, and industrial digitalization to integrate all aspects of a value-adding system. This strategy incorporates computer technology, network communication technology, automation technology, and computer technology (Abdelmajied, 2022). This technology enables rapid technological growth in a variety of industries. Technically integrating CPS into production processes combined with utilizing IoT and services in industrial processes, are, however, heavily influencing the industry 4.0 revolution that is currently taking shape. In consideration of this, this part provides a summary of each important technology driver. The industry 4.0's primary elements are described in the section below:

Cyber Physical System (CPS)

As the name implies, CPS work to combine digital and analogue manufacturing processes, which are crucial to Industry 4.0 deployments. One important property of the systems is its capacity to response to any event. To producing expected results, they offer quick inspection and validation of process feedback. The CPS is intended to communicate with a network and features using a few sensors and actuators. CPSs come with several essential functions, including expedited information availability, maintenance and repairs, pre-defined decision-making, and optimal solution processes. This is divided into three stages:

- **Identification:** The ability to identify individual machines and processes is crucial in the industrial sector. For the identification purpose, a machine speaks in a language is known as unique identification.
- **Sensor and Actuator Integration:** Coupling between sensors and actuators facilitates the control of mechanical motion and the ability of operating machines to detect environmental changes.
- **Development of Sensors and Actuators:** Data analysis and data storage are made possible by sensor and actuator advancements in industrial machinery.

Internet of Things (IoT) and Internet of Services (IoS)

The Internet of Things (IoT) is a novel invention it integrates wide variety of technologies and techniques and is based on the communication between individual objects and the Internet. Recent technological developments have allowed for the expansion of the Internet to a new level known as "smart devices". It enables human problem solving while also connecting machines, devices, and things like sensors and mobile phones. With the development assistance of these kind of integration, CPS can execute and handle issues independently. Nowadays, most electronic items are connected to either the internet or a smart smartphone because of technological improvements. The idea behind the Internet of Services (IoS) will create new opportunities for the service industry by offering a technological and economic framework for the development of business networks between service providers and clients. The growth of IoT in industrial environments and supply chain will present a number of opportunities for consumers, suppliers, and companies, having a substantial impact on a number of industries.

Smart Factories or Smart Manufacturing

A notion derived from IIoT refers to a "Smart Factory", which sees a production environment as a fully automated and intelligent network. It makes it possible for infrastructure, equipment, and logistical networks inside the production facility to be managed without human involvement. Additionally, a smart factory is a space where all these things occur as a result of information exchanges not simply between production machines and equipment but also between all components in the production technology chain. It intends to use cutting-edge functionality to operate and manufacture completely customizable manufacturing at a reasonable speed.

Cloud Systems and Big Data

With the use of the promising technology known as cloud computing, businesses may now more easily reduce expenses while also increasing productivity across a wide range of industries. Through the use of the cloud, businesses could completely eliminate problems with data storage and link installation. As technology advances, more and more devices, data management, and performance characteristics will move away from conventional methods into the cloud-based options. Rapid improvements, performance measurement patterns, and other delivery service are all made possible via the cloud, which makes distribution much faster than with isolated devices. Big Data is a collection of information including both traditional and modern resources both within and outside of an organization, and it serves as just a resource for ongoing research and analysis. Big data is coming from so many other sources at an increasing rate, quantity, and heterogeneity. Big data requires adequate throughput, analysis ability, and information security skills to be efficiently used.

Cyber Security

Communication between machines, sensors, and people is essential for interconnections. To successfully adopt Industry 4.0, communications must be protected. Cybersecurity and communications cannot be viewed as independent processes in Industry 4.0. Manufacturers must be aware of the capabilities and potential threats of Industry 4.0 to fully capitalize on the opportunities it delivers. Data between multiple places flows over an open channel, i.e., the Internet, as in Industry 4.0 based applications, so concerns to security and privacy have extended. Since these applications work with large amounts of data, it is important to take data heterogeneity, data integrity, and data redundancy into account in addition to security and privacy considerations. Despite being the second most frequently attacked industry, the manufacturing sector has weak security. The attack techniques including denial of service (DoS), component tampering, and vulnerability exploitation that other networks are vulnerable to can also be used against smart factories. Additionally, manufacturers find it more challenging to identify and fight against cyberattacks due to the smart factory's enlarged attack surface. Since the recent introduction of the IoT, these risks have evolved to a completely new level and, particularly in the Technology ecosystem, they have the potential to have major physical repercussions.

Popular Attacks on Industry 4.0

Many more industries are moving toward digitalization and automation as part of the Industrial 4.0 Revolution shift. There are a few vulnerabilities that come together with the trend of turning industries into smart sectors. Some of the most common cyber-attacks such as DoS, Spoofing, Eavesdropping, and eavesdropping are highlighted. The Industrial Internet of Things (IIoT) has categorized into four layers in its fundamental design, which is also known as industry 4.0 layered structure. Those layers are Device Layer / Sensing Layer, Network Layer, Service Layer, and Application Layer. All layer is exposed to cybersecurity threats, with associated risks and protective measures. The various layers of industry 4.0 and it cyberattacks are explained in detail in the sections that follow. Figure 1 lists the IIoT layers and potential attacks on each one.

Figure 1. Industrial IoT layers and possible attacks

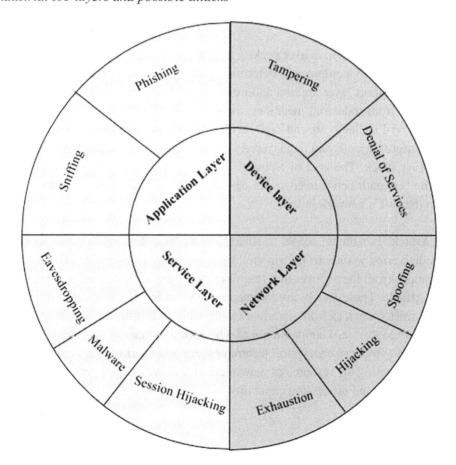

Cyber-Attacks Targeting Device Layer

The device layer includes the devices used to control industrial devices. These include machineries, robotic systems, Programmable logic controllers, actuators, and wearable technologies. The following forms of attacks are made against this layer, which is exposed to direct physical access:

- **Tampering:** A physical modification of the equipment or communication link is made by the attacker. It is possible to identify hardware components, and identities could be taken as well as modified. Such exploit might also be carried out by tampering with the data as it is being transferred from the sender to the receiver. It is possible to prevent interference attempts with tamper-resistant packaging, but even though the process is costly.
- **Denial of Service (DoS):** A DoS attack aims to bring down a devices or sensors so that its intended users are unable to access it. Radio access technology, which operates at the physical layer level, is typically used by IIoT devices to communicate. This wireless connection is susceptible to a DoS attack, which can be carried out either through signal jamming or other means. Monitoring and congestions analysis could be a potential solution.

The consequences of device layer attack is, when an IoT device is exposed to an attacker, the attacker may send the device harmful code or send a message that activates malware. Because of the mentioned incidence, confidential data could be taken, or even encrypted data could be accessed.

Cyber-Attacks Targeting Network Layer

The primary duty of this layer is to deliver packets from the source machinery or IoT equipment's to the destination machinery or IoT equipment's determining the secure or shortest and most efficient path. The edge layer and transport layer are two additional layers that can be created within this layer. The information acquired from industrial machinery is maintained by the edge layer using physical layer protocols including Wi-Fi, Bluetooth, and ZigBee. Control of flow, segmentation, and error handling are provided by the transport layer. By adding layered security controls, this layer aims to reduce the damage in the instance of an attack. The goal of Network Layer cyberattacks is to interrupt routing protocols from selecting the best path between edge devices (Sula, 2018). The next section discusses potential cyber-attacks on the IIoT's network layer:

- **Spoofing Attack:** For illegal access to smart devices, attackers employ this technique. Usually, it involves delivering malicious information from an anonymous source. The device will receive communications from the attacker that resemble those sent to trusted edge devices.
- **Hijacking Attack:** These attacks are simple to carry out but challenging to recognize. Attackers want to stop trusted devices from communicating with each other and begin a new session while posing as a trusted device. The likelihood of a hijacking attempt on a wireless network is great if it does not employ modern encryption techniques and other forms of authentication.
- **Exhaustion:** Targeting the resource of network devices may exhaust network resources including buffers, throughput, and processing capability.

The consequences of network layer attack is, data loss, loss of confidentiality and integrity, disruption to network traffic, inability to access services, all of which result in increased implementation costs and resource wastage.

Cyber-Attacks Targeting Service Layer

This layer is also known as data processing layer. Aggregation and processing of data are typically carried out on the data processing layer. In the data processing layer, the generated data is frequently kept in the cloud. This layer is the target of numerous cyberattacks from end devices, including eavesdropping, session hijacking, insider threats, and other cloud security vulnerabilities. Cyberattacks that aim to compromise the data processing layer's cybersecurity are covered below:

- **Eavesdropping:** One of these privacy concerns with the IIoT system is eavesdropping attacks, particularly because as frequency of transmitting antennas increases. In industries that depend on acquiring and recording information, eavesdropping attacks across the network are regarded as one of the most significant threats. Data transmission between two devices is listened and recorded during an eavesdropping attempt.
- **Malware:** Any program or file that is purposefully created to harm data, services is known as malware, sometimes known as malicious software. In the context of the IIoT, an attacker can access the service account and causes damage regardless the target's system having powerful security mechanisms enabled.
- **Session Hijacking:** Every time a person logs into a service, like the cloud, a session is generated for that specific user. Data breaches in the compression ratio of TLS communications are exploited by session attacks.

In the IIoT and Industry 4.0 context, Malware causes a variety of issues, including system slowdown, identity theft, system crashes, and even taking over the victim's systems. The session hijacking adversely affects the integrity of the victim due to the loss of crucial information.

Cyber-Attacks Targeting Application Layer

Attacks on this layer seek to disrupt the normal operation of the production system. At the time of design, it is exceedingly challenging to forecast and realize how to identify and prevent a physical attack. Threats that haven't yet been addressed are covered in more detail below.

- **Phishing Attack:** It is the most common attack and is used in numerous ways to attack the intended user or system. Phishing refers to a type of "social engineering attack" that is broadly utilized to obtain personal data, including user credentials.
- **Sniffing Attack:** Sniffing attacks are data breaches that have been carried out by packet sniffers that illegally obtain and extract unencrypted data on networks. It is classified as a passive cyber-threat since such intruder is often invisible in this threat.

In the IIoT and Industry 4.0 context, because of obsolete guidelines and policies, the manufacturing sector is extremely susceptible to phishing attack. It checks the target's system for defects and transmits the results to a third-party attacker. In addition, supply chain cyberattacks, IIOT attacks, and theft of proprietary information are frequently directed at manufacturers when a threat actor gains access.

Mostly in era of Industry 4.0, businesses now encounter the following significant security challenges: 1) There is a risk associated with every device connected with the manufacturing. 2) Industrial Control Systems (ICS) have special flaws that make them particularly vulnerable to cyberattacks. 3) The number of attacks grows as Industry 4.0 combines traditionally disconnected systems. 4) In comparison to other sectors, manufacturing does have lesser regulatory requirements norms. The manufacturing sector needs to consider security from a risk perspective (tying business criticality to defense strategies). Maintain an accurate and detailed inventory of all OT resources at all times. Combine the best aspects of IT and OT to develop a complete defense strategy for all attack surfaces. Discover and update obsolete software, unpatched bugs and files that aren't properly encrypted. Utilize legitimate security audits and risk-based management to stay always alert for any potential threats. Make sure that connected device makers and technology vendors adhere to consistent software updates and security patches.

Motivation for Blockchain in Industry 4.0

As stated in the introduction section, Industry 4.0 is a paradigm that is based on a variety of innovative ideas or technologies. IoT and Industry 4.0 have been widely applied in a variety of industrial domains. Industry 4.0 makes use of cloud-based data storage, and connectivity in IoT causes numerous concerns such as delay, single point of failure, and privacy disclosure. IoT's availability and scalability are further limited by the centralized access control (Huaqun Guo et.al., 2022). Blockchain, on the other hand, is an immutable, decentralized, and transparent system, that is trustless and tamper-proof. Therefore, the Blockchain might be the solution for accelerating this transformation by giving industry sectors a reliable and high-quality source of transactional information. The incorporation of blockchain technology into the Industry 4.0 framework benefits business operations by addressing the provenance of products, raw materials, and financial transactions between sectors, customers, stakeholders, and legal compliance. This immutable ledger would provide authentication for the procedure used to create the product and will authenticate that it was done correctly, using the necessary process and materials.

BACKGROUND

The most significant suggestions on Blockchain technologies for Industry 4.0 are covered in this part because of the systematic evaluation. For gathering and sharing competency proof throughout various organizations, a blockchain-based E-Portfolio architecture is presented. This submitted system integrates IPFS, smart contracts, and session management to achieve professional-driven interoperability without sacrificing the cost effectiveness and security (Binbusayyis et al., 2022). The author is suggesting a blockchain-based system that reliably conducts the royalty transactions between the multiple OaG industry participants. One of the main contributions of the suggested method is the secure royalty contract transactions (Mehta et al., 2021). Industry 4.0 is a feasible idea, and the complex nature of these kind of organizations need a stronger security mechanism. The author (Lin et al., 2018) in proposes a novel framework based on a BCT termed BSeIn to protect critical remote authentication process and comprehensive network security for Industry 4.0 uses. The developed model uses the fundamental properties of the BCT together with several cryptographic resources to produce a decentralized, private, and fully transparent system. The authors (Lu et al., 2019) conduct a thorough analysis to examine the potential uses for BCT in the oil and gas sector. The authors (Pal, 2021) suggested that the consensus method will evolve toward a hybrid consensus mechanism to increase efficiency and security, and it will be autonomously modified in accordance with various circumstances in different networking environments or active workflows. Using the information's contextual semantic evaluation, highly efficient processes for identifying security risks can be created. Additionally, the thoughtful analysis of personal information shared between business partners may enhance the capacity of IoT-based industrial organizations. For AGV-based internal logistics, the authors (Mehami et al., 2018) describe manufacturing work on the methodology and system architecture that can support data collection, preprocessing, aggregation, clustering, and other data processing operations. To combining manufacturing records, the system is built using DB-Scan and K-means. With the help of the suggested techniques, it is feasible to identify an undetermined number of clusters, classify incoming observations accurately, keep track of how additional groupings arise, and spot inconsistencies.

Mullet et al. (2022) developed a blockchain-based traceability solution for production plants that offers a successful method for granting transparency to all people concerned with maintaining the anonymity of their individual personal data. The goal is to include encrypted secret information in blockchain operations together with a hash value that was computed prior to encoding. To verify participants validity, the investigators can ask the data owner to grant them access to the private data so they can compare it to the relevant data that has been verified by every participant. Rathee et al. (2021) implemented blockchain system to provide privacy and integrity among the workers and the IIoT devices. According to the experimental analysis, the developed model considerably increased the cybersecurity of wireless sensors by using a blockchain system to compare them to different security parameters. This model is tested against attack success probabilities, how easily an attack may be detected by the system, and falsification attacks. To prevent snoopers and malicious hackers from listening in on conversations in a critical industrial environment, this research suggests a method to use a randomly initialized and master key management approach. The Base station serves as the primary role actor in this method, which generates an initial key determined by the number of accessible sink node, the gateway node, and the participation of a third party. In addition to the above, this system implements innovative blockchain-based security algorithms for IIoT systems to secure and improve the overall efficiency (Sodhro et al., 2020). The healthcare industry has many difficulties in protecting patient sensitive and confidential information from intruders. Hence, method for protecting health information when keeping, retrieving, and distributing it in the cloud is important so that it is not corrupted by authorized or unauthorized members of a network. The model for Electronic Health Records (EHRs) was developed and suggested various cryptography technique by the authors (Mahajan et al., 2022) with the benefits of blockchain.

What Is Blockchain? And Working Principles of Blockchain

Information in blockchain technology is more reliable and widely available, immutable, and distributed in nature (Nakamoto, 2009). Everyone has access to read the data that is available across the distributed network because it is a public ledger, but no one will permit unauthorized alteration. Members of the network must issue new transactions requests if they want to modify a blockchain ledger in any form. Each member of the network will receive a request, which they must all confirm and agree to move forward with the process. As soon as the above transactions were approved by more than 51% of network participants, they were appended to the current ledger. Each new transaction will be stored in a block, which also includes the date of the most recent valid transaction, the hash of the previous block, the current block address, and information about the participating member. The ledger is comprised of several blocks, which are distinguished from one another by their hash values. This technology was initially successfully applied on cryptocurrency, and after some time it expanded to a variety of applications in the financial, healthcare, smart appliance, and supply chain sectors, and many others.

Public blockchains, private blockchains, consortium blockchains, and hybrid blockchains are the three primary categories of blockchain networks. First one, the Public blockchain - Everybody else is encouraged to participate and engage with transactions on this distributed ledger. A copy of the ledger exists for each peer and is non-restrictive in behavior. To maintain the network dynamic and bring more participants, a public blockchain employs an incentive system. It does not permit changing any transactions or records. Private Blockchain - Only those who have received an invitation and had their identification or other necessary information authenticated and validated are allowed to join in this network (Sasikumar et al., 2021). The validation is carried out either by the network operator(s) or by a predetermined set procedure that is implemented using smart contracts as well as other algorithmic authorization approaches. They are typically not accessible to the public and instead operate on a limited network within a company or organization. A closed database that uses distributed ledger technology and cryptographic principles to secure transaction details. Consortium Blockchain - Different private blockchains from various organizations are combined into a consortium blockchain. Each organization maintains its own node or blockchain, but the consortium's members can access, share, and distribute the data inside. Blockchain, which is nothing more than a collection of connected blocks, facilitates inside the storage of data with immutable properties. Four phases must be performed before adding a new block to the chain. Second, other network members must consent to the specified transactions. Following that, a specific block with a distinct identity will be added to the current chain once it has been authorized by the network's participants. Finally, every member's chain will reflect this block.

Key Elements of Blockchain and Its Functionalities

Numerous essential components of blockchain exists, including a ledger, a virtual machine, a consensus mechanism, etc. However, the three most important ones are cryptography, consensus mechanisms, and distributed ledgers.

- **Distributed Ledger:** A database that is regularly updated with all transactions makes up an electronic ledger. This is made up of several blocks that are connected by a chain implementing cryptography. Eliminating the need for a centralized body to process and authenticate transactions is one of ledger's advantages. It offers a verifiable and traceable history of every piece of information stored on the certain collection.
- **Consensus Mechanism:** In decentralized network, it covers a wide range of techniques for establishing security, trust, and agreement. It establishes a set of guidelines for the P2P network so that the nodes may cooperate and agree over which transactions are valid and qualified to be included on the blockchain. It guarantees that the entire system is fault tolerant to reach the necessary agreement and for members to preserve the safe and secure environment.

- **Cryptography:** One of these components makes it possible to maintain the protection, authenticity, and verification of the data in the ledger or the data transferred among end devices. Encryption techniques are primarily broken down into two categories: 1) Symmetric Encryption - In which the same key is used for both data encryption and decryption since key needs to be kept a secret. 2) Asymmetric Encryption - wherein two distinct keys (i.e) public key and private are used for data encryption and decryption.

Consensus Protocols and Merkle Tree

Confidentiality, a fundamental property of blockchain technology, is problematic when it comes to establishing trust. The consensus process is used to validate the transaction and arrive at a conclusion regarding the proposed transaction impact on ledger updates. Consensus is simply agreement to add a new transaction block to the blockchain. It makes use of the similar interests shared by the large majority of blockchain users in maintaining the integrity of the network. As a result, these algorithms can be seen as the brains of all blockchain transactions. There are numerous kinds of consensus algorithms for blockchain technology. This mechanism can be chosen based on the activities of respective applications, the resources that are available, the important and essential factors, and the computing power. According to its working model, the consensus algorithm's process is divided into three phases (Fu et al., 2021). These phases are accountant selection, block addition, and transaction confirmation. In Account selection phase, the process of creating new blocks on the blockchain ledger involves validating transactions, grouping them into a block, and delivering the block towards other peers. In the block adding phase, a node initially checks the account and the transaction upon receiving a block from an accountant. If the accountant and block are both authoritative, the consensus algorithms make sure that most of the participants must agree to add the block to the Blockchain ledger. So, every peer has a personal replica of the Blockchain after completing the first two phases. In the transaction confirmation phase, in accordance with the Blockchain that each node has, transactions are confirmed during third phase. Figure 2 illustrates various blockchain development frameworks and consensus algorithms used by each framework.

Figure 2. Blockchain development frameworks and consensus protocols

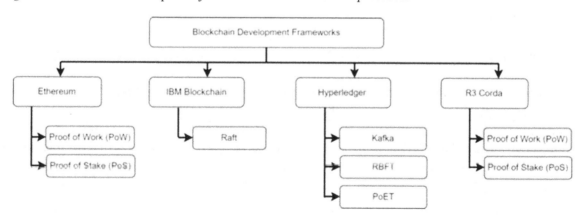

Each block on the blockchain has a transaction, and there are many blocks in aggregate. Verifying all the transactions in this situation is exceedingly challenging. That necessitates additional effort and resources only to perform the verification. The Merkle tree has been incorporated into this technology to address such problems. Merkle trees are implemented mathematical models that quickly and accurately produce results when the verification procedure has been completed. It makes use of certain well-known hashing algorithms, including MD5, SHA-3, and SHA-256. The Merkle root, which is formed by pairing every transaction with every other transaction, is based on the idea of a binary tree. As soon as an encrypted value is obtained, the leaves are coupled to create a new root for those transactions. This procedure will be carried out repeatedly till a confinement root is discovered. The structure of Merkle tree is depicted in Figure 3.

Figure 3. Blockchain's Merkle tree structure

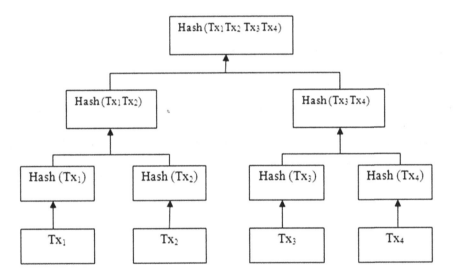

Smart Contracts

A smart contract, like a conventional program, but which executes automatically, in which the terms of a contract between two parties are directly sequenced as system. These contracts enable participants to form trustworthy transactions and negotiations without the need for a centralized authority or an external mechanism. Simple "if/when...then" phrases that are typed into code and placed on a blockchain. A network of computers performs its essential tasks if certain conditions are met or verified. After the transaction is completed, the distributed ledger is updated with the transactions. This indicates that the transaction is finalized and that only participants to whom privilege has been granted can view the transaction.

MAIN FOCUS OF THE CHAPTER

This section discusses industry-specific security and privacy issues as well as the importance of blockchain technology in this generation of industry digitization.

Cyber Security and Privacy Issues and Challenges in Industry 4.0

With its considerable reliance on the Internet and other technologies, Industry 4.0 appears to be a milestone in rapid industrialization. Industry 4.0 is confronted with several difficulties, obstacles, and restrictions that extend beyond the use of new technology and touch on economic and social issues as well. Technical challenges - For enhance the administration and activities of manufacturing environments, Industry 4.0 makes utilization emerging technologies like IoT. Because of the extensive usage of the web and the adoption of new technologies at industry 4.0, there are now more operational challenges and significant issues needs to be address (Aoun et al., 2021). Large volume of data generated by industries like production or instrument design, installation, and control mechanisms, etc. Networks must adjust to an IoT and Big data environment to handle this enormous volume of data. Data security for industry 4.0 is an issue to be addressed, just like it is for every other application in the technology era. Economic challenges - High cost are the second biggest and most important industrial obstacles to the implementation of Industry 4.0 processes. The transition to Industry 4.0 will need a significant commitment of economic resources, which could slow down the process and raise questions about return and profit.

Research by the authors (Mentsiev et al., 2020) was presented to explore numerous industry 4.0-related cybersecurity challenges. Lack of IT/OT Security Expertise - This security issue results from the fact that individuals working on the manufacturing process frequently lack knowledge of the security precautions that must be considered and individuals working on the secure step of the production process. Lack of Policies and Funds - This has been case from the absence or lack of organization - wide guidelines and procedures that guarantee that privacy and security. Lack of Uniform Standardization - In contrast to IoT and certain other emerging applications, Industry 4.0 security has few or no guidelines that are currently available. Technical Constraints of the Devices - Almost majority of these gadgets, whether they are being produced utilizing outdated methods or become currently in use, possess technical limitations that pose several cyber threats. In a review paper, Pereira et al. (2017) found that Industry 4.0's modern and integrated business requirements make it a little more susceptible to computer security. Particularly with regard to programming and functionality that are still extremely simple to replicate. To protect highly valuable data assets, a security strategy to be taken into consideration combines DDoS protection tools with cryptographic algorithms. Supply chain systems contain built-in known vulnerabilities that adversaries take advantage of it. One of the security flaws begins also with provider, who might be targeted by phishing scams and have their protected identities hijacked.

Hajda et al. (2021) employed the security measures used in Industry 4.0 PLC system. Despite the sophisticated technologies that support computer networks, effective cyberattacks frequently are caused by human error. Since internal employees' familiarity and understanding of the manufacturing process, intentional data breaches induced by them are significantly more damaging and difficult to stop against industrial automation. A distinction between proactive and reactive system components can be recognized in network system. Since passive devices often transmit signals without being processed, they don't provide a danger. Active gadgets that are directly connected to the plant's intellectual architecture are the ones most susceptible to hacking attempts. The PLC controllers do not possess any privacy and authentication process, due to the above reason the entire network is susceptible to attacks. PLC contains memory; therefore, a possible attacker may access any connected device and insert a malware into the network. Increasingly interconnected technologies have more vulnerabilities than conventional networks, according to a work published by the researcher Dawson (2018). Researchers are considering new approaches to addressing cybersecurity issues considering recent threats to national infrastructure and electronic criminality. Assume that some goods pass proper inspections, and that the food business uses the wrong amounts of certain nutrients. In such circumstances, equipment interference at an industrial facility may make a whole nation ill.

One of the cornerstones of Industry 4.0 is the IIoT, and the author (Jhanjhi et al., 2021) have highlighted potential cybersecurity risk, associated effects, and mitigation of IIoT. The researchers designed a complete framework based on an investigation of the cybersecurity and privacy challenges in the IIoT. Direct physical assaults are clearly targeted at IIoT's sensing and controller layer. The DoS attack may be conducted through modifying the physical link, disturbance, and blocking, whereas the insufficient verification and improper installation. The authors' perspective is that MITM and DoS are the two primary vulnerabilities that target the network layer. DoS attacks, data extraction, and privilege execution are all directed at the service layer. The possible solution for avoiding service layer attack includes frequent risk assessment and avoiding suspicious communications.

Blockchain Technology Applications for Industry 4.0

This technology enables businesses to test their sense of trust in addition to confidence and innovation. The electronics, cosmetics, and fashion industries are affected by copying their originality, which blockchain can show to be quite beneficial in preventing across all supply-chain segments (Javaid et.al, 2021). The major usage of blockchain in industry sectors are Finance sector, Manufacturing and data production, Product identification and assemblies, information and security, digital purchasing, supply-chain, etc. Currently, the banking and payments industry tends to influence the adoption of blockchain. In data production sector, the blockchain's encryption method can prevent unauthorized access to transferred data, control intellectual assets used to certify copyright, and record licensing rights. In the automobile industry, a variety of activities, partner organizations, procurement data, and other information can all be digitally recorded. In supply chain, businesses are now able to follow a product's history all the way from its starting point to its present location using blockchain technology. In information and security, all data are digitally preserved in blockchain along with how products are made and how they start their journey to market. In contrast to traditional approaches, blockchain secures digital data by utilizing greatest cryptographic algorithms. In actuality, the consensus technique is applied by members in a smart contract as the foundation of BCT. As a result, to maintain the integrity of the blockchain, smart contracts are connected via a hash function. Furthermore, maintaining the data integrity and being able to identify any fraudulent alterations are both possible when utilizing a hash function between the various blocks. Alternatively, integrating a MongoDB with a blockchain network could also impose the security method. Increasing the number of cryptographic approaches protects against different secrecy risks and cyberattacks (Boubecar et al., 2020).

The current IoT food manufacturing sector needs to digitise materials from sources to the complete food manufacturing sector. Blockchain in the IoT can enhance the visibility and life cycle of commodities, particularly traceability in the food manufacturing process. In healthcare sector, due to limited resources, healthcare presents new obstacles for current services. The likelihood of encouraging remote healthcare facilities is increased by recent advancements in wearable medical technology. But still, integrating medical data brings concerns about security, privacy, and confidentiality. To secure patient privacy and ensure the security of their medical records, healthcare networks can successfully be integrated into blockchains. The confidentiality of transaction logs maintained in blockchains is protected by several features built into blockchain technologies. For example, Bitcoin transactions are made with Mac addresses rather than the real identities of the users, ensuring personal identity (Kumar et al., 2022). An eco-industrial park model that fosters resource sharing, material recycling and reuse, and commodity exchange among organizations and neighborhoods has considerable environmental and societal benefits. But there are several technological and economical obstacles to progress. One of the major issues with developing EIPs is a lack of trust, followed by privacy-related and data security issues. By incorporating blockchain technology into EIP development, it becomes difficult or impossible to change or delete a ledger log, protecting transactions and communication (Termizi et al., 2022). The supply chain management is important to people's lives. Agriculture and traditional food supply systems only concern themselves with placing orders and delivering them to their destinations. These systems frequently suffer from single points of failure, data security challenges, and a lack of transparency. It can be efficiently solved via blockchain systems. This system allows to develop decentralized trustful architecture. The accessibility, confidentiality, and privacy of transaction data as well as the organizational information privacy should all be handled by a public supply chain system (Bodkhe et al., 2020).

SOLUTIONS AND RECOMMENDATIONS

This part describes how blockchain will benefit the manufacturing, healthcare, and supply chain industries.

Benefits and Challenges of Blockchain Technology Implementation for Industry 4.0 Application

In its simplest form, Industry 4.0 refers to the adoption of technology to accelerate and improve the production process. Blockchain does, in fact, have a lot to offer in this regard. It increases manufacturing process integrity to a new degree and contributes to the development of a protected and immediate communication. In the context of supply chain management, blockchain offers the safe storing of enormous amounts of data, easily accessible, and great protection. Industry 4.0 CPS must include distributed trust building rather than giving the trust authority to a single entity. A blockchain-based strategy ensures security by providing a certificateless, multiple-signature access control mechanism. This multiple signature system eliminates the single point of failure, protects data against fraudulent activity, and increases confidence. The private or Consortium Blockchain infrastructure transparently verifies and keeps track of device registration. It provides protection from malfunctions by reducing the influence of potentially harmful nodes. Consensus techniques require advanced computing infrastructure and use a lot of electricity. Therefore, creating more effective consensus mechanism remains a difficult task (Rahman et al., 2021).

Blockchain technology allows for the efficient sharing of crucial patient information within the healthcare industry. Instead of storing health information directly, this technology is used to store the addresses of mobile devices and sensor information. The health information collected by these sensors may now be accessed securely utilizing a blockchain-based approach. Over the last few years, there have been significant changes in the power sector. Blockchain technology as a mechanism could speed up by reducing the cost of transactions and running the grid more economically. In addition to being more efficient, immutability characteristics of blockchains makes them important for security and privacy in the power sector. An agriculture sector relies on multiple outside conditions, like the temperature, the quality of the crops, and complicated supply systems, etc. The agricultural sector is made more transparent and identifiable due to blockchain technology (Alladi et al., 2019). With the adoption of IIoT technologies, the industrial sector has entered a new development stage of evolution. For protecting data exchanges in a smart manufacturing system, blockchain offers a solution based on a consensus mechanism. The challenge is, since each manufacturer might implement in several different blockchains, their smooth integration must be standardized and interoperable.

Blockchain technology and smart contracts can be used to create a decentralized Machine to Machine industrial applications. Smart contracts can assist in tracking machine-to-machine interactions, simplifying the traceability of operations as well as resources, and enabling a detailed history of the manufacturing process. Such details are kept in the smart contract for accounting or control purposes. With the option of authenticating content, security and consistency can be increased while forgery risk can be reduced. Blockchain holds opportunity to build modern infrastructure. however, it will continue to come across certain difficulties. Its adaptability could be a key difficulty (Celio et al., 2020). The acquiring, analyzing, and transfer of sensitive data items have grown heavily necessary on the expanding IoT-driven smart devices industry and the impact of risk considerations. The blockchain-based technique generates an initial key using a cryptographic function determined by the number of existing nodes, the cluster head, and the participation. When the initial key and the certificate are combined for authentication, the authorized third party will produce and validate the certificate. A master key is required to execute subsequent processes, but it cannot be obtained if the first key and certificate are not generated. This blockchain-based system is created to prevent snoopers from penetrating the sensitive industrial environment and listening in on communications (Sodhro et al., 2020).

The benefits of blockchain technology on industry 4.0 have so far been covered in this chapter. There have been several difficulties that must be considered while integrating blockchain on industry 4.0 are discussed in this section (Lee et al., 2019). Implementation cost- Consider the expenses of implementation and deployment, as well as the cost of replacing existing infrastructure. Storage Capacity - Massive volumes of data will be produced during the manufacturing operation. The current blockchain architecture cannot store a large amount of data, and the existing blockchain protocols generate a significant amount of congestion. Lack of Knowledge and Infrastructure - Current industrial IoT applications are using security procedures that call for centralized management, which makes the installation of blockchains more complicated. Legal and Compliance Issues - Since many manufacturers, exchange of data about the sector can be a sensitive matter.

This section concludes that blockchain technology is designed with strong encryption that makes it difficult for hackers to gain access to sensitive data. This makes it an ideal technology for Industry 4.0 applications, where data security is paramount. It allows for a transparent and immutable record of transactions, making it easier to track and trace products throughout the supply chain. This can drastically reduce product counterfeiting, which is a major problem for many industries. The distributed ledger technology used in blockchain can make transactions and processes more efficient, reducing time and cost associated with manual processes. Also, it has some limitations too. Implementing This technology can be expensive, making it difficult for smaller companies to take advantage of the technology. The technology is complex and can be difficult for non-technical users to understand and use. There is a limited pool of experts with the skills and knowledge necessary to develop and implement blockchain technology.

FUTURE RESEARCH DIRECTIONS

In-depth information about industry 4.0 and blockchain technology is presented in this chapter. The incorporation of blockchain offers several advantages for improving manufacturing sectors and protecting from cybersecurity threats. However, there have been a few challenges that must be considered while implementing blockchain. This industry offers a wide range of research opportunities. A significant amount of data will be produced by industry sectors. In relation to it, the current consensus protocol is insufficient to manage such large amount of information without congestion. Industry-focused research should also be addressed to overcoming this kind of problem if blockchain technology is to be fully utilized and adaptable.

CONCLUSION

In-depth information on Industry 4.0, blockchain deployment into Industry 4.0, and blockchain technology's opportunities to solve cyber security threats are all provided in this chapter. Industrial revolutions mark revolutionary times that allow for new production processes. Developing the next generation of intelligent industrial systems would be another objective. As a result, Industry 4.0 as a phenomenon might be represented as a technological revolution which incorporates wide range of technologies to develop the manufacturing of the future. It is possible to transform things and machines smarter so they can connect with and learn from one another with the support of new technologies adoption, sensors, and transmissions. One of the key elements of Industry 4.0 is digitization, which enables for business to gain from efficiency in all sectors. And because of being an essential element of industry 4.0 and performing an important function, vulnerabilities are a risk for the IIoT. The IIoT is built on the IoT, inductors, and connectors as well as the cyber-physical system. As part of Industry 4.0, blockchain technology integration is now being introduced. Blockchain's feature makes it simple to share digital design data that is protected by copyright, improving the accuracy and consistency of the production process. However, the interconnectedness, deployment, and connectivity between such wireless devices may also be subject to different cyber threats. Also, it might be quite difficult to send protected information to the desired location. Using timestamps, public audits, and consensus procedures, data is always kept in blockchain technology in an immutable manner. By utilizing these procedures in industry 4.0 security architecture is strengthened and data integrity and privacy are guaranteed.

REFERENCES

Abdelmajied, F. Y. (2022). Industry 4.0 and Its Implications: Concept, Opportunities, and Future Directions. In T. Bányai, Á. Bányai, & I. Kaczmar (Eds.), *Supply Chain - Recent Advances and New Perspectives in the Industry 4.0 Era*. IntechOpen. doi:10.5772/intechopen.102520

Ahmad Termizi, S. N. A., Wan Alwi, S. R., Manan, Z. A., & Varbanov, P. S. (2022). Potential Application of Blockchain Technology in Eco-Industrial Park Development. *Sustainability (Basel)*, *15*(1), 52. doi:10.3390u15010052

Alladi, T., Chamola, V., Parizi, R. M., & Choo, K. K. R. (2019). Blockchain Applications for Industry 4.0 and Industrial IoT: A Review. *IEEE Access : Practical Innovations, Open Solutions*, *7*, 176935–176951. doi:10.1109/ACCESS.2019.2956748

Aoun, A., Ilinca, A., Ghandour, M., & Ibrahim, H. (2021). A review of Industry 4.0 characteristics and challenges, with potential improvements using Blockchain technology. *Computers & Industrial Engineering*, *162*, 107746. Advance online publication. doi:10.1016/j.cie.2021.107746

Bianco, D., Bueno, A., Filho, M., Latan, H., Ganga, G., Frank, A., & Jabbour, C. (2022). The role of Industry 4.0 in developing resilience for manufacturing companies during COVID-19. *International Journal of Production Economics*, *256*, 108728. doi:10.1016/j.ijpe.2022.108728

Binbusayyis & Vaiyapuri. (2022). *A professional-driven blockchain framework for sharing E-Portfolio in the context of Industry 4.0*. ICT Express. doi:10.1016/j.icte.2022.03.010

Bodkhe, U., Tanwar, S., Parekh, K., Khanpara, P., Tyagi, S., Kumar, N., & Alazab, M. (2020). Blockchain for Industry 4.0: A Comprehensive Review. *IEEE Access : Practical Innovations, Open Solutions*, *8*, 79764–79800. doi:10.1109/ACCESS.2020.2988579

Boubecar, S. (2020). A Survey on the Usage of Blockchain Technology for Cyber-Threats in the Context of Industry 4.0. *Sustainability (Basel)*, *12*(21), 19. doi:10.3390u12219179

Dawson, M. (2018). Cyber Security in Industry 4.0: The Pitfalls of Having Hyperconnected Systems. *Journal of Strategic Management Studies*, *10*(1), 19–28.

Ferreira, & Rabelo, Silva, & Cavalcanti. (2020). *Blockchain for Machine-to-Machine Interaction in Industry 4.0*. . doi:10.1007/978-981-15-1137-0_5

Fu, X., Wang, H., & Shi, P. (2021). A survey of Blockchain consensus algorithms: Mechanism, design and applications. *Science China. Information Sciences*, *64*(2), 121101. doi:10.100711432-019-2790-1

Guo, H., & Yu, X. (2022). A Survey on Blockchain Technology and its security. Blockchain. *Research and Applications.*, *3*(2), 100067. doi:10.1016/j.bcra.2022.100067

Hajda, J., Jakuszewski, R., & Ogonowski, S. (2021). Security Challenges in Industry 4.0 PLC Systems. *Applied Sciences (Basel, Switzerland)*, *11*(21), 9785. doi:10.3390/app11219785

Javaid, M., Haleem, A., Singh, R., Khan, S., & Suman, R. (2021). Blockchain technology applications for Industry 4.0: A literature-based review. Blockchain. *Research and Applications.*, *2*(4), 100027. doi:10.1016/j.bcra.2021.100027

Jhanjhi, N., Humayun, M., & Almuayqil, S. N. (2021). Cyber security and privacy issues in industrial internet of things. *Computer Systems Science and Engineering*, *37*(3), 361–380. doi:10.32604/csse.2021.015206

Lakshmana Kumar, R. (2022). A Survey on blockchain for industrial Internet of Things. *Alexandria Engineering Journal, 61*(8), 6001–6022. doi:10.1016/j.aej.2021.11.023

Lee, J., Azamfar, M., & Singh, J. (2019). A Blockchain Enabled Cyber-Physical System Architecture for Industry 4.0 Manufacturing Systems. *Manufacturing Letters, 20,* 34–39. doi:10.1016/j.mfglet.2019.05.003

Lin, C., He, D., Huang, X., Choo, K.-K. R., & Vasilakos, A. V. (2018). BSeIn: A blockchain-based secure mutual authentication with fine-grained access control system for industry 4.0. *Journal of Network and Computer Applications, 116,* 42–52. doi:10.1016/j.jnca.2018.05.005

Lu, H., Huang, K., Azimi, M., & Guo, L. (2019). Blockchain Technology in the Oil and Gas Industry: A Review of Applications, Opportunities, Challenges, and Risks. *IEEE Access : Practical Innovations, Open Solutions, 7,* 41426–41444. doi:10.1109/ACCESS.2019.2907695

Mahajan, H. B., Rashid, A. S., & Junnarkar, A. A. (2022). Integration of Healthcare 4.0 and blockchain into secure cloud-based electronic health records systems. *Applied Nanoscience.* Advance online publication. doi:10.100713204-021-02164-0 PMID:35136707

Mehami, J., Nawi, M., & Zhong, R. (2018). Smart automated guided vehicles for manufacturing in the context of Industry 4.0. *Procedia Manufacturing, 26,* 1077–1086. doi:10.1016/j.promfg.2018.07.144

Mehta, D., Tanwar, S., Bodkhe, U., Shukla, A., & Kumar, N. (2021). Blockchain-based Royalty Contract Transactions Scheme for Industry 4.0 Supply-Chain Management. *Information Processing & Management, 58*(4), 102586. Advance online publication. doi:10.1016/j.ipm.2021.102586

Mentsiev, A., Guzueva, E., & Magomaev, T. (2020). Security challenges of the Industry 4.0. *Journal of Physics: Conference Series, 1515*(3), 032074. doi:10.1088/1742-6596/1515/3/032074

Mullet, V., Sondi, P., & Ramat, E. (2022). A blockchain-based confidentiality-preserving approach to traceability in Industry 4.0. *International Journal of Advanced Manufacturing Technology.* Advance online publication. doi:10.100700170-022-10431-9

Nakamoto, S. (2009). *Bitcoin: A Peer-to-Peer Electronic Cash System.* https://metzdowd.com

Pal, K. (2021). Privacy, Security and Policies: A Review of Problems and Solutions with Blockchain-Based Internet of Things Applications in Manufacturing Industry. *Procedia Computer Science, 191,* 176–183. doi:10.1016/j.procs.2021.07.022

Pereira, T., Barreto, L., & Amaral, A. (2017). Network and information security challenges within Industry 4.0 paradigm. *Procedia Manufacturing, 13,* 1253–1260. doi:10.1016/j.promfg.2017.09.047

Rahman, Z., Khalil, I., Yi, X., & Atiquzzaman, M. (2021). Blockchain-Based Security Framework for a Critical Industry 4.0 Cyber-Physical System. *IEEE Communications Magazine, 59*(5), 128–134. doi:10.1109/MCOM.001.2000679

Rathee, G., Balasaraswathi, M., Chandran, K. P., Gupta, S. D., & Boopathi, C. S. (2021). A secure IoT sensors communication in industry 4.0 using blockchain technology. *Journal of Ambient Intelligence and Humanized Computing, 12*(1), 533–545. Advance online publication. doi:10.100712652-020-02017-8

Sasikumar, R., Karthikeyan, P., & Thangavel, M. (2021). *Blockchain Technology for IoT: An Information Security Perspective.* . doi:10.4018/978-1-7998-5839-3.ch008

Sodhro, A. H., Pirbhulal, S., Muzammal, M., & Zongwei, L. (2020). Towards Blockchain-Enabled Security Technique for Industrial Internet of Things Based Decentralized Applications. *Journal of Grid Computing, 18*(4), 615–628. doi:10.100710723-020-09527-x

Sula, E. (2018). A review of Network Layer and Transport Layer Attacks on Wireless Networks. *International Journal of Modern Engineering Research, 08*(12), 23–27.

KEY TERMS AND DEFINITIONS

Consensus Algorithm: Making decisions about a group of activities.
Cyber Physical System: Integrate computing, networking, and physical components.
Cyber Security: Technique of securing critical infrastructure and sensitive information.
Immutability: The transactions of blockchain are consistent, unaltered, and unmodifiable.
Industrial Internet of Things: Use of smart sensors and actuators to enhance manufacturing.
Industry 4.0: Digital industrial that allow for automation and real-time decision making.
Smart Contract: Software that will run when certain conditions are met.
Smart Manufacturing: Increasing production efficiencies using cutting-edge technologies.

Chapter 17
Securing Advanced Metering Infrastructure Using Blockchain for Energy Trade

Yuvraj Singh
VIT Bhopal University, India

Subhash Chandra Patel
VIT Bhopal University, India

Jyoti Chauhan
VIT Bhopal University, India

ABSTRACT

To effectively regulate the energy supply, advanced metering infrastructure (AMI) deployment is gaining momentum in various parts of the world. Energy distributors, service providers, and consumers must work together to address several issues. All the transactions need to be documented properly and securely. Third parties can be trusted in those transactions by using blockchain. With the deployment of advanced metering infrastructure (AMI) and distributed ledgers, blockchain may aid in safeguarding and facilitating the movement of data. This chapter discusses the viability of utilizing blockchain for advanced metering infrastructure and the security risks and threat landscape.

INTRODUCTION

"If it's smart, it's vulnerable", they say. This study discusses the viability of utilizing blockchain for advanced metering infrastructure and electronic devices that transmit information such as power use, pricing, and advanced metering that serve as the point of contact between homeowners and Distribution System Operators (DSOs). Since it may affect the transaction and billing information, secure communication between the two parties is crucial.

DOI: 10.4018/978-1-6684-8145-5.ch017

Copyright © 2023, IGI Global. Copying or distributing in print or electronic forms without written permission of IGI Global is prohibited.

Smart grids play a vital role in creating and implementing the digital paradise, just as we are on the verge of creating smart cities. The smart grids may be thought of as the basis for the same since smart homes, buildings, streets, and other places include intelligent gadgets that require real-time monitoring and scheduling of power use.

The main purpose of smart meters is to report real-time use, sending the recorded data to the smart grid at frequent intervals. The extra capabilities also include a smart interface to manage electricity consumption in home appliances during peak hours and the ability to analyze usage trends and disconnect customers from electricity usage directly from the smart grid when a problem arises. Many securities may affect this setup like Distributed Denial of Service (DDoS) attacks, Man in the Middle (MITM) attacks, adjusting/altering invoices, stealing payment information, etc. Blockchain technology can be used to address these problems and to have secure and trusted financial transactions.

Blockchain helps to make transactions comprehensive and safe. It is not just restricted to crypto-currency and is being employed in the majority of other sectors as well. Among Distributed Energy Resources (DER) transactions, the demand for blockchain implementation is very high as it facilitates peer-to-peer energy exchanges at microgrids. By monitoring energy consumption, load balancing, and demand-supply at negotiated prices, the distribution system operators enable the sale of excess produced energy to electric cars without the intervention of distributed system operators. With many different applications Blockchain, one such application lays the way for a sustainable environment and a digitally driven society by including an automated smart metering system. It takes into consideration how much energy is used by home appliances to secure Blockchain for producing power use and transparent bill creation. American company Bankymoons was the first to integrate Blockchain technology into a smart grid's smart metering system.

The full implementation of peer-to-peer technology is still fraught with difficulties, but it allows for a secure flow of transactions between Smart Meters and DSOs through the distributed trust that is built up among peers using cryptographic techniques, which ultimately takes care of security attacks like eavesdropping, data tampering, and unauthorized access to data. In this study, we suggest a blockchain based on Ethereum to improve the security of transactions between SMEs and DSOs.

LITERATURE WORKS

Blockchain saves transactions in blocks and through a timestamp and interconnected hash links, each block in Blockchain is linked to the one before it. Hash values ensure that no data or value is ever updated by an unauthorized person. Blockchain is a distributed ledger with no single point of failure since all parties adhere to the no-trust policy. Data is completely decentralized, with no involvement from outside parties. A chain of the ledger made up of several blocks is known as a blockchain. Because no individual block can be changed without also changing the entire chain of blocks, systems are protected from attacks and may carry out transactions in a secure manner without the intervention of a third-party Figure 1. The blockchain serves as a public ledger for all transactions that take place when entities participate in digital activities. The act of mining is known as the creation of new blocks, and a method known as consensus helps the user ensure the reliability and integrity of blocks. A network of linked nodes may be used to create blockchain-enabled systems, and several computer languages are already being utilized to create blockchains (Tama, 2017).

In 2015, the blockchain-based system, Ethereum launched the first smart contracts. Additionally, it offers an interactive environment for creating and deploying smart contracts written in a Turing-complete programming language for the user-defined deployment of robust, effective, and smart contracts. The ability to evaluate the account's current balance, save the address in 20 bytes, and execute it are only a few of its numerous benefits. Ethereum has its cryptocurrency, called ether. Smart contracts and other autonomous agents are utilized for inter-account transactions. To provide a run environment, smart contract prototypes created for smart grids are executed on the EVM (Environment Virtual Machine). New nodes are verified by using the entire nodes that EVM has produced. In Ethereum, blocks are generated every 15 seconds. Gas is used as a transaction charge to stop attacks. The product of gas usage and gas price is the definition of a transaction in Ethereum. Gas consumption can be improved as every transaction uses 5 USD for buyers and sellers. There is a need to develop a more reliant smart contract that might serve the demands and specifications of bidders and auctioneers more generally (Omar, 2021).

Figure 1. Chain of blocks

Hyperledger is a private, permissioned blockchain that was created and is now maintained by the Linux Foundation. It was first implemented as a private network for users to monitor their transactions and communicate with their digital assets. One of the main characteristics of the programming languages known as chain codes that are used on the Hyperledger network is support for distributed applications (Androulaki, 2018). It doesn't have many highly qualified programmers. Additionally, it has failed to provide any use cases. Its architecture is intricate. It has the bare minimum of SDKs and APIs also It is not a fault-tolerant network (Cachin, 2016).

The design makes use of particular elements including ordering, peer, and endorsing nodes as well as client applications. Peers are a type of component that is not restricted to any one particular node; they can act as a committer for certain tasks and an endorser for others for some time. They carry out tasks that are not all that dissimilar from those carried out by miners in other blockchain architectures.

Hash functions might be held accountable for ensuring the robustness and security of blockchain in that instance, however even these hash functions could be compromised by some superfast machines, such as supercomputers or quantum computers. To overcome these challenges consensus algorithms were introduced in the blockchain. Some of the primary consensus algorithms are:

Proof of Work (PoW): As an illustration of a cryptocurrency system protected by a proof of work mechanism, think of Bitcoin. In Bitcoin, each block consists of two components:

- block headers with important characteristics, such as the time the block was created and a reference to the preceding block, and the block of transactions' Merkle tree root
- List of transactions in a block

The SHA-256 algorithm (NIST) is used to hash a block twice, and the resultant integer value is used to reference a specific block $[0, 2^{256} -1]$. With a variable number of inputs and a range of $[0, M]$, the generic hashing function hash () is used to cater to various implementation possibilities.

A single parameter that may be supplied to the SHA-256 hashing function, for instance, can be created by treating the function's inputs as binary strings and merging them all together.

The proof of work protocol makes use of the block reference, which must fall below a particular value for a block to be deemed valid:

$$hash(B) \leq \frac{M}{D} \tag{1}$$

When the intended difficulty is $D \in [1,M]$. There is no other known technique to discover B satisfactory. Continually going over each and every variable in the block header. The greater D value, the to identify a valid block, further iterations are required; the anticipated number of operations is D. The amount of time $T(r)$ required for a miner with equipment that can do r operations per second to $\frac{r}{D}$ is an exponential distribution that describes how to discover a valid block

$$PT(r) \leq t = 1 - exp\frac{rt}{D} \tag{2}$$

Consider n Bitcoin miners with hash rate $r_1, r_2, r_3, \ldots, r_n$. The period of time to find a block T is equal to the minimum value of random variables $T(ri)$ assuming that the miner publishes a found block and It instantly reaches other miners. T is also distributed exponentially in accordance with the characteristics of the exponential distribution:

$$P\{T_{min}(T_1, \ldots, T_n) \leq t\} = 1 - exp\left(\frac{-t}{D} \Sigma_{i=1}^{n} r_j\right); \tag{3}$$

$$P\{T = T_i\} = \frac{r_i}{\Sigma_{i=1}^{n} r_j}$$

The final equation demonstrates that mining is equitable: a miner with a share of mining power p has the same probability of solving a block before other miners with probability *p*. It can be demonstrated that Bitcoin's proof of work meets Conditions 1-3.

Proof of Stake (PoS): Proof of stake algorithms change inequality such that it now depends on the user's possession of the specific coin used with the PoS protocol rather than block attributes.

Think about a user with the addresses A and *bal*(A). An approach for proof of stake that is widely utilized employs a condition as

$$hash\left(hash\left(B_{prev}\right),A,t\right) \le Bal\left(A\right)\frac{M}{D} \tag{4}$$

Where,

- B_{prev} shows the block that the user is currently constructing on,
- *t* is the present timestamp in UTC.

Some cryptocurrencies employ modified versions which we describe in the respective sections, for a variety of reasons.

In contrast (Negris, 1993), the timestamp *t* in the left portion of the equation is the only variable that the user may modify equation (4). The protocol locks the address balance; for instance, the protocol may compute the balance using money that hasn't moved in a day. A PoS cryptocurrency can also operate similarly to Bitcoin by using unspent transaction outputs; in this scenario, the balance is frozen by default. The range of feasible values for *t* is constrained by a proof of stake procedure. A user may try no more than 7200 different choices of t, for instance, if t must not deviate from the UTC time on network nodes by more than an hour. Therefore, proof of stake does not need any expensive calculations.

Block search time for address A has an exponential distribution with rate $bal\left(\dfrac{A}{D}\right)$. As a result, the (4) proof of stake implementation is fair: the likelihood of generating a valid block is proportional to the user's balance of funds and the entire quantity of money in circulation. For the whole network, the time to locate a block is spread exponentially with the rate, $\sum_{bal(d)}^{a} D$. So, if the currency's money supply $\sum_{bal(d)}^{a} D$ is fixed or increases at a predictable rate, the difficulty D must be known beforehand:

$$D = \frac{1}{T_{ex}} \Sigma_a^{bal(a)} \tag{5}$$

with T_{ex} representing the anticipated interval between blocks. Since not all currency owners take part in block minting, *D* must be modified in practice based on recent blocks.

Delegated Proof of Stake (DPoS): "Delegated proof of stake (DPoS) is a generic term describing an evolution of the basic PoS consensus protocols." DPoS is utilized in BitShares, as are other proposed algorithms such as Slasher and Tendermint. In these protocols, blocks are minted by a a predetermined set of users of the system (delegates), who are rewarded for their duty and punished for malicious behavior. Delegates for each block are selected based on stake and blockchain history.

Each participant in the blockchain network casts a vote to choose the delegates who will create blocks. Distributed voting is the foundation of the main concept. Out of the N witnesses chosen, 50% of the stakeholders support decentralization. The data will be included in the following block if the witness is unable to produce a new block, new stakeholder voting will produce a new witness to take the place of the failed witness. Compared to PoS and PoW, this algorithm promises to be more effective and efficient.

Practical Byzantine Fault Tolerance (PBFT): Depending on the technique, 2/3 of the network's nodes must vote in favor of the transaction being included in the next block to be considered legitimate. This approach is often employed in semi-trusted or trusted settings. Hyperledger makes use of the PBFT algorithm. Given that its complexity has been brought down to a polynomial level, it is the most effective and improved method. Byzantine fault-tolerant algorithms will be increasingly important in the future because malicious attacks and software errors are increasingly common and can cause faulty nodes to exhibit arbitrary behavior. Whereas previous algorithms assumed a synchronous system or were too slow to be used in practice, the algorithm described in this paper is applicable: it works in asynchronous environments such as the Internet and incorporates several important optimizations that improve the response time of previous algorithms by an order of magnitude (Andoni, 2019). It comprised five steps, which are:

- The item master node is requested by the client for the collection of timestamps.
- The master node records requests and sends a "per-prepare" message to the server nodes.
- Message of prepare is accepted by server nodes and broadcasted to other nodes.
- The item request message is executed by nodes and sends a commit message. Item client nodes receive a reply from server nodes.

The authors developed a framework for a quantum-secured, permissioned blockchain called Logicontract as a crucial protective measure against this threat (LC). To reach a consensus on the blockchain, LC uses a digital signature system based on Quantum Key Distribution (QKD) methods and a vote-based consensus algorithm. The main contribution of his paper is the creation of (1) a quantum- resistant lottery protocol that demonstrates the utility and use of LC; (2) a scalable consensus protocol used by LC; (3) a logic-based scripting language for the creation of smart contracts on LC; and (4) an unconditionally secure signature scheme for LC that makes it immune to the attack of quantum computers. The programming language with logic-based syntax has certain well-known drawbacks. For instance, it might be challenging to predict how much resources would cost and how long a smart the contract will take to execute. It is necessary to create a more robust smart contract formalism that is similar to Ethereum so that smart contracts on LC can do practically all distributed computing jobs (Sun, 2019).

BLOCKCHAIN IN ENERGY SECTOR

To develop smart energy, a self-maintaining, self-rectifying, robust, and decentralized system is needed.

With improvements in several technologies, the blockchain timeline is illustrated in Figure 2.

A variety of technologies have been combined to create blockchain technology. Blockchain was built on the principles of distributed computing, which were initially discussed in 1982. With the publication of his white paper "Blockchain: A Peer-to-Peer Electronic Cash System" in 2008, Satoshi Nakamoto introduced the first project. Since then, a variety of blockchain technologies have been created, but the real-world use of blockchain only began with the introduction of smart contracts in 2013. Even at that time, a dependable and adaptable platform was still required, so the Linux Foundation introduced.

Figure 2. Timeline of blockchain

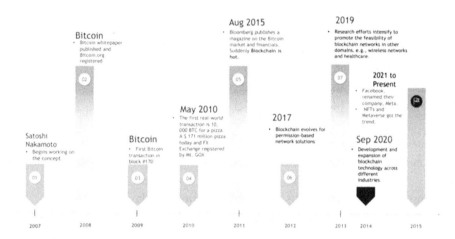

Hyperledger in 2015 to address this issue. Since then, the energy sector has been utilizing blockchain to transform the existing grid infrastructure into intelligent grids.

Blockchain is now seen as a useful technology by an increasing number of companies, independent of bitcoin and other cryptocurrencies. Nevertheless, every year from 2016 to the present has its highs and lows.

2016

- ◦ The word blockchain gained acceptance as a single word, rather than being treated as two concepts, as they were in Nakamoto's original paper.
- ◦ The Chamber of Digital Commerce and the Hyperledger project announced a partnership to strengthen industry advocacy and education.
- ◦ A bug in the Ethereum decentralized autonomous organization code was exploited, resulting in a hard fork of the Ethereum network.
- ◦ The Bitfinex bitcoin exchange was hacked and nearly 120,000 bitcoins were stolen -- a bounty worth approximately $66 million.

2017

- ◦ Bitcoin hit a record high of nearly $20,000.
- ◦ Japan recognized bitcoin as a legal currency.
- ◦ Seven European banks formed the Digital Trade Chain consortium to develop a trade finance platform based on blockchain.

- ○ The Block.one company introduced the EOS blockchain operating system, designed to support commercial decentralized applications.
- ○ Approximately 15% of global banks used blockchain technology in some capacity.

2018

- ○ Bitcoin turned 10 this year.
- ○ Bitcoin's value continued to drop, ending the year at about $3,800.
- ○ The online payment firm Stripe stopped accepting bitcoin payments.
- ○ Google, Twitter, and Facebook banned cryptocurrency advertising.
- ○ South Korea banned anonymous cryptocurrency trading but announced it would invest millions in blockchain initiatives.
- ○ The European Commission launched the Blockchain Observatory and Forum.
- ○ Baidu introduced its blockchain-as-a-service platform.

2019

- ○ Walmart launched a supply chain system based on the Hyperledger platform.
- ○ Amazon announced the general availability of its Amazon Managed Blockchain service on AWS.
- ○ Ethereum network transactions exceeded 1 million per day.
- ○ Blockchain research and development took center stage as organizations embraced blockchain technology and decentralized applications for a variety of use cases.

2020

- ○ Nearly 40% of respondents incorporated blockchain into production, and 55% viewed blockchain as a top strategic priority, according to Deloitte's 2020 Global Blockchain Survey.
- ○ Ethereum launched the Beacon Chain in preparation for Ethereum 2.0.
- ○ Stablecoins saw a significant rise because they promised more stability than traditional cyber currencies.
- ○ There was a growing interest in combining blockchain with AI to optimize business processes.

Over the course of these five years, interest in adopting blockchain for purposes other than cryptocurrencies has grown. As governments and businesses turn to blockchain to address a range of use cases, this trend will continue beyond 2021. This includes the right to vote, real estate, fitness monitoring, intellectual property rights, the internet of things, and the provision of vaccines. Additionally, several cloud providers now provide blockchain as a service, and there is a bigger than ever need for competent blockchain developers.

Utility businesses and decision-makers in the energy sector have claimed that blockchain technology may be able to address some of the problems facing the sector. Blockchain technologies, according to the German Energy Agency, have the potential to boost the effectiveness of current energy practices and procedures. They can also hasten the development of IoT platforms and digital applications and bring about innovation in P2P energy trading and decentralized generation. Additionally, they claim that through enhancing internal procedures, customer services, and prices, blockchain technology can greatly enhance the present practices of energy businesses and utility firms (Burger, 2016).

As distributed energy resources and information and communication technology evolve, energy systems are going through a radical upheaval (ICT). The decentralized and digitization of the energy system, which is a major problem, necessitates the examination, development, and use of innovative paradigms and distributed technologies. Blockchains may offer a potential way to manage and operate complex energy systems including microgrids. A new analysis from Eurelectric claims that the actual transfer of power has prevented wider use of blockchain technology in the energy sector thus far. (Koyunouglu, 2019; Mylrea, 2017; Mustafa, 2016).

Updating network resilience and ensuring supply security are major challenges as RES usage keeps growing. Blockchains might increase network resilience and supply security by simplifying and speeding IoT applications and enabling more effective flexibility markets. In research, the Research Institute of the Finnish Economy makes the case that by providing open and transparent solutions, blockchains might guarantee interoperability in smart grid and IoT applications. Energy market operations may become more open and effective, according to Deloitte. As a result, this may enhance competition, encourage customer mobility, and make it easier to transfer energy providers. If cost-saving potential materializes, we may use technology to address fuel poverty and concerns with energy affordability (Mattila, 2016; Municipality, 2021).

Figure 3. Advanced metering infrastructure architecture

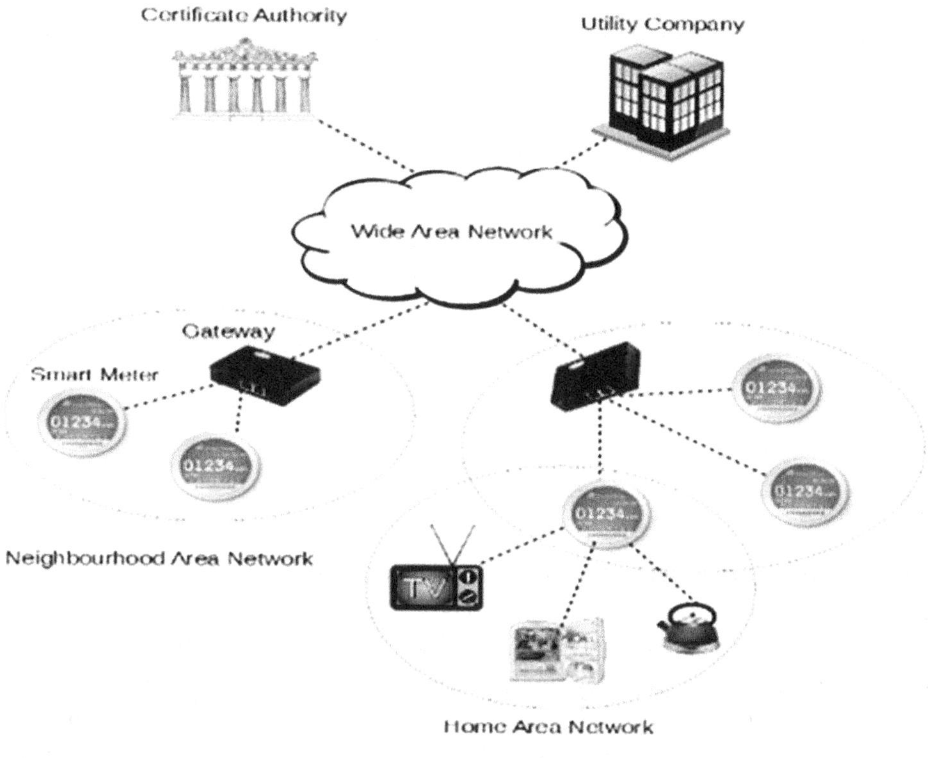

ADVANCED METERING INFRASTRUCTURE OVERVIEW

An AMI is a system that sits in the middle of the utility and user domains. Power pricing and demand-side management are its two key objectives. SMs, DCs, and the central system are the three primary types of components that make up an AMI architecture. These parts are connected by bidirectional communication networks.

Advanced Metering Infrastructure Components

Due to its sophisticated features, an SM is also referred to as a next-generation meter. An SM's primary function is to gather information about an end user's power usage from their location.

Two components make up an SM: (1) A meter keeps track of the energy the consumer uses. The DC receives these meter values. (2) Computing components carry out pre-programmed functions such as remote connection and disconnection, firmware upgrade, tamper and theft detection and prevention, and so on (Cebe, 2018; Shokry, 2022; Gulisano, 2014).

Figure 4. Mind map illustrating the overall structure of the article and its key sections. In addition, the figure highlights the core elements and the sub-sections

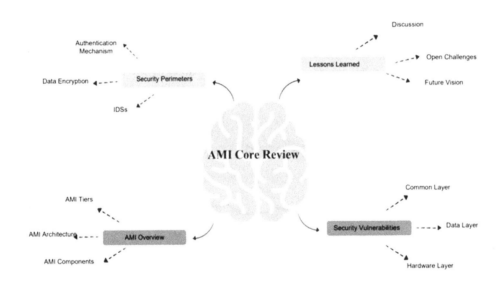

A DC, also known as a smart meter gateway or a data aggregator, has several definitions (Komogortsev, 2015). There are several definitions, but they all serve the same purpose in UCs, which is to serve as an intermediary device between the SM and the data center. A DC carries out two primary tasks: transmitting orders to SMs from the UC and relaying data from SMs to the UC (Ghasempour, 2016)

The data center of a UC. It is often found within the utility company's major buildings. A UC's primary functions include gathering data from SMs, instructing SMs via the DC to carry out certain duties, and monitoring various parts of the SG, including the quantity of power generated, transmission lines, and distribution centers (Khattak, 2019). In an AMI, communication networks are crucial. They are in charge of establishing connections between all of an AMI's major parts, including the UC, DCs, and SMs.

Data is sent from SMs to DCs and subsequently to the UC via bidirectional communication channels. Commands are also sent from the UC to the SMs using these channels. Although the communication methods utilized in an AMI vary greatly, they may typically be divided into two categories: wired and wireless. Due to the volume and sensitivity of the data exchanged across the channel, choosing the appropriate communication mechanism is crucial for AMI's protection (Bae, 2016; Ismail, 2014; Ibrahem, 2021).

Advanced Metering Infrastructure Architecture

An AMI can be implemented using a variety of designs based on the components and communication technologies employed. The major goal of the AMI is to convey data from SMs to DCs, which are subsequently forwarded to the UC over a bidirectional communication channel. This means that the architecture must achieve this goal. AMI architecture may be divided into two basic categories: direct and indirect. Without a DC, a direct architecture connects an SM to the UC through a communication network that may be cable or wireless. The ease of implementation is a benefit of direct architecture. When there are few users and not a lot of data, this form of design is suitable for a limited region.

An indirect architecture would be employed when there are more users and data since a direct design is no longer the best option. Between the SMs and the UC, an intermediate exists in an indirect architecture. The cloud might serve as the middleman, allowing the data to be sent via the internet to the UC. Alternatively, there are DCs between the SMs and the UC in an aggregator-based design (Avancini, 2019; Gungor, 2012).

Figure 5. Advanced metering infrastructure layers

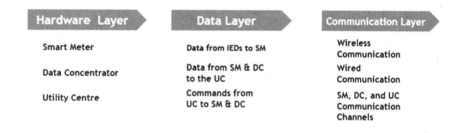

Advanced Metering Infrastructure Tier

The NAN, which can link to several HANs, is the second AMI layer or stage in the AMI architecture. A DC, which obtains information from SMs via the HANs, is the primary element of a NAN. The communication system must be able to transport a large volume of data more securely since a NAN has more consumers than a HAN and its data size is larger. As a result, power line communication systems, optical fibers, and cellular networks (LTE/2G-3G systems) are employed (Popovic, 2022).

The WAN, which links all of the HANs and NANs with the UC, is the final stage in the AMI. The meter data management system is connected to the WAN; it gathers, stores, and analyses the data before sending orders or actions back to the NAN and ultimately onto the HAN. A wired connection is preferable because it can transport the gathered data more quickly and securely over the great distance between the NANs and the UC, which may be in a different city. To connect HANs to NANs and finally NANs to WAN, power line communications are frequently employed (Yan, 2017).

ADVANCED METERING INFRASTRUCTURE VULNERABILITIES

An AMI is a service that the UC offers to the client. Its goal is to improve the customer's power service as well as the SG's performance. Utilizing three characteristics, referred to as the CIA triad—confidentiality, integrity, and availability—the security level and therefore the stability of this service are evaluated (Ghasempour, 2016).

Confidentiality is the first of them, which indicates that only authorized people will be able to access the data and that it won't be shared with anyone else. Only the customer and the UC have access to sensitive data, which includes things like power usage and a client's personal information. The data must not be altered during transmission from the source to the destination, which is the second critical factor. Any alteration would compromise the service's integrity, whether it is related to information sent from the SM to the UC or the other way around. The proportion of time a steady service is offered to the consumer can be used to determine the service's availability. The integration of ICT into conventional power grids has presented new security challenges for such SGs. The AMI, which is a significant part of an SG, as we saw in the previous sections, is made up of several devices. The majority of these components, including the SMs and DCs, are located outside the UC, making them susceptible to both physical and digital assaults (Gopstein, 2021).

Hardware Layer Vulnerabilities

In an AMI system, the hardware layer is made up of both the SMs and the DCs. An SM outside of the UC has several risks due to its nature. Additionally, as we previously explained, a UC can command an SM by sending commands across a bidirectional channel to the device. The UC can connect or disengage an SM using one of these instructions, remote disconnect. This functionality is necessary, but it also leaves the SM open to assault from someone pretending to be the UC. This command can be sent by the attacker to several SMs, which could result in a Denial of Service (DoS) attack.

Table 1. Security vulnerabilities in the AMI hardware layer

AMI Component	Vulnerabilities	Attack	Direct Impact	General Impact
SM	Bidirectional communications between the SM and the customer and between the SM and the UC.	The attacker impersonates a UC and sends malicious code to SMs.	SMs shut down.	Widespread denial of power.
SM	Lack of resources in SM	The attacker performs a buffer overflow attack.	Instability in the operation of the SM.	Localized denial of power.
SM	Customer interference	The attacker sends malicious code to affect the firmware of the SM or the data stored in the SM.	SM shuts down.	Localized denial of power or data theft.
SM	Ability to log on to the SM via a web application	SQL injection, DoS, or DDoS.	Stop the SM.	Localized denial of power.

Since numerous SMs are connected to the UC through a single DC, these attacks against the SM may also be made against a DC, but they may have a greater effect, particularly if the AMI has an indirect or mesh topology design. A DC attack can have an impact on several SMs, resulting in the simultaneous localized denial of power to multiple SMs or the data theft of all customers linked to the hacked DC.

The numerous attacks that may be made against an AMI system are listed in Table 3. Every attack type impacts at least one of confidentiality, integrity, and availability, hence this must be taken into account while designing the AMI. The integrity of the system is impacted by any alteration to the data or apps that are used by the AMI.

The confidentiality and integrity of consumer data are impacted by attacks that compromise such data. Confidentiality, integrity, and availability are all impacted by attacks that break the SM or DC owing to a firmware update.

Communication Layer Vulnerabilities

As previously mentioned, IEDs are connected to SMs within the HAN, SMs to DCs within the NAN, and DCs to UCs inside the WAN through communication channels. As a result, they are the component of the AMI system that is most susceptible to threats and assaults owing to the significance and volume of data sent over the communication channels.

HANs and NANs utilize wireless communication, making the networks vulnerable to attacks on wireless communication channels such as man-in-the-middle (MITM) attacks.

The relationships between the AMI communication layer vulnerabilities, the attacks that take advantage of them, and the effects on the AMI system's performance and parameters are listed in Table 4. Due to their great distance from one another, using wireless transmission media between SMs and DCs poses the most risk to an AMI communication layer. Common threats like session hijacking, MITM, and communication channel failure, which can result in data leakage or fraud, can affect wireless communications.

Table 2. AMI data layer vulnerabilities

Vulnerabilities	Attack	Direct Impact	General Impact
Direct connection between the customer and the SM	The customer makes a fraudulent claim for energy consumption.	Data loss or modification.	High energy losses and compromised privacy of customer usage data.
Remote updating of firmware and direct connection between the customer and the SM.	Firmware manipulation.	Data modification.	SM and DC shut down, leading to a localized denial of power.
Customer interference with SM.	Injection of false data.	Data modification.	The attacker controls the SM and compromises estimates of the power system state.
Remote connection to SM and DC using the IP in the AMI system.	DoS attack.	Denial of data transfer	Localized and widespread denial of power.
Lack of security configuration in the utility data center.	Data manipulation by an internal attacker.	Data fabrication.	Affect the integrity of or steal data

Table 3. Possible security threats and their impacts on an AMI

Threat	Compromised AMI Service	Vulnerabilities	Impact: Integrity (I), Availability (A), Confidentiality (C)
Tamper with application services at AMI nodes	Integrity	Management applications and services remain exposed and available to all nodes.	Disruption of the communication flow due to the rerouting of all traffic to the attacker's node for later manipulation. (I)
Masquerade as the control center.	Integrity & Confidentiality	Lack of authentication or encryption.	Impersonation of the control center to send unauthorized commands to meters or read metering data. (I, C)
Bypass authentication in metering protocols.	Integrity & Confidentiality	Poor implementation of metering protocols.	Manipulation of reading parameters of SMs. (C, I)
Buffer overflow in the AMI meter's firmware	Integrity & Confidentiality	The firmware makes assumptions regarding the data it receives, particularly the size of each message format.	The system becomes unstable or freezes. Parameter values in the memory stack are changed. Arbitrary code is executed. (C, I)
Firmware manipulation	Integrity, Availability, & Confidentiality.	Firmware architecture with poor access controls	An attacker executes a disconnect action and then makes the meter completely unresponsive till it is returned to the manufacturer, thus making it impossible for the network operator to reverse their actions. (C, I, A)

Table 4. Security vulnerabilities in the AMI communication layer

Vulnerabilities	Attack	Direct Impact	General Impact
Wireless communication technology is used.	Firmware update of the SM or DC.	A leak from communication media	Localized and widespread denial of power.
Wireless transmission media	Session hijacking.	A leak from security protocols in the transmission media.	Data theft or manipulation.
Inadequate wireless technology security.	MITM attack.	Failure of a communication channel.	Data theft or manipulation.
Interference with communication channels	Bandwidth loss.	Bandwidth congestion.	Data congestion or loss.

ADVANCED METERING INFRASTRUCTURE SECURITY PERIMETERS

To defend an AMI against an attack, countermeasures must be utilized. Each AMI component can be addressed using a different approach. Encryption and integrity checking for the data layer can protect the data exchanged between the key elements.

AMI components that are physically unprotected end devices and located beyond the boundaries of the energy utility must be kept secure from unwanted access. Additionally, as the AMI communication layer relies on wireless connections to transport data, the data are susceptible to tampering or access by an attacker. As a result, an IDS is the best option for an AMI as a second line of defense because it can find any security flaws in the system.

Communication technology flaws can be used by attackers. An attacker might disable the demand-supply balance and steal or alter consumer energy consumption statistics, for instance, by impersonating a well-known ID or introducing malicious code. In an AMI system, authentication is therefore a crucial mitigating strategy that must be used.

Data Encryption

An essential technique for protecting the data layer of an AMI system is encryption. It can protect the confidentiality of data being transported over the HAN, NAN, or WAN via the AMI. It can defend the AMI against assaults like data sniffing, data hijacking, and MITM.

A feasibility study on the integration of a fully homomorphic encryption (FHE) system with the wireless communication standard IEEE 802.11s was carried out by Tonyali, Saputro, and Akkaya.

They have a technique that can be applied to HAN data transfers. The NS-3 network simulator tool was utilized to research a range of situations. A straightforward node-to-node authentication technique based on electromagnetic signal intensity was presented by Parvez, Islam, and Kaleem. It uses two straightforward servers and two-level encryption without adding to the complexity associated with packet processing. The encryption of data exchanged between the SM and the UC is managed by one server (the master), while randomized data transfers are managed by the other server. Ibrahem et al. presented a monitoring and billing system with effective encryption that protects user privacy (PMBFE).

Hasan and Mouftah proposed SG AMI use a lightweight AMI data encryption solution. In order to safeguard customers' private information and facilitate real-time measurements of power use, Lee et al. presented a system with searchable and homomorphic encryption. A safe and private system based on proxy re-encryption operations and additive homomorphic encryption was proposed by Saxena, Choi, and Grijalva. In order to protect against identity and associated data theft threats, the suggested technique can aggregate metering data without disclosing the actual individual data (identification or energy use) to intermediary firms or any third party.

An authentication and key management system based on reconfigurable ROPUFs built on Xilinx Spartan-3E FPGA boards were suggested by Nath et al. An effective method for mutually authenticating an SM of a HAN and an authentication server in the UC by using a first password was proposed by Nicanfar et al. Based on a certificateless cryptosystem and PKI, Saxena, and Choi created a protocol that offers distributed and mutual authentication across communication organizations. The protocol has a cloud-trusted authority, is integrated, distributed, lightweight, and regulated centrally. For unicast, multicast, and broadcast communications in an AMI, George, Nithin, and Kottayil employed a hybrid encryption technique. It was suggested to use a key management system for hybrid communication channels.

Intrusion Detection Systems

An IDS is a potent tool for protecting an AMI system's data and communication layers from attackers who may otherwise take advantage of unidentified system flaws and cause disruptions. IDS of all stripes have been used to safeguard AMIs. An IDS architecture for an AMI that was installed in SMs, DCs, and the central system (the AMI head end) was proposed by Faisal et al. The criteria for the three components of the AMI were determined via data mining on the open KDD Cup 1999 dataset. This added to the research done by Faisal et al.

Using the KDD Cup 99 and NSL-KDD datasets as their foundation, Yao et al. suggested an AMI intrusion detection model based on the cross-layer feature fusion of convolutional neural networks (CNNs) and long short-term memory (LSTM). For an AMI architecture, Alseiari and Aung created a real-time distributed IDS that makes use of data stream mining in a multi-layer implementation.

An IDS was suggested by Vijayanand, Devaraj, and Kannapiran for the quick identification of dangers to an SG's AMI. To find assaults on an SG's NAN, this IDS uses a multi-SVM classifier with a mutual information-based feature selection approach. Huang suggested an extended regression neural network-based intrusion detection technique (GRNN). Its nonlinear mapping function is outstanding, and its convergence rate is high. The study's analysis and verification of the suggested technique utilized the open intrusion detection dataset NSL-KDD.

The tampering of firmware can be stopped using intrusion detection methods. Using deep learning, Jakaria, Rahman, and Hasan suggested a unique method to identify SMs that are providing false data based on user energy usage trends. They came up with a way to identify relay nodes in an AMI that could be manipulating data before sending it to an aggregator.

SECURING AMI USING BLOCKCHAIN

Blockchain technology could be used to improve the security and privacy of the power grid. The market design framework comprises seven essential elements for the effective functioning of microgrid energy markets based on blockchain technology. These elements include grid connection, information system, market mechanism, pricing mechanism, energy management trading system, and regulation. On an Ethereum network, a smart contract that is implemented defines the electricity market mechanism (Sabounchi, 2017).

SM-DSO INTERACTION IMPLEMENTATION WITH BLOCKCHAIN

With the use of smart meters, customers and DSOs may exchange information about generating, consumption, and energy costs in both directions. The adoption of smart metering infrastructure will be a turning point in the digital revolution of the energy industry. It mainly offers customers access to utilities, so they may consciously take part in real-time energy trading platforms that enable (Cusumano, 1998; Beaird, 2020) transparency in usage and pricing. The infrastructure for smart meters has various security flaws because of these benefits. If an attacker is successful in obtaining illegal access, it may result in complete access to and control of household equipment. Smart Meter sends the data of consumption in an interval of every 15 minutes and in, between that interval, an eavesdropper may access the channel and use the consumption data for malicious purposes (Wang, 57). The attacker can even perform slide attacks (Mbitiru, 2017). The attack's axis may stretch into other domains, like how an attacker may launch grayouts, blackouts, or even modify price details (Case, 2016).

Blockchain technology can be used to address the aforementioned security issues when trading energy between distributed system operators and smart meters (DSO). The blockchain's concatenation like characteristic makes it possible to connect block meters, each of which contains two hash meters for the current block and the other for the preceding block—helping to build a peer-to-peer trust model and guarantee data validity.

As per Figure 5, smart meters authorize the sale and trade of energy contracts with the auxiliary market. For instance, when smart meters submit a tacit request, the system operator replies with a signed copy of the contract. The advantages of using smart contracts for the exchange of energy between smart meters and DSOs are shown in Figure 5.

This data is added to the blockchain as soon as a smart contract between the two DSOs and the Smart meter is formed. A genuine and authorized node must be chosen to create and include a new block in the blockchain. In the presented work, the node for block validation is decided using the proof of stake (PoS) consensus technique.

It is assumed that Ancillary Market SC1, shown in Figure 5, and SM1 enter into a contract. Solc compiler version: "-solc:0.8.17+commit.9c3226ce.Emscripten.clang" was used to compile the contract. The produced bytes of code were installed on SM1, a blockchain node running on Ethereum. Now, SM1 is selected as the validator node after taking into account the consensus PoS process.

In the case shown in Figure 5, SM1 is identified as the authorized 3 nodes for node validation, meaning that it will determine whether to add additional blocks through PoS and then announce its decision to network peers. A copy of the newly created block is distributed to network peers when it is created and added to the system.

Figure 6. Energy trading contracts with ancillary market

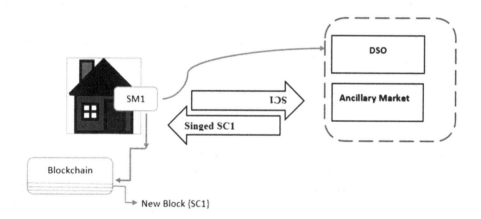

DISCUSSION

The security vulnerabilities to an AMI system are correspondingly rising with the rise of IoT devices like SMs and DCs. The UC receives a substantial quantity of data and information from AMI systems; hence it is critical that the UC be able to defend against many forms of attacks.

The hardware, communication, and data layers make up the three core levels of an AMI system. Each layer has unique traits and qualities and is susceptible to different kinds of attacks. For the hardware layer, since there are more SMs, there are also more attacks on them, such as malicious code injection to steal data or firmware modification to cause a localized DoS.

The major component of the AMI communication layer, the communication connections that bring the AMI components together, has vulnerabilities that may be used to launch attacks including traffic interspersion attacks, MITM attacks, and session hijacking attacks. The data that is exchanged across an AMI network is susceptible to theft, unlawful deletion, and tampering at the data layer.

The AMI data layer can use an encryption countermeasure approach to safeguard the data being sent. Traditional encryption methods require that the encrypted data be first decrypted before any computing operation is carried out. The data becomes vulnerable to both internal and external threats after it has been decrypted. Since computational operations may be conducted to the encrypted data without first having to decode them, homomorphic encryption can aid in protecting the privacy of data in an AMI system and enhancing its security.

The AMI data layer is a good candidate for this encryption method. It improves the safety of the data while it is being stored and transported. As it can recognize malicious behavior, an IDS may be employed as a second line of defense for an AMI communication layer to find outside attackers. In order to stop an attack once it has been discovered, an IPS is now combined with an IDS. Artificial intelligence (AI)-based intrusion prevention systems (IPSs) are crucial because they guarantee the cybersecurity standards of confidentiality, integrity, and availability (CIA). The agent module, analysis engine, and reaction module are the three basic components of an IPS. Analysis engines may be classified into three categories: signature-based, anomaly-based, and specification-based.

The possibility for malicious activity in an AMI system is compared to a specified set of signatures for various threats by a signature-based IPS. Using machine learning or a neural network, an anomaly-based intrusion detection, and prevention system may spot unusual activity in an AMI system. Systems for intrusion detection and prevention that are based on specifications use established policies to dictate how the AMI system should behave normally. There are unresolved difficulties for each tier of the AMI system that remain today and require significant research attention, despite all the potential security countermeasures discussed above and the mitigation procedures outlined in the literature.

FUTURE VISION

For an AMI to work better, several researchers have adapted new technologies, such as speeding up the information collection process. Additionally, modern methods like AI, big data analytics, blockchains, and cloud computing might improve the analysis of the vast amounts of data gathered from SM devices, which may be used to address some of the unresolved issues already described for each tier of an AMI system.

Blockchain

Distributed ledgers come in the form of blockchains. A blockchain may foster trust in an untrustworthy setting, making it a potent new weapon for cybersecurity. Multiple devices' transactions are included in the decentralized ledger. To guarantee data integrity, the data are encrypted and held by blockchain participants.

By decentralizing the administration, a blockchain may be utilized to safeguard the whole AMI system and the devices connected to it. With this method, no device is dependent on a single administrator or authority. By being able to recognize and respond to suspicious commands coming from an unfamiliar network, it increases the security of end devices like SMs.

The use of inadequate authentication and authorization protocols is an open challenge for the AMI hardware layer. Authentication and authorization are vital for safeguarding the main components of an AMI system from unauthorized access. Blockchain technology has recently been used for access control. A blockchain consists of records (blocks) recorded in a decentralized digital ledger, which stores transactions, in contrast to the tables in a relational database.

CONCLUSION

Blockchain technology is attracting interest due to its flexibility in distributed governance and system utilities' superior protection against attacks and data tampering. Blackouts might result from a successful attack on an SG that results in either a localized or broad denial of the power service. In order to provide novel methods for enhancing AMI security, more studies should be done on blockchains, big data analytics, cloud computing, and artificial intelligence (AI). This survey's complete coverage of AMI systems, including security flaws, assaults, and defenses, makes it relevant and distinctive. It exemplifies how the blockchain may be used by smart meters and DSOs. The Solidity platform is used to model smart meter transactions. Blockchain implementation is demonstrated with DSO over the Ethereum network. The experiments indicate that the proposed method can be implemented in DSOs and smart meters as it consumes less gas and provides more security, which opens new doors for future work on less gas consumption and more security. The effective implementation of blockchain for fully distributed peer-to-peer energy transactions can also be extended.

REFERENCES

Andoni, M. (2019). A review on consensus algorithm of blockchain. *Renewable & Sustainable Energy Reviews*, *100*, 143–174. doi:10.1016/j.rser.2018.10.014

Androulaki, E. a. (2018). Hyperledger fabric: a distributed operating system for permissioned blockchains. In *Proceedings of the thirteenth EuroSys conference* (pp. 1-15). 10.1145/3190508.3190538

Avancini, D. B.-M. (2019). Energy meters evolution in smart grids: A review. *Journal of Cleaner Production, 217*, 702-715.

Bae, M. a. (2016). Preserving privacy and efficiency in data communication and aggregation for AMI network. *Journal of Network and Computer Applications, 59*, 333-344.

Beaird, J. a. (2020). *The principles of beautiful web design*. Sitepoint.

Burger, C. a. (2016). *Blockchain in the energy transition. A survey among decision-makers in the German energy industry*. DENA German Energy Agency.

Cachin, C. a. (2016). Architecture of the hyperledger blockchain fabric. In *Workshop on distributed cryptocurrencies and consensus ledgers* (p. 310). Academic Press.

Case, D. U. (2016). Analysis of the cyber attack on the Ukrainian power grid. *Electricity Information Sharing and Analysis Center (E-ISAC), 388*, 1-29.

Cebe, M. a. (2018). Efficient Public-Key Revocation Management for Secure Smart Meter Communications Using One-Way Cryptographic Accumulators. In *2018 IEEE International Conference on Communications (ICC)* (pp. 1-6). IEEE. 10.1109/ICC.2018.8423023

Cusumano, M. A. (1998). Microsoft secrets: How the world's most powerful software company creates technology, shapes markets, and manages people. Simon and Schuster.

Ferreira, J. C. (2018). Building a community of users for open market energy. *Energies, 11*, 2330.

Ghasempour, A. (2016). *Optimizing the advanced metering infrastructure architecture in smart grid.* Utah State University.

Ghasempour, A. a. (2016). Finding the optimal number of aggregators in machine-to-machine advanced metering infrastructure architecture of smart grid based on cost, delay, and energy consumption. In 2016 13th IEEE Annual Consumer Communications \& Networking Conference (CCNC) (pp. 960-963). IEEE. doi:10.1109/CCNC.2016.7444917

Gopstein, A. a. (2021). *NIST framework and roadmap for smart grid interoperability standards, release 4.0. Department of Commerce.* National Institute of Standards and Technology. doi:10.6028/NIST.SP.1108r4

Gulisano, V. a. (2014). Metis: a two-tier intrusion detection system for advanced metering infrastructures. In *International Conference on Security and Privacy in Communication Networks* (pp. 51-68). Springer. 10.1145/2602044.2602072

Gungor, V. C. (2012). A survey on smart grid potential applications and communication requirements. *IEEE Transactions on industrial informatics, 9*, 28-42.

Ibrahem, M. I. (2021). Privacy Preserving and Efficient Data Collection Scheme for AMI Networks Using Deep Learning. *IEEE Internet of Things Journal, 8*, 17131-17146.

Ismail, Z. a. (2014). A game theoretical analysis of data confidentiality attacks on smart-grid AMI. *IEEE journal on selected areas in communications, 32*, 1486-1499.

Khattak, A. M. (2019). Smart meter security: Vulnerabilities, threat impacts, and countermeasures. In *International Conference on Ubiquitous Information Management and Communication* (pp. 554--562). Springer. 10.1007/978-3-030-19063-7_44

Komogortsev, O. V. (2015). Attack of mechanical replicas: Liveness detection with eye movements. *IEEE Transactions on Information Forensics and Security, 10*, 716-725.

Konashevych, O. (2016). *Advantages and current issues of blockchain use in microgrids. Электронное моделирование.*

Koyunouglu, A. S. (2019). Blockchain applications on smart grid A review. Kadir Has University.

Lee, S. a. (2014). A security mechanism of Smart Grid AMI network through smart device mutual authentication. In *The International Conference on Information Networking 2014 (ICOIN2014)* (pp. 592-595). IEEE.

Mattila, J. (2016). *The blockchain phenomenon--the disruptive potential of distributed consensus architectures.* ETLA Working Papers.

Mbitiru, R. a. (2017). Using input-output correlations and a modified slide attack to compromise IEC 62055-41. In *2017 IEEE International Autumn Meeting on Power, Electronics and Computing (ROPEC)* (pp. 1-6). IEEE. 10.1109/ROPEC.2017.8261692

Mengelkamp, E., Gärttner, J., Rock, K., Kessler, S., Orsini, L., & Weinhardt, C. (2018). Designing microgrid energy markets: A case study: The Brooklyn Microgrid. *Applied Energy, 210,* 870–880. doi:10.1016/j.apenergy.2017.06.054

Municipality, D. (2021). UOB-IEASMA-125: Experimental Analysis of Machine Learning Classification Algorithms. In First International IEASMA Conference on Engineering, Applied Sciences and Management (UOB-IEASMA 2021). Academic Press.

Mustafa, M. A. (2016). A local electricity trading market: Security analysis. In 2016 IEEE PES innovative smart grid technologies conference Europe (ISGT-Europe) (pp. 1-6). IEEE.

Mylrea, M. a. (2017). *Blockchain for smart grid resilience: Exchanging distributed energy at speed, scale and security. In 2017 Resilience Week.* RWS.

Mylrea, M. a. (2017). Cybersecurity and optimization in smart "autonomous" buildings. In *Autonomy and Artificial Intelligence: A Threat or Savior?* (pp. 263–294). Springer. doi:10.1007/978-3-319-59719-5_12

Negris, T. (1993). Thin client. In *Wikipedia.* en.wikipedia.org

NIST. (n.d.). SHA-1. In *Wikipedia.* en.wikipedia.org

Omar, I. A. (2021). Implementing decentralized auctions using blockchain smart contracts. *Technological Forecasting and Social Change, 168,* 120786.

Popovic, I. A. (2022). Multi-Agent Real-Time Advanced Metering Infrastructure Based on Fog Computing. *Energies, 15,* 373.

Sabounchi, M. a. (2017). Towards resilient networked microgrids: Blockchain-enabled peer-to-peer electricity trading mechanism. In *2017 IEEE Conference on Energy Internet and Energy System Integration (EI2)* (pp. 1-5). IEEE. 10.1109/EI2.2017.8245449

Shokry, M. a.-E. (2022). Systematic survey of advanced metering infrastructure security: Vulnerabilities, attacks, countermeasures, and future vision. *Future Generation Computer Systems.*

Sun, X. a. (2019). Towards quantum-secured permissioned blockchain: Signature, consensus, and logic. *Entropy, 21,* 287.

Tama, B. A.-H. (2017). A critical review of blockchain and its current applications. In *2017 International Conference on Electrical Engineering and Computer Science (ICECOS).* IEEE. 10.1109/ICECOS.2017.8167115

Troncia, M. a. (2019). Distributed ledger technologies for peer-to-peer local markets in distribution networks. *Energies, 17,* 3249.

Vangulick, D. a. (2018). Blockchain for peer-to-peer energy exchanges: design and recommendations. In 2018 Power Systems Computation Conference (PSCC) (pp. 1-7). IEEE. doi:10.23919/PSCC.2018.8443042

Wang, W. a. (2013). Cyber security in the smart grid: Survey and challenges. *Computer Networks,* 1344-1371.

Yan, L., Chang, Y., & Zhang, S. (2017). A lightweight authentication and key agreement scheme for smart grid. *International Journal of Distributed Sensor Networks, 13*(2), 13. doi:10.1177/1550147717694173

Yan, Y. a. (2013). An efficient security protocol for advanced metering infrastructure in smart grid. *IEEE Network, 27*, 64-71.

Chapter 18
Some Insights of Cyber Physical Systems in the Context of the Tourism and Travel Industry:
A Blockchain–Based Smart Framework for Smart Services

Hariharasitaraman S.
https://orcid.org/0000-0003-2411-6246
VIT Bhopal University, India

Rounak Yadav
VIT Bhopal University, India

Preksha Agrawal
VIT Bhopal University, India

ABSTRACT

Cyber-physical systems (CPS) facilitate the incorporation of humans, objects, and computing systems in their physical environment. These systems operate in real-time and are used to enable the systems and devices to self-organize and reconfigure to respond to their changing environments. They help to realize data-intensive interconnected platforms that allow data streams to run continuously on an autonomous basis. CPSs in the context of tourism and travel are considered important elements for developing efficient and effective smart tourism services. This research explores various facets of CPSs and proposes a blockchain-based framework to offer a smart tourism ecosystem, catering to the dynamic preferences and needs of the tourists. The key idea is to use a novel blockchain-based data security mechanism, which uses a set of policies to enforce data security for smart tourism services.

DOI: 10.4018/978-1-6684-8145-5.ch018

Copyright © 2023, IGI Global. Copying or distributing in print or electronic forms without written permission of IGI Global is prohibited.

1. INTRODUCTION

Cyber Physical Systems (CPS) refer to the integration of physical and digital components that work together in real-time to monitor and control physical processes (Kalluri et al., 2021). In recent years, CPS have gained a lot of attention for their potential to revolutionize various industries, including the tourism and travel industry. The tourism and travel industry is a rapidly growing sector, with billions of people traveling domestically and internationally each year. With the integration of CPS, this industry is poised to experience significant improvements in terms of efficiency, customer experience, and cost reduction. The rise of the Internet of Things (IoT) and Big Data has resulted in increased productivity and the appearance of new business models. The development of new cyber-physical systems that can be used in various industries is also helping to realize the potential of Industry 4.0 (Navickas et al., 2017).

The tourism and travel industry has a large number of physical processes, which includes activities such as guiding, transport, entertainment, shopping, and accommodations (Paraskevas 2022). Many of these processes depend on a large number of human components such as taxi drivers, tour guides, hotel receptionists, and travel agents. The integration of such human components into a digital system will help automate the aforementioned physical processes thereby significantly reducing human errors, increasing efficiency, and reducing costs (Pishdad-Bozorgi et al., 2020).

The future of the tourism and travel industry will greatly rely on the technological advances in the area of CPS. CPSs are being integrated as standard components in manufacturing and service activities. A recent McKinsey report identifies over $15 trillion in economic benefits that will be created as CPS are adopted by industry. In the context of the tourism industry, they hold significant promise for improving the customer experience by improving the safety and efficiency of processes and improving the reliability of services (Smirnov et al., 2017b). This is particularly important in the travel industry where a single incident could result in multiple millions of dollars of economic losses.

As the tourism and travel industry continues to embrace new technologies, their cyber ecosystems are becoming more vulnerable to security threats. These include the vast amount of data they store and the financial transactions they perform. Several prominent organizations in the travel and tourism industry have made headlines in the past couple of years for failing to address the increasing number of security threats (Palmer, 2017).

Recent studies provide insights on the nature of attacks targeting the hospitality industry and advocate the need to invest more efforts in the development of specific solutions. The most common attacks targeting hospitality include malware (Kishore et al., 2020), phishing (Hasbini,2016), denial of service (Cheema et al., 2022), and web-based application attacks (Singh et al., 2019). In addition to the above, cognitive hacking is another threat that the hospitality industry is highly vulnerable. It is a form of an Advanced Persistent Threat (APT) which exploits the human factor to achieve goals on a computer network. The term refers to automated tools that target human behavior, in an effort to exploit an individual's habits and predictability.

Despite the various security standards and solutions that have been proposed to improve the security of smart applications in the hospitality industry, the existing solutions are still not ideal. These include having a single point of failure or high communication and computation costs. Most of the security solutions currently available focus only on a few aspects of the security architecture and fail to address various factors such as network latency, scalability, and data storage (Subasinghe et al., 2020). Blockchain technology can provide better security solutions that overcome these problems and address the requirements of smart applications within the hospitality industry (Morkunas et al., 2019).

This chapter explores the role of blockchain in smart applications within the hospitality industry and suggests an eco-system based security architecture for the same. The benefits of having blockchain technology as an ecosystem include high level of security, efficient communication, improved scalability, reduced latency, automated data collection, and data storage, reduced overheads and costs of cyber security, better data confidentiality, and improved data integrity. This paper proposes a framework called Block Chain based Security Framework for Smart Tourism (BC-SFST) eco-system addressing the above requirements.

The contributions of this research are as below.

1. Deep insights on existing blockchain models in the hospitality industry are provided to understand their characteristics
2. The need for a new secure eco-system is explored to secure smart applications within the hospitality industry
3. A security architecture framework for leveraging blockchain in smart applications within the hospitality industry is proposed, which could also be applicable to other industry verticals.

Rest of this chapter is organized as below. Section 2 presents a detailed review of literature in the context of this research. The requirements of a block chain based eco-system for smart tourism applications are described in Section 3. The requirements of a blockchain ecosystem are presented in Section 4 and the proposed framework is descried in detail in Section 5. The applications of the proposed framework are discussed in Section 6 and the chapter is concluded in Section 7.

2. RELATED WORKS

The use of blockchain technology reduces the risk of network attacks and single point of failure. It allows users to maintain their information in an immutable manner across the network, and it eliminates manual processes such as reconciliation between various administrative and ledger tasks. Due to the use of various linked chains, the level of security and transaction speed of blockchain technology have significantly increased. A number of studies have been conducted by researchers on this technology for Industry 4.0 applications and a comprehensive review is presented by Bodkhe et al. (2020).

Mettler (2016) talks about how blockchain technology has revolutionized healthcare, and presents various open challenges and research gaps. Yli-Huumo (2016) and colleagues have reviewed the current state of blockchain technology, while Ahram and colleagues highlight its immutability and resistance to attacks.

Weiss et al. (2017) discussed the various aspects of blockchain applications for public healthcare. They also talked about its decentralized architecture and how it eliminates the need for a central authority. They additionally analyzed the metrics of such applications. Zhang et al (2017) analyzed the various metrics of decentralized applications and discussed the security and evolution challenges encountered in IoT, smart agriculture and tourism & hospitality industries.

Krieger et al. (2017) explored the various advantages and limitations of blockchain technology for electronic health record systems and discussed the regulatory compliance issues that affect its privacy and security. Duan et al. (2017) explored the various educational applications of blockchain technology. In this paper, they presented a framework that allows an evaluation software to create graduation marks and certificates. They talked about how various components of blockchain technology are used in the verification of transactions, such as blocks, digital signatures, and the Merkle hash tree.

Several companies, such as Expedia, One Shot Hotels, and CheapAir, have already started using blockchain technology for their various operations, such as making payments and booking travel accommodations. With the potential to revolutionize the tourism industry, digital currencies can be integrated with smart contracts.

The potential of blockchain technology to transform the tourism industry is immense due to its ability to create trust and improve the efficiency of the travel-related transactions. It can also help promote the development of new loyalty programs and improve the quality of online travel reviews as evident from the investigations of Rejeb and Karim (2019).

The paper by Pérez-Sánchez et al. (2021) proposed a blockchain based loyalty programme for the tourism industry. It discusses how to create value and build loyalty among customers by using the technology. In this paper, the authors used the blockchain technology to track the transactions in order to create value and build loyalty among customers through various functions such as the tracking of the transactions and the payment functions.

Similarly, the paper by Petrović et al. (2021) proposed a loyalty programme for the travel industry. It was built to monitor the transaction records of the customers and reward the customers on meeting the set criteria in order to enhance the loyalty and the retention of customers. In this paper, the authors have proposed the blockchain to track the transactions of the customers for recording the transaction and making it available in a real-time manner. Similarly, the paper by Ramos (2021) proposed a blockchain technology based tourism management system to maintain the tourism-related records of the customers in order to store the relevant and important information of customers and their preferences for future purposes. The aim of this paper was to facilitate the travel industry by using blockchain technology for tourism data storage and travel experiences.

The use of blockchain technology can help solve various issues related to sustainable tourism. However, there are still many challenges that prevent the implementation of this technology in the tourism industry. A study by Erol et al. (2022) aims to identify these issues through a combination of expert opinions and literature review. The findings of this study were analyzed using a combination of expert opinions and a proposed cross-impact matrix multiplication procedure. It revealed that the lack of interoperability and technical maturity are the most common challenges that prevent the implementation of blockchain technology in the tourism industry.

Blockchain technology can help improve the efficiency and transparency of the integrated system by continuously updating and verifying the information related to various services, such as hotel reservations, car rentals, and airplane tickets (Irannezhad & Mahadevan, 2021). It can also help prevent unauthorized access to the system. The ability to distribute fast and accurate information within the system can help make it easier for people to purchase health insurance.

According to Treiblmaier (2021), blockchain technology will play a central role in the operations of the tourism and hospitality industry in 2021. Its application and innovation are expected to have a huge impact on the industry. However, despite its positive effects, blockchain technology still has a long way to go before it can fully benefit the tourism industry. Due to the complexity of the tourism industry, it is important that various aspects of the blockchain technology are understood and analyzed properly.

The concept of smart cities has gained widespread popularity over the past decade. It has led to the emergence of the Smart Tourism Destination (STD) concept (Tyan et al., 2021). These areas are expected to benefit from the use of ICTs to develop sustainable tourism projects. According to previous studies, various forms of Information and Communications Technologies (ICTs) such as the IoT, cloud computing, and the end-user Internet service system are vital for developing smart tourism destinations.

The technology known as Metaverse (Buhalis et al., 2023) is likely to impact society in the next couple of decades. It enables users to experience both physical and digital worlds through a seamless journey. With digital immersion, users will have the opportunity to travel back in time and experience dangerous and ancient events, such as the eruption of volcanoes. It is an innovative platform that aims to transform the way tourism is marketed and managed. It enables brands and agencies to connect with consumers through digital twins, and it allows them to create and manage effective marketing and promotional campaigns.

Integration of block chain with new technologies evolving in the hospitality industry can potentially unlock new revenue opportunities. One of the primary use case for blockchain in hospitality is digital tokenization of loyalty points and rewards systems (Chen & Tham, 2023). The most well-known companies in this space are Travelport and Worldspan. Travelport's blockchain-based program allows hotels, airlines and retailers to exchange loyalty points between them and offer instant redeemable tickets to frequent flyers using distributed ledger technology. Worldspan offers a blockchain-based loyalty and rewards program called blockchain loyalty to hotels and travel agencies. Blockchain loyalty rewards can be redeemed against hotel stays or against online travel agency bookings.

Despite the increasing number of studies on blockchain technology, the practical implementation in retail is still in its early stages. A study by Dwivedi et al. (2023) aims to identify the factors that prevent retailers from adopting blockchain. The study was conducted using the innovation resistance theory and the dynamic capabilities model. This investigation was conducted on 360 retailers and utilized a single cross-section design. The data collected during the study was analyzed using a structural equation modeling procedure. The results revealed that the biggest factor that prevents retailers from adopting blockchain technology is the ownership of data. The results also indicated that managerial and innovation capabilities can influence the resistance factors that prevent retailers from adopting blockchain.

This research identifies the need for building a security based eco-system to deploy the fullest potential of blockchains in the tourism and travel industry.

3. BACKGROUND

This section presents the basic concepts of blockchain technology for a comprehensive understanding of blockchain enable models and their capabilities.

3.1. Basic Components of Blockchain Networks

Blockchain is a decentralized, distributed ledger that records transactions across multiple nodes. The basic components of a blockchain network include:

1. **Nodes:** Participants in the network who hold a copy of the blockchain ledger and validate transactions.
2. **Blocks:** A collection of transactions that are grouped together and added to the chain.
3. **Cryptographic Hash Functions:** A mathematical function that converts an input into a fixed-size string of characters, used to secure the integrity of the blockchain.

4. **Consensus Algorithm:** A process used by nodes to reach agreement on the current state of the blockchain, ensuring that all nodes have the same information.
5. **Token or Coin:** A unit of value used in the blockchain network, often used to incentivize nodes to participate in the network and validate transactions.
6. **Smart Contracts:** A self-executing program with the terms of the agreement between buyer and seller, directly written into lines of code.

These components work together to form a secure and transparent system for recording transactions and maintaining a consistent state across all nodes in the network.

3.2. Types of Blockchain Networks

Blockchain networks are classified into public and private based on the type of access to its network. In a public network, all users are granted access and anyone can access and view the blockchain. In this type of network, there is a need for consensus because, in its absence the integrity of the blockchain will not be assured. In public blockchain, the nodes in the network have the task of validating and verifying the transaction. For this reason, nodes in a public blockchain are usually paid in order to perform this task. However, there is a need for users to purchase the access using tokens in the case of private blockchain. In order to access the network, the user must first purchase a digital token. As a result of this, in private Blockchain transactions are private and do not require other entities to verify them.

The security of blockchains is different between the private and public types. The former uses computers connected to the internet to create transactions and add blocks to the ledger, while the latter only allows certain organizations to join. Because of this, businesses may not be ideal when it comes to protecting the confidentiality of their data.

3.3. Blockchain Network Structure

The term blockchain refers to a group of blocks, each composed of a body and a header as shown in Figure 1. The header contains information about a particular block, while the body holds the data related to that block. The blockchain is a ledger that records all of the transactions that happen on it, and it is the central pillar of any type of financial transaction. Its decentralized infrastructure ensures that the transactions are tracked and resolved efficiently. The header of a block contains its metadata and the Merkle Root data structure. The current block's hash is derived from the previous block's hash, which serves as a secure connection between the two.

Transactions are carried out through the body of the block, which is structured as a set of records. The number of records per block is specified as a parameter, and each block records the block height and a timestamp. The transactions are also identified with unique IDs in their headers. A blockchain is maintained as a unique and immutable ledger that keeps all of the transactions that have ever happened in a given blockchain in a tamper-proof manner. Since each record can be referred to by other records, the database is able to resolve conflicts, keep the records secure, and trace transactions. In addition to the transactions, the blockchain also includes smart contracts which use programming logic to facilitate contractual agreements that exist on the blockchain. The use of smart contracts enables the application to operate without needing human involvement.

Figure 1. Blockchain network

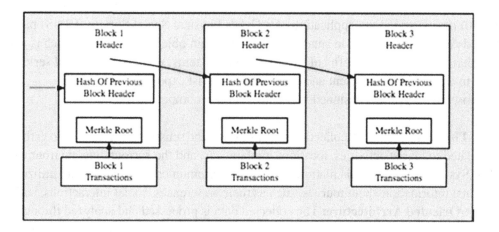

4. CASE STUDIES

This section presents three important case studies on the application of CPS in tourism and travel.

4.1. Infomobility-Based Tourism

Smirnov et al. (2017a) explored the integration of CPSs and context-aware information services to enhance tourist experiences. The proposed framework aims to provide personalized, real-time information for tourists by leveraging the power of IoT devices, sensor networks, and CPS.

The framework consists of four main components:

1. **Context model:** A semantic model representing the tourist's context, which includes preferences, current activities, location, and other relevant factors.
2. **IoT-Based Monitoring System:** A network of IoT devices and sensors responsible for collecting and processing data related to the tourist's context, such as weather, traffic conditions, and local events.
3. **CPS-Based Reasoning Mechanism:** A decision-making module that utilizes context data and predefined knowledge to generate personalized recommendations and services tailored to the tourist's needs and preferences.
4. **Information Service:** A communication layer that delivers personalized information to the tourist through various channels, such as mobile applications or wearable devices.

The authors evaluate the effectiveness of the proposed cyber-physical infomobility framework through a case study involving the creation of a personalized sightseeing tour for a tourist in St. Petersburg, Russia. The case study demonstrates how the system can adapt tour recommendations based on real-time data from IoT devices and sensors, considering factors such as the tourist's interests, time constraints, weather conditions, and traffic information.

4.2. Service Oriented Architecture for Tourism

Ashari (2020) demonstrated the application of a Cyber Physical Social System (CPSS) based on Service Oriented Architecture (SOA) in smart tourism. The main objective of this research is to develop a framework that combines the benefits of cyber-physical systems, social systems, and service-oriented architecture to create a more efficient and personalized tourist experience.

The proposed framework is designed with the following components:

1. **Cyber-Physical Systems:** A collection of IoT devices and sensors are integrated to gather real-time data related to tourist activities, locations, preferences, and the surrounding environment.
2. **Social Systems:** Social media platforms and other communication channels are utilized to collect additional information about tourists, such as their preferences, social interactions, and reviews.
3. **Service-Oriented Architecture:** The collected data is processed and analyzed through a service-oriented architecture, which enables the development of modular and reusable software components for various tourism services.

The case study focuses on the implementation of the CPSS-SOA framework in a smart tourism context. It is demonstrated how the system effectively collects and processes data from various sources, such as IoT devices, sensors, and social media platforms, to provide personalized recommendations and services to tourists. The integration of SOA allows for the flexible and scalable development of tourism services, which can be easily adapted to meet the changing needs and preferences of tourists. The results of the case study indicate that the CPSS-SOA framework can significantly improve the overall tourist experience by providing more accurate and timely information, as well as personalized recommendations and services.

4.3. CPS in Connected Car-Based E-Tourism

Smirnov et al. (2017b) have also explored the application of a CPS in the context of connected car-based e-tourism. The primary objective of this research is to develop a framework that combines the strengths of CPSs, human-computer interaction, and connected car technologies to provide a more efficient and personalized travel experience. The proposed framework consists of the following components:

1. **CPS:** A network of IoT devices, sensors, and connected cars is used to collect real-time data related to the tourists' location, route, and surrounding environment.
2. **Human-Computer Interaction:** An adaptive user interface is developed to facilitate effective communication between the tourists and the CPH system, enabling the provision of personalized recommendations and services.
3. **Connected Car Technologies:** Connected car technologies are integrated to provide a seamless and dynamic travel experience, with features such as route optimization, automatic booking of tourist attractions, and real-time traffic information.

The case study focuses on the implementation of the CPH framework in a connected car-based e-tourism scenario. It is demonstrated how the system effectively collects and processes data from various sources, including IoT devices, sensors, and connected cars, to offer personalized recommendations and services to tourists. The integration of human-computer interaction and connected car technologies allows for a more user-friendly and dynamic travel experience, catering to the individual needs and preferences of tourists.

5. REQUIREMENTS OF BLOCKCHAIN ECO-SYSTEM FOR SMART TOURISM

Industry 4.0 has led to the evolution of Tourism 4.0 which aims to be an integral part of the digital revolution. Tourism 4.0 is centered around smart tourism, digital tourism, cloud, big data, IoT, Service 4.0, smart cities and block chaining. There are three limitations related to security aspects of using CPSs in the tourism and travel industry:

1. **Cybersecurity Risks:** As CPSs are composed of a network of physical and digital devices, they are vulnerable to cyber-attacks such as data breaches, hacking, and malware infections. With sensitive customer data and financial transactions being processed within the tourism and travel industry, cybersecurity is a significant concern. The risk of cyber-attacks can result in significant reputational damage, loss of business, and financial losses.
2. **Privacy Concerns:** The collection and sharing of personal data are necessary for the proper functioning of CPS. However, this poses privacy risks to individuals who may not be aware of the information that is being collected or how it is being used. If not managed properly, such data can be misused and lead to issues like identity theft, stalking, and cyberbullying.
3. **Lack of Standardization and Regulation:** Currently, there are no industry-wide standards for the design and implementation of CPS in the tourism and travel industry. The absence of such standards can lead to inconsistency in cybersecurity protocols and safety measures across different CPS deployments. Additionally, regulatory gaps in this domain can create challenges in managing risks and ensure compliance with legal and ethical frameworks.

Blockchain technology provides solutions to these security concerns. Blockchain's decentralized architecture and use of cryptography make it resistant to cyber-attacks and data breaches. Its immutable and transparent ledger allows for secure sharing of data and ensures that all parties have equal access to information. Moreover, the self-governing nature of blockchain networks ensures that security measures are constantly evolving and improving over time. This research addresses the requirements of a blockchain enabled ecosystem for smart tourism and the following key components are identified.

1. An identity framework for participants

The identity and authentication framework helps participants authenticate to the blockchain in a decentralized environment. This framework is used to facilitate Smart contracts for transactions, which involves digital assets and currency among individuals, companies, and governments, while maintaining a private or public blockchain network. Identity issues are resolved using digital identities to address the privacy, security, and ownership issues of participants, especially when a participant is a multi-national, or governmental entity.

2. Infrastructure for storing, processing and exchanging information about tourists

The infrastructure for processing and storing tourist information includes a digital infrastructure that stores and disseminates digital records of tourist experiences. This infrastructure enables secured exchange of such data between diverse stakeholders such as hotels, car rentals, airlines, insurance companies, travel agencies and cruise lines. This fragmentation makes it difficult to build a consensus among key players and to agree upon the data that need to be shared with external partners such as cities, car rental companies and airlines. Tourism 4.0 aims to achieve consensus across the industry, which will be the foundation of digital trust.

3. A decentralized peer to peer communications network

Blockchain technology enables the creation of P2P, a peer to peer communications network which is self-owned, self-governed, and transparent. It facilitates a decentralized trust infrastructure in a permissionless environment where participants create, store and exchange information. This will enable tourism stakeholders to connect and trade data securely. It is envisaged that this decentralized P2P platform will replace intermediaries in the ecosystem and reduce transaction costs.

4. Cryptographic techniques and data structures for managing and validating transactions

Blockchain based tourism frameworks require secure and transparent data structure for storing and disseminating tourist information, transactions and receipts among stakeholders. It is envisaged that such a decentralized trust infrastructure will be based on a cryptographic framework and blockchain technology. Developers can utilize various advanced cryptographic and computational techniques to create a secure digital trust system using blockchain technology. One of the most important components of this system is the hash function, which is an algorithm that can generate unique IDs. A stored chain can be formatted with hash values to ensure that the data is secure. A digital signature is also used to verify the identities of the receivers and senders in transactions. The consensus mechanism ensures that all computer nodes are involved in the process of protecting the data.

5. A data analytics driven distributed ledger for holding transactions

Transactions regarding tourism services and benefits are stored in a distributed ledger, which is a digital ledger in which transactions are verified and stored in a cryptographically secure manner. This ledger is decentralized, transparent, immutable and open to everyone. Thus, it will enable stakeholders to exchange data securely and effectively. Data analytic tools such as machine learning, predictive analytics, augmented analytics and big data can be used to verify and analyze transactions and to extract relevant information.

6. Cryptographic techniques and data structures for managing and validating transactions

Blockchain based tourism frameworks require secure and transparent data structure for storing and disseminating tourist information, transactions and receipts among stakeholders. It is envisaged that such a decentralized trust infrastructure will be based on a cryptographic framework and blockchain technology. Developers can utilize various advanced cryptographic and computational techniques to create a secure digital trust system using blockchain technology. One of the most important components of this system is the hash function, which is an algorithm that can generate unique IDs. A stored chain can be formatted with hash values to ensure that the data is secure. A digital signature is also used to verify the identities of the receivers and senders in transactions. The consensus mechanism ensures that all computer nodes are involved in the process of protecting the data.

6. PROPOSED BLOCKCHAIN-BASED SECURITY FRAMEWORK FOR SMART TOURISM

The CPSs in Tourism and Travel are expected to be modeled as a set of sub-systems such that each sub-system is composed of multiple components, and each component may contain the sensors and actuators. The major CPSs in Tourism & Travel are the physical systems of the hotel such as the room systems, the kitchen system, the distribution system, the service system, and the transportation system. Each of them in a specific level is composed of the system elements such as human-machine interfaces, computer systems, mobile systems, and other elements. A component of a sub-system is called a level (for example, a floor) in a complex environment where multiple levels exist and the components of each level exchange the information, and each level is also able to control the other levels as shown in Figure 2.

Figure 2. Smart tourism eco-system

6.1. Major Design Considerations

Following are the major design considerations of the proposed Block Chain based Security Framework for Smart Tourism (BC-SFST) eco-system.

1. Integration of physical and digital components

The interaction between the CPS components of a tourism system is based on the communication channels, built on the hardware infrastructure and the software. They rely on existing communication channels such as wired internet, network, mobile networks, or wireless networks. The integration of these communication channels with the digital and physical components of the CPSs can be achieved by establishing the common language among the systems to which the CPSs can send and receive messages in different forms, including text, sound, video, etc. Further communication protocols need to be established between the components that can establish and maintain business-level-to-business-level or business-to-consumer connections. Further, the communication standards and protocols among the existing communication channels and digital components of the CPSs need to be agreed, standardized and deployed for supporting the existing as well as new communication protocols within the ecosystem.

2. Privacy and data preservation in communication

The privacy in communication is an issue of concern because of the growing number of CPSs that may be connected in various ways. The major privacy problems are caused by the identity theft, misdirection of data, and data theft. The data that are transferred between the CPSs are of various types, such as texts, emails, photos, videos, etc. Some of them have personal data such as health status, financial status, marital status, etc. The privacy in communication can be achieved by the establishment of a secure communication link, which can be ensured by the use of digital encryption technologies. These technologies are also useful in detecting and preventing any unauthorized and unwanted intrusion, and in providing protection against malware and data stealing. The authentication and authentication mechanism may be based on the public-private key pairs, the X.509 certificates, and other mechanisms. The digital signature and digital signatures can be used to certify the identity of the sender and authenticity of the information content in a message.

3. Protection of CPSs and data assets from cyber attacks

The cyber security is related to security of CPSs and data assets such as information technology systems (IT), information resources, personal information, data, information, and content. It is achieved by having a layered security approach that provides the different layers of protection to the information and data. It includes the data protection, network security, personal identification, authentication, authorization, privacy, cryptography, anti-malware, firewalls, and intrusion detection and prevention systems.

4. Assurance of trust and legitimacy of data

It is necessary to establish the trust mechanism by establishing the common data format and data encryption methods. The data is trusted if it is authenticated, verified, and signed by the trusted participants in the data communication. The participants include the data providers, data receivers, data maintainers, data access controllers, and data users. The authenticity of a data or message relies on a reliable source that is the major contributor to the generation of the data. The data verification and authentication mechanisms involve a message sender, a message receiver, and a trusted entity. The data integrity ensures that the data is in valid and consistent form. A trusted party is responsible for securing the data access rights, authenticity and confidentiality of the data.

5.   Enforcing policies and procedures

The enforcement of the policies and procedures is the key step to protect the data assets. They should be enforced according to the business requirements, which are established and defined by the business owners and managers. The access control, information security, data confidentiality, data integrity, communication protection, data storage, and data retention policies and procedures must be enforced at multiple levels of granularities in the business models.

6.   Infusion of intelligent decision-making capabilities

The information collected from the different sources can be used to generate the business-level-to-business-level and business-to-consumer messages in the system. As the communication channels between the CPSs are established, the business-level-to-business-level and business-to-consumer messages can be exchanged in the form of information and data. Once the messages are created, the intelligent decision-making capabilities of the smart contract can be used to perform the task. These capabilities can be defined as software modules, services, or data that can be used to trigger the smart contracts in the system, and also to perform decision-making processes. This decision-making capabilities can be based on the historical knowledge and current state of the components. It can also be based on machine learning and deep learning models trained on large datasets.

6.2. Architecture of the Blockchain Ecosystem for Smart Tourism

Smart tourism can be achieved by creating a transparent decentralized network of users, service providers, and third-party providers. The proposed architecture comprises four layers: infrastructure, platform, distributed computing, and application as shown in Figure 3. Each of these layers provides a specific function that enables the efficient and secure operation of the smart tourism system.

1.   **Infrastructure Layer:** This layer provides the necessary hardware and software resources for the proper functioning of the system. It includes networking equipment, servers, and cloud computing resources.
2.   **Platform Layer:** This layer provides the necessary infrastructure for developing and deploying decentralized applications. It includes blockchain technology, smart contract development platforms, and consensus algorithms.
3.   **Distributed Computing Layer:** This layer facilitates the distribution of computing resources and data storage among the nodes in the network. This layer helps to ensure the security and reliability of the system.
4.   **Application Layer:** This layer provides the end-user experience and includes all the applications developed to support smart tourism services such as ticket booking, hotel reservation, and tour management. These applications are built on top of the underlying blockchain technology, making them secure and transparent.

Figure 3. Blockchain ecosystem architecture

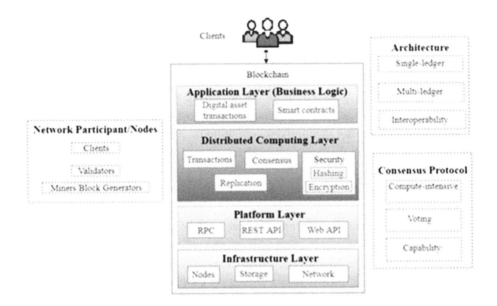

By implementing this architecture, smart tourism can leverage the benefits of blockchain technology such as immutability, transparency, and decentralization to improve the efficiency and security of tourism-related services. Each layer of the blockchain architecture works together to create a secure, decentralized, and transparent platform for data management and transactions.

6.3. Blockchain Generation Process

The blockchain generation process for smart tourism refers to the steps involved in creating and implementing a blockchain-based solution for the tourism industry. The specific steps may vary depending on the specific use case, but the general process typically includes the following steps:

1. **Identifying the Problem:** The first step is to identify the specific pain points and challenges in the tourism industry that can be addressed through blockchain technology.
2. **Defining the Solution:** Based on the identified problem, the next step is to define the solution and determine how blockchain technology can be leveraged to address the issue.
3. **Designing the Architecture:** The architecture of the blockchain solution is designed, including the number of nodes, the consensus mechanism, and the structure of the blockchain.
4. **Developing the Smart Contracts:** Smart contracts are created to define the rules and logic of the blockchain solution. They ensure that the rules are automatically executed when certain conditions are met.
5. **Implementing the Solution:** The blockchain solution is then implemented and tested, including the deployment of nodes, the installation of the consensus mechanism, and the creation of the smart contracts.

6. **Deploying the Solution:** After testing, the blockchain solution is deployed and made available to the users, such as tourists and tourism businesses.

7. **Monitoring and Maintenance:** The blockchain solution is continuously monitored and maintained to ensure its smooth operation and address any issues that arise.

6.4. Implementation of Security Mechanisms

A blockchain can be mathematically represented as a linked list data structure, where each block in the chain contains a hash of the previous block, a timestamp, and transaction data. The blocks are linked together in a linear sequence, forming a chain of blocks as in Figure 1. The hash function used in a blockchain is designed to ensure that once a block is added to the chain, the contents of that block cannot be altered without changing the hash of that block and all subsequent blocks. This creates a tamper-evident and secure ledger of all transactions in the blockchain.

A block chain BC is represented as in (1), where B_i is a block for $i \in [1, k]$ and t_i is the timestamp for block B_i. To add a block B_i to the blockchain, a block proposer picks a random time t_i and calculates the corresponding hash value $H_{B_i}(t_i)$, then B_i is added as a block at t_i. To verify a block, the miner must solve the Proof of Work (PoW) problem.

$$BC: \{(B_1, t_1), (B_2, t_2), \ldots, (B_k, t_k)\} \tag{1}$$

PoW requires a miner to pick a random value r between 1 and some constant k (e.g., 32), and generate a block B_i in which the previous hash value is equal to $H_{B_i}(r)$, and the new hash value is calculated as follows.

A block B_i' is equal to the existing block B_i except for the previous hash value in the block which is equal to $H_{B_i}(r)$, instead of $H_{B_i}(t_i)$. That is, $B_i' = (B_i, H_{B_i}(r), t_i)$. B_i' is then added as a block to the chain BC for t_i. Thus, every block miner that tries to change any content in any block B_i will be able to successfully add one block B_i' into the chain BC with a PoW calculation. Each block proposer who wants to try to change a content in any block B_i will be required to generate a PoW calculation that is significantly greater than the PoW calculation of any block proposer who wants to add one block B_i' into the chain BC during the validation process for the blocks. A blockchain miner C gets rewarded for adding blocks into the blockchain in return for validating new blocks and solving the PoW. It is designed to be the most computationally intensive calculation in the validation process and ensures that the mining of blocks is distributed.

All users must have some computational ability to validate blocks. That is, all users must be able to execute calculations and solve the PoW. This means that users can be limited in their computer resources such as storage space, bandwidth, etc. Since blockchains are very resource intensive, the users of blockchains are often asked to pay a fee to the miner(s) to validate their transactions. Miners are free to mine a block however they like, the only requirement is that miners add their block into the block chain, and it must validate using the PoW calculation. A typical PoW is performed by solving a hash function of a user-defined block, which is more costly and time-consuming than the PoW of a block.

6.5. Services of BC-SFST

The capabilities of the proposed BC-SFST for the smart tourism ecosystem can be used to realize the following services. These services can help to improve the efficiency, security, and transparency of the tourism industry, providing benefits for both tourists and tourism businesses.

1. **Digital Identity Management:** Blockchain can be used to create a secure digital identity for tourists, providing a secure and decentralized way to store and manage personal information.
2. **Ticketing and Reservations:** Blockchain can enable secure and transparent ticketing and reservation systems for tourist attractions, hotels, and flights.
3. **Loyalty Programs:** Blockchain can be used to create and manage loyalty programs for tourists, providing a secure and efficient way to track and reward customers.
4. **Supply Chain Management:** Blockchain can provide visibility into the supply chain for tourism-related goods and services, helping to improve efficiency and reduce costs.
5. **Payment Processing:** Blockchain can provide fast, secure, and low-cost payment processing for tourism-related transactions, including payments for tickets, reservations, and other goods and services.
6. **Data Management:** Blockchain can provide a secure and transparent way to store and manage data related to the tourism industry, such as visitor statistics and travel patterns.

7. BC-SFST APPLICATIONS

The BC-SFST model can be used to enhance the tourism industry in deploying the solutions described in the following subsections.

7.1. Secure and Efficient Payment System

The BC-SFST model can also be used to implement a secure and efficient payment system for tourism-related transactions. The use of blockchain technology can ensure that transactions are transparent, secure, and tamper-proof, making it easier for tourists to make payments and for merchants to receive payments. The requirements of secure payment systems such as user authentication and fraud prevention can be met by relying on blockchain's transparency and decentralization to allow for authentication based on a unique identity. Additionally, the use of credit systems to ensure a user is trustworthy may be achieved by creating a digital reputation system which incorporates a user's transaction history. By implementing blockchain technology, tourists can also be granted the right to receive digital certification for the purchases that they make with other users. The following steps are used to implement a secured payment system with the proposed BC-SFST. The schematic of this system is illustrated with Figure 4.

1. A tourist T_i selects a service provider S_j and initiates a transaction Tr_{ij} for the desired service.
2. The transaction details Tr_{ij} are encrypted using the Encryption Function E, resulting in encrypted transaction data, E_T. This ensures secure and confidential communication between the tourist and the service provider: $E_T \leftarrow E(Tr_{ij})$

3. The encrypted transaction data, E_T, is then verified using the Verification Function (V) to authenticate the transaction and prevent fraud, generating a verified transaction, V_T: $V_T \leftarrow V(E_T)$

4. A Smart Contract, SC_{ij}, is created and deployed using the Smart Contract Function S based on the verified transaction data, V_T. This contract automates and enforces the agreed-upon terms between the tourist and the service provider: $SC_{ij} \leftarrow S(V_T)$

5. The Payment Function φ processes the secure payment P_{ij}, from the tourist T_i to the service provider S_j according to the terms outlined in the smart contract: $SC_{ij}\ P_{ij} \leftarrow \varphi(T_i, S_j, SC_{ij})$

Figure 4. Secured payment system

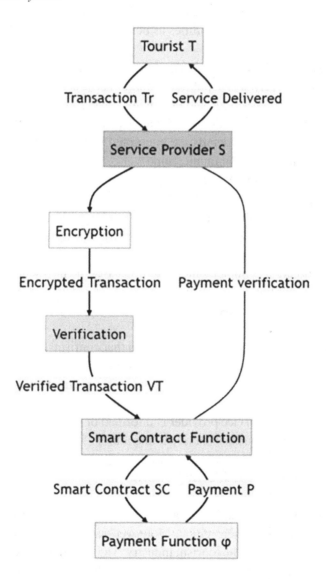

Further, smart contracts can be used to automate all processes involved in the payment transaction, as they can be executed without the intervention of third parties and are verifiable and transparent. This type of technology has the potential to streamline and simplify the entire payment process, while guaranteeing that all transactions are executed in a secure and efficient manner. It should be noted that a unique security feature of the BC-SFST model is its ability to protect against fraud while still ensuring the anonymity of both the customer and merchant. This ability is achieved by employing smart contracts and their ability to generate random identifiers for both parties.

7.1.1. Implementation in Ethereum Platform

The secure payment system using the BC-SFST framework can be implemented on the Ethereum blockchain by leveraging its smart contract capabilities as below.

1. **Ethereum Accounts Creation:** Ethereum accounts are created for both the tourist and the service provider, with associated private and public key pairs. These accounts are used to manage and store Ether (ETH) for making transactions and deploying smart contracts.
2. **Transaction Initiation:** A transaction is initiated by the tourist with the service provider for the desired service. The transaction details are encrypted using a standard encryption algorithm to ensure secure and confidential communication.
3. **Smart Contract Deployment:** A smart contract is written in Solidity, Ethereum's programming language, capturing the agreed-upon terms between the tourist and the service provider. The smart contract should include the following functions:
   a. **Verification:** A function is implemented that verifies the encrypted transaction to authenticate the transaction and prevent fraud.
   b. **Payment:** A function is implemented that processes the payment from the tourist to the service provider according to the terms outlined in the smart contract. This can be done using the transfer or send functions in Solidity to transfer Ether from the tourist's account to the service provider's account.
   c. **Service Delivery:** A function is implemented that confirms the delivery of the service from the service provider to the tourist and updates the smart contract accordingly.
4. **Smart Contract Execution:** Upon deploying the smart contract on the Ethereum blockchain, it is executed automatically when the pre-defined conditions in the contract are met. The payment is processed securely, and the service provider is informed of the successful transaction. The service provider then delivers the requested service to the tourist.

7.2. Integral Platform for Tour Management

In a bid to improve the tourist experience, several governments have developed the tourism industry by introducing tourism destinations in their region. Moreover, various organizations have been created to coordinate the needs and services of the tourism industry. The BC-SFST has the potential to provide an excellent mechanism for the service providers to coordinate their service provision requirements while managing the flow of data among the different entities. The BC-SFST model can be used to provide a centralized platform where all the entities involved in the service provision can share resources and coordinate their activities.

The BC-SFST model can be used to create a single platform for tourists to manage their trips, allowing them to access various tourism-related services such as transportation, accommodation, and attractions. The solution can be deployed using a cloud-based computing platform and offer a central interface to the various tourism-related services. This interface can be presented to tourists either in the form of a mobile application or a browser interface with support for language translation services. The application can be also customized for specific tourist groups and be extended to support various languages.

7.3. Personalized Experience for Tourists

The concept of personalization in the travel and experience industry involves combining the information collected by various agencies and service providers to create customized experiences for each individual traveler. Personalization can be achieved by combining the information collected about a customer's interests, likes, and preferences in order to provide them with the best possible experience. Social media helps in this process by allowing service providers to collect valuable data about their customers. Some of the areas where they can offer this type of service include cruise lines, hotels, and flight travel. The BC-SFST model can also be used to create a secure and efficient solution for the personalization of tourist experiences. This model can track a user's history of locations visited and generate an itinerary based on that history. It can also be used to record and quantify users' activities to create a personalized experience for users based on their unique preferences. Users can then be provided with the recommendations of other users who have similar interests. The combination of the BC-SFST model with blockchain technology makes this process more secure, as transactions are carried out in a transparent and decentralized manner.

7.4. Sustainable Tourism Practices

The goal of sustainable tourism is to ensure that the environment is used in a way that is beneficial to both the development of the tourism industry and the preservation of natural resources. To achieve this, the tourism industry should respect the cultural and traditional values of its host communities. It should also contribute to the development of inter-cultural understanding. The tourism industry should also ensure that its long-term operations are sustainable. This can help provide stable and predictable economic benefits to the various stakeholder groups that it serves.

The development of sustainable tourism requires the participation of all its stakeholders, as well as political leadership that can ensure its continuous success. This process can be carried out through regular monitoring and the introduction of necessary corrective measures. A sustainable tourism experience should provide a high level of satisfaction to its visitors, and it should promote responsible practices and raise awareness about the environment. The BC-SFST allows for complete and verifiable transactions, as well as increased transparency. Transparency encourages responsible behavior and the active participation of stakeholders in environmental protection and sustainable development. The use of smart contracts helps to avoid fraud, while minimizing costs and enhancing efficiency by automating processes and reducing the administrative burden.

7.5. Disaster Relief and Crisis Management

Tourists are vulnerable to disasters and crises which have the potential to impact their safety and satisfaction with their trip. A system of crisis communication between tourists and their concerned parties can be utilized in order to manage crisis situations. Crisis communication is used for the sharing of information, and the use of blockchain technology can help the integration of different communication sources into a centralized system in order to allow for fast and easy access to the necessary information. In addition, BC-SFST can also be utilized to assist in managing the effects of a disaster by providing an open platform for tourism enterprises to provide aid for their customers. This can be achieved by creating a decentralized information exchange system to allow various parties to obtain real-time information regarding the conditions in the affected area. As a result, these parties can easily offer help and assistance to affected areas, especially in the context of travel and tourism.

8. CONCLUSION

This chapter presents a novel Blockchain based CPS called BC-SFST for efficient data collection, security, and exchange. This model helps to realize various smart tourism services with smart contracts using a novel data security framework that is designed to protect users from any breach of security. The proposed framework can be customized to offer dynamic services to the users to suit their individual travel/tourism needs. The use of a tokenized reward system makes the proposed model a self-sustainable ecosystem that supports services such as digital ID management, disaster management, traceability, interoperability etc. Further, the proposed model can be extended to other business verticals such as healthcare and medical tourism, transportation, and entertainment.

REFERENCES

Ahram, T., Sargolzaei, A., Sargolzaei, S., Daniels, J., & Amaba, B. (2017, June). Blockchain technology innovations. In 2017 IEEE technology & engineering management conference (TEMSCON) (pp. 137-141). IEEE. doi:10.1109/TEMSCON.2017.7998367

Ashari, I. F. (2020). Implementation of cyber-physical-social system based on service oriented architecture in smart tourism. *Journal of Applied Informatics and Computing*, 4(1), 66–73. doi:10.30871/jaic.v4i1.2077

Bodkhe, U., Tanwar, S., Parekh, K., Khanpara, P., Tyagi, S., Kumar, N., & Alazab, M. (2020). Blockchain for industry 4.0: A comprehensive review. *IEEE Access : Practical Innovations, Open Solutions*, 8, 79764–79800. doi:10.1109/ACCESS.2020.2988579

Buhalis, D., Leung, D., & Lin, M. (2023). Metaverse as a disruptive technology revolutionising tourism management and marketing. *Tourism Management*, 97, 104724. doi:10.1016/j.tourman.2023.104724

Cheema, A., Tariq, M., Hafiz, A., Khan, M. M., Ahmad, F., & Anwar, M. (2022). Prevention Techniques against Distributed Denial of Service Attacks in Heterogeneous Networks: A Systematic Review. *Security and Communication Networks, 2022*, 2022. doi:10.1155/2022/8379532

Chen, S. H., & Tham, A. (2023). A crypto-tourism case study of agnes water/seventeen seventy, Australia. *Tourism and Hospitality Research, 23*(1), 108–112. doi:10.1177/14673584221085472

Duan, B., Zhong, Y., & Liu, D. (2017, December). Education application of blockchain technology: Learning outcome and meta-diploma. In *2017 IEEE 23rd International Conference on Parallel and Distributed Systems (ICPADS)* (pp. 814-817). IEEE.

Dwivedi, Y. K., Balakrishnan, J., Das, R., & Dutot, V. (2023). Resistance to innovation: A dynamic capability model based enquiry into retailers' resistance to blockchain adaptation. *Journal of Business Research, 157*, 113632. doi:10.1016/j.jbusres.2022.113632

Erol, I., Neuhofer, I. O., Dogru, T., Oztel, A., Searcy, C., & Yorulmaz, A. C. (2022). Improving sustainability in the tourism industry through blockchain technology: Challenges and opportunities. *Tourism Management, 93*, 104628. doi:10.1016/j.tourman.2022.104628

. Hasbini, M. A. (2016). Operation Ghoul: targeted attacks on industrial and engineering organizations. *Securelist-GREAT (Kaspersky Lab), 17*.

Irannezhad, E., & Mahadevan, R. (2021). Is blockchain tourism's new hope? *Journal of Hospitality and Tourism Technology, 12*(1), 85–96. doi:10.1108/JHTT-02-2019-0039

Kalluri, B., Chronopoulos, C., & Kozine, I. (2021). The concept of smartness in cyber–physical systems and connection to urban environment. *Annual Reviews in Control, 51*, 1–22. doi:10.1016/j.arcontrol.2020.10.009

Kishore, P., Barisal, S. K., & Mohapatra, D. P. (2020, September). An incremental malware detection model for meta-feature API and system call sequence. In *2020 15th Conference on Computer Science and Information Systems (FedCSIS)* (pp. 629-638). IEEE. 10.15439/2020F73

Krieger, U., Liu, W., Zhu, S. S., & Mundie, T. (2017). Advanced Block-Chain Architecture for e-Health Systems. In *19th International Conference on E-health Networking, Application & Services (HealthCom): 2nd IEEE International Workshop on*. IEEE Xplore Digital Library.

Mettler, M. (2016, September). Blockchain technology in healthcare: The revolution starts here. In *2016 IEEE 18th international conference on e-health networking, applications and services (Healthcom)* (pp. 1-3). IEEE.

Morkunas, V. J., Paschen, J., & Boon, E. (2019). How blockchain technologies impact your business model. *Business Horizons, 62*(3), 295–306. doi:10.1016/j.bushor.2019.01.009

Navickas, V., Kuznetsova, S. A., & Gruzauskas, V. (2017). Cyber–physical systems expression in industry 4.0 context. *Financial and Credit Activity Problems of Theory and Practice, 2*(23), 188-197.

. Palmer, D. (2017). Hackers are using hotel Wi-Fi to spy on guests, steal data. *ZDNet, Cyberwar and the Future of Cybersecurity), 6*(20), 7.

Paraskevas, A. (2022). Cybersecurity in travel and tourism: a risk-based approach. In *Handbook of e-Tourism* (pp. 1605–1628). Springer International Publishing. doi:10.1007/978-3-030-48652-5_100

Pérez-Sánchez, M. D. L. Á., Tian, Z., Barrientos-Báez, A., Gómez-Galán, J., & Li, H. (2021). Blockchain technology for winning consumer loyalty: Social norm analysis using structural equation modeling. *Mathematics, 9*(5), 532. doi:10.3390/math9050532

Petrović, S., Bjelica, D., & Radenković, B. (2021, September). Loyalty system development based on blockchain technology. In *E-business technologies conference proceedings* (Vol. 1, No. 1, pp. 157-161). Academic Press.

Pishdad-Bozorgi, P., Gao, X., & Shelden, D. R. (2020). Introduction to cyber-physical systems in the built environment. In *Construction 4.0* (pp. 23–41). Routledge. doi:10.1201/9780429398100-2

Ramos, C. M. (2021). Blockchain Technology in Tourism Management: Potentialities, Challenges, and Implications. In Blockchain Technology and Applications for Digital Marketing (pp. 84-109). IGI Global.

Rejeb, A., & Karim, R. (2019). Blockchain technology in tourism: Applications and possibilities. *World Scientific News, 137*, 119–144.

Singh, A., Sharma, A., Sharma, N., Kaushik, I., & Bhushan, B. (2019, July). Taxonomy of attacks on web based applications. In *2019 2nd International Conference on Intelligent Computing, Instrumentation and Control Technologies (ICICICT)* (Vol. 1, pp. 1231-1235). IEEE. 10.1109/ICICICT46008.2019.8993264

Smirnov, A., Shilov, N., & Gusikhin, O. (2017, March). Cyber-physical-human system for connected car-based e-tourism. In *Proceedings of 2017 IEEE Conference on Cognitive and Computational Aspects of Situation Management,* Savannah, GA, USA (pp. 27-31). IEEE.

Smirnov, A., Shilov, N., Kashevnik, A., & Ponomarev, A. (2017). Cyber-physical infomobility for tourism application. *International Journal of Information Technology and Management, 16*(1), 31–52. doi:10.1504/IJITM.2017.080949

Subasinghe, M., Magalage, D., Amadoru, N., Amarathunga, L., Bhanupriya, N., & Wijekoon, J. L. (2020, November). Effectiveness of artificial intelligence, decentralized and distributed systems for prediction and secure channelling for Medical Tourism. In *2020 11th IEEE Annual Information Technology, Electronics and Mobile Communication Conference (IEMCON)* (pp. 314-319). IEEE. 10.1109/IEMCON51383.2020.9284898

Treiblmaier, H. (2021). The token economy as a key driver for tourism: Entering the next phase of blockchain research. *Annals of Tourism Research, 91*, 103177. doi:10.1016/j.annals.2021.103177

Tyan, I., Yagüe, M. I., & Guevara-Plaza, A. (2021). Blockchain Technology's Potential for Sustainable Tourism. In *Information and Communication Technologies in Tourism 2021: Proceedings of the ENTER 2021 eTourism Conference, January 19–22, 2021* (pp. 17-29). Springer International Publishing.

Weiss, M., Botha, A., Herselman, M., & Loots, G. (2017, May). Blockchain as an enabler for public mHealth solutions in South Africa. In 2017 IST-Africa Week Conference (IST-Africa) (pp. 1-8). IEEE. doi:10.23919/ISTAFRICA.2017.8102404

Yli-Huumo, J., Ko, D., Choi, S., Park, S., & Smolander, K. (2016). Where is current research on block-chain technology? A systematic review. *PLoS One*, *11*(10), e0163477. doi:10.1371/journal.pone.0163477 PMID:27695049

Zhang, P., Walker, M. A., White, J., Schmidt, D. C., & Lenz, G. (2017, October). Metrics for assessing blockchain-based healthcare decentralized apps. In *2017 IEEE 19th international conference on e-health networking, applications and services (Healthcom)* (pp. 1-4). IEEE. 10.1109/HealthCom.2017.8210842

Chapter 19
Empirical Study on Cyber-Crime and Cyber Terrorism

Subhash Chandra Patel
VIT Bhopal University, India

Santhoshini Sahu
VIT Bhopal University, India

ABSTRACT

This chapter will give a clear idea of what cyber-crime is and cyber terrorism's causes and types and how these are done and what is the main difference between cyber-crimes and cyber terrorism. It will also explore what precautions can be taken that may help a user with these attacks.

INTRODUCTION

In the era of industry 4.0 many new applications are been developed and socializing of models are also increasing. Based on this the usage of social networks or the internet have been increased very abruptly. Latest advancements in every field can be seen abundantly clear and criminal activities related to internet and computers also have increased like copyright infringement, hacking, child pornography, child exploitation, credit card fraud and many more. Cyber crime has many factors like political, economic and socio-cultural. There are many types of cyber crime like carding, cracking, hacking, etc. Many terrorist groups are working towards this cyber crime which is known as cyber terrorism involves hacking of websites, phishing attacks, injection attacks and many more. There are two main forms of cyber terrorism i.e., hybrid and pure cyber terrorism. These cyber terrorists do not need any bombs or any weapons to destroy any organization or any country economy they can do by just sitting in a computer connected through internet. They just try to find the weak points in confidential network and get themselves involved in the network either by shutting down the network using denial of service or by spoofing the original website and getting access or by attacking the computers in the network with any ransomware and many other attacks may be done. The main motto of doing the attacks by the terrorists is especially gaining

DOI: 10.4018/978-1-6684-8145-5.ch019

Copyright © 2023, IGI Global. Copying or distributing in print or electronic forms without written permission of IGI Global is prohibited.

the benefit from the government or creating huge loss to government. Mainly this chapter objectives are to discuss what are the causes and types of cyber crime and cyber terrorism, in different fields of study how these show their effect and how these can be prevented or detected.

BACKGROUND

Cyber Crime

According to Siburian (2016), Cyber Crime is defined as a crime which involves a computer or a network connected through components or computers. Cyber Crime history started with the evolution of internet. The reported first ever cybercrime is getting information from the simple local network and slowly in late 1990s cybercrime started increasing. Cybercrime is in many forms like ransomware, hacking, and many other forms. Cybercrime is termed as a serious criminal activity because sometimes it involves the profit of the individual, or sometimes the profit of the organization and also sometimes without any profit just with a cause of grudge or any other factor can lead to this crime. Cybercrime is taken into more consideration because it not only damages the computers or networks but also compromise the crucial or sensitive data. Before suspects in crime are justified with physical evidence, considering witness statements and suspects interview on case, but in today's scenario the crime investigation is done with help of digital gadgets and computers. Witness have become computer logs or history of chats or browsing data. The three main components of criminal activities carried out by computers or the internet are:

- For committing of crime, the tool used is computer.
- In the commission of crime, computer is used as repository for information storage or as generator.
- With the intention of damaging the information stored in the computer is the major target so that integrity, availability and or confidentiality is compromised.

According to Alsulami (2022), Crime Triangle describes cybercrime as traditional crime which tells for a cybercrime to occur, they may be three factors namely, opportunity, victim, and a motive. For a crime to occur there must be chance known as opportunity, the intention to do crime is the motive and the person who have to be attacked is the target. The first cybercrime reported was in the year 1970 $1.5 million was taken by chief from many accounts of "New York's Union Dime Saving Bank's" Branch. The first ever cybercrime happened in a large scale was in 1989 from "First National Bank of Chicago" where $70million was stolen.

Table 1. According to Global Cybersecurity Exposure Index (2020) an exposure classification scale

Exposure Classification	Score Range
Very high	0.800-1.000
High	0.600-0.799
Moderate	0.400-0.599
Low	0.200-0.399
Very low	0.00-1.99

Table 2. According to Global Cybersecurity Exposure Index 2020 score of top 10 countries

Country	Rank	Score
Finland	1	0.110
Denmark	2	0.117
Luxembourg	3	0.124
Australia	4	0.131
Estonia	5	0.134
Norway	5	0.134
Japan	6	0.138
United Stated	7	0.145
Austria	8	0.162
Switzerland	9	0.179
New Zealand	10	0.190

Figure 1. Exposure classification country distribution by cyber threat exposure

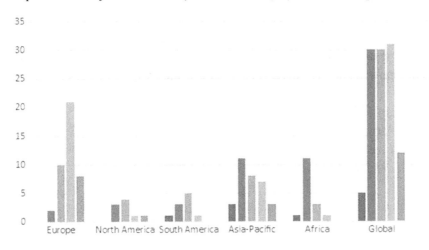

Top 10 countries in the exposure index are shown in the Table 2. According to the observation of the above details Finland is very less exposed to cyber threats among the 108 countries. Europe is very less vulnerable region which has least score of exposure considering all regions. Out of all countries 67.44% of European countries have low and very low number of cyber threats all over. Out of 108 countries Afghanistan is most vulnerable country. Africa is having 0.643 the most exposure level per country. The highest exposure countries around 60% are from Asia-Pacific. The levels of exposure are classified in the Table 1. Figure 1 is designed to show the number of countries with risk of each level in each continent over the world.

Causes of Cyber Crime

According to Siburian (2016), the factors affecting cyber-crime are:

1. **Political Factors:** The enforcement and process taken by the government creates multiple cybercrimes.
2. **Economic Factors:** Increased economic progress makes people to get influenced by the sales of good in online platforms have given scope of many cybercrime cases.
3. **Socio-Cultural Factors:** These factors are formed by the information technology advances, human resources and formation of new community in the cyber space.

Types of Cyber Crime

Some of the types of cyber-crime are:

1. **Phishing:** In this attack, the hacker tries to get the confidential information of users by using communication media illegally.
2. **Pharming:** The attacker directs the user to a fake website and gets their personal information.
3. **Non-Payment/Non-Delivery:** The seller will not receive the amount even after selling the product or shipping the product or does not get the item which you have paid for.
4. **Extortion:** It is gaining money or property from any person or organization using a wrong act like threating or violence or blackmail.
5. **Personal Data Breach:** It is a type of breach of security which leads to loss, change, disclosure, access to any sensitive information.
6. **Identity Theft:** It is a crime where the attacker tries to get the personal information and tries to act like that person whose details he has obtained for his personal gain.
7. **Spoofing:** A person tries to get the loop hole in a program and get illegal access and gain advantage.
8. **Misrepresentation:** These are false claims of which are true that may affect someone's decision in contact with a contract.
9. **Confidence Fraud:** It is attack which is done after gaining the trust of a person or a group.
10. **Threat and Harassment:** It is an unwanted physical, social, verbal or any other rude behaviour by a group or by one person.
11. **Email Account Compromise:** It is one of the "Impersonation attack" where the attacker tries to behave like someone who he is not like CEO, any authority official.
12. **Credit Card Fraud:** It is the one type of identity theft which consists of using credit card in an unauthorized manner by bluffing people for the purpose of adding account, recovering account.
13. **Employment:** In this attack the attacker pretends to give a stable job after paying a amount but actually gives nothing.
14. **Tech Support:** By using social engineering a technical support person takes advantage of the network in an adverse manner.
15. **Real Estate Crime:** In real estate, a person tells false details of related information to another person about the transaction or the person does not give proper information about the other.
16. **Advance Fee:** This scam involves promise of very large amount or property in assurance of advance payment of a small amount.

Table 3. According to Varga (2021) types of cybercrime with count

S.No	Type of Cyber-Crime	2020 Victim Count	% of Total Cybercrime
1.	Phishing and pharming	241342	32.96
2.	Non-payment/non-delivery	108869	14.87
3.	Extortion	76741	10.48
4.	Personal data breach	45330	6.19
5.	Identity theft	43330	5.92
6.	Spoofing	28218	3.85
7.	Misrepresentation	24276	3.32
8.	Confidence fraud	23751	3.24
9.	Threat and harassment	20604	2.81
10.	Email account compromise	19369	2.65
11.	Credit card fraud	17614	2.41
12.	Employment	16879	2.31
13.	Tech support	15421	2.11
14.	Real estate crime	13638	1.86
15.	Advance fee	13020	1.78

Using Digital Forensics to Find Cyber-Crime

According to MacDermott et al. (2020), Digital Forensics is same like computer forensics, where these analysts observe the seized data and explain the present state of the evidence or facts in terms of digital. Some specialist software's like FTK Imager or EnCase Forensic Imager are used for taking static data using digital images. Digital forensics is a challenging work now as there a high increase in digital media and devices. IoT had seen the internet as connection of intelligence, configure of self, with other objects in a global infrastructure which has "Radio Frequency Identification" (RFID) technology, different sensors, etc. So many models are developed to speed up the process of cyber crime investigation. Some such models according to the authors are "Digital Forensics Process Model" or Digital Forensic Methodology which gives a framework how to do digital forensics investigation considering different stages namely, identify, secure, analyse and present, "Advanced Data Acquisition Model" (ADAM) methodology which takes consideration of time constraints and allocated enough time for every stage. Its main aim is to address the potholes found in the last study, "CFSAP" (Computer Forensics-Secure, Analyse, Present) has four main elements in computer forensics by identifying the digital evidence sources, preserving these evidences, analysing these, and presenting them for expert opinion, "Framework for Reliable Exoeriment Design" (FRED) has three different stages like collection, analysis and presentation of evidence and how these levels are based on them the importance is given dependently. According to Yaacoub et al. (2022), in digital forensics the categories as per forensic evidence are Computer based, IoT based, Network based, Mobile based, Cloud based. According to authors IoT based digital evidence is very helpful in the crime scene as many appliances are being used in everyone house and these have many data stored in it and it can be very strong evidence sometimes to prove a crime. A large number of frameworks like building a forensic aware ecosystem for IoT, Prototype for digital forensic readiness, etc. are designed according to the authors which are not applicable for standardization.

Statistics of Cyber Crime up to the Year 2022 Worldwide

According to Griffiths (2023), the number of cybercrime victims per million internet users are highest in UK with 4783 in the year 2022 which is 40 percent more than 2020 figures. USA is the next highest country with 1494 victims which is 13 percent less than 2020. Out of two North American internet users one internet user had a data breach in 2021. More than 50 percent rise is seen than 2020 in the country Netherlands. Over 2020 75 percent of victims have decreased in the country Greece. In the year 2021, an average of 97 data breach victims are there and $787,671 amount is lost every hour.

Figure 2. NCSI comparison of few countries

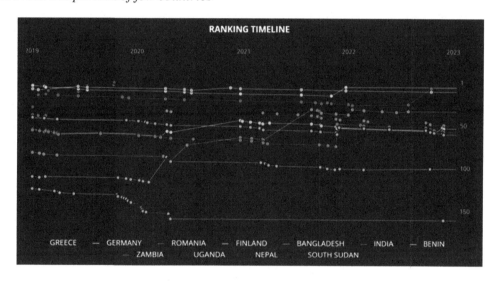

Figure 3. National Cyber Security Index in January 2023 of few countries

In the year 2021, the percentage of attacks happened on the organizations are shown in Figure 3. The percentage of internet users who have experienced cybercrime all over the world is shown in Figure 4.

Figure 4. Percentage of cybercrime cases encountered by internet users over the world by cyber threat encounter rate by country 2017

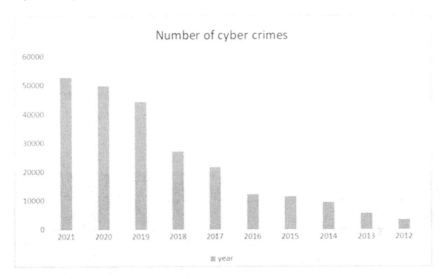

Figure 5. Percentage of attacks against organisation by continent in 2021

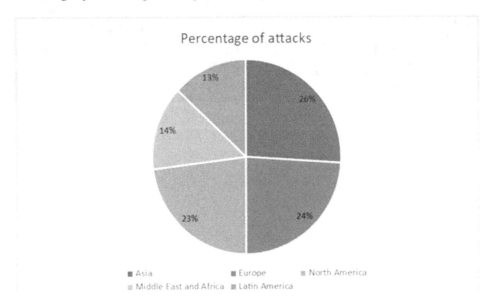

Since the cyber crime is increasing at a large rate, security also plays a vital role her. Security mainly focus on three main things integrity, confidentiality and availability. Many of the cyber crimes occurs because of negligence and unawareness of using network. Mainly the attacks are classified as:

A.   Cryptographic Attack

The attacker tries to get the plaintext without key by discovering the fallibility of the cryptographic algorithm, code or ciphers.

B.   Passive Attack

The attacker tries to listen to the channel silently without the knowledge of the user and uses the data as needed. This type of attack is difficult to find out.

C.   Active Attack

The attacker tries to change or modify the data as he wants to gain authorization or any benefits.

Cyber Warfare

According to Li and Liu (2021), cyber warfare is the highest and most complex type of cyber-attack (cyber operation) carried out against the cyber interests of nation states, with the most serious consequences.
The consequences of cyber warfare may include:

- Simultaneous initiation of physical warfare or ground operations and promotion of the initiation of physical warfare in the near future.
- Catastrophic destruction or damage to international national image.
- Catastrophic destruction or damage to a country's political and economic relations.
- Massive human casualty or threat to public health and safety.
- Internal turmoil.
- Widespread disruption to national administration.
- Destruction of public trust or religious, national, or ethnic beliefs.
- Severe damage to the national economy.
- Widespread destruction or disrupted performance of national cyber resources.

Cyber Terrorism

According to Alava et al. (2020), some of the Digital actions followed by different researchers are:

1. **Slacktivism:** Without any harm a simple way of showing people's opinions based on some emojis for taking a political stand.
2. **Clicktivism:** A simple action of showing consisting modality by clicking hate or like opinions or by just retweeting for giving support.
3. **Hashtivism:** A simple message which adds a hashtag in a message to show stand digitally for a moment or activity.
4. **Online Petition:** A type of digital petition which gets directly delivered to email after signing by the petitioner, used for stopping any activities mostly.

5. **Trolling:** Group of opinions collected voluntarily to provoke other participants and to generate some reaction of them.
6. **Sockpuppeting:** Using fake identity in social media or creating fake pages of person to create rumours or fake news against someone.
7. **Hacktivism:** With the help of viruses, worms, or any other harmful techniques to destroy, block, hijack any website or systems which causes a lot of damage.
8. **Flash Mobbing:** Using the networks and gathering followers to carry out a movement.
9. **Cop Watching:** These people record the videos of cops with people without their knowledge and publish them online to discriminate the duty of cops.
10. **Mail-Bombing:** Tries to block the services provided to and by the institution by overflowing mailbox of the institution with emails to create digital political action.
11. **Cyber-Graffiti:** Involves hacking of website by modifying the source code so that political slogans will be made or making the site down by not allowing accessibility.
12. **Phone Zap:** Action which consist in flooding the switchboard by making continuous calls to a institution or person so that people will discuss on this.
13. **Meme:** A hateful content humorously on internet by photo morphing, GIFs, small videos, procuring jokes to provoke dissemination of information digitally.
14. **Doxing:** To harm people their personal data is been hacked.

CYBER CRIME IN TERMS OF COST AND IMPACT

According to Yaacoub et al. (2020), the term loss comes with very easy words when a cyber crime or cyber terrorism happens because financial loss or data loss is the main problem which occurs in these. Many people with a single link are giving access to their data to a hacker, it may be personal data like photos, usernames, passwords, or any data breach. Now a days financial loss due to cyber crime has much increased because hackers try to bluff people telling to update their personal details, or bank details and get the amount from the user very easily. This is mainly happening because of no proper knowledge in people who are accessing social networks or any bank transactions. Online payments have increased a lot in all over the country as UPI has set a trend of easy payments and many financial losses occurs due to cyber crime. Every day in articles and news paper one or the other cyber cases are reported where people are duped for money. Money is not only the main motto in some cases, some cyber crime cases are reported for personal data breach. Data breach happens where photos are morphed and illegal usage of personal details for doing any criminal activities are increasing now a days. The security attacks may take may forms in terms of cost, some of them are:

- **Delays:** Due to cyber crime, the system which is effected gets service delays until the problem is fixed.
- **Affected Performance:** Due to delay in the system, the performance of the system is also effected and it caused the system to behave abnormally.
- **Financial Losses:** The main cyber attack is Ransomware attack where the user system is hacked and all files are encrypted and finally a ransom amount is asked for decrypting the data. Ransomware attacks are mainly targeting Industrial Control Systems which gives huge loss to the companies.

- **Disclosure of information:** Due to the cyber attacks there is disclosure of personal information or confidential information of the organizations which in turn leads to financial losses.
- **Loss of Life:** Some hackers are using the personal information of people to get benefits in terms of money or property but some people who are unable to pay the hackers are ending their life's which also needs to be considered as a loss.

CYBER CRIME AFFECTS DIFFERENT SECTORS

Cyber Crime has been affecting many people and in the same way it is affecting different organizations and sectors like medical, insurance, and many more. Cyber crime has seen a very high rise during the covid-19. Some of them are discussed below.

Cyber Crime During COVID-19 Pandemic

According to Alsulami (2022), "Severe Acute Respiratory Syndrome Coronavirus-2" (SARS-CoV-2) is a novel virus detected was first noted in humans in 2019 and on 11th February 2020 COVID-19 name was given by WHO (World Health Organisation). Due to the pandemic mostly, all companies have started working online. This became a golden opportunity for hackers as all the databases were connected by home networks. Around "907,000 spam messages, 737 malware-related incidents, and 48,000 malicious URLs related to COVID-19" and it's shown that "average ransomware payment of second quarter compared to first quarter has increased by 60 percentage".

Figure 6. Percentage of feedback given by countries on inflicted cyberthreats during COVID-19

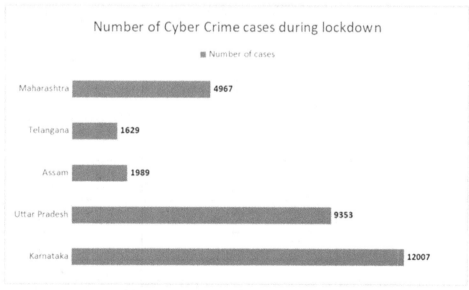

Insurers Towards Cyber-Crime

According to Timofeyev et al. (2022), insurance companies account one of the most essential for country's economic growth and its average insured loss is more than 2.3 million from a cyber incident. So, this threat cannot be taken lightly or ignored because it may create negative impact in people, i.e., customers on the insurance companies.

The group of criminals in the field of insurance are:

1. **Business Email Compromise (CEO Fraud):** Is an attack where the attacker pretends to be any higher official or the CEO of the organization and make the employees do things which are harmful to the organization.
2. **Malware (Ransomware):** Is a software which encrypts the data or block the access of the data until the user pays a ransom amount.
3. **Denial of Service Attacks (DoS Attacks):** Is an attack where continuous requests are made to a server or a single system which makes it unavailable for other users to access.
4. **Phishing:** Is a sort of attack that spoofs a website and directs to a fake look alike website and captures all the sensitive data.

Table 4 shows how Cyber Crime is affecting US businesses over past years these include ransomware, credit card fraud, data leaks, etc. it also shows that from the year 2005 the number of breaches mostly increased. The table concludes that cybercrime is not only a danger for each person as an individual but also gives a great threat to large number of organizations which affect legally and financially.

Table 4. US business affected by data breaches over years

Year	Number of Breaches	Records Exposed in Millions
2005	157	66.9
2006	321	19.1
2007	446	127.7
2008	656	35.7
2009	498	222.5
2010	662	16.2
2011	419	22.9
2012	447	17.3
2013	614	91.98
2014	783	85.61
2015	784	169.07
2016	1106	36.6
2017	1632	197.61
2018	1257	471.23
2019	1473	164.68
2020	1001	155.8

COMPONENTS OF CYBER TERRORISM

The five key components in terms of cyber terrorism are namely target, motive, means, effect, intension by the actor who can be a state, private, non-state or any agency which is going to conduct this activity using cyberspace as weapon or a target. Cyber Terrorism had its impact in the process industry also, the major impacts happened on aurora, Stuxnet. Cyber terrorism is happening in the nuclear power plants also where many incidents have happened in south Korea because of the data leak, or software's which are very vulnerable to attacks.

TOOLS USED IN CYBER CRIME AND CYBER TERRORISM

There are many hacking tools which are used to detect cyber crime or cyber terrorism, some of them are:

1. **Rootkits:** These are special software's used by hackers to get the access of computer in remote location in which he want to perform the attack. Actually, these are designed to fix any problem which happened in a software but these became weapons for hackers.
2. **Keyloggers:** These software's are designed to record each and every key stroke done by the user and intercept and store the details like phone numbers, password, etc., which may be helpful for him.
3. **Vulnerability Scanners:** This system scans large networks to find the weakness and later can exploit it.
4. **Worm, Virus, and Trojan:** These are the malicious programs so they are sent to the network and access of computer are gained.
5. **Botnet:** A series of hacked computers are used to perform DDos (Distributed Denial of Service) attack to bring the specific servers down.

SOLUTIONS AND RECOMMENDATIONS

Many ways are available to detect cyber crime when it is encountered and many ways are available like firewalls, honeypots, etc., to protect the individual or organization before an attack happens. Some of those defence methods are:

1. **Honeypots:** These are the servers which are used to bluff the hacker by creating a fake data which resembles the original data.
2. **Air Gap:** It is system which helps to secure data transferring among two networks.
3. **NAC:** For accessing any network or device in the network this system implements the necessary security protocols.
4. **Encryption System:** Data transferring is encrypted by this system.
5. **Digital Signature:** To identify the sender by allowing proof of identity.
6. **Antivirus:** It detects any malicious file or software entering into the system.

Prevention of Cyber Crime

According to List of Cybersecurity Associations and Organizations (2018) Associations for Industries to prevent cybercrime:

1. **AEHIS:** The Association for Executives in Healthcare Information Security

The Association of Healthcare Information Security Executives (AEHIS) was formed in 2014 to provide a training and networking platform for senior healthcare IT security leaders.

2. **AISA:** Australian Information Security Association

Established in 1999, AISA has become a recognized information security organization in Australia with more than 6,000 individual and business sponsors across Australia..

3. Black Cybersecurity Association

BCA is a welcoming and inclusive non-profit organization dedicated to community building, mentoring, and employment opportunities for underrepresented minorities in cybersecurity.

4. **CLUSIT:** Italian Association for Information Security

CLUSIT is open to anyone and any organization interested in IT security. Awareness, education, ongoing expert updates and exchange of information are the most effective tools to address IT security concerns.

5. **CCMC-COE:** The Cybersecurity Maturity Model Certification Center of Excellence

Honest cyber capabilities that use standards, design experience, and lessons learned from key industry groups, standards bodies, public sector leaders, and the cyber community to improve and strengthen the defence industrial base and the Department of Defence's overall security and supply chain resiliency.

6. **Cyber Florida:** At the University of South Florida

Publicly funded by the University of South Florida, but "hosted", we work with all 12 institutions of the Florida State University system, as well as other dedicated partners in all types of agencies; And the US military accomplishes our mission.

7. Canadian Centre for Cybersecurity

The Cyber Centre is a single, integrated source for expert cybersecurity advice, guidance, service and support for Canada's government, critical infrastructure owners and operators, the private sector and the public.

8.   **CyberNB:** Canada's Epicentre for Cybersecurity

CyberNB has built an extensive network of national and international partners and collaborators in business, government and academia. As a dynamic non-profit organization, we are a bridge and multiplier for the joint development of Canada's booming cybersecurity sector.

9.   **Cyber NYC:** Building New York City's.Cyber Future

Cyber NYC works with all stakeholders in the New York City cyber ecosystem: corporations, venture capitalists, opinion leaders, students, universities, government officials and cyberspace workers.

10. CyberOregon

The Oregon Cybersecurity Advisory Board was formed to develop a shared vision to create a cross-industry cybersecurity center of excellence in collaboration with Oregon's cybersecurity businesses, private sector security professionals, educational institutions, law enforcement agencies, and local governments.

11. UK Cybersecurity Association

The UK Cyber Security Council is for anyone interested in cyber security issues. You might be someone interested in seeking a job in an industry with a large company that needs help and support to protect yourself from cyber threats.

12. German Cyber Security Council e.V.

Members of the Association consist of large corporations, operators of critical infrastructure, numerous federal states (eg North Rhine-Westphalia, Mecklenburg-Vorpommern), large cities (eg Frankfurt) and experts and decision makers in their fields. cyber security.

13. **CSIA:** Cyber, Space, and Intelligence Association

The CSIA provides a critical medium for exchange of ideas between national security leaders in government, industry, and Congress, focusing on the challenges and opportunities in cybersecurity, space, and intelligence.

14. CyberTexas Foundation

Since 1999, our founders have created and spearheaded many successful developments in San Antonio's growing cyber ecosystem. In April 2015 the CyberTexas Foundation was born. Our mission is to advance cybersecurity in San Antonio, Texas through education, workforce development and readiness.

15. Texas Cybersecurity Council

The Texas Cybersecurity Commission represents the recognition that cybersecurity initiatives cannot rely solely on government. Council members represent all areas of the public and private sectors, government agencies, public and private institutions of higher education, and private businesses in Texas.

16. Louisiana Cybersecurity Commission

The Louisiana Cybersecurity Commission is a state partnership made up of key stakeholders, subject matter experts, and cybersecurity experts from the Louisiana public sector, private sector, academia, and law enforcement.

Security Countermeasures

External

According to Bendovschi (2015), many organizations without any profit are fighting against cyber attacks such as "International Association of Cyber Crime Prevention" (IACP) or "Secure Domain Foundation" (SDF) are creating awareness towards the cyber crime, its risks, and how they are caused and how to defend these attacks. Now a days google also started "Project Zero" to find the bugs and attacks on their own. Some financial institutions like AXA Corporate Solutions Company have started a product which has insurance covering all costs needed to recover a cyber attack.

Internal

Continuous Risk Assessment: A series of steps need to be performed by companies based on their size and setup because no two companies are same.

IT Environment Health: All the hardware and software being used in the company must be properly protected with latest updates, patches and see that no exception occurs. The companies also must make sure that there is agreement of maintenance by the third parties to do the maintenance and upgrade services.

Authentication: Access to data and programs in the company depending on risk assessment must be limited only to trusted people or based on roles. Remote access of files needs to be authenticated with at least any two combinations like random PIN or password or biometric or any other authentication technique.

Internal Commitment and Responsibility: Every staff need to take responsibility of the policies and need to be followed properly so that no chance of any vulnerability may occur.

Access to Information: Access permissions needed to be taken care by the company by removing the access of employee who left the organization and after change in roles permissions to access need to be changed accordingly.

Data Retention: To avoid compromising of information the best practice to be followed is to remove the unwanted data and all the servers or archives must be disconnected from the network.

CONCLUSION

This study tells the reader what is cyber-crime. What are its causes, its types and what type of attacks are possible on the digital information. This study also deals with cyber terrorism. This study gives the reader the complete idea behind cyber crime and different organizations over the world helping people to recover from the cyber-crime. This study also tells what countermeasures can be taken externally and internally to prevent cyber-crime.

REFERENCES

Alava, S., Chaouni, N., & Charles, Y. (2020). How to characterise the discourse of the far-right in digital media? Interdisciplinary approach to preventing terrorism. *Procedia Computer Science*, *176*, 2515–2525. doi:10.1016/j.procs.2020.09.324

Alsulami, H. (2022). Implementation analysis of reliable unmanned aerial vehicles models for security against cyber-crimes: Attacks, tracebacks, forensics and solutions. *Computers & Electrical Engineering*, *100*, 107870. doi:10.1016/j.compeleceng.2022.107870

Bendovschi, A. (2015). Cyber-Attacks – Trends, Patterns and Security Countermeasures. *Procedia Economics and Finance*, *28*, 24–31. doi:10.1016/S2212-5671(15)01077-1

Bottazzi, G., & Me, G. (2014). Responding to cyber crime and cyber terrorism—botnets an insidious threat. *Cyber Crime and Cyber Terrorism Investigator's Handbook*, 231–257.

Cho, H. S., & Woo, T. H. (2017). Cyber security in nuclear industry – Analytic study from the terror incident in nuclear power plants (NPPs). *Annals of Nuclear Energy*, *99*, 47–53. doi:10.1016/j.anucene.2016.09.024

Global Cybersecurity Exposure Index. (2020). https://10guards.com/en/articles/global-cybersecurity-exposure-index-2020

Griffiths, C. (2023). *The Latest Cyber Crime Statistics*. AAG IT Support.

Interpol. (2020, August 4). *INTERPOL report shows alarming rate of cyberattacks during COVID-19*. Www.interpol.int

Kaur, J., & Kumar, K. R. R. (2021). *The Recent Trends in CyberSecurity: A Review. Journal of King Saud University*. Computer and Information Sciences.

Kebande, V. R., Mudau, P. P., Ikuesan, R. A., Venter, H. S., & Choo, K.-K. R. (2020). Holistic digital forensic readiness framework for IoT-enabled organizations. *Forensic Science International: Reports*, *2*, 100117.

Kenney, M. (2015). Cyber-Terrorism in a Post-Stuxnet World. *Orbis*, *59*(1), 111–128. doi:10.1016/j.orbis.2014.11.009

Khudhair, A. S. (2020). Internet Addiction. *Scholars Journal of Medical Case Reports*, *08*(04), 505–507. doi:10.36347jmcr.2020.v08i04.025

Lagazio, M., Sherif, N., & Cushman, M. (2014). A multi-level approach to understanding the impact of cyber crime on the financial sector. *Computers & Security, 45*, 58–74. doi:10.1016/j.cose.2014.05.006

Li, Y., & Liu, Q. (2021). A comprehensive review study of cyber-attacks and cyber security; Emerging trends and recent developments. *Energy Reports, 7*(7), 8176–8186. doi:10.1016/j.egyr.2021.08.126

List of Cybersecurity Associations and Organizations. (2018, February 28). *Cybercrime Magazine.*

Lubis, M., & Handayani, D. O. D. (2022). The relationship of personal data protection towards internet addiction: Cyber crimes, pornography and reduced physical activity. *Procedia Computer Science, 197*, 151–161. doi:10.1016/j.procs.2021.12.129

Luiijf, E. (2014). New and emerging threats of cyber crime and terrorism. *Cyber Crime and Cyber Terrorism Investigator's Handbook*, 19–29.

MacDermott, Á., Baker, T., Buck, P., Iqbal, F., & Shi, Q. (2020). The Internet of Things: Challenges and Considerations for Cybercrime Investigations and Digital Forensics. *International Journal of Digital Crime and Forensics, 12*(1), 1–13. doi:10.4018/IJDCF.2020010101

Moslemzadeh Tehrani, P., Abdul Manap, N., & Taji, H. (2013). Cyber terrorism challenges: The need for a global response to a multi-jurisdictional crime. *Computer Law & Security Report, 29*(3), 207–215. doi:10.1016/j.clsr.2013.03.011

Okutan, A., & Çebi, Y. (2019). A Framework for Cyber Crime Investigation. *Procedia Computer Science, 158*, 287–294. doi:10.1016/j.procs.2019.09.054

Plotnek, J. J., & Slay, J. (2021). Cyber terrorism: A homogenized taxonomy and definition. *Computers & Security, 102*, 102145.

Saidi, F., Trabelsi, Z., Salah, K., & Ghezala, H. B. (2017). Approaches to analyze cyber terrorist communities: Survey and challenges. *Computers & Security, 66*, 66–80. doi:10.1016/j.cose.2016.12.017

Servida, F., & Casey, E. (2019). IoT forensic challenges and opportunities for digital traces. *Digital Investigation, 28*, S22–S29. doi:10.1016/j.diin.2019.01.012

Shree, R., Shukla, A. K., Pandey, R. P., & Shukla, V. (2021). A contiguous cyber crime investigation framework to deal with the cyber dependent-cum-cyber enabled crimes. *Materials Today: Proceedings.* Advance online publication. doi:10.1016/j.matpr.2020.12.428

Siburian, H. K. (2016). Emerging Issue in Cyber Crime: Case Study Cyber Crime in Indonesia. *International Journal of Scientific Research, 5*(11), 511–514.

Timofeyev, Y., & Dremova, O. (2022). Insurers' responses to cyber crime: Evidence from Russia. *International Journal of Law, Crime and Justice, 68*, 100520. doi:10.1016/j.ijlcj.2021.100520

Varga, G. (2021, October 25). *Global Cybercrime Report: Which Countries Are Most At Risk? 2022.* SEON.

von Solms, R., & van Niekerk, J. (2013). From information security to cyber security. *Computers & Security, 38*, 97–102. doi:10.1016/j.cose.2013.04.004

Willems, E. (2011). Cyber-terrorism in the process industry. *Computer Fraud & Security, 2011*(3), 16–19. doi:10.1016/S1361-3723(11)70032-X

Yaacoub, J.-P. A., Noura, H. N., Salman, O., & Chehab, A. (2022). Advanced digital forensics and anti-digital forensics for IoT systems: Techniques, limitations and recommendations. *Internet of Things, 19*, 100544. doi:10.1016/j.iot.2022.100544

Yaacoub, J.-P. A., Salman, O., Noura, H. N., Kaaniche, N., Chehab, A., & Malli, M. (2020). Cyber-physical systems security: Limitations, issues and future trends. *Microprocessors and Microsystems, 77*, 103201. doi:10.1016/j.micpro.2020.103201 PMID:32834204

Chapter 20
Cyberbullying:
The Panorama for Prevention and Overcoming Cyberbullying

Sharad Shandhi Ravi

https://orcid.org/0009-0008-7134-013X

VelTech Rangarajan Dr. Sagunthala R&D Institute of Science and Technology, India

ABSTRACT

Children and teens often use the internet today. Because kids and teens are using the internet more frequently, a new kind of bullying (harassment) called cyberbullying has emerged. The schoolyard is no longer a place where harassment is accepted. Cyberbullying is the term used to describe harassment that takes place online. Cyberbullying has commonly been described as a "extreme, deliberate activity or action carried out by an individual or a group utilising electronic forms of contact, repeatedly and over time against a victim who cannot quickly defend himself or herself." In addition to mail, pictures, messages, smartphones, internet, and social media sites, bullying may also happen through other avenues. A 22-year-old girl in Kerala, India, who was a famous TikToker, supported the Kerala minister's approaches towards cyberbullying. Only because of that has she been continuously bullied by her followers. The followers used bad commends and threatened her by saying she will be raped by them. Impact of cyberbullying, preventive measures, and law support are discussed here.

INTRODUCTION

A web-based technology known as social media aims to facilitate social interaction among a large number of individuals via a network .The Internet is a common and widely used network .However, social media platforms can also be used by local networks .The most recent technological revolution has led to the rapid expansion of social media and its inevitable incorporation into everyday life .The increasing use of smart phones is the reason for this stunning growth .With smart phones, it is simple to virtually access any social media platform from anywhere .These social media sites' mobile versions are so user-

DOI: 10.4018/978-1-6684-8145-5.ch020

Copyright © 2023, IGI Global. Copying or distributing in print or electronic forms without written permission of IGI Global is prohibited.

friendly because they are so simple to use. Additionally, the Map services were used extensively on mobile devices to quickly and easily locate locations and directions.

On social media sites, users may exchange information, engage in conversations, and produce digital content. They can design widgets, podcasts, photo and video sharing sites, social media platforms, virtual worlds, blog posts, wikis, micro - blogs, and other types of social media, to name a few. Social media is used by billions of people across the world to connect and exchange information. On a personal level, social media may be used to communicate with loved ones, learn new things, expand your hobbies, and have fun. Social media may be used professionally to network with other business people and deepen your understanding of a certain subject. On a professional level, social media may be used to engage with customers, get feedback, and establish your brand.

Hence a social media has thousands of benefits at the same time it has demerits also. Cyber bullying, one of the most significant drawbacks of social media, is one of its worst features. Cyberbullying is the act of bullying that takes place on social media platforms. The majority of people make fun of other people by using fake social media accounts .They can do whatever they want and can't be found easily. Assuming someone else's identity and creating fraudulent accounts to send damaging messages to other individuals or on their behalf; posting humiliating films or pictures of someone else online; and utilising messaging apps to send threatening, abusive, or insulting photographs, videos, or messages. Bullying and cyberbullying frequently happen together.

This chapter mention some incident, happened recently.

Meera is one of Kerala's most powerful individuals. She is an accomplished author and screenwriter. She was recently honoured by the Kerala government with the Kerala Sahithya Academy Award. Several members of the party harassed her when she commented on an MLA's Facebook post. Subsequently, she was abused again again by some other party members for her support for migrant labour. She was not bothered by the negative experiences she had. She struggled against it. She was a brave lady. All of these instances occurred during COVID-19.

An actress, she was just 18 years old and acted in the movie Thanneermathan. She was subjected to psycho bitching; hence, she posted casual photos on Instagram. Several people were offended by her choice of wearing shorts and wrote hateful comments in the remarks area. It was reported by Manorama news paper on 20/5/2020.

Cyberbullying is a new cultural problem that demonstrates the two-edged nature of modern innovation, which is always balancing between risks and spectacular open doors. In India, the great majority of teenagers have some sort of online connection. More than 87% of fourth- to tenth-graders are now prepared to use the Internet from the convenience of their own homes, and the percentage of kids and teenagers who use the Internet at home is rising quickly. Kids may take part in a variety of online activities including playing games, researching information, and communicating with friends. However, a number of recent allegations of the Web's detrimental societal effects, which occur in both academic work and well-known media, have recently overtaken the list of benefits. Web offences including cyberstalking, sexual exploitation, and cyberbullying, which all endanger the welfare of kids and teenagers who use the Internet, have received a lot of attention. Children's bullying and aggressiveness is a well-known and inescapable societal problem. The unfortunate byproduct of linking young people's hostility with technological communication is cyberbullying, and this phenomenon's growth is cause for alarm. The opportunity to direct research on cyberbullying is good due to its widespread prevalence and the social issue it addresses. When the research is concluded, the personal elements that should be looked at include socioeconomics, personal experiences, vicarious experiences, and protective resources.

They intimidate other individuals by making fun of them and sending them offensive videos and images. Bullying is considerably simpler when done online. They insult others and tease them in numerous ways, which makes other people feel insecure. Young children and teenagers are the primary targets of cyberbullying. Desperation, anxiety, and many other symptoms of stress are all brought on by cyberbullying. On the other side, cyberbullying leaves a digital trail(Foot print) that might be helpful and act as proof to put an end to the abuse.

BACKGROUND

This chapter included five news stories and survey reports, as well as four conference paper reports, in my literature study. With this research review, the ugliness of cyberbullying may be simply determined.

On 8/2/2021, BBC News reported on Phoebe Jameson's terrible ordeal. Around 10,000 obnoxious accounts had been blocked by herself. She was receiving 100 death threats every day on the internet. She was trolled for the first time after sharing torso photographs and words on social media. Phoebe's portrait on International Women's Day in March last year provoked a barrage of criticism and "dozens of remarks" regarding her appearance.

According to McAfee's research on kids, teenagers, and technology,' one in every three Indian young people has suffered the agony of internet abuse, and half have come across classmates who have.

According to recent international research conducted by computer security software company McAfee, 60% of Canadian youngsters as old as 10 had endured some kind of cyberbullying. The global figure is just slightly higher, at 63%. The report, "Cyberbullying in Plain Sight," offers insight on cyberbullying patterns according to poll responses from 11,687 parents and their children last summer in nine countries, notably 1,516 in Canada.

Social media is being used by people of all ages, not just youngsters. Despite the fact that teens use more. They can't imagine their lives before the Internet and social media. That's how addicted they are. They are carving out their own territory and forming networks of like-minded people (Reich,2010). They are exploring social media. They are also exploited at the same time.

According to a poll conducted by UNICEF and the UN Special Representative of the Secretary-General (SRSG), one out of every three young children has been bullied. This poll was carried out in 35 nations. They came to the same conclusion based on the poll.

MAIN FOCUS OF THE CHAPTER

Definition

Harassment that takes place on computers, smartphones, and tablets is known as cyberbullying. Cyberbullying can occur online in web-based entertainment, debates, or games where people can see, participate in, or exchange content via SMS, text messages, apps, or online. The act of expressing unfavourable, nasty, malicious, or cruel statements about another person online is known as cyberbullying. In certain circumstances, it comprises disclosing a person's private or sensitive information in a way that embarrasses or humiliates them. Cyberbullying occasionally veers over into unethical or illegal behaviour.

Table 1. Literature survey

Author	Title	Country	Year	Target	Findings
Iranzo et al. (2020)	Cyberbullying, psychosocial adjustment, and suicidal ideation in adolescence	UK	2020	A senior member	In this study, A group of people with autism participated in this study. On social media, a 15-year-old kid shared a video about a 10-year-old boy. That youngster was bullied by social media users from the start, which caused him to lose confidence.
Kırcaburun et al. (2019)	Problematic online behaviors among adolescents and emerging adults: Associations between cyberbullying perpetration, problematic social media use, and psychosocial factors	UK	2019	902 ages 13-23 and 604 ages 20-47	Someone bullies people who are more engaged on social media in this chapter. Such individuals have less social relationships. They are unconcerned about what is going on outside. One worrisome reality is that if even a minor negative event occurs, those people become sad and isolated.
Janopaul-Naylor & Feller (2019)	Cyberbullying: Harassment at your fingertips	USA	2019		A frequent condition is mentioned in this paper. Who uses social media? Individuals who are subjected to a great deal of bullying, such as extortion, sexual harassment, and so forth.
Nakano et al. (2016)	Analysis of Cyber Aggression and Cyber-bullying in Social Networking	USA	2016		This study examines Ask.fm, a social media platform where people establish accounts and post questions to one another, and analyses hostile user behaviour that may occur.This might result in cyberbullying occurrences

The use of technology to annoy, undermine, disparage, or focus on another person is known as cyber-bullying. Threats made online are taken seriously, as are crude, offensive, or negligent tweets, postings, or comments. It also counts to publish private information, pictures, or recordings with the intention of tormenting or demeaning someone.

With the prevalence of online entertainment and sophisticated gatherings, comments, photos, posts, and other content posted by individuals are commonly seen by both outsiders and coworkers. A person's online content, including both their own content and any offensive, degrading, or harmful content, creates a kind of publicly accessible, permanent record of their beliefs, actions, and behaviour. This free report may be thought of as a web-based standing that may be accessible to employers, colleges, clubs, schools, and other people who may be looking into an individual now or in the future. In addition to the victim of the harassment and those who perpetrate it or participate in it, cyberbullying can harm the online reputations of all parties involved. Cyberbullying has remarkable characteristics in that it tends to be:

Consistent: Experience cyberbullying may have trouble getting assistance since computers allow for instantaneous, continuous communication throughout the day.

Super Durable: Information shared electronically is permanent and accessible to everyone if it isn't disclosed and deleted. A bad online reputation, particularly for those who pose a threat, can have an impact on job interviews, school acceptances, and other regular difficulties.

Difficult to Notice: Understand since instructors and parents might not hear or see cyberbullying taking place.

Why Do People Do It?

In light of the reality that parents and teachers may not be able to make it happen, why do people really make it happen?

How could somebody engage in cyberbullying? Probably as many explanations exist as there are actual threats. Online provocations that appear to be deliberate can turn out to be accidental. It may be challenging to tell whether someone is joking due to the ambiguity of instant chats, postings, and other online forms of communication. Most people are aware when they are being harassed since it involves making repeated threats or insults. The harassers are aware that they have crossed a line. It's anything but a snide remark or an insult; the hazards go beyond the usual tomfoolery poking or a horrifying comment uttered out of annoyance. The majority of the time, cyberbullying happens for the same causes as other forms of tormenting, but because it happens in secret, it could be much more entertaining. Famous individuals and those on the periphery of society are the two groups who are most likely to pose a threat, according to "Stopbullying.gov.

Popular Children or Teenagers Might Pose a Menace

Some people are making an effort to get notoriety by using web-based entertainment as a result of the growing popularity of virtual entertainment. An important part of this is played by Instagram. In today's youth, it's rare to find someone without an Instagram account. Not many of the recordings in this call for social relay. The majority of these are time-lapse or savagery recordings. Today's people find Instagram to be quite enticing. A few studies claim that the average youth constantly spends 3 to 4 hours on it. A lot of YouTube channels are continuously opened. In the meanwhile, some people are uploading contentious recordings to Popular. People often discuss entertainers, and they are more prevalent than missiles. These recordings have a sizable audience. YouTubers are repeatedly documenting this kind of trick after realising this. People that publish such questionable videos become famous and earn a respectable living through YouTube. Such recorders seldom consider how offensive their recordings are to the person they are offending. Some people purposefully create these recordings to insult. Some people willfully distribute blabbermouth recordings in an effort to cause harm to others and find satisfaction.

Kids or Adolescents Who Are Less Socially Effective May Be a Menace

- It helps them adjust to their own lack of confidence.
- It helps them see that there are persons in the public who are ignorant and disparage others. They boost their self-confidence by doing it. It is undoubtedly a psychological issue. No matter how little they may seem, people like these cause issues.
- They believe it will help them and their friends locate a place to live. Peers are people who are comparable to your coworkers and are your age. Peer pressure is what you experience when someone tries to persuade you to act in a certain manner or follow through on a decision. Whether or whether your buddies are limiting you, you should still act like them. Needing to blend in is common. As long as it seems proper for you as well, it's acceptable to share your friends' and

classmates' interests or behaviours. However, acting naturally is the best course of action, even if it means acting differently from your buddies. For instance, if a child in your group makes fun of a child who actually has a disability, you might be held accountable for doing the same. Or, on the other side, you can act in this way out of fear of being shunned from that meeting.

- They have trouble comprehending the people they harm. Additional examples of cyberbullying victimised by harassment Sometimes, after experiencing cyberbullying themselves, bullies turn into threats. They may be doing this in an effort to feel more in control or in response to feeling duped and unable to defend themselves against the first arrogant jerk. Conflicts and Separations' effects cyberbullying between two individuals who were once friends or in a relationship can be brought on by conflicts within the group or the breakup of the relationship. In light of this, it's possible to interpret this type of cyberbullying as motivated by retaliation or envy. It has been suggested that some people engage in cyberbullying out of exhaustion or a desire to judge another online character. Cyberbullying of this kind is frequently enigmatic. Sadness or Segregation Persons who struggle with social isolation or cyberbullying may also be such people. In the unlikely event that they feel ignored by others, they may explode as a way to feel better or as a way to lash out at society. On the off chance that they feel disregarded by others, they might erupt as a method for feeling better or to vent their fury at society.

Aim

When they engage in web-based tormenting, cyberbullies, in large part, expect to do harm to others. In any instance, harassment might occur unexpectedly if a person perceives actions to be risky.

Redundancy

The hallmark of typical cyberbullying is repetition. This refers to ongoing interactions with the dominating jerk as well as the possibility that information posted online might persist a lot longer than the original harassment. This is especially clear in light of the use of sharing personal information or images in cyberbullying.

Power Lopsidedness

The fact that the victims are engaged in a power struggle with their dominant jerk is another characteristic of cyberbullying. On the off event if the harassment takes place during a public conversation, this may be especially noticeable.

Secrecy

Cyberbullies employ secrecy to hide behind their computer screens when they abuse others online. There is no necessity for a power disparity in the relationship between the harasser and the target in this scenario.

How Cyberbullying Differs From In-Person Bullying

Just Kidding(Tease) and Bulling

People can communicate with one another by laughing at each other. It's a social transaction. In order to bond or form relationships, many adults tease each other. When the best cricket player on the team misses a catch and a friend says, "looser" they can both laugh it off. The teasing demonstrates to each other that they can laugh and remain friends. If done with a positive attitude, this banter can be beneficial. The adult learn how to respond to constructive criticism when they tease one another about their clothes, musical preferences, or behavior. It's a part of their relationship.

Teasing can also be used by kids to influence one another and change their behavior. During lunch, friends may question an adolescent who appears to be fixated on a male she likes, "Seriously, are you gazing at Aswin again? Speak to him immediately! Through this taunting, she picks up a social norm (don't gaze too much) and is inspired to act correctly.. However, teasing can also be used to convey negativity. It is frequently used to make a child the "top dog." A group of girls might, for instance, make fun of one of the boys' colour. Or they might tease the kids to get them to do bad things: Abhin, you're such a weakling that you won't even try smoking.

Additionally, what may be amusing to one child may not be amusing to another. In situations like these, teasing can cause hurt feelings. Groups of children can be separated by teasing one another. There might be a few kids playing together. He is told, "No, you can't play with us," when another child comes to join them. Because that is how they have been taught to interact with others, some children make fun of each other. A child is likely to respond the same way if he frequently hears negative comments at home, from friends, or on his favorite television shows. Teasing can be fun as well. Take, for instance, the back-and-forth conversation that occurs in every romantic comedy.

Harassment, defamation, and manipulation are all examples of cyberbullying. These hostile behaviors are extremely harmful and can easily have a significant impact on anyone. They occur on informational websites, social media platforms, and public forums. A stranger might be a cyberbully as well as a well-known person. Cyberbullying is a widespread issue. However, the goal of this action remains the same—to hurt other people. Cyberbullying is a significant issue. It must be handled seriously since it might have a lot of negative consequences for the victim. It also has an impact on someone's tranquilly. Numerous people have reported that depression and cyberbullying are related. They also cause themselves harm. They are less happy as a result of all the nasty comments directed at them. Cyberbullying has an impact on a person's mental health. It has an impact on their mental well-being. Furthermore, it besmirches an individual's reputation.

On account of cyberbullying, the victim for the most part has no way out of the maltreatment and badgering. Unlike genuine experiences, web-based tormenting and the Internet never truly shut down, and harassing can be relentless. This can cause casualties to feel like they have no way out, especially in the event that the harassing includes sharing their own data or when something posted about them becomes famous online. This sort of tormenting can happen over a long period of time. Tormenting is the act of assaulting another person verbally, internally, or physically. In order to establish the harasser's dominance over the target of his abuse, it is anything but a one-time incident and is carried out over an extended period of time. It may very well be completed by a single person or by a group of people in settings including the workplace, homes, churches, neighbourhood, and colleges. Children are more vulnerable to harassment, and a significant number of schoolchildren experience harassment at school. It mostly happens in lobbies, restrooms, school buses, and during bunch exercises. It can be done in remote areas, but it can also happen with people watching. Not just their companions menace schoolchildren; in some cases, even educators and the framework commit unobtrusive maltreatment.

Using technology, such as chats on phones and messages or texts on the Online platform, torment can also happen in the workplace, in the military, and online. This is referred to as "digital harassment," a form of harassment that is hard to pinpoint the perpetrator of since he may surely masquerade as another person. It includes publishing false information about someone to make him feel ashamed as well as communicating scorn, danger, and sexual comments.

Types of Cyberbullying

- **Blazing:** Flaring alludes to utilising fiery language about somebody or broadcasting hostile messages about them with the expectation of inspiring a response. Likewise, "Blazing" is posting individual put-downs and foul and irate words. Flaring is an extreme disagreement that typically occurs on message boards, through texts, or via email. It might likewise happen via virtual entertainment destinations and YouTube. It is an extremely forceful type of terrorism. One model would be Donald Trump's utilisation of the expressions "Warped Hillary" or "Tired Joe Biden."
- **Savaging:** Savaging is the deliberate publication of content or the making of comments with the intent of evoking degrading internet replies. Finally, a savage will say anything negative or unpleasant about a person or group with the intent of enraged others. This type of cyberbully likes sowing havoc and then watching the consequences.
- **Verbally Abusing:** Ridicule includes using angry language to make fun of people. According to reports, 45% of youngsters have been called nasty names on their mobile phone or the Internet.
- **Spreading Bogus Reports:** Cyberbullies who spread misleading tales make up anecdotes about people and then spread these misleading insights on the web. In a similar report, 32% of teenagers said that somebody had spread bogus tales about them on the Internet.
- **Sending Unequivocal Pictures or Messages:** Cyberbullies may likewise send express pictures or messages without the assent of the person in question.
- **Digital Following/Annoying/Actual Dangers:** Some cyberbullies will over and again focus on similar individuals through cyberstalking, digital badgering, or actual dangers. In that equivalent report, 16% of teenagers announced having survived actual dangers on the Web.
- **Outing:** An outing entails posting private or embarrassing information online about someone. This type of cyberbullying typically occurs on a broader scale rather than being organised or in a smaller group.

Why Do People Become Cyberbullies?

While some people are threats both in person and on the internet, others only become threats in the advanced space. Why would that be the situation? How could somebody menace others online when they could never do that in their daily existence? There are numerous potential clarifications for this way of behaving.

Non-Angry and Mysterious

The primary motivation behind why individuals might become menaces online when they wouldn't in their daily existence has to do with the idea of the Web. An individual can menace others on the web and remain totally unknown. Obviously, this is unimaginable with conventional harassing. Furthermore, web-based harassing should be possible in a non-fierce manner, especially in the event that it is mysterious. This implies that a cyberbully may skirt the Web, leaving terrible remarks, and not stay close by to hear the answers.

No requirement for prominence or actual strength.

To be a domineering jerk, you usually need to have some sort of advantage over your victim. This could imply that you are genuinely bigger than them. It could imply that you are better known than them. Or, on the other hand, it could imply that you have a power imbalance over them of some kind or another. Conversely, anyone can be a cyberbully. There is a compelling reason to have actual strength or fame. This implies that individuals who need to threaten can easily do so on the Internet regardless of their actual status.

Section is not hampered. Like the idea that a compelling reason should be prevailing or well known, there is likewise an exceptionally low obstruction to turning into a cyberbully. Anybody with access to the Web can get everything rolling. Companions are characterised freely on the web, which causes what is going on to make it extremely simple to menace others.

There Is No Criticism From Casualty

Finally, the last reason why individuals who do not threaten may engage in cyberbullying is a lack of criticism from their victim. Cyberbullies, for the most part, harass over a long period of time, in part because there isn't generally criticism from the victim, as there would be in an eye-to-eye connection. Somebody who, in actuality, would see the effect on their victim and back off may not do likewise in that frame of mind of cyberbullying.

Major Problems of Cyberbulling

Even at home, it could seem like you're under assault everywhere, when bullying happens online. There may appear to be no way out. The effects can be long-lasting and have many different effects on a person:

Emotional Effect

Cyberbullying victims may suffer as a result of the tremendous stress it creates in their life. According to research, three out of every ten youngsters who are the victim of cyberbullying demonstrate at least one stress-related symptom. losing interest in their favourite activities or feeling humiliated. Bullies may post sensitive details regarding the victim on the Internet, causing significant emotional trauma to the victim. They may feel awful about going online and slandering their relatives and friends. By staying firm with them, you might let the sufferer recognise that it was regrettable and that you have their support.

Mental Effect

Victims may have a different perspective on the world than others when cyberbullying is ongoing. Life can seem hopeless and without purpose for many people. They might spend less time interacting with friends and family and lose interest in activities they used to enjoy. Additionally, depression and suicidal ideation can occur at any time.

Low Self-Worth

Most of the time, cyberbullying targets the aspects of the victims' lives that make them feel the most vulnerable. A child who is embarrassed by a birthmark, for instance, might be bullied as a result. Even if this is not the case, self-esteem can be damaged by online bullying. Victims of bullying may become increasingly dissatisfied with themselves. People may begin to question their own worth as a result. Cyberbullying can result in psychological maladaptation, diminished well-being, and ultimately low self-esteem, according to studies. Young people have a strong psychological need to be accepted by and belong to their peers.

Academic Problems

Cyberbullying may cause children to lose interest in school. As a result, they frequently have much higher absenteeism rates than children who are not abused. They might skip school to avoid being confronted by the children who are cyberbullying them, or they might do so because the messages that were posted online make them feel ashamed and humiliated. They may also see a decline in their grades as a result of their inability to concentrate or study. Additionally, in some instances, children may either abandon school or lose interest in pursuing higher education.

Suicidal Ideation and Self-Harm

Cyberbullying victims occasionally self-harm in response to their intense emotions. Some may, for instance, commit self-harm by cutting or burning themselves. In fact, bullying and self-harm have consistently been linked in research

Anxiety and Depression

Distress, melancholy, and other stress-related disorders can affect victims of cyberbullying. In addition to the added stress of dealing with cyberbullying on a regular basis, they may lose their sense of happiness and fulfilment. It may also worsen feelings of anxiety and loneliness. Cyberbullying may undermine self-esteem and confidence, which can increase anxiety and depression. Research has consistently supported the premise that a rise in cyberbullying is connected with an increase in depression. According to one study, 89% of cyberbullying victims experienced grief, helplessness, and hopelessness.

Physical Effects

Cyberbullying can make you feel a lot of stress and anxiety, which can make you sick with things like sleeplessness, problems with your digestion, and bad eating habits.

Behavioral Effects

Children who are bullied online may show changes in behavior that are similar to those seen in children who are bullied in more traditional ways. For instance, they keep their identities a secret and stop participating in activities. In extreme cases, when cyberbullying continues for an extended period of time, children may even exhibit more significant behavioral changes.

Attributes of Victims

There are for sure a few familiar parts of the casualty that will generally be rehashed, including the accompanying characteristics:

- Teenagers and youthful grown-ups are the most in danger.
- On account of spreading bogus reports and being the beneficiaries of unequivocal pictures, young ladies are bound to be casualties.
- Individuals who are gay, lesbian, sexually open, or transsexual might be casualties on a more regular basis.
- People who are modest, socially off-kilter, or don't fit in effectively may become casualties.

    Individuals from lower-paying families are bound to be casualties.

- People who use the Internet frequently are bound to become victims of online harassers.

    Detailed instructions for managing a digital domain
    If your child is being bullied online, there are several adult and parental strategies you may use to cope with the cyberbully. Each of these problems deserves its own independent investigation.

As a Parent

Assuming your kid is being harassed on the web, the best strategy is to teach them not to answer the web. What's more, advise them to record each occurrence of digital harassment by saving instant messages, messages, photographs, and some other types of correspondence. This should be possible if necessary by using screen captures. Request that your child send this information to you so that you can keep track of everything.

    Then, on the off chance that the harassment is coming from a school contact, report the examples of cyberbullying to the instructor, head, or regulatory staff at your school. You should also report the harassing behaviour to the police if it is outrageous or dangerous.

    At last, it's essential to promise your teenager that they are not to blame for the harassment on the Web. A few casualties might feel that their conduct caused the issue or that they are somehow at fault. Thus, it's vital to ensure your youngster realises that what happened isn't their shortcoming. As a grown-up a large number of similar standards as above will apply to your circumstance as a grown-up managing a cyberbully. Above all else, make certain to track all cases of harassment, whether they come through your instant messages, courier talks, Facebook gatherings, Instagram DMs, or other web-based sources. Take screen captures and keep envelopes on your PC with proof of the cyberbullying.

Then, assuming you know the source of the cyberbullying, decide if there is a strategy you can take with respect to that individual. For instance, assuming it is a work partner or manager, is there somebody in HR at work that you can address? In the event that it is a relative, is there a method for raising this issue with other relatives to request their help? Finally, if it is someone you only know on the internet, could you ever stop and delete them from all your virtual entertainment? The best strategy will be to ignore the cyberbullying to the greatest extent possible.However, if you are receiving threats, you must report this to the police, along with the evidence that you have gathered.

As a Local Area

It isn't enough for victims of cyberbullying to manage their domineering jerks and attempt to track down arrangements. Regularly, these casualties are sincerely upset and unfit to track down help.

It is our responsibility as a community to pursue the development of frameworks that prevent cyberbullying from occurring in any way. A few likely thoughts for drives are recorded underneath.

Children and adolescents who are cyberbullied are still learning how to manage their emotions and social situations. Cyberbullying at this age could have enduring and long-lasting impacts. Emotional wellness assets ought to be set up to help survivors of cyberbullying deal with their psychological well-being.

Cyberbullying flourishes with status and endorsement. Cyberbullies will stop when social dismissal of cyberbullying turns out to be so boundless and common that they never again have anything to acquire. This implies that each example of web-based harassment that is seen (particularly on account of savage remarks) ought to be disregarded. Furthermore, there should be awareness campaigns emphasising that online harassment is not only unacceptable, but also indicative of a weak social position.

Schools are a resource for guardians attempting to help their youngsters who are being cyberbullied. Therefore, schools ought to have projects and conventions set up right away to quickly manage cyberbullying. Guardians shouldn't need to ask on various occasions for help without getting it.

Consider the Possibility That You Are the Cyberbully

What occurs if you are the cyberbully yourself? To stop, you must examine your motivations for harassing others, as this will educate you on your best course of action regarding activity. We should think about each of these and what you could do.

You are struggling with an emotional wellness problem.

In the event that you feel like your psychological well-being isn't looking great and this may be contributing to your cyberbullying behaviour, make a meeting with your primary care physician to examine your choices. For example, if you are dealing with outrage or hostility, you may benefit from an indignation in the executives' program.

In the event that you have little sympathy for other people or relate to the attributes of psychopathy, then it will be more difficult for you to track down understanding and change. Notwithstanding, you could attempt to channel your energy into various pursuits.

For instance, assuming you are cyberbullying somebody since it gives you a rush, is there a side interest you could take up or a business that you could begin that could give you a rush without ramifications for someone else?

You, Too, Were a Victim

If you were once a victim of cyberbullying and this is the reason you are now engaging in cyberbullying yourself, now is the time to investigate your options for change. It may be the case that you have unsettled outrage that should be taken out another way.

You may also feel more remarkable when you menace, which gives you the halting feeling of a casualty. All things considered, you might have to chip away at alternate ways of working on your identity so you can quit feeling defenceless and wild. All things considered, you were once a casualty yourself, and you know how that feels.

As opposed to continuing with a pattern of harassment and exploitation, you get an opportunity to break the cycle and transcend your past. You'll almost certainly need assistance, most likely expert assistance, to manage your past.

You Had a Controversy or Separation

On the off chance that you are cyberstalking somebody in light of a disagreement you had with them or a terrible separation, it's an opportunity to rethink your way of behaving. What do you expect to accomplish from your cyberstalking? Once more, you might require the assistance of an expert to manage your sentiments that have prompted this way of behaving.

You Are Alone or Confined

Consider the possibility that you are simply desolate, and this is the explanation why you have turned to cyberbullying. This kind of harassment falls into the field of individuals who might feel like the world has cruised them by. Or, on the other hand, every other person is out there appreciating life while you are separated from everyone else.

Find ways to expand your in-person friendly associations in this situation. Join a club, volunteer somewhere, or take up a side interest to meet others like yourself.

You've Had Enough

On the off chance that you are cyberbullying in light of the fact that you are exhausted (and you're not a maniac), then you'll need to consider the reason why you think it is satisfactory to hurt another person in return for making yourself less exhausted.

Unquestionably, many people are exhausted on the planet, but they never cyberbully. Take up a side interest, get familiar with a subsequent language, or track down something to do.

Common Online Bullying Sources Include

1. Websites for social media, including Instagram, Facebook, Snapchat, YouTube, and Twitter
2. Instant messaging apps like Telegram and WhatsApp
3. SMS, Email

Cyberbullying: Laws and Policies in India

According to the legislation, cyberbullying consists of three key components: The US National Crime Prevention Council defines cyberbullying as "the practise of using the Internet, mobile phones, or other devices to email or post text or photographs meant to hurt or disgrace another person." Cyberbullying is the word used to describe harassment of a person who uses the Internet, a mobile phone, or other digital devices. It include doing things like humiliating the victim publicly, revealing private information online, sending unpleasant text messages, etc.

1. Using abusive language
2. Making an effort to humiliate, abuse, or degrade the victim
3. Express the aforementioned via digital or informational communication technologies.

Unfortunately, India is quickly becoming the centre of the world's cyberbullying. These research highlight issues regarding this threat.

- In a 2012 Microsoft Corporation study of 25 nations, India came in third for the number of reported incidences of internet bullying.
- The Internet security company McAfee performed a research in 2014 that found that "Half of the youngsters in India had some experience with cyberbullying."

India Has Anti-Cyberbullying Legislation

Despite the fact that India lacks specific law to handle cyberbullying, Section 66A of the Information Technology Act does so. The consequences for delivering offensive, abusive, or insulting communications utilising digital and information communication technologies are laid forth in this Act.

Below is a list of additional laws that can be used to stop cyberbullying:

- Sending or publishing pornographic material - Section 67
- Publishing or sending sexually obscene content online in violation of Section 67A
- A word, gesture, or action that is meant to offend a woman's modesty - Section 509
- Sending libelous e-mails in violation of Section 499 IPC
- Printing, selling, or promoting obscene or defamatory material or anything meant to be used as leverage - Section 292A
- Contacting or trying to contact a lady while stalking her - Section 354D
- Making sexually suggestive comments is considered sexual harassment under Section 354 A.
- Privacy violation – Section 66E
- Sec. 507 - Criminal intimidation by anonymous communication

- A word, gesture, or action that is meant to offend a woman's modesty - Section 509
- Sending libelous e-mails in violation of Section 499 IPC.
- Techniques used to combat cyberbullying in other nations
- It is untrue to claim that India is the only country where cyberbullying is rife. Even nations like the USA, Canada, and the UK that have strict rules and regulations struggle to manage cyberbullying. In contrast to India, people in these nations prioritise combating cyberbullying, particularly when the victims are young students. Schools have policies in place to address cyberbullying. In order to cope with cyberbullying, school administrators and teachers are not the only ones who become involved. Counselors and, in some circumstances, legal authorities as well.
- There is discussion regarding whether parents may be held accountable for their children's improper usage of technology. Even in the context of India, this is a crucial factor to take into account.

How Can Bullying at Work Be Stopped?

Tell the bullies to stop in a conversation. They continue after that too. Speak with your manager or the HR department. Have plenty of proof with you and talk about your legal rights. Talk to your coworkers and discuss this with them. If they are also targets of bullying, document every instance in a report. In meetings, bring them up. Additionally, have a backup plan; if, despite your best efforts, the problem persists, quit your employment. However, seek for other employment before quitting; there are a number of chances.

- **Incorrect Provisions in the Employment Agreement:** The Industrial Disputes Act of 1947, namely Chapter 5A, outlines the procedures that companies must follow when terminating employees and retrenchment.
- **Maternity Benefit Act, 1961:** This law protects pregnant women from discrimination and stipulates that postpartum mothers can receive maternity benefits.
- The People with Disabilities Act of 1995's Section 24A prohibits discrimination in the workplace.
- **No Sex-Discrimination in Wages:** Employers are required to pay all employees the same amount for performing the same amount of work in accordance with Article 39(d) of the Constitution and Section 2(h) of the Equal Remuneration Act of 1976. Male and female employees are both subject to this requirement.

Anti-Bullying Tools

You can pick who can view your posts or leave comments on them, who can add you as an automatic friend, and how to report bullying events on each social networking site (see those that are available below). For blocking, muting, or reporting cyberbullying, many of them feature simple processes. We advise you to look into these. Social media companies also offer teaching materials and guidance on how to stay safe online to parents, teachers, and children.

You can also serve as the first line of defence against online bullying. Think about the instances of cyberbullying in your neighbourhood and how you may get involved by raising awareness of the issue, speaking up, calling out bullies, or contacting the appropriate parties. A tiny act of kindness could have a significant impact. The first line of defence against cyberbullying might be you. If you are worried about your safety or something that has happened to you online, talk to a trusted adult right immediately. In many countries, you can phone a specialised helpline for free and speak with someone anonymously.

Instagram/Facebook

To help keep kids safe, there are number of tools, including:

- You may covertly guard your account without that individual knowing by using Instagram's Restrict function.
- Your own postings may be subject to comment moderation.
- On Instagram, we'll send notifications to users when they're about to post something that might violate our Community Guidelines, urging them to think twice.
- You can modify your settings to limit direct messaging to people you follow solely.
- Instagram's Hidden Words feature assists in removing remarks and message requests that don't go against our Community Guidelines but can be interpreted as inappropriate or insulting. You can also construct your own word list.
  - For more tips on how to be proactive and have fun on Instagram, check out our guide on the platform, or look through our resources on Facebook's and Instagram's anti-bullying hubs.

TikTok

In addition to the work of our safety staff to prevent harassment and assault off our website, it provides a variety of options to let you control your TikTok experience. All of these are available on our Safety Centre. These are some key points:

- **Restrict Who Comments:** You may choose to have no one, only your friends, or everyone comment on your movies (we've eliminated the everyone selection for users under the age of 16).
- **Filter All Comments:** You may filter out all comments or only the ones that include a certain set of keywords. When we find spam or inappropriate comments, we automatically hide them from users.
- Multiple comment deletions or reports are available, as well as the ability to block users that repeatedly post offensive or otherwise objectionable comments (up to 100 at a time).
- **Comment Prompt:** A comment prompt reminds users of our Community Guidelines, urges them to pause before posting potentially offensive or harsh remarks, and provides them the chance to edit their comments before publishing.

Twitter

- On Twitter, we want everyone to feel secure. We keep releasing and improving tools so that individuals may feel safer, have more control, and manage their online presence. One can use the following security techniques on Twitter:
- **Select Who Can Reply to Your Tweets:** Choose whether anybody, just the individuals you follow, or only the persons you mention may react to your Tweets.

- **Mute:** This feature hides Tweets from a certain account from your timeline without unfollowing or banning that user.
- **Block:** Prevents certain accounts from getting in touch with you, viewing your Tweets, and following you.
- **Report:** Reporting abusive behaviour is one way to stop it.
- **Safety Mode:** A new function that momentarily disables accounts when they use language that might be dangerous or send frequent, unwanted responses or remarks.

How to File a Report

Using the Report link next to the material itself is the best way to report spam or abusive content on Facebook. Examples of how to report material to us are provided below. Find out more about filing abuse reports. Find out what you can do if you don't have an account or if you can't view the content you want to report (say, because someone blocked you). Content for reports profiles.

To Report a Profile
1. Locate the profile you want to report by searching for it or clicking on its name in your Feed.
2. Select Find support or report by clicking to the right.
3. Select the response option that most accurately reflects how this profile violates our Community Standards to offer feedback.
4. After receiving comments, you might be able to send a report to Meta. We don't require reports for some sorts of material, but we still utilise your comments to improve our systems. Select "Done".

You may block or unfriend someone on Facebook if they are bugging you.

To Report a Post
1. Start by going to the post you wish to report.
2. Click on the post's upper right corner.
3. Select Report post or Find assistance.
4. To provide comments, select the one that most accurately reflects how this post violates our Community Standards. Choose Next.
5. After receiving comments, you might be able to send a report to Meta. We don't require reports for some sorts of material, but we still utilise your comments to improve our systems. Select "Done"

Posts on Your Timeline
1. On Facebook, click your profile image in the upper right corner.
2. Click on the top right corner of the post.
3. Select the option that best explains how this post violates our Community Standards by clicking Find support or report post, and then click the next button.

Additionally, you have the option of blocking the author of this Facebook post.

To Report a Photo or Video

1. To enlarge the image or video, click on it. Click Find support or report photo if the profile is closed and you can't see the full-sized photo.
2. Select the image or video by clicking to the right.
3. Select Find support or Report Photo or Report Video, respectively, for images or videos.
4. Choose the one that most accurately reflects the problem, then follow the on-screen directions. Please use the report links after logging in from a computer if you're having difficulties reporting something.

To Report a Message That Goes Against Our Community Standards

1. Click on the top right corner of any Facebook page.
2. Check out the email.
3. Click if you see the notice as a pop-up window. Click whether the message was opened in message view.
4. Click There's a problem.
5. Select the response option that most accurately reflects how this communication violates our Community Standards to offer feedback.
6. You might then be able to submit a report to Meta depending on your feedback. We don't require reports for some sorts of material, but we still utilise your comments to improve our systems.

Please follow these specific guidelines if you wish to report a private discussion. You can inform us if you believe that a communication you received violates our Community Standards.

Additionally, you may report it using the Messenger app. Visit the Messenger Help Centre to find out how to report chats in the Messenger app. Find out more about the resources and tools for Facebook safety. Contact your local police if you ever feel that you or someone you know is in danger right away.

Pages

1. Click on the name of the Page you wish to report in your Feed or do a search for it.
2. Tap the area underneath the Page's cover image.
3. Click Report Page or Find Support.
4. To provide feedback, choose the one that most accurately reflects how this Page violates our Community Standards.
5. After receiving comments, you might be able to send a report to Meta. We don't require reports for some sorts of material, but we still utilise your comments to improve our systems.

Consider asking a friend to report the Page if you are unable to do it yourself.

Groups

In order to report a group you are a part of:

1. Locate the group you wish to report by typing its name into your search bar or clicking on its name in your Feed.
2. Click beneath the group's profile picture.
3. Choose the Report group.

To Report an Event

1. Click Events in the left menu from your Feed to report an event.
2. Visit the event you wish to report about.
3. Select Report event by clicking.
4. Select the response option that most accurately reflects how this profile violates our Community Standards to provide feedback.
5. After receiving comments, you might be able to send a report to Meta. We don't require reports for some sorts of material, but we still utilise your comments to improve our systems.

CONCLUSION

The amazing ability of the digital environment to combine proximity and remoteness raises new issues about how young people make personal and societal decisions. If there is to be some degree of limitation, instructors must provide students with the information and skills they need to manage risk sensibly, protect themselves, and assist vulnerable persons who are being harassed electronically. In other words, while penalties will always be essential, they will not be effective unless they are balanced by the opposing force of addressing the sentiments that underpin all of our connections with others. Being online connected to a community is an important component of young people's social reality. Its importance as a significant component of all young people's everyday activities cannot be overstated.

Most states have implemented legislation to prevent bullying, including cyberbullying, which has lately become increasingly prevalent. A growing number of community and educational leaders recognise the value in developing policies and implementing programmes that address both these behaviours and children's social norms and beliefs. All students must be taught how to respond appropriately to cyberbullying, and potential bullies must realise that their acts may result in severe consequences such as academic sanctions, legal action, and criminal prosecution.

REFERENCES

Fredrick, K. (2010). Mean girls (and boys): Cyberbullying and what can be done about it. *School Library Media Activities Monthly*, *25*(8), 44–45.

Iranzo, B., Buelga, S., Cava, M. J., & Ortega-Barón, J. (2019). Cyberbullying, psychosocial adjustment, and suicidal ideation in adolescence. *Intervención Psicosocial*, *28*(2), 75–81. doi:10.5093/pi2019a5

Janopaul-Naylor, E., & Feller, E. (2019). Cyberbullying: Harassment at your fingertips. *Rhode Island Medical Journal*, *102*(9), 7–9. PMID:31675779

Kırcaburun, K., Kokkinos, C. M., Demetrovics, Z., Király, O., Griffiths, M. D., & Çolak, T. S. (2020). Problematic Online Behaviors among Adolescents and Emerging Adults: Associations between Cyberbullying Perpetration, Problematic Social Media Use, and Psychosocial Factors. *International Journal of Mental Health and Addiction*, *17*(4), 891–908. doi:10.100711469-018-9894-8

Lanktree, C., & Briere, J. (1991, January). *Early data on the trauma symptom checklist for children (TSC-C)* [Paper presentation].The meeting of the American Professional Society on the Abuse of Children, San Diego, CA, United States.

McLoughlin, L. T., Spears, B. A., Taddeo, C. M., & Hermens, D. F. (2019). Remaining connected in the face of cyberbullying: Why social connectedness is important for mental health. *Psychology in the Schools*, *56*(6), 945–958. doi:10.1002/pits.22232

Nakano, T., Suda, T., Okaie, Y., & Moore, M. J. (2016, February). Analysis of cyber aggression and cyber-bullying in social networking. In *2016 IEEE Tenth International Conference on Semantic Computing (ICSC)* (pp. 337-341). IEEE. 10.1109/ICSC.2016.111

Chapter 21

Data Breach in the Healthcare System:
Enhancing Data Security

R. Parkavi
Thiagarajar College of Engineering, India

M. R. Jeya Iswarya
Thiagarajar College of Engineering, India

G. Kirithika
Thiagarajar College of Engineering, India

M. Madhumitha
Thiagarajar College of Engineering, India

O. Varsha
Thiagarajar College of Engineering, India

ABSTRACT

Computers, mobile devices, tablets, and other electronic devices are essential in our daily lives so the data plays a major role in it. Data is a valuable thing that might be stolen or leaked. Our ability to secure emerging technology is outpacing their development. Data storage is a critical component in any industry. Data security must be ensured across all industries, which is crucial. Data breaches, with an emphasis on the healthcare industry, are still on the rise as a result of inefficient data storage techniques like paperwork. Digital data storage is therefore becoming more secure. To store the data digitally, the proper software is needed. EHR (electronic health records) is the relevant program; information about patients, doctors, and medical histories is kept in the EHR. Blockchain technology might offer a way to safeguard this software, in particular if you desire more data security. The secure sharing of electronic data with patients, other doctors, and healthcare providers is made possible by blockchain-powered EHR systems.

DOI: 10.4018/978-1-6684-8145-5.ch021

Copyright © 2023, IGI Global. Copying or distributing in print or electronic forms without written permission of IGI Global is prohibited.

INTRODUCTION

The term "data breach" refers to a security lapse in which unauthorized people copy, hack, view, or access sensitive data. Data is a crucial consideration when determining the needs of a business in today's technology world. Government, healthcare, financial services, insurance, and other large-scale industries, as well as smaller ones like social media, have all experienced data breaches on a regular basis and are subject to severe repercussions as a result. With some technical measures, this kind of data breach is stopped. Hackers can access via bluetooth, text messaging, the internet, or any online services we utilize. One may be online or offline, it makes no difference to them. The two primary sources of data breaches are technological flaws and user behavior. Because of the stored sensitive data, the health care industry consistently ranks among the top five according to statistics of data breaches in various industries. There are numerous websites accessible for reporting the most recent data breaches in order to aid healthcare organizations in bolstering their cyber resilience.

The Office of the National Coordinator for Health Information Technology (ONC) is in charge of the administration's health IT initiatives and serves as a resource for the entire healthcare system. It supports the use of health information technology and the creation of a national, standardised health information exchange in an effort to enhance healthcare. Organizationally, ONC is housed under the Office of the Secretary of the U.S. Department of State. Data breaches frequently require more than a few password changes to be fixed. The reputation, wealth, and other things of an individual or group could suffer long-term as a result of a data leak. Particularly for for-profit businesses, a data breach can have disastrous effects on a company's reputation and financial health. One example of a company that has experienced a data breach is Equifax, another is Target. And now, rather than recalling those companies for their actual business operations, more people link or associate those companies with the incidence of the data breach. Compromised data may expose extremely private information to third parties for government agencies. Armed conflict, shady political dealings, and knowledge of vital national infrastructure are all potential threats to a government and its citizens. Prior to data protection, new technologies are evolving more quickly. The increase in data breaches is also caused by the usage of digital tools, features, and products with insufficient security testing. Data breaches are becoming more common as a result of certain individuals' bad digital practices. Individuals who are the victims of data breaches are at serious risk from identity theft. Data leaks can reveal anything, including banking and social security details. Once they get these details, a criminal can commit any kind of fraud using your name as a cover. Combating identity theft, which can harm your credit and get you in trouble with the law, is difficult. Breaches are widely observed in the healthcare sector.Based on the problems formulated (McLeod & Dolezel, 2018), the objectives are promoting consistency in how the healthcare organizations handle data; Keep the data safe, yet easy enough accessible to users (Patients and Doctors); Setting the risk tolerance among the organization; To prevent and detect fraud access; Ensuring confidentiality of patient and organization data; Promoting knowledge about data security among people; Promoting the idea of pre-planned methods for data security among the healthcare organization and to enhancing data security at certain periods, The main objective of this article is to advance Data Security in software used in the domain of Healthcare and to make use of Electronic Health Records in an efficient way; Enabling quick and safe access to patient records for more coordinated, efficient care; Ensuring data security that should tackle the vulnerability.

BACKGROUND

Patients, families, communities, and populations benefit from healthcare services. The hospital, surgery center, doctor polyclinics, doctor consultation clinic, and nursing home, pharmacy, and primary healthcare center are the major categories of healthcare service facilities. A health information system (HIS) is a platform designed to manage patient data. This includes the systems that collect, store, manage, and disseminate patient medical records as well as the day-to-day operations of a hospital. Clinical notes, social security numbers, administrative data, demographic data, a patient's diagnosis, course of treatment, prescription medications, laboratory test results, information on physiologic monitoring, hospitalization, patient insurance and so forth are all included in the information acquired. These kinds of PHI (Personal Health Information) are more valuable on the black market than Generally Ascertainable Information or credit card information. In order to safeguard the confidentiality, security, and integrity of protected health information, health care organisations must instill a HIPAA compliance mindset throughout their operations. Administrative, physical, and technological safeguards are the three cornerstones of HIPAA's approach to protecting protected health information. The three healthcare security safeguard themes are also referred to as these three foundations. Healthcare data collection frequently involves complex procedures and is subject to very strict rules. The majority of healthcare data gathering organizations employ a number of forms, such as health assessment forms, patient intake forms, authorization forms, and forms for evaluating treatments, among others. As soon as the data is gathered, that information may be accessed in the backend, it often goes through a manual data entry process. Examples of methods used to gather healthcare data include questionnaires, observations, and document inspection. Electronic, paper-based, or a hybrid format may be used to store medical records. Nowadays, the majority of data is gathered via digital means, including a wide variety of apps that are readily available. The most popular are listed below are the resources for gathering health information: The term "Customer Relationship Management" refers to a system for managing client relationships that creates, controls general data, produces reports and carries out different analyses (Chen et al., 2019); EHR stands for electronic health record system, it collects and examines patient data to generate more thorough understanding. Interactive Personal Health Records, often known as PHRs, are an expansion of the Electronic Health Records (EHR) that give individuals the ability to handle many facets of their own healthcare while also making it simpler for doctors to comprehend their patients' needs; CPOE, also known as computerized physician order entry, enables doctors to enter treatment-related orders and instructions directly into networked systems, and the information is then distributed to organizations and medical staff; Mobile applications are programmes that operate on mobile devices and link doctors and patients, as well as gather and retrieve data from various databases. Innovative computer systems called patient data management systems, or PDMS, make an effort to combine administrative duties and clinical decision making. Studies based on real-world data (RWD) are quicker to undertake than randomized controlled trials. Routinely gathered data, such as data from EHR, permits assessment of the benefits and dangers examines the relative effectiveness of pharmaceuticals in the actual world as well as the effectiveness of various medical therapies. Although technological advancements have made it possible to store and secure data more effectively, each method has specific drawbacks. Thus, the only security breaching systems are on the rise, to address that, improvements in already available securing technologies will be created using improved approaches. A form of medical database that is frequently used is the EHR. However, 80% of critical access and rural hospitals reported employing at least a basic EHR system. Larger hospitals are more likely to deploy complex EHR systems, such as those provided by Epic and Cerner. AI-powered EHR platforms offer solutions with a range of functions and seamless integration. The search for documents and information in huge databases can be improved with the aid of machine learning and Natural Language Processing (NLP). The secure exchange of electronic data with patients, other clinicians, and healthcare providers is made possible by an EHR system incorporating Blockchain. Blockchain is a new technology that is being used in many industries, including healthcare, to develop creative solutions. To store and share patient data between hospitals, diagnostic labs, pharmacy companies, and doctors, the healthcare system uses a blockchain network. In the area of medicine, blockchain applications can precisely identify serious errors, including dangerous ones. As a result, it can enhance the efficiency, security, and openness of the exchange of medical data within the healthcare system. With the aid of this technology, medical institutions can better understand and analyse patient data. The blockchain technology and its major advantages in healthcare were studied for this essay. Diagrams are used to describe the various capabilities, enablers, and unified workflow process of blockchain technology to support global healthcare. The promise of this technology is to increase data efficiency for healthcare, and blockchain plays a critical role in handling fraud in clinical trials. In addition to supporting a distinctive data storage pattern at the highest degree of security, it can assist in avoiding the worry of data manipulation in healthcare. It offers adaptability, connectivity, responsibility, and data access authentication. Health data must be protected and kept private for a variety of reasons. Blockchain helps healthcare organisations secure patient data in a decentralised manner and prevent certain threats. Username, password, and an existing QR code are used for login authentication. Due to the possibility of unlawful access, these characteristics are less effective in terms of security. Therefore, since each eye can be recognized uniquely, accurately, and quickly, login authentication utilizing biometrics like eye recognition may be the future work with effective results. In conclusion, preserving data security is crucial in any industry.

THE DIFFICULTIES IN PROTECTING ELECTRONIC HEALTH RECORDS

Security of electronic health data may prove difficult and expensive, especially if many parties may be liable for keeping the data up to date. The European Committee for Standardization has developed and published a framework for the secure storage and sharing of health data using a set of information security standards. Any information on health systems should comply with the four requirements for global security, which are availability, confidentiality, integrity, and accountability, in accordance with European standards. For electronic health record systems to work well, the information must be accessible. Users who have the necessary access to resources, the details must be able to do so in order to carry out the obligations. The need-to-know principle should be applied in this situation. According to this assumption, users must be permitted to gain entry to an individual's electronic health record in order to comply with the organization's access and security criteria, gather the information required to finish a task. Amount of importance of the data that is accepted determines whether the need to know principle is in play. Relevance, however, is a vague word that depends on the context in which the data is produced and the goals for which it is made available. In any event, the data retrieved must be enough and useful to deliver healthcare services. Therefore, accurate user authentication is essential to that data is only used, updated, and modified by people who are authorized to do so. In a complicated setting like the healthcare industry, finding the ideal balance between the need for security and the accessibility of information is essential. Although adding too many security measures may result in user authentication procedures that are less effective, require more time to complete, and are less user-friendly, this is a factor that must be taken into account. The relationship between a patient and a doctor is significantly influenced by confidentiality, as are worries over the privacy of patients. The concept of protecting patient privacy has always been ingrained in the relationship between patient and doctor. However, in a setting of shared care, the conventional notion of patient-physician confidentiality is less obvious. Nowadays, providing healthcare is a multifaceted endeavour that calls for the involvement of numerous players with the purpose of protecting the confidentiality of the widely dispersed electronic health information as well as the details of the treatments, administering security services that provide privacy when accessing sensitive information becomes a serious hurdle for protecting EHR in these conditions. Digital health records integrity and the capacity to deliver accurate data for the sake of accountability are threatened by security lapses. Information integrity is ensured by making certain that only authorised users are able to view, add to, or edit stored information as well as by implementing extra security measures intoor to protect a communication link within the system. Controlling who has access to finding knowledge becomes a challenging and time-consuming endeavour in shared care circumstances. The accuracy and reliability of the data are in reality threatened by the simple fact that current authentication techniques, such PINs or passwords, permit the illegitimate delegation of access permissions. When unauthorized people can access and modify data while not having the rights to do so, information accountability is likewise compromised. A significant factor in every decision involving the implementation of security technologies is the amount of investment and cost connected with their use. In reality, the level of commitment and expense needed to set up and uphold security procedures makes the deployment of electronic health information systems more difficult. The Internet will undergo a complete change thanks to the Internet of Things. IoT-based smart healthcare, smart cities, smart retail, smart agriculture, and IoT systems are emerging, thanks to blockchain technology, which offers advantages like reliable data traceability, security, audit, and provenance, as well as transparency and tamper-proof storage. The privacy issue needs to be addressed first in a list format, and the advancements in the healthcare system need to be separated. In order to improve the data quality of data breach reporting and raise awareness of the data breach environment, this research's findings can be used by government agencies, regulatory bodies, security and data quality researchers, businesses, and managers. Viewed is the framework that defines the elements favouring blockchain-based data sharing across healthcare organizations (Argaw et al., 2019). There are three categories: blockchain factors, security factors, and healthcare systems factors. The fundamental theoretical ideas, background information, and present uses of blockchain have been examined. The state of electronic medical record research has advanced, as have the application possibilities. Through the usage of off-chain record storing, it discusses the present scalability issue that blockchain technology as a whole is currently experiencing. This architecture (Seh et al., 2020) offers the EHR system the benefits of a blockchain-based solution that is scalable, safe, and integrative.

MAIN FOCUS OF THE CHAPTER

An EHR is the name given to the electronic health record. We are approaching the fourth industrial revolution, as is well known. We must be prepared to work with data for that. Data are a valuable resource in today's society. In addition, medical data faces security difficulties despite its importance. This security is insurmountable for any system. The global economy is significantly impacted by crucial in the current worldwide market for data. Significant changes have been made to modern medicine as a result of the EHR revolution. Before this, people could not access their medical records via their devices. This technology enables people from all around the world to access their medical information via websites. Innovative website with features likes distinct profiles for patients and doctors, for instance. Through the blockchain network, they can communicate with one another. The ability of the nodes to store information and the chains connecting them can serve as a straightforward definition of a blockchain system (Jetley & Zhang, 2019), the information is in the block, and can be provided by an ordered list of the nodes and links used. It guarantees the data privacy; each block has been integrated with the others. The medical data cannot be easily altered by anyone either. The foundation for trust is supplied by blockchain technology's improved security, more transparency, and quick traceability in accordance with the blockchain security ecosystem. Beyond problems with trust, blockchain offers a plethora of other benefits for businesses. Take the cost reductions resulting from increased automation, efficiency, and speed. By doing away with the need for third-party or middleman authentication of transactions, blockchain significantly reduces overhead and transaction costs. This is made feasible via blockchain, which greatly reduces errors and paperwork. All across the world, research is conducted using electronic health records (Butpheng et al., 2020). One particular and special benefit is the ability to almost immediately see actual patient outcomes, which is not achievable with other technologies, whether prospective costs and ease of retrospective assessment exist. Existing data is more practical and affordable. The price and practicality of producing anything curated by people. Given the sort of data being collected and the ongoing advancements in the ability to extract information from recordings, the potential of EHR in study is practically limitless. Inflation and expansion of the EHR are happening gradually. Increasingly, researchers are turning to making research more accessible than to electronic health data. The protection of electronic medical data (EMD) from outside theft has been the goal of everything done thus far. Integrity and privacy protection ensure that sensitive data is not merely exposed to outside intrusions. Additionally, it covers data breaches that could happen during an organization shift. We guarantee the accuracy and dependability of the information. Technology has been at the centre of data collection ever since, it provides open verification capabilities that are tamper-proof. The information included in a block cannot be changed in any way, even if the attacker changes some portions of the ledger. The apparatus will identify the error and make a temporary correction. The author (Almulihi et al., 2022) also mentioned that enemies may try to do this to cause network congestion, send out a lot of requests for endorsements at once. It resembles denial of service (DoS) attacks in several ways. As an endorser, it serves no purpose. Check that the data is there before responding to a client request. The client signed the document; even though it takes a lot of work. The system's minimal effect nodes might potentially come under attack, be damaged, or be turned against one another. Encryption is a very good technique to safeguard patient privacy. Blockchain architecture and peer-to-peer network of nodes are effectively handle various interoperability standards using a robust network architecture, protected health information (PHI) can be sent to patients and other recipients who have given their consent using secure, confidential, and tamper-proof email addresses. As previously stated, the consolidation approach makes sure that a record, i.e., an attempt to update an existing one; blocks are readily discernible to spectators. Keys for patients and healthcare professionals are also stored in Meta Mask. Chrome, Firefox, and Microsoft Edge are all compatible with the bitcoin wallet known as Meta Mask. Two additional bitcoin wallets are Enthralled and My Crypto. Making connections to the Ethereum network as simple, dependable, and safe as feasible is Meta Mask's aim. In our work, Meta Mask has shown to be a beneficial tool. It refers to a system that complies with an EHR system's security, privacy, interoperability, and performance standards. As long as the patient gives consent, the proposed technique can be used to share patient data anytime, anyplace. Existing research addresses the aforementioned EHR system criteria. To guarantee patient data security and privacy, interoperability, and performance criteria are met, all of these factors are considered in this effort. Our study uses blockchain technology to meet these requirements because it uses a sophisticated and durable cryptographic method to enable data sharing between healthcare providers while providing patients control over their data. It is recommended to use an electronic transaction technique that is independent of participant confidence. Starting with the current standard design of digitally signed coins, which allows for strict ownership control but is unsatisfactory due to its absence of a mechanism to prevent double-spending Since it keeps a public history of transactions and makes it challenging for an attacker to change the history if honest nodes control the majority of the processing power, a proof-of-work network was proposed as a solution to this issue. The network has a very long lifespan because of its chaotic simplicity. According to PHR, its straightforward user interface enables you to rapidly browse the following options: You can schedule appointments with your doctor and modify or cancel them as necessary. Your prescription, allergy, medical history, and immunization data are all listed in your health history file. You may simply view the records of claims that have been filed on your behalf by using the claims history tool. Additionally, by giving you access to a database that has all of the lab results for the tests you have run, it could be able to save you time and effort. It is simple to interact directly and securely with your supplier using secure messaging services (Algarni et al., 2021).

Cost of Implementation

The cost of implementing an EHR shouldn't come as a surprise. The planned capital budget includes a sizeable amount for EHR selection, implementation, and optimization. An EHR system can cost anywhere between $15,000 and $70,000 per provider to buy and implement, according to one research study. Generally speaking, there are five parts that make up the implementation process: setup fees for hardware and software, assistance with deployment, staff training costs, recurring network fees, and maintenance. Implementation expenditures that weren't anticipated can also arise. One of the major challenges, particularly for smaller institutions, is obtaining money to deploy an EHR.

Lack of Usability

When an EHR system doesn't work with a provider's current workflow, they find it difficult to adopt. For example, the work flows of a therapist and a cardiologist do not suit this EHR system's one-size-fits-all principles. EHR software is less usable due to design problems or insufficient training. Health effects of compromised patient data may be fatal.

Data Privacy

The community of patients and providers' privacy concerns is another significant EHR difficulty. The prospect of data loss as a result of disasters or cyberattacks usually causes concern among stakeholders. National guidelines for the confidentiality of personal health information are mandated by federal regulations. Organizations that experience security breaches may have to pay millions of dollars on legal fees and dispute resolution. As a result, the provider now has a top priority to ensure the EHR system's data security.

Interoperability

To enable information sharing with hospitals and healthcare providers, interoperability is the process of making integrated healthcare data available. To give better treatment and care, interoperability enables practitioners and providers to organize and integrate access to patient data. EHR interoperability remains one of the biggest obstacles to proper data transfer in electronic health records, despite being crucial to comprehend a patient's entire medical history. The coordination of care may be hampered by the lack of interoperability, and poor health outcomes may make it harder to pinpoint the origins of medical problems.

Data Migration

It's a logistical nightmare for employees to export paper works to digital files. Data entry might be laborious and time-consuming for workers because there are so many patients' history documents available. One of the main obstacles in the hospital's EHR installation is this, and if the old system hadn't been set up correctly, the effort would be multiplied.

Issues, Controversies, Problems

The most frequent cyber-attacks in the healthcare industry, or any other industry, may be brought on by nefarious insiders, misplaced or stolen gadgets, or nefarious outside criminals. Some criminally exploitable vulnerabilities are items that are simple to remedy, like a computer's password. Like a person's social security number, other weaknesses cannot be addressed. Data breaches frequently result from weak passwords. If your login information is stolen, thieves can quickly access your email, websites, bank accounts, and other sensitive data. Additionally, malware assaults might undermine the security protocols on your computer, granting unauthorized access. Finally, malware that accesses your work email and files to steal personal information might infiltrate mobile devices.

1. Inadvertent Insider
   An illustration would be:
   - An employee viewing files on a co-worker's computer while not authorized to do so. Unauthorized person access would be seen as occurring even though it was inadvertent and no information was transmitted.
   - A worker who leaves a mobile device with sensitive data that isn't encrypted in an open area.
   - Hackers can also be found, and they employ a range of cyber-attack methods to get information from a network or a specific person.
2. Nefarious Insider
   - This individual intentionally obtains or discloses data with the intent to harm a person or business. A dishonest insider could be the legitimate party.
3. Lost or Stolen Devices
   - Any item that could contain sensitive information is reported missing, including a laptop or an open, unencrypted external hard drive.

EHR ISSUES

To provide effective healthcare and ensure the security and privacy of patient data there are few challenges presented by current EHR models (Koczkodaj et al., 2018). Few of the challenges are:

1. Data Storage

In today's models, shared secrets are saved in frequently updated passwords that are kept in potentially hazardous clouds. This strategy has resulted in widely reported attacks, such the one that took place in December 2014 when hackers infiltrated the servers of American health insurer Anthem and stole the personal data of 80 million clients and staff members. A hack of this kind is less possible under the blockchain paradigm because data are not stored centrally.

2. Data Exchange

The push, pull, and view models are often used by healthcare businesses to promote the interoperability of medical data in a world without blockchain. One provider to another transmits medical information via a push method (e.g., from an emergency room physician to a primary care doctor). In a pull paradigm, a provider requests data from another source (for instance, a cardiothoracic surgeon conferring with a primary care physician). Finally, a provider examines the patient record of another provider in the view model. For instance, a cardiologist may examine a patient's X-ray from an urgent care centre.

3. Data Efficiency

Current practise may use a lot of improvement in terms of efficiency. For instance, the push model prevents the new hospital from having access to the information that was "pushed" from the previous hospital in the event that a patient is transferred to a different facility. It could be annoying to frequently provide the same information to many healthcare professionals or others connected to the same healthcare provider. The management of medical records produced by several healthcare facilities is a problem with current methods. Patient data may be lost as a result of data being dispersed throughout numerous medical organizations.

SOLUTIONS AND RECOMMENDATIONS

In a guidance document, the Agency for Cybersecurity and Infrastructure Security (ICAS) suggested that organizations build an overall internal threat.

"Internal threat mitigation programs must be capable of detecting and identifying inappropriate or illegal actions, assessing threats to determine risk levels, and implement solutions to handle and mitigate the potential consequences of an internal incident," CISA said.

"Organizations should establish a multidisciplinary threat management team to prepare an incident response plan, ensure that their response to an internal incident or potential threat is standardized, reproducible and consistently enforced."

Organizations should begin on a small scale by evaluating existing capacities and resources, defining the purpose of the program, and identifying critical assets. Organizations should also build a culture of shared accountability and develop confidential reporting channels for employees to report suspicious events. Finally, organizations should train their employees in the recognition of internal threat indicators. Along with a thorough risk mitigation program, detection analysis, and post-breach forensics, there are numerous ways in which healthcare organizations can prevent insider threats:

- Revision and updating of cyber security regulations.
- Data backup and deployment of data loss prevention technologies.
- Management of USB devices across the corporate network.
- Strictly enforcing role-based access control and limiting privileged access.
- Putting MFA and zero-trust models into practise.

Healthcare businesses should think about putting systems in place to detect and react to insider threat activities, including as logging and auditing, user activity monitoring, and User and Entity Behaviour Analytics (UEBA).

To further understand how blockchain can handle security and privacy problems, Take identity and access management, which entails regulating data like patient identity on computer networks, into consideration (not only those connected to EHR).

There are three types of data:

1. Information used to confirm an individual's identification;
2. The data that describes the data (meta-data); and
3. The actions that different individuals are permitted to be aware of and take part in.

In a blockchain paradigm, a patient's complete medical records might be encrypted with their private key and stored in a blockchain ledger's key ring. A blockchain-based system is seen as being more secure than the majority of other systems in use today, however it is not completely impenetrable (a person's private key could be stolen, for example). Audit trails, which serve as a record of the actions taken in connection with the production, modification, and deletion of electronic documents, enable transparency. A decentralised record management system based on blockchain called MedRec was developed by researchers from Boston's Beth Israel Deaconess Medical Centre and the MIT Media Lab to manage EHR. Accountability, confidentiality, and data exchange are all managed by MedRec. With the use of this technology, patients can access their medical records from various healthcare institutions and treatment centres. Every transaction involving a patient's information is recorded in an immutable log that is given to the patient. Instead, then keeping patient health records on file, MedRec's system keeps a blockchain-based copy of the signer of the document. The seal ensures that the single duplicate that is attainable is the original, unaltered copy of the record. Patients may determine where their records can go and retain ownership and ultimate control of their information using blockchain. Consequently, the patient gains control, shifting the locus of control away from the medical facility. Service organizations may develop to allow patients to assign such work to them if they do not wish to handle their data. The most difficult part of deploying blockchain-based models in EHR in most nations is making sure that healthcare practitioners only authorize the proper people. Nations can increase the effectiveness of such models through the use of a unique digital ID for patient identification and authentication. Additionally, by doing this, they can raise administrative effectiveness, stop insurance fraud, and boost healthcare quality. Recent years have seen a sharp rise in EHR adoption rates. Since then, healthcare IT administrators and professionals have created innovative approaches to deal with the problems that providers frequently encounter while putting EHR into practise. Here is a list of solutions that will make the procedure simpler and easier to handle if you are a healthcare professional constructing an effective EHR system for others.

1. Make a strategic plan: The first stage in implementing an EHR is to create an extensive strategic strategy for upcoming actions. Team members should be given tasks and responsibilities, and the best doctors should be chosen. Interdependence and support should also be encouraged. A backup strategy should be in place for your team. Productivity among the workforce can deteriorate. Work flows may get chaotic during the implementation stage, and even patients may grow irate. Planning is crucial for his good EHR installation, which is the most important thing to keep in mind in this scenario.

2. Clinical research support: Clinical research is based on the well-established concept that data on patients' health and conditions is extremely significant. The chain of care's data interoperability is substantially improved by the seamless installation of EHR systems. Access to the data that clinical researchers require is simple, and interoperability frameworks enable providers to exchange this data with scientists and researchers in order to advance understanding.

3. Improve productivity: In the healthcare industry, achieving EHR interoperability can be difficult, but doing so can help cut costs, time, and effort. Reduced workload, increased productivity, and the ability to keep delivering superior healthcare services are all advantages of EHR deployment. Redundancy is reduced by digitizing data, which also has the effect of accelerating the handling of patient data and the dissemination of information to service providers.

4. Consider consulting clients as partners: EHR adoption is a team endeavour that requires commitment from all parties involved, including consultants, staff, doctors, vendors, IT vendors, and more, make it a shared objective for all those involved and share a bigger picture of the process. Digital health record will enable you to easily, quickly, and within budget complete your deployment.

5. Demonstrate strong leadership: The team leader must be aggressive and adept at change management to get the group on board with the organization's EHR deployment process. Establish a subcommittee of executives who have experience leading teams to successfully integrate new IT systems across several industries. The adoption of EHR technology and systems can be strengthened by securing strong leadership.

6. Ensure an improved patient experience: When deciding whether to deploy an EHR, think about the advantages that patients will receive. Patient wishes are of the utmost importance in a value-based healthcare system. Patients are, after all, the majority of EHR system users. Therefore, by improving EHR interoperability and ensuring data privacy, you can increase patient loyalty to your company and maintain a better relationship with your patients. This also helps improve the patient experience and improves patient-provider communication on health outcomes.

7. Patient is priority one: Consider the advantages that patients will experience when deciding whether to install an EHR. Patients' desires take precedence in a value-based healthcare system. The majority of users of EHR systems are, after all, patients.

8. Follow the timeline: While going through the EHR implementation process, it might be challenging to meet deadlines. To reduce scheduling delays, make a practical plan. Vendors, partners, and the EHR installation team estimate the cost of a single day's delay. Provide thorough improving efficiency and streamlining processes are the objectives of deploying an EHR, according to training. Targets will be missed and patient satisfaction will suffer if employees do not use the system properly and stick with the old procedures. Create a thorough training programme that explains to your team how patient care will be aided by the new technology, which will make their work easier and more efficient. Boost them up by praising their accomplishments or taking into account additional compensation for overwork.

9. Work with experts: Engage the help of a specialist with extensive understanding of the workflow at the hospital and the interoperability standards of EHR system to guarantee the installation of EHR is successful. Discover how leaders that EHR system to guarantee the installation of EHR is successful. You can then prepare for and quickly overcome potential roadblocks thanks to this.

FUTURE RESEARCH DIRECTIONS

Improvements in Patient Access

Data is converted into knowledge via EHR. It opens the door to health care that is more intelligent, secure, and easily accessible. Even though the public has easy access to the electronic health records, only 50% of people use them. And the majority of them only do it once a year.

More people should be encouraged to access this information in the upcoming years to boost engagement. Furthermore, it is crucial that the SaaS system providers employ a more straightforward user interface.

The Establishment of Unified Standards

Hospital CIOs, developers, and vendors are going to start working on creating a standardised format for medical data in the upcoming years, which will make it easier to share and process data. With EHRs, you may transmit prescriptions to the pharmacist, share notes digitally, and easily access patient lab results. The records ought to operate smoothly in theory. However, interoperability—the capacity for the systems to communicate effectively—remains a significant problem. Only 25% of healthcare companies are able to locate, share, and receive medical data at the moment. Only 40% of hospitals also link the data with their EHR system.

Hospital CIOs, programmers, and vendors will begin to collaborate on creating a consistent standard of medical data in the next 4-5 years. This will simplify the processing and sharing of information.

Cloud-Based EHR Technology Will Grow

The corporate world is not a newcomer to using cloud computing for data processing and storage. With the EHR, the storage and flow of information have significantly improved, which is the most noticeable shift. In order to justify their decision to utilise cloud technology, medical organisations currently point to the costs of infrastructure and software. They will soon understand that cloud-hosted EHR software is less expensive.

The Use of More Accurate Drugs and Treatments

The future of EHRs appears bright as medical digital technology develops. The technology for electronic medical records will rely more on automation using deep learning and AI. Additionally, its decision support systems will give clinicians access to their patients' information and aid them in making better judgements through the use of supporting informatics tools.

There Will Be a Greater Use of Precise Medications and Treatments

EHRs' future appears bright as digital technology advances in the medical field. AI and deep learning will be used to automate tasks more frequently in electrical medical records technology. Additionally, its decision support systems will give doctors access to patient data and support them in making wiser judgements by providing them with accompanying informatics tools.

Patient Engagement Will Rise

Before their records are delivered to the doctor's office, patients will have their questions addressed. Additionally, they have the option of immediately scheduling the appointment. The patient portal will become more user-friendly as a result, and participation will rise.

Using Biometrics to Encrypt Medical Data

A technological option that improves security over encrypted data is biometric encryption. Since the sensitive information in this scenario is encrypted using a biometric characteristic, only the individual who possesses the biometric characteristic can access it. Utilizing this technology to protect medical data would be a positive move since biometric encryption may be seen of as a more potent method of securing and controlling access to sensitive data. For instance, utilising a biometric profile to generate a safe crypto key to encrypt private information, or using a biometric profile to decrypt information using a biometric attribute using fuzzy identity-based encryption (Yaqoob et al., 2021). Doctors and other medical professionals can gain access by using biometric encryption, which offers a safe way to protect medical information like electronic health records.

Maintaining the proper amount of accessibility to medical records is a concern when utilizing biometrics to encrypt personal health information. The need-to-know concept becomes less evident and more challenging to administer when bio-metrics are used to encrypt electronic health records. The implementation of biometric encryption could jeopardise the information's accessibility, which is essential for functional electronic health records. The inability to create the same feature vector for the same feature characteristic under many exposures to a biometric sensor further restricts the use of biometric technologies. Direct encryption of medical data is rather difficult due to a biometric component. A frequent solution to this issue is to conceal the crypto key within the biometric profile. In order to release the encrypted data and confirm the user's identity, a biometric matching system compares scores from the user's biometric profile. A secure database can be used to hold the crypto key that is part of the biometric profile, making it accessible to both authorized employees and patients who need to encrypt or decode the data. As a result of this idea, biometric technology may be used to encrypt sensitive data that is stored in databases or communicated between parties during communication, in addition to being used to confirm a person's identity and grant access authorization to stored data. The use of encryption based on biometric techniques can improve security during the release of information.

Before being given to anyone save individuals who have the biometric feature that identifies the data's intended recipient, personal health records can also be encrypted. For instance, before being shared, medical information can be encrypted. In these circumstances, private medical information can be encrypted and decrypted using fuzzy identity-based encryption. The Identity Based Encryption that was first developed is the foundation of the Fuzzy Identity Based Encryption (IBE) technique. Utilizing an identity and the IBE scheme, a sender can encrypt a message without using a public key certificate. In this instance, the identification is viewed as a string of characters that serve as the user's public key, such as the user's name, email address, or phone number. With this method, it is not necessary for the recipient to be online at the time the message is created or for the user to validate their public key. Fuzzy inputs, such as biometric inputs, can be used as IDs in the Fuzzy Identity Based Encryption technique, a form of Identity-based Encryption (IBE), to encrypt messages. According to the Fuzzy IBE approach, the identity is a group of descriptors that are used to encrypt and decode the message. The use of a biometric as an identification property is permitted by the fuzzy IBE scheme's error tolerance (sometimes referred to as the scheme's fuzziness, which refers to the tolerance that the scheme may provide). When identity attributes are "near" to one another as determined by the "set overlap" distance metric, as is the case in this example, a secret key, SK, is used to decrypt a cypher text, ID, that has been encrypted with identity attributes. The error-tolerance will allow the decryption of a message if the disparity determined by the difference between the identity characteristics is within the permitted bounds, or, to put it another way, if the noise of a sampled biometric identity is taken into consideration inside the scheme. With the aid of a private key, the message must be decrypted.

The Private Key Generator (PKG), a reputable organization charged with creating the private key, is required under the scheme (SK). After the user has been correctly identified, the PKG will only give out such a private key. The cipher text received originally from the sender can then be decrypted using the created key. According to this scenario, the biometric owner can "authenticate" some information, and that information can then be confirmed using the biometric that the "signer" is in possession of. It has already been mentioned that switching from a fuzzy identity-based strategy to a fuzzy authentication scheme is straightforward. An essential aspect of EHR systems is the capacity to remotely access relevant health information from any place and at any time. When exchanging medical information, data encryption is employed. However, in order to have an integrated, functional EHR, the protection of patient privacy and confidentiality must be taken extra care when information is available remotely for both main and secondary purposes. In a system of shared care, it is anticipated that numerous healthcare institutions engaged in the therapeutic process will keep track of medical records. Medical information is really developed and maintained by numerous organizations in the contemporary healthcare environment because various healthcare units within an organization or in a healthcare network with multiple players offer distinct care services. It is necessary to create complete security systems that permit data interchange while simultaneously ensuring patient privacy is protected in order to securely disclose and share electronic health records through unreliable channels, including the Internet. The authentication of users and data encryption are both made possible by biometric technologies. Utilizing their biometric profiles, users of a share care scenario can access and recover information remotely. A public key identification can be used to encrypt the extracted data during information transmission, and the user's biometric profile can be used to decode it afterwards. As a result, the only person who could access the data would be the owner of the biometric profile. The following analysis may helpful in implementing biometrics with compared to existing models.

Table 1 Comparative analysis of authentication methods

Basis	Prevailing Models	Utilizing Biometrics
User friendly and healthcare environment	Passwords and PINs must be remembered. Not suitable for a very demanding medical environment.	The process of authentication is quick and simple, suitable for the majority of medical environments. For some medical situations, certain biometric technologies are inappropriate. The difficulty to obtain a good biometric template, positioning of the biometric future, temperature, humidity, and deterioration of the biometric feature can all have an impact on accuracy. Age, skin tone, injury, or the absence of a biometric trait can all have an impact on enrolment.
Requirements for international security	There are inherent security problems with using PINs, passwords, or smart cards, such as the ability to transmit information without authorization and delegate access rights. Unintentional loss of an access code. Potential for impersonation User is more likely to be able to contest electronic transactions.	Security is improved, unauthorised account access is deterred and detected, and impersonation is avoided. Additionally, it lessens the chance that confidential data will be accessed unlawfully. It is impossible to distribute or assign biometric futures. Transactions using biometrics are hard to challenge.
Atmosphere of shared care	Share care environment possibilities are being investigated in current research and practise.	Local networks have been the focus of recent study and application.
Costs	Maintenance cost will be higher.	Decreases the expense of upkeep and high initial outlay.

CONCLUSION

There is a significant amount of electronic health data, according to a study of data breaches in the healthcare industry. It is frequently a target for attackers, leaving it vulnerable. According to a long-term analysis of data breaches, health records have been exposed as a result of internal and external attacks, including hacking, theft/loss, illegal internal disclosure, and irresponsible disposal of unnecessary yet sensitive materials data. However, a quick examination showed that the most frequent attack techniques used by an attacker were IT incidents and hacking. Additionally, in a short examination, the top locations where private health information is lost are network servers and e-mail accounts. This was the result of cost analysis. Particularly, the cost of data breaches involving health information is substantially higher than the global average. Both the data breach and its effects were shown via a time series study. In the future, the price will rise. Therefore, research worker should prioritize preventive measures safety professionals and health agencies. The electronic health record with blockchain technology made everything easier and more comfortable. Also, the entered data and information more accurate and safety. The major disadvantage is the implementation since this EHR technology is high-cost. In India, the National Health Policy (NHP) was created in 2017 with the intention of ensuring the wellbeing of all Indian people and ensuring that everyone has unrestricted access to high-quality medical treatment. NHP plans to establish a digital health technology environment among many other objectives. The security of user data and privacy rights, as well as data gathering, storage, and sharing, will be essential to its establishment. In order to safeguard patients' privacy and the security of their health information, the Digital Information Security in Healthcare Act (DISHA) was drafted in 2017. By standardising and regulating the overall data retrieval process, preserving users' rights, and streamlining electronic health records for individuals with easy access, DISHA is projected to do so in the future. In this sense, a federated permissioned Blockchain network connected with the health information exchange (HIE) paradigm could close the gap between the creation of laws and regulations and their actual implementation. In order to maintain the security of the shared information, blockchain technology needs a high computing and processing capacity, which necessitates the use of several servers located in various locations. To address this shortcoming, the public and private sectors can collaborate, which could hasten the adoption of blockchain technology in the healthcare industry as well as other industries. India has made some early progress in this approach.

REFERENCES

Algarni, A. M., Thayananthan, V., & Malaiya, Y. K. (2021). Quantitative Assessment of Cybersecurity Risks for Mitigating Data Breaches in Business Systems. *Applied Sciences (Basel, Switzerland)*, *11*(8), 3678. doi:10.3390/app11083678

Almulihi, AAlassery, FIrshad Khan, AShukla, SKumar Gupta, BKumar, R. (2022). Analyzing the Implications of Healthcare Data Breaches through Computational Technique. Intelligent Automation &amp. *Soft Computing*, *32*(3), 1763–1779. doi:10.32604/iasc.2022.023460

Argaw, S. T., Bempong, N.-E., Eshaya-Chauvin, B., & Flahault, A. (2019). The state of research on cyberattacks against hospitals and available best practice recommendations: A scoping review. *BMC Medical Informatics and Decision Making*, *19*(1), 10. Advance online publication. doi:10.118612911-018-0724-5 PMID:30634962

Butpheng, C., Yeh, K.-H., & Xiong, H. (2020). Security and Privacy in IoT-Cloud-Based e-Health Systems—A Comprehensive Review. *Symmetry*, *12*(7), 1191. doi:10.3390ym12071191

Chen, L., Lee, W.-K., Chang, C.-C., Choo, K.-K. R., & Zhang, N. (2019). Blockchain based searchable encryption for electronic health record sharing. *Future Generation Computer Systems*, *95*, 420–429. doi:10.1016/j.future.2019.01.018

Jetley, G., & Zhang, H. (2019). Electronic health records in IS research: Quality issues, essential thresholds and remedial actions. *Decision Support Systems*, *126*, 113137. doi:10.1016/j.dss.2019.113137

Koczkodaj, W. W., Mazurek, M., Strzałka, D., Wolny-Dominiak, A., & Woodbury-Smith, M. (2018). Electronic Health Record Breaches as Social Indicators. *Social Indicators Research*, *141*(2), 861–871. doi:10.100711205-018-1837-z

McLeod, A., & Dolezel, D. (2018). Cyber-analytics: Modeling factors associated with healthcare data breaches. *Decision Support Systems*, *108*, 57–68. doi:10.1016/j.dss.2018.02.007

Seh, A. H., Zarour, M., Alenezi, M., Sarkar, A. K., Agrawal, A., Kumar, R., & Ahmad Khan, R. (2020). Healthcare Data Breaches: Insights and Implications. *Health Care*, *8*(2), 133. doi:10.3390/healthcare8020133 PMID:32414183

Yaqoob, I., Salah, K., Jayaraman, R., & Al-Hammadi, Y. (2021). Blockchain for healthcare data management: Opportunities, challenges, and future recommendations. *Neural Computing & Applications*, *34*(14), 11475–11490. doi:10.100700521-020-05519-w

Section 3
Industry 4.0 Technologies

Chapter 22
Introduction to Augmented Reality

U. Annaamalai
Thiagarajar College of Engineering, India

A. Dhiyaneshwar
Thiagarajar College of Engineering, India

Indira Suthakar
Thiagarajar College of Engineering, India

S. Karthiga
Thiagarajar College of Engineering, India

Nisha Angeline C. V.
Thiagarajar College of Engineering, India

ABSTRACT

Recently, augmented reality (AR) has gained a lot of popularity. The fundamental tenet of augmented reality is to effectively facilitate interactive communication between people and computers. With the aid of specific tools, a person in the real world can enter the electronically produced reality. These days, this technology is included in every mobile filter we use, including those seen in Pokémon Go and the Instagram and Snapchat apps. Wearable versions of numerous miniature augmented reality models have been created. Numerous industries have been investigated using AR technology, including those in the realms of medicine, education, business, architecture, commerce, tourism, navigation, translation, the visual arts, fitness, flying training, the military, industrial manufacturing, etc. The roots of AR in Industry 4.0 are deepening day by day. The immense potential of AR can be utilized in an infinite number of ways to fulfill the objectives of Industry 4.0. This chapter shows the impact of AR in our society.

DOI: 10.4018/978-1-6684-8145-5.ch022

Copyright © 2023, IGI Global. Copying or distributing in print or electronic forms without written permission of IGI Global is prohibited.

INTRODUCTION

In this highly competitive world of technology, immersive technologies like Augmented realities, Virtual realities, and mixed realities have brought up major changes and serve as a key to shaping the future of mankind. Due to VR and AR, we can anticipate significant changes in how we work, are amused, and communicate within the next five to ten years. The direction in which our society is moving will be dramatically altered by these technologies. These technologies are called immersive technologies as they tend to immerse our minds into another reality often created virtually. These technologies take us to a separate dimension that is created virtually. They may put on a headset and feel as though they are at a soccer stadium thousands of kilometers away when they are simply sitting on a couch at home. They may slip on a set of cutting-edge glasses and have a friend who lives on another continent appear as a fully realistic holographic avatar and converse with them. From their house, they might attend a live performance by one of their favorite artists. These technologies tend to simulate users' senses through the combinations of various hardware. The potential of AR, VR, and MR has been utilized effectively in various sectors from manufacturing to medicines. As these technologies serve as a bridge to the future many tech giants like Apple, Microsoft, Google, and Facebook(meta) have been interested in these fields and invested a lot. In 2020, the global augmented reality market was estimated to be 4.16 billion USD and it was predicted to reach up to 97.76 billion USD in a period between 2021-2028. Everyday innovations have been welcomed to increase the efficiency of the process. The environment in AR is not completely synthetic as in VR but is a combination of real-world and digital world entities. The basic purpose of AR is to improve the user experience and to provide some additional digital information over real-world components.

Augmented Reality (AR) is one of the biggest growing technologies right now and is ever expanding. AR superimposes digital information like text, images, video or audio, etc.. over a real-world object. It does not simply display those data over real-world entities but makes those virtual components a part of the natural environment using immersion. More simply it is the overlaying of virtual components on the objects of the real world.AR seems to be a tool that helps mankind to excel in various fields. It has spread its wings in almost all possible fields following the Industrial Revolution4.0. AR increases the production process efficiency, reduces the occurrence of errors, digitalizes information, and improves the overall performance of an industry. AR find its applications in entertainment military and tourism to medicines. AR makes itself an important key to the future and will change everyone's life with no doubt. The purpose of AR is to take mankind next level with the help of such advanced technology. Nowadays all the filters that we use on mobiles such as Snapchat filters, Instagram filters, and a lot more have incorporated this technology. Games such as Pokémon Go, Ingres, Zombie Run, etc have used this technology. Many Miniature AR models have been developed as wearables such as Smart AR glasses, and Head Mounted Tablet(HMT). Even smartphones these days can generate AR. Many Tech giants such as Apple, Microsoft, Samsung, Facebook, Google, Niantic, etc.. have been interested in this field and have invested a lot in this field as it is the future of technologies. A private survey has calculated that the value of AR in the global markets will reach up to 78.4 Billion dollars by 2025 in the Medical field alone. This technology is extensively being used in the commerce field. In 2018 Apple announced that iPhones and pads with iOS 12 will support AR files, Shopify announced AR quick look integration, and Twinkl released a free AR classroom application. Cosmetic companies like L'Oréal, Sephora, Tilbury, etc have also utilized AR. Figure 1 shows the gameplay view of the Pokémon Go game.

Figure 1. Gameplay of Pokémon Go

While generating an AR system the developer should keep the following aspects in mind: combinations of the real world and virtual world, registration in 3D, interactivity in real-time, and most importantly portability. An AR application should be portable and should not be restricted due to device limitations. To develop an AR scene the following three components are essential: Scene generator, tracking, and display. The scene generator generates the scene or 3D objects which need to co-exist with the real-world entity. Tracking is very important in AR as it ensures the proper alignment of 3D objects over real entities, any errors occurring in tracking will ultimately lead to the collapsing of the two worlds and affects the illusion. Hence accurate registration of 3D objects is a must. As proposed in Anand Nayyar et al. (2018). Display devices that we use in AR are mostly HMD (Head Mounted Display) while other devices are also available. To this day display seems to be a constraint for AR technologies as they have many limitations. The major challenges in the display are the weight of the device, resolution, contrast, design, size, and cost. Based on different AR displays we can create various AR experiences that are described as follows. Marker-based AR, where the marker is recognized using an image recognition process through the camera and provide result once the camera senses the marker. A marker is nothing but an image that is loaded to generate certain results. It only works when the marker is detected. Secondly, we have markerless-based AR. It is also known as location-based or GPS-based AR. They act like miniature versions of a GPS tracker and can be used for navigation purposes. They provide the result only if they are placed at the correct position or location and orientation of the device. Next, we have projection-based AR where artificial light is sent into the real world. 3D holograms are the best examples of this type. Finally, we have superimposed AR which replaces the original view of the object with the virtually created augmented object.

BACKGROUND

The idea of AR dates back to 1901 when L. Frank Baum proposed the concept of AR fictionally in his novels. Long after in 1957 Morton Heilig, a cinematographer invented a device called Sensorama. Heilig prepared a variety of short films for the Sensorama, an arcade-style mechanical cabinet designed to stimulate the senses. It had several of the characteristics found in contemporary VR headgear, including stereo speakers, a stereoscopic 3D display, and haptic input provided by chair vibrations. It provides visuals, sounds as well as smells to the user. However, it was not supported by any sort of computer technology. Soon after developing the Sensorama, Heilig also created the Telesphere Mask, the first head-mounted display (HMD) to offer stereo sound and stereoscopic 3D images. Compared to the Sensorama's large sitting form factor, this (relatively) tiny HMD more closely matches modern consumer VR headsets. In 1968 a computer scientist named Ivan Sutherland creates a head-mounted display and he regards it as the "Window into the virtual world". Figure 2 shows the picture of sensorama.

Figure 2. AR in the manufacturing sector

Figure 3. First AR Glass developed in 1968

Figure 3 shows the first AR glass developed by Ivan Sutherland. The invention of video place (an artificial reality laboratory) by Myron Krueger in 1975 marks a milestone in the development of AR. In 1980 Steve Mann created the world's first wearable computer such as Eye tap. Since then there were some minor contributions by various developers and innovators to this field. The first time the phrase "Augmented Reality" was used was in 1990 by Thomas P. Caudell, a former researcher for Boeing. In 1992, Louis Rosenberg created Virtual Fixtures, the world's first functioning AR system at the United States Air Force Research Laboratory (USAFRL). At the Consumer Electronics Show in 1993, Sega, a gaming company riding high after the introduction of its wildly successful Sega Genesis, unveiled the Sega VR headgear for the Sega Genesis (CES). In the fall of 1993, Sega had initially planned to sell the gadget for $200, which was at the time a reasonably reasonable price. The system, however, struggled during development and was never made available to the general public. Tom Kalinske, the CEO of Sega at the time, claimed that the Sega VR's catastrophic first attempt at consumer VR gaming was abandoned because testers had severe headaches and motion sickness. Another seasoned member of the gaming business opted to present its take on VR gaming at the same time. The first portable device that could show stereoscopic 3D images was the Nintendo Virtual Boy, which was introduced. By encouraging further innovation in game production beyond the conventional 2D screen space with the Virtual Boy, Nintendo intended to capitalize on novel technology and solidify its position as an inventor. However, the Virtual Boy also had development problems. According to reports, early color LCD tests produced jerky pictures, which is why Nintendo decided to stick with the red LEDs for the Virtual Boy's final design. In addition, the Virtual Boy originally consisted of a head-mounted system tracking. However, Nintendo altered the head-mounted device due to worries about motion sickness and the potential for kids to acquire diseases like lazy eye up to table top size. The system was condemned by critics. It could never reach sales goals and within a year they were no longer available. Early failures like this, along with subsequent failed attempts to produce mass-market VR gadgets, drove VR advancements back into research labs and over several decades, in academics. In the subsequent years' various innovations such as CMOS active-pixel sensors, demonstration joining live AR-equipped vehicles and manned simulators, augmented reality theatre production, a vision-based system using monocular cameras to track objects, a system for projecting information from 3D CAD models into the real world and a lot more have been made. In 1999 NASA made x-38 spacecraft to fly with the help of augmented reality, it was the first time that NASA had properly and completely used AR technology. In 2000 Sony introduced the concept of AR on the gaming side when it released the eye tap color webcam in its PlayStation 2. In 2004 helmet-mounted AR systems and Human Interface Technology Laboratory was introduced by Trimble navigation. In 2006 world's first immersive AR entertainment was experienced. Palmer Luckey, a tech entrepreneur, was dissatisfied with the VR head-mounted displays that were already available on the market in 2010. The majority of them had very bad end-user experiences because of their exorbitant prices, excessive weight, narrow fields of vision (the whole viewing area a user can see), and significant latency (delays between user input and the display updating to reflect those activities). In response to these problems, Luckey developed several prototype head-mounted displays (HMDs), concentrating on developing a cheap, low-latency, wide-field-of-view, and pleasantly weighted headgear. He advertised his sixth-generation device, the Oculus Rift, as the Rift Development Kit 1 on the crowdfunding platform Kickstarter (DK1). The Kickstarter effort was a resounding success, earning $2.4 million, or about 980% of the initial goal. More significantly, the Kickstarter initiative helped raise consumer interest in virtual reality to an all-time high. In 2013 Google takes its first step into the AR field and launched the first generation of Google Glass. However, it faced many criticisms like privacy issues and cost issues.

Google suspended its production in 2015. In May 2019, google announced the Google Glass Enterprise Edition 2. In 2015 another tech giant Microsoft announces HoloLens augmented reality headset and Windows holographic. 2016 was the biggest breakthrough for AR when Niantic released Pokémon go for iOS and Android smartphones, where you can find and capture Pokémon around us. The game became very popular and there were more than 500 million downloads of the game by the end of 2016. By May 2018, the game had almost 147 million active users and by early 2019 the game surpassed almost 1 billion downloads. Even though the game had many public critics like it had created many public nuisances the game was a profitable one with annual revenue of 6 Billion dollars by 2020. Rewinding to 2017, augmented reality (AR) saw its biggest rise in popularity since its inception as both Apple and Google built their own versions of the technology for their various portable mobile devices that ran either iOS or Android. Estimates place the number users with ARKit- or ARCore-capable devices at roughly a quarter billion by the end of 2017., despite neither company providing precise figures. In 2019 Microsoft announced HoloLens 2 with significant changes to the prior version. Developers rushed to provide content for the massive market that AR, which had previously been operating in relative obscurity, had suddenly opened up. Applications that overlay turn-by-turn directions or points of interest on the real world's maps are some examples, as are AR gaming programs, tools that place 3D objects inside actual rooms for interior design planning, and programs that translate signs in foreign languages by simply pointing a mobile device's camera at them.

IMPACTS OF AR

Augmented reality has the potential to impact a wide range of industries and applications.AR has the potential to enhance the user experience by providing more engaging and interactive content that includes product demonstrations, virtual navigations, and an interactive gaming experience.AR can be used to increase efficiency and productivity in a wide range of industries.AR has the potential to enhance learning that would be more engaging and effective. AR provides training simulations that allow gaining experience in a safe and controlled environment. AR can be used to improve communication and collaboration in a range of industries.AR can provide remote workers with real-time access to information and data that gives effective collaboration with colleagues in different locations.AR can be used to enhance sales and revenue in a range of industries that are used to provide virtual product demonstrations allowing them to experience products before they purchase.AR can be used to improve the accessibility of people with disabilities. AR is creating a lot of impacts in various fields and these are explained below in very detail on various fields that include military, navigation, entertainment, marketing, etc.,

APPLICATIONS OF AR IN VARIOUS FIELDS

Although augmented reality has been around for a while, it wasn't until Android and iOS devices got GPS, cameras, and AR capabilities that its appeal to the general public really began to grow. Augmented reality is a technology that combines virtual reality with the real world. It takes the form of live-streaming imagery that has been digitally altered with computer-generated graphics. Users are able to interact with augmented reality through two different interfaces: wearable headgear and mobile device displays.

Developers have the tools they need to include AR features into their apps thanks to the several AR software development kits available for Android smartphones and Apple's AR Kit for its mobile devices.

Want to see before you buy how a retailer's virtual furniture will appear in your space? An AR app will be available shortly for that. Want to spruce up your dining room table with your favorite locations and characters from action-adventure games? You may.

There are now a plethora of AR apps available for iPhone and Android smartphones, and they aren't only for games anymore. Retailers are very interested in the potential of AR.

The uses of augmented reality are far more varied than their early gaming-focused PC, smartphone, and tablet applications may have suggested. The military supports soldiers who are performing repairs in the field by using augmented reality. AR is used by medical staff to be ready for operations. Applications for business and education are virtually endless.

Military

When it comes to military uses of the technology, the Heads-Up Display (HUD) is the standard illustration of augmented reality. The jet pilot is looking directly at a clear display. Along with other crucial information, the pilot often sees altitude, airspeed, and the horizon line displayed. Because the pilot can get the information he needs without having to glance down at the aircraft's equipment, the phrase "heads-up" is appropriate. As stated in Shumaker and Lackey (2014).

Ground soldiers employ Head-Mounted Displays (HMD). The soldier might be given crucial information, such as the position of the adversary, inside their line of sight. Simulators are also employed using this technology for training reasons.

Navigation

AR may be used to navigate between cities. You can quickly recognize and travel around locations like malls, museums, and parks thanks to this technology. For efficient navigation, AR makes path logistics and visual orienting easier. Applications for augmented reality (AR) can highlight and superimpose directions and instruction points for easy reading of what your camera views.

In an emergency, one may also utilize AR to locate your way. Because it employs optimization modes for successful steering, augmented reality is more useful in disaster situations. Considering that it lessens cognitive stress, this is preferable to traditional navigation techniques.

AR may also be used to calculate speed. An augmented reality application may track how fast your car is moving in comparison to other cars and give you recommendations on maneuvers like turns and passes. Performance is increased, and driving safety is increased. It may also be used to maintain and repair vehicles.

The user's position through GPS, the first camera measurement, and the location of the item is only a few of the inputs used by AR-enabled navigation applications. They keep track of how things move. This data is gathered by sensors and connected to the IMUs of the moving objects. About the user's movement in real-time, the data is utilized to create and overlay components.

Navigational AR integration is not without its difficulties. Before businesses throughout the world integrate augmented reality into navigation plans, there are still a few difficulties to be resolved.

User acceptability is one scenario. Being a new technology, many people are ignorant of the advantages of AR. For businesses looking to use it, this poses a marketing issue since they could have concerns about how it is seen and used.

It also presents some cyber security difficulties. You might need to adhere to stringent restrictions since AR apps are recording client locations. This implies that before the product launch, you might have to go through several administrative processes.

Costs associated with integrating AR at a geographic level across the various locales are similarly high. To create such apps, you'll require a lot of resources, notably competent AR engineers, who could be hard to find.

Sightseeing

In the tourist and sightseeing sectors, augmented reality has a variety of uses. It makes sense to utilize the technology to provide statistics to a live view of exhibits at a museum. As mentioned in Anand Nayyar et al. (2018).

Using augmented reality, sightseeing has been improved outside. Tourists may stroll past historical locations while viewing information and numbers displayed as an overlay on their live screen using a smartphone with a camera. These programs employ picture recognition and GPS to search for information in an internet database. Applications that look back in time and depict how the area seemed 10, 50, or even 100 years ago are also available in addition to information on historical sites.

Figure 4 shows the enhanced view of a monument.

Figure 5. shows how a monument is seen with the assistance of AR technology.

Figure 4. AR sightseeing view

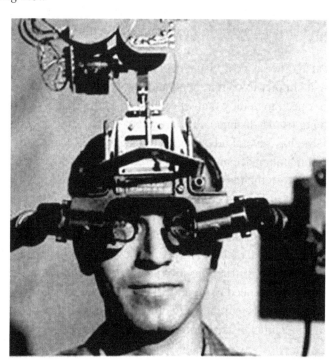

Figure 5. Improvised AR view of a place

Maintenance and Repair

Every industrial operation places a high priority on maintenance and repair since they have an impact on the overall performance and productivity of the company. With Industry 4.0, we have witnessed several technological and industry improvements, but we all agree that Augmented Reality (AR) has changed the game.

Industries benefit from it since it reduces costs and time for businesses. It offers a hands-on environment where technicians may interact with the real thing in front of them and all of its digitally enhanced parts. Additionally, the technician may view the equipment required for the job and even receive AR instructions.

The form of AR tags also offers a clear visual depiction of what is taking place with the machine and its usage history, making it simpler to comprehend and resolve issues.

Because they no longer need to deploy their specialists into the field, AR also helps businesses save money. For problem-solving from a distance, they leverage AR-powered visual aid and collaboration. In this field, augmented reality has several advantages. Because of this, industrial businesses are quickly implementing AR-enabled maintenance and repair procedures.

The majority of technicians in the manufacturing sector are required to physically inspect each machine part. When AR goods are utilized to complete these activities, it's not the case. While AR has been utilized for a while in a variety of sectors, its practical applicability is currently being expanded to assist workers in diagnosing and resolving issues more quickly. The repair instructions may be superimposed over the actual issue using augmented reality. The position of the technician and the equipment are taken into account in the digital overlay of instructions provided by AR technology. As they work on the repair, they may use this to see where they need to go and what they need to accomplish.

Nevertheless, augmented reality is facilitating. Companies can also produce instructions with illustrations and animations, which technicians can utilize to complete tasks.

Since most businesses only employ a small number of specialists, it is important to retain them on hand for the worst-case circumstances. They also frequently have to go to repair locations. They spend most of their time traveling. With AR, specialists can direct technicians from any location at any time; they are only a phone call away. Experts can see everything in 3D in real-time and may instruct personnel on the necessary fixes. Numerous businesses currently make use of augmented reality technology to offer fast, on-demand customer help. The time and money that would otherwise be spent on an expert's consultation or travel expenses will be saved by using it more frequently in the future.

Workers can be trained to perform their tasks more successfully and efficiently using augmented reality. Immersive training using augmented reality helps keep employees on board. Teams may acquire new skills and adjust to the shifting dynamics of their sector by presenting them with real-life scenarios during training. Compared to more passive and uninteresting traditional teaching techniques, it is more participatory. With AR, learning or upgrading skills may be done actively by carrying out actual maintenance or assembly tasks. The tools that employees will use in the field are practiced by them. They may learn more quickly and comprehend the equipment better in this way.

Advertising and Promotions

There are approximately 4.5 billion active internet users worldwide. Marketers and advertisers have a tonne of work to do. It is understandable why the market for digital advertising is rising given that global expenditure on digital advertising is anticipated to increase from 283 billion in 2018 to $517 billion by 2023.

And while early adopters have been the main users of augmented reality advertisements so far, this will change when more people start using the technology. According to Statista, the size of the AR market will more than double from around 3.5 billion in 2017 to more than 198 billion in 2025.

Because augmented reality advertisements are immersive, they aid businesses in forging an emotional bond with consumers. AR advertisements are dynamic and lifelike, in contrast to static pictures or banners, allowing users to view and even engage with them.

Imagine, for instance, a striking billboard promoting a recently released film. Consider what the power of AR may accomplish: passers-by can view the trailer on their smartphone displays by simply pointing their smartphone cameras at the billboard. Which of these two tactics (an AR ad or a billboard) is most likely to generate interest? Customers will almost certainly choose AR advertisements.

Customers who interact with AR advertisements experience it as though they are playing a fun video game. Customers are moved emotionally by this, which makes them more likely to buy. An emotional connection is a powerful strategy for raising brand recognition. AR advertisements are ideal for driving sales as well as for enhancing a company's reputation since people are more likely to remember companies whom they have favorable associations with.

This tactic was applied by Coca-Cola and the World Wide Fund in their Arctic Home Campaign. An augmented reality event was part of the campaign, which sought to safeguard polar bears and their natural environment. It was held at the Science Museum in London. The ability to engage with virtual animals in their natural habitat was available to visitors. The Coca-Cola business used this occasion to help customers develop strong emotional bonds with the brand.

Advertising in augmented reality is typically far cheaper and more immersive than print advertising. A simple AR ad can cost roughly $5,000 to design, while a complex AR campaign with eye-catching visuals may cost up to $100,000. Of course, the price for an AR ad fluctuates based on its quality.

Launching an AR marketing campaign is typically far less expensive than buying print space in a popular print publication. Additionally, many campaigns can use the same AR application.

Entertainment

The 2022 entertainment sector thinks that AR presents a sizable marketing potential since it allows entertainment firms to seamlessly integrate their branded content with the personalities that audiences identify with the most. Those characters may be comical, idealistic, revolutionary, or analytical, depending on the amount of interest displayed by the audience at the moment. The most well-known augmented reality entertainment applications are Snap chat, Google Lens, and Augment, while there are many others. With their user-friendly emoticons, stickers, and eye-catching effects, each software may curatively enhance the fun. These all serve as active representations of the times you spend with your loved ones.

Additionally, the 2022 entertainment industry experts support more regularly integrating the chronological stories of these entertainment applications to enrich the realism of entertainment. It is possible for them to create content and effectively integrate it with their marketing initiatives whenever and wherever they choose whether they are visiting various locations or taking in some comedy acts. They must keep object orientation in real-time in mind while they develop the content. If the same is not given adequate attention, it will have a detrimental effect on their mission statement, which they are using to raise awareness about items whose attributes have not yet been found by the accounts of premium members.

Public Safety

Public safety simply refers to defending the populace from disasters, criminal activity, and other possible threats to their safety. Safety is something you can't compromise on, whether you work in the customer service industry or for a narcotics enforcement organization. The developers of the software KOVA corp. realized this and as a consequence, they released the AR-based Silent Partner program, which instantly and securely records images or videos of unforeseen situations like disasters from your cell phones. Later, you (or public safety personnel or law enforcement personnel) can send any geotagged films or images that can be found anywhere. Additionally, this program contains a speech analysis feature that enables investigators to get the voice content to protect the public.

Drivers can utilize the iOnRoad Augmented Driving Lite App, another AR application that combines GPS, sensors, and native cameras on their smartphones to identify cars and alert drivers before a collision. Additionally, if the driver misses the collision notice, an audio-visual warning will sound, instructing them to use the brakes or slow down the vehicle so they may arrive at the designated locations safely and on time. These applications are a great help to responsible persons working for law enforcement or transportation corporations because they prevent them from considering plans that are inappropriate from the standpoint of public safety.

Manufacturing

Information-intensive and time-consuming manufacturing operations include system maintenance and product assembly. Training employees to carry out such responsibilities might be time-consuming and fruitless. AR may be utilized successfully in assembly planning operations, although VR technology is typically employed in the early stages of an assembly station's life cycle, whereas AR is more in the control and maintenance stages. AR can improve a person's awareness of their surroundings and comprehension of the activities involved in assembling a product. Graphical assembly instructions and animation sequences may be pre-coded for common tasks using an AR method at the design stage. On-demand, these sequences can be communicated and virtually superimposed on the finished goods at the production lines. The animations and instructions may automatically adjust to the conditions that exist on the production lines because they are conditional. These instructions and animated sequences may occasionally be updated with the most recent information from the creators. By using this tactic, assembly operators' training requirements and information overload can be reduced. It could cut down on how long it takes to put something together. Tang et al. investigated three instructional media in an assembly system employing a head-mounted display in 2003: a printed manual, computer-assisted instruction (CAI) using a monitor-based display, and CAI utilizing a laptop computer.

Education

Teachers and instructional designers have faced both creative possibilities and problems as a result of the quick development of new digital devices and technologies. Augmented Reality (AR), one of the most recent forms of digital media, will spread widely. Numerous fields, including medicine, the military, engineering maintenance and repair, and entertainment, have used this kind of technology. With the help of evolving technology, augmented reality (AR) may enhance interactive constructivist learning settings and provide a range of learning possibilities. The majority of research in the field of augmented reality is focused on technology, therefore the demands and efficacy of the educational applications are yet unmet and of modest consequence. Countless initiatives and numerous predictions have been made over the past 20 years addressing the eventual replacement of physical books with digital counterparts like electronic books, as discussed in Dejian Liu et al. (2017).

We no longer have to make a conscious decision about whether to pick electronic books or printed books thanks to the introduction of augmented reality books, which integrate digital material with actual analogy books. Recently, there have been more instances of both Korean and foreign computer science laboratories researching and developing augmented reality books. But the studies frequently pay more attention to the technical, rather than the instructional, components of AR books. Because of the quick advancement of information and communication technology, not just smartphones but also head-mounted, portable, and PC devices now have the display, marker, and camera characteristics needed for augmented reality books. As a result, it is getting simpler to employ AR books for instructional reasons.

Robotics and Tele-Robotics

The user of the system can be helped by an augmented display in the field of robotics and telerobotics.

A visual representation of the remote workspace is used by a telerobotic operator to control the robot. As it is when the operator is looking at the scene, annotation of the view would be helpful. Additionally, adding wireframe illustrations of the view's structures can make it easier to see the distant 3D geometry.

If the operator wants to rehearse a move, they can use a virtual robot that is imagined as an addition to the actual picture. After viewing the results, the operator can determine whether to carry with the move. The robot motion may thus be carried out immediately, which would minimize oscillations brought on by lengthy delays at the remote site in a telerobotics application. Remote medical operations are another use for robots and AR.

Collaborative AR

Two key concerns with collaboration are addressed by AR: seamless integration with current tools and methods, and improving practice by enabling distant and co-located tasks that would otherwise be impractical.

Projectors, portable, and head-worn displays have all been used to create collaborative augmented reality systems. Users are free, can see each other's eyes, and are assured to perceive identical augmentations by employing projectors to enhance the surfaces in a collaborative setting.

Both see-through head-worn displays and see-through portable displays are examples of collaborative AR systems that utilize see-through screens.

Medicine

As said in Dac-Nhuong Le et al. (2018), E-Health is the most recent application of VR/AR technology in healthcare, and it offers several useful features to support health care, such as allowing patients to more clearly describe their symptoms, enabling nurses to locate veins, pharmaceutical companies to provide innovative drug information, and allowing surgeons to get help. It can also be used to treat post-traumatic stress disorder and to support physical therapy, pain management, doctor or hospital visits, and surgical training.

According to predictions, VR and AR will permeate reality more and more, improving mankind both now and in the future. Since the majority of healthcare concerns use both technologies to combat clinical practices, medical training, surgery, phobia, rehabilitation, and emergency medicine since 2008, the topic of how successfully healthcare services and apps capitalize on VR/AR is posed here. However, there is still plenty of room to create appropriate applications utilizing AI and IoT because the healthcare industry needs precise, accurate, adaptable, reliable, and efficient agents, expert systems, gadgets, apps, software, and hardware to not only meet societal demands but also to flourish the working environment of an organization to implement radical change. Additionally, it is required that individuals possess computer science knowledge and comprehension of the possible effects of these technologies, which may enable them to imagine practice in their area of interest.

VR/AR has significant implications for medical education and is thought to be extremely helpful for students learning and/or healthcare training programs. There are several software programs (apps) that the public may use on smartphones for instant instruction, education, and emergency medical care. The medical training program offers a selection of medical interventions from which healthcare professionals might choose. Once a measure has been chosen by a medical professional, the screen will show the tracking pattern located inside the patient's body and search for it. Additionally, the training application will display a three-dimensional animated animation solution illustrating when, where, and under what circumstances certain exercises should be performed. By shifting the mobile device back and forth, the user may also change the mock-(up's simulation's) point of view.

Medical studies primarily focus on medical imaging and its associated fields, which fall under the category of image processing and computer vision. This will aid the development of new VR/AR applications for the improvement of healthcare concerns that are specially designed to operate on mobile devices by inexperienced VR/AR professionals.

The ability to colorize medical photos is a crucial feature when requesting a specific medical image from a database. This concept and method have been put out and are accessible for creating VR/AR apps. When requesting a specific medical picture from a database, the capability to colorize medical images is essential. This idea and approach have been made public and are available for building VR/AR applications.

The surgical team can use augmented reality to observe the CT or MRI data appropriately recorded on the patient in the operating room as the surgery is being carried out. The surgical team will perform better if the pictures can be correctly registered at this stage, and the uncomfortable and complicated stereotactic frames that are presently employed for registration will no longer be necessary.

Ultrasound imaging is a further use for augmented reality in the medical field. The ultrasound technician may examine a volumetric-generated picture of the fetus superimposed on the pregnant woman's belly using an optical see-through display. As the user advances, the picture is accurately displayed and seems to be inside the abdomen. Figure 6 shows a doctor examining a human body.

Figure 7 shows a doctor observing the hypothalamus gland of a patient.

Figure 6. AR in studying human organs

FUTURE OF AR AND ITS LIMITATIONS

Future technologies have many possibilities to incorporate AR in many fields and improve its features in existing fields. There are certain possible developments we could see in the future of AR that includes more advanced AR Hardware such as AR Glasses and AR Headsets and there will be greater adoption in industries that continues to improve even more adoptions in other industries.

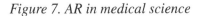

Figure 7. AR in medical science

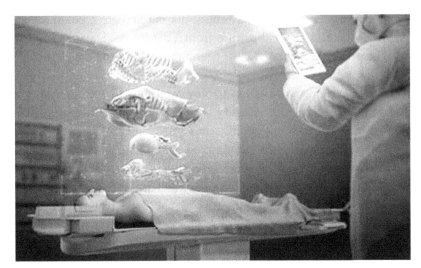

There is a possibility of integration with AI technologies that offer many personalized and intelligent experiences, for example, AR could be used to provide a real-time map and real-time language translation based on our location and preferences.AR Cloud is also an emerging one that would overlay the real world enabling users to interact with virtual objects and information that enables a new form of communication, entertainment, and commercial usage.AR enhances gaming experiences in the future with the most sophisticated graphics and gameplay mechanics. Overall future of AR looks promising that could make a greater revolution in technology.

In talking about its limitations there are various possibilities for facing certain difficulties that include Hardware limitations, Software limitations, Real-world data limitations, and Safety and security issues. One of the biggest limitations of AR is the need for specialized hardware that includes cameras, sensors, and powerful processors to track the user's movements and do certain functionalities. There is a lack of standardized software even now that makes AR developers face challenges in creating applications and also there are limited devices and platforms that limit the availability of AR experiences. The lack of standardization also makes it difficult for developers to create high-quality AR experiences. Another limitation is real-world data limitations such as location data or object recognition to provide the most accurate and appropriate information. Hence the limitations in availability and accuracy in data quality of AR product is also affected. AR applications can collect personal data which must be highly preventive but there is a limitation in data loss or data inaccuracy. Hence despite many positive aspects it also possesses some limitations that could be avoided in the coming generations.

AR DEVICES AND THEIR COMPONENTS

Augmented reality (AR) devices and components are essential for creating and experiencing AR content and it has some key components.AR uses transparent displays that allow users to see the real world by superimposing digital content. Some AR devices use HMDs also to cover the entire field of view and some also use smaller and discrete displays in applications like smart glasses. Cameras are essential for

AR to track users' movement and superimpose digital content in the real world and sensors are used to detect the user's movement. AR requires a powerful processor to handle complex algorithms hence the powerful processor is required to analyze sensor data and render virtual content.

Many AR devices require an internet connection to access cloud-based services and AR devices require batteries to power the device. Examples of AR devices include Microsoft HoloLens, Google Glass, etc.,

MAKING A SIMPLE AR APPLICATION: TECHNICAL SIDE

AR Applications can be done using software named UNITY. Marker-based AR Applications can be developed easily. First Install UNITY Software for free from the internet. Create a New project and name it and select the 3D Core option. Now we are going to do a marker-based AR Application. Marker-based AR is nothing but we set an image target and once we scan it we can find the objects initialized in Unity software for that specific image target. To set up this image target first we need to log in to the website Vuforia Engine. After registering, Click Add Vuforia engine to a Unity project, and after downloading double click it and add it to your unity software by clicking the Import option. To verify right click the Hierarchy panel and you'll find the option Vuforia engine by clicking it select AR Camera. After adding it deletes the main camera which is the default.

Licensing and Setting Up Image Target

In the "Project Window", go to Assets > Resources and double-click "Vuforia Configuration" to view its properties in the inspector panel. Here we should add our license. To add the license key, go to your Vuforia Development Portal License Manager and click "Get Basic". Give the name of your project and you'll get a license key copy it to the "App License Key" in Unity in the inspector panel.

To add an image target click Target Manager and click Add Database and after naming it add the image target. You can choose any image from your device of a maximum of 2 MB. You'll be getting it along with a rating i.e quality of image target. Click it and download a database from the option given by selecting the unity option. After downloading import it to your unity software. From the Vuforia engine option click Image target and the inspector panel opens select the image from the database and give your downloaded database in it and the image target will be set.

Setting 3D Object Over Image Target

Right-click the Image target and click the 3D object and select any object you want and place it properly over top of the image target. That's it now you can click the play button and check it using the webcam that detects the image target and show the 3D object added. As an apk format to view on mobile Click Build Settings and give a location for apk files to be stored and it starts to convert into apk format and you can visualize it on your mobile phone too with this apk. It can be run on AR-supported devices.

RELATED FIELDS

The term "Extended Reality" (XR) is often used to describe a variety of integrated real-world and virtual immersive settings. A subset of the complete spectrum of the reality-virtuality continuum, related human-machine interaction through computers and wearables includes augmented reality (AR), virtual reality (VR), mixed reality (MR), and their nuanced mixes and variants.

Early adopters and XR technology aficionados in recent years have created a variety of use cases for serious gaming, telepresence, education, and even just pure entertainment and fun connection amongst people all over the world. Even in professional settings, the widespread use of XR tools has been hampered by a certain degree of complexity, and efficient remote collaboration falls well short of technological maturity. The most noteworthy exception is still videoconferencing (telepresence), which was made possible by the necessity to cut back on travel in general. A greater translation of research and experimentation into commercial innovation has been hampered by XR's multifaceted technological complexity and the potpourri of economic and human elements. The most recent advancement in what was formerly referred to as VR or AR is called XR. The fusion of head-mounted displays (such as the Oculus Rift) with camera-enabled technology, such as smart glasses (such as Google Glass) or smartphones, first produced MR, which combined VR and AR into one device, and from there came to XR, which had the goal of releasing the user for interaction and achieving a seamless transition between the virtual and the real worlds. This seamlessness was made feasible by two different technologies: wall-sized projection and motion detection combined with powerful, lightweight equipment like CAVE systems and Microsoft HoloLens.

Virtual Reality Continuum

As proposed in Carlos Flavion (2019), a scale called the virtuality continuum is used to gauge how real or virtual technology is. The entirely virtual is at one end of the scale, while the completely genuine is at the other. XR covers the whole range of this scale, from beginning to conclusion. Therefore, the continuum between reality and virtuality includes all conceivable modifications and combinations of tangible and intangible items. Although it has been referred to as a notion in new media and computer science, it falls within the category of anthropology. Paul Milgram was the first to present the idea. In a continuum, nearby regions are essentially indistinguishable from one another, while the extremes differ greatly. As a result, it is not quite apparent what each term's precise boundaries are.

It's crucial to distinguish between the various extended reality (XR) technologies and the components of the virtuality continuum. A conceptual framework is called the virtuality continuum. How many real elements vs. digital elements are displayed is defined by moving from the left end of the continuum—the real environment—where 100% of what is displayed are real or physical objects and 0% are digital elements—to the right end—the virtual environment—where 100% of the objects displayed are digital and 0% are physical objects.

Virtual Reality

As it is stated in Jason Jerald (2016), the term "virtual reality" (VR) is frequently used in the media to refer to made-up worlds that only exist in our thoughts and on computers. But let's be more specific and explain the phrase. Pose tracking and 3D near-eye displays are used in virtual reality (VR), a simulated experience, to provide users with an immersive sense of a virtual environment. Virtual reality has applications in business (such as virtual meetings), education (such as medical or military training), and entertainment (especially video games).

Present-day standard virtual reality systems either make use of virtual reality headsets or multi-projected environments to deliver convincing sights, audio, and other sensations that simulate a user's physical presence in a virtual world. When using virtual reality technology, a user may view around the virtual world, move around in it, and interact with virtual features or items. However, the effect is most usually created by VR headsets, which feature a head-mounted display with a small screen in front of the eyes. The impression can also be created by specially constructed rooms with numerous enormous monitors. Haptic technology may provide for various types of sensory and tactile feedback in virtual reality, in addition to the usual auditory and visual input.

Mixed Reality

Your perception of the actual world may be combined with computer-generated material that may interact with it in mixed reality (MR). Alternatively, it may take a completely digital environment and link it to physical items. This is how MR can occasionally work like VR and occasionally behave like AR. In AR-based MR, the digital material may interact with the actual environment as if it were a part of it rather than being passively layered on top of it. You can even interact with some digital items as though they were physically there, giving the impression that they are there. You might be able to launch a virtual rocket from your coffee table or bounce a virtual soccer ball off the real-world floor and walls.

The combination of a real-world environment with a computer-generated one is referred to as mixed reality (MR). In mixed reality settings, physical and virtual things may coexist and communicate in real time. Augmented reality and mixed reality are often used interchangeably.

Visuo-haptic mixed reality is another name for a mixed reality that integrates haptics. A "Dual Reality" state, in which the motion of the two pendula is uncorrelated, and a "Mixed Reality" state, in which the pendula display stable phase-locked motion that is strongly correlated, are the two stable states of motion for this system.

Ubiquitous Computing

Mobile phones, sensors, and home automation systems are just a few instances of many different devices that share intelligence and computer networking in ubiquitous computing. A "Mixed Reality" state, in which the motion of the two pendula is correlated, and a "Dual Reality" state, in which the motion of the two pendula is uncorrelated, are the two stable states of motion for this system. The idea was first put up by Mark Weiser in 1988, who predicted that technology will permeate daily activities to the point where it would be hard to detect. Just as Weiser anticipated, as computers become more prevalent and sophisticated, it smoothly integrates into our daily activities (like driving or turning on the lights).

In software engineering, hardware engineering, and computer science, ubiquitous computing, sometimes known as "ubicomp," is the idea that computers may now exist everywhere and at any time. With ubiquitous computing, any device, anywhere, and in any format may be used, in contrast to desktop computing. The user interacts with the computer, which may take on many different forms, including laptops, tablets, cellphones, and terminals built into everyday objects like a refrigerator or a pair of glasses. Some of the core technologies enabling ubiquitous computing include the Internet, sophisticated middleware, operating systems, mobile code, sensors, microprocessors, novel I/O and user interfaces, computer networks, mobile protocols, location and positioning, and new materials. The concept of ubiquitous computing is the automated use of small, inexpensive, internet-connected computers to help with daily chores. For instance, a household ubiquitous computing system may connect biometric monitoring woven into clothes to lighting and environmental controls, enabling continuous, imperceptible modulation of lighting and temperature in a space. Theoretically, refrigerators may be "conscious" of the food within them and be able to design a variety of dinners using the food they already have on hand as well as alert users to expired or rotten food.

Devices develop more intelligence as they learn to interpret the massive volumes of data that they consume. Complex data processes become increasingly flexible and scalable until they are reduced to straightforward Bluetooth operations or modest sensor activities. The seamless, intelligent character of ubiquitous computing is improved by artificial intelligence: machines learn to advise their users, carry out tasks without being asked to, and keep track of preferences and habits. However, many people are still concerned about excessive data acquisition. Advanced machine learning and artificial intelligence have many advantages, but they also raise privacy issues and reluctance about how much our computers know about us and how that data may be exploited.

SUMMARY

Unquestionably, augmented reality is one of these cutting-edge technologies that turns science fiction into a reality. Like in the Star Wars and Marvel movies, holograms are already ubiquitous in the real world, delivering an immersive experience that transcends simple entertainment. The use of augmented reality in business is increasingly effective. Despite the several recent developments in AR, there is still more work to be done. Utilizing readily available libraries can aid in the building of applications. One of these is ARToolkit, which offers computer vision algorithms to determine the location and orientation of a camera concerning marked cards so that virtual 3D objects may be precisely superimposed on the markers. For the purpose of helping to solve a number of business problems, augmented reality is used in a wide range of diverse industries, including retail, business, gaming, healthcare, and even the military. It's essential to monitor these technologies if you want to know where the industry is headed. As a result, we covered the fundamentals, effects, applications, restrictions, and potential future developments of AR here.

REFERENCES

Flavion, C. (2019). The impact of virtual, augmented and reality technologies on the customer experience. *Journal of Business Research*, *100*, 547–560. doi:10.1016/j.jbusres.2018.10.050

Jerald, J. (2016). *The VR Book Human-Centered Design for Virtual Reality*. ACM Books.

Le, Le, Tromp, & Nguyen. (2018). Emerging Technologies for Health and Medicine. Scrivener Publishing.

Liu, Dede, Huang, & Richards. (2017) Virtual, Augmented and Mixed Realities in Education. Springer.

Nayyar, Mahapatra, Le, & Suseendran. (2018). Paper. *International Journal of Engineering & Technology, 7*(2),150-160.

Shumaker & Lackey. (2014). Virtual, Augmented and Mixed Reality Applications of Virtual and Augmented Reality. Springer.

Chapter 23
Internet of Things:
Architectures, Applications, and Challenges

Kaustubh Laturkar
Michigan State University, USA

Kasturi Laturkar
Validation Associates LLC, USA

ABSTRACT

With the internet of things (IoT) growing steadily, a wide range of application fields are being offered. These include monitoring health, weather, smart homes, autonomous vehicles, and so on. The result is the incorporation of solutions in various commercial and residential areas and the eventual emergence of them as ubiquitous objects in everyday life. Due to such circumstances, cybersecurity would be essential to mitigate risks, such as data exposure, denial of service efforts, malicious system exploitation, etc. A large majority of entry-level IoT consumer devices lack adequate protection systems, which makes them susceptible to a wide range of malicious attacks. The chapter discusses IoT architectures in depth, along with an analysis of potential applications. A detailed and thorough analysis of challenges in the IoT domain is provided, emphasizing flaws in current commercial IoT solutions and the importance of designing IoT solutions with security and privacy in mind.

INTRODUCTION

Internet of Things (IoT) refers to an interconnected network of intelligent devices (Bhat et al., 2007). It is now possible for a wide array of devices to gather, transmit, record, analyze, and store large amounts of data, which can include autonomous vehicles, integrated platforms, and intelligent monitoring systems, among others (Cirani, 2019). The advent of IoT has made it possible for every industry to rely on them, from food production to medicine, transportation and defense. Using IoT, physical objects can be converted into smart objects that can sense their surroundings, communicate with the rest of the smart objects, perform reasoning, and respond to changes in their environment as they occur (Tripathy, 2018).

DOI: 10.4018/978-1-6684-8145-5.ch023

Copyright © 2023, IGI Global. Copying or distributing in print or electronic forms without written permission of IGI Global is prohibited.

Users could benefit from using these devices in a variety of ways by integrating them into their lives. Some of these smart gadgets people have in their homes include smart cameras that alert them on their smartphone when there is movement during atypical hours, automatic doors that open remotely, smart fridge that notify them if milk is running low etc. It is predicted that smart meters will soon be installed in every home to monitor and control energy consumption, heating, and lighting, if they do not already exist there. As convenient as the Internet of Things is, it also comes with new security risks and privacy concerns that must be taken into account (Mahmoud et al., 2016). Failure to pay attention to these concerns regarding security and privacy can have serious consequences on every aspect of people's lives, from how they live in their homes, to how they drive to work, and even their physical and mental health.

Due to the fact that traditional IoT infrastructures contain a great deal of confidential and proprietary information, cybercriminals are interested in them because the potential for monetary gain is enormous. There is no doubt that safeguarding such massive amounts of data can be challenging in an IoT infrastructure ecosystem with extensive information sets and multiple repositories (Rani et al., 2021). Managing and analyzing data privacy can be complicated given the large volume of diverse information contained in this type of data (Tawalbeh et al., 2020). Dispersed infrastructure and the size of the IoT network are among the most prevalent concerns associated with IoT. The identifying, acquiring, and maintaining of accurate data records is a critical component of IoT and big data research (Wang et al., 2019). Criminals might exploit IoT equipment and networks to gain an advantage over competitors by exploiting IoT equipment and networks. In order to prevent this, IoT and big data analysis require a high level of security. Detecting cybersecurity vulnerabilities can be carried out effectively by combining data analysis and cybersecurity protection policies. Therefore, it is critical to have reliable and high-quality cybersecurity monitoring solutions (Rani et al., 2021).

Security flaws in smart meters and gadgets may enable attackers to gain a significant amount of control over these devices. Cyber-attacks in the IoT era will directly affect all the physical objects that individuals use every day as well as all of the information they contain. As an example, the rapid expansion of wireless control capabilities and the ever-increasing number of sensors in smart cars make them vulnerable to these attacks. Consequently, anyone who hacks into a car will be able to control the windshield wipers, the radio, door locks, and even the brakes and steering wheel of the car (Payne, 2019). If precautions are not taken, then people will be exposed to these kind of cyber-attacks. It is even possible for attackers to control surgically implanted and wearable health devices remotely (e.g., insulin pumps and heart pacemakers) by hacking the communication link between that device and the control and monitoring system that links them together. The attacker might be able to modify the insulin dose, for instance, causing serious health complications that may even result in the death of the patients who wear these smart health devices (Thompson et al., 2018). It is pertinent to note that IoT devices used in enterprise settings can also pose serious security risks. It is possible for attackers to exploit the sensing capabilities of smart objects used in big businesses to turn them into surveillance devices, which can be used to spy on their employees (Cusack & Tian, 2017). The cyber-attacks of this type can not only steal information regarding revenues and other financial aspects, but also employee data, proprietary business documents, and many different types of confidential records (Lin & Bergmann, 2016).

It is expected that in the near future, smart devices will be monitoring people's activities wherever they go, recording them as they occur. Sensors have been found to be able to detect human movements, facial expressions, and speech patterns. Therefore, data sensed by these sensors can reveal personal information that can be misused without adequate security. By aggregating the meta-data from the multiple hacked objects that surround a person over a considerable period of time, an outsider has the ability to gain a great deal of insight into the individual's personal life. Due to the advent of IoT and the proliferation of connected devices, people must find ways to preserve their privacy to ensure their safety in a digital age (Bahirat et al., 2018; Chong et al., n.d.).

This chapter provides an overview of some of the architectural options related to the IoT paradigm. Additionally, the application of IoT is discussed in several sectors and examples are provided to illustrate its use. The chapter also discusses the challenges and requirements of IoT security as well as some countermeasures that can be taken to mitigate these challenges. The last section of this chapter concludes with suggestions for future directions in IoT security research.

IoT ARCHITECTURES

In the context of IoT, architecture is a structure that specifies technical elements, the design and layout of the system, information hierarchy, and operational guidelines. It consists of devices, communication networks, and cloud solutions that enable IoT equipment to communicate (Chanal & Kakkasageri, 2020; Mahmoud et al., 2016). Since IoT embraces a wide array of technologies, there are no universal protocols or standardized designs. As a result, it cannot be employed for all types of use cases, since it is not a simple, straightforward model. Depending on its configuration, it can differ considerably, but it should be sufficiently adaptable with flexible protocol capabilities to facilitate a variety of computing processes. In the absence of a reliable IoT framework, IoT systems would be unusable, undermining the primary purpose of its development. Following is a description of some of the architectural types on which IoT can be deployed.

1. Three Layer Architecture

The three layer architecture system is composed of the perception, network, and application layers (Burhan et al., 2018). Several elements in the IoT network require identification, which is accomplished through the perception layer. As part of this process, RFID cards, detectors, CCTV cameras, and other similar equipment are used to collect information and data associated with each object. A network layer is the backbone of the Internet of Things, and it is responsible for connecting various intelligent systems, telecommunications equipment, and data centers. Aside from this, it also relays data acquired by the perception layer. By using the application layer, consumers can access IoT functionality and capabilities. The application layer outlines a range of use cases related to IoT, such as intelligent homes, interconnected communities, IoT-enabled healthcare, smart automation and more, demonstrating how IoT can be effectively incorporated into various applications (Chanal & Kakkasageri, 2020). While the three-layer architecture represents the foundation for IoT, it is not sufficient to support future IoT applications.

2. Middle-Ware-Based Architecture

This architecture integrates several different software modules and applications that are already available in the industry, and are often sophisticated and multifaceted. Due to its inherent flexibility, IoT has made it possible for just about any object to be linked and transmit data via a digital infrastructure without requiring any additional effort on the part of the user (Tripathy, 2018). In the IoT ecosystem, middleware facilitates data communication between large numbers of digital devices. This is accomplished by creating a network interface for devices, as well as for the application layers that delivers functionality that allows them to communicate and work together reliably. IoT infrastructure built on middleware consists of the following layers: Edge technology, Access gateway, Network layer, Middleware and Application layer (Chanal & Kakkasageri, 2020). The edge technology is more commonly referred to as the hardware layer, which is the layer containing integrated platforms, RFID devices, sensing devices, and other types of hardware components, which provide detection information in a variety of formats (Ramadan, n.d.). This layer essentially obtains information from a platform or infrastructure, processes it, and facilitates its exchange. The exchange of data between different systems is managed through the access gateway layer. This facilitates the flow of information between these systems, allows entities to access their resources, and streamlines message distribution. Depending on the monitoring tool used, the network layer enables data to be reliably transferred and secured from sensors to the core data management platform, enabling effective and efficient data management (Kraijak & Tuwanut, 2015). In the middleware layer, a number of essential features are supported, such as gathering and cleaning irrelevant information acquired from electronic equipment. These features enable integrated programs to manage access to devices based on a variety of parameters. In the middleware layer, there are interface protocols that facilitate functional compatibility between applications by taking advantage of similar networking techniques in order to achieve functional compatibility. Through the use of device abstraction, it supports lexical and conceptual interoperability between multiple systems. Based on the data processed by the middleware layer, the application layer is responsible for the comprehensive management of software. These platforms enable sophisticated applications and end users to interact intuitively and seamlessly (Kraijak & Tuwanut, 2015).

3. Five Layer Architecture

In the era of exponential advancements in IoT, three-layer architectures are no longer adequate. Consequently, a five-layered approach has been put forward as a possible solution (Mashal et al., 2015). Perception, Network, Middleware, Application, and Business layers make up the five-layer IoT framework. The following is a brief description of each of the layers within the architecture

a. **Perception Layer:** Each element of an IoT network has an underlying significance, which is defined by the perception layer (Kumar et al., 2020; Zhong et al., 2016). It utilizes a multitude of detectors and sensors to record relevant data such as location, temperature, vibration, moisture content, pH level, humidity, etc. The primary objective of the system is to gather external data, and relay it to a centralized data management platform using the network layer, while ensuring that all information is kept confidential.

b. **Network Layer:** The purpose of this interface is to serve as a bridge between the perception and middleware layers, as implied by its name. By utilizing communication channels like Wi-Fi, GSM, Universal Mobile Telecommunications Framework, Infrared, and so on, this layer receives information from the perception layer and transmits it to the middleware layer (Kumar et al., 2020; Zhong et al., 2016). Due to its role as the information exchange gateway between perception and middleware, it is sometimes called the communication layer. In each case, the exchange of information is done in a confidential manner, protecting the recorded data from unauthorized access at all times.

c. **Middleware Layer:** There is an array of functions that can be performed by objects in the IoT ecosystem once they have been connected and synchronized. The Middleware Layer has a number of high-level capabilities that it offers its users, such as archiving, data processing, analysis, and the execution of tasks (Chanal & Kakkasageri, 2020; Ungurean et al., 2016). A system identifier and label are used to determine which information is transmitted to the corresponding component based on the data it gathers. In addition, it is capable of taking decisions depending on data obtained from the sensors in order to perform the required tasks.

d. **Application Layer:** The application layer is responsible for managing software applications by handling data that has been evaluated by the middleware layer. It is also responsible for the implementation of numerous types of programming functions. IoT applications can be developed and deployed using this layer using a variety of IoT solutions, which can have a wide range of applications, including intelligent surveillance, digital healthcare, autonomous vehicles, smart wearables like glasses and watches, connected homes, assisted living, automated food production, and so on (Karagiannis et al., 2015; Nebbione & Calzarossa, 2020).

e. **Business Layer:** In general, the effectiveness of an electronic product depends not only on the technologies embedded in it, but also on how it is presented to its customers. The scope of business layer services encompasses the full spectrum of IoT solutions and capabilities (Vashi et al., 2017). In addition to graphical depictions and corporate model representations, it can generate process diagrams, summarized management reports, etc. Information management activities will depend on the volume of reliable information acquired from the lower layers, as well as the efficiency of the operation (Chanal & Kakkasageri, 2020). By providing accurate and thorough evaluation information, it is possible to make better informed decisions related to objectives, plans, and future directions concerning application and device developments in a more efficient and effective manner.

IoT APPLICATIONS

Due to the extensive number of industries that have integrated IoT into their processes, the ubiquitous presence of IoT has become an integral part of modern life (Bhat et al., 2007; Kraijak & Tuwanut, 2015). IoT technologies can be used in a variety of ways, especially as they can be easily adapted to virtually any system that can transmit pertinent data regarding internal processes, operational efficiency, and external factors. The tracking and management of these parameters can be carried out remotely, allowing informed decisions to be made. Depending on the sector in which IoT technology is being used, the benefits and specifications of the technology will differ. The IoT applications in the industrial, defense, medical, and automotive sectors will be discussed in this section. Figure 1 illustrates a summary of IoT applications in the aforementioned sectors.

1. **Industrial Applications**

IoT integration into industrial processes is often referred to as Industrial Internet of Things (IIoT) (Chanal & Kakkasageri, 2020). One of the advantages of IIoT is that it allows organizations to collect, compile, and analyze data collected from sensors that track device performance in order to improve the efficiency of their business processes as a whole. These devices are commonly used in production management, automated measurement, robotics control systems, preventative maintenance, and equipment maintenance, among other applications (Chen et al., 2014). A proper IIoT interface will be able to facilitate the current hardware environment to effectively communicate with any commercial environment in a reliable manner. A data-driven edge computing approach facilitates rapid information exchange and real-time information processing, helping to improve the speed at which problems can be resolved. In order to address the challenges of data management and operational systems, IoT network clustering assists in keeping the reliability of cloud-based communications and information retention in order to keep the network up and running. Implementing and managing equipment synchronization and expanding its use is crucial to the success of business enterprises. In order for businesses to be able to establish, manage, and connect their peripheral equipment as well as other devices effectively, they need to be able to establish the connection quickly and accurately. Further, they require precise maintenance of the system configuration in order to facilitate reliable remote authentication of devices and to resolve errors by keeping track of the notifications sent out by the system (Kwon et al., 2016).

There are a multitude of challenges businesses face when making the move to incorporating IoT into their operations. These include interoperability, privacy, analytics, data transmission, as well as optimizing corporate operations and technological capabilities. Devices used in operations are particularly vulnerable, and even minor breaches can lead to catastrophic results. The trustless concept is essential for an effective defense system. It would be necessary to catalog and describe the endpoints that are associated with such a framework for trust guidelines to be defined. To ensure that the infrastructure continues to be secure and reliable, it is segmented into compartments and monitored closely to keep it updated as necessary. In the event that any abnormal activity is detected that could indicate that an endpoint has been compromised, the necessary countermeasures are implemented as soon as possible in order to minimize any potential threat to the system (Sisinni et al., 2018). There is a significant need for regular monitoring and surveillance of IIoT equipment, components, and systems in order to ensure that these devices remain in proper working order and function as intended. Such insight will enable these organizations to immediately identify potential problems that may affect business processes, personnel safety, and financial performance, thereby increasing their ability to deal with them much more effectively.

2. Defense Applications

There are a number of existing military operations that are confronted with convoluted, peculiar, and unpredictable circumstances, particularly in conjunction with unexpected and unforeseen threats that have the potential to pose significant challenges to the missions (Fraga-Lamas et al., 2016). For the military to effectively make the most informed decisions, they will need an accurate understanding of the environment they operate in, since they will have relatively limited opportunities to acquire such information to develop the best possible options and strategies. In addition to this, they should seek input from every channel possible to ensure that they can obtain the complete, most comprehensive and accurate assessment of the situation in a timely manner and that they are cognizant of the consequences of their actions and strategies. These needs can be met by integrating IoT into the security sector. As modern tactical defense technologies have evolved, these devices are increasingly equipped with surveillance and data communication capabilities, which can be used to monitor or control military devices to meet specific requirements. In order to ensure seamless integration into the information architecture of defense equipment systems, the sensors and actuators embedded within the devices are required to support sophisticated data protocols. The safety measures, standardized protocols, and scalable capabilities should be in place as part of the efforts to achieve seamless interoperability (Payal et al., 2021). As a result of integrating these processes, it is anticipated that the end result could be an electronic equipment configuration that is seamless and comprehensive in every aspect. For IoT solutions developed for the military to be reliable and scalable, they must be designed with a decentralized architecture, networking integration, flexibility, and privacy protection. These systems could be used for surveillance, healthcare services, supply chain management, emergency response, combat information transfer, critical communications, asset tracking and monitoring, threat recognition, incident assessment, personnel readiness training, and many more. However, the deployment of IoT in the military environment is accompanied with underlying concerns regarding security and reliability (Iyer & Patil, 2018). It is possible for unknown intruders to gain access to IoT systems if they are not adequately protected. In this case, information can be controlled, prevented, or disrupted, and automated operations can be affected or compromised. A Trusted Platform Module is designed for military IoT platforms in order to ensure data transmissions are protected from unauthorized access or disclosure. It is based on a crypto algorithm concept, which provides robust authorization and encryption.

3. Medical Applications

Across the healthcare landscape, the need for IoT-enabled diagnostics, intelligent monitoring, and equipment syncing is on the rise (Haghi Kashani et al., 2021; Milovanovic & Bojkovic, n.d.). The growth of these technologies is expected to accelerate in the coming years due to their inherent advantages. IoT can simplify a patient's consultation and treatment by improving their ability to devote more time to communicating with their medical professional, thereby facilitating a better chance of a successful outcome. Although this is the case, the sheer amount of interconnected devices and the massive amount of digital data that is being collected can make it quite challenging to protect data and deal with personal information in a confidential manner. Among the most critical issues faced by IoT in the healthcare industry is the safety and confidentiality of patient data. Despite the fact that IoT connected smart sensors may be able to provide users with real-time information, the majority of these do not comply with established guidelines or industry requirements. It is extremely challenging to collate and analyze information in order to find relevant observations and findings, given the diversity of information and data transfer methodologies in use today (Akan et al., 2016). To be certain that the information generated by IoT is effectively processed, it is imperative to group the inputs into segments in order to avoid information overload and ensure that the inputs are more reliable in order to provide optimal results. When considering investing and developing IoT based health-care mobility solutions, one of the most significant concerns that must be considered is whether the amount of information available in the healthcare industry will have a lasting impact on the selection process in the care facilities. There are a number of potential risks related to IoT devices as far as data security and confidentiality are concerned. These include security breaches, Denial of Service (DoS) attacks, badge duplication, account spoofing, radio frequency interference and cloud-based data harvesting (Bhuiyan et al., 2021; Chanal & Kakkasageri, 2020). As a result of privacy concerns in relation to healthcare data, some patients may be hesitant to reveal their medical records to organizations outside of their own system. Prior to taking advantage of wireless IoT equipment and electronic devices and using radio communication technology such as WiFi, NFC, and Bluetooth, etc. for the healthcare sector, it is imperative to implement a set of safeguards against hacking attacks, phishing attempts, and backdoor intrusions in order to protect these devices.

Figure 1. Summary of the IoT applications in the different sectors

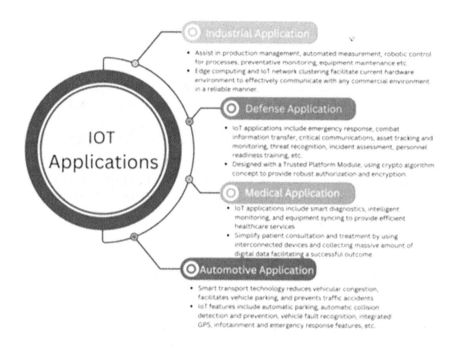

4. Automotive Applications

IoT integration in automotive applications has a number of advantages and use cases. Road congestion could be controlled in cities using electronic detection devices and smart transportation management technologies that could improve the efficiency of traffic flow. A smart transportation system is primarily intended and designed to solve three problems: reducing vehicular congestion, facilitating parking, and preventing traffic accidents (Pourrahmani et al., 2022). The technological achievements that underpin these types of services include GPS receivers that provide location information, accelerometers that measure motion, stabilizing systems that assist in steering, RFID tags that identify automobiles, thermal detectors that monitor individuals and vehicles, and recording devices that monitor automobile growth and road traffic. The cloud-connected automotive vehicles are linked to the network and are connected to a diverse array of IoT devices (Rahim et al., 2021). It is possible to use these devices in the evaluation of traffic patterns in a number of urban sprawls, interstate highways, and metropolitan areas. In recent years, many new vehicle IoT features have been developed, such as automatic parking, automatic collision detection and prevention, vehicle fault recognition, integrated GPS, navigation, emergency response features, etc. As a result of the vast number of vehicle monitoring devices on the road, packet mismatches could occur, excessive bandwidth could be consumed, congestion could occur and vital information could be lost. As the number of smart devices in vehicles increases exponentially, it is becoming even more crucial that cybercriminals are not able to gain access to this information because they can retrieve Individually Recognizable Data from the vehicle's data collection equipment. A consumer's data can include information regarding a trip, vehicle location, their interests in entertainment, their monetary details, etc. In spite of the fact that security measures can protect the administrative interfaces on the end-user device, they should ideally be handled and configured separately from the end-product or system configuration. Implementing a Trusted Computing Base protects the systems and software from duplication and impersonation and ensures that authentic elements are contained within the applications (M.S. Beg et al., 2022). Since, cybercriminals are interested in monitoring network interactions, data integrity should be considered a critical component of every IoT device or application. By encrypting and verifying all exchanges, a network's integrity is preserved, and all exchanges can be securely communicated, thereby preventing unauthorized third parties from altering, hacking, forging the information stored within, and ensuring that the reliability and security of the network can be maintained. A verification is also conducted to ensure that external applications will not cause interference with other crucial processes. IoT breaches tend to be conducted using mechanical devices so preventing access to these electronic components can be an effective strategy to minimize the possibility of such an intrusion and therefore guarantee a tamper-resistant design for the IoT system (Liu et al., 2012).

CHALLENGES WITH IMPLEMENTATION

Internet of Things offers significant potential, but it also faces a number of challenges that must be overcome through further research. As the need for a more standardized approach to processes, the increase in on-demand functionality, and the requirement to ensure compatibility and interoperability has grown, so has the demand for measures to ensure the safety of applications, devices, and the privacy of users. IoT implementation requires consideration of several critical aspects at the foundational stage, which play a major role in the efficiency of the system. Ideally, these measures need to function with limited memory capacity, a small amount of processing capability, and be reasonably inexpensive both in terms of systems and devices. There are a variety of devices, characterized by a wide range of processing capabilities, and the complexity of the infrastructure, all of which contribute to the necessity of systems that are flexible, lightweight, and comply with a variety of government regulations in order to operate effectively. As part of the development of an IoT privacy policy, it is essential to develop a comprehensive model that can be implemented using a novel approach that will facilitate scalability in the diverse network conditions of the IoT (Chanal & Kakkasageri, 2020; Lawal & Rafsanjani, 2022). There are many research challenges that continue to emerge in the area of implementation of the Internet of Things, and the following section summarizes some of them. Figure 2 summarizes some of the challenges with the implementation of IoT infrastructure.

1. **Authentication**

To protect the information from the hands of malicious third parties, authentication is an extremely important safety concern and it is an imperative requirement in IoT. IoT infrastructure information can be retrieved by any user if they have the right credentials (Shah & Venkatesan, 2018). There are various components in the IoT that need to verify their connection to the local gateway before data can be transmitted. Consequently, the local gateway must validate with the server in order to transmit this kind of data. Considering that there are so many entities that can be involved in the IoT, this method can be very time consuming and complex to implement. This could be the result of execution speed being slow or devices interacting for the first time with each other. Hardware and programming inconsistencies across multiple IoT systems will render it much more difficult to devise an approach that is reliable and efficient. All of this necessitates the development of a mechanism to collaboratively validate objects in every exchange within an IoT framework that also has a fast execution rate (Zhang et al., 2014).

2. Security

A major part of the IoT technology consists of components that are engineered to be deployed on a huge scale. A typical implementation of the Internet of Things consists of a collection of similar devices that share many attributes and are based on similar methods of operation. This close resemblance could result in vulnerabilities in the network being magnified and can have a severe impact if compromised (Tawalbeh et al., 2020). In terms of the connections that exist between the various IoT components, the estimated volume is staggering. In certain cases, some of these devices might form links and exchange information in an erratic manner independently of other devices. To assess the safety of the IoT infrastructure, it will be necessary to examine readily available resources, strategies, and approaches, as well as their relevance. It is possible to exploit a serious vulnerability in IoT devices and applications, both for malicious activities as well as to steal confidential consumer information if a sufficient level of protection is not implemented (Xu et al., 2015). This can occur owing to insufficiently encrypted data transmissions between devices and applications. Furthermore, as IoT devices become more complicated in their integration and connectivity, they also potentially compromise the overall stability and reliability of the network if not properly safeguarded and configured (Zhang et al., 2014). This phenomenon is unavoidably influenced in part by the fact that the use of identical elements of IoT is being broadened and automated at an unprecedented rate. IoT devices have the potential to interact with a wide range of devices directly or indirectly, and it is evident that both consumers and designers of IoT devices share an ethical responsibility for protecting the network users and infrastructure against potential threats. Data integrity is regarded as one of the most vulnerable domains within the context of the security of IoT (Alhalafi & Veeraraghavan, 2019). This is largely a result of the extensive adoption of IoT, as well as the capabilities of these systems to gather a large amount of information without adequate security measures. To formulate a well-balanced and suitable response to these issues, an effective and comprehensive IoT strategy is evidently needed, one that is based on a collective sense of ownership.

3. Confidentiality

The effectiveness of IoT can be demonstrated by the fact that it is capable of protecting individuals against the cybersecurity threats through the multiple steps it undertakes to ensure their anonymity and privacy (Porambage et al., 2016). It is important to consider data privacy in IoT to enable authorization and customization to validate entities through a platform for authorization management and device validation, coupled with an authentication monitoring process. A number of potential challenges such as issues of confidentiality and the possibility of adverse effects that may arise as a consequence of the implementation of IoT are likely to be a significant factor in delaying or hindering the widespread adoption of IoT. The importance of considering the principles of confidentiality and individual anonymity is crucial to maintain consumer trust and confidence in the IoT, connected devices, and software applications that accompany them (Lin & Bergmann, 2016; Weber, 2010). IoT devices are being extensively tested to ensure that the confidentiality of monitoring and tracking information is improved over time as the proliferation of IoT devices increases. The ubiquitous intelligence embedded in devices has given rise to privacy concerns in the context of IoT, since data collection and dissemination are possible practically in all environments. The convenience of communication over the Internet is another integral component that contributes to this issue as there is not a standardized process in place for this purpose. Therefore, it is easier to retrieve private data from almost anywhere in the world. This is a major security concern as it can lead to private data misuse, identity theft, and other malicious activities. For the assurance of privacy, solutions must comply with stringent scalability specifications, be able to accommodate a variety of components and elements, as well as meet the resource constraints of the integrated devices, including their power and processing capabilities (Karale, 2021; Weber, 2015).

4.   Interoperability

Ideally, the IoT system should be able to work with a wide range of equipment, platforms, and applications in order to realize its full potential. As a result, it is imperative that these diverse devices exchange information, communicate data, and coordinate to reach the desired outcome. An interoperable system can be achieved at the network, semantic, and syntactic levels. It is important that IoT systems are aligned with the equipment with which they are exchanging data in order for them to work optimally (Yadav et al., 2018). This can be achieved primarily by adhering to standardized communication guidelines and protocols between these systems and the equipment. Since the proliferation of IoT connected devices has shifted focus and approach, interoperability concerns have increased. The ability to develop and manage an accessible Application Programming Interface (API) is essential for the successful implementation of an IoT initiative. For APIs to be maintained and validated for standardized protocols, a central management interface is usually required. IoT networks also require a lot of energy to exchange data from devices connected to them using shared communication channels. In addition, since it is relatively common to use external security solutions, it is very complicated to implement them for all equipment, since they are not interoperable in some cases (Noura et al., 2019; Suzana Maciel et al., 2016). There is also the possibility that organizations may not support the compatibility of their products and devices due to the deployment of proprietary software in order to maintain their position as competitive players in the market. There are a number of factors that contribute to the incompatibility of some devices, including their intricate design and the multifaceted functions they offer. There may be an inability to synchronize data at the information level due to the lack of hardware and software compatibility. The inadequacy of a structured data and established protocols to interpret the significance of the data, pose a formidable barrier to the exchange of information between IoT devices. Due to the dynamic nature of collected information, it is necessary to handle it in a sophisticated manner in order to ensure its accuracy. Furthermore, access to the information is crucial for users to engage with it, which can be challenging, especially when dealing with large amounts of data spread across a wide range of devices and cloud-based databases (Konduru & Bharamagoudra, 2017).

Figure 2. Challenges with the implementation of IoT infrastructure

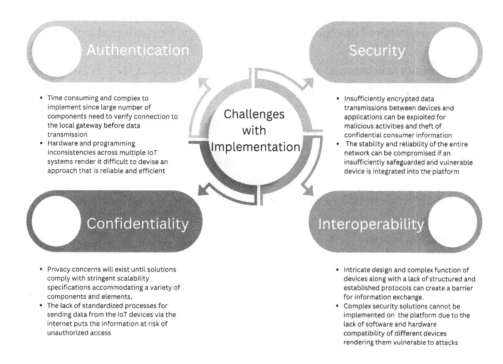

FUTURE DIRECTIONS

Global advancements in technology are causing the world to migrate towards IoT, which will have a profound impact on all aspects of human life in the near future. It will allow businesses to develop innovative products and services, as well as create more efficient processes. A variety of industrial sectors can be transformed by IoT data insights which can be used for real-time analysis. As people's homes and offices become more connected and smarter, it will have a significant impact on their personal lives as well. There will be a complete automation of everything, from home appliances such as refrigerators, ovens, washing machines, to vehicles, homes, large commercial equipment, and even entire cities. Global regulations and standards are expected to be implemented as IoT revolutionizes the world with detailed attention to confidentiality, personal information protection, encryption, permissions, authorization control, security and trust governance. Besides the advancements in sensors and device interconnectivity, lifestyle trends and mobility will also drive IoT adoption. During the next few years, the IoT implementation of connected devices will continue to develop and a number of innovations in this area can be anticipated which are listed below.

1. **Integration of Blockchain in Artificial Intelligence Internet of Things (AIoT)**

A more efficient IoT operation can be achieved with the AIoT through which human-machine interactions and data analysis can be improved. Data from IoT devices can be turned into useful information through artificial intelligence methods, which would increase the overall usability of the system. The tamper-proof nature of blockchain and its ability to provide more security than traditional security mechanisms make it ideal for use in AIoT applications (Kuzlu et al., 2021; Laturkar & Laturkar, 2022; Osuwa et al., 2017). There are a number of directions in which research can be conducted in the future, including:

a. Developing security schemes and analyzing them using techniques such as Automated Validation of Internet Security Protocols and Applications (AVISPA) simulation, Burrows–Abadi–Needham (BAN) logic, and Real-or-Random (RoR) models
b. Enhancing the efficiency of blockchain frameworks by reducing computation power and communications costs
c. Seamless integration of blockchain, artificial intelligence, and IoT tools and technologies
d. Enhancing the privacy of blockchain-based AIoT frameworks
e. Building an AIoT framework based on blockchain that improves data accuracy (Al-Turjman, n.d.)

2. Cloud Internet of Things

The CloudIoT concept refers to the integration of IoT technology with Cloud platforms. CloudIoT provides convenience and functionality in everyday lives; however, most of its working components, such as low-cost sensors and communication chips, are designed without adequate security considerations. In case a malicious attack is executed successfully, the CloudIoT system would be rendered insecure, resulting in loss of sensitive information and catastrophic damage to the infrastructure (Botta et al., 2016). Since the IoT systems are integrated with Cloud platforms, the problem becomes more complex. As opposed to securing a set of devices or cloud, CloudIoT safety involves the integrated framework for cross-platform security of the entire system (Biswas & Giaffreda, 2014). Developing heterogeneous security architectures that allow data generated from disparate sources to be blended is essential to securing CloudIoT systems (Aazam & Huh, 2016). Security requirements and solutions vary depending on the application. In order to create a robust security model, it is imperative to design a security architecture that features similarities across applications.

3. Crowd Sensing

Crowd sensing (CS) enables people to share and extract information related to their interests using mobile devices. In crowd sensing, mobile phones and other wearable devices are emerging as devices for gathering information, computing, and communicating, a process typically referred to as Mobile Crowd sensing System (MCS) (Sisi & Souri, 2021). Mobile computing has the potential to improve the quality of life of people in the fields of healthcare and transportation. Despite MCS' many advantages, it faces several critical challenges that must be addressed in future research. These include data privacy and user trustworthiness (AbualSaud et al., 2019). Additionally, MCS is an effective tool to promote environmental and social sustainability in smart cities. In terms of environmental applications, MCS can be used for a number of purposes, such as measuring pollution levels in cities, monitoring water levels in creeks, and tracking wildlife habitat conditions. Database servers allow users to share their sensed information, which can provide insight into community-related issues (Luo et al., 2019).

4.   Security-by-Design Approach

A security by design approach is used in software and hardware development to emphasize incorporating security features into the initial development process rather than implementing such functionality following an incident resulting from a security breach (Sequeiros et al., 2020). It is essential for IoT applications to implement security by design by following robust development guidelines, adhering to specific standards and best practices, and mapping security requirements to the components' lifecycles (Barbosa et al., 2017). This will ensure the reliability and functionality of IoT components throughout their operational lifetime. This promising approach requires further research, particularly the exploration and implementation of microservice-based security architectures (Beamap et al., 2019; Lam et al., 2022).

5.   The Internet-of-Bio-Nano-Things (IoBNT)

As an emerging information and networking technology framework, IoBNT refers to cross-platform collaboration networks that integrate a wide range of biological and synthetic nanobiological components and equipment symbiotically into the internet infrastructure (Kuscu & Unluturk, 2021). The IoBNT architecture includes bio-nanosensors and devices that perform several functions and processes, including sensing, analyzing, operating, and communicating. Through the use of nanosensors, data can be collected and transmitted to edge nodes for analysis, and used throughout the lifecycle of a service. Data is archived and stored by cloud hosting centers after it has been processed (e.g., ECG, heart rate monitors, oxygen, temperature, and blood pressure sensors) (Akyildiz et al., 2015; Kuscu & Unluturk, 2021). Nevertheless, a group of attackers could use a variety of cyberattacks (such as attacks on cloud data centers, fog nodes, or nanosensors), revealing sensitive data and affecting the smooth operation of the IoBNT networks, including remote patient monitoring and healthcare management. Consequently, wrong medical decisions and treatments could be made, potentially resulting in life-threatening situations and manipulation of medical records (El-Fatyany et al., 2020). IoBNT networks must therefore adequately address security issues, including securing data exchange between parties involved in the healthcare process to maintain patient safety and confidentiality. Furthermore, nanosensors and edge nodes would have to be authenticated and their locations and identities protected in order to ensure system security (Bakhshi & Shahid, n.d.; Kuscu & Unluturk, 2021).

CONCLUSION

Recent years have seen the IoT attract the attention of researchers as businesses, governments, and the general public increasingly use smart technology to solve problems. It has become widely adopted in a number of essential fields due to its capability to provide efficient and effective enterprise applications that are able to perform novel and complex functions more efficiently. Through the IoT, effective communication can be achieved between individuals, thereby bridging an important communication gap. In terms of services and solutions, they provide a wide range of options. IoT sensors and devices are integrated into a wide range of environments, such as commercial vehicles, residential areas, healthcare facilities, industrial operations, etc., making them a vital part of people's daily lives. The development of smart home systems, automated agriculture systems, and a number of other sophisticated technological innovations allows people to live a better and more comfortable life.

While IoT technology has considerable potential, there remains much to be accomplished in terms of research and development before IoT security can be implemented in a comprehensive, decentralized manner. As part of the design process for IoT, it is crucial to take security and privacy into account early on to avoid the common pitfall of addressing them in the late stages of the process. Despite the many benefits of this technology, cybercriminals often misuse it in order to profit from exploitation of IoT systems and sell sensitive information and data for a profit. It is therefore imperative that methods and strategies are developed in order to protect sensitive information transmitted through IoT systems. A great deal of emphasis must be placed on identifying threat models, as well as developing efficient solutions that can be installed on existing infrastructure with all the sensors and devices that are currently available on the market, in order to mitigate cyberattacks. Multi-domain approaches (cloud, fog, and sensing) must be used collaboratively in order to stop or mitigate certain attacks. In addition to the evident reason that different domains can interact and collaborate to stop ongoing malicious activity more effectively, interdomain defensive solutions may also be more cost effective than applying countermeasures to every domain separately. In addition, it is necessary to develop efficient cryptographic techniques that are both computationally efficient and are able to deliver a high level of data confidentiality. It is imperative to adapt the communication protocols for the network to ensure they are compatible with the device constraints.

Due to the internet-connected nature of most devices, the application of IoTs will be severely restricted if issues related to personal information protection and confidentiality are ignored. It is essential that consumers are familiar with the potential safety risks associated with connected devices as well as the need to protect their personal information. Furthermore, organizations must ensure that their systems are reliable and periodically updated in order to prevent potential malicious attacks. It is necessary that privacy and security of connected devices be a priority in order to ensure the successful deployment of IoT technology.

REFERENCES

Aazam, M., & Huh, E. N. (2016). Fog Computing: The Cloud-IoT/IoE Middleware Paradigm. *IEEE Potentials*, *35*(3), 40–44. doi:10.1109/MPOT.2015.2456213

AbualSaud, K., Elfouly, T. M., Khattab, T., Yaacoub, E., Ismail, L. S., Ahmed, M. H., & Guizani, M. (2019). A Survey on Mobile Crowd-Sensing and Its Applications in the IoT Era. In IEEE Access (Vol. 7, pp. 3855–3881). Institute of Electrical and Electronics Engineers Inc. doi:10.1109/ACCESS.2018.2885918

Akan, O., Bellavista, P., Coulson, G., Dressler, F., Ferrari, D., Kobayashi, H., Palazzo, S., Sherman Shen, X., Stan, M., Xiaohua, J., & Zomaya, A. Y. (2016). *eHealth 360° International Summit on eHealth Budapest, Hungary, June 14–16, 2016 Revised Selected Papers*. https://www.springer.com/series/8197

Akyildiz, I. F., Pierobon, M., Balasubramaniam, S., & Koucheryavy, Y. (2015). The internet of Bio-Nano things. *IEEE Communications Magazine*, *53*(3), 32–40. doi:10.1109/MCOM.2015.7060516

Al-Turjman, F. (n.d.). *Transactions on Computational Science and Computational Intelligence Artificial Intelligence in IoT*. https://www.springer.com/series/11769

Alhalafi, N., & Veeraraghavan, P. (2019). Privacy and Security Challenges and Solutions in IOT: A review. *IOP Conference Series. Earth and Environmental Science*, *322*(1), 012013. Advance online publication. doi:10.1088/1755-1315/322/1/012013

Bahirat, P., He, Y., Menon, A., & Knijnenburg, B. (2018). A data-driven approach to developing IoT privacy-setting interfaces. *International Conference on Intelligent User Interfaces, Proceedings IUI*, 165–176. 10.1145/3172944.3172982

Bakhshi, T., & Shahid, S. (n.d.). Securing Internet of Bio-Nano Things: ML-Enabled Parameter Profiling of Bio-Cyber Interfaces. *Proceedings, 22nd International Multi Topic Conference : INMIC'19*. 10.1109/INMIC48123.2019.9022753

Barbosa, M., ben Mokhtar, S., Felber, P., Maia, F., Matos, M., Oliveira, R., Riviere, E., Schiavoni, V., & Voulgaris, S. (2017). SAFETHINGS: Data Security by Design in the IoT. *Proceedings - 2017 13th European Dependable Computing Conference, EDCC 2017*, 117–120. 10.1109/EDCC.2017.33

Beamap, V. V., Guenane Beamap, F., & Mehaoua, A. (2019). Reference Architectures for Security-by-Design IoT: Comparative Study; Reference Architectures for Security-by-Design IoT: Comparative Study. *2019 Fifth Conference on Mobile and Secure Services (MobiSecServ)*.

Beg, M. S., Yusri, I. M., Jamlos, M. F., Azmi, W. H., Badrulhisam, N. H., & Omar, I. (2022). Potential and Limitation of Internet of Things (IOT) Application in the Automotive Industry: An Overview. *International Journal of Automotive and Mechanical Engineering*, *19*(3), 9939–9949. doi:10.15282/ijame.19.3.2022.06.0766

Bhat, O., Gokhale, P., & Bhat, S. (2007). Introduction to IOT. *International Advanced Research Journal in Science. Engineering and Technology ISO*, *3297*(1). Advance online publication. doi:10.17148/IARJSET.2018.517

Bhuiyan, M. N., Rahman, M. M., Billah, M. M., & Saha, D. (2021). Internet of Things (IoT): A Review of Its Enabling Technologies in Healthcare Applications, Standards Protocols, Security, and Market Opportunities. In IEEE Internet of Things Journal (Vol. 8, Issue 13, pp. 10474–10498). Institute of Electrical and Electronics Engineers Inc. doi:10.1109/JIOT.2021.3062630

Biswas, A. R., & Giaffreda, R. (2014). IoT and cloud convergence: Opportunities and challenges. *2014 IEEE World Forum on Internet of Things, WF-IoT 2014*, 375–376. 10.1109/WF-IoT.2014.6803194

Botta, A., de Donato, W., Persico, V., & Pescapé, A. (2016). Integration of Cloud computing and Internet of Things: A survey. *Future Generation Computer Systems*, *56*, 684–700. doi:10.1016/j.future.2015.09.021

Burhan, M., Rehman, R. A., Khan, B., & Kim, B. S. (2018). IoT elements, layered architectures and security issues: A comprehensive survey. *Sensors (Basel)*, *18*(9), 2796. Advance online publication. doi:10.339018092796 PMID:30149582

Chanal, P. M., & Kakkasageri, M. S. (2020). Security and Privacy in IoT: A Survey. In Wireless Personal Communications (Vol. 115, Issue 2, pp. 1667–1693). Springer. doi:10.100711277-020-07649-9

Chen, S., Xu, H., Liu, D., Hu, B., & Wang, H. (2014). A vision of IoT: Applications, challenges, and opportunities with China Perspective. In IEEE Internet of Things Journal (Vol. 1, Issue 4, pp. 349–359). Institute of Electrical and Electronics Engineers Inc. doi:10.1109/JIOT.2014.2337336

Chong, C., Lee, K., & Ahmed, G. (n.d.). Improving Internet Privacy, Data Protection and Security Concerns. In *International Journal of Technology, Innovation and Management (IJTIM)* (Vol. 1, Issue 1). https://journals.gaftim.com/index.php/ijtim/issue/view/1PublishedbyGAF-TIM,gaftim.com

Cirani, S. F. G. P. M. V. L. (2019). *Internet of Things*. John Wiley & Sons Ltd.

Cusack, B., & Tian, Z. (2017). *Evaluating IP surveillance camera vulnerabilities*. doi:10.4225/75/5a84efba95b46

El-Fatyany, A., Wang, H., Abd El-atty, S. M., & Khan, M. (2020). Biocyber Interface-Based Privacy for Internet of Bio-nano Things. *Wireless Personal Communications*, *114*(2), 1465–1483. doi:10.100711277-020-07433-9

Fraga-Lamas, P., Fernández-Caramés, T. M., Suárez-Albela, M., Castedo, L., & González-López, M. (2016). A Review on Internet of Things for Defense and Public Safety. In Sensors (Basel, Switzerland) (Vol. 16, Issue 10). doi:10.339016101644

Haghi Kashani, M., Madanipour, M., Nikravan, M., Asghari, P., & Mahdipour, E. (2021). A systematic review of IoT in healthcare: Applications, techniques, and trends. In *Journal of Network and Computer Applications* (Vol. 192). Academic Press., doi:10.1016/j.jnca.2021.103164

Iyer, B., & Patil, N. (2018). IoT enabled tracking and monitoring sensor for military applications. *International Journal of System Assurance Engineering and Management*, *9*(6), 1294–1301. doi:10.100713198-018-0727-8

Karagiannis, V., Chatzimisios, P., Vazquez-Gallego, F., & Alonso-Zarate, J. (2015). A Survey on Application Layer Protocols for the Internet of Things. Transaction on IoT and Cloud Computing.

Karale, A. (2021). The Challenges of IoT Addressing Security, Ethics, Privacy, and Laws. In Internet of Things (Netherlands) (Vol. 15). Elsevier B.V. doi:10.1016/j.iot.2021.100420

Konduru, V. R., & Bharamagoudra, M. R. (2017). Challenges and Solutions of Interoperability on IoT How far have we come in resolving the IoT interoperability issues. *2017 International Conference On Smart Technology for Smart Nation*. 10.1109/SmartTechCon.2017.8358436

Kraijak, S., & Tuwanut, P. (2015). A survey on IoT architectures, protocols, applications, security, privacy, real-world implementation and future trends. *11th International Conference on Wireless Communications, Networking and Mobile Computing (WiCOM 2015)*. 10.1049/cp.2015.0714

Kumar, P. R., Wan, A. T., & Suhaili, W. S. H. (2020). Exploring data security and privacy issues in internet of things based on five-layer architecture. *International Journal of Communication Networks and Information Security*, *12*(1), 108–121. doi:10.17762/ijcnis.v12i1.4345

KuscuM.UnluturkB. D. (2021). *Internet of Bio-Nano Things: A Review of Applications, Enabling Technologies and Key Challenges*. https://arxiv.org/abs/2112.09249

Kuzlu, M., Fair, C., & Guler, O. (2021). Role of Artificial Intelligence in the Internet of Things (IoT) cybersecurity. *Discover Internet of Things*, *1*(1), 7. Advance online publication. doi:10.100743926-020-00001-4

Kwon, D., Hodkiewicz, M. R., Fan, J., Shibutani, T., & Pecht, M. G. (2016). IoT-Based Prognostics and Systems Health Management for Industrial Applications. *IEEE Access : Practical Innovations, Open Solutions*, *4*, 3659–3670. doi:10.1109/ACCESS.2016.2587754

Lam, K. Y., Mitra, S., Gondesen, F., & Yi, X. (2022). ANT-Centric IoT Security Reference Architecture - Security-by-Design for Satellite-Enabled Smart Cities. *IEEE Internet of Things Journal*, *9*(8), 5895–5908. doi:10.1109/JIOT.2021.3073734

Laturkar, K., & Laturkar, K. (2022, April). Blockchain and the downstream segment: Increasing efficiency through technology. *Hydrocarbon Processing*, 75–78. https://www.hydrocarbonprocessing.com/magazine/2022/april-2022/digital-technology/blockchain-and-the-downstream-segment-increasing-efficiency-through-technology

Lawal, K., & Rafsanjani, H. N. (2022). Trends, benefits, risks, and challenges of IoT implementation in residential and commercial buildings. In Energy and Built Environment (Vol. 3, Issue 3, pp. 251–266). KeAi Communications Co. doi:10.1016/j.enbenv.2021.01.009

le Zhong, C., Zhu, Z., & Huang, R. G. (2016). Study on the IOT architecture and gateway technology. *Proceedings - 14th International Symposium on Distributed Computing and Applications for Business, Engineering and Science, DCABES 2015*, 196–199. 10.1109/DCABES.2015.56

Lin, H., & Bergmann, N. W. (2016). IoT privacy and security challenges for smart home environments. *Information (Basel)*, *7*(3), 44. Advance online publication. doi:10.3390/info7030044

Liu, T., Yuan, R., & Chang, H. (2012). Research on the internet of things in the automotive industry. *Proceedings - 2012 International Conference on Management of e-Commerce and e-Government, ICMeCG 2012*, 230–233. 10.1109/ICMeCG.2012.80

Luo, T., Huang, J., Kanhere, S. S., Zhang, J., & Das, S. K. (2019). Improving IoT data quality in mobile crowd sensing: A cross validation approach. *IEEE Internet of Things Journal*, *6*(3), 5651–5664. doi:10.1109/JIOT.2019.2904704

Mahmoud, R., Yousuf, T., Aloul, F., & Zualkernan, I. (2016). Internet of things (IoT) security: Current status, challenges and prospective measures. *2015 10th International Conference for Internet Technology and Secured Transactions, ICITST 2015*, 336–341. 10.1109/ICITST.2015.7412116

Mashal, I., Alsaryrah, O., Chung, T. Y., Yang, C. Z., Kuo, W. H., & Agrawal, D. P. (2015). Choices for interaction with things on Internet and underlying issues. In *Ad Hoc Networks* (Vol. 28, pp. 68–90). Elsevier B.V., doi:10.1016/j.adhoc.2014.12.006

Milovanovic, D., & Bojkovic, Z. (n.d.). *Cloud-based IoT healthcare applications: Requirements and recommendations*. https://www.iaras.org/iaras/journals/ijitws

Nebbione, G., & Calzarossa, M. C. (2020). Security of IoT application layer protocols: Challenges and findings. In Future Internet (Vol. 12, Issue 3). MDPI AG. doi:10.3390/fi12030055

Noura, M., Atiquzzaman, M., & Gaedke, M. (2019). Interoperability in Internet of Things: Taxonomies and Open Challenges. *Mobile Networks and Applications*, *24*(3), 796–809. doi:10.100711036-018-1089-9

Osuwa, A. A., Ekhoragbon, E. B., & Fat, L. T. (2017). Application of Artificial Intelligence in Internet of Things. *2017 9th International Conference on Computational Intelligence and Communication Networks*, 169–173. https://doi.org/10.1109/CICN.2017.38

Payal, M., Dixit, P., Sairam, T. V. M., & Goyal, N. (2021). Robotics, AI, and the IoT in Defense Systems. In *AI and IoT-Based Intelligent Automation in Robotics* (pp. 109–128). Wiley. doi:10.1002/9781119711230.ch7

Payne, B. R. (2019). Car Hacking: Accessing and Exploiting the CAN Bus Protocol. In Journal of Cybersecurity Education, Research and Practice (Vol. 2019, Issue 1). Academic Press.

Porambage, P., Ylianttila, M., Schmitt, C., Kumar, P., Gurtov, A., & Vasilakos, A. (2016). The Quest for Privacy in the Internet of Things. *IEEE Cloud Computing*, *3*(2), 36–45. doi:10.1109/MCC.2016.28

Pourrahmani, H., Yavarinasab, A., Zahedi, R., Gharehghani, A., Mohammadi, M. H., Bastani, P., & van Herle, J. (2022). The applications of Internet of Things in the automotive industry: A review of the batteries, fuel cells, and engines. In *Internet of Things (Netherlands)* (Vol. 19). Elsevier B.V. doi:10.1016/j.iot.2022.100579

Rahim, M. A., Rahman, M. A., Rahman, M. M., Asyhari, A. T., Bhuiyan, M. Z. A., & Ramasamy, D. (2021). Evolution of IoT-enabled connectivity and applications in automotive industry: A review. In *Vehicular Communications* (Vol. 27). Elsevier Inc. doi:10.1016/j.vehcom.2020.100285

Ramadan, R. A. (n.d.). *Internet of Things (IoT) Security Vulnerabilities: A Review*. https://plomscience.com/journals/index.php/PLOMSAI/index

Rani, S., Kataria, A., Sharma, V., Ghosh, S., Karar, V., Lee, K., & Choi, C. (2021). Threats and Corrective Measures for IoT Security with Observance of Cybercrime: A Survey. In Wireless Communications and Mobile Computing (Vol. 2021). Hindawi Limited. doi:10.1155/2021/5579148

Sequeiros, J. B. F., Chimuco, F. T., Samaila, M. G., Freire, M. M., & Inácio, P. R. M. (2020). Attack and System Modeling Applied to IoT, Cloud, and Mobile Ecosystems: Embedding Security by Design. *ACM Computing Surveys*, *53*(2), 1–32. Advance online publication. doi:10.1145/3376123

Shah, T., & Venkatesan, S. (2018). Authentication of IoT Device and IoT Server Using Secure Vaults. *Proceedings - 17th IEEE International Conference on Trust, Security and Privacy in Computing and Communications and 12th IEEE International Conference on Big Data Science and Engineering, Trustcom/BigDataSE 2018*, 819–824. 10.1109/TrustCom/BigDataSE.2018.00117

Sisi, Z., & Souri, A. (2021). Blockchain technology for energy-aware mobile crowd sensing approaches in Internet of Things. *Transactions on Emerging Telecommunications Technologies*. Advance online publication. doi:10.1002/ett.4217

Sisinni, E., Saifullah, A., Han, S., Jennehag, U., & Gidlund, M. (2018). Industrial internet of things: Challenges, opportunities, and directions. *IEEE Transactions on Industrial Informatics*, *14*(11), 4724–4734. doi:10.1109/TII.2018.2852491

Suzana Maciel, R. P., Maria David, J. N., Barreiro Claro, D., & Braga, R. (2016). Full Interoperability: Challenges and Opportunities for Future Information Systems. Research Challenges in IS in Brazil.

Tawalbeh, L., Muheidat, F., Tawalbeh, M., & Quwaider, M. (2020). IoT privacy and security: Challenges and solutions. *Applied Sciences (Basel, Switzerland), 10*(12), 4102. Advance online publication. doi:10.3390/app10124102

Thompson, B., Leighton, M., Korytkowski, M., & Cook, C. B. (2018). An Overview of Safety Issues on Use of Insulin Pumps and Continuous Glucose Monitoring Systems in the Hospital. In Current Diabetes Reports (Vol. 18, Issue 10). Current Medicine Group LLC 1. doi:10.100711892-018-1056-7

Tripathy, B. K. (2018). *Internet of Things (IoT) Technologies, Applications, Challenges, and Solutions.* CRC Press Taylor & Francis Group.

Ungurean, I., Gaitan, N. C., & Gaitan, V. G. (2016). A middleware based architecture for the industrial internet of things. *KSII Transactions on Internet and Information Systems, 10*(7), 2874–2891. doi:10.3837/tiis.2016.07.001

Vashi, S., Ram, J., Modi, J., Verma, S., & Prakash, C. (2017). Internet of Things (IoT) A Vision, Architectural Elements, and Security Issues. *International Conference I-SMAC*, 492–496. 10.1109/I-SMAC.2017.8058399

Wang, X., Zha, X., Ni, W., Liu, R. P., Guo, Y. J., Niu, X., & Zheng, K. (2019). Survey on blockchain for Internet of Things. In *Computer Communications* (Vol. 136, pp. 10–29). Elsevier B.V. doi:10.1016/j.comcom.2019.01.006

Weber, R. H. (2010). Internet of Things - New security and privacy challenges. *Computer Law & Security Report, 26*(1), 23–30. doi:10.1016/j.clsr.2009.11.008

Weber, R. H. (2015). Internet of things: Privacy issues revisited. *Computer Law & Security Report, 31*(5), 618–627. doi:10.1016/j.clsr.2015.07.002

Xu, T., Wendt, J. B., & Potkonjak, M. (2015). Security of IoT systems: Design challenges and opportunities. *IEEE/ACM International Conference on Computer-Aided Design, Digest of Technical Papers, ICCAD,* 417–423. 10.1109/ICCAD.2014.7001385

Yadav, E. P., Mittal, E. A., & Yadav, H. (2018, November 1). IoT: Challenges and Issues in Indian Perspective. *Proceedings - 2018 3rd International Conference On Internet of Things: Smart Innovation and Usages, IoT-SIU 2018.* 10.1109/IoT-SIU.2018.8519869

Zhang, Z. K., Cho, M. C. Y., Wang, C. W., Hsu, C. W., Chen, C. K., & Shieh, S. (2014). IoT security: Ongoing challenges and research opportunities. *Proceedings - IEEE 7th International Conference on Service-Oriented Computing and Applications, SOCA 2014,* 230–234. 10.1109/SOCA.2014.58

Chapter 24
Internet of Things in the 5G Ecosystem and Beyond 5G Networks

Swati S. Roy
SOA University (Deemed), India

Shatarupa Dash
SOA University (Deemed), India

Bharat Jyoti Ranjan Sahu
SOA University (Deemed), India

ABSTRACT

With the rapid development of technology, the internet of things (IoT) has been an integral part of human society. The expansion and usage of IoT are further being accelerated by the global rollout of 5G cellular technology. The 5G and beyond wireless communications are especially focused on IoT requirements and use cases. One hundred percent coverage and connectivity are promised by the 5G beyond cellular network. The IoT devices may have to connect to any other known or unknown devices for sharing information, which urges different connectivity quality as well as different security and privacy requirements. In this chapter, the authors have explored the usage of 5G network slicing to cater to the diverse IoT connectivity requirement such as latency, bandwidth, and reliability. Moreover, as IoT devices may need to connect to other devices for various purposes, there is a need for trust evaluation among IoT devices. This chapter also discusses the establishment of social relationship among IoT devices to maintain privacy and security requirement through trust management.

DOI: 10.4018/978-1-6684-8145-5.ch024

Copyright © 2023, IGI Global. Copying or distributing in print or electronic forms without written permission of IGI Global is prohibited.

INTRODUCTION

IoT is a framework of interconnected objects or things having unique identities, autonomous configuration capabilities, and performing autonomously. IoT devices accumulate and share data autonomously, which are connected through various technologies and can be controlled remotely. In IoT-based infrastructure, the connected devices act smartly, intelligent processing is carried out, and communication is informative. IoT performs remote monitoring, predictive maintenance, facilities management, efficient manufacturing, connecting with products, and many more things without human intervention. IoT gathers and accumulates essential data autonomously, performs analysis on those stored data for future decision-making, and influences the overall efficiency of the system. It works in different fields including agriculture, government, retail, manufacturing, and transportation. IoT is a dynamic global network of massively interconnected devices, which can communicate with each other to gather and share data as per the requirements, which is very challenging. Furthermore, to manage the communication among devices across the global network, IoT supports interoperable communication protocols including Constraint Application Protocol (CoAP) which enable secure multipoint data transmission in low bandwidth and low energy devices, Message Queuing Telemetry Transport (MQTT) (developed in 1999, initially it was proprietary and now it is open source) which, enable a secure machine to machine (M2M) communication (Sinche, 2019).

Fifth generation (5G) is the first omnipresent connectivity solution that can provide more reliable, faster, and more efficient wireless communication services as compared to existing wireless communication services. Energy consumption, throughput, reliability, scalability, security, and privacy are major concerns for IoT. The revolution in 5G wireless communication technology focuses on IoT requirements i.e., reliable, secure, and faster communication (Chettri, 2019), and (Akpakwu, 2017). The 5G design goal was to overcome the limitations of 4G (Long Term Evolution (LTE)) wireless communication technology basically for massive IoT (Roberts, 2006). The interconnection of billions of smart devices and the exchange of confidential data over the internet poses security challenges including device tampering, spoofing attack, signal jamming, and Denial of Service (DoS) attacks (Mosenia, 2016), and (Puthal, 2019). Increased massive wireless data traffic demands secure and efficient resource allocation. Separate slice allocation for different applications, combined with strong slice isolation mechanisms, can enable data communicated in different slices to be secure and private (Wijethilaka, 2021).

This chapter considers the connection of IoT with 5G wireless communication technology. Various IoT components along with the role of cloud computing, fog computing, and edge computing in IoT environments with their functionalities are contemplated here. Also focus on various short-range communication technologies like Bluetooth, Wireless Fidelity (Wi-Fi), ZigBee, and long-range communication technologies like Long-range Radio (LoRa), Sigfox, 3G, LTE, and 5G used in IoT communication. The role of various technologies like network slicing, and blockchain, with 5G communication technologies to enhance the performance of IoT and SIoT is also discussed. Lastly, the role of 6th generation (6G) wireless communication technology in IoT is discussed.

Internet of Things (IoT)

IoT and the Internet are distinct conceptions. IoT connects devices or objects, accumulates information from the connected objects autonomously, i.e., without human intervention, and stores the collected information in the cloud to be analyzed and used in future decision-making. To put it another way, IoT is the smart infrastructure when compared to the Internet. Due to the huge number of objects in IoT, many challenges come into the picture, including smart connectivity, privacy and security, big data management, data latency reduction, low power consumption, high bandwidth, and complexity. IoT-connected devices must update their characteristics or properties in response to their surroundings and perform with high accuracy while adapting to environmental changes. A massive number of IoT device connectivity, processing, and data sharing among connected devices necessitate standardization, computing, communication technologies, and protocols, which increases complexity (Ismail, 2019).

Unique addresses in IoT allow devices to communicate with one another and collaborate with nearby objects to achieve their desired goal. IoT faces numerous challenges like connectivity, low latency, power consumption, bandwidth, privacy, and security, which must be addressed before the widespread adoption of IoT to improve its efficiency and make it more popular and widely adopted by anyone, anywhere (Atzori, 2010). In IoT, millions of devices are interconnected and communicate among themselves autonomously and collect the required information and utilize services. IoT is intended to interconnect nearly everything in our surroundings and we can access them efficiently and make society smarter. It influences our lives and surrounding environment from various directions such as environmental monitoring, remote access, and monitoring, easy access to devices (Arzo, 2021). Previously Internet communication was limited to desktops, laptops, and mobile phones but currently, various heterogeneous devices can also communicate among themselves in IoT and perform tasks smartly. All those devices will have different service requirements and the current network designs are uniform to each communication. This motivates us to look into IoT communication. Figure 1 represents the overall communication architecture of the IoT infrastructure.

Technologies Used in IoT

An IoT system consists of different components and provides various services including sensing, monitoring, communication, identification, and management. The most prominent components of an IoT system are smart devices, communication, management, services, security, and application.

IoT devices have different activities like sensing, monitoring, and control, and can share data with different applications and other devices connected to the system through different communication technologies like Wi-Fi, and ZigBee. IoT devices can process the accumulated data locally or send it to the cloud server for processing. IoT objects have various interfaces to communicate with other objects, like memory and storage interfaces, input/output (I/O) interfaces, and interfaces for audio or video communication. Various common services in IoT are device modeling, monitoring, controlling, and communication. IoT system provides various modules to analyze and perform decision-making. The most common technologies in IoT are its hardware platforms like processor, clock speed, bus width, and various technologies for communication in different applications (Ray, 2018).

IoT influences a better lifestyle and new industrial opportunities and countless services can be rendered. However, challenges come with opportunities such as the interconnection of the billions of smart devices and the exchange of confidential data over the Internet increases privacy and security challenges (Mosenia, 2016).

Figure 1. Overall communication architecture in the internet of things

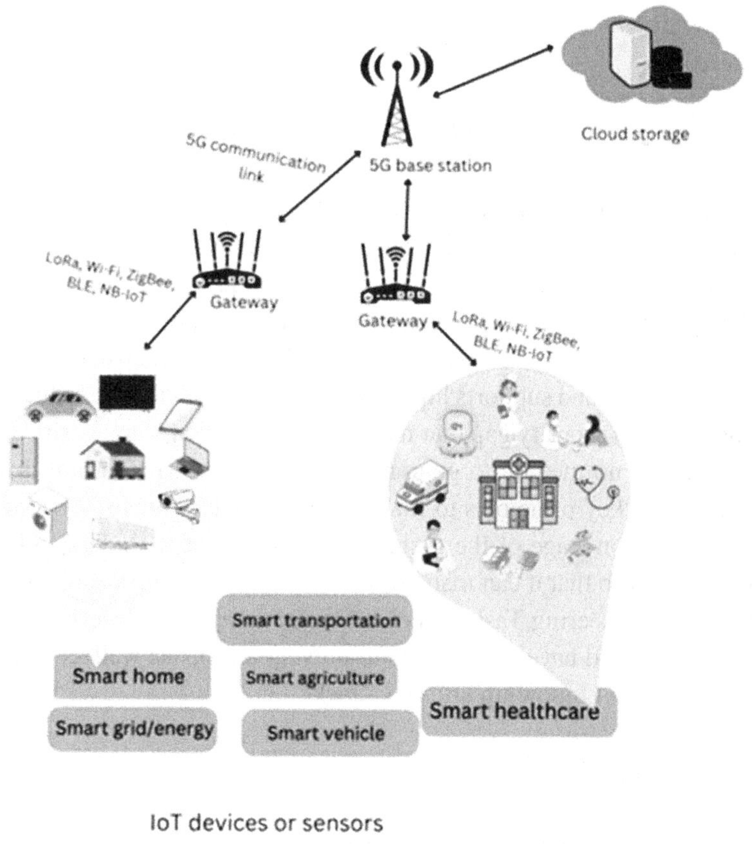

IoT Security

IoT is distributed, heterogeneous, and dynamic as compared to the other networks, therefore it is more complicated to manage and perform. There is no method to guarantee complete security, however different key principles can be used to manage and protect the system. IoT security systems should have real-time monitoring and leak path detection facility to ensure a more efficient security mechanism. It is required to understand system interaction with its different components so that it can manage security. The security architecture in IoT has various methods to prevent attacks as well as respond during attacks, and continue with improvement and follow-up after an attack (Song, 2017; Sattar, 2021; Banerjea, 2021).

Standards for IoT

Standard issues for the development and implementation of IoT are very complex and extensive. Different organizations are responsible for the development of global standards and standards for functionality, compatibility, privacy, and security. The Institute of Electrical and Electronics Engineers (IEEE) is one of the organizations to provide these standards. Organizations are based on consent having characteristics like openness, transparency, balance, provision for appeal, and so on. Generally, standards are based on funding. Standards development organizations (SDO) like IEEE, International Standards Organization (ISO), International Electrotechnical Commission (IEC), and so on cost for the standards, whereas some organizations freely distribute them for instance the European Telecommunications Standards Institute (ETSI) (Violette,2018).

Standardization for Data Transfer and Security

Security in IoT is more complicated as compared to the security environment of Information Technology (IT). As IoT is more distributed, heterogeneous, and dynamic as compared to other computer networks it is more complicated. IoT includes functions of both IT and Operational Technology (OP) to increase efficiency and productivity, because of which IoT security is more challenging as compared to others. By merging the functions of both IT and OP, IoT enables more effective new use cases, opens the flow of data within the network, and supports high-level business decisions to reduce costs and complexities. But this merging creates a security gap that makes cyber criminals target critical data and infrastructure (Kranz, 2018). There is no method to guarantee complete security for any IoT system, nevertheless, companies use different key principles to manage and protect their IoT system which is designed and managed at the conception stage of the system. It is important to understand system interaction with its different components so that it can manage security in a finer approach. Extra security can be added through the Internet Engineering Task Force's manufacturer usage description (IETF MUD) standard. Security architecture should have the features to prevent attacks as well as respond during attacks, and perform improvements and follow-up after an attack.

Benefits and Future of IoT

IoT connects and enables autonomous communications among a large number of interconnected heterogeneous devices. Devices or objects in IoT are smarter and can communicate with each other. Processing in IoT is also smarter; the system performs autonomously based on the received data from the environment and stores the data for analysis to make smart decisions that increase efficiency, productivity, and performance and lower the overall cost.

IoT provides tremendous advantages in various application areas like smart cities i.e., providing convenience to the people in the respective city, healthcare, education; industry by improving production, manufacturing, collaboration with other companies, and in many more essential ways which include analysis, prediction, and decision making aspects, transportation sector; agriculture by improving traditional farming techniques, seed selection, farming methods and various necessary steps for improvement of production; smart grid by utilizing smart energy supply and mitigate energy consumption. IoT act as a key player in the modernization and advancement of society and alleviate human effort with improved and quality work within stipulated time with more efficacy (Swamy, 2020; Cano, 2017; Ploennigs, 2018; Lee, 2017).

IoT is a vast area with different technologies and applications. IoT provides a storage platform for the huge amount of collected data and takes essential steps and performs accordingly to provide the best results as per the user requirements and takes imperative measures for future improvements. IoT spreads over various fields and occupies many different businesses and large industries. It confers platforms to accumulate and analyze data and improves the overall performance of the system which influences and upgrades our lives, this innovation in IoT imparts new challenges to the existing technologies, and this contemplates the future of the IoT.

Issues or Challenges in IoT

IoT enables devices to observe and perceive the environment, induce unified decisions, and accomplish tasks based on observations. To take advantage of IoT in diverse application domains, relevant networking and computing infrastructure are needed to ensure low latency and fast response time (Ammad, 2020). IoT provides scads of benefits and convenience to users. IoT devices have unique identities, self-configuration abilities, and autonomous operating capabilities i.e., without human interference which contributes to IoT becoming more efficient to handle the requirements and provide more experience to the users (Vaezi, 2022). However, IoT has many challenges to performing flawlessly such as security issues, standardization, massive energy consumption (as millions of devices are connected in IoT infrastructure), and the huge amount of heat generated by these large number of devices contribute to global warming (Perera, 2018; Abualigah, 2021; Mittal, 2019), IoT has a massive number of devices, each device will have different connection requirements in IoT, smoothing the functioning of the system standardization is necessary, but the development, maintenance, and functionality of standards are very complicated for such a huge dynamic network of heterogeneous devices and the privacy and security risk is high (sharing of personal data).

COMMUNICATION TECHNOLOGIES IN IoT

IoT uses various wired and wireless communication standards like Wi-Fi, World wide Interoperability for Microwave Access (WiMAX), Low rate Wireless Personal Area Network (LR-WPAN), and mobile communications (2G, 3G,4G,5G) for data transfer and communication among various objects and components of the IoT (Swamy, 2020). Figure 2 represents various wireless communication technologies used for communication in IoT. The connected devices in the IoT system gather and exchange data through sensors. These IoT devices are connected through gateways. There are various standard organizations provide IoT communication standards such as IEEE, Internet Engineering Task Force (IETF), Constraint Restful Environments (CORE), IP wireless Access in vehicular environments (IPWAVE), IPv6 over low power wide area networks (Ip WAN). Bluetooth, Wi-Fi, ZigBee, UWB (Ultra-Wide Band), and IR (Infrared) are various short-range low-power wireless communication technologies. LoRa (long-range Radio), and Sigfox are various long-range communication technologies. Sigfox, LoRa, and NBIoT (Narrowband IoT) are various low-power Wide Area Networks (LPWAN) (Calvanese Strinati, 2019; Verma, 2020; Sodhro, 2020) used for efficacious communication.

Wi-Fi: Wi-Fi or IEEE 802.11 is a wireless local area network (WLAN) standard. It has a 2.4 GHz operating frequency and its range is more than 100m and its transmission power is 1 mW.

ZigBee: In 2002 ZigBee Alliance was established to provide a standard mesh network specification as well as a complimentary application layer standard for IoT. It is a low-power (consume 1mW), low-cost communication standard. ZigBee has an operating range of up to 300 meters with channel bandwidth 1MHz. It has a 250kbps data transfer rate. Applications are energy monitoring, home appliance connections (e.g., thermostats), smart metering, manufacturing, and production automation, smart grid monitoring, and Industry 4.0.

Z-Wave: Z-Wave is a wireless communication standard created by Zensys Inc. and was later acquired by Silicon Labs Inc. The data rate of Z-Wave is up to 100 kb/s. It can support up to 232 devices with 1-3 channels. For security, it employs 128-bit AES encryption. In smart homes, Z-Wave is commonly used to connect door locks, remote controls, smoke detectors, and other home appliances. It allows for the reliable transmission of small data packets with low latency and is optimized for smart home applications, with a communication range of up to 100 meters covering the vast majority of residences (40 m on the 500 Series chip) and will continue to grow.

LoRa and Sigfox: ZigBee and Z-Wave have up to 300m coverage per radio hop. They are not suitable for long-range and low-power wireless communication. For this purpose, LoRa and Sigfox were introduced. Lora WAN was introduced by LoRa Alliance which is an open and non-profit organization, for long-range communication.

Figure 2: Different types of communication technologies

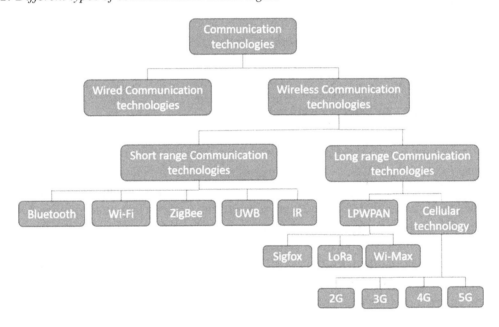

Sigfox is a long-range wireless communication technology on low power and has a low data rate, and operates at 868 MHz/902 MHz LoRa and Sigfox both work on star network topology. Furthermore, they are suitable for several applications including smart grids and smart metering.

Bluetooth: Bluetooth is an IEEE 802.15.1 standard. It is a low-cost, low-power, short-range i.e., within 10m wireless communication technology. It is a personal area network (PAN) communication network. It has a 2.4 GHz frequency band and a data rate of 1 Mbps to 24 Mbps. Bluetooth low energy (BLE) is a low-cost and ultra-low power short-range wireless communication version of Bluetooth. Table 1 represents a comparison of various wireless communication technologies.

Table 1. Comparison of various communication technologies

Communication Technology	Standard	Standardization	Frequency Band	Data Rate	Transmission Range	Energy Consumption
Wi-Fi	IEEE 802.11 a/c/b/d/g	IEEE 802.11	5-60 GHz	1Mbps-6.75Gbps	20-100m	High
Wi-Max	IEEE 802.16	IEEE 802.16	2-60GHz	1Mbps-1Gbps	Up to 50km	Medium
LRWPAN	IEEE 802.15.4	IEEE 802.15	868/915 MHz 2.4 GHz	40-250Kbps	10-20m	Low
Bluetooth	IEEE 802.15.1	IEEE 802.15	2.4GHz	1-24Mbps	8-10m	Bluetooth(medium) BLE(very low)
LoRa	Lora WAN R1.0	LoRa Alliance	868/900MHz	0-50Kbps	<30km	Very low
ZigBee		ZigBee Alliance	2.4GHz(ISM band)	250Kbps	Up to 300m(line of sight)	Very low
Z-Wave		Zensys Inc	908 & 916 MHz (USA) 919 & 921 MHz (AU/NZ/BR) 919–926 MHz (JP/TW/KR/SG)	40Kbps	Up to 75-100m(indoor)	Low
Sigfox		Collaboration of ETSI	868 and 915-928MHz	100Kbps	20km	Low

Source: Ray (2018) and Chettri (2019)

Table 2. Comparison of cellular communication technologies

Wireless Technology	Data Rate	Latency	Services	Bandwidth	Spectrum
1G	2.4 kbps	High	voice	30KHz	
2G	10 -100kbps	High	Voice, data	200KHz	
2.5G	50 kbps/200 kbps	High	Voice, data	200KHz	
3G	3Mbps	Medium	Voice, data, video calling	5-20 MHz	1.8 to 2.5GHz
3.5G	5-30mbps	Medium	Voice, data, video calling	5MHz	
3.75G	100-200mbps	Medium	HD video, peer-to-peer file sharing, web services, online gaming	1.4MHz -20MHz	
4G	DL 3Gbps UL 1.5Gbps	Low	HD video, multimedia, data services with data rate	20 MHz(max 100MHz)	2 to 8 GHz
5G	20-100Gbps	Very low (1ms)	AR/VR, telemedicine	1GHz	
6G	1Tbps	Extreme low (0.1ms)	Holographic communication, telemedicine, robotics, AI	100GHz	

Source: Shafique (2020), Roberts (2006), and Calvanese Strinati (2019)

5G AND BEYOND 5G FOR IOT COMMUNICATIONS

Existing technologies for connectivity like Wi-Fi suffer from collision and congestion; 5G wireless networks can handle these issues with the adoption of new methodologies (Kranz, 2018), including New Radio (NR), Multiple Input Multiple Outputs (MIMO) antennae with beam formation technique. Millimeter wave (mm-Wave) communication technology, and Heterogeneous Networks (HetNet) (Swamy,

2020), (Yan,2020),(Shafique, 2020), and (Roberts, 2006). LTE (4G) has many limitations which can be handled by 5G like multiple device connectivity, high data rate, more bandwidth, low latency, higher quality of service (QoS), and low interference. Table 2 represents a comparison among cellular communication technologies from 1G to 6G.

Narrowband IoT (NB-IoT): NB-IoT is a low-power wide area network (WLAN) introduced by 3GPP for cellular communication among network devices. NB-IoT enhances spectrum utilization, reduces energy consumption, reduces cost, and increases network coverage. NB-IoT has three modes which include standalone, in-band, and guard band. Standalone is used for spectrum reuse; in-band is used for spectrum utilization, and guard band is used for utilization of an unused block. Figure 3 represents different types of NB-IoT.

Figure 3. Different types of NB-IoT

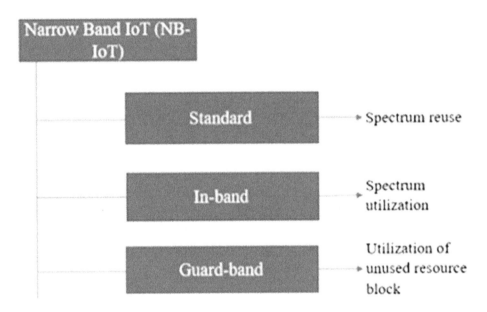

Nowadays, a massive number of devices are connected, and many unmanageable applications, such as Augmented Reality (AR)/Virtual Reality (VR), online games, smart vehicles, autonomous driving, and making everything smarter and emphasizing computation intensive, data-intensive, and delay sensitivity, have entered into the picture. Managing the requirement-specific applications and a huge demand encourages the advancement in communication technology. 5G is not sufficient to support this huge demand which encourages the use of 6G to support very high data rate, widespread coverage, ultra-low latency, accurate localization as well as privacy and security against unauthorized users (Aazam, 2019; Shafique, 2020; Verma, 2020; Guo, 2021). Various necessities of IoT environments are communication technologies, network types, wireless communication technologies, objectives of the infrastructure, characteristics, and various application areas (Vaezi, 2022; Calvanese Strinati, 2019; Sodhro,2020) are reflected in this chapter.

COMPUTING TECHNOLOGIES IN IoT

The IoT is an integrated collection of autonomous objects or things with distinct identities, autonomous configuration capabilities, and autonomous performance. In IoT-based infrastructure, devices are smarter, the processing is more intelligent, and communication is beyond informative. The interconnected devices in the IoT infrastructure communicate with one another and accumulate the necessary data, which is then stored in the cloud. There are various computing techniques such as cloud computing, fog computing, and edge computing used in IoT to enhance efficaciousness in processing, management, and security.

Cloud Computing

Cloud computing is a huge data center collecting the generated data by IoT devices. It is located in different areas on demand. Cloud computing is the distribution of computing resources like storage, databases, applications, networking capabilities, and more through the internet by service providers (known as Cloud Service Providers or CSPs) to their customers. There are different deployment models such as:

1. **Private Cloud:** Also known as internal cloud or corporate cloud and it is of two types, on-premise cloud, and outsourced cloud. Used to build and manage own data centers internally. It's more secure.
2. **Public Cloud:** Anyone can access it. Users can store, access, and manage information using the pay-per-use method, e.g., Google App Engine, Azure, and Microsoft. As it is open to all it has security issues.
3. **Hybrid Cloud:** It is the combination of private and public clouds. The public part has security issues, e.g., Amazon Web Services, Office 365.
4. **Community Cloud:** In the community cloud systems and services can be accessed by a specific organizational community.

Figure 4. Overview of cloud computing

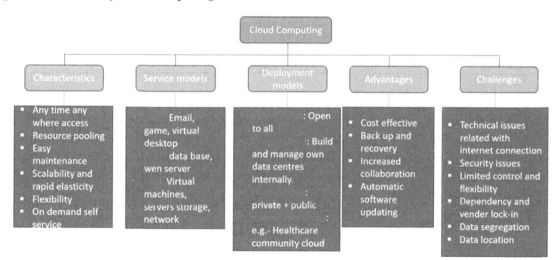

It also has different service modules like:

1. **Software as a Service (SaaS):** It is an on-demand software hosted by CSPs, e.g., Dropbox, BigCommerce, and Google Apps.
2. **Infrastructure as a Service (IaaS):** IaaS is a remote computing infrastructure available through the Internet. It can reduce the cost and complexity to build and manage physical servers and resources available as a service, e.g., Amazon Web Services (AWS), Microsoft Azure, and Google Compute Engine (GCE).
3. **Platform as a Service (PaaS):** It is a cloud computing platform to develop applications, e.g., Windows Azure, Apache Stratos.

Table 3, Comparison of cloud, fog, and edge computing

Features	Cloud Computing	Fog Computing	Edge Computing
Power consumption	High	Low	Low
Computation capacity	High	Low	Low
Storage capacity	High	Low	Low
Network latency	High	Low	Low
Mobility support	No/very low	High	High
Power source	Direct power	Battery/direct power/Green energy, such as solar power	Battery/direct power/Green energy, such as solar power
Context-awareness	No	medium	high
Geo-distribution	Centralized	Distributed	Distributed
Efficiency	Low	High	High
Distance from user	Far	Close	Close
Privacy discloser risk	High	Low	Low
Data processing location	Close to the data center (server)	Locally	Close to the edge(or locally)
Scalability	High	Medium	Low
Bandwidth	Central server	Local server	Data center, internet
Location Awareness	Partially supported	Supported	Supported

With its storage and processing capability, cloud computing has been an integral part of IoT applications. However, due to the remote location of end users, cloud-supported IoT systems face many challenges such as high response time, heavy load on the cloud as it is centralized, and lack of global mobility (Butt, 2019; Aazam, 2020). Figure 4 represents the overview of cloud computing with its characteristics, types, advantages, and challenges.

Fog Computing

Fog computing was introduced by Cisco in 2014 to extend cloud computing and acts as a middleware between cloud and IoT end devices. It provides computing at the network edge and brings the features of the cloud closer to the end devices (Mahmud, 2018; Habibi, 2020; Mosenia, 2016). Fog computing can be used to improve computational power, reduce delay, and can handle the issues caused by cloud computing due to the proliferation of IoT devices. It sends only selected essential data to the cloud for long-term storage and decision-making and is used for low-latency real-time processing. It can mitigate network congestion, and processing time, save network bandwidth, reduce response time, and reduce privacy and security issues (as data is handled locally). Fog computing is not a replacement for cloud computing, it only extends the efficiency of the cloud near the end devices (Aleisa, 2020; Ammad, 2020). However, there are various challenges in fog computing comprising task scheduling, data management, and power consumption (as another layer introduced between IoT and cloud). Various applications of fog computing are patient monitoring, emergency alert, real-time monitoring, parking system management, and so on.

Edge Computing

Edge computing performs computation or processing at the edge, which can reduce energy consumption, increase battery life, lower latency, and increase privacy and security. Edge and fog computing is an extension of cloud computing (Porambage, 2018; Li, 2020; Khan, 2020; Ejaz, 2020). In edge computing, data is processed locally, without the need to pass it to the cloud through a communication medium, which can reduce privacy and security risk. Table 3 represents a comparison of cloud, fog, and edge computing.

IoT APPLICATION AREAS

There are various application areas in IoT including smart transportation, smart grid, industry, agriculture, healthcare, smart home, and smart cities. The smart village is also an important application in IoT (Puthal, 2021; Chanak, 2020). Smart village refers to the advancement of rural areas in education, healthcare, and transportation while minimizing human effort and reducing costs (Li, 2020). Figure 5 represents various application areas influenced by IoT and its components.

Smart Home

Society necessitates smart homes for making life simpler by handling regular household work, convenient setup for autonomous controlling of home appliances, saving energy, and ensuring safety and security. As an example, in the smart home, when the alarm goes off in the morning, IoT can automatically open the window blinds, and switch on the coffee machine, and the water heater. Home automation, indoor air quality monitoring, smart gardening, and security system are various components of smart homes (Park, 2017; Song, 2017; T. Song, 2016).

Figure 5. Various IoT-influenced applications

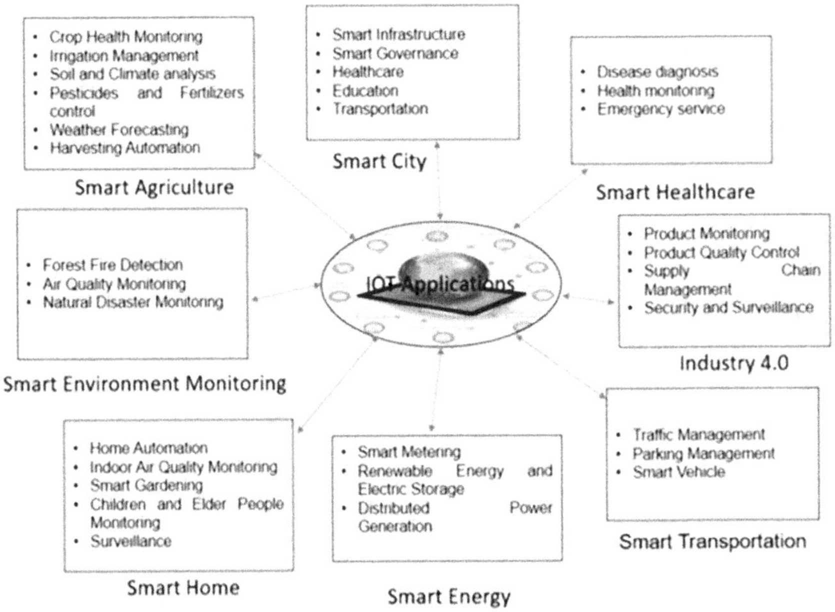

Smart Healthcare

As the world population increases, so do the number and types of diseases, and as a result, patient treatment becomes unmanageable. In this situation, it is very difficult to manage every aspect of the healthcare system according to the traditional methodology. IoT plays a great role to improve the efficiency of the healthcare system by providing anytime, anywhere services. Healthcare is one of the most IoT-influenced areas. Patient treatment, medical diagnosis, drug reference, healthcare awareness, education, and clinical communication are some of the important components of the healthcare system. In IoT-based healthcare infrastructure, healthcare-related data are collected from wearable or sensor devices which are then transferred to the cloud server through the communication gateways and various Artificial Intelligence (AI) and Machine Learning (ML) techniques can be used for the early prediction of diseases like heart attack, cancer, and diabetes (Mohamed, 2022; Habibzadeh, 2019; Mohammed, 2021; Al-Shargabi, 2021; Guo, 2021). Aazam (2019) overviews the combination of IoT and ML that plays a vital role in healthcare, and blockchain is also one of the technologies for the advancement of the healthcare system in terms of privacy and security.

Smart Environment Monitoring

Smart environment monitoring can save lives, products, and resources and reduce costs. Forest fire detection, air quality monitoring, and natural disaster monitoring are various components of smart environment monitoring. IoT enables faster monitoring of the surrounding environment with more accuracy autonomously so that it can be controlled with minimum effort.

Smart Grid/Smart Energy

Excess and careless use of energy may cause scarcity of energy and can harm society. It is imperative to reduce energy consumption, and focus on the best utilization of energy, due to limited energy reserves. IoT plays a vital role in efficient energy utilization and management. Sustainable energy can be generated before being consumed. Energy consumption and generation are in the same quantity referring to the Zero energy system. Smart energy framework includes optimized power consumption, smart inclusion of sustainable energy, and efficient distribution. A most vital part of smart energy is low carbon generation i.e., the use of green energy, biogas, solar, and wind energy, and then efficient distribution of energy is necessary which refers to smart grid, energy trading, and cross-border grids. Optimal energy consumption is also necessary i.e., energy management, energy storage, smart metering, use of the smart device, and so on (Faruque, 2021; Verma, 2020).

Smart Transportation

Rapid growth in population and use of vehicles for transport necessitates smart transportation, which improves the efficiency of vehicle utilization, transport management and also citizens can utilize or choose different transport facilities as per their needs at a low cost with less effort (Mohanty, 2016; Kirimtat, 2020). Intelligent Transport System (ITS) or smart transportation covers all the existing transport systems i.e., air, water, railway, and road transport, and interconnects them. Information and Communication Technology (ICT) and real-time data processing in smart transportation make global airway hubs, intelligent road transport, protected cycle routes, secure pedestrian paths, and intercity railway networks, safer, faster, reliable, and cost-effective transport systems.

Smart traffic management and smart parking system are the most important part of the transportation system. Efficient management of the parking system and traffic flow can improve transportation. Various computation technologies like cloud computing and fog computing can be used to manage transportation systems in a smart society. Various AL/ML techniques and metaheuristic algorithms like Genetic Algorithm (GA), Particle Swarm Optimization (PSO), and Ant Colony Optimization (ACO) can be used for prediction and decision-making to improve transportation efficiency.

Smart City

In recent decades, the world population significantly rose and it is estimated that by the end of 2050, 70% of the population will reside in urban areas, which will consume more energy and generate greenhouse gases (Mohanty, 2016). Thus, it affects the environment adversely and this necessitates the smart city concept. The advancement of technology encourages the merging of cities. However, it requires physical infrastructure, ICT, Big data, and IoT (Kirimtat, 2020; Zanella, 2014; Harrison, 2010). Blockchain can be used for maintaining privacy and security in smart city infrastructure. Various benefits of smart cities are that it improves the Quality of Life (QoL), increase the efficiency of urban operations and services, stimulate competitiveness, reduce energy consumption, reduce water consumption, decrease carbon emissions, regulate requirements of transportation, and manage traffic and city waste effectively (Ammad, 2020).

The establishment of smart cities depends on their vital features, components, and requirements. IoT influences all corners of the cities, improves operation and services, and affects day to day lives of citizens which provides convenience to society (Butt, 2019; Khan, 2020; Choudhary, 2021). There are various security issues in IoT environments, and these issues need to be addressed to build an advanced society (Sattar, 2021).

Smart Agriculture

The increase in global population, limited land, shortage of natural resources, and uncertain climate condition are concerns that motivate society toward advanced and productive smart farming (Elijah, 2018). Soil, climate (humidity, temperature, light), and water are the main components of agriculture. All the components of agriculture need to be managed for smart farming. Sensors, actuators, location tracking, communication, and computing technologies are used for observation, analysis, diagnosis, and decision-making for more productive farming. IoT includes various technologies like RFID (Radio frequency Identification), cloud computing, and fog computing for more advanced agriculture. Crop monitoring, planting, weather forecasting, irrigation management, pesticide and fertilizer control, livestock monitoring, and harvesting automation are the various components of smart agriculture. Unmanned Arial Vehicles (UAV) or drones are used in agriculture for crop monitoring, health assessment, irrigation, and soil analysis. Community farming, waste control, cost reduction, resource management, awareness, security, and fraud prevention are various benefits of smart agriculture. In the agriculture domain connectivity, transport, education, and health are important factors. Dlodlo (2015) focuses on the above factors and discuss how IoT can reduce poverty in rural areas.

Industry 4.0

Industry 4.0 refers to the utilization and expansion of IoT in the industry. It has various components to increase efficiency and productivity in the industrial field. Examples include smart devices with self-configuration capability, remote monitoring, predictive maintenance, equipment management and maintenance, automated modification, product monitoring, product quality control, supply chain management, etc. (Mohanty, 2016; Kirimtat, 2020; Raimundo, 2022). Some of the benefits of IoT in business are,

- Improves the inventory cycle and raises the on-time delivery rate in the industry.
- Reduces build-to-order cycle time and decreases operating costs.
- IoT and predictive maintenance are useful for businesses and industrial growth.
- Solve many existing business issues.
- Used for secure data processing.

5G NETWORK SLICING

Next Generation Mobile Network (NGMN) Alliance first introduced the network slicing concept in 2015. 5G network slicing divides the physical network into multiple logical networks (i.e., network slices) to categorize each slice with specific characteristics and network capabilities. Network slicing is built upon seven main principles: isolation, elasticity, automation, programmability, customization, end-to-end (E2E), and hierarchical abstraction. Multiple networks of different application scenarios can be deployed in parallel under the same network resource pool using Network Functions Virtualization (NFV) technology. Network slicing can satisfy the various networking demands of heterogeneous IoT applications via dedicated slices. Network slicing architecture consists of three layers:

1. **Infrastructure Layer:** Responsible for providing physical or virtual resources such as storage, computing resources, and connectivity.
2. **Network Slice Instance Layer:** It runs on the infrastructure layer and consists of Network Slice Instance (NSI) that forms End to End (E2E) logical network slices.
3. **Service Instance Layer:** It runs over all other layers, and represents end user and business services.

Figure 6. 5G network slicing and IoT applications

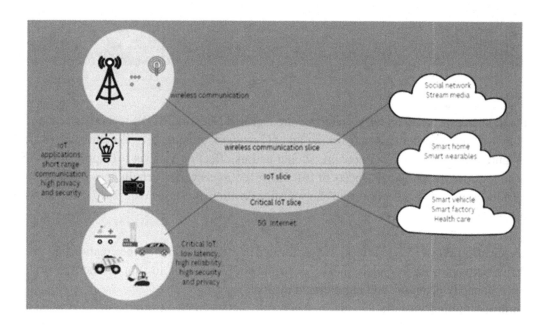

A fully functional network slice can route and control a particular packet over the network without influencing other slices. Slice-paring functions connect the RAN sub slice and core sub slice. A RAN slice can be connected with one or more core slices i.e., paring among slices can be 1:1 or 1:N. Network slicing architecture consists of four segments: RAN sub-slice, Slice-paring functions, Core sub-slice, and Network Slice Management (NSM).

Network slices are divided into different categories based on several models such as vertical and horizontal, Static and Dynamic, and RAN and core network slicing. Vertical network slices are allocated for new applications such as Ultra High Definition (UHD) video, AR/VR, and smart wearables (e.g., medical wearables) with the advancement of 5G wireless communication technology. Horizontal network slicing can reduce high-resource requirements in a device, such as computation, communication, and storage.

Figure 7. 5G network slicing life cycle

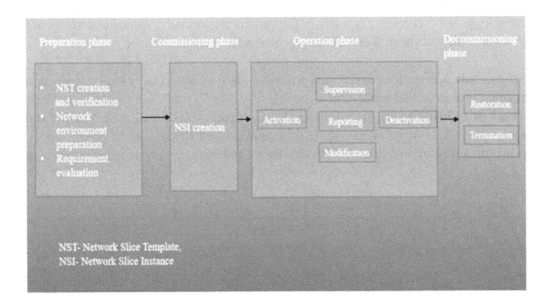

Network slicing is based on NFV and Software Defined Network (SDN) technology, and is the key technology to realize on-demand networking and 5G network architecture (Wijethilaka, 2021; Zhang, 2017). Figure 6 represents the 5G network slicing and its effect on various IoT applications. Network slicing can improve the technical aspects of IoT. However, it has various challenges including optimum resource allocation, access selection, and shorten slice creation duration (Wei, 2017). The network slice life cycle has four phases:

1. **Preparation Phase:** Various tasks are performed in this phase such as the creation and verification of the Network Slice Template (NST), environment preparation to support the network slice life cycle, capacity planning, and requirement evaluation.
2. **Commissioning Phase:** In this phase, a network slice is created from the network slice template. Required resources and network configuration are performed in this phase. After this phase, it will be ready for operation.
3. **Operation Phase:** Required operations are carried out in this phase. It has various sub-tasks such as activation, supervision, Key Performance Indicators (KPI) monitoring, modification, and deactivation.
4. **Decommissioning Phase:** Restoration of dedicated resources and configurations from shared or dependent resources are carried out in this phase. NSI is removed and does not exist anymore after this phase.

Optimum slice allocation can improve the efficiency and performance of the network to handle IoT applications. Figure 7 represents the different phases of the 5G Network slicing life cycle. There are various IoT applications and their requirement varies such as drones, self-driving cars (need ultra-high bandwidth, ultra-low latency), AR/VR (needs highspeed internet), healthcare, financial transactions (need reliability, low latency), smart home (needs medium latency, medium bandwidth). There is a need to manage all these things in such a way that interference, security, privacy, congestion, and latency can be reduced.

SOCIAL INTERNET OF THINGS (SIoT)

In SIoT, the management of relationships among objects is an important part as objects are not intelligent to select a relationship as human beings. Therefore, the main task is the creation, update, and removal of relationships among objects. Figure 8 represents the overall configuration of the Social Internet of Things.

Figure 8. Overall configuration of social internet of things

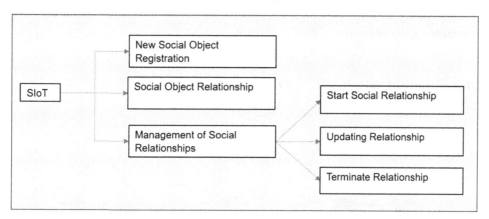

Social Relation

Social relationship among Things depends on various measures like applications, services, and object specifications. Various relationships in SIoT are:

1. **Co-Location Object Relation (CLOR):** It is the relationships between objects in the same location, same workplace, or the same building.
2. **Co-Worker Object Relation (CWOR):** Relationship between objects which work together.
3. **Owner Object Relation (OOR):** Relationship between objects with the same owner.
4. **Social Object Relationship (SOR):** Relationship between devices whose owners are connected in a social network.
5. **Parental Object Relationship (POR):** Relationship between devices created by the same manufacturer.

These relationships are used to identify the boundaries of trustworthy operations in SIoT. Previous transaction history, the centrality of the devices, common neighbors' opinions regarding their experience and transaction with the devices, ratings given to other objects, and ratings received from them can be used for trustworthiness calculations. Social awareness, reputation, and recommendation-based models can improve energy consumption, increase security and reduce data losses. SIoT advances the realization of content and services through the integration of social networking which promotes IoT improvement. For trust value calculation in trust computation and aggregation, trust attributes (social trust, quality of service) are used (Yang, 2022). Figure 9 represents the overall configuration of the SIoT with risk factors. Based on types of feedback (global feedback, feedback from a friend, own opinion on available information) used for trust value calculation, categorizes research as reputation-based, centrality recommendation-based, and knowledge-based. IoT gathers information from the environment, while the social network builds relationships among devices and trust prediction finds the most reliable or trusted node. In the article (Pruthvi, 2019), the author discusses how a college environment can be influenced by SIoT and the way it adds unique social objects and establishes and manages the relationship among objects. SIoT is a community-oriented that detects, chooses, and configures utilities and data from social objects. Better suggestions can be obtained from people connected in the social network when compared to the ones conjured by a single person. Trustworthiness information and reputation information of individuals need to be maintained to enhance security.

Figure 9. Overall configuration of SIoT with risk factor

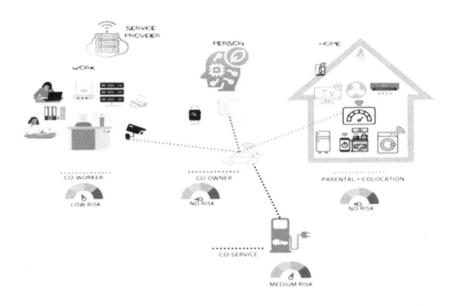

Proposed Model

Here we propose a model to connect IoT devices through social networking and focus on trust management in the SIoT. Social networking with Trust management is the key feature to establishing communication within the cellular network to enhance privacy and security.

Trusting a Device in Public

Trust ranking is a critical component of the SIoT. Feedback and experience from other related devices about a device need to be collected and used to rank the device for trust based on historical data or past transactions. There are different types of responses from other related devices about a particular device:

Positive Response: When a device has a positive experience or a successful transaction with another device, it will send a positive response against that device, increasing its trust ranking.

Negative Response: In the event of an unsuccessful transaction or a negative experience, a device responds negatively to the device. It will lower that device's trust rank.

Neutral Response: In the absence of a positive or negative response, participation in feedback is considered a neutral response.

No Response: A neutral response does not imply that there is no response or connection. A neutral response occurs when a device participates in responding but does not provide a positive or negative response. In contrast, a no-response device will not participate in ranking feedback.

There are numerous other examples of feedback or response about the device from neighboring devices or devices connected to previous transactions, such as:

- The highly disliked node may be well connected, but it should be of low prestige.
- A node with a higher prestige may be just as trustable as another node.
- Every object rate other object and receives ratings from them.
- Opinion of an object about other objects is based on its ratings.
- In the case of an object in isolation, its prestige is determined by the quality of the rating and the truthfulness of the object who has rated it, rather than the number of ratings.

Algorithm 1. More Trustworthy Object Evaluation

```
Input: List of service requests, available objects for communication, trust
rank, object identification
Output: More trustworthy object evaluation
Step-1 Start
Step-2 Find the objects based on their location
Step-3 Find all connected objects of the requested object
Step-4 Evaluate the trust rank and credit rating of each connected object in
the                       network using  Algorithm 2
Step-5 If trust rank value is the largest
            Then more trustworthy
Step-6 Return the identification of the more trustworthy object
Step-7 Stop
```

Algorithm 2. Algorithm to Evaluate Trust Ranking

```
Input: list of linked objects, response
Output: Trust rank evaluation
Step-1 Start
Step-2 Find out the linked objects of the respective device in the network.
Step-3 Identify the unbiased object as per its past response
Step-4 Calculate trust rank as per the response received from the past trans-
action from the unbiased linked devices.
Step-5 if  response = = positive
                Then Increase trust rank
        Else if  response = =negative
                Then Decrease trust rank
        Else if response = = neutral
                Then Less change in trust rank
        Else if response = = no response
                Then No change in trust rank
Step-6 Stop
```

G(V, E) is the communication graph where N number of devices represented as a set of vertices V={v1, v2, ...,vn} and each device has enabled with capillary (Wi-Fi, ZigBee, Bluetooth, etc.) and 5G communications. And communication paths within devices are represented as a set of edges E ={e1, e2, ..., em}. Reliability of the objects evaluated based on direct trust and indirect trust or recommendation trust. Overall trust evaluation consists of three components as trust value of the object itself, the trust value given by other objects directly, and the trust value through recommendation.

$$Overall\_Trust(OT) = Trust\_itself(\alpha)+Trust\_direct(\beta)+Trust\_recommendation(\gamma) \qquad (1)$$

Let the weights of these three components: trust value for itself, trust value directly given and recommended trust value are w1, w2, and w3 respectively.

$$OT =w1\alpha + w2\beta + w3\gamma \qquad (2)$$

w1+w2+w3 =1

w1 represents the trust value of the respective device according to the past transactions (r+, r-), that is the total number of services (T_services) attended concerning successful services given.

w1 = r+/T_services

w2 = direct trust weight

w3 = Θ^i, where i represents the ith trust guarantee for device recommendation, and here 0< Θ <1.

With the increase in the number of services, i value also increases and since biased node trust weight and genuine node trust weight have a greater impact, it is necessary to determine whether a node is biased or unbiased. Equation (1) is used to find out overall trust. And equation (2) finds the overall trust with weight.

In SIoT, social relationships are established among objects to build a social circle which is similar to human beings' social relationships in society. In (Paul, 2016) A. Paul discusses social networking (SN) within IoT devices like human beings' social relationships and dynamically establishing a social relationship within IoT devices and trust management is the main focus of this article. Social networking with trust management is the key factor in social D2D communications in 5G wireless networks.

BLOCKCHAIN

Identity and trust are the two key factors while dealing with network communication. Blockchain has various application areas including e-governance, supply chain management (SCM), healthcare, finance, and so on. Blockchain has various features such as immutability, decentralization, and distributed ledger technology (DLT), which can guarantee the fidelity and security of data records and avoid the need for a third party. However, computation overhead is the major issue in the blockchain. Blockchain can deal with many threats like man-in-the-middle (MITM), Denial-of-service (DoS) attacks, and distributed DoS attacks. Block, node, and transaction are the three main components of Blockchain. Selection of Certificate Authority (CA) is required in each blockchain transaction. This selection process can take a longer time in a large network, which can cause heavy computation overhead. Blockchain has three main platforms such as Ethereum, Hyperledger, and Corda. Again, the Hyperledger is of different types: burrow, fabric, Indy, Iroha, and sawtooth.

In a consensus algorithm, all the peers of the blockchain network reach a common agreement about the present state of the distributed ledger. Due to the presence of the consensus protocol, every transaction in the blockchain is considered to be completely secure, even though there is no central authority present. It can achieve reliability and build trust among peers in the blockchain in a distributed computing environment. Various categories of consensus mechanisms are Proof of Work (Pow), Proof of Stack (PoS), Delegated Proof of Stack (DPoS), Byzantine Fault Tolerance (BFT), Practical BFT, Proof of Authority (PoA), Proof of Activity (PoAc), Proof of Capacity (PoC). Here our objective is to secure the sensitive data in various IoT infrastructures and maintain trust among objects and enable secure communication.

USE OF MACHINE LEARNING IN HEALTHCARE

Advanced computational techniques like artificial intelligence (AI), Machine learning (ML), cloud computing, and communication technologies have proven their potential to deal with big data in the field of making a smart society.

IoT enables healthcare systems to remotely monitor patients and provide improved and better services or treatments. It can be used for smarter management of healthcare infrastructure, and drug delivery which can reduce overall costs. IoT has numerous applications in healthcare, including healthcare monitoring, medical assistance, disease diagnosis, drug referral, and sensing and storing healthcare data (database). ML analyses the collected data from the IoT environment for disease prediction as well as patient healthcare condition prediction using various ML methods. Amani Aldahiri et al. (2021) provide an overview of machine learning technologies for analyzing healthcare datasets for disease prediction and decision-making, as well as the benefits of IoT for medical data generation. People in remote areas face numerous challenges in terms of healthcare because they lack access to diagnostic and treatment facilities. Hameed Kashif et al. (2020) presented a modern low-cost healthcare system based on IoT (Internet of Things) and Machine Learning (ML), which senses a patient's health data and processes it for prediction and decision-making regarding serious health issues and treatment. Sharma et al. (2019) designed algorithms to predict a patient's body conditions as well as the disease by analyzing data generated by the IoT-based healthcare environment. The system collects the patient's body temperature, heart rate, and other data through the IoT devices and which then send this data to the cloud server for the prediction of diseases and health conditions. Data is generated from various sources and healthcare systems to be uploaded to the cloud server. Users can easily access patient information via mobile applications, and the system maintains privacy by utilizing cloud virtual machines. Mohammed Chnar Mustaf et al. (2021) overviewed the uses, challenges, and issues related to the healthcare system with the combination of IoT and machine learning. In Al-Shargabi (2020), the author overviewed the influence of IoT in healthcare and shed light on the different layers in IoT-based healthcare systems such as the perception layer, network layer, process, storage layer, and application layer, along with a focus on the security and privacy of the system.

CONCLUSION AND FUTURE WORK

The 6G technology will bring the network closer to every device. IoT applications, personalized service, cooperative network sharing such as D2D communication, and data processing with Artificial Intelligence for Quality of Experience (QoE) will require users' personal information to be shared over a public network. Moreover, to provide cost-effective and flexible services, different IoT component vendors, IoT servers (apps and subscriptions), network operators, social network servers, and other application service providers may need to exchange user data for better QoE. However, most users do not understand their data privacy and security. Thus, user data privacy and security will become a critical requirement for IoT applications that deal with sensitive information, such as healthcare and military applications. To manage and maintain the privacy and trust of communication, recent approaches like 5G network slicing and SIoT trust management have been discussed in this chapter. IoT and ML together offer superior solutions to the challenges of the traditional system. In the future, improvements in IoT technologies as well as AI methodologies will improve the performance of smart sectors, which could give more benefits and convenience to society. High energy consumption and low life span of the battery of IoT devices might hinder the seamless connection of these devices. Therefore, energy-efficient communication is challenging in IoT. Due to the massive number of IoT devices, centralized authentication is difficult and more complex. As a result, a truly decentralized system that detects and selects trustworthy devices using blockchain becomes more effective. In our future work, we try to establish social networking with the blockchain for more efficient trustworthy device identification as well as trust management.

REFERENCES

Aazam, M., Harras, K. A., & Zeadally, S. (2019). Fog computing for 5G tactile industrial Internet of Things: QoE-aware resource allocation model. *IEEE Transactions on Industrial Informatics*, *15*(5), 3085–3092. doi:10.1109/TII.2019.2902574

Aazam, M., Islam, S., Lone, S. T., & Abbas, A. (2020). Cloud of things (CoT): cloud-fog-IoT task offloading for sustainable internet of things. *IEEE Transactions on Sustainable Computing*, *7*(1), 87–98. doi:10.1109/TSUSC.2020.3028615

Abualigah, L., Diabat, A., Sumari, P., & Gandomi, A. H. (2021). Applications, deployments, and integration of internet of drones (iod): A review. *IEEE Sensors Journal*, *21*(22), 25532–25546. doi:10.1109/JSEN.2021.3114266

Akpakwu, G. A., Silva, B. J., Hancke, G. P., & Abu-Mahfouz, A. M. (2017). A survey on 5G networks for the Internet of Things: Communication technologies and challenges. *IEEE Access : Practical Innovations, Open Solutions*, *6*, 3619–3647. doi:10.1109/ACCESS.2017.2779844

Al-Shargabi, B., & Abuarqoub, S. (2020, November). IoT-Enabled Healthcare: Benefits, Issues and Challenges. In *4th International Conference on Future Networks and Distributed Systems (ICFNDS)* (pp. 1-5). Academic Press.

Aldahiri, A., Alrashed, B., & Hussain, W. (2021). Trends in using IoT with machine learning in health prediction system. *Forecasting*, *3*(1), 181–206. doi:10.3390/forecast3010012

Aleisa, M. A., Abuhussein, A., & Sheldon, F. T. (2020). Access control in fog computing: Challenges and research agenda. *IEEE Access : Practical Innovations, Open Solutions*, *8*, 83986–83999. doi:10.1109/ACCESS.2020.2992460

Ammad, M., Shah, M. A., Islam, S. U., Maple, C., Alaulamie, A. A., Rodrigues, J. J., Mussadiq, S., & Tariq, U. (2020). A novel fog-based multi-level energy-efficient framework for IoT-enabled smart environments. *IEEE Access : Practical Innovations, Open Solutions*, *8*, 150010–150026. doi:10.1109/ACCESS.2020.3010157

Arzo, S. T., Naiga, C., Granelli, F., Bassoli, R., Devetsikiotis, M., & Fitzek, F. H. (2021). A theoretical discussion and survey of network automation for iot: Challenges and opportunity. *IEEE Internet of Things Journal*, *8*(15), 12021–12045. doi:10.1109/JIOT.2021.3075901

Atzori, L., Iera, A., & Morabito, G. (2010). The Internet of things: A survey. *Computer Networks*, *54*(15), 2787–2805. doi:10.1016/j.comnet.2010.05.010

Banerjea, S., Srivastava, S., & Kumar, S. (2021). Data Security in the Internet of Things: Challenges and Opportunities. *Big Data Analytics for Internet of Things*, 265-284.

Butt, A. A., Khan, S., Ashfaq, T., Javaid, S., Sattar, N. A., & Javaid, N. (2019, June). A cloud and fog based architecture for energy management of smart city by using meta-heuristic techniques. In 2019 15th International Wireless Communications & Mobile Computing Conference (IWCMC) (pp. 1588-1593). IEEE. doi:10.1109/IWCMC.2019.8766702

Calvanese Strinati, E., Barbarossa, S., Gonzalez-Jimenez, J. L., Kténas, D., Cassiau, N., & Dehos, C. (2019). *6G: The next frontier.* arXiv e-prints, arXiv-1901.

Cano, J. C., Berrios, V., Garcia, B., & Toh, C. K. (2018). Evolution of IoT: An industry perspective. *IEEE Internet of Things Magazine, 1*(2), 12–17. doi:10.1109/IOTM.2019.1900002

Chanak, P., & Banerjee, I. (2020). Internet-of-Things-enabled smartvillages: An overview. *IEEE Consumer Electronics Magazine, 10*(3), 12–18. doi:10.1109/MCE.2020.3013244

Chettri, L., & Bera, R. (2019). A comprehensive survey on Internet of Things (IoT) toward 5G wireless systems. *IEEE Internet of Things Journal, 7*(1), 16–32. doi:10.1109/JIOT.2019.2948888

Choudhary, P., Bhargava, L., Suhag, A. K., Choudhary, M., & Singh, S. (2021). An Era of Internet of Things Leads to Smart Cities Initiatives Towards Urbanization. *Digital Cities Roadmap: IoT-Based Architecture and Sustainable Buildings*, 319-350.

Dlodlo, N., & Kalezhi, J. (2015, May). The internet of things in agriculture for sustainable rural development. In 2015 international conference on emerging trends in networks and computer communications (ETNCC) (pp. 13-18). IEEE. doi:10.1109/ETNCC.2015.7184801

Ejaz, M., Kumar, T., Ylianttila, M., & Harjula, E. (2020, March). *Performance and efficiency optimization of multi-layer IoT edge architecture. In 2020 2nd 6G Wireless Summit (6G SUMMIT)*. IEEE.

Elayan, H., Amin, O., Shubair, R. M., & Alouini, M. S. (2018, April). Terahertz communication: The opportunities of wireless technology beyond 5G. In *2018 International Conference on Advanced Communication Technologies and Networking (CommNet)* (pp. 1-5). IEEE. 10.1109/COMMNET.2018.8360286

Elijah, O., Rahman, T. A., Orikumhi, I., Leow, C. Y., & Hindia, M. N. (2018). An overview of Internet of Things (IoT) and data analytics in agriculture: Benefits and challenges. *IEEE Internet of Things Journal, 5*(5), 3758–3773. doi:10.1109/JIOT.2018.2844296

Faruque, M. A. (2021, April). A Review Study on "5G NR Slicing Enhancing IoT & Smart Grid Communication". In *2021 12th International Renewable Engineering Conference (IREC)* (pp. 1-4). IEEE.

Guo, F., Yu, F. R., Zhang, H., Li, X., Ji, H., & Leung, V. C. (2021). Enabling massive IoT toward 6G: A comprehensive survey. *IEEE Internet of Things Journal, 8*(15), 11891–11915. doi:10.1109/JIOT.2021.3063686

Habibi, P., Farhoudi, M., Kazemian, S., Khorsandi, S., & Leon-Garcia, A. (2020). Fog computing: A comprehensive architectural survey. *IEEE Access: Practical Innovations, Open Solutions, 8*, 69105–69133. doi:10.1109/ACCESS.2020.2983253

Habibzadeh, H., Dinesh, K., Shishvan, O. R., Boggio-Dandry, A., Sharma, G., & Soyata, T. (2019). A survey of healthcare Internet of Things (HIoT): A clinical perspective. *IEEE Internet of Things Journal, 7*(1), 53–71. doi:10.1109/JIOT.2019.2946359 PMID:33748312

Hameed, K., Bajwa, I. S., Ramzan, S., Anwar, W., & Khan, A. (2020). An intelligent IoT based healthcare system using fuzzy neural networks. *Scientific Programming, 2020*, 2020. doi:10.1155/2020/8836927

Harrison, C., Eckman, B., Hamilton, R., Hartswick, P., Kalagnanam, J., Paraszczak, J., & Williams, P. (2010). Foundations for smarter cities. *IBM Journal of Research and Development, 54*(4), 1–16. doi:10.1147/JRD.2010.2048257

Islam, S. R., Kwak, D., Kabir, M. H., Hossain, M., & Kwak, K. S. (2015). The internet of things for health care: A comprehensive survey. *IEEE Access : Practical Innovations, Open Solutions, 3,* 678–708. doi:10.1109/ACCESS.2015.2437951

Ismail, Y. (Ed.). (2019). *Internet of Things (IoT) for automated and smart applications.* BoD–Books on Demand.

Khan, L. U., Yaqoob, I., Tran, N. H., Kazmi, S. A., Dang, T. N., & Hong, C. S. (2020). Edge-computing-enabled smart cities: A comprehensive survey. *IEEE Internet of Things Journal, 7*(10), 10200–10232. doi:10.1109/JIOT.2020.2987070

Kirimtat, A., Krejcar, O., Kertesz, A., & Tasgetiren, M. F. (2020). Future trends and current state of smart city concepts: A survey. *IEEE Access : Practical Innovations, Open Solutions, 8,* 86448–86467. doi:10.1109/ACCESS.2020.2992441

Kranz, M. (2018). Why industry needs to accelerate IoT standards. *IEEE Internet of Things Magazine, 1*(1), 14–18. doi:10.1109/IOTM.2018.1700011

Lee, S. K., Bae, M., & Kim, H. (2017). Future of IoT networks: A survey. *Applied Sciences (Basel, Switzerland), 7*(10), 1072. doi:10.3390/app7101072

Li, X., Chen, T., Cheng, Q., Ma, S., & Ma, J. (2020). Smart applications in edge computing: Overview on authentication and data security. *IEEE Internet of Things Journal, 8*(6), 4063–4080. doi:10.1109/JIOT.2020.3019297

Mahmud, R., Kotagiri, R., & Buyya, R. (2018). Fog computing: A taxonomy, survey and future directions. In *Internet of everything* (pp. 103–130). Springer. doi:10.1007/978-981-10-5861-5_5

Mittal, M., Tanwar, S., Agarwal, B., & Goyal, L. M. (2019). Energy conservation for IoT devices. *Concepts, Paradigms and Solutions, Studies in Systems Decision and Control,* 1–365.

Mohamed, R. M., Shahin, O. R., Hamed, N. O., Zahran, H. Y., & Abdellattif, M. H. (2022). Analyzing the patient behavior for improving the medical treatment using smart healthcare and IoT-based deep belief network. *Journal of Healthcare Engineering, 2022,* 2022. doi:10.1155/2022/6389069 PMID:35310183

Mohammed, C. M., & Askar, S. (2021). Machine learning for IoT healthcare applications: A review. *International Journal of Science and Business, 5*(3), 42–51.

Mohanty, S. P., Choppali, U., & Kougianos, E. (2016). Everything you wanted to know about smart cities: The Internet of things is the backbone. *IEEE Consumer Electronics Magazine, 5*(3), 60–70. doi:10.1109/MCE.2016.2556879

Mosenia, A., & Jha, N. K. (2016). A comprehensive study of security of internet-of-things. *IEEE Transactions on Emerging Topics in Computing, 5*(4), 586–602. doi:10.1109/TETC.2016.2606384

Park, E., Cho, Y., Han, J., & Kwon, S. J. (2017). Comprehensive approaches to user acceptance of Internet of Things in a smart home environment. *IEEE Internet of Things Journal, 4*(6), 2342–2350. doi:10.1109/JIOT.2017.2750765

Paul, A., Ahmad, A., Rathore, M. M., & Jabbar, S. (2016). Smartbuddy: Defining human behaviors using big data analytics in social internet of things. *IEEE Wireless Communications, 23*(5), 68–74. doi:10.1109/MWC.2016.7721744

Perera, C., Barhamgi, M., De, S., Baarslag, T., Vecchio, M., & Choo, K. K. R. (2018). Designing the sensing as a service ecosystem for the internet of things. *IEEE Internet of Things Magazine, 1*(2), 18–23. doi:10.1109/IOTM.2019.1800023

Ploennigs, J., Cohn, J., & Stanford-Clark, A. (2018). The future of IoT. *IEEE Internet of Things Magazine, 1*(1), 28–33. doi:10.1109/IOTM.2018.1700021

Porambage, P., Okwuibe, J., Liyanage, M., Ylianttila, M., & Taleb, T. (2018). Survey on multi-access edge computing for internet of things realization. *IEEE Communications Surveys and Tutorials, 20*(4), 2961–2991. doi:10.1109/COMST.2018.2849509

Pruthvi, M., Karthika, S., & Bhalaji, N. (2019, February). A Novel Framework for SIoT College. In *2019 International Conference on Computational Intelligence in Data Science (ICCIDS)* (pp. 1-4). IEEE.

Puthal, D., Mohanty, S. P., Bhavake, S. A., Morgan, G., & Ranjan, R. (2019). Fog computing security challenges and future directions. *IEEE Consumer Electronics Magazine, 8*(3), 92–96. doi:10.1109/MCE.2019.2893674

Puthal, D., Mohanty, S. P., Wilson, S., & Choppali, U. (2021). Collaborative edge computing for smart villages (energy and security). *IEEE Consumer Electronics Magazine, 10*(3), 68–71. doi:10.1109/MCE.2021.3051813

Raimundo, R. J., & Rosário, A. T. (2022). Cybersecurity in the Internet of Things in Industrial Management. *Applied Sciences (Basel, Switzerland), 12*(3), 1598. doi:10.3390/app12031598

Ray, P. P. (2018). A survey on Internet of Things architectures. *Journal of King Saud University-Computer and Information Sciences, 30*(3), 291–319. doi:10.1016/j.jksuci.2016.10.003

Roberts, M. L., Temple, M. A., Mills, R. F., & Raines, R. A. (2006). Evolution of the air interface of cellular communications systems toward 4G realization. *IEEE Communications Surveys and Tutorials, 8*(1), 2–23. doi:10.1109/COMST.2006.323439

Sattar, K. A., & Al-Omary, A. (2021). *A survey: Security issues in IoT environment and IoT architecture.* Academic Press.

Shafique, K., Khawaja, B. A., Sabir, F., Qazi, S., & Mustaqim, M. (2020). Internet of things (IoT) for next-generation smart systems: A review of current challenges, future trends and prospects for emerging 5G-IoT scenarios. *IEEE Access : Practical Innovations, Open Solutions, 8*, 23022–23040. doi:10.1109/ACCESS.2020.2970118

Sharma, Y. K., & Khatal Sunil, S. (2019). Health Care Patient Monitoring using IoT and Machine Learning. *IOSR Journal of Engineering*.

Sinche, S., Raposo, D., Armando, N., Rodrigues, A., Boavida, F., Pereira, V., & Silva, J. S. (2019). A survey of IoT management protocols and frameworks. *IEEE Communications Surveys and Tutorials*, *22*(2), 1168–1190. doi:10.1109/COMST.2019.2943087

Sodhro, A. H., Pirbhulal, S., Luo, Z., Muhammad, K., & Zahid, N. Z. (2020). Toward 6G architecture for energy-efficient communication in IoT-enabled smart automation systems. *IEEE Internet of Things Journal*, *8*(7), 5141–5148. doi:10.1109/JIOT.2020.3024715

Song, T., Li, R., Mei, B., Yu, J., Xing, X., & Cheng, X. (2016). A Privacy Preserving Communication Protocol for IoT Applications in Smart Homes. *2016 International Conference on Identification, Information and Knowledge in the Internet of Things (IIKI)*, 519-524. 10.1109/IIKI.2016.3

Song, T., Li, R., Mei, B., Yu, J., Xing, X., & Cheng, X. (2017). A privacy preserving communication protocol for IoT applications in smart homes. *IEEE Internet of Things Journal*, *4*(6), 1844–1852. doi:10.1109/JIOT.2017.2707489

Swamy, S. N., & Kota, S. R. (2020). An empirical study on system level aspects of Internet of Things (IoT). *IEEE Access : Practical Innovations, Open Solutions*, *8*, 188082–188134. doi:10.1109/AC-CESS.2020.3029847

Vaezi, M., Azari, A., Khosravirad, S. R., Shirvanimoghaddam, M., Azari, M. M., Chasaki, D., & Popovski, P. (2022). Cellular, wide-area, and non-terrestrial IoT: A survey on 5G advances and the road toward 6G. *IEEE Communications Surveys and Tutorials*, *24*(2), 1117–1174. doi:10.1109/COMST.2022.3151028

Verma, S., Kaur, S., Khan, M. A., & Sehdev, P. S. (2020). Toward green communication in 6G-enabled massive Internet of Things. *IEEE Internet of Things Journal*, *8*(7), 5408–5415. doi:10.1109/JIOT.2020.3038804

Violette, M. (2018). IoT standards. *IEEE Internet of Things Magazine*, *1*(1), 6–7. doi:10.1109/MIOT.2018.8552483

Wei, H., Zhang, Z., & Fan, B. (2017, December). Network slice access selection scheme in 5G. In *2017 IEEE 2nd Information Technology, Networking, Electronic and Automation Control Conference (ITNEC)* (pp. 352-356). IEEE.

Wijethilaka, S., & Liyanage, M. (2021). Survey on network slicing for Internet of Things realization in 5G networks. *IEEE Communications Surveys and Tutorials*, *23*(2), 957–994. doi:10.1109/COMST.2021.3067807

Yan, L., Han, C., & Yuan, J. (2020, March). *Hybrid precoding for 6G terahertz communications: Performance evaluation and open problems. In 2020 2nd 6G wireless summit (6G SUMMIT)*. IEEE.

Yang, W., Qin, Y., & Li, R. (2022). A Network Embedding-based Approach for Scalable Network Navigability in Content-Centric Social IoT. *IEEE Internet of Things Journal*, *9*(17), 16418–16428. doi:10.1109/JIOT.2022.3151488

Zanella, A., Bui, N., Castellani, A., Vangelista, L., & Zorzi, M. (2014). Internet of things for smart cities. *IEEE Internet of Things Journal, 1*(1), 22–32. doi:10.1109/JIOT.2014.2306328

Zhang, H., Liu, N., Chu, X., Long, K., Aghvami, A. H., & Leung, V. C. (2017). Network slicing based 5G and future mobile networks: Mobility, resource management, and challenges. *IEEE Communications Magazine, 55*(8), 138–145. doi:10.1109/MCOM.2017.1600940

Chapter 25
Applications of Artificial Intelligence in IoT

L. Harish

CMR Institute of Technology, India

D. Rashmi

CMR Institute of Technology, India

ABSTRACT

Artificial intelligence is an excellent solution for handling big data streams and storage in IoT networks. The IoT is becoming more significant with the discovery of high-speed internet networks and lots of superior sensors that may be incorporated into microcontrollers. Internet information streams will now consist of sensor record and user data sent and obtained from workstations. As the range of workstations and sensors keep growing, some information may face reminiscence, latency, channel boundaries, and network congestion problems. Within the last decade, many algorithms were proposed to avoid some of these issues. Amongst all algorithms, AI stays the best solution for data mining, network control, and congestion management.

INTRODUCTION

The IoT refers to Internet-connected things or gadgets that can acquire and process data to make clever choices. The significance of IoT is that theoretical information and knowledge is no way taken into consideration enough for powerful decision making, for this reason the significance of real-time data that allows agencies and people to make more actionable and wise choices. As a result, IoT is developing exponentially in reputation.

Everyday gadgets become "smarter" thanks to the IoT since they can connect with humans as well as other IoT-enabled devices as well as share statistics via the internet. The Internet of Things is rapidly developing into a more intelligent world by merging the physical with the digital.

DOI: 10.4018/978-1-6684-8145-5.ch025

Copyright © 2023, IGI Global. Copying or distributing in print or electronic forms without written permission of IGI Global is prohibited.

All types of statistics systems use the Internet as a powerful tool. The community is accessible almost everywhere, including at home, at work, and on mobile devices (phones, watches). People are starting to expect that practically all commonly used gadgets will be connected to the Internet and will communicate with one another by making simple decisions for people and sustaining their existence. Although it is estimated that there are currently 15 billion connected devices, this number still represents less than 1% of all potential devices that could be connected to the Internet. The next phase is to incorporate artificial intelligence into systems for the Internet of Things (IoT). The IoT is a network of physical "matters" that are implanted with electronics, software, sensors, and connections in order to generate additional revenue and services by exchanging information with the manufacturer, operator, and/or other connected devices. Although each component has an embedded computer that makes it uniquely identifiable, they may all work together inside the current Internet architecture.

As the IoT is described in the definition above, data or records can be transmitted over the internet whether it's from system to device, human to human, or human to computer. Each device will be connected to the internet using its unique identifier number to send or receive priceless data or to provide a service. Things could be sophisticated electrical gadgets that can send or receive signals. With this idea, we want to make things smart and cunning enough to decide whether to reply or to send a signal, like a clinical help message or a stock restock indicator, for example. The concept of AI (Artificial Intelligence) is not new in the context of today's world. Many "things" are created based on this concept, and as IoT and AI combine, more "intelligent matters" that are better at effective dialogue will emerge. In daily life, artificial intelligence is being employed more and more. It is a broad-ranging idea that has applications in a variety of scientific disciplines. It is used in programmes that suggest users to watch movies, take into account their viewing patterns, or identify individuals on tracking recordings. Its distinctive advantage comes from the device learning components, which allow special artificial intelligence approaches to understand a lot of data and show some of their summary. The ability to view a recording of the monitoring in the context of looking for a certain person, for example, is a very significant amenity for someone who does not need to statically check all the data arriving from the necessary gadget (Djenouri et al., 2022).

INTERNET OF THINGS (IoT)

These Internet of Things (IoT) applications have a big influence on the networking, connectivity, and communication protocols used by such web-enabled gadgets. Through the use of AI and machine learning, IoT might make the procedures for gathering data more dynamic and straightforward. IoT enables objects connected to closed, personal internet connections to exchange messages and "these networks come together thanks to the IoT. It makes possible for devices to interact not just among themselves but also with other devices through various forms of networking, making the world much more inter connected."

The IoT can be characterised as an extension of a net and other internet connectivity to various sensors and devices, or "things," giving even basic items like lightbulbs, locks, and vents a higher level of processing and analytical capabilities.

FEATURES OF INTERNET OF THINGS (IoT)

A few most popular features of IoT are:

1. Intelligent
2. Connection
3. Dynamic
4. Huge size
5. Sensing
6. Heterogeneity
7. Security

1. IoT is intelligent because it mixes computer, software, hardware, algorithms, and other elements. Ambient intelligence increases the IoT's capabilities by enabling the devices to react intelligently to various circumstances and carry out specific activities. Despite the ubiquitous use of smart technology, "intelligent" in the context of the Internet of Things only refers to a method of interoperability. Users and devices are communicated with via standard input methods and graphical user interfaces, respectively (Singla, 2020). Algorithms and compute (i.e., software and hardware) combine to provide the "intelligent spark" that gives a product experience intelligence. Consider how the Misfit Shine fitness tracker and the Nest smart thermostat compare. The Shine experience divides compute-intensive processes between a smartphone and the cloud. The AI that gave them their excessive intelligence is less powerful than the Nest thermostat.
2. **Connectivity:** By linking common things, connectivity encourages the growth of the Internet of Things. These devices must be connected for even little interactions to contribute to the collective intelligence of an Internet of Things network. It makes objects accessible via networks and network-compatible. By combining smart things and apps, this connectivity can open up new commercial potential for the Internet of Things. The Internet of Things requires connectivity that goes beyond just putting a WiFi module and calling it a day. Connectivity enables network flexibility and accessibility. Accessibility requires network participation, whereas compatibility gives everyone the same ability to produce and consume data. If this sounds familiar, it's probably because the Internet of Things is subject to Metcalfe's Law.
3. **Dynamic Nature:** Dynamic Data collection from the environment is the Internet of Things' primary purpose, which is made feasible by the constant changes that take place around the devices. The statuses of these devices change dynamically under many circumstances, such as when they are connected or not, sleeping or waking up, and in relation to temperature, location, and speed. The number of gadgets varies dynamically depending on the person, the location, the time, and the condition of each individual gadget. Dynamically changing device context includes things like location and speed as well as connected and/or unconnected states, resting and waking states, and so on. Furthermore, the number of devices may change (Jiang, 2019).
4. **Enormous:** There will be more gadgets that need to be monitored and permitted to speak with one another in addition to those that are now linked to the Internet. It becomes more crucial to process and comprehend the data generated by these devices for application-related reasons. The enormous scope of the Internet of Items is demonstrated by the expected study from Gartner (2015), which projected that there will be 6.4 billion connected devices operating globally in 2016, up 30% from

2015, and that 5.5 million new things would be connected every day. The prediction is that there will be 20.8 billion linked devices by 2020. At least 10 times as many devices will need to be managed and made capable of communication as there are today linked to the Internet. The management of the produced data and its interpretation for application purposes will be even more crucial. This has to do with both effective data processing and data semantics.

5. **Sensing:** Without the usage of sensors, the Internet of Things wouldn't be able to monitor or measure environmental changes, offer information that might be used to report on their condition, or even interact with the environment. The development of skills that faithfully represent our understanding of the real world and the people who inhabit it is now possible because to sensing technologies. Although sensory input only contains analogue information from the physical cosmos, it may nonetheless help us fully understand our complex surroundings. Our capacity to grasp the physical world, other people, and our senses are often taken for granted. With the use of sensing technology, we can design interactions that correctly reflect our understanding of the actual environment and people who reside there Although only an analogue input from the physical world, this can significantly advance our comprehension of our complicated environment.

6. **Heterogeneity:** The Internet of Things requires heterogeneity. Since Internet of Things (IoT) devices can be built on a range of hardware platforms and networks, they can connect to other IoT devices or service platforms over a variety of networks. The IoT architecture should make direct network contact between various networks possible. Scalability, flexibility, extensibility, and interoperability are the guiding principles of the IoT in the development of heterogeneous devices and the ecosystems in which they operate. IoT devices have a heterogeneous character since they are constructed using a number of hardware networks and platforms. They might utilise a variety of networks to talk to other devices or service platforms.

7. **Security:** Security IoT devices are inherently vulnerable to security issues. While we benefit from the IoT's efficiency, novel experiences, and other benefits, it would be a mistake to disregard the security concerns it raises. IoT has serious issues with privacy and transparency. A new security paradigm must be developed in order to safeguard endpoints, networks, and the data transferred between them.

IoT IS CRUCIAL, BUT WHY?

Due to the ioT, people may live shrewdly, effectively, and entirely in control of their life. IoT is vital for business in addition to providing smart home automation devices. With insight about anything between machine performance to supply chain and logistics operations, the IoT enables a real-time perspective of how a company's systems truly function.

By using IoT, businesses may automate processes and save labour costs. Additionally, it enhances customer service, reduces waste, lowers the price of producing and shipping goods, and offers insight into customer interactions.

IoT would continue to increase in importance as one of the important contemporary technologies as more businesses come to realise how connected gadgets may help them remain competitive.

HOW IS IoT IMPLEMENTED?

The IoT ecosystem comprises of smart, network-capable devices that gathers, shares, and act on environmental data using embedded technology including CPUs, sensors, and communication tools. IoT gadgets can process sensor data locally or transfer it to the cloud for processing by connecting to an IoT gateway. These gadgets communicate with one another often, exchanging data, and responding to the information they provide. The devices do the majority of the work on their own, while users may interact with them to set up, provide the commands, or obtain data.

The network, connection, and communication rules utilised for such internet connected devices are significantly impacted by these IoT uses. IoT might make data collecting processes simpler and more dynamic by utilising AI and machine learning (Lin et al., 2019).

Figure 1. An IoT system example

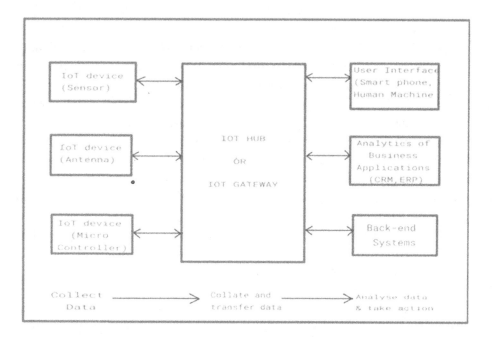

IoT APPLICATIONS

Smart Homes: The creation of smart homes has revolutionised residential home architecture. Energy, time, and money would all be saved by the smart home products. A smart home will allow the owner to manage housekeeping tasks even from a distance. For instance, turning on the heating or air conditioner before getting home, turning on and off the lights, operating the washing machine, etc. Even though these smart houses have been deployed, their high cost remains a significant barrier to their widespread use.

Wearable Devices: These include watches or eyeglasses that have sensors and software built in to gather and analyse data. Such devices have received significant investment from businesses like Google and Samsung. These gadgets largely meet the needs for entertainment, fitness, and health. The need for such systems to be lightweight, compact, and with extremely low power consumption is a big hurdle.

Traffic Monitoring: Vehicles should be able to operate, consume fuel efficiently, reduce pollution, maintain a high level of passenger comfort. A breakthrough would be made if such intelligent traffic could be created, as it would significantly lower the number of fatalities from traffic accidents. Using web applications and sensors, residents can also locate free parking spaces throughout the city.

Industrial Internet: The Industrial Internet of Things, sometimes referred to as Industrial Internet, is the latest trend in the industry (IIoT). Using sensor, software, and big data analytics, it is allowing industrial engineers to create amazing machines. The IIoT offers several opportunities for quality assurance and sustainability. The supply chain's efficiency will increase with the use of tracking applications, real-time inventory information exchange among manufacturers and retailers, and automation delivery.

Smart Cities: The "smart city" is another idea that is gaining ground and increasingly grabbing people's attention. Intelligence surveillance, water distribution, automated transportation, improved energy management systems, urban security, and environment monitoring are some of the uses of the IoT for smart cities. There will be an emphasis on urgent metropolitan challenges including backed-up traffic, air pollution, and a lack of energy resources. When a trash needs to be emptied, gadgets with cellular connection capabilities like Smart Trash will notify municipal services.

Agriculture: With nation's population growing, a reliable food supply is essential. Government helps farmers by implementing cutting-edge methods and research to increase food output. Among the IoT industries that is now developing at the quickest rate is smart farming. Farmers are increasing return on investment by adopting analytical data insights. Simple IoT uses include tracking soil nutrients and moisture, controlling water use for plant growth, and making customised fertilisers. The horticulture industry is using IoT devices or IoT-related gear, such as bright water management system, synthetic level screens and so on. These clever pieces of equipment are used to determine whether the soil and air are suitable for gardening. The use of IoT in farming enables continuous improvement by allowing for constant modification. Ranchers are using IoT approach to produce more and meet the demands of growing populations.

Healthcare: The idea of a connected healthcare system and smart medical equipment holds great promise for businesses as well as for the general welfare of society. According to research, IoT in healthcare will grow rapidly in the upcoming years. IoT in healthcare aims to give people the tools they need to wear connected devices and live better lives. The gathered information will enable individualised health assessments and the creation of disease prevention plans for each individual (Lu et al., 2021).

Advanced Vehicle Sector: This business benefited from the introduction of IoT. Self-propelled vehicles and vehicle GPS systems are two examples of IoT in the automotive industry.

By enabling information communication systems, the Internet of Things (IoT) enables the automotive industry to update the product and respond to ongoing mechanical concerns. IoT aids in enhancing vehicle performance. We can avoid accidents or security issues by using IoT in the automotive industry.

Retail: The Internet of Things has altered the retail sector. E-trade shopping has replaced traditional retail shopping. At the moment, people prefer online purchasing to going to stores. In reaction to the arrival of IoT in the retail sector, markets are also altering their retail strategy.

For instance, to draw customers into their establishments, retailers use Bluetooth signals. These Bluetooth reference points enable businesses to provide their customers location-based services. The customer can receive information about specific products and rebates on their mobile devices when they connect with a retailer application.

Disney's use of behavioural analytics is a fascinating case in point. Through the launch of the IoT-enabled MagicBand, Disney World was able to increase consumer happiness to the highest level possible.

CHALLENGES OF IoT

The primary issues with IoT include:

Infrastructure: To deploy the Internet of Things, advanced infrastructure must be reachable. For practical realisation, the hardware and wireless network should be dependable.

Physical Location: The idea of physical location and position is crucial since the Internet of Items is deeply entrenched in the real world. This is true both for discovering things and for gaining knowledge. As a result, location-based searching must be supported by the infrastructure. The key area of concern is IoT infrastructure. To implement IoT, high-end infrastructure must be available. Hardware and the wireless network should be dependable for practical implementation.

The idea of physical location and position is crucial since the Internet of Items is deeply entrenched in the real world. This is true both for discovering things and for gaining knowledge. As a result, location-based searching must be supported by the infrastructure.

Security and Privacy: Identification, confidentiality, integrity, authentication, and authorization are the main security problems. With the increase in hacking incidents, the IoT application to be developed should be reliable.

Network Issues: The wireless network that IoT employs for communication is essential to its broad use. To make it possible to use the technology effectively, the networking issues must be solved.

IoT'S BENEFITS AND DRAWBACKS

There are several advantages of IoT, a few of which are described below:

- A benefit is having access to data on any device, at any time, from anyplace.
- Increasing connectivity among electronic devices, saving time and money by delivering data packets across linked networks.
- Automating procedures to raise the quality of a company's offerings and minimise the necessity for human interaction.

The following are some of the disadvantages of IoT:

- There is a higher likelihood that a hacker may steal sensitive data when more devices are connected to each other and more data is sent between them.
- It will be challenging to gather and handle data from such a large number of IoT devices (potentially millions) that enterprises may one day have to deal with. If there is a problem with the system, it is possible that all connected devices would get damaged.
- The inability of a worldwide IoT interoperability standard makes it difficult for devices made by different manufacturers to connect to one another.

ARTIFICIAL INTELLIGENCE (AI)

Artificial intelligence simulates way that human mind make decisions and solves problems using computers and other technology. Intelligent systems, machine learning, voice recognition, natural language processing, and machine vision are a few examples of specific AI applications.

HOW DOES AI OPERATE?

Companies are rushing to show how their products and services incorporate AI as interest in the technology grows. Often, when people talk about AI, they just mean one part, like machine learning. Machine learning algorithms need a certain hardware and software foundation to be developed and trained. Some programming languages, such Python, R, and Java, are directly related to AI, but none are. AI systems frequently employ vast amounts of tagged training data to make predictions, then analyse connections and trends before applying them. Similar to how chatbots may pick up on human speech patterns by studying text chat examples, image recognition software analyses millions of instances to identify and describe items in pictures.

AI programming primarily focuses on learning, reasoning, and self-healing.

Learning Strategies: This area of artificial intelligence programming focuses on gathering data and formulating rules to turn it into knowledge.

Reasoning Strategies: A system of rules called an algorithm gives computer hardware precise instructions on how to perform a task. Choosing the right algorithm to achieve a particular result is the main goal of this element of AI programming.

How to Fix Yourself: The goal of this part of AI programming is to constantly improve the algorithms to ensure the highest level of accuracy.

ARTIFICIAL INTELLIGENCE'S SIGNIFICANCE

AI is significant because it occasionally completes tasks more quickly than people and because it can offer previously hidden insights into how businesses function. Particularly for repetitive and detail-oriented jobs like reviewing a large number of legal papers to make sure that crucial fields are filled accurately,

AI systems can do the task swiftly and with few errors. tend to finish. Large organisations saw an improvement in productivity and the creation of whole new business opportunities. Worldwide success has now been achieved by Uber. It was unimaginable to use software to connect people to taxis before the current wave of AI. use potent machine learning algorithms to foretell when locals in a specific location will require a ride, allowing drivers to leave before they are required.

Another example is Google, which has grown to be a significant player in a wide range of online services by using machine learning to analyse user behaviour and then enhance its offers. Google said that in 2017, the company will prioritise artificial intelligence (AI). The largest and wealthiest companies use AI to improve operations and surpass competitors.

AI'S BENEFITS AND LIMITATIONS

Deep learning and artificial neural networks are two AI technologies that are quickly advancing. The fundamental cause of this is because AI is far faster and more accurate than a person at analysing vast amounts of data.

The enormous amount of data collected each day would be too much for a human researcher to process, but AI systems by using machine learning can quickly convert this data into knowledge. The main drawback of employing AI today is the expense of processing the enormous amounts of data that AI programming demands.

BENEFITS

- Available virtual agents powered by AI;
- Effective in occupations requiring meticulousness;
- Reduced time for data-intensive activities;
- Consistent outputs.

LIMITATIONS

- Expensive
- Demanding intense technical knowledge
- Hard to find skilled employees to construct AI implements
- Understands what has been demonstrated
- Lack of transferability between activities

WEAK AI AGAINST STRONG AI

Two categories of AI exist: Strong and Weak. Weak AI, also known as narrow AI, is a kind of artificial intelligence that is built and taught to do a particular job. Strong AI, often known as artificial general intelligence (AGI), is the term used to describe computer programmes that can mimic the cognitive processes of the human brain. Weak AI is demonstrated by commercial robotics and virtual personal assistants like Alexa. Fuzzy logic may be used by an intelligent AI system to convey information from one place to another and automatically generate solutions when faced with a challenging problem. A competent AI software should theoretically be able to pass both the Chinese room and Turing tests.

WHAT ARE THE FOUR DIFFERENT SUBTYPES OF AI?

AI may be categorised into four different subcategories, according to an essay by Arend Hintze, assistant professor of integrative biology, computer science, and engineering at Michigan State University.

These categories vary from sentient systems, which are yet conceivable, through intelligent systems that are now in use and are specialised for a certain task. These are the categories:

- **Reacting Machines:** These AI systems have little memory and concentrate on a particular task. Deep Blue, an IBM chess software which beat Gary Kasparov in the 1990s, serves as an illustration. Although Deep Blue can identify the chessboard pieces and anticipate moves, it lacks memory and is unable to use previous experiences to make forecasts about the future.
- **Inadequate Space:** These AI systems contain memories, which allow them to use the past to influence their actions now. Several of the decision-making techniques used in self-driving cars are developed in this way.
- Psychology used the phrase "theory of mind." It suggests that AI will become capable to correctly identify emotions when applied to the field. This form of AI will be capable to play a crucial part in human teams since it can forecast behaviour and infer human intentions.
- **Self-Awareness:** Computer algorithms with artificial intelligence fall under this heading since they are conscious because they are conscious of who they are. Machines with self-awareness are aware of their own conditions. Such an AI is still hypothetical.

HOW DOES AI IMPACT IoT?

The true potential of IoT is unlocked by artificial intelligence, which enables networks and devices to learn from past activities, predict future actions, and continually improve performance and decision-making skills.

IoT has been steadily adopted by the corporate community over the past ten years. A new era of commercial and consumer technology has begun thanks to the utilisation of IoT devices and their data-gathering capabilities for new or improved business ventures. Now that "artificial intelligence of things," or AIoT, has the potential to be adopted by IoT devices, the next stage has begun.

Adopting and investing in the AIoT will enable consumers, companies, economies, and industries to take use of its capabilities and gain competitive advantages. IoT collects the information, which AI examines to mimic intelligent behaviour and support decision-making with the least amount of human intervention (Talukder & Haas, 2021).

WHY DOES IoT NEED AI?

Devices may communicate with one another and act on these discoveries thanks to IoT. The information that these devices provide determines how beneficial they are. To be useful for making decisions, the data must be gathered, preserved, processed, and examined.

As a result, organisations are faced with a difficulty. As the use of IoT increases, businesses are struggling to efficiently digest the data and use it for insightful decision-making.

These two problems are due to the cloud and data transmission. The cloud cannot scale proportionately to handle all the data that enters from IoT devices due to the limited bandwidth needed to send data from IoT devices to the cloud. No matter how large or complex the communications network is, IoT device data collecting causes latency and congestion.

One IoT application that relies on quick, in-the-moment choices is autonomous vehicles. To be effective and secure, autonomous cars must analyse data and make quick decisions (just like a human being). They cannot be hindered by latency, erratic connectivity, or low bandwidth.

Not all Internet of Things (IoT) applications, such as driverless vehicles, rely on this fast decision-making. IoT devices are already utilised in manufacturing, and latency or delays could have an impact on the processes or limit capabilities in an emergency.

Security regularly uses biometrics to restrict or allow access to specific areas. Without efficient data processing, lags that impact performance and speed are possible, not to mention the dangers in emergency situations. For these applications, high security and extremely low latency are necessary. Processing must therefore be done at the edge. It is impractical to move data back and forth between a local system and the cloud (Zhou et al., 2019).

ADVANTAGES OF AIoT

Each day, one billion terabytes of data are generated by IoT devices. By 2025, there will likely be 42 billion IoT-connected devices on the planet. The networks grow along with the data.

IoT is insufficient since demands and expectations are changing. The abundance of data has produced more obstacles than possibilities. The ideas and potential of all that data are being constrained by obstacles, but intelligent devices may eliminate these obstacles and enable organisations can achieve the full value of their corporate data.

IoT networks and devices can utilise AI to make predictions about the future, analyse past choices, and more to continuously enhance performance and decision-making abilities. Artificial intelligence (AI) is used by the gadgets, allowing them to "think for themselves" and understand data and make decisions in real time without the delays and traffic associated with data transfers.

The AIoT offers a potent solution for intelligent automation, and it has many uses for businesses.

Avoiding Downtime: Some industries, including offshore oil and gas, are hampered by downtime. Inconvenient downtime from unexpected equipment breakdown can be expensive. AIoT can predict equipment breakdowns in order to arrange repairs before the equipment encounters serious problems.

Increasing Operational Efficiency: Massive volumes of data are collected by IoT devices, which AI analyses and uncovers underlying patterns much more quickly than humans. AI and machine learning may boost this competency by predicting operational scenarios and making the right modifications for improved outcomes.

Enabling New and Improved Products and Services: As Natural Language Processing advances, new and better products and services as well as improved human-machine interaction are made possible. AIoT can enhance new or current products and services by enabling greater data processing and analytics.

Enhanced Risk Management: Risk management is crucial for responding to a market environment that is changing quickly. Data may be used by AI and IoT to prioritise the best course of action, anticipate risks, and improve employee safety while lowering cyber threats and financial losses.

AIoT INDUSTRIAL APPLICATIONS

Manufacturing, the car industry and retail are just a few of the industries that the Internet of Things is already changing. Here are a few typical AIoT applications from various industries (Kapoor, 2019).

- **Manufacturing:** IoT is being used by manufacturers to track their equipment. AIoT provides predictive analysis by further fusing the data insights from IoT devices with AI capabilities. Thanks to the Internet of Things, manufacturers can be proactive with warehouse inventory, maintenance, and manufacturing.

- **Robotics:** Robotics could significantly enhance the way production is done. Robots are increasingly being developed with AI and data transfer sensors, allowing them to continuously learn from data to boost output and cut expenses.

- **Sales and Marketing:** Retail analytics tracks customer behavior inside a physical shop using data from cameras and sensors to make predictions about things like how long it will take them to get to the checkout queue. Customers will be happier overall if this is used to boost cashier productivity and suggest staffing levels.

Major retailers may enhance sales by utilizing AIoT technology through consumer analytics. Data from mobile-based user behavior and proximity detection, which increases foot traffic in physical venues, enables customers to get tailored marketing campaigns as they purchase.

- **Automotive:** The AIoT has several applications in the automotive industry, including maintenance and recalls. To decide which components need to be replaced and to offer service checks to customers, the AIoT can anticipate when components may malfunction or break down and include data from recalls, warranties, and safety organisations. As a result, consumers have a more favourable opinion of the reliability of the manufacturer's automobiles.

Autonomous cars are among the most well-known and fascinating AIoT applications. Autonomous cars can predict driver and pedestrian behaviour under a variety of circumstances, making driving safer and more efficient. This is made possible by AI, which gives IoT intelligence.

- **Healthcare:** Providing world-class care to everyone communities is one of the key objectives. Physicians are now seeing fewer patients and are under greater time and effort demands, regardless of how big or sophisticated the healthcare systems are. It might be difficult to deliver high-quality care while handling administrative issues (Merenda et al., 2020; Singla, 2020).

A significant quantity of patient data is also generated and maintained by healthcare facilities, including images and test results. If medical institutions can swiftly access this information to guide diagnostic and therapeutic decisions, it will be essential and vital for providing high-quality patient care.By increasing diagnostic accuracy, enabling telemedicine and remote patient care, and reducing the amount of administrative labour required to monitor patient health at the institution, IoT and AI can successfully solve these concerns. The ability of AIoT to accurately assess patients is mostly because to its ability to identify high-risk patients more quickly than humans can through analysing patient data (Lu et al., 2021).

For predicting the future, AI and IoT are the best technology partners. IoT gets better with AI's intelligent decision-making, and AI gets better with IoT's data interchange. The two will ultimately collaborate to usher in a new era of experiences and solutions that will change enterprises across numerous industries and open up brand-new opportunities (Faid et al., 2022).

- **Accounting:** The benefits of IoT applications in banking and finance are also exciting the accounting sector. The security of the bank and the client has also increased thanks to IoT. It has brought about a lot of improvements in the banking industry, including mobile banking, ATMs, Smart money centres, and so on. Additionally, it has made it possible for customers to move money, save money, and do other financial transactions online using a mobile device or a computer.

For example, Banking IoT solutions like Arimo help detect fraudulent or odd client behaviour using machine learning algorithms that evaluate all the data and point out questionable scenarios.

- **Energy and Utility Sector:** To enhance outcomes, the energy and utility sector is also applying IoT innovation. Oil and gas companies use IoT devices to measure penetration lines. By evaluating the speed of the boring system, these devices improve the cycle and restrict use. A well-known innovation is the brilliant energy network, which rely on IoT devices to ensure communication between the energy grid and clients over a web connection. The application of IoT technology in the energy sector saved money and provided more time and energy.
- **Transportation:** IoT technology is being used in the coordinating and transportation sectors to improve customer experiences. One example of an IoT arrangement in the transportation industry is the GPS tracker. The client can use a GPS tracker to keep track of the item that needs to be delivered to him by connecting the GPS tracker with the route app on his phone. He is able to follow the route of the means of transportation.

Delivery vans are equipped with sensors to monitor temperature, allowing businesses to make sure that their payload is arriving in a safe state. These systems are also employed to check a driver's level of safety while operating a vehicle.

- **Homes and Buildings:** IoT has a significant impact on the residential and commercial real estate sector. With IoT setups, a smart building's presentation is referred to. IoT in the land business includes the home robotization framework, clever door locks, clever heating frameworks, surveillance cameras, and lights. For instance, the Nest thermostat is regarded as the ideal way to change the climate in a home (Zhou et al., 2019).

- **Hospitality:** The astonishing IoT innovations of sensors and feeling recognition cameras enable hotel staff to observe customers' emotions, determine whether they are hungry, and then recommend food based on their preferences and inclinations. This will let the salespeople prepare the client's unique dinners before they ask for them. Hotels like Hilton and Marriott have already tried out hyper-personalized hotel rooms, letting guests use their mobile phones or a tablet given to control amenities like heating, ventilation, and air conditioning.

Two cutting-edge technologies that hold great promise for an intelligent future are AI and the IoT.

HOW QUICKLY IS IoT EXPANDING?

The amount of time spent online is increasing extraordinarily quickly and dramatically. We are all aware of the fact that work is becoming more doable thanks to the Internet.

Let's go on to find out how quickly IoT is developing.

- It's possible that by 2030 there will be 125 billion IoT devices that are connected. The results of the EIU's own IoT Business Index survey are currently being examined in a new report. It includes in-depth interviews with industry leaders that outline the precise extent of the IoT's rapid evolution.
- According to the EIU study, there are three factors driving the IoT's explosive growth. They are a smart-home epidemic.

WHAT IS AIoT?

The phrase "AIoT" refers to the integration of advanced analytics, deep learning, and IoT connection. The foundation of this cutting-edge technology is the integration of AI with IoT infrastructures, which greatly increases the value of the data.

An algorithm that enhances communication and uses predictive skills to provide organisations a competitive edge is made possible by AIoT. Using AI methods like machine learning and deep learning, dispersed nodes' data fuses IoT with AI, to put it simply.

In this way, skills like machine learning are situated closer to the data source. Edge AI, sometimes referred to as Edge Intelligence or edge computing, is an idea that increases the scalability, robustness, and efficiency of the system under consideration (Calo et al., 2017).

POWER OF AI AND IoT CONVERGENCE

Now that we apprehend the abilities of IoT and AI personally, we are able to move on to expertise the need for the intersection of AI and IoT. When AI is blended with the IoT, you get what's referred to as artificial Intelligence of Things (AIoT). The primary purpose for combining AI and IoT is that IoT gadgets are used to acquire all the information and ship it to the cloud or different locations where it can be gathered, normally over the internet, at the same time as AI is the brain of AIoT. Because it's far taken into consideration virtually useful for making choices and simulating what a device might do or react to. To better recognize the decision-making process of those devices, the procedure taken by using AIoT devices are listed below (Firouzi et al., 2022).

1. Data Gathering

Data is gathered using sensors which are connected to IoT devices. These sensors are part of the device and multiple sensors can be attached to the device to gather different types of information. For example, a device may have multiple sensors such as a camera, GPS, and accelerometer to gather different types of information.

2. Data Transmission

Gathered data is transferred to storage, as is usually done in bulk within the cloud. The cloud enables to reduce storage price because organizations don't have to spend more money to have hardware to store large amounts of information.

3. Operation on Data

Storing data in the cloud is not useful with out processing it. Information processing consists of various levels like extraction of relevant information from the cloud, clean it to remove anomalies, transform it into canonical form, and then use algorithms to produce results.

4. Data Prediction

Machine getting to know and deep gaining knowledge of algorithms are important to predicting the future events. After constructing the relevant models, predictions can be made based on the obtained results.

5. Action

The very last step after making a prediction is for thr machine to respond to the generated perception.

IoT OFFERS THE FOLLOWING ADVANTAGES FOR AI

1. IoT data for organization purposes
2. Time and cost saving
3. Automating tasks
4. Reducing human intervention
5. Enhancing the quality of life styles

Figure 2. Block diagram of AI in IoT

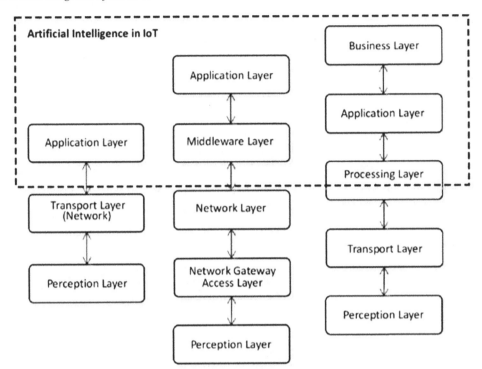

CHALLENGES OF AI IN IoT

Regardless of the various advantages and advancements IoT brings, there are few limitations:

1. Privacy problems
2. Information overflow
3. Bug problem
4. Compatibility troubles

AI AND IoT USE CASES

1. Video Monitoring

Surveillance video for security purposes is significantly more effective and intelligent when AI and IoT are used. Human operators are needed for conventional Video Management Systems (VMS), which need them to view several video streams.

This indicates that the video's subjectivity, restricted attention, and erratic reaction times are its main constraints. AIoT analyses video streams in real-time, identifies objects, and objectively distinguishes persons and events by utilising machine learning algorithms.

In retail, smart video surveillance is quite helpful. For instance, the enormous American grocery chain Walmart employs checkout image recognition camera systems to identify shoplifting. Weapons detection and intrusion event detection are two further deep learning security applications (Singla, 2020).

2. Robots Manufacturing

Manufacturing of robots is one industry that has adopted developing technologies like IoT, AI, face recognition, deep learning, robotics, and others. The intelligence of manufacturing robots is growing as a result of sensors that have been implanted and allow for data exchange. Robots are also equipped with artificial intelligence algorithms that allow them to gain knowledge from new data. With this approach, the production is steadily improved while costs and time are reduced (Djenouri et al., 2022).

3. Unmanned Vehicles

The self-driving cars made by Tesla are the finest illustration of IoT and artificial intelligence functioning together. Artificial intelligence is used by self-driving cars to foresee pedestrian and animal behaviour in a range of circumstances. They are getting smarter with each travel and can, for instance, identify the appropriate speed, the weather, and the state of the roads.

4. Analysis of Retail

Retail analytics uses a large number of camera and sensor data points to watch consumer movements and anticipate when they will reach the checkout line. So that checkout times are shortened and cashier efficiency is increased, the system can suggest dynamic staffing levels.

5. Smart Thermostat

IoT with AI capabilities is superbly shown by Nest's smart thermostat. The integration of smartphones allows users to check and control the temperature from anywhere based on their work schedules and preferred temperatures.

6. Drones Are Used to Monitor Traffic

The urbanisation and city growth did not lead to a corresponding rise in the transportation infrastructures. Thus, as the social costs of driving rose, traffic congestion and road (un)safety have emerged as a social problem. AIoT can provide solutions for traffic management by tracking traffic and making recommendations for changes. Data on traffic flow and potential congestions may be collected and then sent to a centralised platform through IoT. Contrarily, AI has the ability to assess the data and make quick, beneficial decisions, such as rerouting traffic or adjusting speed limits or traffic signal timing to ease congestion and provide a safer and more enjoyable driving experience (Faid et al., 2022).

7. Smart Office Structures

The Internet of Things is already present in many buildings as sensors, cameras, and building controls. The sensors can monitor and adjust the building's lighting and temperature to provide a more cosy and environmentally friendly atmosphere. Additionally, technology like facial recognition and real-time video surveillance are increasingly being utilised to monitor employee performance and conduct while ensuring the safety of the workforce (Rathi et al., 2021).

CONCLUSION

The intersection of AI and IoT has the potential to revolutionize the way we live and work. By combining IoT devices with AI-powered analytics and decision-making capabilities, we can create intelligent systems that can automate and optimize various processes, Leading to increased efficiency, cost savings and improved quality of life.

However, the deployment of AI in IoT also presents significant challenges, such as data privacy and security, ethical concerns and the need for robust and scalable infrastructure. These challenges must be addressed to ensure the responsible and effective deployment of AI in IoT.

Overall, AI in IoT is a rapidly evolving field with tremendous potential to transform various industries and sectors. As the technology continues to mature and more use cases are discovered, we can expect to see significant advances and innovations in the coming years.

REFERENCES

Calo, S. B., Touna, M., Verma, D. C., & Cullen, A. (2017, December). Edge computing architecture for applying AI to IoT. In *2017 IEEE International Conference on Big Data (Big Data)* (pp. 3012-3016). IEEE. 10.1109/BigData.2017.8258272

Djenouri, Y., Belhadi, A., Srivastava, G., & Lin, J. C. W. (2022). When explainable AI meets IoT applications for supervised learning. *Cluster Computing*, 1–11. doi:10.100710586-022-03659-3

Faid, A., Sadik, M., & Sabir, E. (2022). An agile AI and IoT-augmented smart farming: A cost-effective cognitive weather station. *Agriculture*, *12*(1), 35. doi:10.3390/agriculture12010035

Firouzi, F., Farahani, B., & Marinšek, A. (2022). The convergence and interplay of edge, fog, and cloud in the AI-driven Internet of Things (IoT). *Information Systems*, *107*, 101840. doi:10.1016/j.is.2021.101840

Jiang, H. (2019). Mobile fire evacuation system for large public buildings based on artificial intelligence and IoT. *IEEE Access : Practical Innovations, Open Solutions*, *7*, 64101–64109. doi:10.1109/ACCESS.2019.2915241

Kapoor, A. (2019). *Hands-On Artificial Intelligence for IoT: Expert machine learning and deep learning techniques for developing smarter IoT systems*. Packt Publishing Ltd.

Lin, Y. W., Lin, Y. B., & Liu, C. Y. (2019). AItalk: A tutorial to implement AI as IoT devices. *IET Networks*, *8*(3), 195–202. doi:10.1049/iet-net.2018.5182

Lu, Z. X., Qian, P., Bi, D., Ye, Z. W., He, X., Zhao, Y. H., Su, L., Li, S., & Zhu, Z. L. (2021). Application of AI and IoT in clinical medicine: Summary and challenges. *Current Medical Science*, *41*(6), 1134–1150. doi:10.100711596-021-2486-z PMID:34939144

Merenda, M., Porcaro, C., & Iero, D. (2020). Edge machine learning for ai-enabled iot devices: A review. *Sensors (Basel)*, *20*(9), 2533. doi:10.339020092533 PMID:32365645

Rathi, V. K., Rajput, N. K., Mishra, S., Grover, B. A., Tiwari, P., Jaiswal, A. K., & Hossain, M. S. (2021). An edge AI-enabled IoT healthcare monitoring system for smart cities. *Computers & Electrical Engineering*, *96*, 107524. doi:10.1016/j.compeleceng.2021.107524

Singla, S. (2020). AI and IoT in healthcare. *Internet of things use cases for the healthcare industry*, 1-23.

Talukder, A., & Haas, R. (2021, June). AIoT: AI meets IoT and web in smart healthcare. In *13th ACM Web Science Conference 2021* (pp. 92-98). 10.1145/3462741.3466650

Zhou, J., Wang, Y., Ota, K., & Dong, M. (2019). AAIoT: Accelerating artificial intelligence in IoT systems. *IEEE Wireless Communications Letters*, *8*(3), 825–828. doi:10.1109/LWC.2019.2894703

Chapter 26
Smart Precision Agriculture Using IoT and WSN

Anurag Vijay Agrawal
Indian Institute of Technology, Roorkee, India

Lakshmana Phanendra Magulur
Koneru Lakshmaiah Education Foundation, India

S. Gayathri Priya
RMD Engineering College, India

Amanpreet Kaur
Chitkara University Institute of Engineering and Technology, Chitkara University, India

Gurpreet Singh
Chitkara University Institute of Engineering and Technology, Chitkara University, India

Sampath Boopathi
Muthayammal Engineering College, India

ABSTRACT

In precision agriculture (PA), the internet of things (IoT) and wireless sensor networks (WSN) can be utilised to more effectively monitor crop fields and make quick choices. The sensors can be installed in crop fields to gather pertinent data, but doing so uses up some of their limited energy. The use of IoT and WSN for smart precision agriculture necessitates energy-efficient operations, location-aware sensors, and secure localization techniques. In this chapter, agricultural problems are identified using IoT and WSN technologies to rectify them. Pests, a lack of water supply, and leaf diseases can be identified for best solutions through pest identification and classification, soil and water conservation, and leaf issues. The integration of Arduino and various sensors is used in the IoT and WSN to solve the issues automatically. Securing energy conservation can be achieved through IoT and sensor systems using efficient programmes.

DOI: 10.4018/978-1-6684-8145-5.ch026

Copyright © 2023, IGI Global. Copying or distributing in print or electronic forms without written permission of IGI Global is prohibited.

INTRODUCTION

PA is the science of employing more advanced wireless sensors and smart analytics to improve agricultural production and management aspects. It is a ground-breaking concept that has been applied all over the world to boost productivity, reduce labour costs, and guarantee optimal fertiliser and water management. In order to avoid interfering with agriculture activity above ground, WSNs must be deployed underground. They could be used to collect information on variables related to soil, such as nitrate content, moisture content, and other factors. PA makes considerable use of data and information to boost crop output, farming productivity, and agricultural production. PA is a modern approach to crop management and agricultural growth that enables farmers to maximise inputs like water and fertiliser to raise production, quality, and productivity. To aid farmers in managing their operations, a vast amount of data at high spatial resolution is needed, which saves resources and benefits society (Vijayakumar & Rosario, 2011).

1. Field research can have far-reaching effects.
2. Fostering a culture of inquiry and participation.
3. The emphasis of suggestions should be on quantity, administration, knowledge, and spatial flexibility.
4. Advanced results are produced by PA research and development.

By integrating contemporary technologies and lowering the quantity of conventional inputs needed to develop crops, PA seeks to boost agricultural yields and profitability. Farmers can plant crops in more effective patterns and move from point A to point B with more accuracy with the use of GPS devices and lasers. This will help them apply water more effectively and reduce farm effluent discharge. This might lower the cost of agriculture and increase the availability of food. Predictive analytics software uses PA as a technique for obtaining data on crop, soil, and ambient temperature variables to provide farmers with guidance on crop rotation, planting and harvesting schedules, and soil management (Boopathi et al., 2023; Kumara et al., 2023; Vanitha et al., 2023). The digital transformation of the agriculture sector is a top priority to address the numerous difficulties faced in the fields. In order to achieve fine-grid crop management, two strategies—PA and smart farming—that combine cutting-edge technology with conventional agricultural methods may lead in this direction. PA systems might provide farmers with insightful scientific data on their farms, enhancing their competitiveness and earnings. The agriculture industry almost in its entirety may gain from technological improvements (Zhang & Kovacs, 2012).

Time to first node death, time to half node death, time to Last node death, time to ten percent node death, etc. are used to measure the lifespan of WSNs. Clustering is used to divide the network into non-overlapping clusters with one CH in order to optimise economic value. The effectiveness of clustering depends on choosing CHs from among all nodes, which might result in an unbalanced grouping and energy loss, which causes nodes to fail sooner. There have been attempts to balance energy loss across the network, but none of these have been deemed ideal. The performance of present clustering methods is outperformed by fuzziness in network parameters, which is why clustering protocols are not modified based on application requirements (Anand ct al., 2021; Li et al., 2008).

Energy conservation is crucial since sensor nodes run on batteries. Energy-saving routing methods include energy harvesting, energy balancing, energy efficient MACs, and duty cycle scheduling. Energy-efficient routing algorithms must be able to accommodate changes in topology and mobility. QoS-aware WSN routing protocols are suggested. Although there are proposed WSN routing methods for a variety of factors, this work focuses on precision agriculture, which necessitates continuous sensing and transmission as well as real-time monitoring. To enable real-time monitoring of agricultural fields, an energy-efficient routing protocol must be created. Research has been done on sensor network application requirements, such as knowing where you are in a field of interest so you may make an informed decision regarding farming.

By extrapolating the distance between two nodes from the received signal strength indicator, localization without GPS is made possible. Both uncertainty and approximation errors are present in this process. Uncertainty-based problems can be solved using soft computing approaches, including genetic algorithms, fuzzy logic, neural networks, and ant colony optimization. Accuracy, processing overhead, node density, the number of anchor nodes, and other variables all affect how well localization algorithms perform. In WSN, localization algorithms can be distributed or centralised. While distributed algorithms offer better scalability and cheaper communication costs, centralised algorithms are suited for situations that demand the utmost accuracy (S. et al., 2022; Sampath et al., 2022). Localization in ambient and noisy environments, security during localization, localization in mobile wireless sensor networks (MWSN), and localization in three-dimensional space are some of the localization research problems. It is important to consider variables like scalability, mobility, and heterogeneous data traffic. Human society depends heavily on agriculture, which uses a variety of additional strategies and techniques to create food. In order to provide an ideal substitute for gathering and putting information to use to increase agricultural output, innovative methodology and problem-solving approaches might be given in the field of agriculture. Water scarcity and worrisome weather changes call for new and improved methods of mistreating agriculture. In agriculture, WSNs are becoming more commonplace, motivating creative ways to make informed judgments. The development of technology-based precision agriculture has received approval from the International Society of Precision Agriculture (Nayyar & Singh, 2015).

PA collects, uses, executes, and evaluates time-based, spatial, and discrete data in order to assess effectiveness, profitability, quantity, productivity, quality, and stable sustainability. To maximise crop output while reducing environmental impact, agricultural inputs, including water, fertiliser, pesticides, and other chemicals, are applied in precise proportions determined by crop development pattern modelling. Numerous factors, including changes in plant population, nitrogen mineralization, water stress, soil properties, pests, and more, have an impact on fertiliser uptake in a field. Pesticides must be used in accordance with the needs of the crop; otherwise, they risk polluting groundwater and surface water resources. Data from soil sensing and subsequent analysis can be used to comprehend the carbon sequestration process, which is regarded to be a strategy to prevent climate change (Jawad et al., 2017).

Precision Agriculture (PA) in India

The use of precision farming will increase agricultural output while decreasing the use of chemicals, maximising the use of water, mapping yield and soil characteristics, disseminating information about agricultural practises, and minimising resource waste. Smaller plots can be created on uneven terrain, improving resource management and lowering resource waste. PA technology has the potential to boost the Indian economy, boost output, and make better use of resources. enhanced crop quality, profitability, scalability, on-farm living standards, environmental protection, food security, and rural economic expansion. Applications of water, insecticides, and fertilisers can reduce production costs and chemical contamination in plantations growing wheat, cotton, and palm oil. With the help of predictive analytics, farmers may anticipate and avoid issues like water stress, nutritional shortages, and pests/diseases. Agriculture is bringing forth new methods for measuring multi-functional properties and growing prospects for expert service (Mondal, 2011; Mondal & Basu, 2009).

Precision Agriculture-Integrated IoT and WSN

The identification of pests and insects, the management of the environment and water resources, wireless data transmission, and plant disease control are the main topics of this research (Figure 1).

Figure 1. Schematics of smart precision agriculture system using IoT and WSN

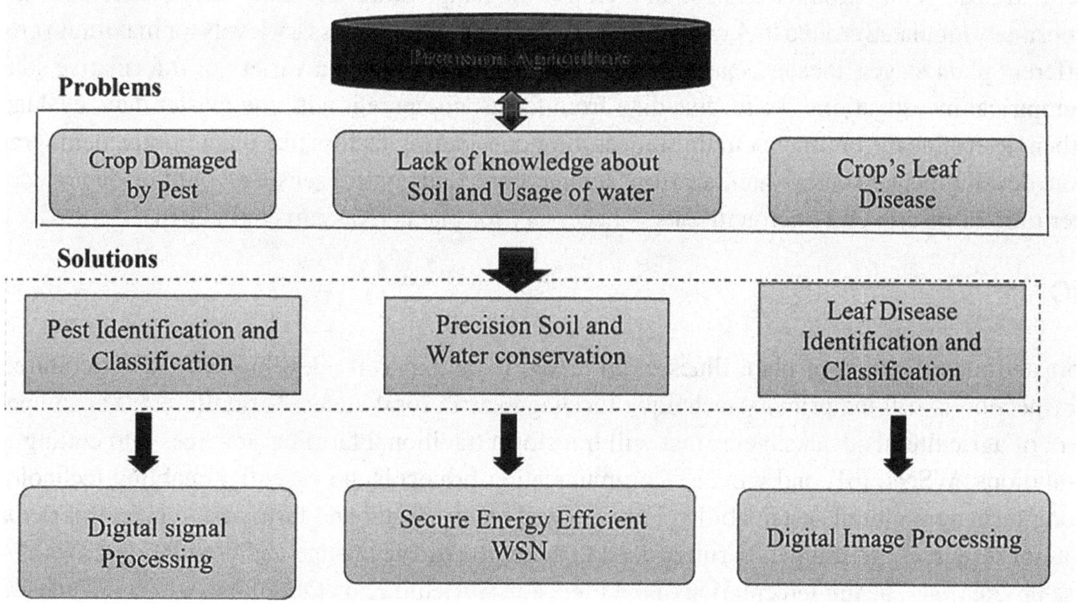

PAPIC

The suggested PA-PIC methodology is a cutting-edge approach to managing and controlling pests and insects. To identify and track resistant and deadly pests early on, it makes use of automatic detection and classification techniques as well as new technology. Farmers can study the spatial-temporal variability of a variety of critical characteristics that affect plant health and productivity using PA approaches. Systems for managing pests are being created to improve insect pest control by using fewer pesticides overall and concentrating on more precise dosage. In order to create a successful pest control strategy, it is also required to gather data on population dynamics and the ecological characteristics that are associated with them. Despite the development of precision farming technologies, horticulture and orchards were ignored in favour of focusing on arable farming. New technologies and autonomous detection traps to find and monitor pests early on. Systems for managing pests are being created to decrease the use of pesticides and increase the precision of treatment. It is important to gather data on population dynamics and the ecological characteristics that are associated with them in order for pest monitoring systems to be as effective as possible (Kasinathan & Uyyala, 2021; Kathole et al., 2022).

PSWCA

The scope of over- and under-irrigated areas, quantities subject to variable rate irrigation control, and the frequency of water management were the main topics of TAKCS. In order to evaluate the depths of water application, uniformity measurements were made using standard rain gauges. To evaluate transition zones, perpendicular evaluation lines to their boundaries were established. To evaluate how plant characteristics, respond to different water depths, grid shape and radial direction assessments were carried out. The most crucial point is that soil and water conservation in Pennsylvania should be taken carefully since young plants require careful nurturing. Additionally, they require moist soil surrounding their roots in order to absorb nutrients and water as well as promote free cell proliferation. A plant will become robust and healthy and produce an abundant crop if the temperature, humidity, and moisture levels are appropriately regulated around it. A comprehensive database of the necessary levels for maximum growth at different plant stages, locales, seasons, etc. would be created using a variety of informative sources and empirical investigations. To receive data from farms, compare it with the master data, evaluate it, and then determine the optimum circumstances after considering factors like plant family, demography, season, developmental stage: water, air flow, temperature, and control sensors would be deployed. The proper ratio of macro- and micronutrients is necessary for plants (Kassam et al., 2014).

PDIC

Automated identification of plant illnesses in leaves is an important development in agriculture, but eye inspection is still the primary technique for diagnosis in rural areas. Agriculture 4.0 is an upcoming era of agricultural advancements that will transform traditional farming practices into cutting-edge PA solutions. WSNs, IoT, and wireless communication protocols are essential enabling technologies for long-term agricultural sustainability. Farmers will require water and farmland to meet this demand, as natural resources are limited. Farmers need to adapt to climate change and population growth to increase production. The implementation of the Precision Agriculture methodology, which includes water conservation, forecasting capabilities, pest and insect management, crop leaf disease identification and classification, the deployment of energy-efficient wireless sensor networks, and secured communication, has a significant technical impact and potential growth for the marketing of agricultural products (Sahana et al., 2022; Sardogan et al., 2018).

Water Conservation and Fertilizer Using WSN

PA is utilising WSN to minimise the environmental impact of fertiliser use and maximise water conservation in order to feed the world's rising population. This idea offers farmers in Pennsylvania a WSN of inexpensive soil moisture sensor nodes to aid in the optimization of irrigation practises. Using ML approaches, a novel cloud-based IoT integration and WSNs methodology for PSWCA is proposed (Sahana et al., 2022; Sardogan et al., 2018).

Energy Efficient Using WSN

The next step in the research is to use the WSN-based IoT to give PA access to SEE-PA-IoT. Based on crucial QoS criteria, WSN applications must simultaneously assure security and energy efficiency. But because security typically reduces QoS, it can be difficult to provide both security and EE with WSNs. While still following security and EE criteria, a technique that is secure and efficient can use less energy (Jawad et al., 2017).

Leaf Disease Identification

The research's final goal is to recognise and categorise leaf diseases using ML. The type of disease that affects the crops is determined by the plant's leaves. Farmers can assess the leaf plant infection and act quickly. Advanced image processing might be a quick, reliable, and accurate way to find leaf plant diseases. For precise and effective diagnosis and classification of plant diseases, several advanced digital images processing approaches, including digital filtering, enhancement, clustering, thresholding, feature extraction, and classification using machine learning (ML), are involved (Jawad et al., 2017).

Current Methodology

The leaves of the plant reveal the type of disease that damages the crops. Farmers can assess the illness in the leaf plant and treat swiftly. Finding leaf plant diseases can be simple, dependable, and accurate with the help of advanced picture processing. The precise and effective detection and classification of plant diseases involves the use of a number of cutting-edge digital image processing techniques, such as digital filtering, enhancement, clustering, thresholding, feature extraction, and machine learning (ML) classification. The lack of information due to a lack of integration is a significant issue for farmers because it affects problem-solving in the greenhouse, SF decision-making, soil condition during plant growth, understanding water level, security, and energy efficiency of agriculture data during transmission, and monitoring well-grown plants from disease attack. This makes farming less profitable because of SF. The system may not be fully deployed for a few years because PA techniques are still being developed and need expert guidance.

PROPOSED METHODOLOGIES

The proposed methodology for Secured Energy Efficient Precision Agriculture is used to deliver precision and efficiency while also providing protection, monitoring, security, and control. It entails protecting the plant from dangerous pests and monitoring and controlling the pests using wireless communication, wireless protocols, wireless sensors, and pest monitoring techniques. To accomplish the goals, research and development are carried out in accordance with 4 organised phases.

Figure 2. Precision soil and water conservation agriculture using IoT

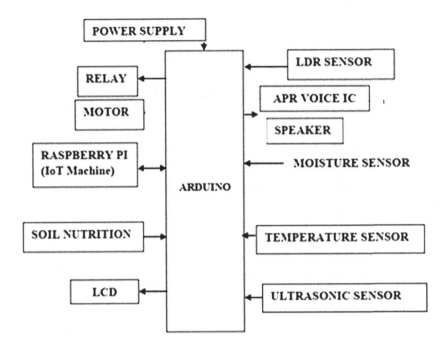

PIC

Ultrasonic acoustic signals from harmful pests and helpful insects would be gathered from different agricultural fields, filtered to remove noise and other disturbances, evaluated using DSP techniques, and then stored in a master database with fixed identification. In order to increase productivity, farmers would benefit from being able to shield seedlings from damaging pests and maintain helpful insects. In order to distinguish between dangerous pests and beneficial insects in greenhouse farming without endangering crops, a unique algorithm called PA-PIC has been presented. It uses an auditory sensor and recording system to assess the fundamental frequency of various pests and insects. To improve quality and eliminate all noise harmonics from noisy acoustic signals, acoustic signal augmentation is employed to filter and enhance the acoustic signal: Devices for recording acoustic signals can only record voice (pest, bug, automobile, wind, and additive white noise). The recording process uses a buffer of 32 GB of SD memory. When used for classification using DL, the MMSE HNE adaptive filter eliminates noise harmonics from the source acoustic signal. PA-PIC classifies audio signals using feature extraction and a noise reduction method called MMSE HNE. The greenhouse is open to the existence of beneficial insects as a form of pest defence (Kasinathan & Uyyala, 2021; Kathole et al., 2022).

PSWCA

To calculate the amount of water and fertiliser plants require, ML techniques, cloud enabled IoT integration, and WSNs are employed. Using the Microcontroller and Raspberry module, the entire PSWCA structure was connected, including each sensor and irrigation system. To predict how much water and fertiliser the plants will need for irrigation, a novel machine learning-based automated irrigation system employing IoT (MLAISIoT) method is suggested (Figure 2). The amount of water and fertiliser required by this MLAIS-IoT strategy is compared to the amount required by planned and automated watering in order to validate the suggested methodology. In this way, water logging can be prevented. The major goal of this study is to use wireless sensors to adopt effective PSWCA techniques in real time to achieve water savings and fertilisation. In contrast to traditional automation techniques, the system now employs ML techniques to accomplish robust automation. The PSWCA incorporates IoT technology to give farmers access to digital data from the agricultural sector. This facilitates remote monitoring and management of the agricultural field. In order to conserve water, the amount of water and fertiliser plants need is determined using the logistic regression (LR) technique and the machine learning (ML) algorithm. Another option is remote access (Mondal, 2011; Vijayakumar & Rosario, 2011).

SEE-PA-IoT

IoT-based WSN has been used in agricultural production to automate PA utilising multiple sensors and monitor yield conditions. In order to validate the suggested methodology, the quantity of water and fertiliser was compared to that required by scheduled and regulated watering. Results showed that the suggested method used less water, fertiliser, and automatic irrigation than expected. The Internet of Things (IoT), which collects and communicates copious amounts of data about tangible and intangible objects, including wireless sensors and physical gadgets, has been studied. WSNs are crucial parts of IoT communication because they gather relevant data and distribute it to users through various IoT communication channels. This method helps plants develop properly and achieves the highest level of conservation possible given the soil and surrounding conditions.

WSN nodes are frequently powered by batteries, which leads to an uneven distribution of energy. The algorithms create continuous adaptive lighting management that satisfies client demands while consuming less energy from lightbulbs. Smart LED lighting with Internet of Things (IoT) capabilities communicates with mobile sensors to determine brightness, colour intensity, or colour temperature. In order to collect data and identify anomalies in real time, IoT sensing devices that can run close sensor ML algorithms have been studied. Methods using near-sensing neural networks may quickly recognise coding moths (Anand et al., 2021; Jawad et al., 2017).

WSNs were suggested as a solution for resource optimization, decision support, and land management in agriculture. They enable PA to increase yield by giving current information about field activity and crop health. To safeguard the sent data, the updated version of precise security and energy efficiency should be used. It is advisable to implement parameters like the likelihood of a false alarm, energy efficiency, detection likelihood, latency, throughput, packet loss, and signal-to-noise ratio. PA seeks to utilise agricultural resources, cut labour expenses, and improve agricultural products' productivity and quality. It makes use of digital technology to identify variations in conditions and modify resource allocations to instantly fulfil crop demands (Anand et al., 2021).

PDIC

Plants can get sick, and there are many different plant diseases that can thwart their organic growth. Reliable disease identification is crucial for accurate plant pathogen diagnosis and control. The existing system uses human input for illness classification and identification, however, computational intelligence-based automatic disease segmentation from photos of plant leaves may be more useful than the current approach. To develop a 2D adaptive digital filter, noises like black-and-white noise, Gaussian noise, random noise, speckle noise, etc. should be eliminated from raw leaf images (2D-ADF). Once all noise has been eliminated, the image should be improved. When developing the segmentation algorithm, the region of interest (ROI) must be segmented (Rothe & Kshirsagar, 2015; Sahana et al., 2022). Different sorts of features should be identified, and DNN testing should be performed to evaluate whether an image is normal, abnormal, mildly abnormal, abnormal, moderately abnormal, or abnormal. The filter is used during pre-processing to take out different sounds from the photos. The Region of Interest is extracted and non-ROI is suppressed using the Hybrid Fast Fuzzy Improved Expectation Maximization Clustering method, while the contrast and brightness of the image are improved. The segmented region of interest is subsequently divided into four classes using deep convolutional neural networks: normal, mild, moderate, and severe. Changing seasonal conditions might cause crops to contract illnesses. The quality and quantity of the crop are impacted by these diseases, which begin by attacking the plant's leaves before spreading throughout the entire plant. Due to the vast number of plants in the field, it is challenging to detect and classify each plant's illness. The significance of early disease identification for maximising agricultural output has been discussed using software to classify groundnut leaf illnesses, the leaf skeletons used to find grape leaf infections. Through image collection, pre-processing, segmentation, extraction, and KNN, KNN increases agricultural productivity. Crop diseases have been identified as a significant barrier to success. This research attempts to produce a more accurate classification system. An ML approach has been used to better diagnose and categorise plant diseases. To improve segmentation, it combines thresholding and morphological techniques.

Benefits

The PA approach increases crop quality and productivity while reducing negative effects on the environment. PA offers an economical solution to categorise pests and insects, use less fertiliser, and boost seed production in agricultural areas. Farmers Edge delivers a high-value solution at a reasonable price to increase yields while reducing costs. By using strip tilling, irrigation, and soil nutrient monitoring to generate higher-quality production, precision farming enhances yields and profit margins. Due to the increased volume of agricultural products, it also boosts profit margins, making it easier to negotiate a higher price when selling the commodity.

PSWCA

A system of constant monitoring and control is advised for plant growth in order to provide high yields. In the past, water supplies relied on the water mill to irrigate the field, which resulted in water waste and crop devastation. However, modern technological developments have made it possible for effective irrigation systems that don't need human assistance. A novel method for cloud-enabled IoT collaboration of WSNs for PSWCA is provided through the use of machine learning (ML) (Vijayakumar & Rosario, 2011).

Wireless Sensors

A wireless sensor is a piece of equipment that gathers sensory information and recognises alterations in the environment, including changes in the air temperature, light levels, soil nutrition, motions, and liquid leaks. It takes extremely little energy for wireless sensors to function, and they can last for years on a single battery. Passive sensors are independent systems that respond to inputs from their environment without the requirement for an external power source. While passive sensors don't need additional electricity to monitor their environment, active sensors do. Environmental variables can be monitored over a vast region with the use of wireless sensors. Gateways fill the gap by acting as both routers and wireless access points (Babu et al., 2022; Boopathi et al., 2022; Chakravarthi et al., 2022; Jeevanantham et al., 2022).

Wireless Air Sensor: Homeowners can detect heating system problems or gauge relative humidity by using active sensors to assess the environment's humidity, temperature, and particles. Air sensors can be used to control room temperature, monitor HVAC operation, and spot problems with refrigeration.

Soil Moisture Sensor: For plants to thrive and regulate their own temperature, soil moisture is necessary. Although roots grow more quickly in moist soil when plants are growing there, excessive soil moisture can also cause air pollution and the spread of soil illnesses.

Temperature and Humidity Sensor: To ascertain the actual level of air humidity at any time and place, humidity sensors, also known as hygrometers, are utilised. They are utilised when the air quality needs to be controlled or when it is extremely bad. Wireless temperature sensors can discover frozen pipes and inform homeowners to potential problems by detecting ambient and material temperatures (Boopathi et al., 2022; Chakravarthi et al., 2022; Gunasekaran et al., 2022; Sampath et al., 2022).

Ultrasonic Sensors: A gadget called an ultrasonic sensor uses high frequency sound waves to measure the separation between two targets and transforms the redirected sound into an electrical signal. In ultrasonic sensors, the broadcaster and recipient are the two most crucial parts. The HVAC system has an air quality sensor that scans the air outside of moving vehicles for pollutants in the form of recoverable or oxidising gases, such as carbon monoxide, compounds, and partially damaged fuel elements. The microcontroller board is equipped with input/output connectors, analogue input pins, crystal clock, a communication device, a power connection, an electronic system, and a restart button. It can be powered by a battery, an AC-to-DC converter, or a USB connection to a computer. The sensors indicate the need for water, and the Arduino microcontroller uses this information to activate a 5-volt DC motor and supply the water to the agricultural field (Boopathi, 2022; Boopathi et al., 2022; Jeevanantham et al., 2022; S. et al., 2022; Sampath et al., 2022).

Wireless Sensor Networks (WSNs)

Self-configuring wireless networks, or WSNs, monitor ambient factors including temperature, sound, acoustic noise, barrier characteristics, mobility, and particles and transmit their data to a centralised site or sink for analysis. A sink is a device that serves as a link between system users, enabling them to request and receive responses from the sink in order to access crucial information from the network. The differential irrigation systems, data and information for watering application, and the effects of variable irrigation. In order to connect sensor nodes with one another, and radio communications. Each sensor node was built with different processing power, storage capacity, and networking capabilities. Sensor nodes self-organize, gather information, follow commands, and sense samples (Jawad et al., 2017).

In their study, the authors explore the idea of "smart monitoring and measurement" (WSN), which has applications in tracking and managing the environment, agriculture, medicine, and mobility. In order to improve network performance and power consumption, a hardware platform that uses radios. PA system with ideal temperature, moisture, soil temperature, humidity, and luminosity ranges to communicate information and explain soil conditions. A smart sensor system with actuators was suggested to improve precision farming performance. The smart board supports action instructions and farm monitoring. In order to boost agricultural productivity to satisfy rising food demand, IoT technology has altered business, particularly smart agriculture and precision agriculture. With downsides, these advances are upending conventional farming methods and creating new opportunities. Farm administration data systems enable the computerization of data collecting, monitoring and regulation, documentation, planning, decision-making, and oversight (Nayyar & Singh, 2015; Nikolidakis et al., 2015).

Novelty of the Proposed Methodology

Inputs and outputs are controlled by an Arduino Uno microcontroller, which utilises a power supply unit to convert 230 V AC electricity to 5 V DC. A microcontroller called Arduino Uno is used to manage wireless sensors like moisture, temperature, soil nutrition, and motors. To control a motor, it is connected to a relay device. The power source for Arduino boards can be a battery, USB cable, AC adapter, or other regulated power source. A rule-based Fertilization and irrigation system was created by Yousif et al. (2018) to track and manage soil quality and plant food supply. The statistics that are currently available to describe PA adoption practises at the national and regional level were evaluated. In-field heterogeneity can be handled with the use of precision agriculture technologies (PATs). The policy and consulting communities have promoted PATs as a strategy to protect natural capital while boosting agricultural land productivity. The level of adoption varies by region and technology, with the majority of studies concentrating on the US or Australia. IoT is the best option, for smart water management systems. Three prediction models to determine soil moisture content in an hour using the IoT and DSS. Agriculture relies heavily on precision irrigation to manage water use and influence crop health, cost, and output. A precision irrigation system for PA-based WSN that helps prevent water wastage and is crucial owing to water scarcity was developed using ML training and testing. A WSN was used to design a specialised irrigation system for crops that controlled water usage according to environmental factors. A soil moisture sensor-based irrigation system is controlled by an ATMEGA 328P on an Arduino UNO board, and sensor data is sent to the cloud and visualised. A website was made to track the water's condition, and a real-time prototype of a personalised irrigation system employed temperature and soil moisture sensors to determine the water level in the soil. A water sprinkler network equipped with temperature, wetness, and moisture sensors is employed to deliver data to the cloud while providing precise irrigation. The placement of the sensor had an impact on accuracy, and ZigBee capabilities were employed for communication. Obstacles, the necessity for software and hardware, ZigBee capabilities, and sensor location all played a role in communication. Real-time irrigation system needs for hardware and software, challenges, and advantages were discussed.

The use of WSN and IoT has been suggested for a number of fertilisation methods. In order to evaluate soil nutrition, wireless sensors are suggested as a part of an automated fertilisation system. There were three components to the system: input, output, and predictive modelling. On the basis of real-time sensory data collected by the sensors, the decision-making support module assessed the right number of fertilisers. An IEEE 802.11 Wi-Fi device and GPS were utilised for connectivity. Real-time information on the soil's humidity, temperatures, conductivity, NO_2, CO_2, and other elements was gathered by a number of sensors.

Data Science Management: To ensure data integrity, sensors on PA must be accurate because false readings can impair process efficiency. To guarantee accuracy, information security procedures must be put in place. Large volumes of data are produced by PA systems, increasing the need for compute and storage. To handle big data sources, new software tools and frameworks are required, and cloud computing is being utilised to combine data administration with IoT.

Learning Adoption of PA: In low-income countries with high rates of illiteracy, farmers plant crops based on their prior knowledge, which decreases their efficiency and hinders them from having access to resources and education.

5G Connectivity: In comparison to 4G networks, 5G networks have the potential to be 100 times quicker, making them perfect for sending data from far sensors and offering real-time data upkeep and decision support.

Compatibility: Device interoperability, which is impeding the adoption and expansion of IoT technologies as well as production efficiency through precision agricultural solutions, is PA's main worry. New strategies and protocols are required to fully realise the potential of machine-to-machine data exchange.

SEE-PA-IoT

The third step is SEE-PA-IoT. With the use of programmable and simple-to-configure environmental sensors, WSN technology has been effectively used to boost network performance. With the help of gateways and CHs, sensor nodes can independently design their own network architecture while in use. Sensor nodes collect the monitoring data, which is then transmitted to the base station, where the CHs gather and forward network packets to the BS. To receive the relevant observational values, end users use web-based applications or the Internet to access the centrally stored BS. However, stationary sensors are not appropriate for large areas or network scalability. Dynamic load balancing techniques are more secure. To improve network speed, resource consumption, and load capacity, IoT technology has been integrated with various industries. As part of the Internet of Things, numerous physical objects are linked to the web.

However, stationary sensors are not appropriate for large areas or network scalability. Dynamic load balancing techniques are more secure. To improve network speed, resource consumption, and load capacity, IoT technology has been integrated with various industries. As part of the Internet of Things, numerous physical objects are linked to the web. To achieve quality of service, security and EE-QoS must be coupled in WSN-based PA (QoS). Environmental sensors gather crucial data as part of a proposed IoT-based WSN infrastructure for PA, and CHs are selected using a multi-criteria classification algorithm. Signal intensity is measured in SNR (signal to noise ratio) in dB, and data transfer from field sensors to the base station (BS) is secure due to stable emission periodicity. The following QoS parameters are enhanced: Peak average power ratio (PAPR) minimization, packet delivery ratio (PDR), packet loss estimation, bandwidth in Mbits/Joules/Sec, and capacity maximisation in Mbits/Sec.

WSNs are a good choice for Software Defined Radio (SDR) networks because of their energy restrictions and effective routing protocols. Clustering is a practical method for making WSNs last longer. A data-driven PA management technique used to increase quality and output. Wireless sensors can be used to create a farming sector that is both extremely effective and environmentally benign. PA can be increased in the field by supplying the proper nutrients and minimising chemical waste for effective weed, insect, and disease control. The WSN, devices, IoT, data science, and analysis tools are being used to design and create a PA system for advanced agriculture with improved power regulation and self-charging capabilities. WSN-SLAP, a secure and lightweight mutual authentication technique that is resistant to security issues and offers full forwarding confidentiality and authentication procedures, was presented. To prove safety, Burrows-Abadi-Needham logic is employed. In IP-enabled WSNs, access management to sensor nodes is required to enhance secure access and protect user access privacy.

Smart applications may now be created thanks to IP technology, however, to ensure safe access and maintain user access secrecy, access control to sensor nodes is required. A CHRotations approach was suggested by Rami Ahmad et al. in 2021 to improve the effectiveness of anomaly detection and assess WSN node traffic. The average predictive performance of 2 percent, 5 percent, and 3 percent was best for the WC classification algorithm. LEACH enhanced with deterministic cluster formation, suggested by Zahid et al. in 2021, surpasses LEACH and direct transmission techniques in terms of network lifetime and congestion overhead. Cluster-Based Energy Optimization with Mobility Sink was proposed by Qian Wei et al. in 2021. (CEOMS). The mobile sink's reflectivity movement efficiency feature enhances the possibility that far-off sensor nodes will be allocated as cluster heads, but CEOMS allocates sensor nodes with higher residual energy as cluster heads. To reduce cluster head allocation at random, the hierarchical clustering technique incorporates the total energy measure and movement performance measure. For cluster-based WSNs, ESPDA is a secure data aggregation method that is coupled with a LEACH-based security system. It has undergone testing for security, connection, and algorithmic analysis complexity.

LEACH-eXtended Message-Passing (LEACH-XMP) was planned to enhance a clustering optimization technique for WSN activities. It considers a nonlinear energy demand model, which makes clustering optimization challenging. The main benefits of the proposed approach are that it can be applied in a practical environment and that it quickly converges to a pretty accurate result. By choosing the least number of sensor nodes for complete coverage, connection, and energy consumption of the sensor network, enhanced genetic algorithm (GA)-based scheduling can maximise efficiency and speed resolution. Two-phase data transmission and cluster heads are chosen using a security framework, and a hybrid technique combining a particle swarm optimization method, Taguchi, RSM, and a genetic algorithm is used to select data transmission channels. Experiments were conducted (Boopathi, 2013, 2022; Boopathi et al., 2021; Boopathi & Sivakumar, 2013; Sampath & Myilsamy, 2021; Yupapin et al., 2022).

LEACH-eXtended Message-Passing is applied to enhance a clustering optimization technique for WSN activities. Clustering optimization is challenging because it considers a non-linear energy demand model. By choosing the fewest number of sensor nodes and the network's complete coverage, connection, and energy usage, improved genetic algorithm (GA)-based scheduling can boost effectiveness and hasten resolution.

The suggested method offers an IoT-based WSN for farmland monitoring and production that is both safe and energy-efficient. The SNR factor is utilised to calculate the wireless signal strength and the permissible sensor packet ratio, and the optimum decision function is used to choose cluster heads. Sensor networking makes use of wireless sensors to gather environmental data and transfer it securely to the BS for wise decision-making. The CHs act as storage or memory buffers for data transmitted to the BS, giving users access to the most recent information possible to make an effective decision with the least amount of farming effort. Agricultural sensors efficiently and securely transmit observational data to BS, enhancing land management and profitability.

BEESP

Wireless sensors for agricultural fields are dispersed over a sizable area, with a cluster head at each place. The CH's role is to collect data from the farmland and convey it responsibly and sparingly to the BS. The proposed method reduces network congestion and latency by allocating agriculture sensors and selecting cluster heads using a multi-criteria classification algorithm. To ensure dependable transmission in the field, it also makes use of encryption technologies.

Uses of BEESP

By combining data and avoiding congestion, BEESP lowers network traffic.

By routing from nodes to cluster heads, BEESP decreases energy consumption, lengthens the lifespan of the wireless sensor network, and is entirely distributed, requiring no external control information or global knowledge. It is an intuitive WSN.

QoS Improvement WSN-Based IoT

In resource-based WSNs, QoS is crucial for increased QoS efficiency and acceptable routing algorithms, just as efficient and acceptable routing depend on dependable and low energy use. To improve the energy efficiency of WSNs and make better use of the constrained energy resources of sensor nodes, a novel algorithm known as BEESP has been proposed. To prevent unnecessary cluster head delivery, BEESP is calculated based on energy usage and compared to traditional methods. In terms of EE, false alarm likelihood, packet transfer to the base station, and curve-based deployment, BEESP performs better than competing protocols. As an application-specific protocol for WSNs, LEACH is suggested. With the use of cluster building and data transmission techniques, the BEESP protocol is proposed to increase the energy efficiency of the WSN by accounting for both the available node energy and the average energy of the network. Compared to non-clustering protocols, cluster-based routing algorithms make greater use of the network's SNs, with the CH in charge of erasing connected data (Jawad et al., 2017).

Cluster-based networking techniques split SNs into several clusters to minimise energy consumption and balance node load, extending network life and boosting energy efficiency. The majority of clustering algorithms use optimal CH selection to prolong the lifespan of the network and prevent SNs from dying too soon. BEESP is a framework protocol stack for WSNs that saves energy but would require more if CH distribution weren't considered. This study suggests a novel enhanced routing method that considers continuous cluster energy and aggregate network energy to enhance EE in the WSN. It ensures the ideal CH count and avoids clusters near the BS from balancing. In order to maximise channel energy utilisation, it also applies a constraint between the sensor network and the CHs to select the CHs, mixing single-hop, multi-hop, and combination connections. The majority of clustering algorithms use optimal CH selection to prolong the lifespan of the network and prevent SNs from dying too soon. BEESP is a framework protocol stack for WSNs that saves energy but would require more if CH distribution weren't considered. This study suggests a novel enhanced routing method that considers continuous cluster energy and aggregate network energy to enhance EE in the WSN. It ensures the ideal CH count and avoids clusters near the BS from balancing. In order to maximise channel energy utilisation, it also applies a constraint between the sensor network and the CHs to select the CHs, mixing single-hop, multi-hop, and combination connections.

SUMMARY

The Internet of Things (IoT) and wireless sensor networks (WSN) can be used in precision agriculture (PA) to more effectively monitor crop fields and make timely decisions. To collect relevant data, the sensors can be deployed in crop fields, although doing so consumes part of their limited energy. Location-aware sensors, safe localization methods, and energy-efficient operations are all required for the application of IoT and WSN in smart precision agriculture. In this chapter, IoT and WSN technologies are used to identify and solve agricultural issues. Through pest identification and categorization, soil and water conservation, and leaf issues, the best solutions to pest problems, a shortage of water supply, and leaf diseases can be found. In the IoT and WSN, the integration of Arduino and other sensors is used to automatically fix problems. Using IoT and sensor systems with effective programmes, energy conservation can be ensured.

REFERENCES

Anand, S. J., Selvi, G. A., Poornima, D., & Vedanarayanan, V. (2021). Iot-Based Secure And Energy Efficient Scheme For Precision Agriculture Using Blockchain And Improved Leach Algorithm. *Turkish Journal of Computer and Mathematics Education*, *12*(10), 2466–2475.

Babu, B. S., Kamalakannan, J., Meenatchi, N., Karthik, S., & Boopathi, S. (2022). Economic impacts and reliability evaluation of battery by adopting Electric Vehicle. *IEEE Explore*, 1–6.

Boopathi, S. (2013). Experimental study and multi-objective optimization of near-dry wire-cut electrical discharge machining process. *Shodhganga@INFLIBNET*. http://hdl.handle.net/10603/16933

Boopathi, S. (2022). Experimental investigation and multi-objective optimization of cryogenic Friction-stir-welding of AA2014 and AZ31B alloys using MOORA technique. *Materials Today. Communications*, *33*, 104937. doi:10.1016/j.mtcomm.2022.104937

Boopathi, S., Arigela, S. H., Raman, R., Indhumathi, C., Kavitha, V., & Bhatt, B. C. (2022). Prominent Rule Control-based Internet of Things: Poultry Farm Management System. *IEEE Explore*, 1–6.

Boopathi, S., Jeyakumar, M., Singh, G. R., King, F. L., Pandian, M., Subbiah, R., & Haribalaji, V. (2022). An experimental study on friction stir processing of aluminium alloy (AA-2024) and boron nitride (BNp) surface composite. *Materials Today: Proceedings*, *59*, 1094–1099. doi:10.1016/j.matpr.2022.02.435

BoopathiS.MyilsamyS.SukkasamyS. (2021). Experimental Investigation and Multi-Objective Optimization of Cryogenically Cooled Near-Dry Wire-Cut EDM Using TOPSIS Technique. *Ijamt Preprint*. doi:10.21203/rs.3.rs-254117/v1

Boopathi, S., Siva Kumar, P. K., Meena, R. S. J., S. I., P., S. K., & Sudhakar, M. (2023). Sustainable Developments of Modern Soil-Less Agro-Cultivation Systems. In Human Agro-Energy Optimization for Business and Industry (pp. 69–87). IGI Global. doi:10.4018/978-1-6684-4118-3.ch004

Boopathi, S., & Sivakumar, K. (2013). Experimental investigation and parameter optimization of near-dry wire-cut electrical discharge machining using multi-objective evolutionary algorithm. *International Journal of Advanced Manufacturing Technology*, *67*(9–12), 2639–2655. doi:10.100700170-012-4680-4

Chakravarthi, P. K., Yuvaraj, D., & Venkataramanan, V. (2022). IoT-based smart energy meter for smart grids. *ICDCS 2022 - 2022 6th International Conference on Devices, Circuits and Systems*, 360–363. 10.1109/ICDCS54290.2022.9780714

Gunasekaran, K., Boopathi, S., & Sureshkumar, M. (2022). Analysis of a Cryogenically Cooled Near-Dry Wedm Process Using Different Dielectrics. *Materiali in Tehnologije*, *56*(2), 179–186. doi:10.17222/mit.2022.397

Jawad, H. M., Nordin, R., Gharghan, S. K., Jawad, A. M., & Ismail, M. (2017). Energy-efficient wireless sensor networks for precision agriculture: A review. *Sensors (Basel)*, *17*(8), 1781. doi:10.339017081781 PMID:28771214

Jeevanantham, Y. A., Saravanan, A., Vanitha, V., Boopathi, S., & Kumar, D. P. (2022). Implementation of Internet-of Things (IoT) in Soil Irrigation System. *IEEE Explore*, 1–5.

Kasinathan, T., & Uyyala, S. R. (2021). Machine learning ensemble with image processing for pest identification and classification in field crops. *Neural Computing & Applications*, *33*(13), 7491–7504. doi:10.100700521-020-05497-z

Kassam, A., Derpsch, R., & Friedrich, T. (2014). Global achievements in soil and water conservation: The case of Conservation Agriculture. *International Soil and Water Conservation Research*, *2*(1), 5–13. doi:10.1016/S2095-6339(15)30009-5

Kathole, A. B., Vhatkar, K. N., & Patil, S. D. (2022). IoT-Enabled Pest Identification and Classification with New Meta-Heuristic-Based Deep Learning Framework. *Cybernetics and Systems*, 1–29. doi:10.1080/01969722.2022.2122001

Kumara, V., Mohanaprakash, T. A., Fairooz, S., Jamal, K., Babu, T., & B., S. (2023). Experimental Study on a Reliable Smart Hydroponics System. In *Human Agro-Energy Optimization for Business and Industry* (pp. 27–45). IGI Global. doi:10.4018/978-1-6684-4118-3.ch002

Li, X., Deng, Y., & Ding, L. (2008). Study on precision agriculture monitoring framework based on WSN. *2nd International Conference on Anti-Counterfeiting, Security and Identification, ASID 2008*, 182–185. 10.1109/IWASID.2008.4688381

Mondal, P. (2011). Critical Review of Precision Agriculture Technologies and Its Scope of Adoption in India. *American Journal of Experimental Agriculture*, *1*(3), 49–68. doi:10.9734/AJEA/2011/155

Mondal, P., & Basu, M. (2009). Adoption of precision agriculture technologies in India and in some developing countries: Scope, present status and strategies. *Progress in Natural Science*, *19*(6), 659–666. doi:10.1016/j.pnsc.2008.07.020

Nayyar, A., & Singh, R. (2015). A Comprehensive Review of Simulation Tools for Wireless Sensor Networks (WSNs). *Journal of Wireless Networking and Communications*, *5*(1), 19–47.

Nikolidakis, S. A., Kandris, D., Vergados, D. D., & Douligeris, C. (2015). Energy efficient automated control of irrigation in agriculture by using wireless sensor networks. *Computers and Electronics in Agriculture*, *113*, 154–163. doi:10.1016/j.compag.2015.02.004

Rothe, P. R., & Kshirsagar, R. V. (2015). Cotton leaf disease identification using pattern recognition techniques. *2015 International Conference on Pervasive Computing: Advance Communication Technology and Application for Society, ICPC 2015*, 1–6. 10.1109/PERVASIVE.2015.7086983

S., P. K., Sampath, B., R., S. K., Babu, B. H., & N., A. (2022). Hydroponics, Aeroponics, and Aquaponics Technologies in Modern Agricultural Cultivation. In *Trends, Paradigms, and Advances in Mechatronics Engineering* (pp. 223–241). IGI Global. doi:10.4018/978-1-6684-5887-7.ch012

Sahana, M., Reshma, H., Pavithra, R., & Kavya, B. S. (2022). Plant Leaf Disease Detection Using Image Processing. *Lecture Notes in Electrical Engineering*, *789*(9), 161–168. doi:10.1007/978-981-16-1338-8_14

Sampath, B., & Myilsamy, S. (2021). Experimental investigation of a cryogenically cooled oxygen-mist near-dry wire-cut electrical discharge machining process. *Strojniski Vestnik. Jixie Gongcheng Xuebao*, *67*(6), 322–330. doi:10.5545v-jme.2021.7161

Sampath, B., Pandian, M., Deepa, D., & Subbiah, R. (2022). Operating parameters prediction of liquefied petroleum gas refrigerator using simulated annealing algorithm. *AIP Conference Proceedings*, *2460*(1), 070003. doi:10.1063/5.0095601

Sampath, B., Yuvaraj, D., & Velmurugan, D. (2022). Parametric analysis of mould sand properties for flange coupling casting. *AIP Conference Proceedings*, *2460*(1), 070002. doi:10.1063/5.0095599

Sampath, B. C. S., & Myilsamy, S. (2022). Application of TOPSIS Optimization Technique in the Micro-Machining Process. In Trends, Paradigms, and Advances in Mechatronics Engineering (pp. 162–187). IGI Global. doi:10.4018/978-1-6684-5887-7.ch009

Sardogan, M., Tuncer, A., & Ozen, Y. (2018). Plant Leaf Disease Detection and Classification Based on CNN with LVQ Algorithm. *UBMK 2018 - 3rd International Conference on Computer Science and Engineering*, 382–385. 10.1109/UBMK.2018.8566635

Vanitha, S. K. R., & Boopathi, S. (2023). Artificial Intelligence Techniques in Water Purification and Utilization. In *Human Agro-Energy Optimization for Business and Industry* (pp. 202–218). IGI Global. doi:10.4018/978-1-6684-4118-3.ch010

Vijayakumar, S., & Rosario, J. N. (2011). Preliminary design for crop monitoring involving water and fertilizer conservation using wireless sensor networks. *2011 IEEE 3rd International Conference on Communication Software and Networks, ICCSN 2011*, 662–666. 10.1109/ICCSN.2011.6014979

Yupapin, P., Trabelsi, Y., Nattappan, A., & Boopathi, S. (2022). Performance Improvement of Wire-Cut Electrical Discharge Machining Process Using Cryogenically Treated Super-Conductive State of Monel-K500 Alloy. *Iranian Journal of Science and Technology - Transactions of Mechanical Engineering*, 1–17. doi:10.1007/s40997-022-00513-0

Zhang, C., & Kovacs, J. M. (2012). The application of small unmanned aerial systems for precision agriculture: A review. *Precision Agriculture*, *13*(6), 693–712. doi:10.100711119-012-9274-5

APPENDIX: ACRONYMS

BEESP: Balanced Energy Efficient Secured Protocol
CH: Cultural Heritage
GPS: Global Positioning System
MACs: Medium Access Control
ML: Machine Learning
PAPIC: Precision Agriculture-Pest Identification and Classification
PDIC: Plant Leaf Disease Identification and Classification
PIC: Pest Identification and Classification
PSWCA: Precision Soil and Water Conservation Agriculture
QoS: Quality-of-Service
SEE-PA-IoT: Secured Energy Efficient Precision Agriculture Using IoT
SF: Smart Farming

Chapter 27
Architecture and Framework for Interfacing Cloud–Enabled Robots

B. Srinivas
Kakatiya Institute of Technology and Science, India

Lakshmana Phaneendra Maguluri
Koneru Lakshmaiah Education Foundation, India

K. Venkatagurunatham Naidu
Guntur Engineering College, India

L. Chandra Sekhar Reddy
CMR College of Engineering and Technology, India

M. Deivakani
PSNA College of Engineering and Technology, India

Sampath Boopathi
Muthayammal Engineering College, India

ABSTRACT

The integration of robot activities with cloud computing and the internet of things is essential to Industry 4.0 implementation. In the chapter, the fundamental principles of cloud computing and integrated robotics are explained. Emergence, characteristics, service delivery models, and computing models of robot-cloud computing principles have been discussed. Classical principles of service-oriented architecture, service models, web services, gSOAP, robotic operating systems, and challenges of robot cloud computing fields were illustrated. The main objective of this chapter is to illustrate cloud computing architecture frameworks. The architecture, platform, setup, and implementation principles of fixed and variable-length strings for cloud robotic frameworks have been briefly illustrated.

DOI: 10.4018/978-1-6684-8145-5.ch027

Copyright © 2023, IGI Global. Copying or distributing in print or electronic forms without written permission of IGI Global is prohibited.

INTRODUCTION

Although there are more applications and uses for mobile robots, their variety of services is constrained by low-power batteries, a lack of software upgrades, and a lack of enough processing and storage. Sharing information and expertise among robots is difficult because they are designed differently. By using the internet to connect a robot to the cloud infrastructure for data processing and storage, a robot's capabilities can be increased. However, because to deployment strategies, architectural design, and other factors, the robot-cloud communication protocol is susceptible to attacks. Additionally, cloud application responses with high latency and low connection speeds may render the robot brainless. A standard command for robots, such as a proxy-based master robot with higher bandwidth, can be used to construct a universal light weight knowledge interchange format, which can be used to address the low speed of robots. This might lessen the redundant data or knowledge produced by diverse robots using various hardware and software. To exchange knowledge data and utilise the computational capacity of the cloud, this suggested study blends robotics with cloud computing technologies. It seeks to provide a generally recognised interface between diverse robots and the cloud while reducing unnecessary code and data for them. Library Assistant as a test bed has been prepared to illustrate the concepts. A test bed for fixed length string communication has been built to test the architecture of mobile robots, and a variable length string is used for testing the architecture. Standard API has been utilised to harness the database and processing capabilities of the cloud. A path or map on a cloud-based architecture has been proposed using KIF, a knowledge interchange protocol. The idea of a variable string has been expanded in order to produce a standard representation for the paths that a robot would use to navigate utilising geographical features. Test bed 3 serves as an illustration of the system architecture of the Cloud Enabled Robotic Framework employing Landmark and Variable Length String.

Enterprises may now invest less in capital expenditures and utilise that money on things like robots thanks to the revolution that cloud computing has brought about in computing and infrastructure management. It offers robust processing, storage, and means to communicate and work together with other robotic systems. Cloud technology can be used by robots to communicate and work together. It is challenging to create software for robots and share data with the cloud due to the diversity of their hardware and operational platforms (Boopathi et al., 2023; Kumara et al., 2023; Vanitha et al., 2023). This is because there isn't a single platform that works with all kinds of hardware, which makes it challenging to reuse code. An open source framework called ROS was developed to make it easier to create strong, complicated robot software behaviour across several platforms. Various communities have contributed to it; however, the robotics communities are opposed to its application. Collections are inscribed and collective, but fail to keep them free of faults, rendering them useless after a predetermined amount of time. Reusing programme code between platforms is challenging, and lack of standard interfaces for robot hardware components is a key challenge (Paraforos & Griepentrog, 2021).

By combining and mapping data from many sources, an ontology can be used to create a new generation of information systems that are accessible to end users as a repository. This idea can be applied to cloud robotics to allow machines to share and reuse information. A networked robotics architecture known as cloud robotics comprises of an infrastructure cloud and an ad-hoc cloud created via machine-to-machine (M2M) interactions. In order to allow task offloading and information sharing, it uses a resilient computing approach to dynamically assign resources from a common pool. To accommodate various applications, many communication protocols and elastic computing models have been proposed. The potential advantages of cloud robotics in many applications have been highlighted through discussions of technical aspects like processing, communication, and security. To facilitate communication between the cloud and robots, researchers have created a variety of cloud robotics system designs, communication protocols, and languages (Batth et al., 2018).

FUNDAMENTAL OF CLOUD COMPUTING

Emergences

Network access to a shared pool of computing resources is made possible by cloud computing and is universal, practical, and on demand.

Parallel, distributed, grid, and utility computing are just a few of the different computing paradigms that have influenced the development of cloud computing. It began in the late 1990s, and as Internet speed increased, more people became interested in cloud computing. In order to make its commercial product available to both people and small businesses, Amazon introduced EC2 in 2006. The emergence of browser-based enterprise cloud applications was sparked by Web 2.0. Offering command line tools, a web interface, and REST APIs, the Google Cloud Platform provides modular cloud-based services and development tools. OpenStack has been a successful initiative for both corporations and developers. Additionally, it has become more well-liked by IT suppliers and producers. It consists of networked compute, storage, network, and management tool components and is managed by the OpenStack Foundation. The networked components of the cloud metaphor stand with various service delivery models (Chen et al., 2010).

Characteristics

Without requiring human assistance, on-demand self-service cloud computing services can be scaled or shrunk as required. Wide network access: Different networks can be utilised to connect heterogeneous computing equipment. Resource pooling: Multi-tenant models serve several customers at once without worrying about the physical servers' locations. Rapid elasticity allows for the speedy introduction, provisioning, and release of capabilities to satisfy consumer demand. Utilize metering services to optimise computing resources with measured service (Babu et al., 2022; Boopathi et al., 2022, 2023; Chakravarthi et al., 2022; Palaniappan et al., 2023; Sampath et al., 2022; Senthil et al., 2023).

Types of Service Delivery Models

Software: On a platform with a cloud infrastructure, the customer accesses applications from the cloud provider with less administrative oversight. The cloud provider is responsible for managing all of the cloud infrastructure and control systems.

Platform: Customers can use programming languages and tools to create, deploy, and manage applications on the infrastructure of cloud providers. They retain control over the deployed programmes and configuration settings, but allow the customer access to the operating systems, computing devices, physical servers, storage, and network.

Infrastructure: Operating systems, basic computing devices, storage, physical servers, hypervisors, and network management capabilities are the utmost privileges granted to the user, enabling them to create, distribute, and operate software.

Control: It is greater and abstraction is less at the core level, whereas abstraction is greater and control is less at the top level. At the bottom level, cost and service management are more important, however they decrease at the top level of the service delivery model.

Types of Cloud Computing Models

Cloud computing models include public, private, community, and hybrid.

Public Cloud: An academic, commercial, or governmental institution owns and manages the cloud infrastructure and computer resources, which are made available to the public across a public network.

Private Cloud: Cloud infrastructure can be maintained with or without a cloud provider and is given to one organisation with exclusive access to and utilisation of computing resources and infrastructure.

Community Cloud: Organizations with shared objectives, such as business needs, cost savings, security concerns, privacy policies, and compliance considerations are provided with cloud infrastructure. It may be owned and managed individually, collectively, or jointly. The management of cloud infrastructure can be done by external solutions.

Hybrid Cloud: A hybrid cloud facilitates data and application portability by combining private, public, or community cloud infrastructures.

Cloud computing in Robotics: Due to its affordability and viability, cloud computing technology is gaining popularity among IT firms and researchers. To optimise the advantages of already-existing robots, it can be utilised to offload computationally intensive operations and significant amounts of data to the cloud.

SERVICE-ORIENTED ARCHITECTURE (SOA)

A loosely connected design known as SOA puts more emphasis on consuming services than on creating them. To accomplish loose coupling, it makes advantage of two architectural constraints: a compact and universal interface to all components, and basic behaviours of messages are given by an extendable schema. Applications built with SOA can be thought of as "black box" components that increase abstraction and enable component reuse (Figure 1). A service in SOA can be added or withdrawn dynamically because it is platform agnostic and self-contained (Doriya et al., 2012).

SOA Components

- Through the translation of transfer protocols, ESB controls message routing and transmission between software components.
- Service provider and customer handshakes are facilitated by SOA Broker.
- The SOA Registry offers comprehensive details about services and locations.
- The SOA Service Manager controls service quality.
- Tools for interacting with the system are provided by Business Process Orchestration Manager.

Systems based on cloud computing require SOA design. A standard protocol, platform independent services, an open standard interface, a searchable repository through the Internet, and reusability are all possible for services. A service can be used to represent each component of a programme. The creation of Web services has been made possible by SOA and cloud computing.

Figure 1. Service-oriented architecture (SOA)

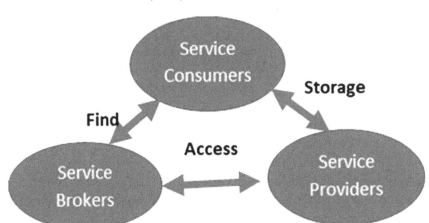

WEB SERVICES

WSDL is a machine-processable format used to describe web services, and SOAP messages are used by other systems to communicate with them (Koubaa, 2014).

XML: For interoperability, encoding systems transform documents into formats that are readable by both humans and machines.

WSDL: Web service specifications are built on XML, which is also used to describe services that are published to a service repository known as UDDI. The web service provider specifies the methods, arguments, and data types, while the WSDL document contains specifics on the location and message format.

SOAP: Web services employ an envelope to send messages, which are then transformed to XML and sent over HTTP.

UDDI: For Web services, WSDL, and distributed registry specifications, there is a platform-independent standard.

Main Components in SOA

- **Service Provider:** This component develops a Web service and provides details about its accessibility, interface, and availability.
- **Service Registry:** The service interface gives the service user access details.

- **Service Consumer:** Using particular communication protocols, service registry connects with service provider. The skills of SOA and Web services complement one another; SOA begins with the definition, implementation, and calling mechanism of an interface, whereas Web services translate to a technical specification. Web service definition language (WSDL) is appropriate for SOA interface specification standards.

Roles: The WSDL format of web services allows for the definition of services and the establishment of communication between service providers and consumers using the SOAP protocol. They offer a platform on which robots can access and perform their functions via a web interface.

gSOAP

Many technological organisations utilise gSOAP, an open source software development toolkit for SOAP/XML-based Web services. It offers the best foundation for developing apps that are dependable, adaptable, trustworthy, and quick. This toolkit offers functions like type-safe serialisation, memory management, concealing unneeded XML data, SOAP-specific details during validity testing. It facilitates the integration of different programming languages and automatically translates XML data types into semantically comparable C/C++ data types. It is appropriate for real-time applications since it produces WSDL and XML as simple, effective code (Hu et al., 2012; Toffetti & Bohnert, 2019).

gSOAP Roles in Robotics

When it comes to managing hardware and software resources, cloud computing technology offers the fundamental building blocks, whereas SOA-based web services explain the process of service definition, service delivery, and publishing & discovery. Data is packaged in XML and sent over HTTP by SOA web services, which use the SOAP protocol to interface with the client. Since XML can not handle big data transfers, providing robotic services is challenging. The gSOAP enters the picture here. It allows for the movement of massive amounts of data and offers a number of capabilities, including the definition of web services, communication methods, publish and discover mechanisms, and the marshalling and unmarshalling of robot data. Additionally, it generates client- and server-side objects for cloud-based robot communication.

ROBOT OPERATING SYSTEM (ROS)

An open source meta operating system called Robot Operating System (ROS) serves as a link between host operating systems, robotic hardware, and robotic software. It offers message forwarding, hardware abstraction, low-level hardware control, implementation of frequently used functionality, and package management. Additionally, it can be used to get, create, write, and execute codes in many languages on various systems (Doriya, 2017; Du et al., 2017; Toffetti & Bohnert, 2019; Zhang & Zhang, 2019). The ROS architecture is shown in Figure 2.

Main Components

- **Middleware:** The XML-RPC API unifies several programming languages into an uniform build and packaging environment and is used for XML-RPC based interprocess communications.
- **Debugging and Visualization Tools:** Separate applications for low-level processing and decision-making are provided by the ROS system, together with visualisation tools like RQT graph, plot, and RXBAG. In order to test various scenarios, it may also capture sensor data and playback it.
- **Robot Controllers:** Motion planning, localization and mapping, computer vision techniques, and 3D data processing are just a few of the common robotic applications that ROS offers as an open source implementation.

Figure 2. ROS architecture

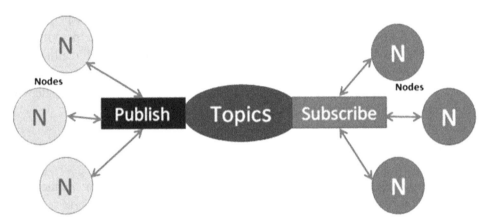

Benefits: Over the host operating system of robots, ROS offers a structured communication layer that enables robots to communicate using a publish-subscribe paradigm and a common HTTP protocol. Additionally, it offers low-level device control and packages sensory data into a portable, user-friendly XML data format, enabling robots to communicate and exchange information with humans and other robots.

ROS Terminologies

Robots can be remotely controlled using Internet Protocol (IP) communication between nodes thanks to ROS.

- **ROS-Master:** It is a centralised XML-RPC server that performs naming service functionality by registering nodes and providing DNS server facilities for them to find one another.
- **Parameter Server:** In ROS-master, storage is utilised to keep data and configuration settings.
- **ROS-Out:** Human-readable log messages are provided via log messages.
- **Nodes:** A robot control system is made up of numerous nodes, which are the core processing units of ROS.
- **Messages:** Data and the data structure that goes with it are transmitted between nodes via messages.

- **Topics:** By publishing a relevant topic, a publish action broadcasts data, and a targeted subscriber programme subscribes to it.
- **Services:** Request/reply instructions are functionally provided by remote procedure calls.

TYPES OF ROBOTS: CLOUD INFRASTRUCTURE

Utilization, knowledge sharing, and service are the three divisions that can be made within cloud robotics.

- **Resource Utilization:** A collection of resources is used to provide the consumer with cloud infrastructure. A cloud server receives an access request from a client robot and checks it for authorization and authentication. If a service is offered, it is made available to the client robot for that specific session.
- **Knowledge Sharing:** Robots can store their data and information about the world they are exploring in a centralised location called a cloud infrastructure. Robots can cooperate by sharing their expertise because they all have unique abilities. A humanoid robot, for instance, can operate an object but lacks the semantics of that object. A humanoid robot can exchange information and semantics with another robot connected to a cloud infrastructure.
- **Robots for Service:** Robot computation and knowledge sharing can be offloaded to cloud infrastructure, enabling service users to work with actual robotic gear through a web interface with a supervisory control. This eliminates the need to buy robotic hardware in order to test tasks like running a specific code, watching the robot's behaviour, and testing a code with particular configuration settings.

CLOUD ROBOTIC SERVICE MODELS

Three robotic services for processing, storage, and applications can be offered by cloud robots. Through the Internet of Things, cloud robotics can offer basic resources like cameras and sensors for sensing and recognising. Robots may store data like photographs, information about barriers, and plans in the cloud and employ computing resources like speech, image recognition, and unlimited storage and processing power. No matter the platform, heterogeneous robots should be able to perform common tasks (Koubaa, 2014; Mateo, 2013).

Robots and cloud computing technology can have a lot of advantages. Robots become lighter, smarter, and more cost-effective thanks to cloud computing, which offers parallel computing on demand for recognition, learning, and motion planning. Additionally, it provides users with access to vast data resources, facilitating knowledge exchange and sharing among numerous robots with different hardware and software.

LIMITATIONS

- The architectural design and implementation, availability and dependability difficulties, data integrity, recovery, and attack vulnerability make the communication protocol used in the cloud insecure.
- Because of their reliance on cloud applications, low speed, device, network, and latency might cause robots to become mindless machines.
- The robotics community must approve of a common framework or platform because two or more robots may not use the same platform.

CHALLENGES AND SOLUTIONS

Challenges: Reliability of Response (RoR) is crucial for off-board computing, Time-to-Response (ToR) should be close to real time, and Data Retrieval Management (DRM) should be compatible with various device kinds. The computational challenges of cloud robotics, such as choosing whether to offload jobs to the cloud, necessitate the use of a framework that can effectively deal with data volume, deadline pressure, and estimate issues. Due to packet loss and communication delays, optimal virtual machine allocation and communication issues are crucial for robotics applications. Robotic behaviour is determined by what has been processed in a virtual machine, and security issues start to surface.

Solutions: Software engineering and information system design can be used to solve cloud computing vulnerabilities, but it can be challenging to develop a security solution that satisfies all the requirements. Since poor network and high latency responses from cloud apps cannot be corrected, a worldwide light weight knowledge interchange protocol can be developed to be followed as a standard command for robots. For low bandwidth devices connected to the robots, a bigger bandwidth master robot based on proxies can be employed. A robotics middleware framework can assist developers in interoperating heterogeneous robots in the cloud, just as middleware has made it possible for software developers to interface with operating systems and apps. Application Programming Interfaces (APIs) are used by robots to recognise objects.

OBJECTIVES

- Cloud enabled robotic framework to reduce redundant code and data.
- KIF and a variable length string are used to create an interface between clouds and robots.
- Provide a suitable platform for robots to navigate using natural landmarks.

ARCHITECTURE

The technology-driven era has a significant role for robots, yet there are no established design guidelines for them. Depending on the work at hand, the availability of resources, and the deployment terrain, many types of robots exist. Despite the fact that the intelligence components needed to do the work appear to be comparable, the robotics community has not been able to establish a standard set of guidelines for the design of robots. ROS is required for cloud robotics applications because it makes it easier for autonomous programmes to share information. For cloud robotics, ROS offers a graph-like structure that enables robot interaction and the sharing of useful data. Real-time information sharing and huge parallel computation are provided via cloud computing. Between the operating system and the software application, ROS serves as an abstraction layer that handles hardware heterogeneity, improves software performance, streamlines software design, and lowers manufacturing costs. It offers a variety of services, including hardware abstraction, message transmission between processes, low-level device control, and many more. A "metaoperating system" for robot software, ROS is not an operating system (Batth et al., 2018; Chen et al., 2010; Doriya, 2017; Gowri et al., 2022; Koubaa, 2014).

ROS enables independent, standalone programmes to communicate with one another by passing a single message or a number of messages. Nodes, messages, topics, and services form its foundation. Nodes have the ability to publish and subscribe to one or more subjects. Robots are built with the help of Cloud Robotics and ROS. The Personal Robot 2 (PR2) is a mobile manipulation platform created with ROS that enables usage of all PR2 features through ROS interfaces. ROS is an open-source, user-friendly, and adaptable framework for developing robot software that is perfect for cloud robotics. ROS is perfect for cloud robotics because it supports code reuse in robotics research and development. By implementing a basic interface that does not compromise on current fabrication techniques, it would make robots more affordable, intelligent, and effective (Boopathi, 2022; Boopathi, Thillaivanan, et al., 2022; Boopathi, Venkatesan, et al., 2023; S. et al., 2022; Sampath et al., 2022).

Since some robots have processors that do not allow interfaces for fast data transfer, the interface shown in this chapter represents a novel attempt to evaluate robots operating in various operating systems. In a real-time setting, the interface unit should be close to the robot to reduce latency. Robots are crucial to technology, yet their design suffers from a serious flaw called redundancy. A robot must be completely recoded or redesigned every time a similar concept needs to be implemented because, unlike computer systems, it does not have any established design standards. Although the robotics community hasn't been able to establish a set of universal design principles, all robot designs share similar intelligence components to complete the mission (Hu et al., 2012).

It may be attempted to use the current hardware-level intelligent component as a vantage point for cloud computing. To reduce duplication in research efforts, this layer can be safely separated and combined. The mathematical model requires that the present robot designs have an equal number of tasks and their corresponding intelligence. If hardware can be abstracted, the intelligence component can be retrieved from the cloud, repurposing the robot designer's skills to create new intelligence components. For cloud robotics applications, ROS, an open source with an inter-programming language header set to promote information transfer across autonomous programmes, is required. ROS provides a graph-like structure for cloud robotics that facilitates robot communication and the exchange of helpful information. Real-time information sharing and huge parallel computation are provided via cloud computing. Middleware Between the operating system and the software application, there is an abstraction layer called Robot that controls hardware heterogeneity, improves software performance, streamlines software design, and lowers production costs. ROS is an open source project that offers a variety of operating system functions, including message transfer between processes, hardware abstraction, and low-level device control. Stanford created it in 2007 and gave it the name Switchyard (Koubaa, 2014).

Independent, individual programmes can exchange data with one another thanks to ROS. Nodes, messages, topics, and services make up ROS. Nodes are computer programmes or processes that exchange messages with one another or pass numerous messages. One message is used for a request, and the other is used for a response. A single subject can be published and subscribed to by nodes. Robots are built with the help of Cloud Robotics and ROS. The Personal Robot 2 (PR2) is a mobile manipulation platform created with ROS that enables usage of all PR2 features through ROS interfaces. ROS is an open-source, user-friendly, and adaptable framework for developing robot software that is perfect for cloud robotics. In cloud robotics, ROS facilitates code reuse, allowing code written for one robot to be used in others. By implementing a simple interface that doesn't infringe on current fabrication techniques, cloud computing techniques can make robots more affordable, intelligent, and effective. Since some robots have processors that do not allow interfaces for fast data transfer, the interface shown in this chapter represents a novel attempt to evaluate robots operating in various operating systems.

Figure 3. Architecture of cloud robots principle

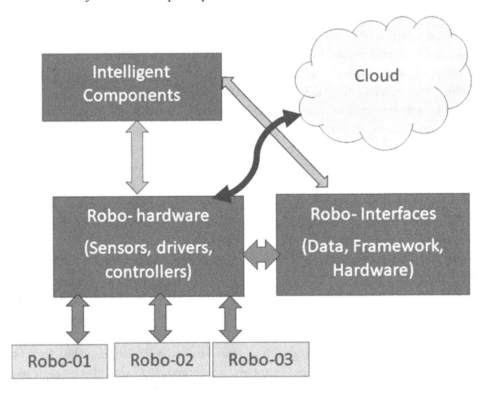

When connecting devices like Bluetooth, WiFi, and GSM, a comparative study of communication mediums and their inadequacies is conducted to compare range, speed, and model of communication. To prevent significant latency in a real-time setting, the proposed interface unit should be close to the robot. Table 2 details the manner in which robots and the cloud communicate, and Table 3 contrasts the various services that a cloud robot might offer. Robots can share intelligence gained through a shared memory on the cloud thanks to the cloud robot, which can store knowledge databases there. This Chapter discusses a generic architecture that enables robots to be connected to multiple communication technologies via the cloud. The concept of exchanging information has already been incorporated in RoboEarth, however there are still difficulties dealing with different processors that don't support ROS or connecting devices with sluggish data transfer rates (Koubaa, 2014).

CLOUD-ENABLED ROBOTIC FRAMEWORK

A middleware interface unit has been designed and created as a test bed for fixed length string communication. A case study of a cloud-enabled robotic framework for a library assistant that serves as a test bed for robots automatically sorting books while utilising a vast database of books from the cloud serves as an illustration of the architecture. Robots Everywhere, a robotic platform control app for Android phones, uses open source software to operate robotic platforms. For Android and Python, Google Inc. has created android robot libraries. An application that can control robots and carry out other duties can be made by bridging the gap between android and robotic applications. To utilise the cloud's database and computational capacity, a cloud architecture consisting of middleware (on an android application) and API has been developed (Batth et al., 2018).

Case 1: Through Fixed Length String

Using middleware and a robot interface, the sorts books by reading barcodes. The middleware part of the system scans a book's barcode and sends it to the cloud for data retrieval in order to track the robot's movements. The shelf number is subsequently transmitted to the robot through Bluetooth serial data transmission. The robot receiver takes serial data from the middleware, picks up the book, lifts it to the appropriate shelf, and places it there. It keeps the book on the shelf and then goes back to its original position.

Fixed Length String: Architecture

The middleware interface and Boebot are the two parts of the experiment. Android programming reads barcodes in the EAN-13 format using a barcode scanner app to identify books in the library. The system is connected to the Google Books API using a private key to scan the barcode and transfer the information to the cloud for retrieval. The cloud then replies with all the data it has about the book, including the author's name, the book's title, its edition, the publisher's name, the year it was published, etc. The Android app organises books into categories and uses Bluetooth to relay shelf numbers to the robot. The main concept is that the robot follows the middleware's (an Android application) movement instructions before returning to its default location. The books are sorted and organised in various shelves by repeating this process. The robot uses an IR LED and an IR sensor to detect and emit radiation (Paraforos & Griepentrog, 2021).

Settings

- **Testing the Boebot:** The Boebot's major components are already attached to the chassis, but to make sure the servomotors are linked and aligned correctly, the internal potentiometer must be set so that PULSOUT 12, 13, and 750 are in the middle using the BASIC stamp programme. The

Boebbot will be prepared to relocate as a result of this. Boebot uses the Easy Bluetooth module to communicate with Android devices.

- **Testing the Android App:** Both Bluetooth communication with the Boebot and the Barcode Scanner programme have been included into the Android application. After barcode scanning was introduced, the Android application was integrated to offer "Preview" capability for the book. The relationships between different modules in the architecture are depicted in Figure 3. To recognise a book and get instructions from the middleware, the middleware uses its Bluetooth and GSM modules to communicate with the cloud.

Implementation: Robots may now access cloud resources and are no longer constrained by their own memories and programmes thanks to an experiment that connected them to the cloud using the Google Books API and book barcodes. The experiment's next step entailed scanning, pairing, and sending data from Bluetooth devices as well as receiving the shelf number from the Boebot and directing it to the appropriate shelf. The final step entailed uniting every module, including the Bluetooth and barcode scanning modules. The Boebot then combed its surroundings for anything resembling a book, stopped to ask for directions, scooped up the book, and dashed back to its starting place. Both high-level programming for Android devices and low-level programming for robots have been used to implement the test. The android application is created using the Eclipse editor, and the robot's CPU is programmed using PBasic. The next section contains the algorithms for the two modules.

Analysis: The IR sensor used by the robots to detect books did not always function, but they were able to find them 80% of the time, and the android device was unable to connect to the robot, yielding an overall success rate of 80%. Due to the fact that it takes less than one second, communication between the middle and the robot is nearly instantaneous. The barcode scanning process takes around a minute. However, due to the internet connection being used at the moment, retrieving information from the cloud takes 3 seconds on average.

Case 2: Cloud Robotic Framework – Variable Length String

Due to its capability to communicate knowledge among various computer programmes, Knowledge Interchange Format (KIF) can be used to exchange knowledge between various systems. Declarative knowledge bases can be effectively translated into and out of different knowledge representation languages thanks to KIF. The implementation of a length string to transfer knowledge across different robots is covered in this chapter. The string, which is kept in the server's shared memory, is an alphanumeric string that represents a robot's journey. The "Robotic Framework for Variable Length String" case study and Test bed II are used to explain the architecture (Hu et al., 2012; Koubaa, 2014; Zhang & Zhang, 2019).

Architecture

A client middleware platform is used by Test bed II to enable server-robot connection. A client computer is linked to a newly constructed server. The website that the server hosts provides the directive for the robot to carry out a certain task. The string is retrieved and processed by the client server. The robot is then given the string and told to act in accordance with it, returning a response. The robot's generated answer reflects the knowledge base or intelligence it has gathered through its navigation in the external world. Robots are fed with the intelligence of the previous robot when they are sent to the same environment with other robots. Extreme care was also made to address the following problems during design. To make maps understandable to all robots, an universal length string is employed to express them. Robots communicate with one another using intermediary computers. Robots must keep track of voltage levels to control supply voltage levels. The projected problems brought on by changes in the geometry of the wheels are taken care of by measuring the circumference of the wheel and ensuring constant voltage from the power source when the robot is moving over a surface with consistent coefficients of friction. The proposed algorithm will be checked, validated, and verified using an open loop control system. Data transfer can be carried out through USB or Bluetooth, and the server and client can communicate utilising an Ad-hoc network or cable connection (Figure 4).

Platform

Software and Hardware platforms are used for the architecture.

Setup

The four parts of Test Bed II are a laptop computer, a Bricx Command Center, a Basic Stamp (Parallax), and Matlab.

- **Virtual Machine:** To function as a middleman between the host and the Boebot and between Lego Mindstorms NXT and the server, virtual machines are made. Ad-hoc is a method of connecting a computer or visitor operating system to a server.
- **Bricx Command Centre:** A bricx command centre is used to programme the Lego Mindstorm, which then locates the robot on its own. The user interface is similar to that of a conventional text editor, with menus and buttons for routine tasks as well as additional menus for more specialised tasks like downloading and developing programmes and collecting data from the robot. It is known as "downloading" the programme when it is converted into binary codes and transferred to the robot over a USB or Bluetooth dongle.
- **Basic Stamp (Parallax):** Because Boebot is written in pbasic, the basic stamp editor must be installed on the development PC. The communication between the debug window are provided by programme and the Basic Stamp 24 pin microcontroller. The debugging output is displayed in the enormous black area of the debug window, and the robot-expected characters are fed into the smaller white box above it.
- **Matlab:** It is used to establish a Bluetooth connection and send the necessary command to the robot.

Implementation

The computer reads a string from a file until the end of the file (EOF) is reached, at which point it delivers the string file to the robot. The robot will begin operating the wheel motors after receiving the string and continue doing so until it locates the stop instruction (S).

Figure 4. Cloud robotic framework: Variable length string

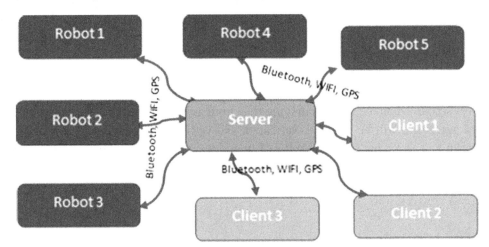

- **Lego Mindstorms NXT:** To make the Lego brick visible to MATLAB, it must be connected with the client computer. The list of Bluetooth devices that are currently available can be found by starting intertwin and using the Remote Names field.
- **Bluetooth Text Format:** The length of a Bluetooth packet is measured without the two length bytes, which are required for messages to indicate how many bytes they include in the first two bytes.
- **Parallax Boebot:** East module is used to open Bluetooth port of Boebot.

Analysis

The test bed 2 has undergone 10 tests, and the results show that less than one second is needed for communication between all of the modules. Since the test bed uses robots intended for research and education rather than industry applications, 1s is regarded as fair. Despite having separate platforms, Boebot and Lego might travel the same path by using the variable string. The test bed 2 was successfully put to the test; the communication lag times with the server and robots were quick, and the variable string was appropriate for sharing and making decisions in real time.

Future Work and Additional Readings

The cloud-based robot programming and controlling optimum path generation and implementation can be done by application of multi-objective and multi-criteria optimization algorithms and experiments might be conducted using Taguchi, surface methodology and mixer method (Boopathi, 2019; Boopathi & Sivakumar, 2013; Haribalaji et al., 2022; Kavitha et al., 2022; Myilsamy & Sampath, 2021; Sampath & Myilsamy, 2021; Yupapin et al., 2022).

SUMMARY

The underlying ideas behind integrated robotics and cloud computing were described in this chapter. Robot-cloud computing principles' emergence, traits, service delivery models, and computing models covered. The challenges of robot cloud computing fields, as well as traditional SOA principles, service models, web services, and gSOAP, were illustrated. This chapter's major goal is to provide examples of cloud computing architecture frameworks. For cloud robotic frameworks, the architecture, platform, setup, and implementation principles of fixed and variable-length strings were briefly illustrated.

REFERENCES

Babu, B. S., Kamalakannan, J., Meenatchi, N., Karthik, S., & Boopathi, S. (2022). Economic impacts and reliability evaluation of battery by adopting Electric Vehicle. *IEEE Explore*, 1–6.

Batth, R. S., Nayyar, A., & Nagpal, A. (2018). Internet of robotic things: driving intelligent robotics of future-concept, architecture, applications and technologies. *2018 4th International Conference on Computing Sciences (ICCS)*, 151–160.

Boopathi, S. (2019). Experimental investigation and parameter analysis of LPG refrigeration system using Taguchi method. *SN Applied Sciences*, *1*(8), 892. doi:10.100742452-019-0925-2

Boopathi, S. (2022). Cryogenically treated and untreated stainless steel grade 317 in sustainable wire electrical discharge machining process: A comparative study. *Environmental Science and Pollution Research International*, 1–10. doi:10.100711356-022-22843-x PMID:36057706

Boopathi, S., Arigela, S. H., Raman, R., Indhumathi, C., Kavitha, V., & Bhatt, B. C. (2022). Prominent Rule Control-based Internet of Things: Poultry Farm Management System. *IEEE Explore*, 1–6.

Boopathi, S., Khare, R., KG, J. C., Muni, T. V., & Khare, S. (2023). Additive Manufacturing Developments in the Medical Engineering Field. In Development, Properties, and Industrial Applications of 3D Printed Polymer Composites (pp. 86–106). IGI Global.

Boopathi, S., Siva Kumar, P. K., Meena, R. S. J., S. I., P., S. K., & Sudhakar, M. (2023). Sustainable Developments of Modern Soil-Less Agro-Cultivation Systems. In Human Agro-Energy Optimization for Business and Industry (pp. 69–87). IGI Global. doi:10.4018/978-1-6684-4118-3.ch004

Boopathi, S., & Sivakumar, K. (2013). Experimental investigation and parameter optimization of near-dry wire-cut electrical discharge machining using multi-objective evolutionary algorithm. *International Journal of Advanced Manufacturing Technology*, *67*(9–12), 2639–2655. doi:10.100700170-012-4680-4

Boopathi, S., Thillaivanan, A., Azeem, M. A., Shanmugam, P., & Pramod, V. R. (2022). Experimental investigation on abrasive water jet machining of neem wood plastic composite. *Functional Composites and Structures*, *4*(2), 025001. doi:10.1088/2631-6331/ac6152

Boopathi, S., Venkatesan, G., & Anton Savio Lewise, K. (2023). Mechanical Properties Analysis of Kenaf–Grewia–Hair Fiber-Reinforced Composite. In *Lecture Notes in Mechanical Engineering* (pp. 101–110). Springer. doi:10.1007/978-981-16-9057-0_11

Chakravarthi, P. K., Yuvaraj, D., & Venkataramanan, V. (2022). IoT-based smart energy meter for smart grids. *ICDCS 2022 - 2022 6th International Conference on Devices, Circuits and Systems*, 360–363. 10.1109/ICDCS54290.2022.9780714

Chen, Y., Du, Z., & Garcia-Acosta, M. (2010). Robot as a service in cloud computing. *2010 Fifth IEEE International Symposium on Service Oriented System Engineering*, 151–158. 10.1109/SOSE.2010.44

Doriya, R. (2017). Development of a cloud-based RTAB-map service for robots. *2017 IEEE International Conference on Real-Time Computing and Robotics (RCAR)*, 598–605. 10.1109/RCAR.2017.8311928

Doriya, R., Chakraborty, P., & Nandi, G. C. (2012). Robotic services in cloud computing paradigm. *2012 International Symposium on Cloud and Services Computing*, 80–83. 10.1109/ISCOS.2012.24

Du, Z., He, L., Chen, Y., Xiao, Y., Gao, P., & Wang, T. (2017). Robot cloud: Bridging the power of robotics and cloud computing. *Future Generation Computer Systems*, 74, 337–348. doi:10.1016/j.future.2016.01.002

Gowri, A. S., ShanthiBala, P., & Ramdinthara, I. Z. (2022). Fog-Cloud Enabled Internet of Things Using Extended Classifier System (XCS). *Artificial Intelligence-Based Internet of Things Systems*, 163–189.

Haribalaji, V., Boopathi, S., Mohammed Asif, M., Yuvaraj, T., Velmurugan, D., Anton Savio Lewise, K., Sudhagar, S., & Suresh, P. (2022). Influences of Mg-Cr filler materials in Friction Stir Process of Aluminium-based dissimilar alloys. *Materials Today: Proceedings, 66*, 948–954. doi:10.1016/j.matpr.2022.04.668

Hu, G., Tay, W. P., & Wen, Y. (2012). Cloud robotics: Architecture, challenges and applications. *IEEE Network, 26*(3), 21–28. doi:10.1109/MNET.2012.6201212

Kavitha, C., Malini, P. S. G., Charan, V., Manoj, N., Verma, A., & Boopathi, S. (2022). (in press). An experimental study on the hardness and wear rate of carbonitride coated stainless steel. *Materials Today: Proceedings*. Advance online publication. doi:10.1016/j.matpr.2022.09.524

Koubaa, A. (2014). A service-oriented architecture for virtualizing robots in robot-as-a-service clouds. *Architecture of Computing Systems—ARCS 2014: 27th International Conference, Lübeck, Germany, February 25-28, 2014 Proceedings, 27*, 196–208.

Kumara, V., Mohanaprakash, T. A., Fairooz, S., Jamal, K., Babu, T., & B., S. (2023). Experimental Study on a Reliable Smart Hydroponics System. In *Human Agro-Energy Optimization for Business and Industry* (pp. 27–45). IGI Global. doi:10.4018/978-1-6684-4118-3.ch002

Mateo, R. M. A. (2013). Scalable adaptive group communication for collaboration framework of cloud-enabled robots. *Procedia Computer Science, 22*, 1239–1248. doi:10.1016/j.procs.2013.09.211

Myilsamy, S., & Sampath, B. (2021). Experimental comparison of near-dry and cryogenically cooled near-dry machining in wire-cut electrical discharge machining processes. *Surface Topography : Metrology and Properties, 9*(3), 035015. doi:10.1088/2051-672X/ac15e0

Palaniappan, M., Tirlangi, S., Mohamed, M. J. S., Moorthy, R. M. S., Valeti, S. V., & Boopathi, S. (2023). Fused Deposition Modelling of Polylactic Acid (PLA)-Based Polymer Composites: A Case Study. In Development, Properties, and Industrial Applications of 3D Printed Polymer Composites (pp. 66–85). IGI Global.

Paraforos, D. S., & Griepentrog, H. W. (2021). Digital farming and field robotics: Internet of things, cloud computing, and big data. *Fundamentals of Agricultural and Field Robotics*, 365–385.

S., P. K., Sampath, B., R., S. K., Babu, B. H., & N., A. (2022). Hydroponics, Aeroponics, and Aquaponics Technologies in Modern Agricultural Cultivation. In *Trends, Paradigms, and Advances in Mechatronics Engineering* (pp. 223–241). IGI Global. doi:10.4018/978-1-6684-5887-7.ch012

Sampath, B., & Myilsamy, S. (2021). Experimental investigation of a cryogenically cooled oxygen-mist near-dry wire-cut electrical discharge machining process. *Strojniski Vestnik. Jixie Gongcheng Xuebao*, *67*(6), 322–330. doi:10.5545v-jme.2021.7161

Sampath, B. C. S., & Myilsamy, S. (2022). Application of TOPSIS Optimization Technique in the Micro-Machining Process. In Trends, Paradigms, and Advances in Mechatronics Engineering (pp. 162–187). IGI Global. doi:10.4018/978-1-6684-5887-7.ch009

Senthil, T. S., Puviyarasan, M., Babu, S. R., Surakasi, R., Sampath, B., & Associates. (2023). Industrial Robot-Integrated Fused Deposition Modelling for the 3D Printing Process. In Development, Properties, and Industrial Applications of 3D Printed Polymer Composites (pp. 188–210). IGI Global.

Toffetti, G., & Bohnert, T. M. (2019). Cloud robotics with ROS. In Robot Operating System (ROS) The Complete Reference (Volume 4) (pp. 119–146). Springer.

Vanitha, S. K. R., & Boopathi, S. (2023). Artificial Intelligence Techniques in Water Purification and Utilization. In *Human Agro-Energy Optimization for Business and Industry* (pp. 202–218). IGI Global. doi:10.4018/978-1-6684-4118-3.ch010

Yupapin, P., Trabelsi, Y., Nattappan, A., & Boopathi, S. (2022). Performance Improvement of Wire-Cut Electrical Discharge Machining Process Using Cryogenically Treated Super-Conductive State of Monel-K500 Alloy. *Iranian Journal of Science and Technology - Transactions of Mechanical Engineering*, 1–17. doi:10.1007/s40997-022-00513-0

Zhang, H., & Zhang, L. (2019). Cloud robotics architecture: trends and challenges. *2019 IEEE International Conference on Service-Oriented System Engineering (SOSE)*, 362–3625. 10.1109/SOSE.2019.00061

APPENDIX: ACRONYMS

API: Application Programming Interface
DNS: Domain Name System
GSM: Global System for Mobile
gSOAP: C and C++ Software Development Toolkit
HTTP: Hypertext Transfer Protocol
RoR: Reliability of Response
RPC: Remote Procedure Call
RXBAG: One of GUI Tool
ToR: Time-to-Response
UDDI: Universal Description, Discovery, and Integration
XML: Extensible Markup Language

Compilation of References

Aazam, M., Harras, K. A., & Zeadally, S. (2019). Fog computing for 5G tactile industrial Internet of Things: QoE-aware resource allocation model. *IEEE Transactions on Industrial Informatics*, *15*(5), 3085–3092. doi:10.1109/TII.2019.2902574

Aazam, M., & Huh, E. N. (2016). Fog Computing: The Cloud-IoT/IoE Middleware Paradigm. *IEEE Potentials*, *35*(3), 40–44. doi:10.1109/MPOT.2015.2456213

Aazam, M., Islam, S., Lone, S. T., & Abbas, A. (2020). Cloud of things (CoT): cloud-fog-IoT task offloading for sustainable internet of things. *IEEE Transactions on Sustainable Computing*, *7*(1), 87–98. doi:10.1109/TSUSC.2020.3028615

Abbas, A. M. (2021). Social network analysis using deep learning: Applications and schemes. *Social Network Analysis and Mining*, *11*(106), 106. Advance online publication. doi:10.100713278-021-00799-z

Abd Aziz, N., Adnan, N. A. A., Abd Wahab, D., & Azman, A. H. (2021). Component design optimization based on artificial intelligence in support of additive manufacturing repair and restoration: Current status and future outlook for remanufacturing. *Journal of Cleaner Production*, *296*, 126401. doi:10.1016/j.jclepro.2021.126401

Abdelazim, K., Moawad, R., & Elfakharany, E. (2020). A Framework for Requirements Prioritization Process in Agile Software Development. *Journal of Physics: Conference Series*, *1454*(1), 12001. doi:10.1088/1742-6596/1454/1/012001

Abdelmajied, F. Y. (2022). Industry 4.0 and Its Implications: Concept, Opportunities, and Future Directions. In T. Bányai, Á. Bányai, & I. Kaczmar (Eds.), *Supply Chain - Recent Advances and New Perspectives in the Industry 4.0 Era*. IntechOpen. doi:10.5772/intechopen.102520

Abdullah, A. S., & Rajalaxmi, R. (2012, April). A data mining model for predicting the coronary heart disease using random forest classifier. In *International Conference in Recent Trends in Computational Methods, Communication and Controls* (pp. 22-25). Academic Press.

Abdullahi, S. I., Habaebi, M. H., & Malik, N. A. (2018). Flood Disaster Warning System on the go. In *Proceedings of the 7th International Conference on Computer and Communication Engineering (ICCCE)*. 10.1109/ICCCE.2018.8539253

Abdulridha, J., Ehsani, R., & Castro, A. (2016). Detection and differentiation between laurel wilt disease, phytophthora disease, and salinity damage using a hyperspectral sensing technique. *Agriculture*, *6*(4), 56. doi:10.3390/agriculture6040056

Abualigah, L., Diabat, A., Sumari, P., & Gandomi, A. H. (2021). Applications, deployments, and integration of internet of drones (iod): A review. *IEEE Sensors Journal*, *21*(22), 25532–25546. doi:10.1109/JSEN.2021.3114266

AbualSaud, K., Elfouly, T. M., Khattab, T., Yaacoub, E., Ismail, L. S., Ahmed, M. H., & Guizani, M. (2019). A Survey on Mobile Crowd-Sensing and Its Applications in the IoT Era. In IEEE Access (Vol. 7, pp. 3855–3881). Institute of Electrical and Electronics Engineers Inc. doi:10.1109/ACCESS.2018.2885918

Adoption, T., & Report, S. (2021). *The First Signpost on the Road from Early Adoption to Widespread Application of Industry 4.0 Technologies 2021 Industry 4.0 Technology Adoption Survey Report*. Academic Press.

Agoramoorthy, M., & Joe, I. P. (2021). Hybrid cuckoo–red deer algorithm for multi-objective localization strategy in wireless sensor network. *International Journal of Communication Systems*. Advance online publication. doi:10.1002/dac.5042

Ahmad Salleh, K., Janczewski, L., & Ahmad, K. (2016). Association for Information Systems AIS Electronic Library (AISeL) Adoption of Big Data Solutions: A study on its security determinants using Sec-TOE Framework Recommended Citation "Adoption of Big Data Solutions: A study on its security determinants usin. *International Conference on Information Resources Management (CONF-IRM)*, 66.

Ahmad Termizi, S. N. A., Wan Alwi, S. R., Manan, Z. A., & Varbanov, P. S. (2022). Potential Application of Blockchain Technology in Eco-Industrial Park Development. *Sustainability (Basel)*, *15*(1), 52. doi:10.3390u15010052

Ahmad, A., Farooq, F., Ostrowski, K. A., Sliwa-Wieczorek, K., & Czarnecki, ́. S. (2021). Application of novel machine learning techniques for predicting the surface chloride concentration in concrete containing waste material. *Materials (Basel)*, *14*(9), 2297. doi:10.3390/ma14092297 PMID:33946688

Ahmed, I., Ahmad, M., Jeon, G., & Piccialli, F. (2021). A framework for pandemic prediction using big data analytics. *Big Data Res*, *25*, 100190. doi:10.1016/j.bdr.2021.100190

Ahram, T., Sargolzaei, A., Sargolzaei, S., Daniels, J., & Amaba, B. (2017, June). Blockchain technology innovations. In 2017 IEEE technology & engineering management conference (TEMSCON) (pp. 137-141). IEEE. doi:10.1109/TEMSCON.2017.7998367

Aiman, M., Bahrin, K., Othman, F., Hayati, N., Azli, N., & Talib, F. (2016). Industry 4.0: A review on industrial automation and robotic. *Jurnal Teknologi, 78*.

Akan, O., Bellavista, P., Coulson, G., Dressler, F., Ferrari, D., Kobayashi, H., Palazzo, S., Sherman Shen, X., Stan, M., Xiaohua, J., & Zomaya, A. Y. (2016). *eHealth 360° International Summit on eHealth Budapest, Hungary, June 14–16, 2016 Revised Selected Papers*. https://www.springer.com/series/8197

Akgun, S., & Greenhow, C. (2021). Artificial intelligence in education: Addressing ethical challenges in K-12 settings. *AI and Ethics*, 1–10. doi:10.100743681-021-00096-7 PMID:34790956

Akpakwu, G. A., Silva, B. J., Hancke, G. P., & Abu-Mahfouz, A. M. (2017). A survey on 5G networks for the Internet of Things: Communication technologies and challenges. *IEEE Access : Practical Innovations, Open Solutions*, *6*, 3619–3647. doi:10.1109/ACCESS.2017.2779844

Akyildiz, I. F., Pierobon, M., Balasubramaniam, S., & Koucheryavy, Y. (2015). The internet of Bio-Nano things. *IEEE Communications Magazine*, *53*(3), 32–40. doi:10.1109/MCOM.2015.7060516

Al Bashish, D., Braik, M., & Bani-Ahmad, S. 2010. A framework for detection and classification of plant leaf and stem diseases. *International Conference on Signal and Image Processing*, 113–118. 10.1109/ICSIP.2010.5697452

Alava, S., Chaouni, N., & Charles, Y. (2020). How to characterise the discourse of the far-right in digital media? Interdisciplinary approach to preventing terrorism. *Procedia Computer Science*, *176*, 2515–2525. doi:10.1016/j.procs.2020.09.324

Aldahiri, A., Alrashed, B., & Hussain, W. (2021). Trends in using IoT with machine learning in health prediction system. *Forecasting*, *3*(1), 181–206. doi:10.3390/forecast3010012

Aleisa, M. A., Abuhussein, A., & Sheldon, F. T. (2020). Access control in fog computing: Challenges and research agenda. *IEEE Access : Practical Innovations, Open Solutions*, *8*, 83986–83999. doi:10.1109/ACCESS.2020.2992460

Alemayehu, D., & Berger, M. L. (2016). Big Data: Transforming drug development and health policy decision making. *Health Services and Outcomes Research Methodology, 16*(3), 92–102. doi:10.100710742-016-0144-x PMID:27594803

Alfaro-Cid, E., Mora, A. M., Merelo, J. J., Esparcia-Alcázar, A. I., & Sharman, K. (2009). Finding relevant variables in a financial distress prediction problem using genetic programming and self-organizing maps. In *Natural computing in computational finance* (pp. 31–49). Springer. doi:10.1007/978-3-540-95974-8_3

Algarni, A. M., Thayananthan, V., & Malaiya, Y. K. (2021). Quantitative Assessment of Cybersecurity Risks for Mitigating Data Breaches in Business Systems. *Applied Sciences (Basel, Switzerland), 11*(8), 3678. doi:10.3390/app11083678

Alhalafi, N., & Veeraraghavan, P. (2019). Privacy and Security Challenges and Solutions in IOT: A review. *IOP Conference Series. Earth and Environmental Science, 322*(1), 012013. Advance online publication. doi:10.1088/1755-1315/322/1/012013

Alharbi, S., Alrazgan, M., Alrashed, A., Alnomasi, T., Almojel, R., Alharbi, R., Alharbi, S., Alturki, S., Alshehri, F., & Almojil, M. (2021). Automatic Speech Recognition: Systematic Literature Review. *IEEE Access : Practical Innovations, Open Solutions, 9*, 131858–131876. doi:10.1109/ACCESS.2021.3112535

Alimam, M. A., Seghiouer, H., Alimam, M. A., & Cherkaoui, M. (2017, April). Automated system for matching scientific students to their appropriate career pathway based on science process skill model. In *2017 IEEE Global Engineering Education Conference (EDUCON)* (pp. 1591-1599). IEEE. 10.1109/EDUCON.2017.7943061

Alkaabi, S. H. A. S., Almulla, H. A. R., Ahli, S. K. A., & Amin, A. H. M. (2022, May). Takhasosi: Career Specialization Guidance System on Permissioned Blockchain Infrastructure for Undergraduate Students. In *2022 8th International Conference on Information Technology Trends (ITT)* (pp. 183-188). IEEE.

Alladi, T., Chamola, V., Parizi, R. M., & Choo, K. K. R. (2019). Blockchain Applications for Industry 4.0 and Industrial IoT: A Review. *IEEE Access : Practical Innovations, Open Solutions, 7*, 176935–176951. doi:10.1109/ACCESS.2019.2956748

Al-madani, A. M., Gaikwad, A. T., Mahale, V., & Ahmed, Z. A. T. (2020). Decentralized E-voting system based on Smart Contract by using Blockchain Technology. *2020 International Conference on Smart Innovations in Design, Environment, Management, Planning and Computing (ICSIDEMPC).* 10.1109/ICSIDEMPC49020.2020.9299581

Almaghrabi, A., & Alhogail, A. (2022). Blockchain-based donations traceability framework. *Journal of King Saud University - Computer and Information Sciences, 34*(10), 9442–9454. doi:10.1016/j.jksuci.2022.09.021

Almalis, I., Kouloumpris, E., & Vlahavas, I. (2022). Sector-level sentiment analysis with deep learning. *Knowledge-Based Systems, 258*, 109954. doi:10.1016/j.knosys.2022.109954

Almamalik, L. (2020). *The Development of the Maturity Model to Assess the Smart Indonesia Manufacturing Companies 4.0 Readiness.* doi:10.2991/aebmr.k.200305.026

Almulihi, AAlassery, FIrshad Khan, AShukla, SKumar Gupta, BKumar, R. (2022). Analyzing the Implications of Healthcare Data Breaches through Computational Technique. Intelligent Automation &amp. *Soft Computing, 32*(3), 1763–1779. doi:10.32604/iasc.2022.023460

Al-Shargabi, B., & Abuarqoub, S. (2020, November). IoT-Enabled Healthcare: Benefits, Issues and Challenges. In *4th International Conference on Future Networks and Distributed Systems (ICFNDS)* (pp. 1-5). Academic Press.

Alsulami, H. (2022). Implementation analysis of reliable unmanned aerial vehicles models for security against cyber-crimes: Attacks, tracebacks, forensics and solutions. *Computers & Electrical Engineering, 100*, 107870. doi:10.1016/j.compeleceng.2022.107870

Al-Taie, M. Z., & Kadry, S. (2017). *Information Diffusion in Social Networks. In Python for Graph and Network Analysis.* Springer. doi:10.1007/978-3-319-53004-8

Al-Turjman, F. (n.d.). *Transactions on Computational Science and Computational Intelligence Artificial Intelligence in IoT.* https://www.springer.com/series/11769

Ameer, I., Bölücü, N., Siddiqui, M. H. F., Can, B., Sidorov, G., & Gelbukh, A. (2023). Multi-label emotion classification in texts using transfer learning. *Expert Systems with Applications*, *213*, 118534. doi:10.1016/j.eswa.2022.118534

Amin, M. S., Chiam, Y. K., & Varathan, K. D. (2019). Identification of significant features and data mining techniques in predicting heart disease. *Telematics and Informatics*, *36*, 82–93. doi:10.1016/j.tele.2018.11.007

Aminul Islam, M. (2022). Industry 4.0: Skill set for employability. *Social Sciences & Humanities Open*, *6*(1), 100280. doi:10.1016/j.ssaho.2022.100280

Ammad, M., Shah, M. A., Islam, S. U., Maple, C., Alaulamie, A. A., Rodrigues, J. J., Mussadiq, S., & Tariq, U. (2020). A novel fog-based multi-level energy-efficient framework for IoT-enabled smart environments. *IEEE Access : Practical Innovations, Open Solutions*, *8*, 150010–150026. doi:10.1109/ACCESS.2020.3010157

Anand, S. J., Selvi, G. A., Poornima, D., & Vedanarayanan, V. (2021). Iot-Based Secure And Energy Efficient Scheme For Precision Agriculture Using Blockchain And Improved Leach Algorithm. *Turkish Journal of Computer and Mathematics Education*, *12*(10), 2466–2475.

Andoni, M. (2019). A review on consensus algorithm of blockchain. *Renewable & Sustainable Energy Reviews*, *100*, 143–174. doi:10.1016/j.rser.2018.10.014

Andrayani, R., & Negara, E. S. (2019). Social Media Analytics: Data Utilization of Social Media for Research. *Journal of Information Systems and Informatics*, *1*(2), 193–205. doi:10.33557/journalisi.v1i2.23

Androulaki, E. a. (2018). Hyperledger fabric: a distributed operating system for permissioned blockchains. In *Proceedings of the thirteenth EuroSys conference* (pp. 1-15). 10.1145/3190508.3190538

Anitha, D., Kavitha, D., Prakash, R. R., & Raja, S. C. (2020). Identification of Opinion Difference in Teaching Learning Methods and Recommendation to Faculty. *Journal of Engineering Education Transformations*, *33*(0), 421–424. doi:10.16920/jeet/2020/v33i0/150197

Ansari, J. A. N., & Khan, N. A. (2020). Exploring the role of social media in collaborative learning the new domain of learning. *Smart Learning Environment*, *7*(9), 9. Advance online publication. doi:10.118640561-020-00118-7

Aoun, A., Ilinca, A., Ghandour, M., & Ibrahim, H. (2021). A review of Industry 4.0 characteristics and challenges, with potential improvements using Blockchain technology. *Computers & Industrial Engineering*, *162*, 107746. Advance online publication. doi:10.1016/j.cie.2021.107746

Aravindaraj, K., & Rajan Chinna, P. (2022). A systematic literature review of integration of industry 4.0 and warehouse management to achieve Sustainable Development Goals (SDGs). In Cleaner Logistics and Supply Chain (vol. 5). Elsevier Ltd. Publishing

Argaw, S. T., Bempong, N.-E., Eshaya-Chauvin, B., & Flahault, A. (2019). The state of research on cyberattacks against hospitals and available best practice recommendations: A scoping review. *BMC Medical Informatics and Decision Making*, *19*(1), 10. Advance online publication. doi:10.118612911-018-0724-5 PMID:30634962

Arnold, C., Kiel, D., & Voigt, K.-I. (2016). How the industrial internet of things changes business models in different manufacturing industries. *International Journal of Innovation Management*, *20*(8), 1–25. doi:10.1142/S1363919616400156

Arzo, S. T., Naiga, C., Granelli, F., Bassoli, R., Devetsikiotis, M., & Fitzek, F. H. (2021). A theoretical discussion and survey of network automation for iot: Challenges and opportunity. *IEEE Internet of Things Journal, 8*(15), 12021–12045. doi:10.1109/JIOT.2021.3075901

Ashari, I. F. (2020). Implementation of cyber-physical-social system based on service oriented architecture in smart tourism. *Journal of Applied Informatics and Computing, 4*(1), 66–73. doi:10.30871/jaic.v4i1.2077

Atici. (2011). Prediction of the strength of mineral admixture concrete using multivariable regression analysis and an artificial neural network. *Expert Systems with Applications, 38*, 9609–9618. https://doi.org/.eswa.2011.01.156 doi:10.1016/j

Atzori, L., Iera, A., & Morabito, G. (2010). The Internet of things: A survey. *Computer Networks, 54*(15), 2787–2805. doi:10.1016/j.comnet.2010.05.010

Avancini, D. B.-M. (2019). Energy meters evolution in smart grids: A review. *Journal of Cleaner Production, 217*, 702-715.

Avdoshin, S., & Pesotskaya, E. (2020). Blockchain in Charity: Platform for Tracking Donations. *Proceedings of the Future Technologies Conference (FTC) 2020, 2*, 689–701. 10.1007/978-3-030-63089-8_45

B, S., Sh, A. S., E, S. K., K, S. N., & S, N. (2022). Blockchain Industry 5.0: Next Generation Smart Contract and Decentralized Application Platform. *2022 International Conference on Innovative Computing, Intelligent Communication and Smart Electrical Systems (ICSES)*. doi:10.1109/ICSES55317.2022.9914151

Babu, B. S., Kamalakannan, J., Meenatchi, N., Karthik, S., & Boopathi, S. (2022). Economic impacts and reliability evaluation of battery by adopting Electric Vehicle. *IEEE Explore*, 1–6.

Bae, M. a. (2016). Preserving privacy and efficiency in data communication and aggregation for AMI network. *Journal of Network and Computer Applications, 59*, 333-344.

Bahirat, P., He, Y., Menon, A., & Knijnenburg, B. (2018). A data-driven approach to developing IoT privacy-setting interfaces. *International Conference on Intelligent User Interfaces, Proceedings IUI*, 165–176. 10.1145/3172944.3172982

Bakhshi, T., & Shahid, S. (n.d.). Securing Internet of Bio-Nano Things: ML-Enabled Parameter Profiling of Bio-Cyber Interfaces. *Proceedings, 22nd International Multi Topic Conference : INMIC'19*. 10.1109/INMIC48123.2019.9022753

Balaji, T. K., Annavarapu, C. S. R., & Bablani, A. (2021). Machine learning algorithms for social media analysis: A survey. *Computer Science Review, 40*, 6–32.

Bandara, S. B. G. J. S., Jayasundera, J. M. K. H., Udayanga, U. H. N., Iloshini, P. A. A., & Pathirana, K. P. P. S. (2018). *Artificial Conversational Agent Based Tour Guide System*. Academic Press.

Bande, S., & Shete, V. V. (2017). Smart flood disaster prediction system using IoT & neural networks. *Proceedings of 2017 International Conference On Smart Technologies For Smart Nation (SmartTechCon)*. 10.1109/SmartTechCon.2017.8358367

Banerjea, S., Srivastava, S., & Kumar, S. (2021). Data Security in the Internet of Things: Challenges and Opportunities. *Big Data Analytics for Internet of Things*, 265-284.

Barbosa, M., ben Mokhtar, S., Felber, P., Maia, F., Matos, M., Oliveira, R., Riviere, E., Schiavoni, V., & Voulgaris, S. (2017). SAFETHINGS: Data Security by Design in the IoT. *Proceedings - 2017 13th European Dependable Computing Conference, EDCC 2017*, 117–120. 10.1109/EDCC.2017.33

Bates, D. W., Saria, S., Ohno-Machado, L., Shah, A., & Escobar, G. (2014). Big data in health care: Using analytics to identify and manage high-risk and high-cost patients. *Health Affairs (Project Hope), 33*(7), 1123–1131. doi:10.1377/hlthaff.2014.0041 PMID:25006137

Batth, R. S., Nayyar, A., & Nagpal, A. (2018). Internet of robotic things: driving intelligent robotics of future-concept, architecture, applications and technologies. *2018 4th International Conference on Computing Sciences (ICCS)*, 151–160.

Beaird, J. a. (2020). *The principles of beautiful web design*. Sitepoint.

Beamap, V. V., Guenane Beamap, F., & Mehaoua, A. (2019). Reference Architectures for Security-by-Design IoT: Comparative Study; Reference Architectures for Security-by-Design IoT: Comparative Study. *2019 Fifth Conference on Mobile and Secure Services (MobiSecServ)*.

Becker, F. G., Cleary, M., Team, R. M., Holtermann, H., The, D., Agenda, N., Science, P., Sk, S. K., Hinnebusch, R., Hinnebusch, A. R., Rabinovich, I., Olmert, Y., Uld, D. Q. G. L. Q., Ri, W. K. H. U., Lq, V., Frxqwu, W. K. H., Zklfk, E., Edvhg, L. V., … Wkh, R. Q. (2015).主観的健康感を中心とした在宅高齢者における 健康関連指標に関する共分散構造分析. *Syria Studies*, *7*(1). https://www.researchgate.net/publication/269107473_What_is_governance/link/548173090cf22525dcb61443/download%0Ahttp://www.econ.upf.edu/~reynal/Civil wars_12December2010.pdf%0Ahttps://think-asia.org/handle/11540/8282%0Ahttps://www.jstor.org/stable/41857625

Beg, M. S., Yusri, I. M., Jamlos, M. F., Azmi, W. H., Badrulhisam, N. H., & Omar, I. (2022). Potential and Limitation of Internet of Things (IOT) Application in the Automotive Industry: An Overview. *International Journal of Automotive and Mechanical Engineering*, *19*(3), 9939–9949. doi:10.15282/ijame.19.3.2022.06.0766

Behmann, J., Steinrücken, J., & Plümer, L. (2014). Detection of early plant stress responses in hyperspectral images. *ISPRS Journal of Photogrammetry and Remote Sensing*, *93*, 98–111. doi:10.1016/j.isprsjprs.2014.03.016

Bendovschi, A. (2015). Cyber-Attacks – Trends, Patterns and Security Countermeasures. *Procedia Economics and Finance*, *28*, 24–31. doi:10.1016/S2212-5671(15)01077-1

Berentsen, A. (2019). Aleksander Berentsen Recommends "Bitcoin: A Peer-to-Peer Electronic Cash System" by Satoshi Nakamoto. *21st Century Economics*, 7–8. doi:10.1007/978-3-030-17740-9_3

Bhanuprakash, C., Nijagunarya, Y. S., & Jayaram, M. A. (2018). An Informal Approach to Identify Bright Graduate Students by Evaluating their Classroom Behavioral Patterns by Using Kohonen Self Organizing Feature Map. *International Journal of Modern Education & Computer Science*, *10*(8), 22–32. doi:10.5815/ijmecs.2018.08.03

Bhat, O., Gokhale, P., & Bhat, S. (2007). Introduction to IOT. *International Advanced Research Journal in Science. Engineering and Technology ISO*, *3297*(1). Advance online publication. doi:10.17148/IARJSET.2018.517

Bhuiyan, M. N., Rahman, M. M., Billah, M. M., & Saha, D. (2021). Internet of Things (IoT): A Review of Its Enabling Technologies in Healthcare Applications, Standards Protocols, Security, and Market Opportunities. In IEEE Internet of Things Journal (Vol. 8, Issue 13, pp. 10474–10498). Institute of Electrical and Electronics Engineers Inc. doi:10.1109/JIOT.2021.3062630

Bianco, D., Bueno, A., Filho, M., Latan, H., Ganga, G., Frank, A., & Jabbour, C. (2022). The role of Industry 4.0 in developing resilience for manufacturing companies during COVID-19. *International Journal of Production Economics*, *256*, 108728. doi:10.1016/j.ijpe.2022.108728

Biba, J. (2018). *20 Top Industrial Robot Companies to Know*. https://builtin.com/robotics/industrial-robot

Bilim, C., Atis,, C. D., Tanyildizi, H., & Karahan, O. (2009). Predicting the compressive strength of ground granulated blast furnace slag concrete using artificial neural network. *Advances in Engineering Software*, *40*(5), 334–340. doi:10.1016/j.advengsoft.2008.05.005

Binbusayyis & Vaiyapuri. (2022). *A professional-driven blockchain framework for sharing E-Portfolio in the context of Industry 4.0*. ICT Express. doi:10.1016/j.icte.2022.03.010

Biswas, A. R., & Giaffreda, R. (2014). IoT and cloud convergence: Opportunities and challenges. *2014 IEEE World Forum on Internet of Things, WF-IoT 2014*, 375–376. 10.1109/WF-IoT.2014.6803194

Bodkhe, U., Tanwar, S., Parekh, K., Khanpara, P., Tyagi, S., Kumar, N., & Alazab, M. (2020). Blockchain for Industry 4.0: A Comprehensive Review. *IEEE Access : Practical Innovations, Open Solutions*, 8, 79764–79800. doi:10.1109/ACCESS.2020.2988579

Boopathi, S. (2013). Experimental study and multi-objective optimization of near-dry wire-cut electrical discharge machining process. *Shodhganga@INFLIBNET*. http://hdl.handle.net/10603/16933

Boopathi, S., Arigela, S. H., Raman, R., Indhumathi, C., Kavitha, V., & Bhatt, B. C. (2022). Prominent Rule Control-based Internet of Things: Poultry Farm Management System. *IEEE Explore*, 1–6.

Boopathi, S., Khare, R., KG, J. C., Muni, T. V., & Khare, S. (2023). Additive Manufacturing Developments in the Medical Engineering Field. In Development, Properties, and Industrial Applications of 3D Printed Polymer Composites (pp. 86–106). IGI Global.

Boopathi, S., Siva Kumar, P. K., & Meena, R. S. J., S. I., P., S. K., and Sudhakar, M. (2023). Sustainable Developments of Modern Soil-Less Agro-Cultivation Systems. In Human Agro-Energy Optimization for Business and Industry (pp. 69–87). IGI Global. doi:10.4018/978-1-6684-4118-3.ch004

Boopathi, S. (2019). Experimental investigation and parameter analysis of LPG refrigeration system using Taguchi method. *SN Applied Sciences*, 1(8), 892. doi:10.100742452-019-0925-2

Boopathi, S. (2022). Cryogenically treated and untreated stainless steel grade 317 in sustainable wire electrical discharge machining process: A comparative study. *Environmental Science and Pollution Research International*, 1–10. doi:10.100711356-022-22843-x PMID:36057706

Boopathi, S. (2022). Experimental investigation and multi-objective optimization of cryogenic Friction-stir-welding of AA2014 and AZ31B alloys using MOORA technique. *Materials Today. Communications*, 33, 104937. doi:10.1016/j.mtcomm.2022.104937

Boopathi, S., Jeyakumar, M., Singh, G. R., King, F. L., Pandian, M., Subbiah, R., & Haribalaji, V. (2022). An experimental study on friction stir processing of aluminium alloy (AA-2024) and boron nitride (BNp) surface composite. *Materials Today: Proceedings*, 59, 1094–1099. doi:10.1016/j.matpr.2022.02.435

BoopathiS.MyilsamyS.SukkasamyS. (2021). Experimental Investigation and Multi-Objective Optimization of Cryogenically Cooled Near-Dry Wire-Cut EDM Using TOPSIS Technique. *IJAMT*. doi:10.21203/rs.3.rs-254117/v1

Boopathi, S., & Sivakumar, K. (2013). Experimental investigation and parameter optimization of near-dry wire-cut electrical discharge machining using multi-objective evolutionary algorithm. *International Journal of Advanced Manufacturing Technology*, 67(9–12), 2639–2655. doi:10.100700170-012-4680-4

Boopathi, S., & Sivakumar, K. (2016). Optimal parameter prediction of oxygen-mist near-dry Wire-cut EDM. *International Journal of Manufacturing Technology and Management*, 30(3–4), 164–178. doi:10.1504/IJMTM.2016.077812

Boopathi, S., Thillaivanan, A., Azeem, M. A., Shanmugam, P., & Pramod, V. R. (2022). Experimental investigation on abrasive water jet machining of neem wood plastic composite. *Functional Composites and Structures*, 4(2), 025001. doi:10.1088/2631-6331/ac6152

Boopathi, S., Venkatesan, G., & Anton Savio Lewise, K. (2023). Mechanical Properties Analysis of Kenaf–Grewia–Hair Fiber-Reinforced Composite. In *Lecture Notes in Mechanical Engineering* (pp. 101–110). Springer. doi:10.1007/978-981-16-9057-0_11

Botta, A., de Donato, W., Persico, V., & Pescapé, A. (2016). Integration of Cloud computing and Internet of Things: A survey. *Future Generation Computer Systems*, *56*, 684–700. doi:10.1016/j.future.2015.09.021

Bottazzi, G., & Me, G. (2014). Responding to cyber crime and cyber terrorism—botnets an insidious threat. *Cyber Crime and Cyber Terrorism Investigator's Handbook*, 231–257.

Boubecar, S. (2020). A Survey on the Usage of Blockchain Technology for Cyber-Threats in the Context of Industry 4.0. *Sustainability (Basel)*, *12*(21), 19. doi:10.3390u12219179

Box, S., & Lopez-Gonzalez, J. (n.d.). *The Future of Technology: Opportunities for ASEAN in the Digital Economy*. Academic Press.

Brownlee, J. (2013). *A tour of machine learning algorithms*. https:// machinelearningmastery.com/a-tour-of-machine-learning-algorithms/

Buhalis, D., Leung, D., & Lin, M. (2023). Metaverse as a disruptive technology revolutionising tourism management and marketing. *Tourism Management*, *97*, 104724. doi:10.1016/j.tourman.2023.104724

Bulchand-Gidumal, J. (2022). Impact of artificial intelligence in travel, tourism, and hospitality. In *Handbook of e-Tourism* (pp. 1943–1962). Springer International Publishing. doi:10.1007/978-3-030-48652-5_110

Burger, C. a. (2016). *Blockchain in the energy transition. A survey among decision-makers in the German energy industry*. DENA German Energy Agency.

Burhan, M., Rehman, R. A., Khan, B., & Kim, B. S. (2018). IoT elements, layered architectures and security issues: A comprehensive survey. *Sensors (Basel)*, *18*(9), 2796. Advance online publication. doi:10.339018092796 PMID:30149582

Butpheng, C., Yeh, K.-H., & Xiong, H. (2020). Security and Privacy in IoT-Cloud-Based e-Health Systems—A Comprehensive Review. *Symmetry*, *12*(7), 1191. doi:10.3390ym12071191

Butt, A. A., Khan, S., Ashfaq, T., Javaid, S., Sattar, N. A., & Javaid, N. (2019, June). A cloud and fog based architecture for energy management of smart city by using meta-heuristic techniques. In 2019 15th International Wireless Communications & Mobile Computing Conference (IWCMC) (pp. 1588-1593). IEEE. doi:10.1109/IWCMC.2019.8766702

Cachin, C. a. (2016). Architecture of the hyperledger blockchain fabric. In *Workshop on distributed cryptocurrencies and consensus ledgers* (p. 310). Academic Press.

Caldeira, M. M., & Ward, J. M. (2002). Understanding the successful adoption and use of IS/IT in SMEs: An explanation from Portuguese manufacturing industries. *Information Systems Journal*, *12*(2), 121–152. doi:10.1046/j.1365-2575.2002.00119.x

Calo, S. B., Touna, M., Verma, D. C., & Cullen, A. (2017, December). Edge computing architecture for applying AI to IoT. In *2017 IEEE International Conference on Big Data (Big Data)* (pp. 3012-3016). IEEE. 10.1109/BigData.2017.8258272

Calvanese Strinati, E., Barbarossa, S., Gonzalez-Jimenez, J. L., Kténas, D., Cassiau, N., & Dehos, C. (2019). *6G: The next frontier*. arXiv e-prints, arXiv-1901.

Cambria, E., & White, B. (2014). Jumping NLP curves: A review of natural language processing research. *IEEE Computational Intelligence Magazine*, *9*(2), 48–57. doi:10.1109/MCI.2014.2307227

Cano, J. C., Berrios, V., Garcia, B., & Toh, C. K. (2018). Evolution of IoT: An industry perspective. *IEEE Internet of Things Magazine*, *1*(2), 12–17. doi:10.1109/IOTM.2019.1900002

Carter-McAuslan, A., & Farquharson, C. (2020). Application of SOMs and k-means clustering to geophysical mapping: Lessons learned. *SEG Technical Program Expanded Abstracts*, *2020*, 3843–3846. doi:10.1190egam2020-w10-01.1

Carvalho, A. R., & Santos, C. (2021). Developing peer mentors' collaborative and metacognitive skills with a technology-enhanced peer learning program. *Computers and Education Open*, 100070.

Case, D. U. (2016). Analysis of the cyber attack on the Ukrainian power grid. *Electricity Information Sharing and Analysis Center (E-ISAC), 388*, 1-29.

Cassel, L., Dicheva, D., Dichev, C., Goelman, D., & Posner, M. (2016). Artificial Intelligence in Data Science. *Lecture Notes in Computer Science, 9883*, 343–346. doi:10.1007/978-3-319-44748-3_33

Cebe, M. a. (2018). Efficient Public-Key Revocation Management for Secure Smart Meter Communications Using One-Way Cryptographic Accumulators. In *2018 IEEE International Conference on Communications (ICC)* (pp. 1-6). IEEE. 10.1109/ICC.2018.8423023

Chae, J., Thom, D., Jang, Y., Kim, S., Ertl, T., & David, S. (2014). Public behavior response analysis in disaster events utilizing visual analytics of microblog data. *Computers & Graphics, 38*, 51–60. doi:10.1016/j.cag.2013.10.008

Chakravarthi, P. K., Yuvaraj, D., & Venkataramanan, V. (2022). IoT-based smart energy meter for smart grids. *ICDCS 2022 - 2022 6th International Conference on Devices, Circuits and Systems*, 360–363. 10.1109/ICDCS54290.2022.9780714

Chanak, P., & Banerjee, I. (2020). Internet-of-Things-enabled smartvillages: An overview. *IEEE Consumer Electronics Magazine, 10*(3), 12–18. doi:10.1109/MCE.2020.3013244

Chanal, P. M., & Kakkasageri, M. S. (2020). Security and Privacy in IoT: A Survey. In Wireless Personal Communications (Vol. 115, Issue 2, pp. 1667–1693). Springer. doi:10.100711277-020-07649-9

Chang, B., Tong, X., Qi, L., & Chen, E. (2018). Study on Information Diffusion Analysis in Social Networks and Its Applications. *International Journal of Automation and Computing, 15*(4), 377–401. doi:10.100711633-018-1124-0

Chang, V., Ramachandran, M., Wills, G., Walters, R. J., Li, C.-S., & Watters, P. (2016). Editorial for FGCS special issue: Big Data in the cloud. *Future Generation Computer Systems, 65*, 73–75. doi:10.1016/j.future.2016.04.007

Chaudhary, K., Alam, M., Al-Rakhami, M. S., & Gumaei, A. (2021). Machine learning-based mathematical modelling for prediction of social media consumer behavior using big data analytics. *Journal of Big Data, 8*(1), 73. doi:10.118640537-021-00466-2

Chaudhary, P., & Chaudhari, A. K. (2012, June). Color transform based approach for disease spot detection on plant leaf. *Int. J. Comput. Sci. Telecomm, 3*(6).

Chauhan, M. (2021, June 8). 8 Applications of IoT in Education. Analytics Steps. In *Smart Education in Industry 4.0: A Systematic Literature Review*. Academic Press.

Cheema, A., Tariq, M., Hafiz, A., Khan, M. M., Ahmad, F., & Anwar, M. (2022). Prevention Techniques against Distributed Denial of Service Attacks in Heterogeneous Networks: A Systematic Review. *Security and Communication Networks, 2022*, 2022. doi:10.1155/2022/8379532

Chen, M., Li, Y., Xu, Z., Huang, X., & Wang, W. (2018). A Blockchain Based Data Management System for Energy Trade. *First International Conference Smart Block 20*, 44-54. 10.1007/978-3-030-05764-0_5

Chen, S., Xu, H., Liu, D., Hu, B., & Wang, II. (2014). A vision of IoT: Applications, challenges, and opportunities with China Perspective. In IEEE Internet of Things Journal (Vol. 1, Issue 4, pp. 349–359). Institute of Electrical and Electronics Engineers Inc. doi:10.1109/JIOT.2014.2337336

Chen, H., Qian, C., Liang, C., & Kang, W. (2018). An approach for predicting the compressive strength of cement-based materials exposed to sulfate attack. *PLoS One*, *13*(1), e0191370. Advance online publication. doi:10.1371/journal.pone.0191370 PMID:29346451

Chen, L., Lee, W.-K., Chang, C.-C., Choo, K.-K. R., & Zhang, N. (2019). Blockchain based searchable encryption for electronic health record sharing. *Future Generation Computer Systems*, *95*, 420–429. doi:10.1016/j.future.2019.01.018

Chen, M., & Hao, Y. (2017). *Disease Prediction by Machine Learning over Big Data from Healthcare Communities*. IEEE. doi:10.1109/ACCESS.2017.2694446

Chen, S. H., & Tham, A. (2023). A crypto-tourism case study of agnes water/seventeen seventy, Australia. *Tourism and Hospitality Research*, *23*(1), 108–112. doi:10.1177/14673584221085472

Chen, S., Yuan, X., Wang, Z., Guo, C., Liang, J., Wang, Z., Zhang, X., & Zhang, J. (2016). Interactive Visual Discovering of Movement Patterns from Sparsely Sampled Geo-tagged Social Media Data. *IEEE Transactions on Visualization and Computer Graphics*, *22*(1), 270–279. doi:10.1109/TVCG.2015.2467619 PMID:26340781

Chen, T. (2020). A simple framework for contrastive learning of visual representations. In *International conference on machine learning*. PMLR.

Chen, Y., Du, Z., & Garcia-Acosta, M. (2010). Robot as a service in cloud computing. *2010 Fifth IEEE International Symposium on Service Oriented System Engineering*, 151–158. 10.1109/SOSE.2010.44

Chettri, L., & Bera, R. (2019). A comprehensive survey on Internet of Things (IoT) toward 5G wireless systems. *IEEE Internet of Things Journal*, *7*(1), 16–32. doi:10.1109/JIOT.2019.2948888

Chew, A. M. K., & Gunasekeran, D. V. (2021). *Social Media Big Data: The Good, The Bad, and the Ugly (Un)truths*. https://www.frontiersin.org/articles/10.3389/fdata.2021.623794/

Cho, H. S., & Woo, T. H. (2017). Cyber security in nuclear industry – Analytic study from the terror incident in nuclear power plants (NPPs). *Annals of Nuclear Energy*, *99*, 47–53. doi:10.1016/j.anucene.2016.09.024

Chong, C., Lee, K., & Ahmed, G. (n.d.). Improving Internet Privacy, Data Protection and Security Concerns. In *International Journal of Technology, Innovation and Management (IJTIM)* (Vol. 1, Issue 1). https://journals.gaftim.com/index.php/ijtim/issue/view/1PublishedbyGAF-TIM,gaftim.com

Chopra, M., Singh, S. K., Sharma, S., & Mahto, D. (2021). Impact and Usability of Artificial Intelligence in Manufacturing workflow to empower Industry 4.0. *CEUR Workshop Proceedings, 3080*.

Choudhary, P., Bhargava, L., Suhag, A. K., Choudhary, M., & Singh, S. (2021). An Era of Internet of Things Leads to Smart Cities Initiatives Towards Urbanization. *Digital Cities Roadmap: IoT-Based Architecture and Sustainable Buildings*, 319-350.

Chou, J.-S., Tsai, C.-F., Pham, A.-D., & Lu, Y.-H. (2014). Machine learning in concrete strength simulations: Multi-nation data analytics. *Construction & Building Materials*, *73*, 771–780. doi:10.1016/j.conbuildmat.2014.09.054

Chuang, S.-P., Liu, A. H., Sung, T.-W., & Lee, H. (2021). Improving Automatic Speech Recognition and Speech Translation via Word Embedding Prediction. *IEEE/ACM Transactions on Audio, Speech, and Language Processing*, *29*, 93–105. doi:10.1109/TASLP.2020.3037543

Cirani, S. F. G. P. M. V. L. (2019). *Internet of Things*. John Wiley & Sons Ltd.

Corsi, A., de Souza, F. F., Pagani, R. N., & Kovaleski, J. L. (2020). Big data analytics as a tool for fighting pandemics: A systematic review of literature. *Journal of Ambient Intelligence and Humanized Computing*, *12*(10), 9163–9180. doi:10.100712652-020-02617-4 PMID:33144892

Cruz, W. M., & Isotani, S. (2014, September). Group formation algorithms in collaborative learning contexts: A systematic mapping of the literature. In *CYTED-RITOS International Workshop on Groupware* (pp. 199-214). Springer. 10.1007/978-3-319-10166-8_18

Cui, L., Yang, S., Chen, Z., Pan, Y., Xu, M., & Xu, K. (2020). An Efficient and Compacted DAG-Based Blockchain Protocol for Industrial Internet of Things. *IEEE Transactions on Industrial Informatics*, *16*(6), 4134–4145. doi:10.1109/TII.2019.2931157

Cusack, B., & Tian, Z. (2017). *Evaluating IP surveillance camera vulnerabilities*. doi:10.4225/75/5a84efba95b46

Cusumano, M. A. (1998). Microsoft secrets: How the world's most powerful software company creates technology, shapes markets, and manages people. Simon and Schuster.

Dai, H.-N., Zheng, Z., & Zhang, Y. (2019). Blockchain for internet of things: A survey. *IEEE Internet of Things Journal*, *6*(5), 1–19. doi:10.1109/JIOT.2019.2920987

Darbellay, F., & Stock, M. (2012). Tourism as complex interdisciplinary research object. *Annals of Tourism Research*, *39*(1), 441–458. doi:10.1016/j.annals.2011.07.002

Darwiesh, A., Alghamdi, M. I., El-Baz, A. H., & Elhoseny, M. (2022). Social Media Big Data Analysis: Towards Enhancing Competitiveness of Firms in a Post-Pandemic World. *Journal of Healthcare Engineering*, *2022*, 1–14. Advance online publication. doi:10.1155/2022/6967158 PMID:35281539

Davenport, T. (2014). *Big data at work: dispelling the myths, uncovering the opportunities*. Harvard Business Review Press. doi:10.15358/9783800648153

Davis, C., Ramirez, S., & Whitmore, D. (2013). *How Does News Diffuse Through Twitter? Predicting spread of information through social media using a Mathematical Model*. https://www.public.asu.edu/~fwang25/poster/Davis2013.pdf

Dawson, M. (2018). Cyber Security in Industry 4.0: The Pitfalls of Having Hyperconnected Systems. *Journal of Strategic Management Studies*, *10*(1), 19–28.

De Aguiar, E. J., Faiçal, B. S., Krishnamachari, B., & Ueyama, J. (2020). A Survey of Blockchain-Based Strategies for Healthcare. *ACM Computing Surveys*, *53*(2), 1–27. doi:10.1145/3376915

de Carvalho, S. D., de Melo, F. R., Flôres, E. L., Pires, S. R., & Loja, L. F. B. (2020). Intelligent tutoring system using expert knowledge and Kohonen maps with automated training. *Neural Computing & Applications*, *32*(17), 13577–13589. doi:10.100700521-020-04767-0

Deep, A., & Sood, M. (2023). Effective Detection of DDoS Attack in IoT-Based Networks Using Machine Learning with Different Feature Selection Techniques. *Proceedings of Data Analytics and Management ICDAM*, *2022*, 527–540.

Demirel, S. T., & Das, R. (2018). Software requirement analysis: Research challenges and technical approaches. *6th International Symposium on Digital Forensic and Security, ISDFS 2018 - Proceeding*, 1–6. 10.1109/ISDFS.2018.8355322

Department of Economic Planning and Development. (2018). *Report of Summary Findings*. Author.

Devadas, R., & Cholli, N. G. (2022). Interdependency Aware Qubit and Brownboost Rank Requirement Learning for Large Scale Software Requirement Prioritization. *International Journal of Computing and Digital Systems*, *11*(1), 625–634. doi:10.12785/ijcds/110150

Dhakate, M., & Ingole, A.B. (2015). Diagnosis of Pomegranate Plant Diseases Using Neural Network. *Fifth National Conference on Computer Vision. Pattern Recognition, Image Processing and Graphics (NCVPRIPG).*

Dhanasekar, V., & Preethi, Y. (2021). A Chatbot to promote Students Mental Health through Emotion Recognition. *2021 Third International Conference on Inventive Research in Computing Applications (ICIRCA)*, 1412-1416. 10.1109/ICIRCA51532.2021.9544838

Dhanasekaran, S., Devi, V. A., Narayanan, S. S., Vijayakarthik, P., Hariharasitaraman, S., & Rajasekaran, S. (2022). A smart digital attendance monitoring system for academic institution using machine learning techniques. *Webology, 19*(1).

Ding, H., & Yuan, Y. (2020). Preface: Industrial Artificial Intelligence. *Zhongguo Kexue Jishu Kexue/Scientia Sinica Technologica, 50*(11), 1413. https://doi.org/ doi:10.1360/SST-2020-0383

Djenouri, Y., Belhadi, A., Srivastava, G., & Lin, J. C. W. (2022). When explainable AI meets IoT applications for supervised learning. *Cluster Computing*, 1–11. doi:10.100710586-022-03659-3

Dlodlo, N., & Kalezhi, J. (2015, May). The internet of things in agriculture for sustainable rural development. In 2015 international conference on emerging trends in networks and computer communications (ETNCC) (pp. 13-18). IEEE. doi:10.1109/ETNCC.2015.7184801

Domakonda, V. K., Farooq, S., Chinthamreddy, S., Puviarasi, R., Sudhakar, M., & Boopathi, S. (2022). Sustainable Developments of Hybrid Floating Solar Power Plants: Photovoltaic System. In Human Agro-Energy Optimization for Business and Industry (pp. 148–167). IGI Global.

Doriya, R. (2017). Development of a cloud-based RTAB-map service for robots. *2017 IEEE International Conference on Real-Time Computing and Robotics (RCAR)*, 598–605. 10.1109/RCAR.2017.8311928

Doriya, R., Chakraborty, P., & Nandi, G. C. (2012). Robotic services in cloud computing paradigm. *2012 International Symposium on Cloud and Services Computing*, 80–83. 10.1109/ISCOS.2012.24

Dorri, Kanhere, & Jurdak. (2016). *Blockchain in internet of things: Challenges and solutions.* arXiv:1608.05187.

Dragomir, O. E., Dragomir, F., & Radulescu, M. (2014). Matlab application of Kohonen Self-Organizing Map to classify consumers' load profiles. *Procedia Computer Science, 31*, 474–479. doi:10.1016/j.procs.2014.05.292

Duan, B., Zhong, Y., & Liu, D. (2017, December). Education application of blockchain technology: Learning outcome and meta-diploma. In *2017 IEEE 23rd International Conference on Parallel and Distributed Systems (ICPADS)* (pp. 814-817). IEEE.

Du, Z., He, L., Chen, Y., Xiao, Y., Gao, P., & Wang, T. (2017). Robot cloud: Bridging the power of robotics and cloud computing. *Future Generation Computer Systems, 74*, 337–348. doi:10.1016/j.future.2016.01.002

Dwivedi, Y. K., Balakrishnan, J., Das, R., & Dutot, V. (2023). Resistance to innovation: A dynamic capability model based enquiry into retailers' resistance to blockchain adaptation. *Journal of Business Research, 157*, 113632. doi:10.1016/j.jbusres.2022.113632

Egert, F., Fukkink, R. G., & Eckhardt, A. G. (2018). Impact of in-service professional development programs for early childhood teachers on quality ratings and child outcomes: A meta-analysis. *Review of Educational Research, 88*(3), 401–433. doi:10.3102/0034654317751918

Egger, R. (2022). *Machine Learning in Tourism: A Brief Overview Applied Data Science in Tourism. Tourism on the Verge.* Springer. doi:10.1007/978-3-030-88389-8_6

Egger, R., & Gokce, E. (2022). Natural Language Processing (NLP): An Introduction: Making Sense of Textual Data. In *Applied Data Science in Tourism: Interdisciplinary Approaches, Methodologies, and Applications* (pp. 307–334). Springer International Publishing. doi:10.1007/978-3-030-88389-8_15

Ejaz, M., Kumar, T., Ylianttila, M., & Harjula, E. (2020, March). *Performance and efficiency optimization of multi-layer IoT edge architecture. In 2020 2nd 6G Wireless Summit (6G SUMMIT)*. IEEE.

Ejnioui, A., Otero, C. E., & Qureshi, A. A. (2012). Software requirement prioritization using fuzzy multi-attribute decision making. *2012 IEEE Conference on Open Systems, ICOS 2012*, 1–6. 10.1109/ICOS.2012.6417646

Elayan, H., Amin, O., Shubair, R. M., & Alouini, M. S. (2018, April). Terahertz communication: The opportunities of wireless technology beyond 5G. In *2018 International Conference on Advanced Communication Technologies and Networking (CommNet)* (pp. 1-5). IEEE. 10.1109/COMMNET.2018.8360286

El-Fatyany, A., Wang, H., Abd El-atty, S. M., & Khan, M. (2020). Biocyber Interface-Based Privacy for Internet of Bio-nano Things. *Wireless Personal Communications*, *114*(2), 1465–1483. doi:10.100711277-020-07433-9

Elijah, O., Rahman, T. A., Orikumhi, I., Leow, C. Y., & Hindia, M. N. (2018). An overview of Internet of Things (IoT) and data analytics in agriculture: Benefits and challenges. *IEEE Internet of Things Journal*, *5*(5), 3758–3773. doi:10.1109/JIOT.2018.2844296

Elsafi, S. H. (2014). Artificial Neural Networks (ANNs) for flood forecasting at Dongola Station in the River Nile, Sudan. *Alexandria Engineering Journal*, *53*(3), 655–662. doi:10.1016/j.aej.2014.06.010

Erol, I., Neuhofer, I. O., Dogru, T., Oztel, A., Searcy, C., & Yorulmaz, A. C. (2022). Improving sustainability in the tourism industry through blockchain technology: Challenges and opportunities. *Tourism Management*, *93*, 104628. doi:10.1016/j.tourman.2022.104628

Esfandiari, M., Jabari, S., McGrath, H., & Coleman, D. (2020). Flood mapping using random forest and identifying the essential conditioning factors; a case study in fredericton, new brunswick, canada. *ISPRS Annals of the Photogrammetry, Remote Sensing and Spatial Information Sciences*, *V-3-2020*, 609–615. doi:10.5194/isprs-annals-V-3-2020-609-2020

Faid, A., Sadik, M., & Sabir, E. (2022). An agile AI and IoT-augmented smart farming: A cost-effective cognitive weather station. *Agriculture*, *12*(1), 35. doi:10.3390/agriculture12010035

Fan, R.-E. (2008). LIBLINEAR: A library for largelinear classification. *Journal of Machine Learning Research*, *9*, 1871–1874.

Farasat, A., Nikolaey, A., Srihari, S. N., & Blair, R. H. (2015). Probabilistic Graphical Models in Modern Social Network Analysis. *Social Network Analysis and Mining*, *5*(1), 1–28. doi:10.100713278-015-0289-6

Farhangian, M., Purvis, M., Purvis, M., & Savarimuthu, T. B. R. (2015, May). The effects of temperament and team formation mechanism on collaborative learning of knowledge and skill in short-term projects. In *International Workshop on Multiagent Foundations of Social Computing* (pp. 48-65). Springer. 10.1007/978-3-319-24804-2_4

Farooq, M. S., Khan, M., & Abid, A. (2020). A framework to make charity collection transparent and auditable using blockchain technology. *Computers & Electrical Engineering*, *83*, 106588. doi:10.1016/j.compeleceng.2020.106588

Faruque, M. A. (2021, April). A Review Study on "5G NR Slicing Enhancing IoT & Smart Grid Communication". In *2021 12th International Renewable Engineering Conference (IREC)* (pp. 1-4). IEEE.

Ferreira, & Rabelo, Silva, & Cavalcanti. (2020). *Blockchain for Machine-to-Machine Interaction in Industry 4.0.* . doi:10.1007/978-981-15-1137-0_5

Ferreira, J. C. (2018). Building a community of users for open market energy. *Energies, 11*, 2330.

Firouzi, F., Farahani, B., & Marinšek, A. (2022). The convergence and interplay of edge, fog, and cloud in the AI-driven Internet of Things (IoT). *Information Systems, 107*, 101840. doi:10.1016/j.is.2021.101840

Fischbach, J., Frattini, J., Vogelsang, A., Mendez, D., Unterkalmsteiner, M., Wehrle, A., Henao, P. R., Yousefi, P., Juricic, T., Radduenz, J., & Wiecher, C. (2023). Automatic creation of acceptance tests by extracting conditionals from requirements: Nlp approach and case study. *Journal of Systems and Software, 197*, 111549. doi:10.1016/j.jss.2022.111549

Flavion, C. (2019). The impact of virtual, augmented and reality technologies on the customer experience. *Journal of Business Research, 100*, 547–560. doi:10.1016/j.jbusres.2018.10.050

Fotovatikhah, F., Herrera, M., Shamshirband, S., Chau, K., Faizollahzadeh Ardabili, S., & Piran, M. J. (2018). Survey of computational intelligence as basis to big flood management: Challenges, Research directions and future work. *Engineering Applications of Computational Fluid Mechanics, 12*(1), 411–437. doi:10.1080/19942060.2018.1448896

Fraga-Lamas, P., Fernández-Caramés, T. M., Suárez-Albela, M., Castedo, L., & González-López, M. (2016). A Review on Internet of Things for Defense and Public Safety. In Sensors (Basel, Switzerland) (Vol. 16, Issue 10). doi:10.339016101644

Fredrick, K. (2010). Mean girls (and boys): Cyberbullying and what can be done about it. *School Library Media Activities Monthly, 25*(8), 44–45.

Furquim, G., Neto, F., Pessin, G., Ueyama, J., de Albuquerque, J. P., Clara, M., Mendiondo, E. M., de Souza, V. C. B., de Souza, P., Dimitrova, D., & Braun, T. (2014). Combining Wireless Sensor Networks and Machine Learning for Flash Flood Nowcasting. *Proceedings of 28th International Conference on Advanced Information Networking and Applications Workshops*. 10.1109/WAINA.2014.21

Furui, S., Kikuchi, T., Shinnaka, Y., & Hori, C. (2004). Speech-to-Text and Speech-to-Speech Summarization of Spontaneous Speech. *IEEE Transactions on Speech and Audio Processing, 12*(4), 401–408. doi:10.1109/TSA.2004.828699

Fu, X., Wang, H., & Shi, P. (2021). A survey of Blockchain consensus algorithms: Mechanism, design and applications. *Science China. Information Sciences, 64*(2), 121101. doi:10.100711432-019-2790-1

Gallén, R. C., & Caro, E. T. (2018). A benchmarking study of K-Means and Kohonen self-organizing maps applied to features of mooc participants. *European Journal of Open, Distance and E-learning, 21*(1).

Ganguli, R., Mehta, A., & Sen, S. (2020). A Survey on Machine Learning Methodologies in Social Network Analysis. *Proceedings of 8th International Conference on Reliability, Infocom Technologies and Optimization (Trends and Future Directions) (ICRITO)*, 484-489. 10.1109/ICRITO48877.2020.9197984

Ganzarain, J., & Errasti, N. (2016). Three stage maturity model in SME's towards industry 4.0. *Journal of Industrial Engineering and Management, 9*(5), 1119–1128. doi:10.3926/jiem.2073

Gao, X., Liu, F., & Liu, C. (2022). Fractional-order rumor propagation model with memory effect. *Social Network Analysis and Mining, 12*(1), 159. doi:10.100713278-022-00988-4 PMID:36321165

García-Pablos, A., Cuadros, M., & Linaza, M. T. (2015). OpeNER: open tools to perform natural language processing on accommodation reviews. In *Information and Communication Technologies in Tourism 2015: Proceedings of the International Conference in Lugano, Switzerland, February 3-6, 2015* (pp. 125-137). Springer International Publishing. 10.1007/978-3-319-14343-9_10

García-Pablos, A., Cuadros, M., & Linaza, M. T. (2016). Automatic analysis of textual hotel reviews. *Information Technology & Tourism, 16*(1), 45–69. doi:10.100740558-015-0047-7

Gartner, Inc. (2020). *Gartner survey reveals 66% of organizations increased or did not change AI investments since the onset of COVID-19*. https://www.gartner.com/en/newsroom/press-releases/2020-10-01-gartner-survey-revels-66-percent-of-orgnizations-increased-or-did-not-change-ai-investments-since-the-onset-of-covid-19

Gavhane, A., Kokkula, G., Pandya, I., & Devadkar, K. (2018, March). Prediction of heart disease using machine learning. In *2018 second international conference on electronics, communication and aerospace technology (ICECA)* (pp. 1275-1278). IEEE. 10.1109/ICECA.2018.8474922

Ghadge, Mogale, Bourlakis, Maiyar, & Moradlou. (2022). Link between Industry 4.0 and green supply chain management: Evidence from the automotive industry. Computers and Industrial Engineering, 169.

Ghasempour, A. a. (2016). Finding the optimal number of aggregators in machine-to-machine advanced metering infrastructure architecture of smart grid based on cost, delay, and energy consumption. In 2016 13th IEEE Annual Consumer Communications \& Networking Conference (CCNC) (pp. 960-963). IEEE. doi:10.1109/CCNC.2016.7444917

Ghasempour, A. (2016). *Optimizing the advanced metering infrastructure architecture in smart grid*. Utah State University.

Ghorpade, P., Gadge, A., Lende, A., Chordiya, H., Gosavi, G., Mishra, A., Hooli, B., Ingle, Y. S., & Shaikh, N. (2021). Flood Forecasting Using Machine Learning: A Review. *Proceedings of 8th International Conference on Smart Computing and Communications (ICSCC)*. 10.1109/ICSCC51209.2021.9528099

Giudici, P. (2018). Fintech Risk Management: A Research Challenge for Artificial Intelligence in Finance. *Frontiers in Artificial Intelligence*, *1*, 1. doi:10.3389/frai.2018.00001 PMID:33733089

Gligor, D. M., & Holcomb, M. C. (2012). Understanding the role of logistics capabilities in achieving supply chain agility: A systematic literature review. *Supply Chain Management*, *17*(4), 438–453. doi:10.1108/13598541211246594

Global Cybersecurity Exposure Index. (2020). https://10guards.com/en/articles/global-cybersecurity-exposure-index-2020

Goh, C. F., Tan, O. K., Rasli, A., & Choi, S. L. (2019). Engagement in peer review, learner-content interaction and learning outcomes. *The International Journal of Information and Learning Technology*.

Gopstein, A. a. (2021). *NIST framework and roadmap for smart grid interoperability standards, release 4.0. Department of Commerce*. National Institute of Standards and Technology. doi:10.6028/NIST.SP.1108r4

Gowri, A. S., ShanthiBala, P., & Ramdinthara, I. Z. (2022). Fog-Cloud Enabled Internet of Things Using Extended Classifier System (XCS). *Artificial Intelligence-Based Internet of Things Systems*, 163–189.

Goymann, P., Herrling, D., & Rausch, A. (2019). Flood Prediction through Artificial Neural Networks: A case study in Goslar. Academic Press.

Gratton, L., & Erickson, T. J. (2007). Eight ways to build collaborative teams. *Harvard Business Review*, *85*(11), 100. PMID:18159790

Greco, C. M., Simeri, A., Tagarelli, A., & Zumpano, E. (2023). Transformer-based language models for mental health issues: A survey. *Pattern Recognition Letters*, *167*, 204–211. doi:10.1016/j.patrec.2023.02.016

Griffiths, C. (2023). *The Latest Cyber Crime Statistics*. AAG IT Support.

Grift, T. (2008). A review of automation and robotics for the bioindustry. *Journal of Biomechanical Engineering*, *1*, 37–54.

Grinblat, G. L., Uzal, L. C., Larese, M. G., & Granitto, P. M. (2016). Deep learning for plant identification using vein morphological patterns. *Computers and Electronics in Agriculture*, *127*, 418–424. doi:10.1016/j.compag.2016.07.003

Guerrero-Rodriguez, R., Álvarez-Carmona, M. Á., Aranda, R., & López-Monroy, A. P. (2021). Studying online travel reviews related to tourist attractions using nlp methods: The case of Guanajuato, Mexico. *Current Issues in Tourism*, 1–16.

Gulisano, V. a. (2014). Metis: a two-tier intrusion detection system for advanced metering infrastructures. In *International Conference on Security and Privacy in Communication Networks* (pp. 51-68). Springer. 10.1145/2602044.2602072

Gunasekaran, K., Boopathi, S., & Sureshkumar, M. (2022). Analysis of a Cryogenically Cooled Near-Dry Wedm Process Using Different Dielectrics. *Materiali in Tehnologije*, *56*(2), 179–186. doi:10.17222/mit.2022.397

Gungor, V. C. (2012). A survey on smart grid potential applications and communication requirements. *IEEE Transactions on industrial informatics*, *9*, 28-42.

Guo, F., Yu, F. R., Zhang, H., Li, X., Ji, H., & Leung, V. C. (2021). Enabling massive IoT toward 6G: A comprehensive survey. *IEEE Internet of Things Journal*, *8*(15), 11891–11915. doi:10.1109/JIOT.2021.3063686

Guo, H., & Yu, X. (2022). A Survey on Blockchain Technology and its security. Blockchain. *Research and Applications.*, *3*(2), 100067. doi:10.1016/j.bcra.2022.100067

Gupta, S. (2013). Using artificial neural network to predict the compressive strength of concrete containing nano-silica. *Civil Engineering and Architecture*, *1*(3), 96–102. doi:10.13189/cea.2013.010306

Gutierrez. (2016). *InsideBIGDATA Guide to Healthcare & Life Sciences*. DellEMC and INTEL.

Habibi, P., Farhoudi, M., Kazemian, S., Khorsandi, S., & Leon-Garcia, A. (2020). Fog computing: A comprehensive architectural survey. *IEEE Access: Practical Innovations, Open Solutions*, *8*, 69105–69133. doi:10.1109/ACCESS.2020.2983253

Habibzadeh, H., Dinesh, K., Shishvan, O. R., Boggio-Dandry, A., Sharma, G., & Soyata, T. (2019). A survey of healthcare Internet of Things (HIoT): A clinical perspective. *IEEE Internet of Things Journal*, *7*(1), 53–71. doi:10.1109/JIOT.2019.2946359 PMID:33748312

Haghi Kashani, M., Madanipour, M., Nikravan, M., Asghari, P., & Mahdipour, E. (2021). A systematic review of IoT in healthcare: Applications, techniques, and trends. In *Journal of Network and Computer Applications* (Vol. 192). Academic Press., doi:10.1016/j.jnca.2021.103164

Hajda, J., Jakuszewski, R., & Ogonowski, S. (2021). Security Challenges in Industry 4.0 PLC Systems. *Applied Sciences (Basel, Switzerland)*, *11*(21), 9785. doi:10.3390/app11219785

Halkiopoulos, C., Dimou, E., Kompothrekas, A., Telonis, G., & Boutsinas, B. (2021, June). The E-tour facilitator platform supporting an innovative health tourism marketing strategy. In *Culture and Tourism in a Smart, Globalized, and Sustainable World: 7th International Conference of IACuDiT, Hydra, Greece, 2020* (pp. 609-623). Springer International Publishing.

Hameed, K., Bajwa, I. S., Ramzan, S., Anwar, W., & Khan, A. (2020). An intelligent IoT based healthcare system using fuzzy neural networks. *Scientific Programming*, *2020*, 2020. doi:10.1155/2020/8836927

Haribalaji, V., Boopathi, S., & Asif, M. M. (2021). Optimization of friction stir welding process to join dissimilar AA2014 and AA7075 aluminum alloys. *Materials Today: Proceedings, 50*, 2227–2234. doi:10.1016/j.matpr.2021.09.499

Haribalaji, V., Boopathi, S., Mohammed Asif, M., Yuvaraj, T., Velmurugan, D., Anton Savio Lewise, K., Sudhagar, S., & Suresh, P. (2022). Influences of Mg-Cr filler materials in Friction Stir Process of Aluminium-based dissimilar alloys. *Materials Today: Proceedings, 66*, 948–954. doi:10.1016/j.matpr.2022.04.668

Harpaz, R., DuMochel, W., & Shah, N. H. (2016). Big data and adverse drug reaction detection. *Clinical Pharmacology and Therapeutics*, *99*(3), 268–270. doi:10.1002/cpt.302 PMID:26575203

Harrison, C., Eckman, B., Hamilton, R., Hartswick, P., Kalagnanam, J., Paraszczak, J., & Williams, P. (2010). Foundations for smarter cities. *IBM Journal of Research and Development*, *54*(4), 1–16. doi:10.1147/JRD.2010.2048257

Hartono, P., & Ogawa, K. (2014, October). Visualizing Learning Management System Data using Context-Relevant Self-Organizing Map. In *IEEE International Conference on Systems, Man, and Cybernetics* (SMC) (pp. 3487-3491). IEEE. 10.1109/SMC.2014.6974469

Healy, M., Hammer, S., & McIlveen, P. (2022). Mapping graduate employability and career development in higher education research: A citation network analysis. *Studies in Higher Education*, *47*(4), 799–811. doi:10.1080/03075079.2020.1804851

HermannM.PentekT.OttoB. (2015). Design Principles for Industrie 4.0 Scenarios: A Literature Review. *Technische Universitat Dortmund*, *1*(1), 4–16. doi:10.13140/RG.2.2.29269.22248

Hoodat, H., & Rashidi, H. (2009). Classification and analysis of risks in software engineering. *World Academy of Science, Engineering and Technology*, *56*(8), 446–452.

Hossain, M., & Aydin, H. (2011). A Web 2.0-based collaborative model for multicultural education. *Multicultural Education & Technology Journal*, *5*(2), 116–128. doi:10.1108/17504971111142655

Hsu, C. M. (2011). A hybrid procedure for stock price prediction by integrating self-organizing map and genetic programming. *Expert Systems with Applications*, *38*(11), 14026–14036. doi:10.1016/j.eswa.2011.04.210

Hu, B., & Li, H. (2020). Research on Charity System Based on Blockchain. *IOP Conference Series. Materials Science and Engineering*, *768*(7), 072020. doi:10.1088/1757-899X/768/7/072020

Huberman, G., Leshno, J., & Moallemi, C. (2017). Monopoly Without a Monopolist: An Economic Analysis of the Bitcoin Payment System. SSRN *Electronic Journal*, 1-56.

Huda, S. (2017). *A Hybrid Feature Selection with Ensemble Classification for Imbalanced Healthcare Data: A Case Study for Brain Tumor Diagnosis*. IEEE.

Hudis, C. A. (2015). Big data: Are large prospective randomized trials obsolete in the future? *The Breast*, *24*, S15–S18. doi:10.1016/j.breast.2015.07.005 PMID:26255742

Hu, G., Tay, W. P., & Wen, Y. (2012). Cloud robotics: Architecture, challenges and applications. *IEEE Network*, *26*(3), 21–28. doi:10.1109/MNET.2012.6201212

Hunter, R. F., Gough, A., O'Kane, N., McKeown, G., Fitzpatrick, A., Walker, T., McKinley, M., Lee, M., & Kee, F. (2018). Ethical Issues in Social Media Research for Public Health. *American Journal of Public Health*, *108*(3), 343–348. doi:10.2105/AJPH.2017.304249 PMID:29346005

Hussain, F., Hussain, R., Hassan, S. A., & Hossain, E. (2020). Machine Learning in IoT Security: Current Solutions and Future Challenges. *IEEE Communications Surveys and Tutorials*, *22*(3), 1686–1721. doi:10.1109/COMST.2020.2986444

Hu, Y., Du, J., Zhang, X., Hao, X., Ngai, E. W. T., Fan, M., & Liu, M. (2013). An integrative framework for intelligent software project risk planning. *Decision Support Systems*, *55*(4), 927–937. doi:10.1016/j.dss.2012.12.029

IBM Cloud. (n.d.). IBM. Retrieved from https://www.ibm.com/cloud

IBM Watson IoT Platform. (n.d.). IBM. Retrieved from https://internetofthings.ibmcloud.com

IBM. (2021). *2021 Digital Transformation Assessment COVID – 19: A Catalyst for change*. https://www.ibm.com/downloads/cas/MPQGMEN9

Ibrahem, M. I. (2021). Privacy Preserving and Efficient Data Collection Scheme for AMI Networks Using Deep Learning. *IEEE Internet of Things Journal, 8,* 17131-17146.

Ing Tay, S., Te Chuan, L., Nor Aziati, A. H., Nur Aizat Ahmad, A., Tay, S., Lee, T., Hamid, N. A., & Ahmad, A. (2018). An Overview of Industry 4.0: Definition, Components, and Government Initiatives Microencapsulation of self-healing agent for corrosion applications View project Biomedical Technology and IR 4.0: Management, Applications & Challenges View project An Overview of Industry 4.0: Definition, Components, and Government Initiatives. *Journal of Advanced Research in Dynamical and Control Systems, 12.* https://www.researchgate.net/publication/332440369

International Labour Organization. (2013). Global employment trends 2013. In Global Employment Trends. ILO.

Interpol. (2020, August 4). *INTERPOL report shows alarming rate of cyberattacks during COVID-19.* Www.interpol.int

Inyang, U. G., Umoh, U. A., Nnaemeka, I. C., & Robinson, S. A. (2019). Unsupervised Characterization and Visualization of Students' Academic Performance Features. *Comput. Inf. Sci., 12*(2), 103–116. doi:10.5539/cis.v12n2p103

Irannezhad, E., & Mahadevan, R. (2021). Is blockchain tourism's new hope? *Journal of Hospitality and Tourism Technology, 12*(1), 85–96. doi:10.1108/JHTT-02-2019-0039

Iranzo, B., Buelga, S., Cava, M. J., & Ortega-Barón, J. (2019). Cyberbullying, psychosocial adjustment, and suicidal ideation in adolescence. *Intervención Psicosocial, 28*(2), 75–81. doi:10.5093/pi2019a5

Irwan, Sukaesih, & Alamsyah. (2020). *Opinion mining using analytics to understand global tourism attraction.* Academic Press.

Islam, M., Dinh, A., Wahid, K., & Bhowmik, P. (2017). Detection of potato diseases using image segmentation and multiclass support vector machine. *IEEE 30th Canadian Conference on Electrical and Computer Engineering (CCECE).* 10.1109/CCECE.2017.7946594

Islam, S. R., Kwak, D., Kabir, M. H., Hossain, M., & Kwak, K. S. (2015). The internet of things for health care: A comprehensive survey. *IEEE Access : Practical Innovations, Open Solutions, 3,* 678–708. doi:10.1109/ACCESS.2015.2437951

Ismail, Z. a. (2014). A game theoretical analysis of data confidentiality attacks on smart-grid AMI. *IEEE journal on selected areas in communications, 32,* 1486-1499.

Ismail, H., Serhani, M., Hussien, N., Elabyad, R., & Navaz, A. (2022). Public wellbeing analytics framework using social media chatter data. *Social Network Analysis and Mining, 12*(1), 163. doi:10.100713278-022-00987-5 PMID:36345490

Ismail, Y. (Ed.). (2019). *Internet of Things (IoT) for automated and smart applications.* BoD–Books on Demand.

Issa, A., Hatiboglu, B., Bildstein, A., & Bauernhansl, T. (2018). Industrie 4.0 roadmap: Framework for digital transformation based on the concepts of capability maturity and alignment. *Procedia CIRP, 72,* 973–978. doi:10.1016/j.procir.2018.03.151

Iyer, B., & Patil, N. (2018). IoT enabled tracking and monitoring sensor for military applications. *International Journal of System Assurance Engineering and Management, 9*(6), 1294–1301. doi:10.100713198-018-0727-8

Jackson, D., & Lambert, C. (2023). Adolescent parent perceptions on sustainable career opportunities and building employability capitals for future work. *Educational Review, 0*(0), 1–23. doi:10.1080/00131911.2023.2182763

Janopaul-Naylor, E., & Feller, E. (2019). Cyberbullying: Harassment at your fingertips. *Rhode Island Medical Journal, 102*(9), 7–9. PMID:31675779

Javaid, Haleem, Singh, & Suman. (2022). Artificial Intelligence Applications for Industry4.0: A Literature-Based Study. *Journal of Industrial Integration and Management, 7*(1), 83–111. Doi:10.1142/S2424862222130004083

Javaid, M., Haleem, A., Singh, R. P., & Suman, R. (2022). An integrated outlook of Cyber–Physical Systems for Industry 4.0: Topical practices, architecture, and applications. In *Green Technologies and Sustainability*. KeAi Publishing.

Javaid, M., Haleem, A., Singh, R., Khan, S., & Suman, R. (2021). Blockchain technology applications for Industry 4.0: A literature-based review. Blockchain. *Research and Applications.*, 2(4), 100027. doi:10.1016/j.bcra.2021.100027

Jawad, H. M., Nordin, R., Gharghan, S. K., Jawad, A. M., & Ismail, M. (2017). Energy-efficient wireless sensor networks for precision agriculture: A review. *Sensors (Basel)*, 17(8), 1781. doi:10.339017081781 PMID:28771214

Jaware, T. H., Badgujar, R. D., & Patil, P. G. (2012). Crop disease detection using image segmentation. *Proceedings of Conference on Advances in Communication and Computing.*

Jeevanantham, Y. A., Saravanan, A., Vanitha, V., Boopathi, S., & Kumar, D. P. (2022). Implementation of Internet-of Things (IoT) in Soil Irrigation System. *IEEE Explore*, 1–5.

Jerald, J. (2016). *The VR Book Human-Centered Design for Virtual Reality*. ACM Books.

Jetley, G., & Zhang, H. (2019). Electronic health records in IS research: Quality issues, essential thresholds and remedial actions. *Decision Support Systems*, 126, 113137. doi:10.1016/j.dss.2019.113137

Jhanjhi, N., Humayun, M., & Almuayqil, S. N. (2021). Cyber security and privacy issues in industrial internet of things. *Computer Systems Science and Engineering*, 37(3), 361–380. doi:10.32604/csse.2021.015206

Jiang, H. (2019). Mobile fire evacuation system for large public buildings based on artificial intelligence and IoT. *IEEE Access : Practical Innovations, Open Solutions*, 7, 64101–64109. doi:10.1109/ACCESS.2019.2915241

Jimenez-Martinez, M., & Alfaro-Ponce, M. (2019). Fatigue damage effect approach by artificial neural network. *International Journal of Fatigue*, 124, 42–47. doi:10.1016/j.ijfatigue.2019.02.043

Joe & Washington. (2018). Art network—A solution for effective warranty management. *Curie J.*

Joe, I. R. P., & Varalakshmi, P. (2016). A Two Phase Approach for Efficient Clustering of Web Services. In M. Senthilkumar, V. Ramasamy, S. Sheen, C. Veeramani, A. Bonato, & L. Batten (Eds.), *Computational Intelligence, Cyber Security and Computational Models. Advances in Intelligent Systems and Computing* (Vol. 412). Springer. doi:10.1007/978-981-10-0251-9_17

Joe, P. (2015). A Survey on Neural Network Models for Data Analysis. *Journal of Engineering and Applied Sciences (Asian Research Publishing Network)*, 10(11), 4872–4876.

Jones, C., & Pimdee, P. (2017). Innovative ideas: Thailand 4.0 and the fourth industrial revolution. *Asian International Journal of Social Sciences*, 17(1), 4–35. doi:10.29139/aijss.20170101

Jorge, J., Gimenez, A., Silvestre-Cerda, J. A., Civera, J., Sanchis, A., & Juan, A. (2022). Live Streaming Speech Recognition Using Deep Bidirectional LSTM Acoustic Models and Interpolated Language Models. *IEEE/ACM Transactions on Audio, Speech, and Language Processing*, 30, 148–161. doi:10.1109/TASLP.2021.3133216

Kabir, M., Ahmed, T., Hasan, M. B., Laskar, M. T. R., Joarder, T. K., Mahmud, H., & Hasan, K. (2023). DEPTWEET: A typology for social media texts to detect depression severities. *Computers in Human Behavior*, 139, 107503. doi:10.1016/j.chb.2022.107503

Kagermann, W., & Helbig, J. (2013). *Recommendations for implementing the strategic initiative INDUSTRIE 4.0*. Final Report of the Industrie 4.0 WG.

Kalluri, B., Chronopoulos, C., & Kozine, I. (2021). The concept of smartness in cyber–physical systems and connection to urban environment. *Annual Reviews in Control*, 51, 1–22. doi:10.1016/j.arcontrol.2020.10.009

Kano, T., Sakti, S., & Nakamura, S. (2020). End-to-End Speech Translation With Transcoding by Multi-Task Learning for Distant Language Pairs. *IEEE/ACM Transactions on Audio, Speech, and Language Processing*, *28*, 1342–1355. doi:10.1109/TASLP.2020.2986886

Kapoor, A. (2019). *Hands-On Artificial Intelligence for IoT: Expert machine learning and deep learning techniques for developing smarter IoT systems*. Packt Publishing Ltd.

Karagiannis, V., Chatzimisios, P., Vazquez-Gallego, F., & Alonso-Zarate, J. (2015). A Survey on Application Layer Protocols for the Internet of Things. Transaction on IoT and Cloud Computing.

Karale, A. (2021). The Challenges of IoT Addressing Security, Ethics, Privacy, and Laws. In Internet of Things (Netherlands) (Vol. 15). Elsevier B.V. doi:10.1016/j.iot.2021.100420

Kasinathan, T., & Uyyala, S. R. (2021). Machine learning ensemble with image processing for pest identification and classification in field crops. *Neural Computing & Applications*, *33*(13), 7491–7504. doi:10.100700521-020-05497-z

Kassam, A., Derpsch, R., & Friedrich, T. (2014). Global achievements in soil and water conservation: The case of Conservation Agriculture. *International Soil and Water Conservation Research*, *2*(1), 5–13. doi:10.1016/S2095-6339(15)30009-5

Kathole, A. B., Vhatkar, K. N., & Patil, S. D. (2022). IoT-Enabled Pest Identification and Classification with New Meta-Heuristic-Based Deep Learning Framework. *Cybernetics and Systems*, 1–29. doi:10.1080/01969722.2022.2122001

Kaur, S., & Singh, M. (2015). Indian Sign Language animation generation system. *2015 1st International Conference on Next Generation Computing Technologies (NGCT)*. 10.1109/NGCT.2015.7375251

Kaur, J., & Kumar, K. R. R. (2021). *The Recent Trends in CyberSecurity: A Review. Journal of King Saud University*. Computer and Information Sciences.

Kausar, N., AliKhan, A., & Sattar, M. (2022). Towards better representation learning using hybrid deep learning model for fake news detection. *Social Network Analysis and Mining*, *12*(1), 165. doi:10.100713278-022-00986-6

Kavitha, D., & Anitha, D. (2016, December). Project Based Learning Using ICT Tools to Achieve Outcomes for the Course'Microcontrollers Based System Design': A Case Study. In *IEEE 4th International Conference on MOOCs, Innovation and Technology in Education (MITE)* (pp. 223-228). IEEE.

Kavitha, C., Malini, P. S. G., Charan, V., Manoj, N., Verma, A., & Boopathi, S. (2022). (in press). An experimental study on the hardness and wear rate of carbonitride coated stainless steel. *Materials Today: Proceedings*. Advance online publication. doi:10.1016/j.matpr.2022.09.524

Kavitha, D., & Anitha, D. (2018). Flipped Classroom Using ICT Tools to Improve Outcome for the Course'Soft Computing'-A Case Study. *Journal of Engineering Education Transformations*, *32*(2), 39–45.

Kavitha, D., & Anitha, D. (2021). Measuring the effectiveness of Individual assessment methods in Collaborative/Co-operative activity in online teaching. *Journal of Engineering Education Transformations*, *34*(0), 637–641. doi:10.16920/jeet/2021/v34i0/157235

Kavitha, D., Zobaa, A. F., Kumar, V. S., & Renuga, P. (2011). NSGA-II Optimized Neural Network Controlled Active Power Line Conditioner under Non-sinusoidal Conditions. *International Review of Electrical Engineering*, *6*(5).

Kayyali, B., Knott, D., & Van Kuiken, S. (2013). *The big-data revolution in US health care: accelerating value and innovation*. McKinsey Co. doi:10.1145/2537052.2537073

Kebande, V. R., Mudau, P. P., Ikuesan, R. A., Venter, H. S., & Choo, K.-K. R. (2020). Holistic digital forensic readiness framework for IoT-enabled organizations. *Forensic Science International: Reports*, *2*, 100117.

Kenney, M. (2015). Cyber-Terrorism in a Post-Stuxnet World. *Orbis*, *59*(1), 111–128. doi:10.1016/j.orbis.2014.11.009

Kersten, W., Blecker, T., Ringle, C. M., Gallay, O., Korpela, K., Tapio, N., & Nurminen, J. K. (2017). Published in: Digitalization in Supply Chain Management and Logistics A Peer-To-Peer Platform for Decentralized Logistics. *Tubdok. Tub.Tuhh.De*, 301–318.

Keum, H. J., Han, K. Y., & Kim, H. I. (2020). Real-Time Flood Disaster Prediction System by Applying Machine Learning Technique. *KSCE Journal of Civil Engineering*, *24*(9), 2835–2848. doi:10.100712205-020-1677-7

Kewalramani, S., Kidman, G., & Palaiologou, I. (2021). Using artificial intelligence (AI)- interfaced robotic toys in early childhood settings: A case for children's inquiry literacy. *European Early Childhood Education Research Journal*, *29*(5), 652–668. doi:10.1080/1350293X.2021.1968458

Khamkar, Kotwal, & Khatri. (2022). CharityChain - A Charity App Built on Blockchain. *International Journal of Scientific Research in Science, Engineering and Technology*, 73–77. doi:10.32628/IJSRSET122933

Khan, A., & Jaffar, M. A. (2015). Genetic algorithm and self organizing map based fuzzy hybrid intelligent method for color image segmentation. *Applied Soft Computing*, *32*, 300–310. doi:10.1016/j.asoc.2015.03.029

Khan, L. U., Yaqoob, I., Tran, N. H., Kazmi, S. A., Dang, T. N., & Hong, C. S. (2020). Edge-computing-enabled smart cities: A comprehensive survey. *IEEE Internet of Things Journal*, *7*(10), 10200–10232. doi:10.1109/JIOT.2020.2987070

Kharche, Bhagat, & Ibrahim. (2019). A Review On Flood Prediction Using Machine Learning based Apache System ML Python Platform. *Journal of Emerging Technologies and Innovative Research*, *6*(1).

Khattak, A. M. (2019). Smart meter security: Vulnerabilities, threat impacts, and countermeasures. In *International Conference on Ubiquitous Information Management and Communication* (pp. 554--562). Springer. 10.1007/978-3-030-19063-7_44

Khudhair, A. S. (2020). Internet Addiction. *Scholars Journal of Medical Case Reports*, *08*(04), 505–507. doi:10.36347jmcr.2020.v08i04.025

Kinkel, S., Baumgartner, M., & Cherubini, E. (2021). Prerequisites for the adoption of AI technologies in manufacturing – Evidence from a worldwide sample of manufacturing companies. *Technovation, 102375*. doi:10.1016/j.technovation.2021.102375

Kırcaburun, K., Kokkinos, C. M., Demetrovics, Z., Király, O., Griffiths, M. D., & Çolak, T. S. (2020). Problematic Online Behaviors among Adolescents and Emerging Adults: Associations between Cyberbullying Perpetration, Problematic Social Media Use, and Psychosocial Factors. *International Journal of Mental Health and Addiction*, *17*(4), 891–908. doi:10.100711469-018-9894-8

Kirimtat, A., Krejcar, O., Kertesz, A., & Tasgetiren, M. F. (2020). Future trends and current state of smart city concepts: A survey. *IEEE Access : Practical Innovations, Open Solutions*, *8*, 86448–86467. doi:10.1109/ACCESS.2020.2992441

Kishore, P., Barisal, S. K., & Mohapatra, D. P. (2020, September). An incremental malware detection model for meta-feature API and system call sequence. In *2020 15th Conference on Computer Science and Information Systems (FedCSIS)* (pp. 629-638). IEEE. 10.15439/2020F73

Kishore, A., Kumar, A., Singh, K., Punia, M., & Hambir, Y. (2018). Heart attack prediction using deep learning. *International Research Journal of Engineering and Technology*, *5*(04), 2395–0072.

Kitchenham, B., & Charters, S. (2007). Guidelines for performing Systematic Literature reviews in Software Engineering Version 2.3. *Engineering (London)*, *45*, 1051–1052. doi:10.1145/1134285.1134500

Kleshcheva, A. (2021). Perception of Dark Tourism. *Zeitschrift für Tourismuswissenschaft, 13*(2), 191–208. doi:10.1515/tw-2021-0014

Knowledgent. (2016). *Big data analytics in life sciences and healthcare: An overview*. Academic Press.

Koczkodaj, W. W., Mazurek, M., Strzałka, D., Wolny-Dominiak, A., & Woodbury-Smith, M. (2018). Electronic Health Record Breaches as Social Indicators. *Social Indicators Research, 141*(2), 861–871. doi:10.100711205-018-1837-z

Kohonen, T. (1990). The self-organizing map. *Proceedings of the IEEE, 78*(9), 1464–1480. doi:10.1109/5.58325

Komogortsev, O. V. (2015). Attack of mechanical replicas: Liveness detection with eye movements. *IEEE Transactions on Information Forensics and Security, 10*, 716-725.

Kon, J. (2019, March 10). Industry 4.0 initiatives to help develop Brunei Digital Economy. *Borneo Bulletin*. https://borneobulletin.com.bn/industry-4-0-initiatives-to-help-develop-brunei-digital-economy/

Konashevych, O. (2016). *Advantages and current issues of blockchain use in microgrids. Электронное моделирование.*

Konduru, V. R., & Bharamagoudra, M. R. (2017). Challenges and Solutions of Interoperability on IoT How far have we come in resolving the IoT interoperability issues. *2017 International Conference On Smart Technology for Smart Nation.* 10.1109/SmartTechCon.2017.8358436

Kostygina, G., Feng, M., Czaplicki, L., Tran, H., Tulsiani, S., Perks, S. N., Emery, S., & Schillo, B. (2021). Exploring the Discursive Function of Hashtags: A Semantic Network Analysis of JUUL-Related Instagram Messages. *Social Media + Society, 7*(4). doi:10.1177/20563051211055442

Koubaa, A. (2014). A service-oriented architecture for virtualizing robots in robot-as-a-service clouds. *Architecture of Computing Systems—ARCS 2014: 27th International Conference, Lübeck, Germany, February 25-28, 2014 Proceedings, 27*, 196–208.

Koyunouglu, A. S. (2019). Blockchain applications on smart grid A review. Kadir Has University.

Kraijak, S., & Tuwanut, P. (2015). A survey on IoT architectures, protocols, applications, security, privacy, real-world implementation and future trends. *11th International Conference on Wireless Communications, Networking and Mobile Computing (WiCOM 2015).* 10.1049/cp.2015.0714

Kranz, M. (2018). Why industry needs to accelerate IoT standards. *IEEE Internet of Things Magazine, 1*(1), 14–18. doi:10.1109/IOTM.2018.1700011

Krieger, U., Liu, W., Zhu, S. S., & Mundie, T. (2017). Advanced Block-Chain Architecture for e-Health Systems. In *19th International Conference on E-health Networking, Application & Services (HealthCom): 2nd IEEE International Workshop on.* IEEE Xplore Digital Library.

Krishnan, S., & Geetha, S. (2019, April). Prediction of Heart Disease Using Machine Learning Algorithms. In *2019 1st international conference on innovations in information and communication technology (ICIICT)* (pp. 1-5). IEEE.

Kulkarni, & Patil. (2012). Applying image processing technique to detect plant diseases. *Int. J. Mod. Eng. Res., 2*(5), 366.

Kumara, V., Mohanaprakash, T. A., Fairooz, S., Jamal, K., Babu, T., and B., S. (2023). Experimental Study on a Reliable Smart Hydroponics System. In *Human Agro-Energy Optimization for Business and Industry* (pp. 27–45). IGI Global. doi:10.4018/978-1-6684-4118-3.ch002

Kumar, N., Gusain, R., Kumar, S., & Sharma, R. (2022). D-Donation: Charity Fraud Prevention using Blockchain. *International Journal for Research in Applied Science and Engineering Technology, 10*(5), 3775–3778. doi:10.22214/ijraset.2022.43222

Kumar, P. R., Wan, A. T., & Suhaili, W. S. H. (2020). Exploring data security and privacy issues in internet of things based on five-layer architecture. *International Journal of Communication Networks and Information Security*, *12*(1), 108–121. doi:10.17762/ijcnis.v12i1.4345

Kumar, S., Saini, M., Goel, M., & Panda, B. S. (2021). Modeling information diffusion in online social networks using a modified forest-fire model. *Journal of Intelligent Information Systems*, *56*(2), 355–377. doi:10.100710844-020-00623-8 PMID:33071464

Kunverji, K., Shah, K., & Shah, N. (2021). A Flood Prediction System Developed Using Various Machine Learning Algorithms. SSRN *Electronic Journal*. doi:10.2139/ssrn.3866524

KuscuM.UnluturkB. D. (2021). *Internet of Bio-Nano Things: A Review of Applications, Enabling Technologies and Key Challenges*. https://arxiv.org/abs/2112.09249

Kuzlu, M., Fair, C., & Guler, O. (2021). Role of Artificial Intelligence in the Internet of Things (IoT) cybersecurity. *Discover Internet of Things*, *1*(1), 7. Advance online publication. doi:10.100743926-020-00001-4

Kwon, D., Hodkiewicz, M. R., Fan, J., Shibutani, T., & Pecht, M. G. (2016). IoT-Based Prognostics and Systems Health Management for Industrial Applications. *IEEE Access : Practical Innovations, Open Solutions*, *4*, 3659–3670. doi:10.1109/ACCESS.2016.2587754

Lagazio, M., Sherif, N., & Cushman, M. (2014). A multi-level approach to understanding the impact of cyber crime on the financial sector. *Computers & Security*, *45*, 58–74. doi:10.1016/j.cose.2014.05.006

Lakshmana Kumar, R. (2022). A Survey on blockchain for industrial Internet of Things. *Alexandria Engineering Journal*, *61*(8), 6001–6022. doi:10.1016/j.aej.2021.11.023

Lakshmanarao, A., Swathi, Y., & Sundareswar, P. S. S. (2019). Machine learning techniques for heart disease prediction. *Forest*, *95*(99), 97.

Lam, K. Y., Mitra, S., Gondesen, F., & Yi, X. (2022). ANT-Centric IoT Security Reference Architecture - Security-by-Design for Satellite-Enabled Smart Cities. *IEEE Internet of Things Journal*, *9*(8), 5895–5908. doi:10.1109/JIOT.2021.3073734

Lanktree, C., & Briere, J. (1991, January). *Early data on the trauma symptom checklist for children (TSC-C)* [Paper presentation].The meeting of the American Professional Society on the Abuse of Children, San Diego, CA, United States.

Larson, D. B., Broder, J. C., Bhargavan-Chatfield, M., Donnelly, L. F., Kadom, N., Khorasani, R., Sharpe, R. E. Jr, Pahade, J. K., Moriarity, A. K., Tan, N., Siewert, B., & Kruskal, J. B. (2020). Transitioning from peer review to peer learning: Report of the 2020 Peer Learning Summit. *Journal of the American College of Radiology*, *17*(11), 1499–1508. doi:10.1016/j.jacr.2020.07.016 PMID:32771491

Lasi, H., Fettke, P., Kemper, H. G., Feld, T., & Hoffmann, M. (2014). Industry 4.0. *Business & Information Systems Engineering*, *6*(4), 239–242. doi:10.100712599-014-0334-4

Laturkar, K., & Laturkar, K. (2022, April). Blockchain and the downstream segment: Increasing efficiency through technology. *Hydrocarbon Processing*, 75–78. https://www.hydrocarbonprocessing.com/magazine/2022/april-2022/digital-technology/blockchain-and-the-downstream-segment-increasing-efficiency-through-technology

Lauriola, I., Lavelli, A., & Aiolli, F. (2022). An introduction to deep learning in natural language processing: Models, techniques, and tools. *Neurocomputing*, *470*, 443–456. doi:10.1016/j.neucom.2021.05.103

Lavanya, Rani, & GaneshKumar. (2020). An automated low cost iot based fertilizer intimation system for smart agriculture. *Sustain. Comput.: Inf. Syst.*

Lawal, K., & Rafsanjani, H. N. (2022). Trends, benefits, risks, and challenges of IoT implementation in residential and commercial buildings. In Energy and Built Environment (Vol. 3, Issue 3, pp. 251–266). KeAi Communications Co. doi:10.1016/j.enbenv.2021.01.009

le Zhong, C., Zhu, Z., & Huang, R. G. (2016). Study on the IOT architecture and gateway technology. *Proceedings - 14th International Symposium on Distributed Computing and Applications for Business, Engineering and Science, DCABES 2015*, 196–199. 10.1109/DCABES.2015.56

Le, Le, Tromp, & Nguyen. (2018). Emerging Technologies for Health and Medicine. Scrivener Publishing.

Lee, J., Azamfar, M., & Singh, J. (2019). A Blockchain Enabled Cyber-Physical System Architecture for Industry 4.0 Manufacturing Systems. *Manufacturing Letters*, *20*, 34–39. doi:10.1016/j.mfglet.2019.05.003

Lee, J., Davari, H., Singh, J., & Pandhare, V. (2018). Industrial Artificial Intelligence for industry 4.0-based manufacturing systems. *Manufacturing Letters*, *18*(September), 20–23. doi:10.1016/j.mfglet.2018.09.002

Lee, S. a. (2014). A security mechanism of Smart Grid AMI network through smart device mutual authentication. In *The International Conference on Information Networking 2014 (ICOIN2014)* (pp. 592-595). IEEE.

Lee, S. K., Bae, M., & Kim, H. (2017). Future of IoT networks: A survey. *Applied Sciences (Basel, Switzerland)*, *7*(10), 1072. doi:10.3390/app7101072

Lee, Y. (2019). Using self-organizing map and clustering to investigate problem-solving patterns in the massive open online course: An exploratory study. *Journal of Educational Computing Research*, *57*(2), 471–490. doi:10.1177/0735633117753364

Letier, E., Stefan, D., & Barr, E. T. (2014). Uncertainty, risk, and information value in software requirements and architecture. *Proceedings - International Conference on Software Engineering. International Conference on Software Engineering*, *1*, 883–894. doi:10.1145/2568225.2568239

Liang, A., & McQueen, R. J. (2000). Computer assisted adult interactive learning in a multicultural environment. *Adult Learning*, *11*(1), 26–29. doi:10.1177/104515959901100108

Liang, S., Zuo, W., Shi, Z., Wang, S., Wang, J., & Zuo, X. (2022). A multi-level neural network for implicit causality detection in web texts. *Neurocomputing*, *481*, 121–132. doi:10.1016/j.neucom.2022.01.076

Li, H., Cui, J., & Ma, J. (2015). Social influence study in online networks: A three-level review. *Journal of Computer Science and Technology*, *30*(1), 184–199. doi:10.100711390-015-1512-7

Li, J., Yuan, Y., Wang, S., & Wang, F. (2018). Transaction Queuing Game in Bitcoin Blockchain. *IEEE Intelligent Vehicles Symposium*, 1–6.

Li, M., Wang, X., Gao, K., & Zhang, S. (2017). A Survey on Information Diffusion in Online Social Networks: Models and Methods. *Information (Basel)*, *8*(4), 118. Advance online publication. doi:10.3390/info8040118

Li, N., Huang, Q., Ge, X., He, M., Cui, S., Huang, P., Li, S., & Fung, S.-F. (2021). A Review of the Research Progress of Social Network Structure. *Complexity*, *6692210*, 1–14. Advance online publication. doi:10.1155/2021/6692210

Lin, C., He, D., Huang, X., Choo, K.-K. R., & Vasilakos, A. V. (2018). BSeIn: A blockchain-based secure mutual authentication with fine-grained access control system for industry 4.0. *Journal of Network and Computer Applications*, *116*, 42–52. doi:10.1016/j.jnca.2018.05.005

Lin, H., & Bergmann, N. W. (2016). IoT privacy and security challenges for smart home environments. *Information (Basel)*, *7*(3), 44. Advance online publication. doi:10.3390/info7030044

Lin, Y. W., Lin, Y. B., & Liu, C. Y. (2019). AItalk: A tutorial to implement AI as IoT devices. *IET Networks*, *8*(3), 195–202. doi:10.1049/iet-net.2018.5182

Li, Q., Li, S., Zhang, S., Hu, J., & Hu, J. (2019). A review of text corpus-based tourism big data mining. *Applied Sciences (Basel, Switzerland)*, *9*(16), 3300. doi:10.3390/app9163300

Li, R., Song, T., Mei, B., Li, H., Cheng, X., & Sun, L. (2018). Block chain for Large-Scale Internet of Things Data Storage and Protection. *IEEE Transactions on Services Computing*, 1–11. doi:10.1109/TSC.2018.2789893

List of Cybersecurity Associations and Organizations. (2018, February 28). *Cybercrime Magazine.*

Li, T., Sun, G., Yang, C., Liang, K., Ma, S., & Huang, L. (2018). Using self-organizing map for coastal water quality classification: Towards a better understanding of patterns and processes. *The Science of the Total Environment*, *628*, 1446–1459. doi:10.1016/j.scitotenv.2018.02.163 PMID:30045564

Liu, Dede, Huang, & Richards. (2017) Virtual, Augmented and Mixed Realities in Education. Springer.

Liu, T., Yuan, R., & Chang, H. (2012). Research on the internet of things in the automotive industry. *Proceedings - 2012 International Conference on Management of e-Commerce and e-Government, ICMeCG 2012*, 230–233. 10.1109/ICMeCG.2012.80

Liu, D., Yan, E. W., & Song, M. (2014). Microblog information diffusion: Simulation based on SIR model. *Journal of Beijing University of Posts and Telecommunications*, *16*, 28–33.

Li, X., Chen, T., Cheng, Q., Ma, S., & Ma, J. (2020). Smart applications in edge computing: Overview on authentication and data security. *IEEE Internet of Things Journal*, *8*(6), 4063–4080. doi:10.1109/JIOT.2020.3019297

Li, X., Deng, Y., & Ding, L. (2008). Study on precision agriculture monitoring framework based on WSN. *2nd International Conference on Anti-Counterfeiting, Security and Identification, ASID 2008*, 182–185. 10.1109/IWASID.2008.4688381

Li, Y., & Liu, Q. (2021). A comprehensive review study of cyber-attacks and cyber security; Emerging trends and recent developments. *Energy Reports*, *7*(7), 8176–8186. doi:10.1016/j.egyr.2021.08.126

Lodders, N., & Meijers, F. (2017). Collective learning, transformational leadership and new forms of careers guidance in universities. *British Journal of Guidance & Counselling*, *45*(5), 532–546. doi:10.1080/03069885.2016.1271864

Lubis, M., & Handayani, D. O. D. (2022). The relationship of personal data protection towards internet addiction: Cyber crimes, pornography and reduced physical activity. *Procedia Computer Science*, *197*, 151–161. doi:10.1016/j.procs.2021.12.129

Lu, H., Huang, K., Azimi, M., & Guo, L. (2019). Blockchain Technology in the Oil and Gas Industry: A Review of Applications, Opportunities, Challenges, and Risks. *IEEE Access : Practical Innovations, Open Solutions*, *7*, 41426–41444. doi:10.1109/ACCESS.2019.2907695

Luiijf, E. (2014). New and emerging threats of cyber crime and terrorism. *Cyber Crime and Cyber Terrorism Investigator's Handbook*, 19–29.

Luo, J., Savakis, A. E., & Singhal, A. (2005). A Bayesian network-based framework for semantic image understanding. *Pattern Recognition*, *38*(6), 919–934. doi:10.1016/j.patcog.2004.11.001

Luo, T., Huang, J., Kanhere, S. S., Zhang, J., & Das, S. K. (2019). Improving IoT data quality in mobile crowd sensing: A cross validation approach. *IEEE Internet of Things Journal*, *6*(3), 5651–5664. doi:10.1109/JIOT.2019.2904704

Lu, Y. (2017). Industry 4.0: A survey on technologies, applications and open research issues. *Journal of Industrial Information Integration*, *6*, 1–10. doi:10.1016/j.jii.2017.04.005

Lu, Z. X., Qian, P., Bi, D., Ye, Z. W., He, X., Zhao, Y. H., Su, L., Li, S., & Zhu, Z. L. (2021). Application of AI and IoT in clinical medicine: Summary and challenges. *Current Medical Science*, *41*(6), 1134–1150. doi:10.100711596-021-2486-z PMID:34939144

MacDermott, Á., Baker, T., Buck, P., Iqbal, F., & Shi, Q. (2020). The Internet of Things: Challenges and Considerations for Cybercrime Investigations and Digital Forensics. *International Journal of Digital Crime and Forensics*, *12*(1), 1–13. doi:10.4018/IJDCF.2020010101

Madilla, S. S., Dida, M. A., & Kaijage, S. (2021). A Review of Usage and Applications of Social Media Analytics. *Journal of Information Systems Engineering & Management*, *6*(3), 1–10. doi:10.21601/jisem/10958

Mahajan, H. B., Rashid, A. S., & Junnarkar, A. A. (2022). Integration of Healthcare 4.0 and blockchain into secure cloud-based electronic health records systems. *Applied Nanoscience*. Advance online publication. doi:10.100713204-021-02164-0 PMID:35136707

Mahakittikun, T., Suntrayuth, S., & Bhatiasevi, V. (2021). The impact of technological-organizational-environmental (TOE) factors on firm performance: Merchant's perspective of mobile payment from Thailand's retail and service firms. *Journal of Asia Business Studies*, *15*(2), 359–383. doi:10.1108/JABS-01-2020-0012

Mahmoud, R., Yousuf, T., Aloul, F., & Zualkernan, I. (2016). Internet of things (IoT) security: Current status, challenges and prospective measures. *2015 10th International Conference for Internet Technology and Secured Transactions, ICITST 2015*, 336–341. 10.1109/ICITST.2015.7412116

Mahmud, R., Kotagiri, R., & Buyya, R. (2018). Fog computing: A taxonomy, survey and future directions. In *Internet of everything* (pp. 103–130). Springer. doi:10.1007/978-981-10-5861-5_5

Malaka, R., & Zipf, A. (2000). Deep Map: Challenging IT research in the framework of a tourist information system. In *Information and Communication Technologies in Tourism 2000: Proceedings of the International Conference in Barcelona, Spain, 2000* (pp. 15-27). Springer Vienna.

Malathy, E. M., Praveen Joe, I. R., & Ajitha, P. (2021). Miniaturized Dual-Band Metamaterial-Loaded Antenna for Heterogeneous Vehicular Communication Networks. *Journal of the Institution of Electronics and Telecommunication Engineers*, 1–10. doi:10.1080/03772063.2021.1892539

Malik, V., & Singh, S. (2020). Artificial intelligent environments: Risk management and quality assurance implementation. *Journal of Discrete Mathematical Sciences and Cryptography*, *23*(1), 187–195. doi:10.1080/09720529.2020.1721883

Mamodiya, U., & Sharma, P. (2014). Article. *Journal of Electrical and Electronics Engineering*, *9*, 33–38.

Mandal, P. (2017). Artificial neural network prediction of buckling load of thin cylindrical shells under axial compression. *Engineering Structures*, *152*, 843–855. doi:10.1016/j.engstruct.2017.09.016

Manikantan, V., & Latha, S. (2013). Predicting the analysis of heart disease symptoms using medicinal data mining methods. *International Journal of Advanced Computer Theory and Engineering*, *2*, 46–51.

Marasco, J. (2007). Software requirements. In Dr. Dobb's Journal (Vol. 32, Issue 9). Pearson Education. doi:10.1201/b12149-5

Marrese-Taylor, E., Velásquez, J. D., Bravo-Marquez, F., & Matsuo, Y. (2013). Identifying customer preferences about tourism products using an aspect-based opinion mining approach. *Procedia Computer Science*, *22*, 182–191. doi:10.1016/j.procs.2013.09.094

Mashal, I., Alsaryrah, O., Chung, T. Y., Yang, C. Z., Kuo, W. H., & Agrawal, D. P. (2015). Choices for interaction with things on Internet and underlying issues. In *Ad Hoc Networks* (Vol. 28, pp. 68–90). Elsevier B.V., doi:10.1016/j.adhoc.2014.12.006

Maspo, N.-A., & Bin, H. (2020). Evaluation of Machine Learning approach in flood prediction scenarios and its input parameters: A systematic review. *IOP Conference Series. Earth and Environmental Science, 479*(1), 012038. doi:10.1088/1755-1315/479/1/012038

Mateo, R. M. A. (2013). Scalable adaptive group communication for collaboration framework of cloud-enabled robots. *Procedia Computer Science, 22*, 1239–1248. doi:10.1016/j.procs.2013.09.211

Matt & Rauch. (2020). SME 4.0: The Role of Small - and Medium - Sized Enterprises in the Digital Transformation. In Industry 4.0 for SMEs (pp. 3-36). Palgrave Macmillan.

Mattila, J. (2016). *The blockchain phenomenon--the disruptive potential of distributed consensus architectures.* ETLA Working Papers.

Mbitiru, R. a. (2017). Using input-output correlations and a modified slide attack to compromise IEC 62055-41. In *2017 IEEE International Autumn Meeting on Power, Electronics and Computing (ROPEC)* (pp. 1-6). IEEE. 10.1109/ROPEC.2017.8261692

McCarthy, J. (2007). From here to human-level AI. *Artificial Intelligence, 171*(18), 1174–1182. doi:10.1016/j.artint.2007.10.009

McLeod, A., & Dolezel, D. (2018). Cyber-analytics: Modeling factors associated with healthcare data breaches. *Decision Support Systems, 108*, 57–68. doi:10.1016/j.dss.2018.02.007

McLoughlin, L. T., Spears, B. A., Taddeo, C. M., & Hermens, D. F. (2019). Remaining connected in the face of cyberbullying: Why social connectedness is important for mental health. *Psychology in the Schools, 56*(6), 945–958. doi:10.1002/pits.22232

Mehami, J., Nawi, M., & Zhong, R. (2018). Smart automated guided vehicles for manufacturing in the context of Industry 4.0. *Procedia Manufacturing, 26*, 1077–1086. doi:10.1016/j.promfg.2018.07.144

Mehta, D., Tanwar, S., Bodkhe, U., Shukla, A., & Kumar, N. (2021). Blockchain-based Royalty Contract Transactions Scheme for Industry 4.0 Supply-Chain Management. *Information Processing & Management, 58*(4), 102586. Advance online publication. doi:10.1016/j.ipm.2021.102586

Mehta, N. K., Prasad, S. S., Saurav, S., Saini, R., & Singh, S. (2022). Three-dimensional DenseNet self-attention neural network for automatic detection of student's engagement. *Applied Intelligence, 52*(12), 13803–13823. doi:10.100710489-022-03200-4 PMID:35340984

Mendes, C., Osaki, R., & Da Costa, C. (2017). Internet of Things in Automated Production. *European Journal of Engineering Research and Science, 2*(10), 13. doi:10.24018/ejers.2017.2.10.499

Mengelkamp, E., Gärttner, J., Rock, K., Kessler, S., Orsini, L., & Weinhardt, C. (2018). Designing microgrid energy markets: A case study: The Brooklyn Microgrid. *Applied Energy, 210*, 870–880. doi:10.1016/j.apenergy.2017.06.054

Mentsiev, A., Guzueva, E., & Magomaev, T. (2020). Security challenges of the Industry 4.0. *Journal of Physics: Conference Series, 1515*(3), 032074. doi:10.1088/1742-6596/1515/3/032074

Merenda, M., Porcaro, C., & Iero, D. (2020). Edge machine learning for ai-enabled iot devices: A review. *Sensors (Basel), 20*(9), 2533. doi:10.339020092533 PMID:32365645

Mettler, M. (2016, September). Blockchain technology in healthcare: The revolution starts here. In *2016 IEEE 18th international conference on e-health networking, applications and services (Healthcom)* (pp. 1-3). IEEE.

Mhlanga, D. (2021). Artificial intelligence in the industry 4.0, and its impact on poverty, innovation, infrastructure development, and the sustainable development goals: Lessons from emerging economies? *Sustainability (Basel), 13*(11), 5788. Advance online publication. doi:10.3390u13115788

Miah, S. J., Vu, H. Q., Gammack, J., & McGrath, M. (2017). A big data analytics method for tourist behaviour analysis. *Information & Management, 54*(6), 771–785. doi:10.1016/j.im.2016.11.011

Mian, S. H., Salah, B., Ameen, W., Moiduddin, K., & Alkhalefah, H. (2020). Adapting universities for sustainability education in industry 4.0: Channel of challenges and opportunities. *Sustainability (Basel), 12*(15), 6100. doi:10.3390u12156100

Mich, L. (2022). AI and Big Data in Tourism: Definitions, Areas, and Approaches. In *Applied Data Science in Tourism: Interdisciplinary Approaches, Methodologies, and Applications* (pp. 3–15). Springer International Publishing. doi:10.1007/978-3-030-88389-8_1

Milovanovic, D., & Bojkovic, Z. (n.d.). *Cloud-based IoT healthcare applications: Requirements and recommendations.* https://www.iaras.org/iaras/journals/ijitws

Mittal, M., Tanwar, S., Agarwal, B., & Goyal, L. M. (2019). Energy conservation for IoT devices. *Concepts, Paradigms and Solutions, Studies in Systems Decision and Control*, 1–365.

Moeuf, A., Pellerin, R., Lamouri, S., Tamayo-Giraldo, S., & Barbaray, R. (2018). The industrial management of SMEs in the era of Industry 4.0. *International Journal of Production Research, 56*(3), 1118–1136. doi:10.1080/00207543.2017.1372647

Mohamed, R. M., Shahin, O. R., Hamed, N. O., Zahran, H. Y., & Abdellattif, M. H. (2022). Analyzing the patient behavior for improving the medical treatment using smart healthcare and IoT-based deep belief network. *Journal of Healthcare Engineering, 2022*, 2022. doi:10.1155/2022/6389069 PMID:35310183

Mohammed, C. M., & Askar, S. (2021). Machine learning for IoT healthcare applications: A review. *International Journal of Science and Business, 5*(3), 42–51.

Mohammed, E. A., Far, B. H., & Naugler, C. (2014). Applications of the MapReduce programming framework to clinical big data analysis: Current landscape and future trends. *BioData Mining, 7*(1), 22. doi:10.1186/1756-0381-7-22 PMID:25383096

Mohan, S., Thirumalai, C., & Srivastava, G. (2019). Effective heart disease prediction using hybrid machine learning techniques. *IEEE Access : Practical Innovations, Open Solutions, 7*, 81542–81554. doi:10.1109/ACCESS.2019.2923707

Mohanty, S. P., Choppali, U., & Kougianos, E. (2016). Everything you wanted to know about smart cities: The Internet of things is the backbone. *IEEE Consumer Electronics Magazine, 5*(3), 60–70. doi:10.1109/MCE.2016.2556879

Molinero, X., & Riquelme, F. (2021). Influence decision models: From cooperative game theory to social network analysis. *Computer Science Review, 39*(1), 100343. Advance online publication. doi:10.1016/j.cosrev.2020.100343

Molokwu, B. C., & Kobti, Z. (2020). Social Network Analysis using RLVECN: Representation Learning via Knowledge-Graph Embeddings and Convolutional Neural-Network, *Proceedings of the Twenty-Ninth International Joint Conference on Artificial Intelligence (IJCAI-20)*, 5198-5199. 10.24963/ijcai.2020/739

Mondal, P. (2011). Critical Review of Precision Agriculture Technologies and Its Scope of Adoption in India. *American Journal of Experimental Agriculture, 1*(3), 49–68. doi:10.9734/AJEA/2011/155

Mondal, P., & Basu, M. (2009). Adoption of precision agriculture technologies in India and in some developing countries: Scope, present status and strategies. *Progress in Natural Science*, *19*(6), 659–666. doi:10.1016/j.pnsc.2008.07.020

Morkunas, V. J., Paschen, J., & Boon, E. (2019). How blockchain technologies impact your business model. *Business Horizons*, *62*(3), 295–306. doi:10.1016/j.bushor.2019.01.009

Mosavi, A., Ozturk, P., & Chau, K. (2018). Flood Prediction Using Machine Learning Models: Literature Review. *Water (Basel)*, *10*(11), 1536. doi:10.3390/w10111536

Mosenia, A., & Jha, N. K. (2016). A comprehensive study of security of internet-of-things. *IEEE Transactions on Emerging Topics in Computing*, *5*(4), 586–602. doi:10.1109/TETC.2016.2606384

Moslemzadeh Tehrani, P., Abdul Manap, N., & Taji, H. (2013). Cyber terrorism challenges: The need for a global response to a multi-jurisdictional crime. *Computer Law & Security Report*, *29*(3), 207–215. doi:10.1016/j.clsr.2013.03.011

Muijs, D., Aubrey, C., Harris, A., & Briggs, M. (2004). How do they manage? A review of the research on leadership in early childhood. *Journal of Early Childhood Research*, *2*(2), 157–169. doi:10.1177/1476718X04042974

Müller, J. M., Buliga, O., & Voigt, K. I. (2018). Fortune favors the prepared: How SMEs approach business model innovations in Industry 4.0. *Technological Forecasting and Social Change, 132*, 2–17. doi:10.1016/j.techfore.2017.12.019

Müller, J. M., Buliga, O., & Voigt, K. I. (2021). The role of absorptive capacity and innovation strategy in the design of industry 4.0 business Models - A comparison between SMEs and large enterprises. European Management Journal, 39(3), 333–343. doi:10.1016/j.emj.2020.01.002

Mullet, V., Sondi, P., & Ramat, E. (2022). A blockchain-based confidentiality-preserving approach to traceability in Industry 4.0. *International Journal of Advanced Manufacturing Technology*. Advance online publication. doi:10.100700170-022-10431-9

Municipality, D. (2021). UOB-IEASMA-125: Experimental Analysis of Machine Learning Classification Algorithms. In First International IEASMA Conference on Engineering, Applied Sciences and Management (UOB-IEASMA 2021). Academic Press.

Mustafa, M. A. (2016). A local electricity trading market: Security analysis. In 2016 IEEE PES innovative smart grid technologies conference Europe (ISGT-Europe) (pp. 1-6). IEEE.

Myatt, G. J. (1969). Making sense of data I: a practical guide to exploratory data analysis and data mining (2nd ed.). Academic Press.

Myilsamy, S., & Boopathi, S. (2017). Grey Relational Optimization of Powder Mixed Near-Dry Wire Cut Electrical Discharge Machining of Inconel 718 Alloy. *Asian Journal of Research in Social Sciences and Humanities*, *7*(3), 18. doi:10.5958/2249-7315.2017.00157.5

Myilsamy, S., & Sampath, B. (2021). Experimental comparison of near-dry and cryogenically cooled near-dry machining in wire-cut electrical discharge machining processes. *Surface Topography : Metrology and Properties*, *9*(3), 035015. doi:10.1088/2051-672X/ac15e0

Mylrea, M. a. (2017). *Blockchain for smart grid resilience: Exchanging distributed energy at speed, scale and security. In 2017 Resilience Week*. RWS.

Mylrea, M. a. (2017). Cybersecurity and optimization in smart "autonomous" buildings. In *Autonomy and Artificial Intelligence: A Threat or Savior?* (pp. 263–294). Springer. doi:10.1007/978-3-319-59719-5_12

Naiknavare, M. (2022). Blockchain based Transparent and Genuine Charity Application. *International Journal for Research in Applied Science and Engineering Technology, 10*(5), 4232–4248. doi:10.22214/ijraset.2022.42839

Nakamoto, S. (2009). *Bitcoin: A Peer-to-Peer Electronic Cash System.* https://metzdowd.com

Nakamura, S., Markov, K., Nakaiwa, H., Kikui, G., Kawai, H., Jitsuhiro, T., Zhang, J.-S., Yamamoto, H., Sumita, E., & Yamamoto, S. (2006). The ATR Multilingual Speech-to-Speech Translation System. *IEEE Transactions on Audio, Speech, and Language Processing, 14*(2), 365–376. doi:10.1109/TSA.2005.860774

Nakano, T., Suda, T., Okaie, Y., & Moore, M. J. (2016, February). Analysis of cyber aggression and cyber-bullying in social networking. In *2016 IEEE Tenth International Conference on Semantic Computing (ICSC)* (pp. 337-341). IEEE. 10.1109/ICSC.2016.111

Naseem, R., Shaukat, Z., Irfan, M., Shah, M. A., Ahmad, A., Muhammad, F., Glowacz, A., Dunai, L., Antonino-Daviu, J., & Sulaiman, A. (2021). Empirical assessment of machine learning techniques for software requirements risk prediction. *Electronics (Basel), 10*(2), 1–19. doi:10.3390/electronics10020168

Naveen, M., & Ponraj, A. S. (2020). Speech Recognition with Gender Identification and Speaker Diarization. *2020 IEEE International Conference for Innovation in Technology (INOCON).* 10.1109/INOCON50539.2020.9298241

Navickas, V., Kuznetsova, S. A., & Gruzauskas, V. (2017). Cyber–physical systems expression in industry 4.0 context. *Financial and Credit Activity Problems of Theory and Practice, 2*(23), 188-197.

Nayyar, Mahapatra, Le, & Suseendran. (2018). Paper. *International Journal of Engineering & Technology, 7*(2),150-160.

Nayyar, A., & Singh, R. (2015). A Comprehensive Review of Simulation Tools for Wireless Sensor Networks (WSNs). *Journal of Wireless Networking and Communications, 5*(1), 19–47.

Nebbione, G., & Calzarossa, M. C. (2020). Security of IoT application layer protocols: Challenges and findings. In *Future Internet* (Vol. 12, Issue 3). MDPI AG. doi:10.3390/fi12030055

Negris, T. (1993). Thin client. In *Wikipedia.* en.wikipedia.org

Neme, A., Pulido, J. R. G., Muñoz, A., Hernández, S., & Dey, T. (2015). Stylistics analysis and authorship attribution algorithms based on self-organizing maps. *Neurocomputing, 147*, 147–159. doi:10.1016/j.neucom.2014.03.064

Netexplo. (n.d.). A Brief Review of New Ways of Learning in the Digital Era, Human Learning in the Digital Era, UNESCO Publishing. PROFINET system description: Technology and application, ''PROFIBUS Nutzerorganisation e. V. (PNO) PROFIBUS & PROFINETInternational (PI), Karlsruhe, Germany. *Tech. Rep., 4*, 132.

Nevo, S., Morin, E., Gerzi Rosenthal, A., Metzger, A., Barshai, C., Weitzner, D., Voloshin, D., Kratzert, F., Elidan, G., Dror, G., Begelman, G., Nearing, G., Shalev, G., Noga, H., Shavitt, I., Yuklea, L., Royz, M., Giladi, N., Peled Levi, N., ... Matias, Y. (2022). Flood forecasting with machine learning models in an operational framework. *Hydrology and Earth System Sciences, 26*(15), 4013–4032. doi:10.5194/hess-26-4013-2022

Newman, M. E. (2005). Threshold effects for two pathogens spreading on a network. *Physical Review Letters, 95*(10), 108701. doi:10.1103/PhysRevLett.95.108701 PMID:16196976

Nikhar, S., & Karandikar, A. M. (2016). Prediction of heart disease using machine learning algorithms. *International Journal of Advanced Engineering. Management Science, 2*(6), 239484.

Nikolidakis, S. A., Kandris, D., Vergados, D. D., & Douligeris, C. (2015). Energy efficient automated control of irrigation in agriculture by using wireless sensor networks. *Computers and Electronics in Agriculture, 113*, 154–163. doi:10.1016/j.compag.2015.02.004

Nirmala Devi & Priya. (2016). *Invoicing and analytics for small and micro manufacturing enterprises 2016*. Academic Press.

NIST. (n.d.). SHA-1. In *Wikipedia*. en.wikipedia.org

Noura, M., Atiquzzaman, M., & Gaedke, M. (2019). Interoperability in Internet of Things: Taxonomies and Open Challenges. *Mobile Networks and Applications*, *24*(3), 796–809. doi:10.100711036-018-1089-9

Novo, O. (2018). Blockchain Meets IoT: An Architecture for Scalable Access Management in IoT. *IEEE Internet of Things Journal*, *5*(2), 1184–1195. doi:10.1109/JIOT.2018.2812239

Noymanee, J., Nikitin, N. O., & Kalyuzhnaya, A. V. (2017). Urban Pluvial Flood Forecasting using Open Data with Machine Learning Techniques in Pattani Basin. *Procedia Computer Science*, *119*, 288–297. doi:10.1016/j.procs.2017.11.187

Noymanee, J., & Theeramunkong, T. (2019). Flood Forecasting with Machine Learning Technique on Hydrological Modeling. *Procedia Computer Science*, *156*, 377–386. doi:10.1016/j.procs.2019.08.214

Nurek, M., & Michalski, R. (2020). Combining Machine Learning and Social Network Analysis to Reveal the Organizational Structures. *Applied Sciences*, *10*(1699), 1-43.

Odo, C., Masthoff, J., & Beacham, N. (2019, June). Group formation for collaborative learning. In *International Conference on Artificial Intelligence in Education* (pp. 206-212). Springer.

Okunlaya, R. O., Syed Abdullah, N., & Alias, R. A. (2022). Artificial intelligence (AI) library services innovative conceptual framework for the digital transformation of university education. *Library Hi Tech*, *40*(6), 1869–1892. Advance online publication. doi:10.1108/LHT-07-2021-0242

Okutan, A., & Çebi, Y. (2019). A Framework for Cyber Crime Investigation. *Procedia Computer Science*, *158*, 287–294. doi:10.1016/j.procs.2019.09.054

Okwu, M. O., & Tartibu, L. K. (2020). Sustainable supplier selection in the retail industry: A TOPSIS- and ANFIS-based evaluating methodology. *International Journal of Engineering Business Management*, *12*, 1847979019899542. doi:10.1177/1847979019899542

Oliveira, T., Thomas, M., & Espadanal, M. (2014). Assessing the determinants of cloud computing adoption: An analysis of the manufacturing and services sectors. *Information & Management*, *51*(5), 497–510. doi:10.1016/j.im.2014.03.006

Omar, I. A. (2021). Implementing decentralized auctions using blockchain smart contracts. *Technological Forecasting and Social Change, 168*, 120786.

Osornio, R. A., & Prieto, M. D. (2020). New Trends in the Use of Artificial Intelligence for the Industry 4.0. New Trends in the Use of Artificial Intelligence for the Industry 4.0. doi:10.5772/intechopen.86015

Osuwa, A. A., Ekhoragbon, E. B., & Fat, L. T. (2017). Application of Artificial Intelligence in Internet of Things. *2017 9th International Conference on Computational Intelligence and Communication Networks*, 169–173. https://doi.org/10.1109/CICN.2017.38

Othman, A. (2020, October 31). MSMEs drive Brunei's economy. *Borneo Bulletin*. https://borneobulletin.com.bn/msmes-drive-bruneis-economy/

Oztemel & Gursev. (2018). Literature review of Industry 4.0 and related technologies. Journal of Intelligent Manufacturing, 31, 127-182.

Oztemel, E., & Gursev, S. (2020). Literature review of Industry 4.0 and related technologies. *Journal of Intelligent Manufacturing*, *31*(1), 127–182. doi:10.100710845-018-1433-8

Pacheco, A., & Reis, J. C. (2019, October). A small-scale educational workbench for Industry 4.0. In *IECON 2019-45th annual conference of the IEEE industrial electronics society* (Vol. 1, pp. 3127-3132). IEEE.

Padil, K. H., Bakhary, N., & Hao, H. (2017). The use of a non-probabilistic artificial neural network to consider uncertainties in vibration-based-damage detection. *Mechanical Systems and Signal Processing*, *83*, 194–209. doi:10.1016/j.ymssp.2016.06.007

Pagan, N., & Dörfler, F. (2019). Game theoretical inference of human behavior in social networks. *Nature Communications*, *10*(1), 5507. doi:10.103841467-019-13148-8 PMID:31796729

Palaniappan, M., Tirlangi, S., Mohamed, M. J. S., Moorthy, R. M. S., Valeti, S. V., & Boopathi, S. (2023). Fused Deposition Modelling of Polylactic Acid (PLA)-Based Polymer Composites: A Case Study. In Development, Properties, and Industrial Applications of 3D Printed Polymer Composites (pp. 66–85). IGI Global.

Palenzuela, Á. J. J., Frasincar, F., & Truşcǎ, M. M. (2022). Modeling Second Language Acquisition with pre-trained neural language models. *Expert Systems with Applications*, *207*, 117871. doi:10.1016/j.eswa.2022.117871

Pal, K. (2021). Privacy, Security and Policies: A Review of Problems and Solutions with Blockchain-Based Internet of Things Applications in Manufacturing Industry. *Procedia Computer Science*, *191*, 176–183. doi:10.1016/j.procs.2021.07.022

Panchalingam, R., & Chan, K. C. (2021). A state-of-the-art review on artificial intelligence for Smart Buildings. *Intelligent Buildings International*, *13*(4), 203–226. doi:10.1080/17508975.2019.1613219

Paraforos, D. S., & Griepentrog, H. W. (2021). Digital farming and field robotics: Internet of things, cloud computing, and big data. *Fundamentals of Agricultural and Field Robotics*, 365–385.

Paraskevas, A. (2022). Cybersecurity in travel and tourism: a risk-based approach. In *Handbook of e-Tourism* (pp. 1605–1628). Springer International Publishing. doi:10.1007/978-3-030-48652-5_100

Park, C., Seo, J., Lee, S., Lee, C., Moon, H., Eo, S., & Lim, H. (2021). BTS: Back TranScription for Speech-to-Text Post-Processor using Text-to-Speech-to-Text. *Proceedings of the 8th Workshop on Asian Translation (WAT2021)*. 10.18653/v1/2021.wat-1.10

Park, E., Cho, Y., Han, J., & Kwon, S. J. (2017). Comprehensive approaches to user acceptance of Internet of Things in a smart home environment. *IEEE Internet of Things Journal*, *4*(6), 2342–2350. doi:10.1109/JIOT.2017.2750765

Parra, X., Tort-Martorell, X., Ruiz-Viñals, C., & Álvarez-Gómez, F. (2019). A maturity model for the information-driven SME. *Journal of Industrial Engineering and Management*, *12*(1), 154–175. doi:10.3926/jiem.2780

Pastorsatorras, R., & Vespignani, A. (2001). Epidemic spreading in scale-free networks. *Physical Review Letters*, *86*(14), 3200–3203. doi:10.1103/PhysRevLett.86.3200 PMID:11290142

Patil, P. D., Mhatre, D. J., Gharat, N. H., & Tinsu, J. (2022). Transparent Charity System using Smart Contracts on Ethereum using Blockchain. *International Journal for Research in Applied Science and Engineering Technology*, *10*(4), 743–748. doi:10.22214/ijraset.2022.41339

Paul, A., Ahmad, A., Rathore, M. M., & Jabbar, S. (2016). Smartbuddy: Defining human behaviors using big data analytics in social internet of things. *IEEE Wireless Communications*, *23*(5), 68–74. doi:10.1109/MWC.2016.7721744

Paul, A., & Das, P. (2014). Flood Prediction Model using Artificial Neural Network. International. *Journal of Computer Applications Technology and Research*, *3*(7), 473–478. doi:10.7753/IJCATR0307.1016

Payal, M., Dixit, P., Sairam, T. V. M., & Goyal, N. (2021). Robotics, AI, and the IoT in Defense Systems. In AI and IoT-Based Intelligent Automation in Robotics (pp. 109–128). Wiley. doi:10.1002/9781119711230.ch7

Payne, B. R. (2019). Car Hacking: Accessing and Exploiting the CAN Bus Protocol. In Journal of Cybersecurity Education, Research and Practice (Vol. 2019, Issue 1). Academic Press.

Pereira, T., Barreto, L., & Amaral, A. (2017). Network and information security challenges within Industry 4.0 paradigm. *Procedia Manufacturing*, *13*, 1253–1260. doi:10.1016/j.promfg.2017.09.047

Perera, C., Barhamgi, M., De, S., Baarslag, T., Vecchio, M., & Choo, K. K. R. (2018). Designing the sensing as a service ecosystem for the internet of things. *IEEE Internet of Things Magazine*, *1*(2), 18–23. doi:10.1109/IOTM.2019.1800023

Peres, R. S., Jia, X., Lee, J., Sun, K., Colombo, A. W., & Barata, J. (2020). Industrial Artificial Intelligence in Industry 4.0 -Systematic Review, Challenges and Outlook. *IEEE Access : Practical Innovations, Open Solutions*, *8*, 220121–220139. doi:10.1109/ACCESS.2020.3042874

Perez, C., & Karmakar, S. (2023). An NLP-assisted Bayesian time-series analysis for prevalence of Twitter Cyberbullying during the COVID-19 pandemic. *Social Network Analysis and Mining*, *13*(1), 51. doi:10.100713278-023-01053-4 PMID:36937491

Pérez-Sánchez, M. D. L. Á., Tian, Z., Barrientos-Báez, A., Gómez-Galán, J., & Li, H. (2021). Blockchain technology for winning consumer loyalty: Social norm analysis using structural equation modeling. *Mathematics*, *9*(5), 532. doi:10.3390/math9050532

Petrović, S., Bjelica, D., & Radenković, B. (2021, September). Loyalty system development based on blockchain technology. In *E-business technologies conference proceedings* (Vol. 1, No. 1, pp. 157-161). Academic Press.

Pishdad-Bozorgi, P., Gao, X., & Shelden, D. R. (2020). Introduction to cyber-physical systems in the built environment. In *Construction 4.0* (pp. 23–41). Routledge. doi:10.1201/9780429398100-2

Ploennigs, J., Cohn, J., & Stanford-Clark, A. (2018). The future of IoT. *IEEE Internet of Things Magazine*, *1*(1), 28–33. doi:10.1109/IOTM.2018.1700021

Plotnek, J. J., & Slay, J. (2021). Cyber terrorism: A homogenized taxonomy and definition. *Computers & Security*, *102*, 102145.

Polyzos, G. C., & Fotiou, N. (2017). Blockchain-assisted information distribu- tion for the Internet of Things. *2017 IEEE International Conference on Information Reuse and Integration (IRI)*, 75–78. 10.1109/IRI.2017.83

Popovic, I. A. (2022). Multi-Agent Real-Time Advanced Metering Infrastructure Based on Fog Computing. *Energies*, *15*, 373.

Porambage, P., Okwuibe, J., Liyanage, M., Ylianttila, M., & Taleb, T. (2018). Survey on multi-access edge computing for internet of things realization. *IEEE Communications Surveys and Tutorials*, *20*(4), 2961–2991. doi:10.1109/COMST.2018.2849509

Porambage, P., Ylianttila, M., Schmitt, C., Kumar, P., Gurtov, A., & Vasilakos, A. (2016). The Quest for Privacy in the Internet of Things. *IEEE Cloud Computing*, *3*(2), 36–45. doi:10.1109/MCC.2016.28

Pourrahmani, H., Yavarinasab, A., Zahedi, R., Gharehghani, A., Mohammadi, M. H., Bastani, P., & van Herle, J. (2022). The applications of Internet of Things in the automotive industry: A review of the batteries, fuel cells, and engines. In *Internet of Things (Netherlands)* (Vol. 19). Elsevier B.V. doi:10.1016/j.iot.2022.100579

Praveen Joe, Malathy, Aishwarya, Akila, & Akshaya. (2022). A Hybrid PSO-ACO Algorithm to Facilitate Software Project Scheduling. *International Journal of e-Collaboration*. doi:10.4018/IJeC.304039

Praveen Joe, I. R., & Varalakshmi, P. (2019a). An Analysis on Web-Service-Generated Data to Facilitate Service Retrieval. *Applied Mathematics & Information Sciences, 13*(1), 47–55. doi:10.18576/amis/130107

Praveen Joe, I. R., & Varalakshmi, P. (2019b). A Multilayered Clustering Framework to build a Service Portfolio using Swarm-based algorithms. *Automatika (Zagreb), 60*(3), 294–304. doi:10.1080/00051144.2019.1590951

Preface. (2021). *The ultimate guide for artificial intelligence (AI) for kids.* https://www.pr eface.ai/blog/kids-learning/ai-for-kids

Prieto, M. D., Sobrino, Á. F., Soto, L. R., Romero, D., Biosca, P. F., & Martínez, L. R. (2019, September). Active learning based laboratory towards engineering education 4.0. In *2019 24th IEEE international conference on emerging technologies and factory automation (ETFA)* (pp. 776-783). IEEE.

Pruthvi, M., Karthika, S., & Bhalaji, N. (2019, February). A Novel Framework for SIoT College. In *2019 International Conference on Computational Intelligence in Data Science (ICCIDS)* (pp. 1-4). IEEE.

Purbasari, I. Y., Puspaningrum, E. Y., & Putra, A. B. S. (2020, July). Using Self-Organizing Map (SOM) for Clustering and Visualization of New Students based on Grades. *Journal of Physics: Conference Series, 1569*(2), 022037. doi:10.1088/1742-6596/1569/2/022037

Puthal, D., Mohanty, S. P., Bhavake, S. A., Morgan, G., & Ranjan, R. (2019). Fog computing security challenges and future directions. *IEEE Consumer Electronics Magazine, 8*(3), 92–96. doi:10.1109/MCE.2019.2893674

Puthal, D., Mohanty, S. P., Wilson, S., & Choppali, U. (2021). Collaborative edge computing for smart villages (energy and security). *IEEE Consumer Electronics Magazine, 10*(3), 68–71. doi:10.1109/MCE.2021.3051813

Qalati, S. A., Yuan, L. W., Khan, M. A. S., & Anwar, F. (2021). A mediated model on the adoption of social media and SMEs' performance in developing countries. *Technology in Society, 64*(January), 101513. doi:10.1016/j.techsoc.2020.101513

Qiang, Z., Pasiliao, E. L., & Zheng, Q. P. (2019). Model-based learning of information diffusion in social media networks. *Applied Network Science, 4*(1), 111. doi:10.100741109-019-0215-3

Qu, X., Yang, L., Guo, K., Ma, L., Sun, M., Ke, M., & Li, M. (2021). A survey on the development of self-organizing maps for unsupervised intrusion detection. *Mobile Networks and Applications, 26*(2), 808–829. doi:10.100711036-019-01353-0

Raghupathi, W., & Raghupathi, V. (2014). Big data analytics in healthcare: Promise and potential. *Health Information Science and Systems, 2*(1), 3. doi:10.1186/2047-2501-2-3 PMID:25825667

Rahim, M. A., Rahman, M. A., Rahman, M. M., Asyhari, A. T., Bhuiyan, M. Z. A., & Ramasamy, D. (2021). Evolution of IoT-enabled connectivity and applications in automotive industry: A review. In *Vehicular Communications* (Vol. 27). Elsevier Inc. doi:10.1016/j.vehcom.2020.100285

Rahman, Z., Khalil, I., Yi, X., & Atiquzzaman, M. (2021). Blockchain-Based Security Framework for a Critical Industry 4.0 Cyber-Physical System. *IEEE Communications Magazine, 59*(5), 128–134. doi:10.1109/MCOM.001.2000679

Raimundo, R. J., & Rosário, A. T. (2022). Cybersecurity in the Internet of Things in Industrial Management. *Applied Sciences (Basel, Switzerland), 12*(3), 1598. doi:10.3390/app12031598

Ramadan, R. A. (n.d.). *Internet of Things (IoT) Security Vulnerabilities: A Review.* https://plomscience.com/journals/index.php/PLOMSAI/index

Ramos, C. M. (2021). Blockchain Technology in Tourism Management: Potentialities, Challenges, and Implications. In Blockchain Technology and Applications for Digital Marketing (pp. 84-109). IGI Global.

Rani, S., Kataria, A., Sharma, V., Ghosh, S., Karar, V., Lee, K., & Choi, C. (2021). Threats and Corrective Measures for IoT Security with Observance of Cybercrime: A Survey. In Wireless Communications and Mobile Computing (Vol. 2021). Hindawi Limited. doi:10.1155/2021/5579148

Rathee, G., Balasaraswathi, M., Chandran, K. P., Gupta, S. D., & Boopathi, C. S. (2021). A secure IoT sensors communication in industry 4.0 using blockchain technology. *Journal of Ambient Intelligence and Humanized Computing*, *12*(1), 533–545. Advance online publication. doi:10.100712652-020-02017-8

Rathi, V. K., Rajput, N. K., Mishra, S., Grover, B. A., Tiwari, P., Jaiswal, A. K., & Hossain, M. S. (2021). An edge AI-enabled IoT healthcare monitoring system for smart cities. *Computers & Electrical Engineering*, *96*, 107524. doi:10.1016/j.compeleceng.2021.107524

Ray, P. P. (2018). A survey on Internet of Things architectures. *Journal of King Saud University-Computer and Information Sciences*, *30*(3), 291–319. doi:10.1016/j.jksuci.2016.10.003

Reid, E. R., & Kelestyn, B. (2022). Problem representations of employability in higher education: Using design thinking and critical analysis as tools for social justice in careers education. *British Journal of Guidance & Counselling*, *50*(4), 631–646. doi:10.1080/03069885.2022.2054943

Rejeb, A., & Karim, R. (2019). Blockchain technology in tourism: Applications and possibilities. *World Scientific News*, *137*, 119–144.

Revelo, R. A., & Baber, L. D. (2018). Engineering Resistors: Engineering Latina/o Students and Emerging Resistant Capital. *Journal of Hispanic Higher Education*, *17*(3), 249–269. doi:10.1177/1538192717719132

Reyna, C., Martín, C., Chen, J., Soler, E., & Díaz, M. (2018). On Blockchain and its integration with IoT Challenges and opportunities. *Future Generation Computer Systems*, *88*, 173–190. doi:10.1016/j.future.2018.05.046

Rezaeianzadeh, M., Tabari, H., Arabi Yazdi, A., Isik, S., & Kalin, L. (2013). Flood flow forecasting using ANN, ANFIS and regression models. *Neural Computing & Applications*, *25*(1), 25–37. doi:10.100700521-013-1443-6

Ricci, F. (2022). Recommender systems in tourism. In *Handbook of e-Tourism* (pp. 457–474). Springer International Publishing. doi:10.1007/978-3-030-48652-5_26

Roberts, M. L., Temple, M. A., Mills, R. F., & Raines, R. A. (2006). Evolution of the air interface of cellular communications systems toward 4G realization. *IEEE Communications Surveys and Tutorials*, *8*(1), 2–23. doi:10.1109/COMST.2006.323439

Rodrawangpai, B., & Daungjaiboon, W. (2022). Improving text classification with transformers and layer normalization. *Machine Learning with Applications*, *10*, 100403. doi:10.1016/j.mlwa.2022.100403

Rothe, P. R., & Kshirsagar, R. V. (2015). Cotton leaf disease identification using pattern recognition techniques. *2015 International Conference on Pervasive Computing: Advance Communication Technology and Application for Society, ICPC 2015*, 1–6. 10.1109/PERVASIVE.2015.7086983

Roy, G. (2023). Travelers' online review on hotel performance–Analyzing facts with the Theory of Lodging and sentiment analysis. *International Journal of Hospitality Management*, *111*, 103459. doi:10.1016/j.ijhm.2023.103459

Rozario, A., & Zhang, C. (2022). The Effects of Artificial Intelligence on Firms' Internal Information Quality. SSRN *Electronic Journal*. doi:10.2139/ssrn.3850823

S., P. K., Sampath, B., R., S. K., Babu, B. H., & N., A. (2022). Hydroponics, Aeroponics, and Aquaponics Technologies in Modern Agricultural Cultivation. In *Trends, Paradigms, and Advances in Mechatronics Engineering* (pp. 223–241). IGI Global. doi:10.4018/978-1-6684-5887-7.ch012

Sabounchi, M. a. (2017). Towards resilient networked microgrids: Blockchain-enabled peer-to-peer electricity trading mechanism. In *2017 IEEE Conference on Energy Internet and Energy System Integration (EI2)* (pp. 1-5). IEEE. 10.1109/EI2.2017.8245449

Sadia, H., Abbas, S. Q., & Faisal, M. (2019). Volatile requirement prioritization: A fuzzy based approach. *International Journal of Engineering and Advanced Technology*, 8(5), 2467–2472.

Sadia, H., Abbas, S. Q., & Faisal, M. (2023). A Bayesian Network-Based Software Requirement Complexity Prediction Model. In *Lecture Notes on Data Engineering and Communications Technologies* (Vol. 139, pp. 197–213). Springer. doi:10.1007/978-981-19-3015-7_15

Sadiq, M., & Jain, S. K. (2013). A fuzzy based approach for requirements prioritization in goal oriented requirements elicitation process. *Proceedings of the International Conference on Software Engineering and Knowledge Engineering, SEKE*, 54–58.

Sahana, M., Reshma, H., Pavithra, R., & Kavya, B. S. (2022). Plant Leaf Disease Detection Using Image Processing. *Lecture Notes in Electrical Engineering*, 789(9), 161–168. doi:10.1007/978-981-16-1338-8_14

Saher, N., Baharom, F., Romli, R., Bikki, S., Saher, N., Baharom, F., Romli, R., & Bikki, S. (2018a). A Review of Requirement Prioritization Techniques in Agile Software Development. *Knowledge Management International Conference (KMICe)*, 25–27. http://www.kmice.cms.net.my/ProcKMICe/KMICe2018/pdf/CR63.pdf

Saher, N., Baharom, F., Romli, R., Bikki, S., Saher, N., Baharom, F., Romli, R., & Bikki, S. (2018b). A Review of Requirement Prioritization Techniques in Agile Software Development. *Knowledge Management International Conference (KMICe)*, 25–27.

Saidi, F., Trabelsi, Z., Salah, K., & Ghezala, H. B. (2017). Approaches to analyze cyber terrorist communities: Survey and challenges. *Computers & Security*, 66, 66–80. doi:10.1016/j.cose.2016.12.017

Saini, K. (2021). Blockchain Foundation. *Essential Enterprise Blockchain Concepts and Applications*, 1–14. https://doi.org/1 doi:10.1201/9781003097990-

Salais-Fierro, T. E., Saucedo Martínez, J. A., & Pérez-Pérez, B. I. (2020). A decision making approach using fuzzy logic and anfis: A retail study case. *EAI/Springer Innovations in Communication and Computing*, 155–172. doi:10.1007/978-3-030-48149-0_12

Saleh, H., Avdoshin, S., & Dzhonov, A. (2019). *Platform for Tracking Donations of Charitable Foundations Based on Blockchain Technology. In 2019 Actual Problems of Systems and Software Engineering.* APSSE. doi:10.1109/APSSE47353.2019.00031

Samikannu, R., Koshariya, A. K., Poornima, E., Ramesh, S., Kumar, A., & Boopathi, S. (2022). Sustainable Development in Modern Aquaponics Cultivation Systems Using IoT Technologies. In *Human Agro-Energy Optimization for Business and Industry* (pp. 105–127). IGI Global.

Sampath, B. C. S., & Myilsamy, S. (2022). Application of TOPSIS Optimization Technique in the Micro-Machining Process. In Trends, Paradigms, and Advances in Mechatronics Engineering (pp. 162–187). IGI Global. doi:10.4018/978-1-6684-5887-7.ch009

Sampath, B., & Myilsamy, S. (2021). Experimental investigation of a cryogenically cooled oxygen-mist near-dry wire-cut electrical discharge machining process. *Strojniski Vestnik. Jixie Gongcheng Xuebao*, 67(6), 322–330. doi:10.5545v-jme.2021.7161

Sampath, B., Pandian, M., Deepa, D., & Subbiah, R. (2022). Operating parameters prediction of liquefied petroleum gas refrigerator using simulated annealing algorithm. *AIP Conference Proceedings*, *2460*(1), 070003. doi:10.1063/5.0095601

Sampath, B., Sureshkumar, M., Yuvaraj, T., & Velmurugan, D. (2021). Experimental investigations on eco-friendly helium-mist near-dry wire-cut edm of m2-hss material. *Materials Research Proceedings*, *19*, 175–180. doi:10.21741/9781644901618-22

Sampath, B., Yuvaraj, D., & Velmurugan, D. (2022). Parametric analysis of mould sand properties for flange coupling casting. *AIP Conference Proceedings*, *2460*(1), 070002. doi:10.1063/5.0095599

SAP. (n.d.). *What is Industry 4.0?* https://www.sap.com/india/insights/what-is-industry-4-0.html

Saranya, S., Muvvala, S. P., Chauhan, V., & Satwik, R. (2022). Crowdfunding Charity Platform Using Blockchain. *2022 International Conference on Inventive Computation Technologies (ICICT)*. 10.1109/ICICT54344.2022.9850562

Saravanan, M., Vasanth, M., Boopathi, S., Sureshkumar, M., & Haribalaji, V. (2022). Optimization of Quench Polish Quench (QPQ) Coating Process Using Taguchi Method. *Key Engineering Materials*, *935*, 83–91. doi:10.4028/p-z569vy

Sardogan, M., Tuncer, A., & Ozen, Y. (2018). Plant Leaf Disease Detection and Classification Based on CNN with LVQ Algorithm. *UBMK 2018 - 3rd International Conference on Computer Science and Engineering*, 382–385. 10.1109/UBMK.2018.8566635

Sasikumar, R., Karthikeyan, P., & Thangavel, M. (2021). *Blockchain Technology for IoT: An Information Security Perspective*. . doi:10.4018/978-1-7998-5839-3.ch008

Sattar, K. A., & Al-Omary, A. (2021). *A survey: Security issues in IoT environment and IoT architecture*. Academic Press.

Savchenko, A. V., Savchenko, L. V., & Makarov, I. (2022). Classifying emotions and engagement in online learning based on a single facial expression recognition neural network. *IEEE Transactions on Affective Computing*, *13*(4), 2132–2143. doi:10.1109/TAFFC.2022.3188390

Schaupp, E., Abele, E., & Metternich, J. (2017). Potentials of Digitalization in Tool Management. *Procedia CIRP*, *63*, 144–149. doi:10.1016/j.procir.2017.03.172

Schlick, J. (2012, May). Cyber-physical systems in factory automation-Towards the 4th industrial revolution. In *2012 9th IEEE International Workshop on Factory Communication Systems* (pp. 55-55). IEEE.

Schuckert, M., Liu, X., & Law, R. (2015). Hospitality and tourism online reviews: Recent trends and future directions. *Journal of Travel & Tourism Marketing*, *32*(5), 608–621. doi:10.1080/10548408.2014.933154

Seh, A. H., Zarour, M., Alenezi, M., Sarkar, A. K., Agrawal, A., Kumar, R., & Ahmad Khan, R. (2020). Healthcare Data Breaches: Insights and Implications. *Health Care*, *8*(2), 133. doi:10.3390/healthcare8020133 PMID:32414183

Senthil, T. S., Puviyarasan, M., Babu, S. R., Surakasi, R., & Sampath, B. (2023). Industrial Robot-Integrated Fused Deposition Modelling for the 3D Printing Process. In Development, Properties, and Industrial Applications of 3D Printed Polymer Composites (pp. 188–210). IGI Global.

Senthil, T. S., Puviyarasan, M., Babu, S. R., Surakasi, R., Sampath, B., & Associates. (2023). Industrial Robot-Integrated Fused Deposition Modelling for the 3D Printing Process. In Development, Properties, and Industrial Applications of 3D Printed Polymer Composites (pp. 188–210). IGI Global.

Senthilkumar, R. (2021). Prognostic System for Heart Disease using Machine Learning: A Review. *Journal of Science Technology and Research*, *2*(1).

Senthilkumar, S. A., & Bharatendara, K. (2018). Big data in healthcare management: A review of literature. *Am. J. Theor. Appl. Bus.*, *4*(2), 57–69. doi:10.11648/j.ajtab.20180402.14

Sequeiros, J. B. F., Chimuco, F. T., Samaila, M. G., Freire, M. M., & Inácio, P. R. M. (2020). Attack and System Modeling Applied to IoT, Cloud, and Mobile Ecosystems: Embedding Security by Design. *ACM Computing Surveys*, *53*(2), 1–32. Advance online publication. doi:10.1145/3376123

Servida, F., & Casey, E. (2019). IoT forensic challenges and opportunities for digital traces. *Digital Investigation*, *28*, S22–S29. doi:10.1016/j.diin.2019.01.012

Setiadi, H., Saptono, R., Suryani, E., & Agnestya, N. R. (2019, December). Recommendation System Using Self Organizing Map (SOM) for Thesis Examiners and Preceptors of Universitas Sebelas Maret-Department of Informatics. In *IEEE 6th International Conference on Engineering Technologies and Applied Sciences (ICETAS)* (pp. 1-7). IEEE.

Seyidov, J., & Adomaitienė, R. (2016). Factors influencing local tourists' decision-making on choosing a destination: A case of Azerbaijan. *Ekonomika (Nis)*, *95*(3), 112–127. doi:10.15388/Ekon.2016.3.10332

Shafique, K., Khawaja, B. A., Sabir, F., Qazi, S., & Mustaqim, M. (2020). Internet of things (IoT) for next-generation smart systems: A review of current challenges, future trends and prospects for emerging 5G-IoT scenarios. *IEEE Access : Practical Innovations, Open Solutions*, *8*, 23022–23040. doi:10.1109/ACCESS.2020.2970118

Shah, T., & Venkatesan, S. (2018). Authentication of IoT Device and IoT Server Using Secure Vaults. *Proceedings - 17th IEEE International Conference on Trust, Security and Privacy in Computing and Communications and 12th IEEE International Conference on Big Data Science and Engineering, Trustcom/BigDataSE 2018*, 819–824. 10.1109/TrustCom/BigDataSE.2018.00117

Shah, S. M. S., Batool, S., Khan, I., Ashraf, M. U., Abbas, S. H., & Hussain, S. A. (2017). Feature extraction through parallel probabilistic principal component analysis for heart disease diagnosis. *Physica A*, *482*, 796–807. doi:10.1016/j.physa.2017.04.113

Shakila, U. K., & Sultana, S. (2021). A Decentralized Marketplace Application based on Ethereum Smart Contract. *2021 24th International Conference on Computer and Information Technology (ICCIT)*. 10.1109/ICCIT54785.2021.9689879

Shakirov, V., Solovyeva, K. P., & Dunin-Barkowski, W. L. (2018). Review of State-of-the-Art in Deep Learning Artificial Intelligence. *Optical Memory and Neural Networks (Information Optics)*, *27*(2), 65–80. doi:10.3103/S1060992X18020066

Sharabov, M., & Tsochev, G. (2020). The Use of Artificial Intelligence in Industry 4.0. *Problems of Engineering Cybernetics and Robotics*, *73*, 17–29. doi:10.7546/PECR.73.20.02

Sharma, Y. K., & Khatal Sunil, S. (2019). Health Care Patient Monitoring using IoT and Machine Learning. *IOSR Journal of Engineering*.

Shaukat, Z. S., Naseem, R., & Zubair, M. (2018). A dataset for software requirements risk prediction. *Proceedings - 21st IEEE International Conference on Computational Science and Engineering, CSE 2018*, 112–118. 10.1109/CSE.2018.00022

Shi, L., Du, J., Liang, M., & Kosrtm, F. (2019). A Sparse RNN-Topic Model for Discovering Bursty Topics in Big Data of Social Networks. *Journal of Information Science and Engineering*, *35*(4), 749–767.

Shokry, M. a.-E. (2022). Systematic survey of advanced metering infrastructure security: Vulnerabilities, attacks, countermeasures, and future vision. *Future Generation Computer Systems*.

Shree, R., Shukla, A. K., Pandey, R. P., & Shukla, V. (2021). A contiguous cyber crime investigation framework to deal with the cyber dependent-cum-cyber enabled crimes. *Materials Today: Proceedings*. Advance online publication. doi:10.1016/j.matpr.2020.12.428

Shruthi, J, Sumathi, M S, Srivatsa Raju, S, & Vidya, R Pai. (2020). Forecasting & Detection Of Flood Using Random Forest Learning Method. *European Journal of Molecular and Clinical Medicine*.

Shumaker & Lackey. (2014). Virtual, Augmented and Mixed Reality Applications of Virtual and Augmented Reality. Springer.

Shwartz-Ziv, R., & Armon, A. (2022). Tabular data: Deep learning is not all you need. *Information Fusion*, *81*, 84–90. doi:10.1016/j.inffus.2021.11.011

Siburian, H. K. (2016). Emerging Issue in Cyber Crime: Case Study Cyber Crime in Indonesia. *International Journal of Scientific Research*, *5*(11), 511–514.

Sinche, S., Raposo, D., Armando, N., Rodrigues, A., Boavida, F., Pereira, V., & Silva, J. S. (2019). A survey of IoT management protocols and frameworks. *IEEE Communications Surveys and Tutorials*, *22*(2), 1168–1190. doi:10.1109/COMST.2019.2943087

Singapore Economic Development Board. (2019). *The Smart Industry Readiness Index*. https://www.edb.gov.sg/en/about-edb/media-releases-publications/advanced-manufacturing-release.html

Singh, A., Rajak, R., Mistry, H., & Raut, P. (2020). Aid, Charity and Donation Tracking System Using Blockchain. *2020 4th International Conference on Trends in Electronics and Informatics (ICOEI)*, (48184). 10.1109/ICOEI48184.2020.9143001

Singh, A., Sharma, A., Sharma, N., Kaushik, I., & Bhushan, B. (2019, July). Taxonomy of attacks on web based applications. In *2019 2nd International Conference on Intelligent Computing, Instrumentation and Control Technologies (ICICICT)* (Vol. 1, pp. 1231-1235). IEEE. 10.1109/ICICICT46008.2019.8993264

Singla, S. (2020). AI and IoT in healthcare. *Internet of things use cases for the healthcare industry*, 1-23.

Sinha, A., & Kumar, P. (2021). Information diffusion modeling and analysis for socially interacting networks. *Social Network Analysis and Mining*, *11*(1), 11. doi:10.100713278-020-00719-7 PMID:33456625

Sirisha, N. S., Agarwal, T., Monde, R., Yadav, R., & Hande, R. (2019). Proposed Solution for Trackable Donations using Blockchain. *2019 International Conference on Nascent Technologies in Engineering (ICNTE)*. 10.1109/ICNTE44896.2019.8946019

Sisinni, E., Saifullah, A., Han, S., Jennehag, U., & Gidlund, M. (2018). Industrial internet of things: Challenges, opportunities, and directions. *IEEE Transactions on Industrial Informatics*, *14*(11), 4724–4734. doi:10.1109/TII.2018.2852491

Sisi, Z., & Souri, A. (2021). Blockchain technology for energy-aware mobile crowd sensing approaches in Internet of Things. *Transactions on Emerging Telecommunications Technologies*. Advance online publication. doi:10.1002/ett.4217

Sivamoorthy, T., Ansari, A. M., Sivakumar, D. B., & Nallarasan, V. (2022). Flood Prediction Using ML Classification Methods on Rainfall Data. *International Journal for Research in Applied Science and Engineering Technology*, *10*(4), 499–502. doi:10.22214/ijraset.2022.41297

Smirnov, A., Shilov, N., & Gusikhin, O. (2017, March). Cyber-physical-human system for connected car-based e-tourism. In *Proceedings of 2017 IEEE Conference on Cognitive and Computational Aspects of Situation Management,* Savannah, GA, USA (pp. 27-31). IEEE.

Smirnov, A., Shilov, N., Kashevnik, A., & Ponomarev, A. (2017). Cyber-physical infomobility for tourism application. *International Journal of Information Technology and Management*, *16*(1), 31–52. doi:10.1504/IJITM.2017.080949

Sodhro, A. H., Pirbhulal, S., Luo, Z., Muhammad, K., & Zahid, N. Z. (2020). Toward 6G architecture for energy-efficient communication in IoT-enabled smart automation systems. *IEEE Internet of Things Journal, 8*(7), 5141–5148. doi:10.1109/JIOT.2020.3024715

Sodhro, A. H., Pirbhulal, S., Muzammal, M., & Zongwei, L. (2020). Towards Blockchain-Enabled Security Technique for Industrial Internet of Things Based Decentralized Applications. *Journal of Grid Computing, 18*(4), 615–628. doi:10.100710723-020-09527-x

Song, T., Li, R., Mei, B., Yu, J., Xing, X., & Cheng, X. (2016). A Privacy Preserving Communication Protocol for IoT Applications in Smart Homes. *2016 International Conference on Identification, Information and Knowledge in the Internet of Things (IIKI)*, 519-524. 10.1109/IIKI.2016.3

Song, T., Li, R., Mei, B., Yu, J., Xing, X., & Cheng, X. (2017). A privacy preserving communication protocol for IoT applications in smart homes. *IEEE Internet of Things Journal, 4*(6), 1844–1852. doi:10.1109/JIOT.2017.2707489

Sremac, S., Tanackov, I., Kopic, M., & Radovic, D. (2018). Anfis model for determining the economic order quantity. *Decision Making: Applications in Management and Engineering, 1*(2), 81–92. doi:10.31181/dmame1802079s

Srilakshmi, G., & Praveen Joe, I. R. (2023). A-DQRBRL: Attention based deep Q reinforcement battle royale learning model for sports video classification. *Imaging Science Journal*, 1–20. Advance online publication. doi:10.1080/13682199.2023.2180022

Standards for Industry 4.0. (2019). http://standardsi40.sg/

Stentoft, J., Jensen, K. W., Philipsen, K., & Haug, A. (2019). Drivers and Barriers for Industry 4.0 Readiness and Practice: A SME Perspective with Empirical Evidence. *Proceedings of the 52nd Hawaii International Conference on System Sciences, 6*, 5155–5164. 10.24251/HICSS.2019.619

Stolcke, A., Chen, B., Franco, H., Gadde, V. R. R., Graciarena, M., Hwang, M. Y., ... Zhu, Q. (2006). Recent innovations in speech-to-text transcription at SRI-ICSI-UW. *IEEE Transactions on Audio, Speech, and Language Processing, 14*(5), 1729–1744. doi:10.1109/TASL.2006.879807

Strijbos, J. W., Martens, R. L., Jochems, W. M. G., & Broers, N. J. (2004). The Effects of Functional Roles on Group Efðciency: Using multilevel modeling and content analysis to investigate computer-supported collaboration in small groups. *Small Group Research, 35*(2), 195–229. doi:10.1177/1046496403260843

Su, J., Yu, C., & Ng, D. T. K. (2022). A meta-review of literature on educational approaches for teaching AI at the K-12 levels in the Asia-Pacific region. *Computers and Education: Artificial Intelligence*, Article 100065.

Subasinghe, M., Magalage, D., Amadoru, N., Amarathunga, L., Bhanupriya, N., & Wijekoon, J. L. (2020, November). Effectiveness of artificial intelligence, decentralized and distributed systems for prediction and secure channelling for Medical Tourism. In *2020 11th IEEE Annual Information Technology, Electronics and Mobile Communication Conference (IEMCON)* (pp. 314-319). IEEE. 10.1109/IEMCON51383.2020.9284898

Sula, E. (2018). A review of Network Layer and Transport Layer Attacks on Wireless Networks. *International Journal of Modern Engineering Research, 08*(12), 23–27.

Sun, X. a. (2019). Towards quantum-secured permissioned blockchain: Signature, consensus, and logic. *Entropy, 21*, 287.

Supriyanto, G., Abdullah, A. G., Widiaty, I., & Mupita, J. (2019). Career guidance web-based expert system for vocational students. *J. Eng. Sci. Technol, 14*(4), 1865–1877.

Suzana Maciel, R. P., Maria David, J. N., Barreiro Claro, D., & Braga, R. (2016). Full Interoperability: Challenges and Opportunities for Future Information Systems. Research Challenges in IS in Brazil.

Swamy, S. N., & Kota, S. R. (2020). An empirical study on system level aspects of Internet of Things (IoT). *IEEE Access : Practical Innovations, Open Solutions, 8*, 188082–188134. doi:10.1109/ACCESS.2020.3029847

Tajudeen, F. P., Jaafar, N. I., & Ainin, S. (2018). Understanding the impact of social media usage among organizations. *Information & Management, 55*(3), 308–321. doi:10.1016/j.im.2017.08.004

Talukder, A., & Haas, R. (2021, June). AIoT: AI meets IoT and web in smart healthcare. In *13th ACM Web Science Conference 2021* (pp. 92-98). 10.1145/3462741.3466650

Tama, B. A.-H. (2017). A critical review of blockchain and its current applications. In *2017 International Conference on Electrical Engineering and Computer Science (ICECOS)*. IEEE. 10.1109/ICECOS.2017.8167115

Tan, Q., Liu, N., & Hu, X. (2019). Deep Representation Learning for Social Network Analysis. *Frontiers in Big Data. Frontiers in Big Data, 2*(2), 2. Advance online publication. doi:10.3389/fdata.2019.00002 PMID:33693325

Tan, Z. X., Thambiratnam, D. P., Chan, T. H. T., & Razak, H. A. (2017). Detecting damage in steel beams using modal strain energy based damage index and artificial neural network. *Engineering Failure Analysis, 79*, 253–262. doi:10.1016/j.engfailanal.2017.04.035

Tawalbeh, L., Muheidat, F., Tawalbeh, M., & Quwaider, M. (2020). IoT privacy and security: Challenges and solutions. *Applied Sciences (Basel, Switzerland), 10*(12), 4102. Advance online publication. doi:10.3390/app10124102

Taxidou, I., & Fischer, P. (2013). Realtime Analysis of Information Diffusion in Social Media. *Proceedings of the VLDB Endowment International Conference on Very Large Data Bases, 6*(12), 1416–1421. doi:10.14778/2536274.2536328

Thirumoorthy, K., & Muneeswaran, K. (2021). An elitism based self-adaptive multi-population Poor and Rich optimization algorithm for grouping similar documents. *Journal of Ambient Intelligence and Humanized Computing*, 1–15.

Thomas & Schaefer. (2017). Industry 4.0: An Overview of Key Benefits, Technologies, and Challenges. In Cybersecurity for Industry 4.0: Analysis for Design and Manufacturing (pp. 1-33). Springer Publishing.

Thompson, B., Leighton, M., Korytkowski, M., & Cook, C. B. (2018). An Overview of Safety Issues on Use of Insulin Pumps and Continuous Glucose Monitoring Systems in the Hospital. In Current Diabetes Reports (Vol. 18, Issue 10). Current Medicine Group LLC 1. doi:10.100711892-018-1056-7

Thuraisingam, T., Ean, T. C. G., & Singh, P. K. H. (2019). Impact of Peer Assessment Intervention on Student Motivation and Learning in Composition Classes. *International Journal of Education, Psychology and Counseling, 4*(30), 225–236.

Timofeyev, Y., & Dremova, O. (2022). Insurers' responses to cyber crime: Evidence from Russia. *International Journal of Law, Crime and Justice, 68*, 100520. doi:10.1016/j.ijlcj.2021.100520

Toffetti, G., & Bohnert, T. M. (2019). Cloud robotics with ROS. In Robot Operating System (ROS) The Complete Reference (Volume 4) (pp. 119–146). Springer.

Torky, A. A., & Aburawwash, A. A. (2018). A deep learning approach to automated structural engineering of prestressed members. *International Journal of Structural and Civil Engineering Research, 7*, 347–352. doi:10.18178/ijscer.7.4.347-352

Treiblmaier, H. (2021). The token economy as a key driver for tourism: Entering the next phase of blockchain research. *Annals of Tourism Research, 91*, 103177. doi:10.1016/j.annals.2021.103177

Trifiro, B., Clarke, M., Huang, S., Mills, B., Ye, Y., Zhang, S., Zhou, M., & Su, C. C. (2022). Media moments: How media events and business incentives drive twitter engagement within the small business community. *Social Network Analysis and Mining, 12*(1), 174. doi:10.100713278-022-01003-6 PMID:36505398

Trilles Oliver, S., Torres-Sospedra, J., Belmonte, O., Zarazaga-Soria, F.J., González Pérez, A., & Huerta, J. (2019). *Development of an open sensorized platform in a smart agriculture context: A vineyard support system for monitoring mildew disease.* Academic Press.

Tripathi, P., Kumar, S., & Rawat, P. (2022). Paradigm Shift in the Functioning of the Tourism and Hotel Industry Using NLP, Digital Assistant, and AI Models. In Artificial Intelligence for Societal Development and Global Well-Being (pp. 196-210). IGI Global.

Tripathy, B. K. (2018). *Internet of Things (IoT) Technologies, Applications, Challenges, and Solutions.* CRC Press Taylor & Francis Group.

Trojovský, P., Dhasarathan, V., & Boopathi, S. (2023). Experimental investigations on cryogenic friction-stir welding of similar ZE42 magnesium alloys. *Alexandria Engineering Journal, 66*(1), 1–14. doi:10.1016/j.aej.2022.12.007

Troncia, M. a. (2019). Distributed ledger technologies for peer-to-peer local markets in distribution networks. *Energies, 17*, 3249.

Tyan, I., Yagüe, M. I., & Guevara-Plaza, A. (2021). Blockchain Technology's Potential for Sustainable Tourism. In *Information and Communication Technologies in Tourism 2021: Proceedings of the ENTER 2021 eTourism Conference, January 19–22, 2021* (pp. 17-29). Springer International Publishing.

Ujakpa, M. M., Nghipundjwa, O., Hashiyana, V., Mutalya, A. N., André, P., & Ndevahoma, I. (2021, May). An Investigation of the Use of Career Guidance App by Undergraduate Students: Case Study of Namibia. In 2021 IST-Africa Conference (IST-Africa) (pp. 1-9). IEEE.

Ungurean, I., Gaitan, N. C., & Gaitan, V. G. (2016). A middleware based architecture for the industrial internet of things. *KSII Transactions on Internet and Information Systems, 10*(7), 2874–2891. doi:10.3837/tiis.2016.07.001

UNIDO. (2016). Opportunities and Challenges of the New Industrial Revolution for Developing Countries and Economies in Transition. *Department of Trade, Investment and Innovation*, 6–7. https://www.unido.org/sites/default/files/2017-01/Unido_industry-4_NEW_0.pdf

Unterberger, P., & Müller, J. M. (2021). Clustering and Classification of Manufacturing Enterprises Regarding Their Industry 4.0 Reshoring Incentives. *Procedia Computer Science, 180*, 696–705. doi:10.1016/j.procs.2021.01.292

Vaezi, M., Azari, A., Khosravirad, S. R., Shirvanimoghaddam, M., Azari, M. M., Chasaki, D., & Popovski, P. (2022). Cellular, wide-area, and non-terrestrial IoT: A survey on 5G advances and the road toward 6G. *IEEE Communications Surveys and Tutorials, 24*(2), 1117–1174. doi:10.1109/COMST.2022.3151028

Vaidya, S., Ambad, P., & Bhosle, S. (2018). Industry 4.0 - A Glimpse. In Procedia Manufacturing (pp. 233 - 238). Elsevier B.V. Publishing.

Van Gassen, S., Callebaut, B., Van Helden, M. J., Lambrecht, B. N., Demeester, P., Dhaene, T., & Saeys, Y. (2015). FlowSOM: Using self-organizing maps for visualization and interpretation of cytometry data. *Cytometry. Part A, 87*(7), 636–645. doi:10.1002/cyto.a.22625 PMID:25573116

Vangulick, D. a. (2018). Blockchain for peer-to-peer energy exchanges: design and recommendations. In 2018 Power Systems Computation Conference (PSCC) (pp. 1-7). IEEE. doi:10.23919/PSCC.2018.8443042

Vanitha, S. K. R., & Boopathi, S. (2023). Artificial Intelligence Techniques in Water Purification and Utilization. In *Human Agro-Energy Optimization for Business and Industry* (pp. 202–218). IGI Global., doi:10.4018/978-1-6684-4118-3.ch010

Varga, G. (2021, October 25). *Global Cybercrime Report: Which Countries Are Most At Risk? 2022.* SEON.

Vashi, S., Ram, J., Modi, J., Verma, S., & Prakash, C. (2017). Internet of Things (IoT) A Vision, Architectural Elements, and Security Issues. *International Conference I-SMAC*, 492–496. 10.1109/I-SMAC.2017.8058399

Vassileva, J., Wang, Y., & Vassileva, J. (2017). Bayesian Network-Based Trust Model Bayesian Network-Based Trust Model. *Proceedings IEEE/WIC International Conference on Web Intelligence (WI 2003)*, 372–378.

Venkatesan, R., Kathrine, G. J. W., & Ramalakshmi, K. (2018). Internet of things based pest management using natural pesticides for small scale organic gardens. *Journal of Computational and Theoretical Nanoscience, 15*(9–10), 2742–2747. doi:10.1166/jctn.2018.7533

Vennila, T., Karuna, M. S., Srivastava, B. K., Venugopal, J., Surakasi, R., & Sampath, B. (2022). New Strategies in Treatment and Enzymatic Processes: Ethanol Production From Sugarcane Bagasse. In Human Agro-Energy Optimization for Business and Industry (pp. 219–240). IGI Global.

Verma, S., Kaur, S., Khan, M. A., & Sehdev, P. S. (2020). Toward green communication in 6G-enabled massive Internet of Things. *IEEE Internet of Things Journal, 8*(7), 5408–5415. doi:10.1109/JIOT.2020.3038804

Vijayakumar, S., & Rosario, J. N. (2011). Preliminary design for crop monitoring involving water and fertilizer conservation using wireless sensor networks. *2011 IEEE 3rd International Conference on Communication Software and Networks, ICCSN 2011*, 662–666. 10.1109/ICCSN.2011.6014979

Vindhya, L., Beliray, P. A., Sravani, C. R., & Divya, D. R. (2020). Prediction of Heart Disease Using Machine Learning Techniques. *International Journal of Research in Engineering, Science and Management, 3*(8), 325–326.

Violette, M. (2018). IoT standards. *IEEE Internet of Things Magazine, 1*(1), 6–7. doi:10.1109/MIOT.2018.8552483

von Solms, R., & van Niekerk, J. (2013). From information security to cyber security. *Computers & Security, 38*, 97–102. doi:10.1016/j.cose.2013.04.004

Wanda, P. (2022). RunMax: Fake profile classification using novel nonlinear activation in CNN. *Social Network Analysis and Mining, 12*(1), 158. doi:10.100713278-022-00983-9

Wang, W. a. (2013). Cyber security in the smart grid: Survey and challenges. *Computer Networks,* 1344-1371.

Wang, W., Chau, K., Qiu, L., & Chen, Y. (2015). Improving forecasting accuracy of medium and long-term runoff using artificial neural network based on EEMD decomposition. *Environmental Research, 139*, 46–54. doi:10.1016/j.envres.2015.02.002 PMID:25684671

Wang, X., Zha, X., Ni, W., Liu, R. P., Guo, Y. J., Niu, X., & Zheng, K. (2019). Survey on blockchain for Internet of Things. In *Computer Communications* (Vol. 136, pp. 10–29). Elsevier B.V. doi:10.1016/j.comcom.2019.01.006

Wang, Y., & Hajli, N. (2017). Exploring the path to big data analytics success in healthcare. *Journal of Business Research, 70*, 287–299. doi:10.1016/j.jbusres.2016.08.002

Weber, R. H. (2010). Internet of Things - New security and privacy challenges. *Computer Law & Security Report, 26*(1), 23–30. doi:10.1016/j.clsr.2009.11.008

Weber, R. H. (2015). Internet of things: Privacy issues revisited. *Computer Law & Security Report, 31*(5), 618–627. doi:10.1016/j.clsr.2015.07.002

Wei, H., Zhang, Z., & Fan, B. (2017, December). Network slice access selection scheme in 5G. In *2017 IEEE 2nd Information Technology, Networking, Electronic and Automation Control Conference (ITNEC)* (pp. 352-356). IEEE.

Weiss, M., Botha, A., Herselman, M., & Loots, G. (2017, May). Blockchain as an enabler for public mHealth solutions in South Africa. In 2017 IST-Africa Week Conference (IST-Africa) (pp. 1-8). IEEE. doi:10.23919/ISTAFRICA.2017.8102404

Wendel, J., & Buttenfield, B. P. (2010). *Formalizing guidelines for building meaningful self-organizing maps. GIScience.* Short Paper Proceedings.

Wesley, P. W., & Buysse, V. (2010). *The quest for quality: Promising innovations for early childhood programs.* Paul H. Brookes Publishing Company.

Wijethilaka, S., & Liyanage, M. (2021). Survey on network slicing for Internet of Things realization in 5G networks. *IEEE Communications Surveys and Tutorials, 23*(2), 957–994. doi:10.1109/COMST.2021.3067807

Willems, E. (2011). Cyber-terrorism in the process industry. *Computer Fraud & Security, 2011*(3), 16–19. doi:10.1016/S1361-3723(11)70032-X

Williams, R., Park, H. W., Oh, L., & Breazeal, C. (2019a). Popbots: Designing an artificial intelligence curriculum for early childhood education. *Proceedings of the AAAI Conference on Artificial Intelligence, 33,* 9729–9736. 10.1609/aaai.v33i01.33019729

Wu & Cheng. (2017). Omic and electronic health record big data analytics for precision medicine. *IEEE Transactions, 64*(2).

Wu, Lin, & Weng. (2004). Probability estimates for multi-classclassification by pairwise coupling. *JMLR, 5,* 975–1005.

Wu, H., & Zhu, X. (2020). Developing a Reliable Service System of Charity Donation During the Covid-19 Outbreak. *IEEE Access: Practical Innovations, Open Solutions, 8,* 154848–154860. doi:10.1109/ACCESS.2020.3017654 PMID:34812351

Xiao, X., Wu, Z. C., & Chou, K. C. (2011). A multi-label classifier for predicting the subcellular localization of gram-negative bacterial proteins with both single and multiple sites. *PLoS One, 6*(6), e20592. doi:10.1371/journal.pone.0020592 PMID:21698097

Xie, Y. (2015). *Predicting Days in Hospital Using Health Insurance Claims.* IEEE.

Xu, H., & Lv, Y. (2022). Mining and Application of Tourism Online Review Text Based on Natural Language Processing and Text Classification Technology. *Wireless Communications and Mobile Computing, 2022,* 2022. doi:10.1155/2022/9905114

Xu, T., Wendt, J. B., & Potkonjak, M. (2015). Security of IoT systems: Design challenges and opportunities. *IEEE/ACM International Conference on Computer-Aided Design, Digest of Technical Papers, ICCAD,* 417–423. 10.1109/ICCAD.2014.7001385

Xu, X. (2012). From cloud computing to cloud manufacturing. *Robotics and Computer-integrated Manufacturing, 28*(1), 75–86. doi:10.1016/j.rcim.2011.07.002

Yaacoub, J.-P. A., Noura, H. N., Salman, O., & Chehab, A. (2022). Advanced digital forensics and anti-digital forensics for IoT systems: Techniques, limitations and recommendations. *Internet of Things, 19,* 100544. doi:10.1016/j.iot.2022.100544

Yaacoub, J.-P. A., Salman, O., Noura, H. N., Kaaniche, N., Chehab, A., & Malli, M. (2020). Cyber-physical systems security: Limitations, issues and future trends. *Microprocessors and Microsystems, 77,* 103201. doi:10.1016/j.micpro.2020.103201 PMID:32834204

Yadav, E. P., Mittal, E. A., & Yadav, H. (2018, November 1). IoT: Challenges and Issues in Indian Perspective. *Proceedings - 2018 3rd International Conference On Internet of Things: Smart Innovation and Usages, IoT-SIU 2018.* 10.1109/IoT-SIU.2018.8519869

Yadav, K. K., Sharma, A., & Badholia, A. (2021). Heart disease prediction using machine learning techniques. *Information Technology in Industry, 9*(1), 207-214.

Yakimov, P., & Iovev, A. (2019). *Towards Industry 44.0 Oriented Education.* . doi:10.1109/ET.2019.8878609

Yan, L. X., & Subramanian, P. (2019). A review on exploiting social media analytics for the growth of tourism. In *Recent Trends in Data Science and Soft Computing: Proceedings of the 3rd International Conference of Reliable Information and Communication Technology (IRICT 2018)* (pp. 331-342). Springer International Publishing. 10.1007/978-3-319-99007-1_32

Yan, Y. a. (2013). An efficient security protocol for advanced metering infrastructure in smart grid. *IEEE Network, 27*, 64-71.

Yang, W., Qin, Y., & Li, R. (2022). A Network Embedding-based Approach for Scalable Network Navigability in Content-Centric Social IoT. *IEEE Internet of Things Journal, 9*(17), 16418–16428. doi:10.1109/JIOT.2022.3151488

Yan, L., Chang, Y., & Zhang, S. (2017). A lightweight authentication and key agreement scheme for smart grid. *International Journal of Distributed Sensor Networks, 13*(2), 13. doi:10.1177/1550147717694173

Yan, L., Han, C., & Yuan, J. (2020, March). *Hybrid precoding for 6G terahertz communications: Performance evaluation and open problems. In 2020 2nd 6G wireless summit (6G SUMMIT).* IEEE.

Yaqoob, I., Salah, K., Jayaraman, R., & Al-Hammadi, Y. (2021). Blockchain for healthcare data management: Opportunities, challenges, and future recommendations. *Neural Computing & Applications, 34*(14), 11475–11490. doi:10.100700521-020-05519-w

Yli-Huumo, J., Ko, D., Choi, S., Park, S., & Smolander, K. (2016). Where is current research on blockchain technology? A systematic review. *PLoS One, 11*(10), e0163477. doi:10.1371/journal.pone.0163477 PMID:27695049

Yoo, S., Lee, S., Kim, S., Hwang, K. H., Park, J. H., & Kang, N. (2021). Integrating deep learning into CAD/CAE system: Generative design and evaluation of 3D conceptual wheel. *Structural and Multidisciplinary Optimization, 64*(4), 1–23. doi:10.100700158-021-02953-9

Yuan, H., Xu, H., Qian, Y., & Li, Y. (2016). Make your travel smarter: Summarizing urban tourism information from massive blog data. *International Journal of Information Management, 36*(6), 1306–1319. doi:10.1016/j.ijinfomgt.2016.02.009

Yupapin, P., Trabelsi, Y., Nattappan, A., & Boopathi, S. (2022). Performance Improvement of Wire-Cut Electrical Discharge Machining Process Using Cryogenically Treated Super-Conductive State of Monel-K500 Alloy. *Iranian Journal of Science and Technology - Transactions of Mechanical Engineering*, 1–17.

Yupapin, P., Trabelsi, Y., Nattappan, A., & Boopathi, S. (2022). Performance Improvement of Wire-Cut Electrical Discharge Machining Process Using Cryogenically Treated Super-Conductive State of Monel-K500 Alloy. *Iranian Journal of Science and Technology - Transactions of Mechanical Engineering*, 1–17. doi:10.1007/s40997-022-00513-0

Zaidi, I., Nazmudeen, M. S., & Mohiddin, F. (2019). Identifying Factors Contributing to the Level of Industry 4. 0 Technologies Adoption among SMEs in Different Countries. Academic Press.

Zaidi, I., Nazmudeen, M. S., & Mohiddin, F. (2021b). K-Means Clustering Approach to Categorize the Maturity Level of Industry 4.0 Technology Adoption of MSMEs in Brunei Darussalam. *3rd International Conference on Business, Economics and Finance (ICBEF) Proceedings*, 76. https://doi.org/https://doi.org/10.36924/20220

Zaidi, I., Nazmudeen, M. S., & Mohiddin, F. (2021a). A Comparative Study on IR4. 0 Technologies and its Maturity Level on Small, Medium Enterprises in Developed and Developing Countries. *ICBIM*, 1–16.

Zakaria, N. (2021). Action network: A probabilistic graphical model for social simulation. *Simulation, 98*(4), 335–346. doi:10.1177/00375497211038759

Zanella, A., Bui, N., Castellani, A., Vangelista, L., & Zorzi, M. (2014). Internet of things for smart cities. *IEEE Internet of Things Journal, 1*(1), 22–32. doi:10.1109/JIOT.2014.2306328

Zehra, N. (2020). Prediction Analysis of Floods Using Machine Learning Algorithms (NARX & SVM). *International Journal of Sciences, Basic and Applied Research*, *49*(2), 24–34. https://www.gssrr.org/index.php/JournalOfBasicAndApplied/article/view/10719

Zhang, L., Dabipi, I.K., & Brown Jr, W.L. (2018). Internet of things applications for agriculture. IoT A to Z. *Technol. Appl.*, 507–528.

Zhang, P., Walker, M. A., White, J., Schmidt, D. C., & Lenz, G. (2017, October). Metrics for assessing blockchain-based healthcare decentralized apps. In *2017 IEEE 19th international conference on e-health networking, applications and services (Healthcom)* (pp. 1-4). IEEE. 10.1109/HealthCom.2017.8210842

Zhang, Z. K., Cho, M. C. Y., Wang, C. W., Hsu, C. W., Chen, C. K., & Shieh, S. (2014). IoT security: Ongoing challenges and research opportunities. *Proceedings - IEEE 7th International Conference on Service-Oriented Computing and Applications, SOCA 2014*, 230–234. 10.1109/SOCA.2014.58

Zhang, C., & Kovacs, J. M. (2012). The application of small unmanned aerial systems for precision agriculture: A review. *Precision Agriculture*, *13*(6), 693–712. doi:10.100711119-012-9274-5

Zhang, H., Liu, N., Chu, X., Long, K., Aghvami, A. H., & Leung, V. C. (2017). Network slicing based 5G and future mobile networks: Mobility, resource management, and challenges. *IEEE Communications Magazine*, *55*(8), 138–145. doi:10.1109/MCOM.2017.1600940

Zhang, H., & Zhang, L. (2019). Cloud robotics architecture: trends and challenges. *2019 IEEE International Conference on Service-Oriented System Engineering (SOSE)*, 362–3625. 10.1109/SOSE.2019.00061

Zhang, J. (2021). The Application and Thinking of Big Data in the Career Planning Education of College Students. *2nd International Conference on Information Science and Education (ICISE-IE)*, 868-871. 10.1109/ICISE-IE53922.2021.00198

Zhang, M., Akiyama, M., Shintani, M., Xin, J., & Frangopol, D. M. (2021). Probabilistic estimation of flexural loading capacity of existing RC structures based on observational corrosion-induced crack width distribution using machine learning. *Structural Safety*, *91*, 102098. Advance online publication. doi:10.1016/j.strusafe.2021.102098

Zhan, Z., Fong, P. S., Mei, H., & Liang, T. (2015). Effects of gender grouping on students' group performance, individual achievements and attitudes in computer-supported collaborative learning. *Computers in Human Behavior*, *48*, 587–596. doi:10.1016/j.chb.2015.02.038

Zheng, X., Luo, Y., Sun, L., Zhang, J., & Chen, F. (2018). A tourism destination recommender system using users' sentiment and temporal dynamics. *Journal of Intelligent Information Systems*, *51*(3), 557–578. doi:10.100710844-018-0496-5

Zhou, J., Wang, Y., Ota, K., & Dong, M. (2019). AAIoT: Accelerating artificial intelligence in IoT systems. *IEEE Wireless Communications Letters*, *8*(3), 825–828. doi:10.1109/LWC.2019.2894703

Zong, C. (2013). *Statistical Natural Language Processing*. Tsinghua University Press.

About the Contributors

Thangavel Murugan is serving as an Assistant Professor in the Department of Information Systems and Security, College of Information Technology, United Arab Emirates University, Abu Dhabi, United Arab Emirates. He received Doctorate from Madras Institute of Technology (MIT) Campus, Anna University – Chennai. He received Post Graduate degree as M.E. Computer Science and Engineering from J.J. College of Engineering and Technology, Trichy under Anna University – Chennai (University First Rank Holder & Gold Medalist) and Bachelor's degree as B.E. Computer Science and Engineering from M.A.M College of Engineering, Trichy under Anna University – Chennai (College First Rank Holder & Gold Medalist). He presently holds 10+ years of Teaching and Research experience from various academic institutions. He has published 10+ articles in International Journals, 15+ book chapters in International Publishers, 25+ in the proceedings of International Conferences and 3 in the proceedings of national conferences /seminars. He has been actively participating as reviewers in the international journals and conferences. He has attended 100+ Workshops / FDPs/Conferences in various Higher Learning Institutes like IIT, Anna University. He has organized 50+ Workshops / FDPs /Contests/Industry based courses over the past years of experience. He has been a technical speaker in various Workshops/ FDPs/Conferences. His research specialization is Information Security, High Performance Computing, Ethical Hacking, Cyberforensics, Blockchain, Cybersecurity Intelligence and Educational Technology.

E. Nirmala received her doctorate from Anna University in Chennai, Madras Institute of Technology Campus. She has been a teacher in the academic profession for more than 18 years. worked as an assistant professor, Associate professor, and HOD for top institutions. She is an expert in big data analytics, cloud security, and layered security. She is currently working on a project to safeguard the people of Assam in drowning water with a team of students. She has led numerous faculty development programmes and seminars funded by ISTE and Anna University. She has worked as a trainer for IBM RAD and DB2 as well as a resource person for EMC2. She has worked as a visiting faculty member at Anna University, Periyar University, MS University, and Tamil Nadu Open University. She has given guest lectures in colleges in Tamil Nadu and Andhra Pradesh. She has been working as an Assistant Professor Senior for SCSE at VIT Bhopal University, holding a significant number of publications in journals both national and international. She excels academically as well as by giving lectures and providing public exposure on start-ups through the Entrepreneurship Development Institute of India (EDI. Dr.E. Nirmala is a life member of the ISTE (Indian Society for Technical Education). Being an optimist, she would clutch the fingers of her student to dream for Big India.

* * *

Vivek A. R. is currently a sophomore pursuing Bachelor of Technology in Information Technology at Thiagarajar College of Engineering Madurai. He has completed HSC in the year 2021 with 95.8% score and SSLC in the year 2019 with 93% score at St.John's English School and Junior College Besant Nagar Chennai. His research interests include website analysis, machine learning and software development.

A. M. Abirami is presently working as Associate Professor in the Department of Information Technology, Thiagarajar College of Engineering, Madurai, India. She received her PhD Degree in the area of Text Analytics and Semantic Web from Anna University Chennai in 2018. Her Research Interest includes Data Analytics, Text Analytics, Programming, Semantic Web Technologies, and Education Technology. She has nearly 15 national/international conference publications, 10 national/international journal publications, and 3 book chapters in the area of text analytics and engineering education. She is interested in improving Teaching Learning methodologies of Engineering Education. She has earned "Cambridge International Certificate for Teachers and Trainers", trained by Wipro's Mission10x programme. She is a Professional Member of ACM Professional Society (Association of Computing and Machinery), and IET Professional Society. She is a trained auditor for ISO 9001:2015 by TUV SUD South Asia Ltd. Chennai. She is a Member of Internal Quality Assurance Cell (IQAC) of TCE.

Anurag Vijay Agrawal (Senior Member, IEEE) has been associated as Consultant with Electronics & ICT Academy IIT Roorkee, an initiative supported by MeitY, Govt of India. He has more than 20 years of academic, research and consultancy experience. He received B.E. degree in Electronics and Communication Engineering from MJP Rohilkhand University, Bareilly, Uttar Pradesh, India and M.E. degree in Electronics and Communication Engineering from Panjab University, Chandigarh, India in 2000 and 2010 respectively. He completed Ph.D. from the Department of Electronics and Communication Engineering with Wireless and Mobile Communications Specialization at Indian Institute of Technology Roorkee, Roorkee, India in 2021. His more than 30 IPR and other research contributions include German/Indian patents, designs, copyrights, books, book chapters, international/national journals and conference publications. He was recipient of IEEE Uttar Pradesh Section Young Professional Star Award in 2021. Dr. Agrawal is nominated member of Blockchain and Distributed Ledger Technologies Sectional Committee, Bureau of Indian Standards, India. In October 2022, he got inclusion in Panel-6 (Blockchain Use Cases) of the Committee. He has been part of the Technical Program Committee of several IEEE Conferences and organized special track sessions in IEEE international conferences. His current research interests are in the areas of MIMO/Massive MIMO communications, digital predistortion, energy efficiency, transportation engineering, high-speed Railways communications, Intelligent Transportation Systems, 5G/6G Signal Generation & Enhancement, Deep Learning, Machine Learning, Blockchain and Internet of Things.

Sampath B. completed his undergraduate in Mechanical Engineering and postgraduate in the field of Engineering Design. He completed his Ph.D. from Anna University, Chennai, Tamil Nādu, India.

Subbulakshmi Balasubramanian is currently working as Assistant professor in the department of Computer Science and Engineering at Thiagarajar College of Engineering, Madurai, Tamil Nadu, India. She has 20 years of teaching and research experience. She has completed her Ph.D from Anna University, Chennai in the year 2019. She is a life member in Computer Society of India (CSI). She has published research papers in various reputed journals and conferences. She is guiding under graduate and post graduate students in the area of sentiment analysis, data analytics and machine learning. Her research interest includes Databases, Data mining, Machine Learning and Data Analytics. She has authored several chapters in the refereed edited books of springer and acting as Reviewer in International Journals from IEEE, Springer.

Sampath Boopathi () completed his undergraduate in Mechanical Engineering and postgraduate in the field of Computer-Aided Design. He completed his Ph.D. from Anna University and his field of research includes Manufacturing and optimization. He published 60 more research articles in Internationally Peer-reviewed journals, one Patent grant, and three published patents.He has 16 more years of academic and research experiences in the various Engineering Colleges in Tamilnadu, India..

Jeyamala Chandrasekaran is currently associated with the Department of Information Technology at Thiagarajar College of Engineering. She is a post graduate in Computer Science and Engineering and has pursued her doctoral degree from Anna University, Chennai in the domain of Information Security. Her research works have been published in reputed international journals and international conferences. She possesses a teaching experience of fifteen years. Other areas of her interest include Artificial Intelligence, Cryptography and Network security, Computer Programming and Computer Networks and Educational Technology. She has served as a reviewer in various reputed international journals and conferences.

Jyoti Chauhan is an Assistant Professor at School of Computing Science and Engineering at VIT Bhopal University, Dr Jyoti has 9 Years of Teaching Experience. She has published research papers in reputed journals and conferences with Scopus and SCI indexing. Dr Jyoti is having expertise and interest in IoT, Healthcare and AI.

Anitha D. is working currently as an assistant professor in the Department of Computer Applications, Thiagarajar College of Engineering, Madurai, Tamilnadu, India. Her academic qualifications include PhD and Master of Computer Applications from Anna University, Tamilnadu. She has been part of the teaching fraternity since 2004, guiding postgraduate Computer Applications students. Her research interests are higher education and engineering education. Her publications include six international journals and 14 international conferences. She is very curious about using different teaching learning methodologies that improves learning and usage of technology in learning.

Kanishta G. is a final year student pursuing B.Tech Information technology in Thiagarajar College of Engineering, Madurai. Her personal interests area are Data Analytics and Programming Languages.

Kirithika G. is a second year student pursuing B.Tech Information technology in Thiagarajar college of engineering, Madurai. Her personal interests area are Cyber Security and Programming Languages.

Naga Nivedithaa G. is a student of CSE department of TCE. She is pursuing her III year. in B.E. She participated in many contests, her area of interest includes data Science and Analytics. She is good in producing novel idea which are useful for society.

Riddhi G. is a final year student pursuing B.Tech Information technology in Thiagarajar College of Engineering, Madurai. Her personal interests area are Data Analytics and Programming Languages.

Rajeev Goyal holds a Doctorate and M.Tech in Computer Science and Engineering. With over 21 years of experience in both academia and industry, he has worked with reputable national and international universities such as VIT and AMITY. Dr. Goyal's expertise is reflected in his 8 publications in renowned academic databases such as Scopus and Web of Science. I am an authorized instructor for CCNA Introduction to Networks and cyber Ops Associate. Additionally, I hold international certifications from Juniper Networks Certified Associate and Microsoft Certified Security Compliance. My teaching expertise has been recognized with the Award for Excellence in Teaching in Higher Education, which was presented to me by Edwin Incorporation in partnership with JYD, International Higher Education Institutes in Thailand. In addition to his academic pursuits, Dr. Goyal is a member of several professional and industrial organizations, including ISTE, IAENG, IET, IRJIE, IRJIET (Reviewer Board Membership), and MTTF. He has also demonstrated his expertise as a speaker at various Faculty Development Programs and has been an active organizer of conferences, workshops, and short-term courses. Currently, Dr. Goyal's area of research is focused on the analysis of online social networks and recommender systems and Federated Learning.

Deepak Gupta (affiliated with LMISTE) received the B.E., M.TECH., and Ph.D. degrees in Computer Science and Engineering. He is currently working with ITM, Gwalior, Madhya Pradesh, India, as an Associate Professor. He has more than 20 years of experience. He has presented many research articles in international journals and conferences and organized various FDPs, events, conferences, and workshops.

Shyam Sunder Gupta (affiliated with LMISTE) received the B.E., M.TECH., and Ph.D. degrees in Computer Science and Engineering. He is currently working with Amity University Madhya Pradesh, Gwalior, Madhya Pradesh, India, as an Associate Professor. He has more than 20 years of experience. He has presented many research articles in international journals and conferences and organized various FDPs, events, conferences, and workshops. He holds two patents and two copyrights to his credit. His research interests include the area of soft computing, machine learning, big data analytics, and healthcare.

Sandeep Kumar Hegde obtained his B.E and MTech degree in Computer Science and Engg from VTU University, India. He completed PhD from VTU University. He has published research papers in various international journals and conferences. Presently he is working as assistant professor in the Department of Computer Science and Engg at NMAMIT, Nitte. His area of interest includes big data analytics, machine learning and computational intelligence. He is a life member of ISTE.

W. Jaisingh is an Associate Professor in the School of Information Science, at Presidency University, India. He received a Doctorate from Anna University, Chennai in the year 2013, a Master of Philosophy in Computer Science from Alagappa University in 2005, and the Master of Computer Applications from Bharathiar University in 2001. He has got 22 years of Teaching and Research experience. He has published more than 20 papers in International refereed journals, 30 papers in International Conferences, and contributed chapters to the books. He has received "Indian Book of Records" and "Asia Book of Records" for contributing as an author in the book titled "Covid 19 and its Impact". The book has been selected for the record "maximum authors contributing to a book". He is a Lead Editor in Maximum Authors Contributing for a Book on "Covid 19 and its impact", 2021. His area of Research Interest includes Data Science, Machine Learning, Data Mining, Data Analytics, Image Processing, and Deep Learning. He is a lifetime member of professional societies such as the International Association of Computer Science and Information Technology (IACSIT), the Computer Science Teachers Association, and the Indian Society for Technical Education (ISTE).

R. K. Kavitha holds a doctoral degree in Computer Applications from Anna University, Chennai. She has been involved in teaching Postgraduate Computer Applications students for more than 20 years. She has completed her M. Phil (Computer Science) and MCA from Bharathiar University, Coimbatore. Her research interest includes Software Engineering, Knowledge Management, and Educational Data Mining. She has attended many National and International Conferences where she has presented papers and has published papers in international research journals. Her personal interest includes conducting E-Literacy Programmes. Her hobbies include reading books and exploring new things around. She is a team player, continuous learner, friendly, and a passionate teacher.

Kasturi Laturkar is currently working as a Validation Engineer for Validation Associates LLC. She graduated with a M.S. in Chemical Engineering from Syracuse University and a B.Tech in Chemical Engineering from Guru Gobind Singh Indraprastha University, Delhi, India. She has more than 3 years of experience working in commissioning, qualification and validation of upstream and downstream bioprocessing equipment and critical utilities.

Kaustubh Laturkar is currently working as an engineer at the Facility for Rare Isotope Beams, Michigan State University which is a US-DOE project after completing his M.S in chemical engineering from University of Florida and B.E. in chemical engineering from Panjab University, Chandigarh, India. He has more than 8 years of experience working in the field of process engineering, refinery operations, utility systems design and operation with a special focus on design and commissioning of engineering systems.

Gautham M. is a second year student pursuing B.Tech Information technology in Thiagarajar College of Engineering, Madurai. His personal interests are working in data engineering and cyber security.

Madhumitha M. is a second year student pursuing B.Tech Information technology in Thiagarajar college of engineering, Madurai. Her personal interests area are Security based learning and programming.

Nirmala Devi M. has 16 years of teaching experience and 14 years of research experience and She produced 22 publications. She has 105 google scholar citations and 72 Scopus citations for my publications. She completed her Ph.D. on "Improving the performance of data mining algorithms for the prediction of Chronic diseases and Medline documents". She secured Top Percentile, Expert Badge, and Honor Code for attending 2-8 weeks of workshops/Training in Course era, IBM cognitive Class, NPTEL, IIT Bombay, IUCEE EPICS, and ATAL. She handled Skill Training and delivered 10 lectures on Data Science and Analytics in association with NPIU and NASSCOM for students and Outside Faculty. She is a Life member of ISTE and member of ACM.

Poorani Marimuthu is currently working as an Assistant Professor at Information and Science Engineering Department of CMR Institute of Technology, Bengaluru. She completed her Ph.D. degree and Masters in Engineering at MIT Campus, Anna University. She has published her works in many reputed journals and conferences. Her area of interest are soft computing, NLP and IoT.

Jeya Iswarya M. R. is a second year student pursuing B.Tech Information technology in Thiagarajar College of Engineering, Madurai. Her personal interests area are Security based learning and programming.

Lakshmana Phanendra Magulur was awarded Ph.D. in Computer Science and Engineering from Annamalai University, Chidambaram. Post Graduation in Information Technology from Gandhi Institute of Technology and Management, Vishakapatnam Under Graduation in Computer Science and Engineering from Seshadri Rao Gudlavalleru Engineering College formerly known as Gudlavalleru Engineering College Automation Anywhere Certified Advanced RPA Professional 2022 ServiceNow Certified System Administrator Microsoft Certified: DevOps Engineer Expert Microsoft Certified: Azure Developer Associate Microsoft Certified: Azure Data Fundamentals Microsoft Certified: Azure AI Fundamentals Microsoft Certified: Azure Fundamentals Oracle Cloud Infrastructure Foundations 2021 Associate AWS Certified Cloud Practitioner TensorFlow Developer Certificate UI-PATH Certified RPA Developer Member of Professional Bodies of Computer Society of India (CSI), Indian Society for Technical Education (ISTE), Institution of Engineers (India) [IEI], Institution of Electronics and Telecommunication Engineers (IETE). Currently Working as an Associate Professor at Koneru Lakshmaiah Educational Foundation (K L Deemed to be University) Formally Worked as Assistant Professor in the CSE Dept. of Gudlavalleru Engineering College, Gudlavalleru from July-2013-May-2016 (2.8 years) JNTUK Ratified. Authorized 39 International/National Research papers which are indexed in reputed databases like Scopus, Web of Science, IEEE Xplore, Springer Link, and ACM Digital Library. Sound Laboratory Experience in C, Oops through C++, Python, and R Programming. Passion to learn Cutting Edge technologies and transfer the knowledge as a part of the teaching-learning process. Have an aptitude and understanding of technology. Self-starter, Life long learner and take ownership of assignments. Drive to learn new technologies and turn around quickly to execute identified work.

H. Mickle Aancy is Assistant Professor, Department of Management Studies, Panimalar Engineering College Chennai. She has about 15 years of experience in teaching both Engineering and Management Studies. Her area of research includes Marketing, Management, Administration and Management Technology. She has published more than 10 articles in National and international journals and also present more than 20 papers in seminars, conferences and workshops.

Fadzliwati Mohiddin, BA Management Studies (Universiti Brunei Darussalam); MBA (Lancaster University, UK); PhD Information Systems (Curtin University of Technology, Western Australia), is the Dean and a Senior Assistant Professor at the School of Business, Universiti Teknologi Brunei (UTB). Prior to joining UTB she was the Chief Information Officer, the Director of ICTC and the Dean of the Faculty of Business and Management Sciences Universiti Islam Sultan Sharif Ali (UNISSA). She was also holding the post of Deputy Dean at the Faculty of Business, Economics and Policy Studies, Universiti Brunei Darussalam from 2009-2010. She lectures in Business Information Systems and General

Management. She was involved with several ICT projects that include Knowledge Management Systems and E-Learning Systems for the Ministry of Education. And she has been appointed to judge for several business and ICT competitions such as the Asia Pacific ICT Award (APICTA), the Brunei ICT Award (BICTA) since 2010, and the Brunei National Innovation Award of the Prime Minister's Office. Her current research interest includes Information Systems Success, Knowledge Management, E-Government, Leadership, National Culture and General Management.

Sampath N. is a final year student pursuing B.Tech Information technology in Thiagarajar College of Engineering, Madurai. His areas of interest include blockchain and IoT.

K. Venkatagurunatham Naidu completed his Bachelor of Technology in Computer Science and Engineering from K.S.R.M College of Engineering, Kadapa Affiliated to Sri Venkateswara University, Tirupati. He had completed his Master of Technology in Computer Science and Engineering from Bharath University, Chennai and Present Pursuing Ph.D. in Computer Science and Engineering at Dr. M.G.R Educational and Research Institute, Chennai. Currently He is working as a Assistant Professor in the Department of Computer Science and Engineering at Guntur Engineering College, Guntur, AP, India. He has over 11 years of Teaching experience in reputed engineering colleges in A.P. His main areas of interest include IoT,IoT Forensics, Internet of Everything, Data Science, Web Technologies, Cloud Computing, and Image Processing.

Varsha O. is a second year student pursuing B.Tech Information technology in Thiagarajar college of engineering, Madurai. Her personal interests area are System Administration and Data Engineering.

Karthikeyan P. is currently working as an Associate Professor in Thiagarajar College of Engineering, Madurai from 2007 onwards. He has completed the Ph.D. programme in Information and Communication Engineering under Anna University, Chennai, Tamilnadu, India in the year 2015. He published 25 papers in refereed international journals and conferences. He received the B.E. degree in Computer Science and Engineering from Madurai Kamaraj University, Madurai, Tamilnadu, India in the year 2002. He also received his M.E. degree in Computer Science and Engineering from Anna University, Chennai, Tamilnadu, India in the year 2004. His research interests include computational intelligence and educational technology.

Sanjai P. is a final year student pursuing B.Tech Information Technology in Thiagararajar College of Engineering, Madurai. His areas of interest include blockchain and IOT.

Subhash Chandra Patel received his PhD degree in CSE from IIT (BHU), Varanasi in 2018 and M.Tech. degree in Information Security from the Guru Gobind Singh Indraprashtha University, New Delhi in 2010. B.Tech in CSE in 2006. Currently he is working as an Assistant Professor in the School of Computer Science and Engineering at VIT University Bhopal. He reviewed various paper for Transactions on Cloud Computing Journal. His research interests include Cloud Computing Security, Information Security, Internet of Things and Software Engineering.

Rajalaxmi Prabhu B. obtained her B.E and MTech degree in Computer Science and Engg from VTU University, India. She pursuing PhD from VTU University. She has published research papers in various international journals and conferences. Presently she is working as assistant professor in the Department of Computer Science and Engg at NMAMIT, Nitte. Her area of interest includes big data analytics, machine learning and computational intelligence. She is a life member of ISTE.

Parkavi R. is working as an Assistant Professor, Department of Information Technology, Thiagarajar College of Engineering, Madurai. She currently pursuing Ph.D. in Information and Communication, Anna University, Chennai. Her research interests include Educational Technology, Learning Analytics, and Information Security. She is a member of IEEE. She has published research papers, best practices in international journals. She also presented papers in reputed educational conferences. Recently she completed IIEECP certification and got ING.PAED.IGIP title from IGIP, Austria.

Swathi R. is a student of CSE department at Thiagarajar College Engineering. She is pursuing her III year. B.E(CSE). She participated in many contests; her area of interest includes data Science and Analytics. She is good in producing novel ideas which are useful for society.

Arun Kamaraj S. is a second year student pursuing B.Tech Information technology in Thiagarajar College of Engineering, Madurai. His personal interests are working in data engineering and cyber security.

Hariharasitaraman S. is presently serving as Assistant Professor Grade-II in the School of Computer Science and Engineering. He completed his doctorate on the topic of analyzing data integrity schemes in cloud computing from KARE. His doctorate dissertation outlines various research directions and opened up future avenues in designing secure data integrity protocols. He completed his Masters of Engineering in Computer Science and Engineering from Anna University in the year 2005, in master's dissertation outlines in Designing and analyzing software infrastructures for the internetworking environment. He has completed a Bachelor of Engineering in the field of Computer Science & Engineering in the year 2003. He has more than 28 publications and 1 book chapter in National, International Conference, and peer-reviewed International Journal proceedings indexed in Scopus, SCIE, and SCI databases. He has more than 13 years of teaching experience and 2 years of Industry experience as a Lead Quality Analyst from top NIRF-ranked Institutions. He is a Certified Software Testing Professional (CSTP), EMC2 Cloud Infrastructure Services Associate (CIS), and Microsoft Certified Cloud Associate (MTA). He is a resource person and technical trainer for conducting hands-on workshops/ Industrial Seminars/FDPs in technical, research, and quality domains targeted for various levels of audience. He is the recipient of Elsevier Publons certified journal reviewer Award, and reviewer for Springer-Journal of SuperComputing, Achieved Grand Master position in Jedis rank towards generating open-sourced data to support speech and language technologies in Indian languages for "Crowdsourcing for Language Processing (CLAP)", Project funded by MHRD and DST, Govt. of India under the IMPRINT 2 scheme, IIT Bombay, Synerg, Department of CSE along with that he is the recipient of Best Paper Awardee- INCODS security Conference, Best teacher awardee, Best mentor, Best faculty advisors for two consecutive academic years. He successfully headed various administrative positions in organizations he worked like University level IQAC Coordinator – Academic Quality Assurance, Coordinator for Extension/ Outreach Activities, and Programme Coordinator for Corporate Relations. He is an active member of various technical national and international bodies like the Information Security Awareness Council, MeitY, GoI, ACM, IEEE, ISTE, CSI, and IAEng. His research area of interest is Computing, Security, Ambient, and Artificial Intelligence.

Karthikeyan S. is a second year student pursuing B.Tech Information technology in Thiagarajar College of Engineering, Madurai. His personal interests are working in data engineering and cyber security.

Uma S. is a professor in the Department of Computer Science and Engineering at Hindusthan College of Engineering and Technology, Coimbatore, Tamil Nadu, India. She received her B.E., degree in Computer Science and Engineering (CSE) in First Class with Distinction from P.S.G. College of Technology, M.S. (By Res.) degree from Anna University, Chennai, Tamil Nadu. She received her Ph.D., in the faculty of Information and Communication Engineering from Anna University, Chennai with High Commendation. She has 31 years of academic experience and organized many National and International seminars, workshops and conferences. She has published many research papers in National and International Conferences, Journals, Book Chapters, Patents and Books. She is a potential reviewer of International Journals and Member of Professional Bodies like ISTE, CSI, IEEE, IAENG, etc., She is a recipient of "Bharath Jyoti", "Certificate of Excellence" and "Best Citizen of India" Awards. Her research interests are Programming, Pattern Recognition and Analysis Of Nonlinear Time Series Data, Artificial Intelligence, and Digital Analytics.

Vigneshwaran S. is a final year student pursuing B.Tech Information technology in Thiagarajar college of engineering, Madurai. His areas of interest include blockchain and IOT.

Santhanalakshmi S. T. is working as Associate Professor in the Department of Computer Science and Engineering at Panimalar Engineering College, Chennai, Tamil Nadu, India. She is pursuing her Ph.D Degree in the Department of Data Analytics at Saveetha School of Engineering (SIMATS), Saveetha University, Chennai, Tamil Nadu, India. She has earned her Master of Engineering in Information Technology from Sathyabama University, Chennai, Tamil Nadu, India. She has finished her Bachelor of Engineering Degree in Computer Science and Engineering from Bharathiyar University, Coimbatore, Tamil Nadu, India. She is having 18 years of teaching experience. Her research interests include Deep Learning, Data Science and Data Analytics in Computer Vision and Computer Networks. She has published around 12 papers at various National and International Journals. She has presented papers at various National and International Conferences.

Santhoshini Sahu is a research scholar in School of Computing Science and Engineering at VIT Bhopal University. Her research interests includes Cyber Security, Machine Learning and Deep Learning.

Mohamed Saleem is a Senior Assistant Professor at the UTB School of Business. He has 23 years of experience in teaching and research in the field of Information Technology, especially in Data Science for Business and Analytics. Currently, he has been teaching undergraduates and postgraduates in Business Intelligence and Analytics and also supervising postgraduate students in the area of analytics. He has also conducted various executive training programs for middle and senior management officers in the area of Business Analytics. His research interests are in the area of HR Analytics, Smart Cities, the Internet of Things, Preventive maintenance of industrial equipment using machine learning and IR 4.0 adoption and its impact on SMEs.

Sharad Shandhi Ravi is a well-educated man who has had significant accomplishments in the profession of teaching. He was born in India and spent his youth in a tiny town in the country's south. He has a lifelong interest in studying and was always ready to enhance his knowledge. He pursued a Master of Technology (M.Tech) degree from a top institution in India after finishing higher secondary. He succeeded in his studies and post graduated with honours, obtaining numerous academic prizes.

Yuvraj Singh is a 3rd year student under Integrated M.Tech program in School of Computing Science and Engineering at VIT Bhopal University, His research interests included Blockchain Technology, Cyber Security and Machine Learning.

S. Sumitra is presently working as an Associate Professor in IIST Trivandrum, India. She completed her PhD in Machine Learning, Department of Automatic Control & Systems Engineering, The University of Sheffield, UK. She is Interested in the development of theoretical frame work for Machine Learning algorithms and its application to real world problems. She has more than 10 publications in the reputed journals and more than 10 conference publications.

Saranya V. is in the field of lecturing engineering graduates since 2011 .She was awarded as Doctorate of Philosophy (Ph.D) by Anna University in the year 2019. She has published papers in various international journals like Springer under the topics Resource Management in sensor networks and routing in self organizing networks. She has been awarded for "Best Paper Publication" in the year 2018. She has published many research papers in National and International Conferences, Journals, Book Chapters and Patents. She has reviewed an ample number of papers in IGI Global, Springer and so on. Her research interests include block chain technology in smart education systems, AI, deep learning and mobile networks. She is an active member of Professional Bodies like ISTE, IAENG, MISTE, IACSIT and IRED.

Nurul Izzati Naqibah Binti Zaidi is a PhD Candidate in Management at the UTB School Of Business. She has been studying business courses from Higher National Diploma to Bachelor Of Degree in Business and Technology Management. Her research area is on IR4.0 and impact on SMEs.

Index

S

T

U

V

W

Y

Recommended Reference Books

IGI Global's reference books are available in three unique pricing formats:
Print Only, E-Book Only, or Print + E-Book.

Order direct through IGI Global's Online Bookstore at
www.igi-global.com or through your preferred provider.

ISBN: 9781799895862
EISBN: 9781799895886
© 2022; 427 pp.
List Price: US$ 215

ISBN: 9781668439425
EISBN: 9781668439449
© 2022; 281 pp.
List Price: US$ 250

ISBN: 9781668463116
EISBN: 9781668463123
© 2022; 1,027 pp.
List Price: US$ 765

ISBN: 9781668439210
EISBN: 9781668439234
© 2022; 313 pp.
List Price: US$ 250

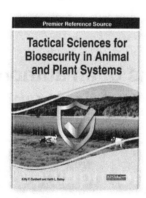

ISBN: 9781799879350
EISBN: 9781799879374
© 2022; 454 pp.
List Price: US$ 215

ISBN: 9781668445587
EISBN: 9781668445600
© 2022; 273 pp.
List Price: US$ 250

Do you want to stay current on the latest research trends, product announcements, news, and special offers?
Join IGI Global's mailing list to receive customized recommendations, exclusive discounts, and more.
Sign up at: **www.igi-global.com/newsletters.**

Publisher of Timely, Peer-Reviewed Inclusive Research Since 1988

www.igi-global.com   ✉ Sign up at www.igi-global.com/newsletters   f facebook.com/igiglobal   t twitter.com/igiglobal   in linkedin.com/igiglobal

Ensure Quality Research is Introduced
to the Academic Community

Become an Evaluator for IGI Global Authored Book Projects

Premier Reference Source

Tax Audit and Taxation
in the Paradigm of
Sustainable Development

Premier Reference Source

Controlling Epidemics
With Mathematical and
Machine Learning Models

Premier Reference Source

School-Museum
Relationships and
Teaching Social Sciences
in Formal Education

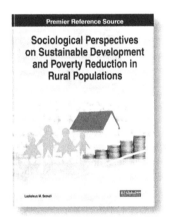
Premier Reference Source

Sociological Perspectives
on Sustainable Development
and Poverty Reduction in
Rural Populations

The overall success of an authored book project is dependent on quality and timely manuscript evaluations.

Applications and Inquiries may be sent to:
development@igi-global.com

Applicants must have a doctorate (or equivalent degree) as well as publishing, research, and reviewing experience. Authored Book Evaluators are appointed for one-year terms and are expected to complete at least three evaluations per term. Upon successful completion of this term, evaluators can be considered for an additional term.

If you have a colleague that may be interested in this opportunity,
we encourage you to share this information with them.

Easily Identify, Acquire, and Utilize Published Peer-Reviewed Findings in Support of Your Current Research

IGI Global OnDemand

Purchase Individual IGI Global OnDemand Book Chapters and Journal Articles

For More Information:
www.igi-global.com/e-resources/ondemand/

Browse through 150,000+ Articles and Chapters!

Find specific research related to your current studies and projects that have been contributed by international researchers from prestigious institutions, including:

- Accurate and Advanced Search
- Affordably Acquire Research
- Instantly Access Your Content
- Benefit from the InfoSci Platform Features

"It really provides an excellent entry into the research literature of the field. It presents a manageable number of highly relevant sources on topics of interest to a wide range of researchers. The sources are scholarly, but also accessible to 'practitioners'."

- Ms. Lisa Stimatz, MLS, University of North Carolina at Chapel Hill, USA

Interested in Additional Savings?

Subscribe to

IGI Global OnDemand *Plus*

Learn More

Acquire content from over 128,000+ research-focused book chapters and 33,000+ scholarly journal articles for as low as US$ 5 per article/chapter (original retail price for an article/chapter: US$ 37.50).

7,300+ E-BOOKS.
ADVANCED RESEARCH.
INCLUSIVE & AFFORDABLE.

IGI Global
PUBLISHER of TIMELY KNOWLEDGE

IGI Global e-Book Collection

- **Flexible Purchasing Options** (Perpetual, Subscription, EBA, etc.)
- Multi-Year Agreements with **No Price Increases** Guaranteed
- **No Additional Charge** for Multi-User Licensing
- No Maintenance, Hosting, or Archiving Fees
- Continually Enhanced & Innovated **Accessibility Compliance Features** (WCAG)

Handbook of Research on Digital Transformation, Industry Use Cases, and the Impact of Disruptive Technologies
ISBN: 9781799877127
EISBN: 9781799877141

Handbook of Research on New Investigations in Artificial Life, AI, and Machine Learning
ISBN: 9781799886860
EISBN: 9781799886877

Handbook of Research on Future of Work and Education
ISBN: 9781799882756
EISBN: 9781799882770

Research Anthology on Physical and Intellectual Disabilities in an Inclusive Society (4 Vols.)
ISBN: 9781668435427
EISBN: 9781668435434

Innovative Economic, Social, and Environmental Practices for Progressing Future Sustainability
ISBN: 9781799895909
EISBN: 9781799895923

Applied Guide for Event Study Research in Supply Chain Management
ISBN: 9781799889694
EISBN: 9781799889717

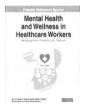

Mental Health and Wellness in Healthcare Workers
ISBN: 9781799888130
EISBN: 9781799888147

Clean Technologies and Sustainable Development in Civil Engineering
ISBN: 9781799898108
EISBN: 9781799898122

Request More Information, or Recommend the IGI Global e-Book Collection to Your Institution's Librarian

For More Information or to Request a Free Trial, Contact IGI Global's e-Collections Team: eresources@igi-global.com | 1-866-342-6657 ext. 100 | 717-533-8845 ext. 100

Are You Ready to
Publish Your Research

PUBLISHER of TIMELY KNOWLEDGE

IGI Global offers book authorship and editorship opportunities across 11 subject areas, including business, computer science, education, science and engineering, social sciences, and more!

Benefits of Publishing with IGI Global:

- Free one-on-one editorial and promotional support.

- Expedited publishing timelines that can take your book from start to finish in less than one (1) year.

- Choose from a variety of formats, including Edited and Authored References, Handbooks of Research, Encyclopedias, and Research Insights.

- Utilize IGI Global's eEditorial Discovery® submission system in support of conducting the submission and double-blind peer review process.

- IGI Global maintains a strict adherence to ethical practices due in part to our full membership with the Committee on Publication Ethics (COPE).

- Indexing potential in prestigious indices such as Scopus®, Web of Science™, PsycINFO®, and ERIC – Education Resources Information Center.

- Ability to connect your ORCID iD to your IGI Global publications.

- Earn honorariums and royalties on your full book publications as well as complimentary content and exclusive discounts.

Join Your Colleagues from Prestigious Institutions, Including:

Australian National University

Massachusetts Institute of Technology

JOHNS HOPKINS UNIVERSITY

HARVARD UNIVERSITY

TSINGHUA UNIVERSITY ~1911~

COLUMBIA UNIVERSITY IN THE CITY OF NEW YORK

Learn More at: www.igi-global.com/publish

or Contact IGI Global's Aquisitions Team at: acquisition@igi-global.com

Printed in the United States
by Baker & Taylor Publisher Services